Contemporary China
in the Post–Cold War Era

About the Editors

Dr. Bih-jaw Lin is the former director of the Institute of International Relations in Taipei and a professor of international relations at the National Chengchi University. He is the author or editor of numerous books and articles, including *Kuo-chi cheng-chih yü wai-chiao cheng-ts'e* (International politics and foreign policy, 1990), *Education in Mainland China: The Literary Perspective* (1991), *Forces for Change in Contemporary China* (1993), *Asia and Europe: A Comparison for Developmental Experiences* (1993), and *Contemporary China and the Changing International Community* (1994). In 1994 Dr. Lin assumed the post of deputy secretary-general of the National Security Council of the Republic of China.

James T. Myers is director of the Center for Asian Studies and professor of government and international studies at the University of South Carolina. He is the author or editor of numerous works in the field of contemporary China studies, including *Enemies without Guns: The Catholic Church in the People's Republic of China* (1991), *Forces for Change in Contemporary China* (1993) and *Contemporary China and the Changing International Community* (1994) (the last two with Bih-jaw Lin). Dr. Myers is also a co-editor of *Chinese Politics: Documents and Analysis,* vols. one (1983), two (1986), three (1995) and four (1996), all published by the University of South Carolina Press.

Contemporary China in the Post–Cold War Era

Edited by
Bih-jaw Lin and James T. Myers

UNIVERSITY OF SOUTH CAROLINA PRESS

Published in Columbia, South Carolina, by the
University of South Carolina Press

Manufactured in the United States of America

00 99 98 97 96   5 4 3 2 1

Library of Congress Cataloging-In-Publication Data

Contemporary China in the post–Cold War era / edited by Bih-jaw Lin
and James T. Myers.
    p.   cm.
    "Composed of papers delivered at the 23rd Sino-American Conference
on Contemporary China held in Taipei on June 7–8, 1994" —Introd.
    Includes bibliographical references and index.
    ISBN 1–57003–093–6 (cloth : alk. paper)
    1. China—History—1976– —Congresses. 2. Taiwan—History—1975–
—Congresses. I. Lin, Bih-jaw. II. Myers, James T. III. Sino-
American Conference on Contemporary China (23rd : 1994 : Taipei,
Taiwan)
DS779.16.c66   1996   95–19948
951.05'9—dc20   CIP

Contents

Introduction, *James T. Myers*   xi

Part I. Ideological and Political Changes in Mainland China

1. The Problems of Isms: Pragmatic Orthodoxy
   and Liberalization in Mainland China
   Brantly Womack   3

2. The Political Implications of the CCP's
   "Socialist Market Economy" Proposal
   An-chia Wu   22

3. Generational Change, Institutional Pluralism, and
   Decision-making in Teng's China
   Suisheng Zhao   41

Part II. Economic and Social Changes in Mainland China

4. Mainland China's Economic System:
   A Study in Contradictions
   Jan S. Prybyla   57

5. Mainland China's Transition from a Planned to a
   Market Economy: New Breakthroughs and Hurdles
   Chu-yuan Cheng   85

6. Reemergence of Chinese Nonstate Enterprises:
   Trends, Fluctuation, and Regional Variations
   Belton M. Fleisher, Wen Lang Li, and Jian Chen   102

7. Migration and Politics on the Shanghai Delta
   Lynn T. White III   117

Part III. Trends in Taiwan

8. Trends in Taiwan: A Political Perspective
   Shelley Rigger   149

9. Trends in Taiwan: An Economic Perspective
   Cal Clark   169

Part IV. Mainland China's Military and Security Policy

10. The PRC's National Security Objectives in the
    Post-Cold War Era and the Role of the PLA
    Ralph A. Cossa   199

11. The PRC's Military and Security Policy in the
    Post-Cold War Era
    Harlan W. Jencks   225

Part V. Mainland China's Foreign Policy and Foreign Relations

12. Mainland China in a Changing Asia-Pacific
    Regional Order
    Samuel S. Kim   263

13. How Flexible Is Peking's Foreign Policy?
    Chih-yu Shih   306

14. Peking's Post-Tienanmen Foreign Policy:
    The Human Rights Factor
    John F. Copper   328

Part VI. Cross-Strait Relations

15. Cross-Strait Relations and Their Implications for the
    United States
    Robert G. Sutter   353

16. Cross-Strait Economic Relations and Their Implications
    for Taiwan
    Ramon H. Myers and Linda Chao   379

17. Mainland China's Economic Policy Toward Taiwan:
    Economic Needs or Unification Scheme?
    Yu-Shan Wu   393

    Contributors   413

Tables

1.1 Chinese Public Opinion, 1987   13

1.2 Is Party Leadership Necessary?   18

2.1 The Division of Fiscal Revenue and Administrative Power Between the Central and Local Governments Under the Proposed Tax-Sharing System   35

2.2 Ratios of Central and Local Government Revenues and Expenditures in Mainland China (1978-92)   36

3.1 Membership Changes in the CCP Central Committee   43

3.2 Generational Data of the Fourteenth Politburo Members   45

3.3 Career Pattern of the Fourteenth Politburo Members   49

6.1 Dependent Variable Percentage Growth of Nonagricultural Real GDP per Nonagricultural Population, by Province, 1978-89 (%)   110

6.2 Dependent Variable Mean Nonstate/Total Manufacturing Output Ratio 1978-89, by Province (%)   112

7.1 Migration to and from Shanghai   121

7.2 Migration to and from Shanghai Delta Cities: Shaohsing and Hsiashih   129

7.3 Transient Populations of PRC Cities in Mid-Reform   138

8.1 Success Rate for KMT and Non-KMT Candidates   163

9.1 Indicators of Economic Development Level   171

9.2 Indicators of Social Outcomes   176

9.3 Composition of Exports   180

9.4 Importance of ROC-Hong Kong Trade by Commodity, January-May 1992   183

9.5 Indicators of Social Development   186

9.6 Indicators of State's Economic Role   189

11.1 Official PRC Defense Budget   232

17.1 Taiwan's Trade Surplus Dependency on Mainland China (1990-93)   401

17.2 Cross-Strait Trade Through Hong Kong (1979-93)   404

Figures

6.1 Social Labor Force (Employment) by Type of Industry   105

6.2 Nonagricultural Social Labor Force (Employment) by
     Ownership   108

6.2a Percentage of Gross Output Value of Manufacturing
     Sector by Ownership   108

6.3 Annual Growth Rate of Staff and Workers by
     Ownership and Industry (1978-91)   109

6.4 Annual Wage by Ownership   114

6.5 Percentage of Individual Ownership by Industry   115

6.6 Individual Ownership vs. Percentage of Nonagricultural
     Labor by Provinces (1991)   115

17.1 Taiwan's Indirect Trade Dependency on Mainland China
     (1979-93)   406

17.2 Mainland China's Indirect Trade Dependency on Taiwan
     (1979-93)   406

17.3 Cross-Strait Trade Through Hong Kong (1979-93)   407

FOREWORD

The end of the Cold War has created a new regional and global setting for the two sides of the Taiwan Strait to pursue their respective economic, political, and strategic interests. Both Taipei and Beijing have significantly adapted their ideology, domestic politics, economic development strategy, and foreign policy to meet these changes. This is the context in which "Contemporary China in the Post–Cold War Era" was chosen as the theme of the 23rd Sino-American Conference on Contemporary China held in June 1994 in Taipei.

The papers presented at the conference analyzed recent changes in politics, economics, foreign relations, and the general security environment in Taiwan and mainland China. Discussion was lively, and presenters have taken into account these thoughtful exchanges and revised their papers accordingly.

As editors, we would like to extend our deep appreciation to our respective institutions for their sponsorship and support. The Institute of International Relations at National Chengchi University in Taipei, Taiwan, now under the directorship of Dr. Yu-ming Shaw, looks forward to hosting and sponsoring future gatherings of this kind, which have become important occasions for scholars and experts from the United States and the Republic of China to share their insights into developments in mainland China, Taiwan, and Hong Kong.

Bih-jaw Lin
Deputy Secretary-General
National Security Council
Republic of China

Contemporary China
at the End of the Cold War

James T. Myers

The end of the Cold War, the dissolution of the Soviet Union, and the demise of communism in all but a few scattered outposts are among the most significant events of the past ten years. The current volume seeks to explore various aspects of conditions in Mainland China and Taiwan in light of these historic developments. The chapters that follow are papers delivered at the 23rd Sino-American Conference on Contemporary China held in Taipei on June 8, 1994. Topics covered include the sweeping changes taking place in the People's Republic of China (PRC) as well as the mounting problems that have accompanied policies of reform and opening to the outside world. Also considered is the rapidly changing political scene in the Republic of China (ROC) on Taiwan and the continuing problems and prospects of cross-Strait relations between the PRC and ROC.

In part 1, three scholars consider ideological and political changes in the PRC. Brantly Womack defines ideology as an enforced system of thought—an orthodoxy. He cites three contradictions in the present system: 1) between the pragmatic content of Deng Xiaoping's thought and the authoritarian form of that thought; 2) between control of political discourse and growth of other forms of discourse which impinge on political discourse; and 3) between consequences of liberalization and consequences of political control. Liberalization, suggests Womack, involves a change in the relationship between state and society, not simply a change in the structure of the regime.

An-chia Wu in chapter 2 discusses the ideological and political significance of the idea of "socialist market economy." He looks at the effects on the bureaucracy of the PRC and asserts that the huge public official sector can only be reduced gradually. As to the effects on the centrally planned economy, Wu suggests that the growth of the private sector must imply a decline of the state sector of economy. In terms of the problem of central-local relations, Wu notes the desire of the government for stronger central control to promote social stability, but such control, he believes, if it is achieved, will have a negative impact on economic growth. Wu also notes that the introduction of market reforms has been related to rising rural unrest and to the growth of corruption.

In chapter 3, Suisheng Zhao discusses generational change, institutional pluralism, and decision making in Deng's China. He writes that massive generational change was begun at the 12th National Congress of the Communist Party of China (CPC) in 1982 and largely completed by the 14th CPC Congress in 1992. Zhao notes that the new generation of leaders is better educated and that the new leaders tend to come to power through narrow career paths; the power of younger leaders tends to be institutional while the power of older leaders is highly personal. A kind of institutional pluralism is developing in the leadership representing different governmental organizations. With regard to the policy implications of these developments, Zhao asserts that any major change in the institutional representation structure of the ruling Politburo will bring about different policy outcomes according to the institutional model.

Part 2 deals with economic and social changes in the PRC. In chapter 4, Jan S. Prybyla sees the PRC economic system as a study in contradictions. Prybyla observes that mixed public-private, planned-market type systems can exist and are not uncommon. Yet, for this arrangement to be successful, one type must clearly dominate the economic landscape. The system must be either public-planned or private-market in its essence. Furthermore, writes Prybyla, marketization without legal privatization of property and a rule of law or civilized legal order can bring economic growth and development in the short run but represents a serious danger to the market-private property order in the long run. Prybyla contrasts economic development in the PRC with the Taiwan model and suggests that corruption which is both deep and pervasive may be the biggest problem facing the PRC. Finally, Prybyla suggests that the PRC has left unsolved two of the most difficult problems, namely extension of the economic pluralism to the political system and creation of private property.

In chapter 5 Chu-yuan Cheng discusses the problems of transition from a planned to a market economy. He asserts that the reform program addresses the core of the economic structure and that it has therefore encountered increasing resistance. Because of the success of private-market reforms, suggests Cheng, without a thorough reform of the system, the collapse of the state enterprise seemed imminent. The new reform program adopted by the CPC Central Committee in November 1993 addressed a number of important areas of the economy. At the heart of the new agenda, writes Cheng, was the effort to invigorate the floundering state enterprises. The program also sought to reform the market system, reform the banking system, reform the taxation system, reform the investment system, reform the planning system, reform the foreign trade system, and rationalize the system of income distribution and the social security system. Discussing the socio-economic consequences of this sweeping plan, Cheng cites resistance from local authorities, labor unrest, bureaucratic sabotage, and market disturbance. Looking toward the future, Cheng sees no turning back for the PRC despite these problems. Economic development and reform have been stop-and-go, one step forward, two steps back, yet there will be no return, in his view, to the old system of planning.

In chapter 6, Belton M. Fleisher, Wen Lang Li, and Jian Chen consider the development of Chinese nonstate enterprises. The authors note that the "denationalization" of the Chinese economy involves the decline in the number of state-owned enterprises relative to the number of collectively owned enterprises (COE), joint ventures and individually owned businesses. The fastest growth has occurred in the COE sector, especially among the township and village enterprises (TVEs). The authors theorize that the rise of a strong middle class is related to the rise of political liberalization. They point out, however, that the most important sector of the nonstate economy is the COEs rather than individually owned businesses, and that while the role of the central government in the Chinese economy is diminishing, provincial, municipal and village governments have taken the lead in industrialization in the reform era. Thus, they conclude, the development of a strong middle class and corresponding progress toward a more liberal or democratic political system may be a very slow process.

Lynn T. White III begins chapter 7 with the observation that the "largest quick urban migration in all human history" has occurred in China over the last two decades. The causes of this enormous shift of population have been primarily attributable to the economic attraction of city employment. White asserts that the migration of large numbers of workers to Shanghai has been a mixed blessing. The migrants have provided low-cost labor and services to the city at low prices, thus fighting inflation. Yet, for a variety of reasons, this migration has been unpopular with the permanent Shanghai residents. White does not see the large population of "blind drifters" as a political threat because he believes that they bring their conservative attitudes with them from the countryside. Whatever the cost-benefit analysis of urban migration, White sees the phenomenon as a concomitant of modernization and concludes with the observation that in any case the Chinese government has lost most of its previous ability to control where people live.

Part 3 of the present volume considers trends in Taiwan. In chapter 8

Shelley Rigger considers Taiwan in the stage of "normalization" of politics. She notes the development of a competitive party system, both between and within parties. Rigger cites the campaign against corruption as an example of confronting old ways of doing things. The author also discusses the liberalization of the media, the shift from machine-based politics to issue politics, and the marginalization of extremely conservative positions in political dialogue.

Also addressing the changing situation in Taiwan, Cal Clark in chapter 9 looks at trends in Taiwan from an economic perspective. He credits the leadership of the ROC with flexible and rapid response to changes in economic environment. Likewise, he sees a "virtuous cycle" of positive reinforcements between social and economic developments. Clark also notes the generally balanced and complementary economic roles of the public and private sectors.

In part 4 we turn to a consideration of Mainland China's military and security policy. In chapter 10 Ralph A. Cossa looks at the question of the PRC's national security objectives in the present era and at the role of the People's Liberation Army (PLA). Cossa writes that, while the post–Cold War security environment has been something of a mixed blessing for the PRC, on balance the situation has been viewed by Peking as positive. In the present era, the author postulates six main national-security objectives of the PRC: "(1) maintenance of internal stability and control; (2) preservation of regional stability; (3) development of the national economy; (4) reunification with Hong Kong and Taiwan; (5) international respect and recognition; and (6) development of a modern military." Cossa writes that one cannot be sure where these objectives will take China in the coming years, but he suggests several courses of action which he believes the PRC must take if China is to become a stable and responsible member of the community of nations.

In chapter 11 Harlan W. Jencks cites four major goals of Chinese military and security policy: maintenance of internal political stability; maintenance of external security against invasion; achievement of "hegemony" over its near neighbors; and achievement of "great power" status. Jencks suggests that the most significant middle- and long-term military threat to China seen by leaders of the PRC is from Japan. Conversely, according to the author, "the gravest threat the PRC poses to Asia—indeed to the world—is its own internal breakup." Jencks stresses China's desire to be a "great power," and he cites what he describes as the PRC's "fundamental assumptions" about China's special status in Asia. In his view, China wants to be friendly and cooperative but at the same time the PRC assumes it should be the dominant power in the region and that others should recognize and defer to what China believes to be its regional interests.

In part 5 three authors consider Mainland China's foreign policy and foreign relations. Samuel S. Kim in chapter 12 writes of Mainland China in a changing Asia-Pacific regional order. Kim describes China's behavior as a "puzzle." China, he asserts, is experiencing the "deepest international peace" of the century, yet Beijing acts "as if it were faced with the greatest external security threat" by building up its military power and greatly increasing military spending in a period in which global military spending has been declining. Citing the "thoroughly intermeshed" relationship between PRC domestic and foreign policies, Kim surveys the entire range of PRC relations in the Asia-Pacific region. Finally, Kim surveys the serious internal problems facing the PRC and concludes that China today is a "weak, Balkanizing state"; in a conclusion similar to that made by Jencks, Kim suggests that the main danger to regional stability stems from Beijing's domestic weakness.

In chapter 13 Chih-yu Shih discusses the question of the "flexibility" of Chinese foreign policy, while in chapter 14 John F. Copper turns his attention to the question of the human rights factor in post-Tiananmen PRC foreign policy. Copper asserts that in the wake of the 1989 Tiananmen incident, foreign criticism of China's human rights policies became a major issue in Beijing's foreign policy considerations for the first time. Copper discusses three types of response by Beijing to foreign criticism and suggests that the one he calls the "offensive" policy has been relatively successful. He believes that in the future Beijing may more often adopt such a policy when confronted with human rights complaints. In conclusion, Copper writes, "The perspective in Peking appears to be that China can win the human rights debate because Asia is the center of the world's economic development and because other Asian nations as well as Third World countries generally agree with Beijing on the definition of human rights."

Part 6 of the volume concerns relations between the PRC and ROC. In chapter 15 Robert G. Sutter considers cross-Strait relations and their implications for the United States. Sutter surveys the changes in PRC-ROC relations since the Korean war and then looks at the varied interests of the three actors—PRC, ROC, USA. In the concluding section he reviews US policy options in cross-Strait relations.

Ramon H. Myers and Linda Chao discuss cross-Strait economic relations and their implications for Taiwan in chapter 16. The authors discuss the new patterns of Taiwanese business activity on the Mainland and the growing integration of the PRC and ROC economies. In the final section of the chapter Myers and Chao discuss the implications and increasing costs for Taiwan of the integration of the two economies. These costs include: 1) socio-legal costs, including lack of legal protection for ROC citizens and businessmen in the

PRC as well social costs and family problems created by extramarital relations between ROC men and PRC women; 2) rising opportunity costs of trade and investment, including outflow of resources from the ROC, rising interest rates for loans, and loss of tax revenues; 3) rising transaction costs of monitoring ROC-PRC economic relations, including policing, regulating, preventing smuggling, costs of hijacking and entry of illegal labor from the PRC. According to the authors, these costs may already exceed economic benefits of the trade and are likely to become polarizing political issues in the ROC in the future.

In the final chapter of the present volume Yu-Shan Wu discusses Mainland China's economic policies toward Taiwan. Wu makes the "economic reform argument," namely that economic reform has assumed paramount importance on the PRC political agenda. He asserts that the survival of the communist regime hinges on the success of the reform program. From Beijing's point of view, writes Wu, the cross-Strait economic relationship has its most important meaning in serving the needs of the economic development on the Mainland. Therefore, PRC economic policy will vary with PRC economic needs. Wu contends that the "unification" argument—that the PRC is trying to lure the ROC into a relationship which can be used as a lever against the ROC—is not valid. Wu does not exclude the possibility that the Mainland might some day attempt to use economic ties to push for unification with Taiwan but asserts that current decisions regarding cross-Strait relations are made primarily on economic grounds.

The picture which emerges from these chapters does not predict a very positive future for the PRC in the short- to mid-term. The PRC faces an identity and leadership crisis; post-Deng leaders must also contend with a decline of central power and control. Writers point to internal problems that include social disorder, rising crime, rampant corruption, rural unrest, workers' unrest, and an army of "blind drifters" which has invaded China's large cities.

The leadership must also deal with the implications of the loss of control over information brought on by the proliferation of fax machines and satellite dishes. This "cultural pollution" is also accompanied by real chemical pollution and a serious degradation of China's natural environment. Perhaps most significant in the short run (at the time of this publication) is the looming succession crisis which many scholars believe will accompany the passing of Deng Xiaoping.

In terms of foreign affairs, the chapters in this volume have suggested that the most serious danger to the region lies in the uncertainties of China's domestic politics. A weak and fragmented China is certain to be less predictable than a strong and unified one. Under such circumstances it is difficult to know whether China's next generation of leaders will be able successfully to cope with the mounting list of problems. It is similarly difficult to predict how or if China will fit into a peaceful new regional or world order.

Contemporary China in the Post–Cold War Era

Part I

Ideological and Political Changes in Mainland China

1

The Problems of Isms: Pragmatic Orthodoxy and Liberalization in Mainland China

Brantly Womack

"Teng Hsiao-p'ing (Deng Xiaoping) Thought" is not a contradiction in terms, but as an officially enforced ideology of pragmatism it is a contradiction in functions. Throughout his career Teng's characteristic style has been pragmatism. Not just pragmatism in the service of ideological ends—something that could also be attributed to Mao Tse-tung (Mao Zedong)—but pragmatism as opposed to doctrinal politics. In his early days in France he was known as the "doctor of the mimeograph machine." He became famous and then infamous (during the Cultural Revolution) for his remark, "Black cat, white cat, what difference does it make as long as it catches mice." And he came back to power in 1978 with the slogan that "practice is the only criterion for determining truth."

Teng Hsiao-p'ing's pragmatic attitude has prevailed since 1978, and his political direction and leadership have been praised fulsomely. But ever since 1978 Teng's political thought has played an authoritative role similar in function to that of Mao's political thought. Moreover, the authoritative role of Teng's thought has not been a transitional phenomenon, strongest in the 1970s and fading in the 1980s. From the time of the Fourteenth Party Congress in 1992 the attempt has been made to reassert Teng Hsiao-p'ing's thought as a new orthodoxy for mainland China. A particularly apt example is the devotion of the entire first page of the *People's Daily* on November 6, 1993 to remarks by Teng Hsiao-p'ing made in January and February 1992 in Wuchang, Shenzhen, Zhuhai, and Shanghai.[1]

---

[1] Also available in *Teng Hsiao-p'ing wen-hsüan* (Selected works of Teng Hsiao-p'ing), vol. 3 (Nanning: Kwang-si jen-min ch'u-pan-she, 1994), 370-83.

The text was not printed as news (too old for that), nor as documentation (clearly it is an edited collation), and it certainly is not merely one opinion among many. Rather, it is political thought that is meant to be directive for the Party. Its publication implicitly asserts that the viewpoints presented are beyond public question. In fact, of course, Teng's speeches from his southern trip signaled an important setback for Li P'eng (Li Peng) and Ch'en Yün (Chen Yun), and they were warmly welcomed by progressives inside and outside mainland China. However, the pragmatic content of the orthodoxy stands in ironic contrast to its dogmatic form.

The contradiction between the pragmatic content and the doctrinaire form of "Teng Hsiao-p'ing Thought" sets first level of questions to be addressed by this essay. We will not address the fascinating question of the content and internal consistency of Teng's politics per se, because that topic would be a considerable research project in its own right. Instead, we will focus on the relationship of content and form. Clearly the form of orthodoxy has continuities with the orthodoxy of "Mao Tse-tung Thought" and earlier with Leninism and traditional Chinese politics. Indeed, I will argue that it is best considered a neo-traditional orthodoxy in contrast to Mao's revolutionary orthodoxy. Therefore the question of the continuity and differences between Maoist orthodoxy and Teng's pragmatic orthodoxy must be examined.

There is clearly a profound difference between Mao's "struggle between two lines" after 1957 and Teng's enforcement of boundaries of orthodoxy against the unpermitted left ("uphold modernization and openness") and against the unpermitted right ("uphold the four fundamental principles").[2] Teng's position creates a limited space for public discourse, while Mao's approach led to an absolute repression of intellectual differences. Since the content of Teng's politics has discouraged the interference of politics in other societal questions, especially economics, there have been very real developments in what can be said in mainland China.

One might describe three, or three and one-half, ranges of discourse: politics, policy, and private opinion. The additional one-half would be external political discourse, opinions about Chinese politics that originate from persons outside mainland China and insulated from its political sanctions. Given the changes in public, political discourse and the emergence of expert, private, and external discourse, the second major set of questions to be addressed here centers on mapping the new intellectual territory of the Teng era.

---

[2]The shift is best analyzed in Tang Tsou, "Political Change and Reform: The Middle Course," in Tang Tsou, *The Cultural Revolution and Post-Mao Reforms* (Chicago: University of Chicago Press, 1986), 219-59.

Politics, the public discussion of overtly political questions, is still restricted, and in this public realm of discourse open challenge and debate are not permitted. The zigzag of liberalization and repression of political discourse in the 1980s demonstrates both the limited, indirect, and vulnerable nature of political discourse and the gradual progress made in this area.

Policy, the consideration of concrete problems and solutions with a bearing on public interests, has increasingly allowed the expression of expert opinion. Expert opinion can be radically challenging of specific policies in the expert (largely *nei-pu*—internal, limited circulation) press, and variably bold or cautious in the public media. Thus the realm of expert discourse has expanded enormously in the 1980s.

Private concerns, and private opinions that do not attempt to become public and political, are largely left alone in the post-Mao era. Private discourse includes opinions and rumors about politics, and few visitors have not been impressed with the increasing variety and boldness of such opinions.

The external realm of discourse includes overseas Chinese, diplomatic problems with domestic implications such as Hong Kong, and external attention to Chinese political affairs such as American interest in human rights and the activities of Amnesty International.

The third and last set of questions to be considered here concentrates on the challenge posed by liberalization to any orthodoxy, that of Teng Hsiao-p'ing included. Far from relieving pressure on politics, mainland China's new fields of discourse press on the current boundaries of what is permitted, regardless of where those boundaries are set and whether or not the content of the orthodoxy is reasonable. The imposition of an orthodoxy creates a sense of alienation among those who submit to it, and the alienation results from the fact of imposition rather than from the details of the content of orthodoxy or the level of sanctions. Thus liberalization is more likely to increase the risk of political challenge rather than simply satisfy and coopt increasing numbers of intellectuals. But liberalization is also an inexorable pressure sanctioned by the content of Teng's pragmatic orthodoxy, and it will seem even less avoidable to his successors. The possibility of crisis cannot be excluded, even though there are many reasons for all sides to avoid crisis.

Since the primary audience of this essay is already well familiar with contemporary Chinese politics, this essay will concentrate on trying to present the theoretical questions outlined above as clearly as possible rather than presenting a detailed narration of China's ideological history.

From Revolutionary Orthodoxy to Pragmatic Orthodoxy

The primary difference between Maoist orthodoxy in the 1957-76 period and that of Teng Hsiao-p'ing is that Mao's politics was structured by a future-oriented revolutionary mission while Teng is oriented toward maximizing the opportunities at hand. This is more basic than differences in pragmatism or in attention to economics, because differences in these areas can be derived from the fundamental difference in orientation. The difference in orientation also determines the vast differences in political function of the two orthodoxies.

Maoist Orthodoxy

With the accomplishment of socialist transition in 1956, Mao was faced with reorienting his politics toward the next historic task of achieving Communism.[3] But the achievement of Communism was a much more ideologically-defined goal than his previous targets of revolutionary success (achieved in 1949) and socialist transition. Moreover, unlike the previous two phases, the Soviet Union could not be used as a model of success. On the contrary, the emergence of revisionism in the Soviet Union demonstrated how desperately difficult the new historic task would be. Domestically, the strategy of a united front to reach a shared goal was no longer applicable, because the former class allies, the national bourgeoisie, petty bourgeoisie, and so forth, could only distract and derail the proletariat as it tried to transform the given political economy and culture. Indeed, the bad influence of classes rooted in a society of exploitation reached beyond its members and into the Chinese Communist Party (CCP) itself, in the form of "Party persons in power going the capitalist road."

During the revolutionary struggle before 1949, correct leadership centered on the practical task of understanding the concrete political situation and mobilizing maximum popular support. At this time Mao defined correct leadership in terms of becoming well-informed about the local situation and of avoiding the mistakes of being too cautious ("empiricism," "opportunism," "tailism,") on the one hand, and too adventurous ("subjectivism," "voluntarism," "putchism," "blind adventurism") on the other. However, after 1956 mainland China was at the edge of history, and all error was seen as constraining its forward progress toward Communism. Obstruction and derailment of the socialist mission was objectively in the interests of capitalism. Therefore Mao Tse-tung Thought after 1956 was engaged in a "two-line struggle" with capitalist tendencies rather than occupying a pragmatic middle ground between excessive caution and excessive risk-taking. The division between correctness and error

---

[3]The leftist transition in Mao's politics is discussed in more detail in Brantly Womack, "Where Mao Went Wrong," *Australian Journal of Chinese Affairs*, no. 16 (July 1986): 23-40.

became one with the division between left and right.

Of course, the economic and political crises induced by the Great Leap Forward and the Cultural Revolution required pragmatic action oriented toward present crises rather than future goals. But the fact of failure was not acknowledged publicly, and the rationale of the pragmatic policies was not incorporated into the orthodoxy. As a result, the pragmatic policies (and the pragmatists themselves) were doubly vulnerable: their failure could be blamed on lack of vision and revolutionary nerve, while their success did not prove the validity of pragmatism but rather created the opportunity for new leftist interventions.

The ultimate absurdities of leftist orthodoxy were the arcane campaigns of the early 1970s, most notably the critique of Confucius and Lin Piao (Lin Biao) and the critique of *Water Margin*. In these the posture of mortal struggle with capitalism was maintained, but the justifying orientation toward the Communist future disappeared. Leftist orthodoxy in the 1970s was fighting a defensive action in the political present against Chou En-lai's (Zhou Enlai's) sponsorship of returning pragmatists, most notably Teng Hsiao-p'ing. The logic of Gang of Four leftism was simple: if to be left was to be correct, then the task of political orthodoxy could be reduced to exposing the non-left. The problems of production, modernization, and so forth, were only camouflage for rightists. In other words, exerting the "all-round dictatorship" of the proletariat would necessarily be correct, because the only possible mistake would be that of not being left enough.

Pragmatic Orthodoxy

The reversal of leftist orthodoxy in 1978 was so complete that it appeared that orthodoxy was simply replaced by pragmatism. The new orthodoxy of Teng Hsiao-p'ing differed fundamentally from leftism not only in its content but also in its retreat from the pervasive penetration of ideological concerns into all aspects of life. However, Teng did not repudiate Marxism-Leninism, or even Mao Tse-tung Thought. More importantly, an orthodoxy was necessary for the direction and legitimacy of the CCP's role of political leadership. Thus, not only did pragmatism become a new orthodoxy, but it was pragmatic to do so. Instead of the leadership following the orthodoxy, the orthodoxy followed the leadership.

Teng could not repudiate the idea of a Communist future and remain a Marxist, but he could establish an intermediate goal of economic modernization that would provide practical direction for all policy. In effect, the ultimate goal that drove Mao's leftism was postponed indefinitely. Chao Tzu-yang (Zhao Ziyang) announced at the Thirteenth Party Congress in 1987 that mainland China was still in the primary stage of socialism, and it would remain at this stage for a hundred years. The message here was not one of humility. The primary stage of socialism permitted other forms of economic organization, including capitalism, and a hundred years duration implied that there was no need at present to be concerned about historical progress and transition to higher levels of socialism. While Mao's leftism might be described as "no here and all hereafter," post-Mao orthodoxy was "all here and no hereafter."

Without the pressure of progress toward Communism, policy could be set by the tangible benefits that it promised. Moreover, the harsh egalitarian and anticommercial strictures derived from Marx's description of Communism could be replaced by the promotion of a socialist market economy. Theorists returned to the Marxist classics to reassert the priority of economics over politics, and "socialist economics" was redefined as whatever policies were most productive under mainland China's present conditions.

The new political orthodoxy was described as a struggle on two fronts rather than as a two-line struggle, but the ideological struggle became sporadic and defensive. An oscillation began between demands that thought be freed and "forbidden zones" be opened up and attacks on various signs of bourgeois liberalization and spiritual pollution. Since the harshness of earlier ideological campaigns had been condemned, the mode of conduct and penalties applied in post-Mao ideological conflicts were quite mild by comparison. Nevertheless, the principle was carefully maintained that the regime's political trajectory could not be criticized by the left, while its political structure could not be questioned by the right.

While Teng Hsiao-p'ing's pragmatism has certainly been a progressive influence on Chinese politics, his pragmatic orthodoxy might be considered conservative or even "neo-traditional" for a number of reasons.[4] This is hardly surprising, since as Michel Oksenberg has pointed out most of the world's "great reformers" have been conservative in significant respects.[5] First, in contrast to the future orientation of revolutionary orthodoxy, it is primarily concerned with maintaining the existing political leadership, policy, and structure. The regime has patronized reform, but it has not countenanced the challenging of its power. It is a "neo"-traditional orthodoxy rather than merely a traditional one because it aims to preserve societal structures while encouraging growth in its material level and

---

[4]See Lowell Dittmer, *China's Continuous Revolution* (Berkeley: University of California Press, 1987), 267-68, for a similar analysis.

[5]Michel Oksenberg and Bruce J. Dickson, "The Origins, Processes, and Outcomes of Great Political Reform: A Framework for Analysis," in *Comparative Political Dynamics: Global Research Perspectives*, ed. Dankwart Rustow and Kenneth Erickson (New York: Harper Collins, 1991), 235-61.

capacities. The tragedy of June 4, 1989 demonstrated both the real effects of reform and the unreformed essence of power at the center. Secondly, it is clearly a passive orthodoxy of an elderly leadership, even if its policy content is progressive and the societal effects of its policies undermine the old order. It is more daring in its permissiveness than in its active leadership. Moreover, politics of the post-Mao era has been increasingly dominated by that most traditional of concerns, the problem of anointed succession.

It is ironic that a future-oriented revolutionary orthodoxy could produce a relative stagnation of society, while a present-oriented neo-traditional orthodoxy has presided over the most rapid and sustained economic growth in China's modern history. Teng's new orthodoxy deserves credit for permitting China's material transformation, but the material transformation poses challenges to the structure of his pragmatic orthodoxy.

Fields of Discourse in Post-Mao China

Teng Hsiao-p'ing's pragmatic orthodoxy has had transformative effects on the intellectual world of mainland China even if the role of orthodoxy itself has remained unchallenged. Political discourse has been transformed in its content and to a lesser extent in its breadth and rules of engagement. More impressive has been the emergence of expert discourse related to specific policy issues, and of private opinion. Lastly, there is a much greater role for external political discourse, especially with the international condemnation of the June 4 massacre and the impending reversion of the sovereignty of Hong Kong.

Political Discourse

In one respect political discourse has been totally transformed under Teng Hsiao-p'ing. What could be said with impunity during the Cultural Revolution cannot be said now, and what is orthodoxy now was condemned in the Cultural Revolution. A clear marker of the reversal was the disappearance of the term "revisionism" in early 1980. The fact that this once common term of abuse cannot be used in political discourse in the post-Mao era is, paradoxically, also a sign of continuities. Just as in the Maoist period, political discourse is reserved for the support of the official orthodoxy. No challenge is permitted, though it must be said that the current regime is far less trigger-happy in detecting deviations.

Political discourse is difficult to define, and the distinction that I will draw between political discourse and policy discourse is intended to sketch a frontier between two general arenas and styles of discussion

rather than a thin line between two completely disjunctive categories.[6]
The difference is that political discourse brings into the discussion the
purposes and direction of public action and merits of public officials,
while policy discourse assumes agreement on purposes and assumes the
competence of officials, and it concentrates on the practical evaluation
of policy effects, problems, and alternatives. In a democracy, the ultimate
audience for political discourse is the citizenry itself, while the audience
for policy discourse is the policymakers.

In mainland China, there is no citizenry, even though individual
citizen rights have improved. The difference between a citizenry and "the
masses" is that the interests of the masses are presumed to be in harmony
with the leadership, and political discourse consists of persuading the
masses to be enthusiastic about current policies and leaders. Even though
the general discussion of policy alternatives has been proposed by such
diverse leaders as P'eng Chen (Peng Zhen) in 1984 and Wan Li in 1986,
the structure of the Party's media monopoly would make it very difficult
to permit even a limited public political forum. As a result, even though
the content of political discussion varies over time, and has changed completely since the mid-seventies, at any particular time it appears that everyone is in agreement. The road winds, and it may go in the right direction,
but it remains narrow. Of course, oblique but clear political differences
do emerge in the press, but the fact that the disputes remain oblique shows
that the primary audience is within the leadership, and that the structure
of the media prevents open questioning.

Policy Discourse

In contrast to the continuing narrowness of political discussion, the
realm of policy discussion has mushroomed in the post-Mao era. Perhaps
the best illustration of the extent and range of different opinions in policy
discourse are the discussions of economic policy analyzed by Joseph Fewsmith in his *Dilemmas of Reform in China*.[7] The policy arena is one of
fact and expertise. It questions the relative efficiency of black and white
cats and the extent of the mouse problem in Szechwan (Sichuan); it does
not look at the cat from the point of view of the mouse. It advises the
leadership from the side; it does not stand between the leadership and

---

[6]Besides the ambiguity of the relationship between political discourse and policy discourse,
Professor Lynn White has quite rightly raised the question of the relationship between
intellectual, articulated politics and practical, unarticulated politics. This problem cannot
be addressed without a much broader discussion of ideology and politics than the scope
of the present essay permits.

[7]Joseph Fewsmith, *Dilemmas of Reform in China* (Armonk, N.Y.: M. E. Sharpe, 1994).

the people. There has been an explosion in the public specialist media, but the most interesting advice is provided internally in the *nei-pu* media. There can be a broad range of implicit and explicit disagreement among experts, even in public forums, and new factual perspectives can be raised that call into question existing policies.

The importance of the pragmatic character of Teng Hsiao-p'ing's orthodoxy is clear in the expansion of policy discourse. While the range of political discourse remains narrow, the domain of public concerns completely dominated by political concerns has been reduced by nine-tenths. Even such major questions as the adoption of new economic reforms or the continuation of the current population policy can be dissolved into practical concerns of efficiency and be argued by experts. Public conflict among experts is avoided, and even policy discussion becomes more sensitive as it approaches the implicit critique of current policy, but both conflict and critique do occur.

Private Opinion

Ultimately, private opinion has probably seen the greatest expansion of discourse. Due to the confluence of several factors, Mao Tse-tung achieved what was probably the highest level of control over private opinion in modern history, and it was especially strong in urban areas and among intellectuals. Teng Hsiao-p'ing is not interested in maintaining control in such matters; as long as it does not become political, private opinion fits into the realm that Tang Tsou has called the "zone of indifference." Since the state's tolerance of private opinion is based on indifference rather than citizen rights, it can be arbitrary if its attention is roused. The best recent example is the self-confessions required of broad reaches of the urban population in the aftermath of the Tienanmen (Tiananmen) massacre. However, in general the state's interest in private opinion has subsided, and its invasive capacity has weakened.

The claims just made are difficult to prove, since private opinions remain private. But beyond anecdotal evidence, there is the evidence of opinion polls that show a broad divergence of opinion from official media, and significant differences among different groups of people. I would argue that if people were afraid to talk to one another, and did not do so, they would tend to articulate the media viewpoint both because they would not have the chance to formulate their own point of view (except to themselves) and because they would not be likely to trust a pollster if they did not trust their friends.

The most amazing political opinion survey that I have seen was a national survey of a stratified sample of almost two thousand people carried out in July 1987 and published as a two hundred and fifty page book under the editorship of Wen Ch'i (Wen Qi).[8] The respondents are differentiated by occupation, age, education, party affiliation, and urban/ rural residence, and they show very interesting confluences and differences. I reproduce only a tiny portion of the opinions in table 1.1 in order to show the variety of opinion in 1987, that is, before the major inflation of 1988-89 and the events of 1989.

The table demonstrates clearly that in 1987 there was a considerable alienation of people from the government despite a fairly high level of support for policies over the previous ten years. Criticism of the attitude of officials was even more prominent, and there was a fair amount of understanding for the student demonstration. The general unwillingness in 1987 to participate in demonstrations under any circumstances shows the powerful effect of the Tienanmen events on Chinese political culture. The opinions of the local people's congresses imply that they are of some use, but they are not looked on as the bastions of popular government. Another question indicates that there is considerably greater hope for the people's congress system as a whole.[9]

The main point for our present purposes is that private opinion in mainland China, even on political questions too sensitive to be raised in the media, is fairly well developed. It is also rather critical of the government, though it shares the government's values of stability and, at least in 1987, was not inclined toward political action.

External Political Discourse

The last field of discourse to be considered is that of external political discourse, namely, discussion of Chinese politics aimed at influencing Chinese politics but originating beyond the government's control. This arena has also seen much development, with special advances in 1977-79 and after 1989. In the first period, reformers supporting Teng Hsiaop'ing had close relations with parts of the Hong Kong media, and the "insider stories" reported in *Cheng Ming* and *Ch'i-shih nien-tai* (The Seventies) influenced domestic politics in turn. External reporting played a major, complicated role in the Tienanmen demonstrations and their world effect. Since June 4, however, external political discourse has had a greatly increased significance, though it is impossible to know at this point what long-term effect it will have on Chinese politics.

---

[8]Wen Ch'i, *Chung-kuo cheng-chih wen-hua: Min-chu cheng-chih nan-ch'an te she-hui hsin-li yin-su* (Chinese political culture: The social psychological elements in the difficult birth of democratic politics) (Kunming: Yun-nan jen-min ch'u-pan-she, February 1989).
[9]Ibid., 66.

Table 1.1
Chinese Public Opinion, 1987

Questions:

1. What is your view and attitude toward the government? (Trust/Distrust)
2. Do you think that the political system needs to be reformed now? (Necessary/Unnecessary)
3. What is the citizen judgment of the political situation over the last ten years? (Satisfied/Dissatisfied)
4. How do you judge the utility of the local people's congress? (Very useful/Somewhat useful/No use)
5. How do citizens view the 1986 student demonstrations? (Tolerant/Critical)
6. No matter what I would not participate in a demonstration. (True/False)

Occupation	Question 1		Question 2		Question 3		Question 4			Question 5		Question 6	
	Trust	Distrust	Nec.	Unnec.	Satisf.	Dissat.	Very useful	Some useful	No use	Tolerant	Critical	True	False
Worker	68.39	21.27	57.39	23.21	68.94	6.06	15.89	47.12	20.82	48.49	33.67	61.96	38.04
Self-employed	69.66	18.37	44.82	28.45	65.89	5.43	26.67	34.58	17.50	51.28	25.21	47.72	52.28
Intellectual	68.33	19.22	78.89	12.66	66.24	9.90	8.45	46.13	28.87	66.90	16.34	66.78	33.22
Cadre	85.34	7.76	80.41	13.28	75.99	4.28	11.17	68.19	14.62	53.16	39.32	75.00	25.00
Peasant	56.73	37.30	56.17	23.94	70.09	9.00	16.56	32.70	28.67	48.91	26.56	52.85	47.15

Source: Wen Ch'i, *Chung-kuo cheng-chih wen-hua: Min-chu cheng-chih nan-ch'an te she-hui hsin-li yin-su* (Chinese political culture: The social psychological elements in the difficult birth of democratic politics) (Kunming: Yun-nan jen-min ch'u-pan-she, February 1989) 64, 68, 77, 83, 125.

Three major venues of external political discourse should be mentioned. The intellectuals and overseas students who enthusiastically supported the Tienanmen events and who were exiled or have not returned to mainland China comprise the core of the first. Regardless of its immediate domestic impact, this group has affected the attitude of host countries toward mainland China, and its reform plans for democracy and federalism may well become important articulations of radical progressive policies. The second venue is foreign concern about human rights and related issues. Because these concerns have linked domestic politics with foreign policy, they have forced the government to deal publicly with issues that it might otherwise have avoided. On the other hand, such foreign interference complicates some issues by adding an external dimension. The third venue was given special prominence by Governor Chris Patten's proposals for democratic reforms in Hong Kong. Because Hong Kong presents a unique case of external, insulated politics in the process of becoming internal (but still somewhat insulated) politics, Hong Kong would have been a very interesting outpost for Chinese political developments in any case. Governor Patten's proposals leaned heavily on the current, external situation, highlighting Peking's (Beijing's) current lack of control and making questions of political transition more problematic.

Even if external political discourse cannot persuade the political leadership to change, it can affect its agenda of issues that require public positions to be formulated, and, as domestic politics changes, such agenda-setting might set the horizons of future politics. However, while the external venue protects the participants, it also complicates their relationship to the mainstream of Chinese politics. On the one hand, they are outsiders in a political culture that has usually had an internal orientation. On the other hand, their proposals may become too rigid and too remote from the practical realities of politics.

If we summarize the changes in all four fields of discourse, it is clear that the pragmatic character of the post-Mao era has effected basic changes in mainland China's ideological and intellectual environment despite its continuing control over political discourse. Moreover, the four fields of discourse mentioned above are not so separate in reality. There is no great wall between policy advice and political pushing and shoving. Policy research institutes played a special role in the politics of the Peking Spring, and they suffered as a result. Even more obvious is the fact that the growth of private opinion will spill over into both public action (such as participation in demonstrations) and it will also induce a new style of public-oriented politics among the leadership. Although the relative freedom granted to expert discourse and private opinion reduces the oppressiveness of the continuing control of political discourse, it ultimately creates an intellectual context in which there are political pressures from all sides that want to express themselves.

Orthodoxy and Liberalization

Professor Adam Przeworski describes a democratic transition as the outcome of a bargain between two sides, each with two players.[10] On the government side there are the conservatives and the reformers, while on the societal side there are the moderates and the radicals. Democratic transition has two preconditions: the reformers and the moderates must come to an agreement, and they must control their respective camps; that is, the reformers must secure the compliance of the conservatives, and the moderates must secure the compliance of the radicals. Then a transition from an authoritarian regime to a democratic one can take place, with the reformers and the moderates both hoping to do well in the new elections, the conservatives receiving assurances that they will not be victims of the new regime, and the radicals accepting the transition as a necessary first step to their ultimate goals.

There is one fundamental problem in applying this model to a regime with a political orthodoxy: the bargain cannot take place. The orthodoxy does not permit the articulation of the societal positions, and there is no mechanism for discussion between government and opposition. The regime must be in a situation of prolonged weakness in order for societal forces to articulate themselves, and the very act of meeting and bargaining with the opposition already amounts to an acknowledgment of their right to participate in politics, and therefore is already an abandonment of the political orthodoxy. These conditions existed in Poland. The strength the Catholic Church there prevented a consolidation of Communist orthodoxy, and labor movements were handled by a mixture of concessions and control. The "Round Table" bargaining of early 1989, which included Solidarity and worked out the compromises for the upcoming election (held on June 4, 1989), was the only democratic transition in the Communist world to fit the Przeworski model of bargaining. The events in mainland China on June 4 put mainland China at the other end of the spectrum, and explicit bargaining is perhaps the least likely scenario for democratization.

The two major possibilities for democratic transition in mainland China are the two that have occurred in Communist countries other than

---

[10]Adam Przeworski, *Democracy and the Market* (Cambridge: Cambridge University Press, 1991).

Poland. The first is a process of reform and liberalization that culminates in the Communist party adopting democratic measures, and the other is the occurrence of a political crisis in which the regime chooses to compromise with the demonstrators rather than suppress them. The two possibilities are not exclusive, but it is worth noting that in Europe it has been the more authoritarian regimes that have ended in crisis (East Germany, Romania, Czechoslovakia), while the more reformist regimes have had smoother transitions. A tentative conclusion from the European experience would be that liberalization does reduce and channel disruptive societal pressures, even if it does not dissolve systemic alienation. Oppression increases the potential for a disruptive crisis.

The problem of whether or not liberalization in mainland China could gradually cross a democratic threshold seemed much easier before 1989.[11] Clearly the repression exercised on June 4 created a greater alienation of many people from the leadership. Also, the rejection of Communist regimes in elections and demonstrations throughout Europe raises the question of how alienated the Chinese public might be from the current regime, and what might they do if given a chance to express themselves politically.

Liberalization and Systemic Alienation

The view of liberalization held by most reformers within the leaderships of European Communist countries and by most informed observers before 1989 was that, as the leadership adopted more popular and less repressive policies, it would receive greater popular approval. As its popularity grew, it could then risk a relatively free election and expect to win. The electoral victory of reform Communism would then allow it to move even closer to the nonauthoritarian policies and methods of social democratic parties. This proved not to be the case. Although the existing leaderships of both countries were responsible for the adoption of democratic reforms, they lost badly in the ensuing elections. In the case of Hungary, the reform communists lost to groups who were not well organized and who did not have well-known leaders. In Mongolia, Bulgaria, and Romania the reform communists did better in the first rounds of elections, but they lost control of the political agenda and in Bulgaria they were defeated in later elections. Reform communists have come back into power in later elections in Lithuania, Poland, Hungary, and Russia, but under vastly different conditions of societal crisis. They could not recreate a smooth transition.

---

[11]See Brantly Womack, "Party-State Democracy: A Theoretical Exploration," *Issues & Studies* 25, no. 3 (March 1989): 37-57.

Why were the voters so ungrateful to the reformers? Why did they take the most radical alternatives available to them, rather than the more prudent course of gradual change? It is easy to say that they were rejecting totalitarian government, but in fact the governments they rejected were far from oppressive, and these same "totalitarians" had themselves introduced democratic elections. Part of the reason lies in the particular politics of each country, but I think that a general cause was a lack of identification with a political system that did not permit meaningful participation.

The logic of systemic political alienation would be as follows. If the citizens do not feel that they have participated in selecting the leadership, then they do not view the current leaders and their policies in terms of alternatives that they have rejected. Even if policies are liberalized and conditions are good, the public simply sees this as good luck rather than as the accomplishment of current leaders, because it is out of their control and they have not considered alternatives. By contrast, in democratic countries the leadership is rewarded and punished even for economic situations that are clearly beyond its control. The public in Communist countries does not like this situation of lack of political control, even if it appreciates the reformers as individuals. Therefore, given the chance to express itself, it rejects the reformers not because they are reformers but because of their continuity with the past. Meanwhile, the public is inexperienced and naive vis-à-vis the non-Communist alternatives presented by democratic politics, and so it is impressed by the novelty of new parties and media figures and by the magnificence of their promises.

Mainland China also faces the problem of systemic alienation. Even if people are impressed by the economic progress of the last fifteen years, they do not necessarily attribute successful policies to the current leaders. The demonstrations of 1989 were complicated phenomena, but they certainly showed that the public was not conservative in considering alternatives.

The 1987 opinion survey cited earlier asked whether or not the Party's leadership was necessary. The responses were obtained as listed in table 1.2.

On the one hand, the table shows a high degree of acceptance of Party leadership. Roughly 90 percent of respondents consider it necessary. But 10 percent in each category are already dissatisfied, and another 30 percent are only in favor of Party leadership at the present time. When does "the present stage" change? When an alternative is available? When a crisis occurs? The middle category can be considered a swing opinion group. Undoubtedly the whole spectrum of opinion has shifted significantly away from the Party since 1989 because of the large-scale public demonstrations that the center ultimately suppressed. Even if the

Table 1.2
Is Party Leadership Necessary?

Answers:	Worker	Self-employed	Intellectual	Cadre	Peasant
1. Always necessary	63.42	63.68	45.93	50.00	65.51
2. Necessary for this stage but maybe not in future	25.50	18.91	43.54	44.76	25.31
3. Used to be necessary but not now	11.07	17.41	10.53	5.24	9.18

Source: Wen, *Chung-kuo cheng-chih wen-hua*, 104.

demonstrators were not hostile to the government at the time, the fact that they had identified themselves with a movement that was negated by the regime must have increased systemic alienation.

Fear of Alternatives

Counterbalancing the effect of systemic alienation is a factor that was largely absent in the collapse of European Communism, namely, fear of what might happen if the current political system is rejected. There are three reasons why this fear would be more lively in mainland China than in Europe. First, the fact that the European economies were stagnant while mainland China's is booming means that people might think twice before approving of radical changes in policy. Secondly, the Cultural Revolution was a fairly recent reminder that chaos is possible, that students are not always right, and that criticizing the Party can lead to trouble. Lastly, the example of what has happened to European Communism since 1989, and especially the collapse of the Soviet Union, certainly gives Chinese citizens reasons to be concerned about the casual abandonment of their political system.

It is impossible to know how these concerns might interact with or counterbalance systemic alienation. Certainly political order and avoidance of chaos is a high value in Chinese political culture, but would it lead to more cautious public attitudes and participation if the public had an opportunity for participation? It is hard to guess in advance to what extent concerns about the future might translate into support for the present political structure. Perhaps people would simply be more worried. A sense of threat does not necessarily lead to a willingness to compromise. But it must be remembered that the East Europeans, especially the Poles, expected massive Western assistance and improved economic performance, and these will not be factors for the Chinese public. Regardless of whether the experience of European Communism will make the public more cautious, it almost certainly will make reformers within the government more cautious.

It can be expected that liberalizers do not want to put their own power at risk, and after the unexpected outcomes in European Communist transitions, the risks involved in transition, both for national welfare and for the liberalizers themselves, must seem greater than before. Nevertheless, as we have seen in the area of public discourse, liberalization creates societal pressures that push it forward. The closer the regime comes to the edge of democratization, the greater its own doubts must be, and yet the greater the societal (and world) pressure to keep on going and to cross the threshold. After the collapse of European Communism, the leap from the last stage of liberalization, in which the regime anticipates societal interests but maintains control to the first stage of democratization, in which the regime puts itself at risk, but under favorable conditions, must seem larger, more threatening, and less attractive. Under these tense circumstances it is not surprising that a crisis can become the midwife of a new political situation.

Crisis and Liberalization

It is impossible to predict the likelihood or outcome of a major popular demonstration like that of spring 1989. On the one hand, the difficulty and risk of participation has been proven, and better preparations have been made for crowd control. In addition, some unique factors occurred in succession in 1989—the death and funeral of Hu Yao-pang (Hu Yaobang), the May Fourth anniversary, and Mikhail Gorbachev's visit—that provided an unusually long inhibition of exercising government control. On the other hand, it is quite imaginable that situations will occur in which the central government will appear to be unable or unwilling to control demonstrations. There are certainly some people willing to take the risk of leadership, and once a demonstration starts the risk of merely participating is rather small. Moreover, it is rather easy to imagine a division within the government on how to handle demonstrations, and it is also possible that the media would again give mixed signals to the rest of the country concerning the official acceptability of demonstrations.

The basic challenge of popular demonstrations is that they confront a regime that is authoritarian in its structure and gradualist in its policies with a force that is popular and unstructured and makes demands that require radical policy changes. As Tang Tsou's analysis of Tienanmen makes clear, it can easily happen that no compromise is really possible, in that the minimum conditions of each side do not overlap.[12] On the

---

[12]Tang Tsou, "The Tiananmen Tragedy: The State-Society Relationship, Choices, and

other hand, neither side will want to repeat the tragedy, and so both sides in future popular crises now have a model both of what to do and what not to do.

Conclusion:
Dilemmas of the Self-Limited State

The existence of a liberal democratic state is as much an expression of the relationship between a limited public power and other societal interests as it is a question of the internal constitution of the state. A totalistic state, one in complete control of all societal activities, may be benign, but it cannot be liberal.

Teng Hsiao-p'ing's pragmatic orthodoxy has led the Chinese party-state to give rein to material incentive and initiative in Chinese society, and in the half-generation since 1979 this has produced remarkable growth and diversification in Chinese society. The mechanism of the reforms has been that of Party leadership rather than compromise with other societal forces, but the Party's leadership options are continually reshaped by the outcomes of its previous policies. The CCP now confronts a society that is still structured around its political leadership, but the material life and strength of the society has grown immeasurably more complex. The Party's options are limited by this new context even if it has no "social contract" with what it has created.

In the sphere of ideology, the Party's continuing monopoly of political discourse is conditioned by the emergence of expert discourse, private opinion, and external political discourse. Even if we ignore for the moment the considerable changes in the content and range of political discourse, the general intellectual function of political discourse has been transformed since the days when the words of "three newspapers and one magazine" set the language of every study group in mainland China. This is most clear in the few cases where the regime has tried to mimic the ideological control of earlier times, for instance, in the rural "socialist ideological education campaign" of 1990-92.[13] Political orthodoxy has become an empty church for at least six days of the week, and not everyone is listening on the seventh.

Mechanisms in Historical Perspective," in *Contemporary Chinese Politics in Historical Perspective*, ed. Brantly Womack (Cambridge: Cambridge University Press, 1991), 265-328. This essay is available in Chinese in Tsou Tang, *Erh-shih shih-chi Chung-kuo cheng-chih* (Chinese politics in the twentieth century) (Hong Kong: Oxford University Press, 1994), 135-203.

[13]Weixing Chen, "The CCP's Socialist Ideology Education Campaign 1990-92: A Funeral for Ideology?" *Issues & Studies* 29, no. 5 (May 1993): 70-88.

The diminution of the salience of political orthodoxy is appropriate for the pragmatic content emphasized by Teng Hsiao-p'ing. His "second revolution" is quite a bit different from the first.[14] It avoids abruptness, engages in institutional development, and rarely backtracks from reforms once they are adopted. His emphasis on economic development and on seeking truth from facts justifies a greater role for expertise in policy advising, and it turns public scrutiny away from private matters. There is not as much need for ideological purity at the primary stage of socialism, and the next stage does not arrive for a hundred years. The gradualness of reform is natural to pragmatism because a pragmatic ideology is less certain of and less committed to its next step than a more dogmatic ideology. If one is searching for the next step to take, it should be a relatively small one. The resulting societal diversification would be difficult to reverse, and in any case Teng Hsiao-p'ing has not shown any inclination to reverse it.

Nevertheless, a pragmatic orthodoxy is still an orthodoxy in form. It reflects the Party's political monopoly in the arena of ideology, and by requiring compliance from the public it prevents a sense of citizen participation and responsibility in politics. Even though the public is happy about the new policies and would rather concentrate on economic matters, the Party's political and ideological tutelage creates a systemic alienation. In turn, systemic alienation makes the public's behavior less predictable and therefore makes the transition from Party monopoly to democratic forms more risky. Neither continued gradual reform nor popular crisis presents an easy solution to the problem of democratic transition, but of course gradual reform is more desirable since it does not risk chaos. The transition from orthodoxy to a more open political arena remains a leap.

So the very difficult challenge of the politics of ideas in mainland China, from the point of view of an enlightened center, is how to expand the political realm and decrease the oppressiveness of orthodoxy while at the same time minimizing challenge and preventing crises. Clearly there is no easy solution. The question is whether the theoretical impossibility of squaring the circle can be resolved into a practical process of infinite approximation.

---

[14]Indeed, in Teng's first usage of the term "second revolution" to describe his policies he contrasts his reforms with the violence of the Cultural Revolution: "I consider reform to be a kind of revolution, although certainly not a revolution like the Cultural Revolution." See *Teng Hsiao-p'ing wen-hsüan* 3:82.

2

The Political Implications of the CCP's "Socialist Market Economy" Proposal

An-chia Wu

The idea of creating a "socialist market economy" was first proposed at the Chinese Communist Party's (CCP's) Fourteenth National Congress in October 1992 after long years of discussion and debate among CCP theoreticians. In March the following year, at the First Session of the Eighth National People's Congress (NPC), it was decided that the socialist market economy should be written into mainland China's constitution to serve as a guiding principle for economic structural reform. This chapter examines the background of the socialist market economy proposal and its ideological and political significance.

Historical Background

It was Lenin, rather than Marx or Engels, who first used the terms "commodity economy," "market economy," and "planned economy." On many occasions in the period shortly after the Russian Revolution, Lenin proposed that the commodity economy be eliminated. He maintained that capitalism would inevitably be replaced by socialism and that the new society would have a planned economy. Nevertheless, he admitted that to rely entirely on state planning would be unrealistic. Under his New Economic Policy (NEP), free trade was permitted and the commercial principle (also known as the market principle) was observed by state-run enterprises. However, the NEP was suspended at the end of the 1920s and Stalin switched to a planned economy. From that time on, the commodity economy has been regarded as the antithesis of a planned economy. Although Stalin also spoke about commodity production and the law of value, he nevertheless strictly limited their application.

The CCP adopted the Stalinist model of economic development and restricted the role of the market. This situation only began to change after December 1978, when the Third Plenary Session of the CCP's Eleventh Central Committee decided to permit a market element in the planned economy.[1] Then, in June 1981, the CCP admitted that the production and exchange of commodities could also exist in a socialist society,[2] and that the law of value should be observed. No mention was made of a commodity economy, however, as it was still regarded as a capitalist phenomenon based on the system of private ownership.

There was still no mention of a market economy at the CCP's Twelfth National Congress in September 1982, which simply called for the planned economy to be "supplemented" by market regulation.[3] However, the market economy was already a topic of academic discussion in mainland China, and some scholars had mentioned the concept of a "socialist market economy."[4] The first official document to accept the concept of a "commodity economy" was the "Decision on Reform of the Economic Structure" adopted at the Third Plenary Session of the CCP's Twelfth Central Committee in October 1984. This defined the socialist economy as a "planned commodity economy based on public ownership."[5] This statement marked a theoretical breakthrough for the CCP, and by October 1987, at the Party's Thirteenth National Congress, Chao Tzu-yang (Zhao Ziyang) formally proposed the development of a "socialist planned commodity economy" which would integrate planning with the market.[6]

---

[1] Ch'en Yün, "Questions Concerning Planning and the Market" (March 8, 1979), in *San-chung-ch'üan-hui i-lai chung-yao wen-hsien hsüan-pien* (A collection of selected important documents issued since the Third Plenary Session) (Changchun: Kirin People's Publishing House, 1982), 68-71. This is an outline of Ch'en's speech at the Third Plenary Session of the CCP's Eleventh Central Committee.

[2] "On Questions of Party History—Resolution on Certain Questions in the History of Our Party Since the Founding of the People's Republic of China," *Beijing Review* 24, no. 27 (July 6, 1981): 37. The Resolution said that it is necessary to have a planned economy and at the same time give play to the supplementary, regulatory role of the market on the basis of public ownership. It also urged the promotion of commodity production and exchange on a socialist basis.

[3] Hu Yaobang [Hu Yao-pang], "Create a New Situation in All Fields of Socialist Modernization," *Beijing Review* 25, no. 37 (September 13, 1982): 19-20.

[4] *Ch'iu-so* (Exploration) (Changsha), 1993, no. 6:17-19. The idea of a socialist market economy had been suggested at two symposiums in 1979, one in March in Chengtu (Chengdu), Szechwan (Sichuan) and one in April in Wusih (Wuxi), Kiangsu (Jiangsu). However, the term was not accepted by the leadership which at that time preferred the rather vague concept "planned commodity economy."

[5] The Decision states that the "full development of a commodity economy is an indispensable stage in the economic growth of society." *Beijing Review* 27, no. 44 (October 29, 1984): vii.

[6] Zhao Ziyang, "Advance Along the Road of Socialism with Chinese Characteristics," *Beijing Review* 30, no. 45 (November 9-15, 1987): xi-xii.

Although Chao did not say which was to be given priority—planning or the market—considerable emphasis was obviously given to the market, as the Congress passed a decision to the effect that the market should be guided by the state and enterprises should be guided by the market.

The Thirteenth Congress sparked off a long debate over the relationship between planning and the market which focused on two questions: whether the economic reform should be market-oriented and whether it should be aimed at building a socialist market economy. Some scholars expressed the fear that economic reform was generating capitalism in mainland China. Teng Hsiao-p'ing (Deng Xiaoping) addressed these questions during his tour of South China in early 1992:

> Whether there should be more planning or more market factors is not the essential difference between socialism and capitalism. The planned economy is not equivalent to socialism because there is planning under capitalism too, and the market economy is not equivalent to capitalism because there is a market under socialism too.[7]

A formal proposal to establish a socialist market economy was finally put forward at the Party's Fourteenth Congress in October 1992. It was pointed out that the establishment of a socialist market economy would involve changes in mainland China's economic structure and the readjustment of certain policies. In view of this, it was suggested that a general plan be drawn up and carried out step by step.[8]

At a plenary session of the Politburo held in May 1993, it was decided to set up a working group to draft regulations for the new system. At the first meeting of the working group, Chiang Tse-min (Jiang Zemin) said that the regulations should be formulated under the guidance of Teng's theories on the building of a socialist market economy and the Political Report delivered at the Fourteenth Congress. After eight revisions, the draft was adopted at the Third Plenary Session of the Party's Fourteenth Central Committee on November 14, 1993 under the title, "Decision of the CCP Central Committee on Some Issues Concerning the Establishment of a Socialist Market Economic Structure."[9] The preliminary framework of

---

[7]Deng Xiaoping, "Gist of Speeches Made in Wuchang, Shenzhen, Zhuhai and Shanghai" (From January 18 to February 21, 1992), *Beijing Review* 37, no. 6-7 (February 7-20, 1994): 11.

[8]Jiang Zemin, "Accelerating Reform and Opening-Up," *Beijing Review* 35, no. 43 (October 26-November 1, 1992): 18.

[9]Tsou Ai-kuo and Cheng Ch'ing-tung, "The Grand Program Toward the New Century," *Fu-yin pao-k'an tzu-liao—Chung-kuo kung-ch'an-tang* (Reprinted Newspaper and Magazine Materials—The Chinese Communist Party) (Peking), December 1993, no. 12:26-28. For the full text of the "Decision on Some Issues Concerning the Establishment of a Socialist Market Economic Structure," see *Beijing Review* 36, no. 47 (November 22-28, 1993): 12-31.

the new system is supposed to be in place before the end of the century. At the Second Session of the Eighth NPC in March 1994, the CCP leadership reaffirmed its decision to set up a socialist market economy.

Ideological Revolution

The creation of a socialist market economy involves a theoretical and ideological struggle within the CCP, and will only be possible after the Party has cast off its "leftist" shackles. The antileftist argument was presented in three important books published in mainland China in 1992 and 1993—*Li-shih te ch'ao-liu* (The trend of history), *Fang-"tso" pei-wang-lu* (Memorandum on guarding against "leftism"), and *Chung-kuo tso-huo* (The leftist disaster in China)[10]—which provided an insight into the heated debate within the Party over the orientation, speed, and scope of reform. While touring South China in 1992, Teng had hoped to call a halt to this debate when he said:

> At present, Rightist tendencies are affecting us, as are "Leftist" ones. But it is the "Leftist" tendencies that are deep-seated. Some theorists and politicians try to scare the public with political labels. That is not Rightist, but "Leftist." "Leftism" carries a revolutionary color, giving the impression that the more "Left," the more revolutionary. "Leftist" tendencies led to dire consequences in the history of the Party. Some fine things were destroyed overnight. Rightism may ruin socialism, so can "Leftism." China should maintain vigilance against the Right but should primarily guard against the "Left." The Right exists as displayed in the turmoil. The "Left" also lives. To regard reform and opening as introducing and developing capitalism and to see the danger of peaceful evolution coming mainly from areas of the economy are "Leftist" tendencies.[11]

Teng's remarks to a certain extent helped to build a consensus within the Party on the establishment of a market economy in mainland China. What remains to be done is to eliminate the old ideological bonds which hinder the establishment of the new system.

The CCP regime has not yet worked out how it will resist Western influence, both ideological and political, during the course of establishing a socialist market economy. Although the new system will facilitate the absorption of more capital, technology, and management expertise from the Western capitalist countries, it is also creating confusion among Party

---

[10]*Li-shih te ch'ao-liu* (The trend of history) (Peking: Chinese People's University, April 1992); Chao Shih-lin, ed., *Fang-"tso" pei-wang-lu* (Memorandum on guarding against "leftism") (Taiyuan, Shansi: Shu-hai ch'u-pan-she, 1992); Wen Yü, *Chung-kuo tso-huo* (The leftist disaster in China) (Peking: Chao-hua ch'u-pan-she, February 1993).

[11]Deng, "Gist of Speeches," 13.

members as to whether they are supposed to be practicing socialism or capitalism. Some fear that increased emphasis on the market will lead to the collapse of the Communist regime, as reform led to the demise of Communism in the Soviet Union and Eastern Europe. In an effort to clear away this ideological confusion, the CCP authorities have explained the downfall of Communism in Moscow and Eastern Europe as the result of economic failure. The CCP leaders also attribute political changes in these countries to the West's efforts at "peaceful evolution." They maintain that the reforms undertaken in the Soviet Union and Eastern Europe were not aimed at reforming socialism but at effecting a transition from socialism to capitalism.[12] Government corruption is another reason put forward by the CCP for the collapse of Communism. Indeed, the main emphasis is on internal factors as the main cause of the collapse of Communism in Europe; "peaceful evolution" is seen as a secondary, external factor.[13] Nevertheless, the leaders still urge a protracted war against peaceful evolution,[14] though they realize that it is essential to gain a thorough understanding of the West's peaceful evolution efforts so that the measures taken to counter them do not have an adverse effect on mainland China itself, especially on its economic development. Rapid economic growth through accelerated reform and opening-up is seen as the most effective way of countering peaceful evolution.[15]

Actually, the CCP authorities have admitted that the "socialist" market economy is no different from a "capitalist" one, although Party members are still required to pay lip service to socialism. As Ting Kuan-ken (Ding Guangen) has pointed out, in both systems, all economic activities are directly or indirectly related to the market, and the market mechanism is essential for the circulation of the major elements of production and for the allocation of resources; enterprises have full autonomy and are free to participate in the market and manage production as they wish; the government regulates enterprises by adjusting levels of taxation, prices, and the money supply rather than intervening directly in production; and businesses are run in accordance with the law.[16]

---

[12]Ch'ang Yen-t'ing, "Some Questions Concerning Rectifying the Work Style of the Party and the Building of a Clean Government" (Part I) (June 15, 1992), *Chung-kuo ta-lu yen-chiu* (Mainland China Studies) (Taipei) 36, no. 8 (August 1993): 91.

[13]Ibid., 92; "Ch'iao Shih's Speech at the Commencement of the Central Party School" (January 6, 1993), *Issues & Studies* (Taipei) 30, no. 3 (March 1994): 136.

[14]Jiang, "Accelerating Reform and Opening-Up," 29.

[15]Ting Kuan-ken, "A Few Words on Studying the Report to the Party's Fourteenth Congress" (A document circulated within the CCP). Ting is a member of the Politburo and the Central Committee Secretariat.

[16]Ibid.

However, although the CCP leaders have deliberately played down the differences between socialism and capitalism, they are realistic about applying capitalist methods. For example, Ting Kuan-ken had this to say on the subject:

> In order to emancipate people's minds and speed up the pace of reform and opening-up, we should have a correct understanding of capitalism, boldly absorb and draw lessons from all the fruits of civilization created by human society, and absorb and draw lessons from the various countries in the world, including the developed capitalist countries, from their advanced management and administration methods which manifest the general rule of modern social production and commodity economy. We should neither blindly worship capitalism nor stubbornly discriminate against it. Instead, we should understand and utilize it correctly and critically inherit it. More than seventy years ago, Lenin criticized the ideology of refusing to learn from capitalism. He said: "We cannot imagine any kind of socialism other than the one built on the basis of the experiences and lessons obtained from the enormous capitalist culture." In building socialism, we should absorb and draw lessons from the useful things of capitalism, and build the "mansion" of socialism with the "materials" of capitalism. Only by boldly absorbing and drawing lessons from the fruits of the civilization of human society will socialism be able to create a labor productivity higher than that of capitalism and claim a superiority over capitalism and eventually defeat it.[17]

Believing that persuading Party members and cadres to accept Teng's theory of "socialism with Chinese characteristics" is the key to political stability in mainland China, the CCP leadership is working hard to promote Teng's theory. The CCP Central Committee document, "The Main Points of Propaganda Work in 1993," laid great stress on Teng's theory and called for the latest volume of Teng's works to be published within the year. Also on the agenda were a "study program" for "socialism with Chinese characteristics," a "simple reader" on the subject for grassroots-level Party members, two national meetings on propaganda work, two national theoretical conferences based on the summary of Teng's theory contained in Chiang Tse-min's report to the Party's Fourteenth Congress, and seminars for provincial department-level cadres and propaganda department heads.[18]

Prominent members of the leadership have always been ready to heap praise on Teng's line on reform and opening-up. In his speech at the commencement of the CCP Central Party School on January 6, 1993, Ch'iao Shih (Qiao Shi) described Teng's socialism with Chinese characteristics

---

[17]Ibid.

[18]"The Main Points of Propaganda Work in 1993," *Issues & Studies* 30, no. 2 (February 1994): 116-27.

theory as rich in content and a creative development of Marxism. He urged Party members to study the theory in earnest and not merely use it as a slogan.[19] In another speech at the Central Party School the following month, Ch'iao urged the whole Party to "arm itself" with Teng's theory which he said would ensure success in socialist modernization.[20] In November, Chiang Tse-min stressed the connection between Teng's theory and Marxism-Leninism and Mao Tse-tung (Mao Zedong) thought,[21] while at a mass rally in December, he simply referred to Teng's theory as the heir to Mao thought.[22]

In order to establish Teng's theory as the guiding principle for the reforms, all the ideas and policies advanced by Teng since the Third Plenary Session of the CCP's Eleventh Central Committee in 1978 were written into the revised constitution adopted at the March 1993 session of the Eighth NPC, although Teng was not referred to directly. Then, at the Third Plenary Session of the CCP's Fourteenth Central Committee in November that year, Teng's theories of "emancipating people's minds" and "seeking truth from facts" were reaffirmed as the guiding principles for the reform and opening-up policy and for the Party as a whole.

However, since reform of the economic structure entails a profound revolution in the economic base and many aspects of the superstructure, it is bound to upset the various interest ties that were either inherent in the old structure or are products of the transition from old to new. Difficulties and obstructions of one kind or another are unavoidable. In other words, as the regime itself admits, some of the inconsistencies and problems that have arisen in economic development stem from the fact that the drawbacks of the old structure have not been thoroughly eradicated and the new structure has yet to take shape.[23] One manifestation of such problems is the way that some people claim that reform and opening-up has deviated from Mao Tse-tung thought and fear an increase in foreign influence. In his speech to the Central Party School in February 1993, Ch'iao Shih

---

[19]"Ch'iao Shih's Speech at the Commencement," 138.

[20]Ch'iao Shih, "Persist in Arming the Whole Party with the Theory of Building Socialism with Chinese Characteristics—Speech at the Opening Ceremony of the CCP Central Party School in the Spring of 1993" (February 23, 1993), a document circulated within the CCP.

[21]Chiang Tse-min, "Speech at the Meeting on Studying the Third Volume of *Selected Works of Teng Hsiao-ping*" (November 2, 1993), *Ch'iu-shih* (Seeking Truth) (Peking), November 11, 1993, 5.

[22]Chiang Tse-min, "Speech at a Mass Rally in Commemoration of the Centenary of Mao Tse-tung's Birth," *Ta Kung Pao* (Hong Kong), December 27, 1993, 7.

[23]"Decision on Some Issues Concerning the Establishment of a Socialist Market Economic Structure," 12.

mentioned this problem and prescribed intensified theoretical study as a way of persuading cadres that this is not the case.[24]

In his speech at the mass rally mentioned above, Chiang Tse-min described Teng as a loyal comrade-in-arms of Mao Tse-tung and the most prominent successor and developer of Mao Tse-tung thought. He stressed the way that both Teng and Mao formulated their policies in line with the specific situation in China. To support this argument, Chiang said that mainland China had deliberately avoided patterning its version of the market after the Western model in order to prevent the intrusion of decadent Western ideology. As further proof of Teng's credentials as Mao's ideological heir, he pointed to the way Teng Hsiao-p'ing had, like Mao, emphasized self-reliance for mainland China.[25]

From the above, it is clear that no mainland Chinese leader dares to openly admit deviating from Mao Tse-tung thought, which is the theoretical basis of the regime's legitimacy. Of course, this does not mean to say that they are not selective when it comes to "inheriting" Mao's doctrines. In fact, major parts of Mao's thought have been discarded, including the theory of class struggle, the use of political movements to promote economic development, and Mao's blind xenophobia. All that has been preserved is nationalism, self-reliance, and "seeking truth from facts." Mao's theories are now applied in a pragmatic way, and in particular they are used as a rallying point for safeguarding national sovereignty and dignity. The greater the challenge from without, the more frequent the references to Mao's thought.

Although the leadership is trying to link Teng's theories with Mao's thought, there are remarkable differences between the two. For example, some of Teng's innovations, such as the market economy, the shareholding system, the bankruptcy law, stock markets, and the toleration of the non-state sector, can by no stretch of the imagination be described as developments of Mao's thought, but are rather negations of Mao's ultraleftist ideology. What Teng shares with Mao are the ideals and goals of socialism, a conviction of the need to maintain state sovereignty and keep the military under Party control, and a belief in grooming successors. Among these Maoist doctrines, nationalism is the one that is most consistently upheld, being used to suppress demands for democracy in mainland China and attempts by the West to shape mainland China in its own image.[26]

---

[24]See note 20 above.

[25]See note 22 above.

[26]Chiang Tse-min, "Speech at the 1993 National Conference on Judicial Work" (December 24, 1993), a document circulated within the CCP.

Political Implications of the Revolution

The shift from a planned economy to a socialist market economy will have a number of important political implications for mainland China. It will be increasingly difficult for the CCP to maintain Party operation and discipline, there will be a strong demand for legislation and legislative supervision, and a need to cut back the bureaucracy. The public sector of the economy will decline, relations between the central and local governments will likely become increasingly strained, and the change will entail a drastic transformation in the thinking of the military. What is more, mainland China's links with the international community will become closer.

Impact on the Party

Party cadres have yet to adjust their thinking to cope with the demands of the reform policy. The Party organization and its activities are all products of the planned economy, with its centralization of power, lack of democracy, integration of Party and government functions, and prevalence of formalism and bureaucratism. All these will be obstacles to the establishment of a market economy. To cope with the new economic structure, Party members will have to adjust their way of thinking and change the Party's organizational structure and type of activities.

The second challenge the Party will face is how it is to define its role. The CCP has long seen itself as the vanguard of the working class, cherished an ideal of modesty, honesty, and selflessness, and advocated collectivism and Communism. However, the growth of the market economy has encouraged some types of mentality which are the exact opposite of Communism, including money-worship, a change in the relationship between inferiors and superiors to one simply between employer and employee, and a growth of individualism. The problem for the Party is how to preserve its traditional position as the vanguard of the working class while advocating a socialist market economy.

Another problem the Party faces is how to deal with Party cadres who use their political power to enrich themselves.

Legal Aspects

A proper legal system is essential if the market economy is to develop smoothly. The NPC Standing Committee has given top priority to economic legislation, and it aims to pass a complete body of laws necessary for the operation of the socialist market economy before the end of the current NPC in 1998. Major areas of legislation include regulating the operation of the market and maintaining market order, strengthening the government's ability to exercise macroeconomic control, the institution of a social security system, and the development of basic industries. Both Ch'iao Shih and T'ien Chi-yün (Tian Jiyun), respectively chairman and vice chairman of the NPC Standing Committee, have emphasized the importance of the NPC's role in supervising the government. For example, at a meeting for chairmen and vice chairmen of NPC special committees in April 1993, Ch'iao underlined the importance of the law, saying that things will go wrong if they are not supervised by the law.[27] Later, in conversation with leaders of local people's congress standing committees on July 3, he called for more efforts to be made in supervising the various levels of the government, the courts, and the procuratorate.[28] Echoing Ch'iao's remarks, T'ien Chi-yün said that all state organizations and their staffs should accept supervision and that it is a "decadent feudalistic mentality" to hold the view that one's power should not be restricted, because history has proved that unrestricted power will result in corruption and even good cadres may go to the bad if they are not constantly supervised. He also criticized the ineffectiveness of the people's congresses' supervisory work and the failure of law enforcement personnel to abide by the law themselves, saying that he had heard many complaints about this.[29]

The State Council is also paying close attention to the legal aspects of the socialist market economy. In its "Decision on Strengthening Government Legal Work," the State Council lists the major tasks thus: strengthening leadership cadres' consciousness of the law; the introduction of a legal framework for administration in order to raise efficiency and ensure consistent and stable policy implementation; correct handling of the relationship between legal work and reform so as to lay a good foundation for the reform measures; discontinuation of the practice of exempting certain departments or localities from the need to abide by the law; improvement of the interpretation and collation of administrative rules and regulations; and supervision of the government at all levels by the Party, the people's congresses, the judiciary, the political consultative conferences, the democratic parties, public opinion, and the masses.[30]

The creation of a proper legal system is beneficial not only to the establishment of a socialist market economy but also to political stability in general. It will help smooth the way for the reform measures and

---

[27]*People's Daily* (Overseas edition), May 1, 1993, 1.

[28]Ibid., July 5, 1993, 1.

[29]*Wen Wei Po* (Hong Kong), July 4, 1993, 3. T'ien's remarks were reprinted in the *People's Daily* on July 5 though some of his more hard-hitting comments were omitted.

[30]"Decision on Strengthening Government Legal Work," a classified State Council document *Kuo-fa* (1993) No. 72 (October 9, 1993).

various economic development projects and this will lay a good foundation for economic growth. It will also prevent individual leaders from abusing their power for private gain or acting in a dictatorial fashion, thus helping to allay people's dissatisfaction with CCP rule.

One obstacle to this task is the way that cadres tend to handle their work by administrative means, without regard for the law. Besides this, the Party committees still have a lot of influence and the Party always overrides the law.

Cutting the Bureaucracy

Reform of the bureaucracy is an essential prerequisite for further market-oriented economic reform. Efforts are to be made to change the functions of government agencies, sort out their relations with each other, streamline the administration, reduce staff, and improve efficiency. Enterprise management is to be separated from government administration, so that enterprises can become autonomous entities operating according to market principles. Meanwhile, regulatory functions are also to be shifted to the market so that it can play a better role in resource allocation.

Chiang Tse-min has described this reform as a revolution, and he has pointed out that it will take some time to complete.[31] Mainland China has over 34 million government employees, and the number increases by about one million each year.[32] Salaries for these people consume an average of 40 percent of total government revenue. These numbers cannot be reduced at a sweep, however, as throwing large numbers of people out of work would cause enormous social problems.

Decline of the Planned Sector of the Economy

It is the failure of the planned economy—the very foundation of the CCP's one-party dictatorship—that has prompted the move toward a socialist market economy. As the role of the market increases, the planned sector is sure to decline. A planned economy is applicable only under certain historical conditions—for example, when the economy is underdeveloped and construction is carried out on a small scale (such as during the period of the First Five-Year Plan); when there is only a simple economic and industrial structure (when the nonpublic sector is small and heavy industry is emphasized); when there is a single develop-

---

[31]"Chiang Tse-min's Speech at the National Work Conference on Government Restructuring" (July 23, 1993), a document circulated within the CCP, translated in *Issues & Studies* 30, no. 6 (June 1994): 119-33.

[32]Lan Yeh, ed., *Chung-kuo cheng-fu ta ts'ai-yüan* (The great streamlining of the Chinese government) (Chungking: Chungking University Press, March 1993), 17.

ment goal (in wartime or under threat of war, or in order to guarantee food supply); at a time of serious natural disaster or economic crisis; or when the country is following a policy of isolation. Since these conditions do not exist today, the allocation of resources should be decided by the market instead of by administrative planning.[33]

Although the CCP still claims that the public ownership system should predominate in the economy, the public sector is obviously declining. According to mainland Chinese statistics, the public sector was responsible for 54.6 percent of total industrial output in 1990, compared to 77 percent in 1978. In the period 1980-92, public sector industrial output grew by only 8 percent, while the nonpublic sector showed an 18 percent increase. It was the nonpublic sector that was responsible for the high growth rate of the mainland Chinese economy in the 1980s, and since the reforms began, the ratio of the output growth rates in the public, collective, and other sectors of the economy has been 1:1.2:2.2. The growth rate of the nonpublic sector is more than double that of the public sector. In some places, the introduction of the shareholding system is causing the public sector to merge to some extent with the nonpublic sector. As a result, some public sector enterprises are less than 51 percent state-owned. These developments cause some people to speculate that further progress toward a market economy will make it impossible for the CCP to support the myth that the public sector is the mainstay of the economy. Some argue for outright privatization, though there are still some dogmatists who believe that in order to preserve socialism it is necessary to restrict the growth of the nonpublic sector and maintain the supremacy of public sector by, for example, decreeing that the state should hold not less than a 51 percent share in all state-owned enterprises.[34] The socialist market economy policy will only exacerbate the decline of the public sector and so it is actually a "capitalist" reform under socialist guise.

Strained Central-Local Relations

The distribution of revenue between the central and local governments has varied as policy has veered from centralization to decentralization and between regulation and deregulation. The traditional, highly-centralized socialist system did succeed in mobilizing resources for industrialization

---

[33]Liu Kuo-kuang, "Questions Concerning the Socialist Market Economy" (October 28, 1992), a document circulated within the CCP.

[34]Yang Shang-te and Yen K'a-lin, "How to Understand 'Taking the Public Ownership System as the Main Body'," *Ching-chi jih-pao* (Economic Daily) (Peking), November 2, 1993, 1.

in mainland China, but it had a fatal weakness in that it encouraged inefficiency and resources were poorly distributed.

Although the reforms have helped to improve efficiency and enhance economic results, the decentralization measures have limited the state's financial resources and reduced its ability to exercise overall control over the economy. This has led to a rethink of the roles and functions of the central and local governments.

The decline in central power is mainly due to the local governments' newfound autonomy and the lack of regulations that would allow the central government to exercise effective control over them. Using their new powers, some localities have even engaged themselves in activities that violate central government policy. For example, construction projects are needlessly duplicated, investment is undertaken without due consideration, development zones are created at will, and local protectionism is rife. This has created disorder in society.

The respective functions and powers of the central and local governments have not been clearly defined, with Article 3 of mainland China's constitution merely stipulating that the initiative of local governments should be brought into play under the unified leadership of the central government. This vagueness inevitably results in conflicts between the two levels of government. On the one hand, the central government interferes in affairs that should be decided by the localities, and on the other, local governments sometimes disregard central policies in order to protect their own interests. Under these circumstances, the central government tends to redefine the functions of local governments at will, while the local governments, fearing that central policy may change at any time, pursue short-term gains.

Another factor that has had an adverse effect on central-local relations is the center's lack of consistency in enforcing control over the economy. When the center is keeping the economy on a tight rein, local governments and enterprises find it difficult to pursue their own interests, but once restrictions are removed, the economy quickly heats up and gets out of control. The CCP leaders are well aware of the dangers of strained central-local relations. Chiang Tse-min has pointed out that the major problems in economic matters should be solved quickly to avoid great disasters.[35]

Central-local conflict is currently reflected in controversy over the latest tax reform proposals. In March 1994, the Second Session of the

---

[35]Chu Ta, "Chiang Tse-min Gave out Signs of Warning," *Kuang-chiao ching* (Wide Angle) (Hong Kong), no. 250 (July 1993): 6.

Table 2.1
The Division of Fiscal Revenue and Administrative Power Between the Central and Local Governments Under the Proposed Tax-Sharing System

	Fixed fiscal revenue	Administrative responsibility
Central government	Customs duties; consumption tax; income tax of state-owned enterprises; product tax; revenues from banks, railways and insurance companies; income tax paid by financial organizations licensed by the Peopel's Bank of China; special income from the increase of tax on tobacco	National defense, foreign relations, armed police force, key construction projects; administrative expenditures of state organs; repayment of capital and interest on domestic and foreign debts
Local governments	Business tax; income tax of local enterprises; individual income tax; agricultural trade tax; tax on urban maintenance and construction; market trade tax; bonus tax	Local political, economic, cultural, and security affairs
Shared by central and local governments	Value-added tax; resources tax (marine resources tax paid to central government); stock transaction tax; industrial and commercial consolidated tax	—

Source: "The Product of Reconciliation and Compromise, Resistance from the Coastal Areas Is Still Strong," *Ming Pao* (Hong Kong), November 29, 1993, A9, cited in Chen Te-sheng, "Peking's Economic Policy After the Third Plenum of the CCP's Fourteenth Central Committee," *Issues & Studies* (Taipei) 30, no. 2 (February 1994): 23.

Eighth NPC decided to change the current system under which local authorities are responsible for their own finances after handing over a fixed proportion of their revenues to the state. The main innovations in the tax reform are a revenue-sharing system based on a rational division of functions and powers between the central and local authorities, a system under which certain taxes will be paid to the central government and others to the local authority, and the establishment of separate central and local taxation systems. Under the new system, there will be a turnover tax of which the main component will be a value-added tax (see table 2.1).[36] These are only regulations in principle and the authorities may encounter problems when they put them into force. The central government's share of total revenue decreased sharply during the Fourth and Fifth Five-Year Plan periods, though it started to rise again during the Sixth Five-Year

[36]Li Peng, "Report on the Work of the Government," *Beijing Review* 37, no. 14 (April 4-10, 1994): viii.

Table 2.2
Ratios of Central and Local Government Revenues and Expenditures in Mainland China (1978-92)

Unit: %

Year	Revenue ratio		Expenditure ratio	
	Center	Localities	Center	Localities
The First Five-Year Plan period	45.4	55.6	74.1	25.9
The Second Five-Year Plan period	22.7	77.3	48.1	51.9
1963-65	27.6	72.4	59.7	40.3
The Third Five-Year Plan period	31.2	68.8	61.1	38.9
The Fourth Five-Year Plan period	14.7	85.3	54.2	45.8
The Fifth Five-Year Plan period	15.6	84.4	49.4	50.6
The Sixth Five-Year Plan period	30.6	69.4	48.8	51.2
The Seventh Five-Year Plan period	39.5	60.5	39.6	60.4

Source: *Chung-kuo t'ung-chi nien-chien 1991* (Statistical yearbook of China 1991) (Peking: Chung-kuo t'ung-chi ch'u-pan-she, August 1991), 221, cited in *Chung-kuo kuo-chia neng-li pao-kao* (A report on the national capacity of China), ed. Wang Shao-kuang and Hu An-kang (Shenyang: Liaoning People's Publishing House, December 1993), 36.

Notes:
1. Revenue includes foreign loans.
2. Central and local revenues listed here are actual amounts collected, not figures calculated according to the financial system.

Plan period (see table 2.2). Whether the new system will work depends on whether it gains the support of local governments.

The CCP's current policy is to strengthen the power of the central government in order to maintain social stability. But overconcentration of power is likely to hamper rapid economic growth and thus lead to further instability. Only greater local autonomy will ensure that living standard rise, thus guaranteeing long-term social stability.

Impact on the Military

The military, just like the civilian population, has been affected by the changes in the economic structure. Many soldiers have begun to regard business as a more attractive profession than military service. Eager to make more money, they collect information about economic affairs and read books such as *Cheng-ch'üan chih-shih* (Knowledge about negotiable securities), *Ku-p'iao ju-men* (The ABC of stocks), and *T'ou-tzu chih-nan* (A guide to investment). Their interest in money-making has led some of them to abuse their power for private gain.[37] In some places, the military has accumulated formidable economic power which has enabled it to build close ties with local political and economic elites. The craze for making money has created difficulties with discipline and morale within the armed forces and also hampered recruitment.

Closer Links with the World Economy

Market-oriented reforms will inevitably increase mainland China's involvement in the global economy, and its business operations will have to be brought in line with international norms. Ch'ien Ch'i-ch'en (Qian Qichen), Peking's vice premier and foreign minister, made the following remarks in this regard:

> In foreign trade, we need to gain access to the international market for a wide range of our products and to enable our enterprises to compete on the international market. We should become familiar with international conventions and international trade rules and regulations, and must abide by them. On the other hand, we should learn to use international conventions, rules, and regulations to protect ourselves. Therefore, our enterprises must compete on the international market.[38]

The development of a market economy will force enterprises to improve their production and management methods. For example, if mainland China joins the General Agreement on Tariffs and Trade (GATT), it will have to open its markets, forcing domestic enterprises to improve product quality in order to enhance their competitiveness. Mainland China will no longer be able to adopt an isolationist policy. The closer its relations with the outside world, the more it will be affected by the outside world.

---

[37]*Cheng-kung chuan-k'an* (Political Work Journal) (Sian), 1993, no. 3:7-8.

[38]"Ch'ien Ch'i-ch'en's Report on the International Situation" (September 5, 1992), *Issues & Studies* 30, no. 1 (January 1994): 115.

Conclusion

The shift from a planned economy to a socialist market economy will have a far-reaching impact on mainland China's political, economic, social, and ideological development; indeed, the CCP leaders have admitted that the transition will be "a profound social transformation."[39] Such a transformation will inevitably bring about a great change in people's ideology, mentality, and lifestyle.

As mainland China discards the old system for the new, an ideological divergence has appeared among the leadership. Some fear that intensified reform will result in a wholesale adoption of capitalism, and some who have noticed the increasing foreign influence caution against possible deviation from a policy of independence and self-reliance. To dispel these suspicions, Chiang Tse-min has made great efforts to elaborate Teng Hsiao-p'ing's theory on building socialism with Chinese characteristics and to emphasize that Teng is a true successor of Mao Tse-tung. This is a good illustration of the kind of problems the CCP is facing as it tries to promote economic growth. It remains to be seen whether the leadership can clear away confusions about values, the economic structure, and moral principles after the market economy comes into full operation.

Whether the socialist market economy can be established will to a large extent depend on whether political stability can be maintained in mainland China. From documents issued by the CCP and from news reports published on the Chinese mainland, it is clear that future political developments will be decided by the following factors: whether the Chiang Tse-min leadership can consolidate its position; whether the central-local differences can be resolved; whether peasants' discontent with the government can be allayed; whether official corruption can be overcome; and whether social disorder resulting from the reform and opening-up policy can be checked.

At both the Party's Fourteenth Congress in October 1992 and the First Session of the Eighth NPC in March 1993, Chiang managed to keep all his positions in the Party, the government, and the military. In name at least, he is the successor of Teng Hsiao-p'ing, but whether he is in a strong enough position to cope with the challenges he will encounter after Teng's death remains to be seen. Factors that may affect Chiang's leadership position include the attitude of the military, his relations with the other third-generation leaders in the Politburo, and the results of the reform and opening-up policy. Chiang can only play the role of a negotiator and

---

[39]"The Main Points of Propaganda Work in 1993," 117.

mediator in policy decisions. Take the reform of state-owned enterprises as an example. Although he has followed Teng's instructions by calling for continued reform, Chiang has also promised state firms more government assistance. One may understand this as an effort to reduce dissatisfaction among enterprise employees. Compared to Chiang, Chu Jung-chi (Zhu Rongji) has assumed a quite uncompromising attitude toward state-owned enterprises, telling them to promote, not impede, the reform policy and urging that badly-managed ones should be closed down.

Central-local conflict may also undermine political stability. After the CCP's Fourteenth Congress, Chiang Tse-min made a series of speeches on the subject of strengthening central government control over the regions. Relations between the center and the localities may have to be adjusted as a result of the new taxation reforms, as local governments which deliver more tax revenues to the center will surely have more bargaining power. Balancing the need for a stable source of revenue against the need to encourage economic development in the localities will present the CCP regime with serious problems in the future.

Dissatisfaction among farmers concerning certain aspects of rural policy will also have an adverse impact on social stability. Although mainland China's economic reforms started in the rural areas, farmers have not benefitted from them as much as other groups of late. They are dissatisfied with the exorbitant taxes and levies, the fall in the government's grain purchase price, and cadres' diversion of funds earmarked for grain purchases toward investment in the nonagricultural sector. In addition, the growth of the market has provided peasants with an excuse to criticize continued government control of the price of farming implements and fertilizers. If these questions cannot be solved, peasant riots like that in Jenshou (Renshou) County, Szechwan (Sichuan) Province, may occur at any time.

Rampant corruption presents yet another threat to political stability. This is a longstanding problem that will not be solved overnight. The introduction of market-oriented reforms has provided increased opportunities for corruption, as there are insufficient laws and regulations governing economic transactions. Many cadres abuse their power, squander government funds, exploit legal loopholes to pursue private gain, and indulge in corruption under the guise of promoting local interests. If corruption continues to develop unchecked, the CCP will forfeit the trust of the people and eventually lose power.

Despite the very real possibility that popular distaste for corruption will destabilize the regime, many cadres lack the will to fight corruption. Some are said to argue that market-oriented reforms make corruption inevitable and that corruption is common in almost all countries. Others believe that economic development should come before fighting corruption.

Many units have covered up instances of corruption in order to preserve their reputations. The problem is that the emphasis on profits in a market economy has been mistaken for a license to pursue private gain in all circumstances. What is more, inadequate laws and regulations also hamper the anticorruption drive.

Obviously, the Chiang Tse-min leadership still has many problems after the Third Plenary Session of the CCP's Fourteenth Central Committee. Its chief task now is to maintain political stability while working for further economic growth.

The Decision adopted at the Third Plenary Session reiterated the regime's policy that public ownership should predominate in mainland China's economy, something that is crucial to the regime's survival. This should allay suspicions that the leadership favors private ownership, while at the same time stopping calls from some cadres for a radical change in the ownership system. Despite these efforts to bolster the role of the public sector, its stake in the economy is becoming progressively smaller, as state-owned firms issue shares or are transferred to collective or individual ownership, and the establishment of new private or collective sector firms outstrips that of state-owned enterprises. As this tendency grows, more and more state property is likely to be transferred into private hands by unofficial means.

Shaking off the bondage of an outworn ideology is the key to successful reform in mainland China, and there is still much to be done in this respect. For example, reliance on economic planning is still widespread, and during an inspection tour of Hainan Province in September 1993, Chu Jung-chi complained that many leaders were still shackled by old doctrines. All in all, an ideological revolution is under way in mainland China which will sooner or later result in the demise of socialism.

3

Generational Change, Institutional Pluralism, and Decision-making in Teng's China

Suisheng Zhao

In an attempt to understand the decision-making process in the People's Republic of China (PRC), scholars have developed a wide variety of theories, models, and approaches. Early attempts focused on ideological differences and political strife among individual leaders.[1] In recent decades, however, scholars have challenged the ideological and power struggle paradigm and emphasized the structural and institutional environment and process that constrains the policy choices of Chinese leaders. The structural features of formal decision-making institutions, such as the Politburo and the Central Committee of the Chinese Communist Party (CCP), have increasingly become one of the new focuses of scholarly scrutiny.[2]

---

[1]The titles of many early works on Chinese politics indicate this focus. See, for example, Franz Schurmann, *Ideology and Organization in Communist China* (Berkeley: University of California Press, 1966); A. Doak Barnett, *Cadres, Bureaucracy, and Political Power in Communist China* (New York: Columbia University Press, 1967); John W. Lewis, *Leadership in Communist China* (Ithaca, N.Y.: Cornell University Press, 1963); Harry Harding, "Maoist Theories of Policy-Making and Organization: Lessons from the Cultural Revolution," in *The Cultural Revolution in China*, ed. Thomas W. Robinson (Berkeley: University of California Press, 1971), 113-64; Andrew J. Nathan, "A Factional Model for Chinese Politics," *China Quarterly*, no. 53 (January-March 1973): 34-66; and Lucian W. Pye, *The Dynamics of Chinese Politics* (Cambridge, Mass.: Oelgeschlager, Gunn, and Hain, 1981).

[2]In a path-breaking study of mainland China's reform policymaking process, Susan Shirk argues that institutional rules now matter more than before. "In the history of economic reform policy decisions, communist politicians were obviously concerned as much with winning the support of the groups well represented in the CCP Central Committee, especially local officials, as with winning the approval of the retired elderly leaders who no longer had formal institutional positions." See Susan Shirk, *The Political Logic of Economic*

This research will analyze the demographic and career patterns of the Central Committee and Politburo members elected at the CCP's Fourteenth National Congress in October 1992 as a means of understanding the structure of the leadership in Teng Hsiao-p'ing's (Deng Xiaoping's) China. It will argue that a genuine generational change in the mainland Chinese leadership took place after the Party's Twelfth Congress in 1982. Not only were the leaders of the new generation relatively young and well-educated, but most of them had joined the Communist Party since 1949 and proved their worth during the years of reform. Their careers tended to be concentrated in a single and more or less established bureaucratic sector, which, as a salient feature of their career pattern, made their authority base different from that of the older revolutionary generations. Because of this narrow career path, their policy positions tended to reflect the parochial concerns (or interests) of the bureaucratic institutions or localities in which they had worked for most of their careers rather than some vague national consensus position in the policy process.[3] Thus, an institutional pluralism, to borrow Jerry Hough's apt phrase,[4] has developed along with the emergence of the new generation of leaders in Teng's China.

A New Generation of Leaders

The massive generational change in the Central Committee and the Politburo started at the Party's Twelfth National Congress in 1982. This

---

Reform in China (Berkeley: University of California Press, 1993), 9. David Bachman also argues that "the [Chinese] political system is institutionalized in the sense that it is generally governed by norms and dominant in the sense that the system fundamentally constrains leadership choice." See David Bachman, "The Limits on Leadership in China," *Asian Survey* 32, no. 11 (November 1992): 1046.

[3]Interest representation in mainland China and other Soviet-type states has always been a controversial issue among scholars. Gordon Skilling's idea that quasi-autonomous groups legitimately articulated and pursued their interests in the political system challenged the dominant totalitarian model in the 1950s and 1960s. This was followed by the application of corporatist theories of state to Communist systems in the 1970s. A study of Chinese bureaucratic politics in the late 1980s by Kenneth Lieberthal and Michel Oksenberg suggested that Chinese leaders and bureaucratic agencies represented different interests because they were assigned different tasks. Their study resulted in a new "fragmented authoritarianism" model for the Chinese system. See H. Gordon Skilling, "Interest Groups and Communist Politics," *World Politics* 18, no. 3 (April 1966): 435-51; Andrew Janos, "Group Politics in Communist Society: A Second Look at the Pluralistic Model," in *Authoritarian Politics in Modern Society*, ed. Samuel P. Huntington and Clement H. Moore (New York: Basic Books, 1970), 204-38; Kenneth Lieberthal and Michel Oksenberg, *Policy Making in China: Leaders, Structures, and Process* (Princeton, N.J.: Princeton University Press, 1988); and Kenneth Lieberthal and David M. Lampton, eds., *Bureaucracy, Politics, and Decision Making in Post-Mao China* (Berkeley: University of California Press, 1992).

[4]Jerry Hough, *The Soviet Union and Social Science Theory* (Cambridge, Mass.: Harvard University Press, 1977), 22.

Table 3.1
Membership Changes in the CCP Central Committee

	14th Congress (1992)					13th Congress (1987)	
	FM		AM		FM + AM		FM + AM
Newly elected	55	29.1%	95	73.2%	150	47.0%	43 + 61	36.5%
Promoted from AM to FM	28	14.8%	—	—	28	8.8%	20	7.0%
Promoted in 1989 (AM to FM)	1	0.5%	—	—	1	0.3%	—	—
Elected in 1987 (13th Congress)	40	21.2%	22	16.9%	62	19.5%	—	—
Elected in 1985 (National Party Conference)	39	20.7%	7	5.4%	46	14.4%	51 + 17	23.9%
Elected in 1982 (12th Congress)	18	9.5%	4	3.0%	22	6.9%	41 + 29	24.5%
Already a member before 12th Congress	8	4.2%	2	1.5%	10	3.1%	20 + 3	8.1%
Total:	189	100%	130	100%	319	100%	175 + 110	100%

Note: FM: Full Member; AM: Alternate Member.
Source: *China News Analysis* (Hong Kong), no. 1471 (November 1, 1992): 6.

took place in accordance with Teng Hsiao-p'ing's plan for *chi-t'i chieh-pan* (collective succession), which was unveiled at a Central Committee plenum on February 29, 1980, arranged to start preparations for the Twelfth Congress. Teng's words on that occasion were: "We stress collective leadership, and when we discuss succession nowadays we mean collective succession."[5] Under Teng's direction, the Twelfth Congress set up a "model of collective succession."[6] More than two-thirds of the Twelfth Central Committee members were newly elected.[7]

The massive generational change was accelerated at the Thirteenth Congress in 1987 and largely completed at the Fourteenth Congress in 1992. By this time, the old generation of revolutionary leaders had almost completely departed. As table 3.1 indicates, 8.1 percent of full and alternate members who entered the Central Committee before the Twelfth Congress were still there at the Thirteenth Congress. This group of old

---

[5] *Selected Works of Deng Xiaoping (1975-1982)* (Peking: Foreign Languages Press, 1984), 267.
[6] Chung Chün, *Kai-ke tsung-she-chi-shih* (The general designer of reform) (Peking: Chung-kung chung-yang tang-hsiao ch'u-pan-she, 1993), 482.
[7] Ibid.

leaders was reduced to only 3.1 percent of the entire committee at the Fourteenth Congress. Correspondingly, 95.8 percent of the full members and 98.5 percent of the alternate members, or 96.9 percent of the total membership, joined the Fourteenth Central Committee in 1992. There were 83 newcomers and 65 departures in this Central Committee. The majority of the full members who left the Central Committee were those who had reached the age limit, set officially at 65. In the new Central Committee, of the 177 full members whose birth dates are available, only 17 were over 66 years old, 75 were between 61 and 65, 57 between 56 and 60, 19 between 51 and 55, and 9 were 50 or below.[8] The longest-serving members were Hua Kuo-feng (Hua Guofeng, age 71), the only former Party leader still present in the Central Committee, and Ni Chih-fu (Ni Zhifu, age 59), chairman of the Federation of Trade Unions, both of whom joined the Central Committee in 1969.

The Fourteenth Politburo is composed of a birth cohort with an average age of 62 (as of 1992), 2.05 years younger than that of its predecessor, the Thirteenth Politburo (64.05). If we borrow William Strauss and Neil Howe's definition of a generation of leaders as a cohort whose length is approximately 20-25 years,[9] it is clear that a large majority (86.36 percent) of the Fourteenth Politburo belongs to one generation, born during the twenty-year period 1916-36 (see table 3.2). This is in spite of the fact that a significant age gap of 26 years separates the oldest member, Liu Hua-ch'ing (Liu Huaqing), born in 1916, and the youngest, Hu Chint'ao (Hu Jintao) and Wen Chia-pao (Wen Jiabao), both born in 1942.[10]

In general, this new generation of leaders is well-educated. As indicated in table 3.2, among the twenty-two Politburo members, one obtained a postgraduate degree; fifteen received college degrees from domestic and foreign universities; five, without formal college education, participated in a variety of nondegree professional training programs; and only one has nothing more than a high school diploma. Most of these leaders attended school between the late 1940s and the early 1960s. Among the eleven domestic college graduates, three were at college during the 1940s, five in the 1950s, and three in the 1960s (before the Cultural Revolution).

---

[8]*China News Analysis* (Hong Kong), no. 1471 (November 1, 1992): 4.

[9]A generation is defined by William Strauss and Neil Howe as "a cohort-group whose length approximates the span of a phase of life and whose boundaries are fixed by peer personality." See William Strauss and Neil Howe, *Generations: The History of America's Future, 1584 to 2069* (New York: Quill William Morrow, 1991), 60.

[10]As table 3.1 shows, full and alternate members of the Fourteenth Politburo were born in three distinct periods: six between 1916 and 1928, before the split in the CCP-Kuomintang united front; thirteen between 1928 and 1936, prior to the anti-Japanese war; and three between 1936 and 1942, during the anti-Japanese war.

Table 3.2

Generational Data of the Fourteenth Politburo Members

Name	Year of birth	Year joined the CCP	Education (schools, years, and fields)
Standing Members			
Chiang Tse-min	1926	1946	Shanghai Chiaotung Univ., Engineering (1943)
Li P'eng	1928	1945	Moscow Motive Power College, Engineering (1948-54)
Ch'iao Shih	1924	1940	One-year training, Huatung United Univ., Chinese Literature (1944-45)
Chu Jung-chi	1928	1949	Tsinghua Univ., Engineering (1947-51)
Liu Hua-ch'ing	1916	1935	Trained at USSR Navy Institute (1950s)
Li Jui-huan	1934	1959	Six-year evening program, Peking Construction School, Engineering (1960s)
Hu Chin-t'ao	1942	1964	Tsinghua Univ., Engineering (1959-65)
Full Members			
Ting Kuan-ken	1929	1956	Shanghai Chiaotung Univ., Business Management (1946-51)
T'ien Chi-yün	1929	1945	One-year Business Accounting (1947)
Li Lan-ch'ing	1932	1952	Futan Univ., Business Management (1952)
Li T'ieh-ying	1936	1955	Charles Univ., Czechoslovakia, Engineering (1955-59)
Yang Pai-ping	1920	1938	The PLA Political Academy (1958-60)
Wu Pang-kuo	1941	1964	Tsinghua Univ., Engineering (1960-66)
Tsou Chia-hua	1926	1944	Moscow Advanced College of Industrial Engineering (1948-54)
Ch'en Hsi-t'ung	1930	1949	Peking Univ., Chinese Literature (1946-49)
Chiang Ch'un-yün	1930	1947	A correspondence college, in Chinese Literature
Ch'ien Ch'i-ch'en	1928	1942	One-year training, Soviet Komsomol Central School (1954)
Wei Chien-hsing	1931	1949	Dairen College of Industry (1952), USSR, Engineering (1953-57)
Hsieh Fei	1932	1949	High School
T'an Shao-wen	1929	1955	Northwest Engineering Institute, Textile Engineering (1952)
Alternate Members			
Wang Han-pin	1925	1941	Southwest Univ., History (1942-46)
Wen Chia-pao	1942	1965	Peking Geology College (1960-64), graduate degree (1965-68)

Sources: *Chung-kuo ying-ts'ai* (China's Talents) (Peking), nos. 37-74, 1992-93; *Chung-kung yen-chiu* (Studies on Chinese Communism) (Taipei), vol. 26, no. 10 to vol. 27, no. 9 (October 1992 to September 1993).

Since a majority of them finished their education between the foundation
of the PRC and the beginning of the Cultural Revolution, they were, in
Chinese political terminology, products of the "seventeen-year educational
system."[11] This system was dominated by Liu Shao-ch'i's (Liu Shaoqi's)
line, and supposedly trained them to be "red experts," that is, to have
technical or professional skills combined with a kind of rustic Marxism
and loyalty to the CCP.[12]

The year of joining the CCP is also often used to rank cadres according to revolutionary seniority. There are four distinctive groups:
ch'ang-cheng kan-pu (cadres who joined the Party during the Long March
period or the years before 1936); *san-pa-ssu kan-pu* (those who joined
during the anti-Japanese war of 1937-45); *chieh-fang chan-cheng kan-pu*
(those whose membership dates back to the civil war period of 1945-49);
and *chieh-fang-hou kan-pu* (those who have joined the Party since 1949).
We find that among the twenty-two Politburo members, only one—Liu
Hua-ch'ing—is a *ch'ang-cheng kan-pu*; seven are *san-pa-ssu kan-pu*; six
are *chieh-fang chan-cheng kan-pu*; and eight are *chieh-fang-hou kan-pu*
(see table 3.2). The fact that there is only one *ch'ang-cheng kan-pu* left
in this group of leaders is an important indicator of the generational transition. Although *san-pa-ssu kan-pu* and *chieh-fang chan-cheng kan-pu*
still constitute a majority in the group, this does not necessarily mean
that the CCP leadership is still largely composed of those who fought
in the revolutionary war under Mao Tse-tung (Mao Zedong), as most of
these *san-pa-ssu* and *chieh-fang chan-cheng kan-pu* were actually in school
when they joined the Party and very few of them have any real military
experience. Thus, these college student *san-pa-ssu* and *chieh-fang chan-
cheng* leaders, along with *chieh-fang-hou kan-pu*, have become the core
of the leadership, indicating a handover from the revolutionary war generation to the new peacetime generation. Most members of this group worked
their way up the bureaucratic ladder in the 1950s and 1960s, and proved
their worth during the years of reform in the 1980s and 1990s.

The election of the Fourteenth Central Committee and its Politburo
clearly marked the emergence of a new generation of leaders. They have
been described in the Chinese official media as the *k'ua-shih-chi chieh-*

---

[11]The "seventeen years" are from 1949 to 1966.

[12]A well-educated background does not necessarily give a cohort group identity. In fact,
differences in educational background have produced cleavages among this group of leaders.
For example, leaders trained in the Soviet Union (the *liu-Su p'ai*) form a group in the
Fourteenth Politburo. A balance has been maintained between the *liu-Su p'ai* and domestic
college graduates, as well as between technicians and those with a background in the humanities and management. As yet, there have been no Western-educated Politburo members.

pan-jen (trans-century successors) and the *ti-san-tai ling-tao* (the third generation leaders).[13]

Career Patterns and Institutional Pluralism

Besides being a birth cohort most of whose members received college education and joined the CCP in colleges or after the founding of the PRC, the new generation of leaders is also characterized by the different and often very narrow career paths its members followed to the top. These narrow career paths made it difficult for them to build broad power bases, like those of the old revolutionary leaders, and also hampered the establishment of transformational or transcendent goals. Constrained by their career experiences and the structure of the political system, they have often become interest advocates of the institutions that they have worked through or have been in charge of for most of their careers. This has resulted in the development of an institutional pluralism within the CCP leadership structure.

In simple terms, the top echelon of the political leadership is composed of two types of individuals: (1) influential but elderly revolutionary leaders who have retired or semiretired from their official posts; and (2) top officeholders who have climbed the established bureaucratic ladder to their current positions. Roughly speaking, the authority of the first type of leader is essentially personal, deriving from the charisma of the individual, while the authority of the second type is relatively institutional, deriving from and being constrained by impersonal organizational rules. In an ideal type of authority, the latter rests not on an individual's charisma but on his or her formal position in an institutional setting.

Why do the retired elders possess personal authority while the officeholders are forced to rely on institutional authority? One answer to this question is simply that they have followed different career paths. As war heroes and founders of the PRC, the former Party and military leaders who helped Mao Tse-tung seize power not only have personal charisma but also maintain broad and deep connections throughout the power structure. For example, Teng Hsiao-p'ing served as political commissar in one of the four People's Liberation Army (PLA) field armies during the revolutionary war. He also held positions in the CCP's Central Military Commission in the 1950s, 1960s, and 1980s. He was the director of the

---

[13]Mainland China's leaders have been officially divided into three generations: the first generation represented by Mao Tse-tung, the second represented by Teng Hsiao-p'ing, and the third represented by the current Party general secretary, Chiang Tse-min.

CCP's Central Organization Department in the early 1950s and its secretary-general from 1954 until the beginning of the Cultural Revolution. In the 1970s and early 1980s, Teng was a vice premier in the State Council. This broad career path gave him a vast network of connections in the government, the Party, and the army.

Leaders of the new generation cannot match the broad career paths of the elders. A good deal of their time has been spent rising through the ranks of the bureaucracy and building ties vertically within their own organizations. Their careers tended to be concentrated in a single field, often being associated with just one type of work or one bureaucratic sector. Whereas the revolutionary elders actually helped build the Chinese bureaucracy and institutions and hence stand above the state, the younger generation leaders are products of the state structure, and rooted within it.

The career patterns of members of the Fourteenth Politburo exemplify the narrow path to power followed by the new generation of leaders. An examination of the career experiences of Politburo members indicates that few of them have crossed the boundary between the central government bureaucracy and central Party organs, or the boundaries between military, government, and Party organs, or those between local government and central Party organs. Fourteen of the twenty-two Politburo members spent their whole careers before election in only one of the four institutional clusters.[14] There is a small group of eight Politburo members who have had experience in two clusters of governing institutions. Of these, six moved vertically between the central government bureaucracy and local government and two worked in both the central Party organs and the central government bureaucracy. The only Politburo member whose career has spanned three clusters of institutions is Wei Chien-hsing who worked in the central Party organs, central government agencies, and local government (see table 3.3).

A majority (63.6 percent) of Politburo members have experience of only one cluster of governing institutions.[15] As specialists rather than

---

[14]Seven Politburo members worked only at local level before being promoted to the central leadership, and another seven work only in the central government and Party bureaucracy.

[15]Some China scholars use the broad concept of technocracy to describe the tendency toward specialist rule in mainland China. For example, William deB. Mills finds that Teng and his associates used the Party's Twelfth Congress to begin the replacement of the old revolutionary generation by a technocratic elite. Li Cheng and Lynn White find that elite transformation reached a peak at the Thirteenth Congress in 1987. See William deB. Mills, "Generational Change in China," *Problems of Communism* 32, no. 6 (November-December 1983): 16-35; Li Cheng and Lynn White, "The Thirteenth Central Committee of the Chinese Communist Party: From Mobilizers to Managers," *Asian Survey* 28, no. 4 (April 1988): 371-99, and "Elite Transformation and Modern Change in Mainland China and Taiwan: Empirical Data and the Theory of Technocracy," *China Quarterly*, no. 121 (March 1990): 1-35.

Table 3.3

Career Pattern of the Fourteenth Politburo Members

	Year entered the CC	Central Party experience	Central govt. experience	Military experience	Local experience
Standing Members					
Chiang Tse-min	1982	—	Yes	—	Yes
Li P'eng	1982	—	Yes	—	—
Ch'iao Shih	1982	Yes	—	—	—
Chu Jung-chi	1987	—	Yes	—	—
Liu Hua-ch'ing	1982	—	—	Yes	—
Li Jui-huan	1982	—	—	—	Yes
Hu Chin-t'ao	1985	—	—	—	Yes
Full Members					
Ting Kuan-ken	1987	Yes	Yes	—	—
T'ien Chi-yün	1982	—	Yes	—	Yes
Li Lan-ch'ing	1987	—	Yes	—	Yes
Li T'ieh-ying	1982	—	Yes	—	Yes
Yang Pai-ping	1987	—	—	Yes	—
Wu Pang-kuo	1987	—	—	—	Yes
Tsou Chia-hua	1977	—	Yes	—	Yes
Ch'en Hsi-t'ung	1982	—	—	—	Yes
Chiang Ch'un-yün	1987	—	—	—	Yes
Ch'ien Ch'i-ch'en	1982	—	Yes	—	—
Wei Chien-hsing	1982	Yes	Yes	—	Yes
Hsieh Fei	1982	—	—	—	Yes
T'an Shao-wen	1992	—	—	—	Yes
Alternate Members					
Wang Han-pin	1987	—	Yes	—	—
Wen Chia-pao	1987	Yes	Yes	—	—

Sources: Same as table 3.2.

generalists, these leaders are usually effective in making policy decisions in their own fields and tend to pursue policies of which they have special knowledge. They also tend to become policy advocates of particular governing institutions, sectors, or local governments.

    This tendency is reinforced by a system of functional division of responsibility among the top leaders. Politburo members and members of the Central Secretariat are assigned as leaders of special leadership groups in charge of one sector of administration, such as economic and financial affairs, ideological and cultural work, foreign affairs, or legal and political affairs.[16] Teng Hsiao-p'ing has described this system of division of responsibility thus: "There should be a collective leadership in settling major issues. But when it comes to particular jobs or to decisions affecting a particular sphere, individual responsibility must be clearly defined and each person should be held responsible for the work entrusted to him." He believed that one way to enhance efficiency was to assign specific tasks to particular persons who were given broad powers and allowed to handle matters independently.[17]

In addition to the system of division of responsibility in the Politburo and the Central Secretariat, Central Committee members are also elected horizontally along sectoral lines or vertically along the lines of central and local governments. Most ministries and important offices in the State Council and all provinces have their own Central Committee members. In the Fourteenth Central Committee, with the exception of Hupeh (Hubei) and Tsinghai (Qinghai) which are represented by only one full member each, all other provinces are represented by two or (in the cases of Peking [Beijing], Kwangtung [Guangdong], and Sinkiang [Xinjiang]) three full members, who usually include both the provincial Party secretary and the governor. Policy advocacy is thus built into the leadership structure through the division of responsibility and resources among individual leaders who have had career experience in only a narrow cluster of governing institutions. They have to become specialists in the job to which they are assigned or the sectors and localities from whence they came.

To the extent that the Central Committee and Politburo contain a group of political leaders who are specialists in different governmental organizations and institutions, an institutional pluralism has developed in the mainland Chinese political system. This pluralism clearly differs from the classical pluralism of the West, which allows all citizens to choose between the policy programs of competing elites in elections and to form new pressure groups or parties to advance their political interests. In mainland China, pluralism is primarily confined within the political elite and the official domain. With a few exceptions, those who want to present their interests in the policymaking process have to work through personal connections with top leaders or work within the bureaucratic institutional apparatus. Although any citizen can make appeals or sug-

---

[16]For an excellent study of this functional division, see Carol Lee Hamrin, "The Party Leadership System," in Lieberthal and Lampton, *Bureaucracy, Politics, and Decision Making in Post-Mao China*, 95-150.

[17]*Selected Works of Deng Xiaoping (1975-1982)*, 267.

gestions regarding official policies, the leading participants in the policy-making process are top bureaucratic leaders. Under institutional pluralism, individual leaders with very narrow political career paths advocate the interests of their own bureaucratic institutions, sectors, or localities. These leaders must be reckoned with not only according to the strength of their personal influence but also according to the institutional resources provided by their offices or institutional connections.[18]

Specialty Representation Under Institutional Pluralism

Policy outcomes can be partially explained by the structural features of specialty representation in the top decision-making institutions such as the Politburo and the Central Committee. An analysis of the representation structure of the Fourteenth Politburo highlights the policymaking process under institutional pluralism.

In accordance with their career paths, the membership of the Fourteenth Politburo may be broken down into five groups of specialists: (1) industrial technocrats with careers primarily in industrial and technological sectors (Chiang Tse-min, Li P'eng, Ting Kuan-ken, Li T'ieh-ying, Wu Pang-kuo, Tsou Chia-hua, and Wen Chia-pao); (2) central bureaucrats whose careers were concentrated in economic, diplomatic, or legal areas (Chu Jung-chi, T'ien Chi-yün, Li Lan-ch'ing, Ch'ien Ch'i-ch'en, and Wang Han-pin); (3) local bureaucrats who spent most of their careers as local government and Party leaders (Li Jui-huan, Hu Chin-t'ao, Ch'en Hsi-t'ung, Chiang Ch'un-yün, T'an Shao-wen, and Hsieh Fei);[19] (4) military leaders who served as active officers for most of their lives (Liu Hua-ch'ing and Yang Pai-ping); and (5) Party controllers who worked mainly in the Party's central personnel and ideological control organs (Ch'iao Shih and Wei Chien-hsing).

---

[18]The emergence of institutional pluralism does not mean that the new generation of leaders can make all decisions without interference from the elders. Teng and several other elders still have a final say in all major political decisions. The institutional pluralism model can mostly be applied to routine economic policy decisions. For an analysis of the relationship between leadership involvement levels and issue-areas, see Suisheng Zhao's concluding chapter in *The Decision Process in Deng's China*, ed. Carol Lee Hamrin and Suisheng Zhao (Almond, N.Y.: M. E. Sharpe, forthcoming).

[19]Xiaowei Zang distinguishes technocrats from bureaucrats and defines technocrats as "those in power who have college degrees in finance, engineering, and other applied sciences and have worked in factories, industrial bureaus, and economic planning agencies." He defines bureaucrats as "state and party cadres who have worked in the government system, the party hierarchy, mass organizations, the PLA, or other agencies." See Xiaowei Zang, "The Fourteenth Central Committee of the CCP: Technocracy or Political Technocracy?" *Asian Survey* 33, no. 8 (August 1993): 787-803. Obviously, in this study, technocrats and bureaucrats are used in an even narrower sense than in Zang's article.

Although the five groups of specialists represent a wide range of important institutions, a careful study of the structure of the Politburo reveals that two traditionally well-represented groups of specialists are either not represented or underrepresented here: agricultural specialists and Party controllers.

Agricultural specialists, cadres with extensive rural work experience, were well-represented in both the Twelfth and Thirteenth Politburos. These two Politburos issued a central directive each year in the name of the Party Central Committee and the State Council to set policy guidelines for agricultural reform, and these policy directives were usually very instrumental in guiding agricultural reform. Although about 80 percent of the population in mainland China is still rural, there is no single Politburo member with specialized knowledge of agriculture or career experience in rural work. Policy decisions on agricultural and rural issues made by the current Politburo often reflect this lack of knowledge and are ineffective in implementation, a problem that is reflected in the growing unrest in mainland China's rural areas. Since the mid-1980s, government taxation and levies on the rural population have increased dramatically, and the situation has only worsened in recent years. A report in *Chung-kuo ch'ing-nien pao* (China Youth Daily) reveals that Changshou County in Szechwan (Sichuan) Province levied 2,426 kinds of fees on farmers in late 1992. A farmer had to pay eight different types of fees to the local government just to build a house.[20] Since 1992, riots provoked by heavy government taxation and other levies have been reported in Szechwan, Anhwei (Anhui), and Kweichow (Guizhou) provinces. To cope with the problem, a series of Politburo and State Council meetings were convened in early 1993. The outcome was a directive (*wen-chien*) issued jointly by the Party Central Committee and the State Council on July 22, 1993, which announced the abrogation of more than thirty types of nationwide fees in rural areas, including contributions to public health and villagers' public funds (*kung-i-chin*).[21] Just before the directive was issued, the Ministry of Health submitted a report to the State Council, suggesting that the lack of health insurance for farmers and other rural residents made it necessary to collect public health fees of this kind and that this should not be treated as an extra burden. Premier Li P'eng (Politburo Standing Committee member) read the report and passed it on to Vice Premier Chu Jung-chi (Politburo Standing Committee member) for con-

---

[20]Quoted from *Min-chu Chung-kuo* (Democratic China), no. 18 (November 1993): 41.

[21]Wang Yüan, "Heavy Burden to Peasants, Bottomless Holes of Extra Fees," *Chung-kuo ta-lu* (Mainland China Monthly), November 1993, 50.

sideration. Chu read the report and wrote his comments on it. Two weeks later, however, the directive was issued without any revision. As a Chinese official indicated, this incident showed that mainland China's top decision-makers lack a comprehensive understanding of rural society.[22]

One group of specialists well-represented in previous Politburos and Central Committees but underrepresented in the present leadership is the Party controllers. Although the two Party cadres in the Politburo (Ch'iao Shih and Wei Chien-hsing) had extensive careers in the Party control organ (the Central Organization Department), they do not have a reputation for expertise in theoretical and ideological control over the Party and government; rather, they are known for their pragmatic approach to reform and Party affairs. The underrepresentation of Party controllers, especially the ideological experts, reflects the domination of Teng Hsiao-p'ing's pragmatic approach over the policymaking arena. After a long struggle during which he was forced to sacrifice a number of his associates—including Hu Yao-pang (Hu Yaobang) and Chao Tzu-yang (Zhao Ziyang)—Teng successfully ended an ideological debate on mainland China's reform policy and blocked the ideologues from entering the leadership just before the Party's Fourteenth Congress.[23] But having stripped the CCP of its Communist ideology, Teng has deprived it of the means to control its members and keep them united. Indeed the confidence crisis (*hsin-yang wei-chi*) has its origins at the very start of the reform era in the late 1970s. Party leaders with ideological expertise in previous Politburos tried very hard to restore confidence in the Party by reestablishing the dominance of orthodox Communist ideology. Their failure and expulsion from the leadership has left the Party without leaders capable of using the official ideology to justify the Party's policy, and ideology as an instrument of control has largely given way to organizational and disciplinary control, as symbolized by the presence of two Party controllers in the Politburo.

Further analysis reveals that leaders with career experience in inland provinces are not represented in the Fourteenth Politburo. The Twelfth Politburo had two leading members from inland provinces (Chao Tzu-yang from Szechwan and Wan Li from Anhwei), while the Thirteenth Politburo added another (Yang Ju-tai [Yang Rudai]). However, all of the five local bureaucrats in the Fourteenth Politburo come from coastal provinces. The imbalance of development between coastal areas and in-

---

[22]This official is a personal friend of the author and would like to remain anonymous.

[23]This was during his tour of South China in early 1992. See Suisheng Zhao, "Deng Xiaoping's Southern Tour: Elite Politics in Post-Tiananmen China," *Asian Survey* 33, no. 8 (August 1993): 746.

land China since the reforms were launched has been a serious problem and a source of both economic and political tension. Lack of representation at the top, however, means that the complaints and demands of inland provinces do not always receive due consideration. It is not surprising that most of the peasant riots of recent years occurred in densely populated inland areas. Excessive taxation imposed by local governments is, of course, one of the most important causes of these riots. But a more fundamental reason is the lack of firm and positive political action on the part of the central government to restore the balance. Instead, as the prosperity gap between coastal and inland areas has increased, the central government has played a more and more passive role in the matter. As a result, provincial leaders in these areas tend to work out their own ways of dealing with their problems. Along with the increase in autonomy that the reform policies have given provincial governments, most provincial leaders have established horizontal ties with each other to cope with the central leadership in Peking. For instance, the governor of coal-rich Shansi (Shanxi) Province, Hu Fu-kuo (Hu Fuguo), ignoring Peking's planning on coal allocation, arranged an exchange of coal for investment with other provinces. This seriously disrupted the nation's allocation of an important economic resource. During the period of economic austerity imposed by Chu Jung-chi in mid-1993, the central work teams which were sent to the provinces to enforce the Central Committee's austerity directive encountered unprecedented disobedience. The teams had to be escorted by cadres from the Central Organization Department whose job it was to force local leaders to comply with the central directive.[24]

In sum, a new generation of leaders emerged at the CCP's Fourteenth Congress in 1992. Most of these form a birth cohort of well-educated bureaucrats who have worked their way up through the system. One important feature of these leaders is the narrowness of their careers; they are more specialists than generalists. The functional division of power among top leaders has reinforced their tendency to act as policy advocates of the central or local government institutions or sectors from whence they came, and the result is the development of an institutional pluralism.

---

[24]This information was obtained from personal interviews with friends in the Peking government.

Part II

Economic and Social Changes in Mainland China

4

Mainland China's Economic System: A Study in Contradictions

Jan S. Prybyla

Chinese Economic Reforms in Historical Perspective

Since 1949 the economy of mainland China has undergone two reforms and four adjustments. By "reforms" I mean fundamental changes in the institutional structures of coordination and property and in the positive and normative economic theories that analytically explain and morally justify those structures. The first of these reforms consisted in tearing down the earlier market and traditional coordination mechanisms and private/tenant property regime, and replacing them with bureaucratic coordination (central administrative command planning) and public (state and collective) property on the Soviet model. Begun in the early 1950s, the reform, carried out by means of mass mobilization campaigns, was completed in 1956 at which time the Chinese economic system could be described as "classical socialist," at a low developmental level.[1] Its analytical-ethical infrastructure was Marxist-Leninist-Stalinist. The second reform was launched at the end of 1978 and is still in progress. It consists in the piecemeal, nonviolent dismantling of the bureaucratic coordination mechanism, or what was left of it in the wake of the Cultural Revolution, and of state and collective property, and replacing them with market coor-

---

[1] The term "classical socialism" is Kornai's. Janos Kornai, *The Socialist System: The Political Economy of Communism* (Princeton, N.J.: Princeton University Press, 1992). I have used the term "classical plan" or "Stalinplan" to describe the same phenomenon. Jan S. Prybyla, *Market and Plan Under Socialism: The Bird in the Cage* (Stanford, Calif.: Hoover Institution Press, Stanford University, 1987).

dination and various property combinations leaning toward the private. The analytical-ethical infrastructure is at this stage somewhat schizophrenic: officially, it is Marxist-Leninist-Maoist (the so-called "Four Basic Principles": socialist road, dictatorship of the proletariat, Party leadership, and Marxism-Leninism-Mao Tse-tung Thought); in everyday practice it is catch-as-catch-can "pragmatism."

In between there were four intrasystemic adjustments—what one might describe as moving the deck-chairs around on the *Titanic*: two shuffles to the starboard and two to the port-side. The rightward neo-Khrushchevian adjustments took place from October 1956 to June 1957 (a by-product of the Hundred Flowers interlude), and again from December 1960 to November 1965, the so-called "Policy of Readjustment, Consolidation, Filling-Out, and Raising Standards." Both were liberalizing in the sense that they used distorted and disjointed markets and highly restricted private property rights to get socialism out of trouble—to "perfect" it was the official phrase. At the theoretical level there was some timid theorizing along Libermanistic lines (e.g., Sun Yeh-fang, Yang Chien-pai, Ho Chien-chang, Chang Ling), but not much to speak of.[2] The two leftward adjustments were the Great Leap Forward (1958-60) and the Cultural Revolution (1966-76), both of them tumultuous exercises in extreme left Stalinist Maoism. They were designed to, and in the event did, eliminate all vestiges of market coordination and private property. Curiously enough, they were also intended to, and did in fact, destroy or seriously weaken much bureaucratic coordination (the central planning apparatus) and they communized state/collective property.[3] The result was systemic void or organized anarchy. The leftward swings traumatized the nation and many Party regulars. With benefit of hindsight, one could argue that the 1961-65 rightward adjustment (carried out, among others, by Teng Hsiao-p'ing) could perhaps have evolved into a true marketizing and privatizing reform of the economic system, anticipating the current systemic changes by nearly

---

[2]The reference is to Y. Liberman's proposals published in *Pravda* (September 7, 1962, and September 20, 1964), and to the more sophisticated market-tending ideas of V. Nemchinov (*Pravda*, September 21, 1962, and *Kommunist*, 1964, no. 5). Alec Nove, *The Soviet Economic System*, 3rd ed. (Boston: Allen & Unwin, 1986), 319-22, "Soviet Reformers and Their Models."

[3]In the absence of market prices, a statistical apparatus for the collection and processing of vast amounts of data is an indispensable prerequisite for bureaucratic coordination (central planning). At the height of the Great Leap Forward there were a dozen practicing statisticians left in mainland China. The State Statistical Bureau was rebuilt during the 1961-65 rightward adjustment, and then destroyed again in 1966. Jan S. Prybyla, *The Political Economy of Communist China* (Scranton, Penn.: International Textbook Company, 1970). The deficiency of mainland Chinese statistics today is in part attributable to these recurrent bouts of madness.

two decades, had Mao been effectively neutralized in July 1959 at the Central Committee meeting in Lushan, during which he was severely criticized by his colleagues for the economic catastrophe caused by the Leap. On the other hand, perhaps it took the added disaster of the Cultural Revolution, which hit the leaders, high and low, as hard as the "masses," plus the death of Mao and the collapse of Soviet and East European socialism, to transform the Party from within and make real "capitalist-roaders" out of most Communist leaders. In a sense Mao sowed the seeds of the current reforms by tearing apart, in pursuit of a higher and purer socialism, the institutions of socialist economic coordination and property and along the way discrediting the ideology associated with them, first during the Leap, then again in the Cultural Revolution. One lesson drawn from the two left adjustments by the survivors was that there was only one direction the economy could take to get out of the morass, and that was toward the market. Another lesson was that teleological leaps in economics could be calamitous and should be replaced by ideological de-emphasis ("ideology cannot supply rice"—Teng), and pragmatic gradualism-cum-cautious experimentation ("crossing the river while groping for the stones"—a de-ideologized twist on Mao's "learning by doing"). However, the lesson was incompletely learned, as illustrated by the investment zealotry that gripped the country following Teng Hsiao-p'ing's obiter dictum about the need for speed ("low speed development is equal to stagnation or even retrogression") during his famous southern expedition in January-February 1992.

Nevertheless, at the beginning, in the late 1970s and early 1980s (and rhetorically at least to this day), the reformers did not intend to replace bureaucratic coordination with market coordination, and public with private property. Their stated and, I believe genuine, intent was to perform a transplant operation on the ailing body of the plan: to cautiously marketize and quasi-privatize the more diseased organs in order to improve the circulation of information and stimulate incentives in the service of a few fundamental and overarching statist ends, such as increased efficiency (less waste motion), assured state revenues and, above all, social stability, but not to bring about a systemic transmutation and metempsychosis of socialism into capitalism and, god forbid, of Party autocracy into political pluralism.[4]

Mao's actions during the two leftward adjustments of mainland China's underdeveloped classical socialism also inadvertently contributed

---

[4]Dorothy J. Solinger, *China's Transition from Socialism: Statist Legacies and Market Reforms, 1980-1990* (Armonk, N.Y.: M. E. Sharpe, 1993).

to the post-Mao reforms by decentralizing the classical socialist system that mainland China had adopted from the Soviets between 1953 and 1956. The Maoist decentralizations were administrative and largely, although not altogether, the unintended consequence of the organized anarchy of the Great Leap and the Cultural Revolution during parts of which Chinese society reverted to an almost cellular state.[5] They were administrative in the sense that they relaxed the vertical bureaucratic linkages that are the essential form of coordination in the centrally planned Soviet-type system, and thereby significantly increased the decision-making powers of regional authorities located at the level of provinces and below. That such decentralizations were an intrasystemic adjustment, not a systemic reform, is borne out by the fact that they did not transfer decision-making powers to actual buyers and sellers (producing enterprises and consumers), and did not permit the establishment of horizontal contractual linkages (direct exchange relations arbitrated by market prices) between such competing buyers and sellers. Nonetheless, they legitimized the dispersion of bureaucratic power and adumbrated the very high degree of economic initiative displayed after 1978 by provincial, township, and village governments, an entrepreneurship that has been one of the driving forces of rapid industrial growth under the reform.

Thus, mainland China's post-1978 market-oriented reforms may be seen as the result of an evolutionary process—in both institutions and the learning process—to which many of Mao's defining thoughts and policies contributed in an unintended way. Not long ago a good case could be made for regarding classical socialism ("Communism" in the vernacular) as a unique historical phenomenon incapable of fundamentally (that is, systemically), incrementally, and peacefully transforming itself from within. The Chinese institutional and intellectual experience since 1978 in economics, and the Russian and East European experiences in economics and politics after 1989-91 suggest that classical socialism can be seen, more accurately perhaps, as merely one of many historical social formations not immune to internal pressures for structural transformation in response to accelerating changes in environmental values and technologies.[6]

---

[5]In part Maoist decentralizations were deliberate, stemming from Mao's idiosyncratic conceptions of defense strategy in which self-contained, self-sufficient local units (right down to the people's communes) figured prominently.

[6]On environmental pressures or the world techno-economic revolution, see my "The ROC's Role in Building a Global Economy," *Issues & Studies* (Taipei) 28, no. 11 (November 1992): 1-17.

Key Elements in the Transformation of
Mainland China's Economic System

Concepts

The two key questions posed by all economic systems are: First, how arc decisions made as to what should be produced, how, and for whom, and how should what is produced be distributed? And second, who owns what? The first question concerns the system's mechanism of internal and external coordination, the second concerns the system's property rights.

In capitalism, coordination is achieved through spontaneously generated, workably competitive market prices (market coordination) or the price mechanism, a term frequently used as a synonym for the market system. Internal prices comprise prices of goods and factors (wages, interest rates, rents). External prices comprise exchange rates, and the prices of goods and services traded internationally. In classical socialism coordination is achieved deliberately through administrative planning (bureaucratic coordination). Market coordination involves voluntary response of the transactors to price signals. Bureaucratic coordination, or central planning, involves unconditional commands cast in physical or monetary terms (input and output quotas) directed by superiors to executors. A synonym for classical socialism is "administrative command system."

In capitalism private ownership (rights of use, transfer, and residual income vested in individuals or voluntary associations of individuals) is the dominant form of property. In classical socialism the bulk of property is public, that is, in practice state or collective (direct or indirect government ownership).

Mixtures of market and bureaucratic coordination and private and public property are not only possible but common. From the standpoint of a system's coherence and internal consistency, it is important that one or the other form of coordination and property should be unequivocally dominant: coordinating mechanisms and property rights should not generate contradictory signals to economic actors. While absolute purity in coordination and property is neither possible in practice nor desirable, the internal logic of a system requires that there be a critical minimum mass of compatible vital organs. Unfortunately what constitutes such a critical minimum mass escapes precise quantification.

Concepts Applied to Mainland China

Mainland China's movement away from dominant bureaucratic coordination and public property ("growing out of the plan") toward market coordination and various permutations of nonstate property after 1978, is explained by Teng Hsiao-p'ing in the following terms: "Capitalism and socialism have no direct bearing on the planned economy and the market economy . . . planned economy and market economy are both economic measures [i.e., instrumentalities]. Socialism's real nature is to liberate productive forces, and the ultimate goal of socialism is to achieve common prosperity."[7] ("It doesn't matter whether a cat is black or white so long as it catches mice.") Such a reformist definition of socialism as an economic phenomenon is healthier than a class warfare-based one, but it does exact a price in credibility. In fact, ever since the Bolshevik Revolution in Russia, and doctrinally much longer than that, the abolition of market coordination and private property and their replacement by bureaucratic coordination and state property ("ownership by the whole people") have been absolute values, integral parts of the new, historically superior stage of socialism, not, as Teng now explicates, discardable and interchangeable tools in the service of common prosperity. "The opinion," Teng continues, "which equates reform and opening [up to the outside world] to ushering in and developing capitalism, and which holds that the danger of peaceful evolution [to democracy] mainly comes from the economic field, precisely represents 'leftism'."[8] This is good polemical sparring for it places the onus of proof on the defenders of the faith, now hatted with the label of reactionary leftists. Nevertheless, "once the idea that certain features of capitalism need somehow imitating or incorporating into socialism begins to pervade officialdom, the system is departing from its classical state."[9] As an economic entity, socialism loses not only its institutional foundations, but its belief system as well.[10] The soul goes out of it. There seems to be nothing left.

No, not quite. What is left is the unswerving determination of all Communist Party factions, right reformers and their relatives, left reactionaries and their relatives, and establishment intellectuals alike, to hold onto undivided political power which now brings with it not just psychic power rents (as it did under poorer demonetized Maoism) but generous

---

[7] Teng Hsiao-p'ing during his tour of southern China, January 18-February 21, 1992, in: British Broadcasting Corporation, *Summary of World Broadcasts*, Part 3: *The Far East*, 1326 (1992).

[8] U.S. Foreign Broadcast Information Service, *Daily Report: China*-92-063-S (April 1, 1992).

[9] Kornai, *The Socialist System*, 52. "The official ideology of classical socialism reflects a belief that [socialism's economic] superiority follows from the system itself. Socialism achieves greater accomplishments not because the population makes great sacrifices when required, nor because economic policy is better advised than in the capitalist countries, but because of the system's basic properties, which guarantee that sooner or later, once the initial disadvantage has been overcome, its superiority will plainly emerge." Ibid.

[10] To the question: "What principles do you follow in your work?" Hu Yanchou, president of Shanghai Cable TV, replies: "We have just two principles. One is satisfying demand. The other is making money." *Wall Street Journal*, December 2, 1993, A11.

money incomes as well. Classical socialism had three basic elements, two economic, and one political: central planning, public property, and Communist party monopolitics, the last theoretically explained by the concept of the "leading role of the party," a Leninist formulation of Marx's historical materialism at the socialist stage.

Today the official justification for the continuance of Communist Party monopoly contains two arguments. First, only the Communist Party can carry out a successful economic transplant surgery, marketizing and privatizing those socialist organs it considers dysfunctional, without sliding into capitalism. Only the Party in monopoly power, backed by the gun when necessary, can prevent "peaceful evolution" on the cultural and political fronts, and combat what Li P'eng in his opening speech to the National People's Congress (March 1994) identified as "money-worship, ultra-individualism, and decadent lifestyles" (bourgeois spiritual pollutants), not least among Party members. Second, only the Communist Party in undivided control of the political sphere can assure "social stability" and prevent chaos: "Après nous le *luan!*"

The old-fashioned tacit social contract between the Communist Party and the masses was that the people kept out of politics and did what they were told, and in return the Party guaranteed full employment, price stability (no open inflation), rough distributional equality (of income, not power), and better living standards in the future conditional (the "catchup with the advanced" promise, implying consumption postponement in the present). The new social contract's first clause (people keeping out of politics) remains unchanged, as demonstrated on June 3-4, 1989 in Tienanmen Square. The change is in the second clause: in return, the people can do what it takes to grow rich in the market ("to get rich is glorious"). This has the additional advantage of keeping their minds off politics. But for most people there is no longer any guarantee of employment security, price stability, and income equality. Unemployment, inflation, and a bulging Lorenz curve (highly skewed income distribution) concentrate the mind on perceived injustices, unfairness, and corruption, and are in this sense subversive of social stability, particularly during cyclical recessions.[11]

---

[11]A secret Chinese government report leaked to Hong Kong in early April 1994, counted 6,000 strikes in mainland China in 1993 (all strikes are illegal) and more than 200 riots. Many of them were protests against layoffs and unpaid wages in state-owned industries where the employment guarantee still holds, more or less. Patrick E. Tyler, "Discontent Mounts in China, Shaking the Leaders," *New York Times*, April 10, 1994, 3. In Kwangtung (Guangdong), an estimated 500,000 child laborers are allegedly working under sweatshop conditions. They are part of the province's 8 million transient workers. For the country as a whole, some estimates point to a "floating" population of some 100 million surplus

Key Attributes of Mainland China's Reform Accomplishments

Mainland China's post-1978 economic reforms have been highly successful in several respects. There have also been failures and an accumulation of potentially very dangerous problems. On the whole, the reforms and their results have been appraised positively by foreign traders and private investors who put their own money on the line; bankers, governments, and international financial agencies who put other people's money on the line; and "China watchers" (especially political scientists writing on economics), journalists, academics, and sundry political pilgrims in search of "capitalism with a human face" who have no money, only their reputations. The reaction of Hong Kong and Taiwan businessmen, and of many monied Chinese expatriates in other countries, has been for the most part euphoric. The vision of "Greater China" comprising the southern provinces of the Chinese mainland, Taiwan, and Hong Kong, peopled by millions of moderately affluent consumers, is the talk of the town. Some governments (e.g., the ROC government on Taiwan, or sections of it) and many professional economists specializing on China have been more cautious for a variety of what appear to be cogent reasons.[12]

The successes as well as the failures of mainland China's economy can be attributed in some measure to the reforms that in the 1980s and early 1990s moved the economy away from central administrative command planning and state-collective property, a long way toward, but not quite to, market coordination and private property. A particularly significant element of this transition has been the partial marketization and privatization of mainland China's external economic relations, known as the policy of the "open door," which has initiated a process of gradual integration of the Chinese economy in the world market system.

Coordination Reforms

Retreat from classical socialism has been greatest on the internal and

---

laborers seeking work. Industrial accidents, involving tens of thousands of workers, more than doubled in 1993 according to figures by the Labor Ministry. The official *Legal Daily* blames large income gaps in the countryside for the breakdown of social order in some rural areas: "Village social order," it says, "is out of control." Rapes, kidnappings, and thefts are attributed to rapid growth of consumerism amid widespread low incomes and to the corrupt and tyrannical attitudes of local rural officials who monopolize ("leading role of the party") land, water, and other resources, while bandits and feuding clans run rampant. *Wall Street Journal* May 4, 1994, A9. Voices have been raised, and promptly silenced, urging the formation of independent labor unions and the drawing up of a charter of labor rights.

[12]This caution is much in evidence in the analyses contained in a survey of "The Chinese Economy in the 1990s," *China Quarterly*, no. 131 (September 1992).

external coordination fronts, less impressive, but not unimportant on the property front.

In the early 1980s, 70 percent of the value of all commodities was accounted for by rigid state-set prices. Allocation of the bulk of producer goods was done by physical orders (theoretically producer goods were excluded from "commodity" market transactions), and many consumer goods, including most basic necessities, were physically rationed with the help of subsidized prices. By 1990 two-thirds of agricultural products, over 80 percent of manufactured consumer goods, almost all services, and one-third of producer goods were being traded at market prices.[13] In 1979, 700 kinds of producer goods were physically allocated by the plan; 20 in 1992.

At the beginning of the reform the exchange rate of the *jen-min-pi* (*yuan*) was fixed by the government well above its value on the world market, making most exports unprofitable and causing excess demand for foreign exchange, which was dealt with by an elaborate system of administrative exchange controls. From the mid-1980s on, the *yuan* was repeatedly devalued, somewhat erratically some claim, to make it conform more closely to its world market price. The exchange rate adjustments have become more frequent since 1991. Exporters are now allowed to retain a portion of their foreign currency earnings and to convert it into local currency on swap markets. Since 1991 four-fifths of all foreign exchange in mainland China has been priced at the swap market rate: "In short, China appears to be within striking distance of achieving internal convertibility of the [*jen-min-pi*] in trade transactions."[14] What at first looked like an administrative decentralization of foreign trade management through the replacement of a small number of very large product-specific monopolistic foreign trade corporations by some 4,000 smaller ones in the early 1990s, turned out to be in large part genuine economic liberalization as these entities competed among themselves for foreign sales and imports and based their decisions increasingly on world market prices. By 1991, according to Lardy, more than 90 percent of all imported goods were based on world market prices, and by the late eighties 80 percent of exported goods were influenced by such international prices.

---

[13]K. C. Yeh, "Macroeconomic Issues in China in the 1990s," *China Quarterly*, no. 131 (September 1992): 540. In 1988, according to urban household survey data, urban households bought 80, 57, 60, 76, 63, and 69 percent of their fresh vegetables, pork, beef and mutton, chicken, eggs, and fish, respectively, in free markets. Joseph C. H. Chai, "Consumption and Living Standards in China," ibid., 731.

[14]Nicholas R. Lardy, "Chinese Foreign Trade," ibid., 710. See also Nicholas R. Lardy, *China in the World Economy* (Washington, D.C.: Institute for International Economics, 1994).

Whereas in 1978 planned export commodities numbered 3,000, by 1988 their number had dropped to 112.[15]

Unlike administrative decentralization of decision-making introduced, as we have seen, in part by default during the left Maoist adjustments of 1958-60 and 1966-76, decentralization by free market price is reformist in the sense that it hands over the exercise of effective choice about entry, exit, and allocation of resources from the monoparty's planning bureaucracy to actual competing buyers and sellers, consumers and producers, households and firms, creating in effect relatively sovereign decision-making spheres outside the purview of state commands. Concurrently, it privatizes property, in fact if not always in law, by vesting those in charge of assets, whether as private persons or managers of state/collective enterprises, with the rights to use and transfer (buy, sell, rent, merge, break-up) assets, and dispose of net income, subject only (or mainly) to a market-determined hard budget constraint. Marketization with de facto, but without legal privatization of property rights (i.e., clear specification of what belongs to whom) and without the rule of law or civilized legal order (predictability and absence of whim and arbitrariness in law), can invigorate and rationalize the economy for a while, perhaps for a long while, but it represents, I think, a serious danger to the market-private property order over the longer term. Just as democracy and civil society are two sides of the same coin, so is market coordination and legally articulated, unambiguously recognized, and constitutionally conceived and protected private property.[16]

---

[15]Lardy, "Chinese Foreign Trade," 704-5.

[16]The view that what really matters is to give transactors a considerable degree of autonomy from government intervention within a credibly competitive market setting has recently gained ground. "An appropriate ownership system may be very important as a prerequisite for dynamic markets. The question of whether public ownership is inherently inimical to such markets remains open; some counterexamples do exist. What clearly is dangerous is aspects of public ownership that interfere with the autonomy of market transactors, free entry, and competition." Of the essence is "widespread participation, voluntary interactions, and flexible prices." To this end, "developing and maintaining buyers' markets [buffered equilibrium] for industrial products is important because it provides firms with strong incentives to be responsive to the demand side and to improve efficiency." William A. Byrd, *The Market Mechanism and Economic Reforms in China* (Armonk, N.Y.: M. E. Sharpe, 1991), 42, 219, 224. A somewhat similar but broader-gauged thesis is propounded by another World Bank-connected economist, Inderjit Singh, in "Is There Schizophrenia About the Two-Track Approach?" World Bank, *Transition*, July-August 1991, 3-4. Notice that Byrd's definition of the market mechanism lacks a specific reference to private property: "Markets entail voluntary exchange of goods by self-interested individuals or entities for each other or for money. The autonomy of transactors is a crucial element. They are free to enter and exit the market and to accept or refuse transaction offers. Another important element is decentralization of information and its flow through horizontal rather than vertical channels. A third is the existence of market prices. Finally, the motivation of self-interest on the part of transactors is an integral element." Byrd, *The Market Mechanism*

Simulation of private property behavior by Weberian bureaucrats, the recurrent dream of Walresian market socialists, is not sufficient to ensure the continued vitality, dynamism, and efficiency of the market order, and may be, in fact, an obstacle to this end.

Property Reforms

The notion of "growing out of the plan" is illustrated by the evolution since 1978 of mainland China's property forms.[17] There has been so far no privatization of large state-owned property and only a very hesitant movement toward the "corporatization" of such property, involving the issuance of shares to workers, managers, and various state authorities in the affected firms. There has also been some leasing of medium-sized state industrial and commercial enterprises or parts of them to private individuals and mixed private-cooperative groups. One hundred state-owned enterprises—0.001 percent of the total—were scheduled for corporatization in 1994. As of the end of the first quarter of the year none had been corporatized. Central and local state-owned large and medium-sized industrial firms above the township and village levels still employ 70 percent of the urban labor force (ca. 70 million workers), own two-thirds of total fixed industrial assets, account for 80 percent of the volume of freight traffic, and are the state's major source of tax revenues and concurrently a heavy drain on state expenditures.[18] In 1990 state industrial enterprises accounted for 77 percent of all losses, and half their gross profits were offset by losses. In 1990 these losses were more than seven times those of 1982. All the same, whereas in 1980 central and local state-sector firms accounted for 75.5 percent of total gross industrial output value, by 1990 (in 1980 constant prices) their share had fallen to 48.5 percent

---

and Economic Reforms in China, 22-23. Dwight Perkins notes four conditions that must be met for a market system to work well in a reforming centrally planned economy: (1) goods must be made available through the market rather than through administrative allocation; (2) prices must reflect long-run relative scarcities rather than the dictates of the plan; (3) competition must exist; no monopolists, otherwise no productivity gains; and (4) managers must behave according to the rules of the market, rather than those of the state bureaucracy. Notice, here too, the absence of explicit, clearly articulated laws defining private property rights. *The Economist* (London), A Survey of China, November 28, 1992, 7.

[17] "[T]here is no frontal attack on the planning system or attempt to abolish mandatory planning outright, but its share in economic activity declines because the portion subject to planning does not grow with the economy as a whole." Byrd, *The Market Mechanism and Economic Reforms in China*, 203. I include state/collective property as an integral and crucial element of the "plan," whereas Byrd seems to limit the definition of plan to what I term "coordination."

[18] State Statistical Bureau, Peking, *Statistical Yearbook of China 1992*, 230.

and the decline has continued since.[19]

How so? Because of the relatively rapid growth rates of output in the nonstate multi-ownership sector of the industrial economy: old socialist collective, new cooperative, individual, joint collective-individual, joint foreign, overseas Chinese, foreign private, etc., particularly at the township level and below (township and village: predominantly collectively-, cooperatively-, and individually-owned entities—the least regulated industries). Between 1980 and 1990 (in 1980 prices) state-sector industrial output doubled; the output of the collective-cooperative sector grew 5 1/2 times; that of private (individual) firms grew 1,300 times, albeit from a minuscule base; and that of other firms (joint state-collective, joint state-individual, joint collective-individual, joint foreign, overseas Chinese, foreign owned) 35 1/2 times. Except for firms in 100 percent foreign or overseas Chinese ownership, fully private enterprises are small in size and represent not quite 6 percent of the gross value of industrial output (1991). Still, private ownership is the fastest growing property form, although the growth takes place from very modest beginnings. A mid-1993 survey by the Chinese Academy of Social Sciences found that there were 184,000 such private businesses—41 percent of them service firms—with a total of 3 million employees and a registered capital of US$5.2 billion, an increase of 225 percent from the year before.[20] Many of the township and village collective and cooperative enterprises lean toward an "as if" private ownership form, at least in the sense that they purchase most of their inputs and sell the bulk of their output on the more or less free market, often in stiff competition with one another. But given the multiple-tier economic system that mainland China has today and the murkiness of Chinese commercial law as regards both property and coordination, purchasing inputs and selling outputs on the market does not exclude and often requires resort to personal-bureaucratic connections or *kuan-hsi* leavened by informal transfers of income from private to public pockets at all levels of cadredom.

In short, what we see on the Chinese industrial landscape, particularly in the southern provinces with their large inflows of foreign and Chinese overseas capital, and in some of the larger cities such as Shanghai, Peking, and Tientsin, is the quasi-privatization of property from below, or better, the diversification of property forms outside the state-owned sector and

---

[19]Robert Michael Field, "China's Industrial Performance Since 1978," *China Quarterly*, no. 131 (September 1992): 595.

[20]Ibid., 604; *China Statistical Yearbook 1992; Wall Street Journal*, April 7, 1994, A11.

the progressive marginalization of that sector by rapid growth of output in the nonstate sphere. I believe that the main reason for the authorities' foot-dragging on reform of the ownership structure of the state industrial sector has less to do with ideology than with fear of the short-run economic consequences of such action, specifically of the massive urban unemployment that would surely result from the imposition of a hard budget constraint on the firms as part of the property reform. The Decision of the Third Plenary Session of the Chinese Communist Party's Fourteenth Central Committee (November 1993) left open a loophole that advocates of the privatization of state property could use in the future if they prevail in the political succession battles. The Decision emphasizes public ownership, but also notes that such ownership need not necessarily be dominant in certain regions and industries. Nevertheless, unlike the successor republics of the Soviet Union and some ex-socialist countries of Eastern Europe, mainland China has left the most difficult problem of denationalization of the largest industrial enterprises to the last.

In the countryside, changes in the ownership structure came early (before 1984) in the form of decollectivization and the creation of what in essence is a household tenancy system. The land remains publicly owned, but farm households have extensive rights of use to their assigned land plots, including the right to transfer these use rights with permission of the authorities. They also possess the right to net income from the land, i.e., right to appropriate the portion of income remaining after payment of costs, taxes, and other fiscal charges, which reportedly are often levied by local cadres with a good deal of capriciousness. Households can own farm implements and machines (e.g., hand tractors), livestock, draft animals, and means of local transportation. Individuals have also gained increased property rights in their own persons: they can legally move within the countryside and millions of them (some estimates put the "floating" population at 100 million) have illegally migrated to the larger cities in search of employment. Legalization of rural migration to metropolitan areas is on the agenda. There is apparently concern among the peasants about the firmness of the authorities' commitment to even the incomplete privatization that obtains in the countryside. Such concern tends to sap household incentives to invest in the land. The recurrent talk by officials about the need to introduce a "two-tier operational system" that would combine "decentralized household-based farming with a collectively-organized 'socialized service system'," may have more to do with economic rationality (the need for infrastructural capital formation, improved marketing, and technical transformation which individual households either cannot or will not do) than with ideology, although ideological impulses are not absent. However that may be, the "both sides of the mouth" character of such talk understandably worries the farmers.[21]

The Taiwan Model: Yes and No

Mainland China had to address two formidable economic problems, development and systemic reform, where other East Asian societies of kindred cultures—Taiwan, Hong Kong, Singapore, and South Korea—had to tackle only one: development. The developmental problem has been solved by these four societies over a period of some three decades (1960s-1980s) in exemplary fashion. Now mainland China, too, is breaking the back of underdevelopment and its accomplishments to-date in this regard are directly related to its systemic transformation. The ongoing transformation appears to be headed for something akin to the "Taiwan Developmental Model," a subspecies of "East Asian Model." Strictly speaking, there are two East Asian models, the difference between them turning on the role of the state in the economy: the Hong Kong model of active noninterventionism or quasi laissez-faire, and the Taiwan-Singapore-South Korea-Japan model of industrial and trade policies pursued by highly activist governments. Except for Japan where democracy was implanted by the occupation authorities at the end of World War II (and promptly transformed by the Japanese into one-party democracy), all governments of the East Asian model, the unelected "soft" Hong Kong government included, were in various degrees authoritarian during the economic takeoff (1950s-1960s) and the early parts of self-sustaining growth (1970s-1980s). They all shared, though with differing emphases, a pragmatic developmental philosophy "guided by two principles. One [was] the maintenance of private property and the market mechanism in an environment favoring private enterprise. The other [was] the maintenance of a balance between economic growth and stability and of an equitable distribution of income as society becomes more affluent and the standard of living and quality of life improve."[22] Mainland China still has a distance

---

[21]"Pledges to preserve contractual arrangements with individual farm households and to deregulate more prices suggest accelerated reform. But the simultaneous advocacy of two-tier management and the maintenance of dual-track pricing indicate a more ambiguous attitude towards agricultural development policy." Robert F. Ash, "The Agricultural Sector in China: Performance and Policy Dilemmas During the 1990s," *China Quarterly*, no. 131 (September 1992): 572. I have noted the peasants' concern in my "*Pao-kan Tao-hu*: The Other Side," *Issues & Studies* 22, no. 1 (January 1986): 74-75.

[22]K. T. Li, *Economic Transformation of Taiwan, ROC* (London: Shepheard-Walwyn, 1988), xi. "I have always believed that government can serve only as a guide and catalyst in the process of economic development—that it can help establish the type of environment needed for economic development to take root, but that the true success of any national develop-

to go to rid itself of the legacy of teleological dogma, and given the uncertainties of the imminent leadership succession, there are no guarantees that the journey will not be interrupted. But the process of ideological attrition is far advanced, in part because of the loss of faith in the old Marxist-Leninist verities by the people and officials alike.

What then are the major characteristics of the Taiwan developmental model? Have the mainland reforms drawn on that model, and if so, in what particular respects?

Characteristics of the Taiwan Model

1. Taiwan's economic system is "mixed" in the sense that the government actively participates in the economy both in matters of coordination and property. The crucial stipulation here is that despite a relatively generous conception of the legitimate economic functions of government, (1) at all developmental stages market coordination and private property rights are dominant and "the most important function of the government is to provide an institutional framework and environment in which the market mechanism is allowed to function freely,"[23] and (2) that the evolutionary direction of the model is toward greater individual decision-making freedom (implying an enlargement of personal responsibility, not license), competitively arrived at voluntary buyer-seller agreement as the basic organizing principle, and the expansion of private ownership as the dominant form of property rights. As noted before, the government's economic philosophy is strongly growth-oriented.

The form of government is authoritarian, but there is a commitment to eventual democratization of the political system and the rule of law, which is actually carried out.

---

ment effort depends vitally on the will and the commitment of the people." Ibid., iv. K. T. Li, now special assistant to the President of the Republic of China on Taiwan, was one of the leading architects of Taiwan's "economic miracle."

[23]Chi-ming Hou, "Relevance of the Taiwan Model of Development," *Economic Review* (Taipei), September-October 1989, 1-20; Chu-yuan Cheng, "The Taiwan Developmental Model: Its Essence, Performance, and Implications," *American Journal of Chinese Studies*, October 1992, 305-24; K. T. Li, "The Economic Transformation of the Republic of China: A Model of Success," *Economic Review*, March-April 1991, 1-7; Fredrick F. Chien, "The Economic Development of Taiwan, Republic of China: An Economic Success Story," ibid., November-December 1989, 1-7; Jan S. Prybyla, "Economic Developments in the Republic of China," in *Democracy and Development in East Asia: Taiwan, South Korea, and the Philippines*, ed. Thomas W. Robinson (Washington, D.C.: American Enterprise Institute Press, 1991), 49-73; Jan S. Prybyla, "Taiwan as a Model of Economic Growth and Development: The Contributions of Chiang Ching-kuo," *American Asian Review*, Spring 1994, 182-98; "The Titan Stirs," *The Economist*, A Survey of China, November 28, 1992, 3-6; *The East Asian Miracle: Economic Growth and Public Policy* (Washington, D.C.: World Bank, 1993).

Last but not least, partly as a result of lessons learned from the disastrous experience on the mainland before 1949, observance by civil servants of high standards of personal integrity is required. John Stuart Mill was right: "It really is of importance not only what men do, but also what manner of men they are who do it."

2. A peaceful (not class struggle-inspired) land reform aimed at creating entrepreneurial farmer-owners.

3. Balanced sectoral growth with emphasis on "useful" growth that benefits consumers in the here and now.

4. Export orientation and openness to foreign direct investment as a source of capital and technological/managerial know-how. In the early stages export promotion is combined with import substitution, with outward (export) orientation gaining ground, the movement being in a direction that allows "market forces to function freely without any bias either against or in favor of imports or exports," i.e., progressive liberalization and internationalization of the economy.[24] At the theoretical level, rejection of dependency theories.

5. Emphasis on stability in the midst of growth, specifically stability of the price level and employment (avoidance of inflation, activity cycles, and unemployment).

6. Equitable income distribution.

7. High priority accorded to investment in human capital.

Mainland Reform and the Taiwan Model

1. Mixed system. After nearly sixteen years of reform, mainland China's economy is "mixed" as regards coordination and property. Although internal and external coordination is now to a significant degree carried out by market or market-influenced prices, many of the markets are very imperfect, most of them riddled with ad hoc administrative regulations, restrictions, and other often arbitrary interferences by unaccountable local potentates. Consequently, the resulting prices are distorted, there is still dual pricing for some key goods and services, as well as pockets of state pricing—a "multicultural" price arrangement, so to speak, better than the old system of rigid state-fixed nonprices, but still not very conducive to allocative rationality.[25] The property system is also varied and

---

[24]Hou, "Relevance of the Taiwan Model," 19.

[25]"[S]o far the leadership has been unwilling to let go of a system of administered prices because changes in the price level affect government revenue, the distribution of profits, and the urban cost of living—all of which set off political and bureaucratic struggles." Field, "China's Industrial Performance," 601. Y. Y. Kueh, "Foreign Investment and Economic Change in China," *China Quarterly*, no. 131 (September 1992): 657 and 664,

legally ill-defined, hence subject to the whim of officialdom. The best that can be said for it at this stage is that it is increasingly nonstate. Still, the lines of division between private, quasi-private, cooperative, collective, and state are fuzzy, there is a good deal of incompatible overlap, and a widespread feeling that the commitment to privatization, a central feature of the Taiwan model, is lacking.[26] Despite these doubts, if the reform is not interrupted, the share of state-sector industrial output in the gross value of industrial output in the year 2000 is expected to fall to 25 percent from just under 50 percent now. By and large, the government's economic philosophy, still by no means free of Marxist-Leninist ideological preconceptions, has become relatively results-oriented.

The economy's growth has been rapid but much more erratic than Taiwan's. The real growth rate of gross national product (GNP) in the decade 1980-90 was 8.9 percent, or 7.4 percent per capita (10.1 and 8.7 percent respectively in 1980-85). The headlong pace has continued into the early 1990s (13 percent in 1993). The mainland growth rates compare favorably with those of Taiwan between 1963 and 1973 (11.1 percent overall, 8.6 percent per capita) and Taiwan's highest rate of 13.7 percent in 1976. The gross value of mainland industrial output (in 1980 constant prices) rose at an average annual rate of 12.6 percent from 1980 through 1990, but also in spurts ranging from 4.3 percent (1981) to 21.7 percent (1985). The gross value of real agricultural output averaged 6.4 percent per annum from 1981 through 1990 (3.4 percent for grains). An initial upsurge in 1981-85 was followed by stagnation or sharply lower growth rates in 1986-90 for grain, cotton, oil seeds, sugar, and meat (pork, beef, mutton).[27] The relative severity of the mainland's activity cycles is attributable in large measure to the concurrent pursuit of growth and institutional restructuring (reform) of the economy, a good deal of it being of an ad hoc, unintegrated, and compromise nature. The financial mechanisms of macroeconomic intervention in the emerging market economy are still quite rudimentary, particularly as regards monetary controls involving both

---

calls the exchange rate adjustments made by Chinese authorities in the 1980s and the 1986 devaluation, "erratic."

[26]In the 1960s, 48 percent of Taiwan's industrial output value originated in the state-owned sector. By 1992 the share had been reduced, largely through the more rapid growth of private-sector output, to 18 percent. Council for Economic Planning and Development, Republic of China, *Taiwan Statistical Data Book 1993*, 84.

[27]Yeh, "Macroeconomic Issues"; Field, "China's Industrial Performance"; Ash, "The Agricultural Sector," 502, 588, 547-48; *Taiwan Statistical Data Book 1993*, 26-32. The authors of the *China Quarterly* analyses warn against the many problems involved in dealing with Chinese mainland statistics. The statistical situation is better than before the reform, but far from good.

central and commercial banking, but in other respects (e.g., the tax system) as well. Formal market linkages are often overridden by informal personal-bureaucratic networks that distort or paralyze monetary and fiscal policies. Investment hunger and easy money are stimulated by the continued presence of soft budget constraints over large areas of the state-owned economy, by the banks' high degree of responsiveness to the apparently unquenchable thirst for funds of local Party-government officials, and by the bad habit, acquired in Mao's time, to go on a spending spree every time the paramount leader makes a pronouncement of the "growth is good!" genre. In these circumstances, when the economy overheats, the authorities resort to administrative means of cooling it down, usually bringing about a recession and occasionally (e.g., 1989) social instability.

I have argued at length elsewhere that from being totalitarian, market- and private property-phobic, the Chinese government has evolved into a market-friendly, private property-tolerant "Chinochet" authoritarianism, by reason of its devolution of several decision-making powers to relatively autonomous transactors in the market segments of the economy.[28] Also, because of the breakdown of the belief system, the onslaught of alternative values by reason of the information revolution, and the bulldozing of inner city neighborhoods, the realm of what one might broadly call "culture" has been detotalitarianized. Despite the continued crackdown on open political dissent, the old household registration system and its inner core, the neighborhood networks of socialist morality police, have been considerably weakened.

The Taiwan model's requirement of personal integrity on the part of civil servants has been lacking. The mainland reforms are noted for widespread corruption from the top down. This represents, in my view, a most serious threat to the whole reformist undertaking.

2. Peaceful land reform. The decollectivization of agriculture and the introduction of the household responsibility system represent an important, peaceful and, by and large, successful in terms of production and factor productivity, reform of the land tenure system. Unlike the Taiwan model's land tenure adjustment, which between 1950 and 1963 transferred very broad property rights of use, transfer, and net income to farm families, the mainland reform stopped at the tenancy stage at which the Taiwan reform began. Like much else, it is an incomplete reform, recurrently raising doubts about its permanence and bona fides.

3. Balanced growth. The mainland reforms have brought about

---

[28] Jan S. Prybyla, "Chinese Puzzle," *Working Paper*, 1-94-2 (The Pennsylvania State University, University Park, Penn.), 19-23.

greater balance to a once sectorally highly skewed economic structure, but infrastructural facilities and the energy sector continue to lag behind. They have also modernized that structure in terms of the respective contributions to total output and employment of the agricultural, industrial, and services sectors. A significant shift of resources from low to high productivity employments—from agriculture to industry and services—has occurred. Concurrently a dramatic structural change has taken place within agriculture from crop cultivation to other tasks, especially animal husbandry and fisheries.[29] Combined with rapid growth, these modernizing structural changes have benefitted large numbers of Chinese people in terms of living standards and quality of life indices (e.g., more balanced diet, ownership of consumer durables, etc.). The average annual growth rate of material consumption per head from 1978 to 1990 was 7 percent (9.1 percent from 1978 to 1985, reflecting a fall in the rate of accumulation). Per capita disposable income in 1980 prices rose at an average annual rate of 7.2 percent, four and a half times the rate in 1957-78.[30] By and large the Taiwan model applies. The London *Economist* (November 28, 1992), a journal not normally given to hyperbole, puts it this way: "China's economic performance since [December 1978] has brought about one of the biggest improvements in human welfare anywhere at any time."

4. Exports and foreign investment. The Taiwan model has been replicated in mainland China's abandonment of inward-oriented policies, its combination of import substitution and export promotion, devaluation of the foreign exchange rate, the setting up of special economic zones (SEZs) for the express purpose of attracting foreign capital, technology, and managerial expertise, and various measures of trade liberalization aimed at invigorating domestic activity by importing competition and integrating the domestic economy in the world market. One should not, however, go overboard on this. A European Community trade official cited by the *Far Eastern Economic Review* (May 13, 1993) sums it up quite nicely and not surprisingly, since the European Community has not been averse to doing things along similar lines: "We're told that China has a socialist market economy. So far, our experience is that the market bits are on exports and the socialist bits are on imports." Exports and foreign direct investment have soared since the mid-1980s and are now, together with domestic marketization and property reforms, the engines propelling the economy's takeoff. Between 1980 and 1993 (Chinese customs data) exports and imports each increased by five times. From 1980 through 1991

---

[29]Yeh, "Macroeconomic Issues," and Ash, "The Agricultural Sector," 527, 551-52.
[30]Chai, "Consumption and Living Standards in China," 722, 723.

(customs data) the average annual rate of growth of foreign trade was 12.3 percent compared with world trade growth of 5.5 percent per annum. In 1993 exports rose 8 percent from the previous year and imports 29 percent (reflecting mainland China's investment boom). As a percentage of GNP, foreign trade has risen from about 10 percent in the late 1970s to 38 percent in 1992.[31] As was the case with Taiwan, the United States is the largest purchaser of Chinese-made exports (inclusive of reexports through Hong Kong). As had been the case with Taiwan, the United States has been registering (since 1983) a sizeable and growing deficit on its trade with mainland China (US$24 billion in 1993, expected to reach US$30 billion in 1994), resulting in the sort of trade tensions that accompany the Taiwan (and more broadly East Asian) development model. The evolution of the structure of Chinese exports broadly follows the lines of the Taiwan model.

Foreign direct investment (FDI), both contracted (pledged) and actual (realized), rose sharply after the mid-1980s, buoyed by investments from Hong Kong and Taiwan, that is, "overseas" Chinese capital inflows in search of cheaper land rental and labor costs, quite undeterred by the occasional brusque reassertion of the Communist Party's claim to monopoly political power (e.g., June 3-4, 1989). The absolute and relative importance of outside (Hong Kong, Taiwan) Chinese capital in total FDI in mainland China is a phenomenon unique in history. For example, FDI from Hong Kong accounted for roughly 60 percent of all realized FDI in mainland China in the period 1984-90. If Taiwanese contributions are included, the ratio rises to almost 75 percent. While such a high FDI concentration ratio makes excellent business sense in the present, it also poses delicate problems for the future. Even though near-abroad Chinese private investors have not been spooked by the Tienanmen massacre (which from a purely business standpoint restored a measure of social stability to the country), any sizeable mishandling of Hong Kong's looming reintegration with China or any rough play with Taiwan could very quickly shut off the investment spigot. Contracted FDI in mainland China during 1979-93 was US$221 billion, of which US$111 billion in 1993 alone: *that's* euphoria! Actually utilized FDI came to a cumulative total of around US$60 billion by 1993, US$25.8 billion of it (43 percent) in 1993. By the end of that year there were 167,500 foreign-invested firms in the coun-

---

[31]Lardy, "Chinese Foreign Trade," 694-95; "Statistical Communique of the State Statistical Bureau [SSB] of the People's Republic of China on the 1993 National Economic and Social Development" (February 28, 1994), *Beijing Review* 37, no. 11 (March 14-20, 1994): 23; *Business America*, February 1994, 14.

try, 50 percent more than the year before.[32]

A reviewer of mainland China's opening up concludes that "it is difficult to see the first ten years of China's 'open door' policy towards DFI [direct foreign investment] as anything other than a resounding economic success. . . . DFI has played a positive and significant role in the process of reducing the costs of catching up with the more developed economies. The Chinese goals of increased exports and technology transfer have been met, although not exactly as China's policy makers intended."[33]

5. Price and employment stability. The Taiwan development model is one of rapid and relatively smooth growth with price and employment stability. Over the twenty-eight-year period 1965-92 there were only three years on Taiwan in which the rate of increase in the consumer price index exceeded 10 percent, all three reflecting the steep increases in world oil prices (the two oil shocks). The unemployment rate on Taiwan since 1966 has never exceeded 3 percent, and for eighteen out of the twenty-seven years (1966-92) it has been below 2 percent.[34] Mainland China's growth in the reformist eighties and early nineties has been rapid but uneven, subject to recurrent inflationary surges, and attended by sizeable unemployment, both open and disguised, the latter mainly in state-owned industry. Chinese policymakers, in both Taiwan and on the mainland, have been at all times extremely sensitive to inflation and unemployment, for historical reasons (pre-1949 hyperinflation) and because inflation and unemployment erode much of the gain from growth by causing declines in personal real incomes, which in turn can translate into social and political unrest. Price indices for the mainland economy are not very informative or reliable. Official figures indicate an average annual rate of increase in market-determined prices of roughly 10 percent for the period 1980-89 with two inflationary spurts in 1985 (17 percent) and 1988 (32 percent). The average annual rate of increase in retail prices (prices of goods sold through the state's commercial channels and partly—12-15 percent—distributed through the "free" [but often government-constricted] market) for the period 1980-91 is put at 7.3 percent. Both figures probably understate the real situation by rather wide margins. In April 1993, the annual inflation rate was put at 17

---

[32] "Statistical Communique of the SSB," 23, and other Chinese government figures.

[33] Richard Pomfret, *Investing in China: Ten Years of the Open Door Policy* (Ames: Iowa State University Press, 1991), 137. The author, presumably writing under the impact of the Tienanmen Square massacre, concludes that in the light of this event, even "potential foreign investors are now reassessing their attitude towards China" (p. 144). Not so. Potential foreign (including foreign-Chinese) investors responded in a way to suggest that they are allergic to any democracy movements that disrupt the conduct of everyday business.

[34] *Taiwan Statistical Data Book 1993*, 16.

percent in the thirty-five largest cities compared to 20 percent in 1988, the year before Tienanmen. In March-April 1994 it had risen to an annual 23-26 percent, much higher for certain key foods and an estimated 30 percent in the countryside. In February 1994, the prices of vegetables, staple grains, and meat were respectively 54, 40, and 33 percent higher than a year before. In the absence of effective, preferably nonadministrative, anti-inflationary measures, inflation could accelerate to an annual rate of more than 50 percent by year's end.[35] One side-effect of the inflation has been to make real interest rates negative, this despite official increases in the interest rate on one-year bank deposits. This has tended to discourage personal savings and encourage occasional outbursts of hoarding of such valuables as gold and jewelry.

There are two major reasons why mainland China has had difficulty in achieving rapid growth with price and employment stability on the model of Taiwan. First, there are what one might call the "ordinary" developmental difficulties of coordination and property experienced by all developing market- and private property-oriented economies: problems caused by money wages rising faster than increases in labor productivity, monetary expansion fueling excess demand, ineffective monetary and fiscal policies, inadequate transportation and communications infrastructures, a sprawling underpaid and venal officialdom, difficulties involved in moving people from lower to higher value-added employments ("industrialization") compounded by high population growth rates or relatively low rates but high absolute numbers of people added every year (the Chinese case), and more. Second, there are "extraordinary" difficulties that originate in the effort to transform a bureaucratically coordinated, state/collective property-dominated system into one dominated by market coordination and private property. In other words, the second set of difficulties is caused by systemic transition from socialism to capitalism—by economic reform—and it compounds and often overlaps the ordinary developmental tribulations of countries growing out of a rudimentary to a more mature level of basically the same, market and private property-oriented system. These extraordinary difficulties have been experienced by all countries making the transition after the collapse of the Soviet system. Mainland China is not unique in this respect, except that it steadfastly denies what it is in fact doing, that is, abandoning classical socialism, and that, some foreign investors say, so far it has handled the mechanics of the economic transition better than others.[36]

---

[35]*Far Eastern Economic Review*, May 27, 1993, 68-69; *New York Times*, April 10, 1994, 3.

[36]The transition from socialism to a private property-dominated market-coordinated system

One cause of inflation, which seems to sit astride the "ordinary-extraordinary" divide, but is mostly attributable to an incomplete and often contradictory reform, is the state's apparent loss of (or at least much lessened) control over the money supply, which constitutes another departure from the Taiwan model. The demand-pull which caused the money to flow was mainly due to rapid growth of investment expenditures (one-third to one-half of the growth in aggregate demand in the 1980s) by newly more autonomous local governments, firms, and farm households which borrowed from financial institutions (extrabudgetary investment), whereas formerly their investment outlays would have been financed primarily through the state budget. Another reason for the rapid expansion of the money supply (M1, M2, and M3) throughout the 1980s and early 1990s—at two-digit levels, well above the growth rate of GNP—was the central government's need to cover its annual budgetary deficits (caused by expenditures rising more rapidly than revenues) with overdrafts from the People's Bank of China. While total government revenue in 1980-90 rose at an annual rate of 10.7 percent, current expenditure increased at an annual rate of 18.6 percent (subsidies alone at 12.1 percent).[37] The causes of this disparity are traceable to the reform, one of them being the increasing unwillingness and ability of the richer provinces to transmit locally collected tax revenues to the center. On this question of budgetary deficits, mainland China's reforms deviate from the Taiwan model's conservative fiscal policies characterized by budgetary surpluses in most years.

Mainland China's unemployment problem has been serious and due

---

is made "extraordinarily" difficult by socialist derivative values, such as security, equality, and stability, which have been internalized by large segments of the population and which tend to conflict with market ethics. The market system, as demonstrated by the Taiwan model, can work toward reducing insecurity, inequality, and instability by providing participants with rough equality of opportunity at the outset and by fine-tuning the market through monetary and fiscal policies, but it cannot automatically produce security, equality, and stability, nor guarantee them. These values have wide popular appeal that antedates and transcends socialist ideology and, as illustrated by post-socialist Poland, Hungary, Lithuania, Russia, and Ukraine, to name only a few, they remain deeply entrenched even when the absolute socialist values of central planning (bureaucratic coordination), public property, and the exercise of monopoly political power by the Communist party have been rejected by the people. In some societies that have not experienced socialism, traditional secular philosophies or religious value systems may also present obstacles to the acceptance of the ethics of the market system. Marketization is as much a state of mind as a matter of institutions. But institutions do matter, and socialist institutional arrangements (comprehensive state property, central physical command planning, and the notion of the firm as a social-cum-police security unit rather than an economic value-adding entity) have been more damaging to people's material welfare and more resistant to modernization than the most primitive tribal institutional arrangements.

[37]Yeh, "Macroeconomic Issues," 517, 534-37.

to the two sets of causes. Some of it is caused by demographic factors common to many developing countries (except that in mainland China they are more massive): rapid population growth and the growth in the numbers of working age people—697 million in 1990, an estimated 781 million in the year 2000, an increase of 84 million of whom 74 million will be looking for jobs. Add to this 12 million now unemployed or underemployed urban workers (a conservative figure), and 20 million redundant workers in state-sector enterprises and government organizations (a systemic or "extraordinary" problem that I would put at 30-35 million), plus at least 100 million surplus agricultural workers (some Chinese projections put that surplus at 200-350 million)—and you come up with a minimum grand total of 206 million job-seekers in the 1990s seeking the 125 million jobs that the economy is likely to generate in that period—on the assumption that the annual growth rate of GNP will be 6 percent and that the elasticity of employment with respect to income remains the same as in 1978-90. Such huge unemployment would certainly slow down the reforms (e.g., retard the application of bankruptcy laws to state firms, strengthen the tendency to set up regional protectionist barriers to the movement of labor from high unemployment areas, and delay capital deepening needed for productivity growth).[38]

6. Equity of income distribution. In Taiwan the ratio of the income of the highest fifth of households to the lowest fifth which was 11.6 in 1961 (20.5 in 1953), fell steadily to 4.2 in 1981 and rose gradually thereafter to 4.97 in 1991, still a very equitable spread by any standard.[39] The widening spread in the late eighties and early nineties has been due to stock exchange speculation and steep increases in real estate prices.

The mainland reforms have introduced the quasi-market distributional

---

[38]Ibid., 522. A high degree of labor mobility within and among industries, occupations, regions, firms, and business sizes is a characteristic of the Taiwan model. "There have been virtually no barriers to entry into any occupation or industry. Also, there has been a high degree of inter-generational mobility among the population." Hou, "Relevance of the Taiwan Model," 3. There is evidence that despite legal and illegal barriers to labor mobility on the mainland, the degree of such mobility has been rising since the beginning of the reforms. Large numbers of men have migrated from the countryside to the cities in search of work or better paid work. As a result, women now account for 70 percent of the rural labor force, a proportion expected to rise to 77 percent by the year 2000 (185 million) with only 55 million men left on the land at that time. Women have migrated mostly to nearby townships, where they now account for one-third of the work force in township industrial enterprises. *Wall Street Journal*, March 10, 1994, A13.

[39]*Taiwan Statistical Data Book 1990*, 61-62, and *1993*, 62-63. The lowest and second fifths of households had 21 percent of total household income in Taiwan in 1991, compared to 12 percent in developing countries. One might note, however, that official statistics on income distribution in Taiwan perhaps understate the disparities because of the existence of sizeable unreported incomes in certain segments of the economy.

principle of "from each according to his ability, to each according to his [in the countryside mostly her] work," which if adhered to results in widening income disparities. Several other forces have also contributed to this trend. One is the government's deliberate policy to increase income spreads so as to sharpen work incentives. Another is the side-by-side existence of market and planned economies with planned, relatively inflexible wages in the latter and many income enhancing possibilities in the former. Officials and others with access to both the market and planned segments (and the free and fixed prices in them) can, and do, engage in arbitrage activities thereby greatly benefitting their personal and extended household (i.e., their relatives') incomes. Following a small reduction in income inequality and in the incidence of poverty during the early phase of the reforms (1978-84), both rose during the later phase (1985-93). The growing income and wealth disparities are interpersonal, interregional (between the coastal and inland provinces), and intersectoral (between urban and rural earners) and are defended by trickle-down theories: some people get rich first, then their prosperity seeps down to the rest. It is thought that today the per capita income of the "gold coast" provinces is as much as ten times higher than that of the poorest inland regions. In 1980 the per capita income of peasants around Shanghai was more than three times that of peasants in the poor province of Kansu, rising to more than four times in 1990. Rural incomes are on average less than 40 percent of urban ones and the incidence of poverty is much higher in rural than in urban areas. A survey carried out by the State Statistical Bureau reveals that the bank deposits of mainland China's richest 3 percent exceeded the combined savings of the country's 800 million peasants.[40] Particularly galling is the perception of injustice. Despite a rising overall income level, there is a widespread feeling that many "undeserving" people are growing rich too quickly and not always in conformity with the principles expounded by marginal revenue product theories. Some of this feeling may be due to simple human envy. Some, no doubt, stems from deeply ingrained socialist notions of equality. But much comes from the simple observation that corrupt people in positions of monopolistic political power take advan-

---

[40] *The China Monitor*, January/February 1994, 12; Chai, "Consumption and Living Standards in China," 737-43; Wang Xiaoqiang and Bai Nangeng, *The Poverty of Plenty* (Houndsmills, Basingstoke, England: Macmillan, 1991). Reporting on peasant households in Szechwan Province the London *Economist* (May 8, 1993, 43) says: "It is unusual in the West to find people living next door to each other with so large (1 to 1/15 of income) differences between their incomes." Perhaps it was not so unusual in the West in the early decades of capitalist development. Taiwan during its early development phase apart, it is not unusual in market-oriented developing countries.

tage of the cracks between emerging markets and disappearing plan to appropriate ("privatize") monetary rents that were formerly collected in the form of nonmonetized privileges of power.

7. Investment in human capital. A key element of the Taiwan model has been heavy investment in developmentally relevant education. The story is well known and need not be repeated. In this respect mainland China has an enormous self-created handicap to overcome. Much has been done since 1978 to undo the ravages of the Cultural Revolution and earlier mind-shrinking ideological campaigns, but the problem will not quickly go away. Students in the hard, applied, and social sciences have been sent for study abroad (mainly to the United States) in large numbers and there has been a significant reduction in the ideological content of school curricula. However, the teaching profession, indeed the whole educational sector, are to all appearances not high priority funding areas. The share of educational expenditure in GNP fell steadily after the mid-1980s (3.1 percent in 1986, 2 percent in 1990) as did school enrollment. The latter may be attributed in large part to higher returns on work in the economy's market sector than on education under the reforms. Teachers are underpaid and their pay is frequently late in coming, and educational facilities remain underdeveloped. Illiteracy rates in the countryside are on the rise. Research and development (R&D) funding as a percentage of GNP declined after the mid-1980s (from 1.4 percent in 1984 to 0.7 percent in 1990), as did the numbers of R&D personnel.[41] The neglect of investment in human capital in the eighties and early nineties cannot long continue without producing negative effects on the economy's future "modern" (factor productivity improvement-driven) growth.

Conclusion

Mainland China's systemic transformation since 1978 may be likened to the growth path of a teenager who suddenly shoots up and looks ungainly because all the proportions are wrong. The juices are flowing and the hormones are acting up, which often makes him obnoxious. The rapid growth and the undisputed improvement in the material condition of very large numbers of people are due to the progressive abandonment of bureaucratic coordination (central planning) and the diminished role of state

---

[41]Yeh, "Macroeconomic Issues," 524-25; Raymond P. Byron and Evelyn Manaloto, "Returns to Education in China," *Economic Development and Cultural Change*, July 1990, 738-96. Taiwan's domestic R&D expenditure as share of GNP was 1.7 percent in 1991, after trailing at lower levels for a long while.

property, and their progressive replacement by market coordination and mixed, increasingly nonstate property forms inclined toward de facto private. The developmental success has also been due in large measure to mainland China's half door opening to the world market and the enthusiastic response to that aperture by foreign, particularly Hong Kong and Taiwan Chinese traders and investors. In this, as in some aspects of the internal reform, mainland China has reproduced elements of the Taiwan developmental model, albeit with many departures and exceptions, which is not surprising given the many objective (e.g., size) and subjective (e.g., ideology) differences between the two societies.

The systemic transformation of mainland China's economy is far from complete, and in fact, such evolutions have no preordained ending. Market coordination is beginning to emerge as the dominant force, but the markets are highly imperfect, much controlled and interfered with by cross-dressed entrepreneur-officials and official entrepreneurs, many of them crooked. Private property is impure, legally ill-defined, and poorly protected, and subject to the arbitrary incursions of Communist transvestites in an environment notable still for the absence of the rule of law. But, as nature would have it, the theoretically messy arrangement of highly uncertain gender has worked so far, neither better nor worse than Western capitalism years ago during its teenage transition to maturity. This fact, especially when contrasted with the transitional travails of Russia and the East European countries, has given rise to something approaching euphoria abroad. But great caution rather than great optimism is in order. Notwithstanding initial spectacular achievements in growth and raising living standards from low socialist levels, mainland China faces daunting objective (e.g., demographic) and systemic obstacles on its way to procuring a "comfortably well-off" standard of living for its people by the end of this century. The many reform-connected or partly reform-connected problems mainland China has experienced over the last sixteen years are due primarily to the insufficiency, haphazardness, and inconsistencies of the reform and in some respects to the reform's much-vaunted gradualness. The unevenness of growth; the post-1984 incentive problems in agriculture; heavy burden of subsidies paid to prop-up large loss-making state enterprises; recurrent inflation; open and disguised unemployment; the growing income and wealth gaps among households, regions, and sectors of the economy; the neglect of investment in human capital; and pervasive corruption of officials at all levels—insofar as all these are connected with systemic transition, they point, I believe, to the need to push forward with marketizing coordination and privatizing property. What mainland China has now is a loose arrangement, a collage, rather than a coherent seamless market system. This arrangement could easily become mired in a big Peru-like mercantilistic bog, if the distortions in price coordination and the ambiguities and uncertainties of the property structure are not removed and unambiguously clarified. Not least, the problem of reconciling pluralism in economics with political monopoly remains starkly posed.

5

Mainland China's Transition from a Planned to a Market Economy: New Breakthroughs and Hurdles

Chu-yuan Cheng

After fifteen years of incessant trial-and-error and several changes of course, mainland China's economic reform has reached a critical point. In November 1993, in the wake of Teng Hsiao-p'ing's (Deng Xiaoping's) 1992 "whirlwind,"[1] a "Decision on Some Issues Concerning the Establishment of a Socialist Market Economic Structure" was adopted by the Third Plenary Session of the Chinese Communist Party's (CCP's) Fourteenth Central Committee initiating an ambitious reform program. The new program shifts policy emphasis from the dismantling of the old, ossified system to the building of a new dynamic structure. The program also has been expanded from a single-item thrust to a more comprehensive, co-ordinated advance. The reform program involves the establishment of a modern enterprise system; a unified, open, and competitive market structure; a system of macroeconomic control; a more rational social distribution system; and a stratified social security system. Essentially, it is a grand plan, often referred to as "the Decision," to move mainland China away from the Stalinist central planning model to a market economy quite similar to the Western paradigm.[2]

---

[1]The Teng "whirlwind" refers to Teng Hsiao-p'ing's spring 1992 South China talks which swept the country like a whirlwind and infused fresh vigor into its reform and opening-up program. The remarks made historic contributions to mainland China's transition from a planned to a market economy.

[2]"Decision of the CPC Central Committee on Some Issues Concerning the Establishment of a Socialist Market Economic Structure" (Adopted on November 14, 1993 by the Third Plenary Session of the Fourteenth Central Committee), *Beijing Review* 36, no. 47 (November 22-28, 1993): 12-13. Hereinafter cited as the "Decision."

Because the reform program addresses the core of the economic structure, it has encountered increasing resistance. In recent months, the overheating of the economy and other side-effects of reform have triggered the reemergence of numerous social and economic maladies. The most blatant are double-digit inflation, widespread unemployment, rampaging corruption, and mounting rural and urban unrest. Signs of deep discontent are beginning to erode the confidence of the leadership. When the National People's Congress (NPC) convened in March 1994, the top leaders in Peking (Beijing) struck a note of caution and called for a balance among growth, stability, and reform.[3] With "stability" as the new watchword, the pace of the reform has slowed down considerably. However, the trend toward privatization, marketization, and globalization appears to be irreversible and inevitable.

The Reform Process

The reform program of the past fifteen years has followed an uneven path. The entire process can be roughly divided into three stages.

The initial stage, 1978 to 1984, focused on rural reform with the abolition of the communes and institution of the contract responsibility system. This first stage resulted in the institution of peasant incentives and a rapid resurgence in agricultural production. The advent of the new system ushered in significant changes to agricultural operations and the emergence of 20 million village and township industrial firms of all different sizes. By 1993, the village industries were employing more than 100 million workers and generating one-third of mainland China's gross national product (GNP).[4]

The second stage commenced with the adoption of the "Decision on Reform of the Economic Structure" by the Third Plenary Session of the CCP's Twelfth Central Committee in October 1984, which extended the reform to the urban areas. The highlight of the second phase involved the delegation of greater authority to individual enterprises in order to transform them into relatively independent economic units, responsible for their own successes and failures. Another major urban economic reform concerned the revamping of the price structure through the adoption of

---

[3]Li Peng, "Report on the Work of the Government" (Delivered at the Second Session of the Eighth National People's Congress on March 10, 1994), ibid. 37, no. 14 (April 4-10, 1994): ii, and *Wall Street Journal*, March 11, 1994, 6.

[4]For detailed analysis of the early reform, see Chu-yuan Cheng, "Economic Reform in Mainland China: Consequences and Prospects," *Issues & Studies* (Taipei) 22, no. 12 (December 1986): 13-44.

a two-tier pricing system. For most industrial intermediaries, this system involved a state-planned price for national allocation within the state plan and a negotiated price well above the planned price. The dual-level pricing system, while providing some incentives for producers, created unjustified disparities in competitiveness among enterprises. The new price system produced steep rises in the prices of basic materials, triggering a series of price hikes throughout the industrial sector and an inflationary spiral in the economy as a whole.

The third major measure during the second stage was the delegation of greater discretionary authority to local governments. Each province, after fulfilling its tax quotas, could retain most of its revenue. The retention of revenues at the local level drastically curtailed state revenues. In fact, they declined sharply as a percentage of national income from 37.2 percent in 1978 to 19.2 percent in 1988, a drop of 18 percentage points in ten years. The share of central revenues to total revenues also fell steadily, from 70 percent in 1952-57 to only 47.2 percent in 1988.[5] The decrease in state revenues and the increase in state subsidies for agriculture, foreign trade, and state enterprises created a huge state deficit. Between 1979 and 1988, the total state deficit exceeded 160 billion *yuan* (US$43 billion at the 1989 official exchange rate). To finance the deficit, the state resorted to heavy issuance of currency, which, in turn, accelerated inflation.

Moreover, the lax macro-management also led to a shift of capital investment authority from central control to local control. The portion of capital investment outside the central government budget grew from 16.7 percent in 1978 to 67 percent in 1988. The dispersion of funds resulted in an overextension of the scale of capital investment, distorted the allocation of capital, and underlay the rapid growth of inflation during those years. Widespread speculative activity, notably by state commercial units and government offices, exacerbated the inflationary spiral. The prevalence of "official profiteering" (*kuan-tao*) and the rise of a new privileged class contributed to popular resentment, culminating in bloodshed at Tienanmen (Tiananmen) Square.[6]

The Tienanmen incident severely set back economic reform by depriving the reformers of their brain-trust and halting all reform programs, which were either suspended or dismantled. The system of hierarchial control and egalitarianism remained basically intact. No separation between the government administration and the state enterprises existed, and state enterprises

---

[5]*Nan-k'ai ching-chi yen-chiu* (Nankai Economic Studies), 1990, no. 1:79-80.
[6]Chu-yuan Cheng, *Behind the Tiananmen Massacre: Social, Political, and Economic Ferment in China* (Boulder, Colo.: Westview Press, 1990), 13-25.

still lacked responsibility for their own profits and losses. The system often described as "everyone eating from the same pot" continued to dominate. The entire economic structure remained highly bureaucratic and inefficient. In the wake of the Tienanmen massacre, economic decision-making power was still consolidated in the hands of the hard-liners, who favored strengthening central planning and slowing the pace of economic growth.

The third stage began in late January 1992, when mainland China's paramount leader Teng Hsiao-p'ing, after a year of seclusion, suddenly reappeared to make a tour of Kwangtung (Guangdong) followed by a nineteen-day stay in Shanghai. In his southern tour, Teng made a series of speeches calling for bolder economic reforms and a broader opening-up policy. He especially stressed economic growth and the adoption of "useful elements of capitalism."[7]

Behind Teng's "southern offensive," a new wave of support for the acceleration of reform soon swept over the country. The reformist economists, after years of deliberation, reached a new consensus that it was time to discard the existing central planning system in favor of a capitalist-type market economy. With this new consensus, the CCP's Fourteenth National Congress in October 1992 adopted a "socialist market economy" as mainland China's new economic system. While the general guidelines were conceptualized during the Party Congress, the detailed program was not formulated until November 1993 at the Third Plenary Session of the Fourteenth Central Committee. Since that time, the reform has regained its viability; the reform program is expected to hit full stride in 1994.

In retrospect, the reform of the previous fifteen years has produced mixed economic results.

While the state enterprises suffered a steady deterioration, nonstate economic sectors grew rapidly. Village industries, private firms, individual businesses, and foreign-invested firms now account for more than 50 percent of the national economy. The rise of nonstate sectors helped to bolster economic growth. During the 1978-92 period, gross domestic product (GDP) increased 233 percent at an average annual growth rate of 9 percent, far exceeding the 6.1 percent annual growth rate of the preceding twenty-six years (1953-78). Industrial output scored a 320 percent increase at an average annual growth rate of 10.8 percent. Domestic and foreign trade also greatly expanded. Retail sales of commodities rose 8.5 percent a year, and foreign trade increased by 16 percent per annum. Total im-

---

[7]See Deng Xiaoping, "Gist of Speeches Made in Wuchang, Shenzhen, Zhuhai and Shanghai" (From January 18 to February 21, 1992), *Beijing Review* 37, no. 6-7 (February 7-20, 1994): 9-20.

port/export value jumped from 32nd place in the world in 1978 to 11th place in 1992. In general, standards of living have significantly improved, especially in the coastal areas.[8]

However, in terms of stability, efficiency, and equity, the reform program failed to achieve its goals. Since the 1950s, despite a central planning system, mainland China's economy has been susceptible to regular business cycles similar to those of Western market economies. Seven such cycles, each lasting an average of 4.6 years, have been completed to this date.[9] Underlying the business cycles are the capital investment cycles. Statistics show that from 1978 to 1992, measuring from peak to peak, the economy has completed three cycles; the peak rates of growth were 14.7 percent in 1984, 11.3 percent in 1988, and 13 percent in 1992. The three troughs of the cycles were 4.4 percent in 1981, 8.1 percent in 1986, and 4.1 percent in 1990.[10] The peak growth rates were three times the trough rates, indicating weak macroeconomic control.

Low efficiency has been a chronic flaw for the Chinese state enterprises. Reforms of the past fifteen years failed to make significant improvements. Large numbers of industrial firms, as well as enterprises in commerce and foreign trade, suffered losses. In recent years, 37 percent of state industrial enterprises operated at losses, 33 percent with "hidden losses," and only 30 percent made profits.[11] In 1992, state subsidies for the losses in industry, transports, commerce, food, agriculture, and construction exceeded 50 billion *yuan*, creating an unbearable burden on the state budget.

As a part of the reform, the government encouraged a segment of the population to enrich themselves, hoping that their affluence might stimulate others to emulate them. The policy led to the emergence of many new millionaires and widened the gap in income distribution. The opening-up policy also enlarged the income disparities between coastal and interior regions, causing the rise of localism.

By 1993, the mainland Chinese economic system was fettered by many structural impairments. Without a thorough reform of the system, the collapse of the state enterprise system seemed imminent.

The New Reform Programs

The Decision adopted by the Third Plenary Session of the CCP's

---

[8]Qin Hongyu, "China: 15 Years of Reform," ibid. 36, no. 43 (October 25-31, 1993): 20-24.
[9]Hiroyuki Imai, "China's Business Cycles," *China Business Review* (Washington, D.C.), January-February 1994, 14-16.
[10]Ibid.
[11]The PRC State Statistical Bureau, *Statistical Yearbook of China, 1993*, 31-32.

Fourteenth Central Committee on November 14, 1993 covers ten major aspects which are subdivided into fifty categories. Each category involves many detailed guidelines. The gists of several selected programs are presented in the following section with brief analyses and comments.

Reform of State Enterprises

The focal point of the new reform agenda is the effort to invigorate the floundering state enterprises. The first step was the adoption of a set of new regulations to clarify the relationship between the state and the enterprises. A set of Regulations on Transforming the Management Mechanism of Industrial Enterprises Owned by the Whole People was announced in July 1992. The Regulations grant enterprises fourteen detailed rights encompassing a wide range of freedoms in enterprise management. The new stipulations delineate the legal status of state-owned enterprises and abrogate the subordinate role of enterprises to government administrative organs. Each enterprise can now become an independent economic unit responsible for its own financial well-being. Efforts have been made to reform systems for labor, personnel, and wages throughout the country, involving 60,000 enterprises with 30 million workers and staff.

To convert state enterprises into autonomous entities requires separating the state and the enterprises. The crux of the transformation involves the issue of property rights. Under the new definition of property, although the state owns the assets of state-owned enterprises, the enterprises, as legal entities, possess all rights over the assets created by investment and have rights and responsibilities under law. The Decision encourages the establishment of standard shareholding companies and experimentation with the corporate system.[12]

While the stipulations give only guidelines, the recent changes in ownership structure among large and medium-sized state-owned industrial enterprises in Shanghai provide more concrete examples.

In 1993, one-third of large and medium-sized industrial enterprises in Shanghai transformed their ownership structures. During the conversion, a group of enterprises was selected for transformation into various company forms on the basis of property structures. This was done in accordance with five traits of modern enterprise systems: autonomous management, sole responsibility for profits and loses, self-development, self-restraint, and business achievements.

Large and medium-sized state-owned enterprises which record re-

---

[12]*Chung-kuo hsin-hsi pao* (China Information News) (Peking), February 14, 1994, 1.

markable progress after transformation can be reorganized into companies with sole investment following verification of the amount of assets held by the enterprise. Enterprises with different forms of ownership are encouraged to turn into joint-stock corporations.

In the process of transformation, large enterprises may become conglomerates integrating industry, business, scientific research, and finance. Small firms should become specialized. Well-performing businesses should change into corporations and loss-incurring firms should be eliminated through merger, auction, or declaration of bankruptcy.[13]

In short, according to the Decision, enterprise reform aims to gradually transform the backward, inefficient state enterprises into Western-type corporations and to sell or lease those small and medium-sized firms to private or foreign investors.

Reform of the Market System

In line with the enterprise reform is a series of new guidelines to revamp the market system. These guidelines attempt to establish a unified, open, competitive, and orderly market system. Major measures toward these ends include: (1) developing monetary, labor force, real estate, technology, and information markets; (2) revamping the price system—though price reforms have been conducted for more than ten years, much work remains to be done, including the abolition of the existing dual-pricing system and the marketization of prices for production factors; (3) developing wholesale markets and experimenting with the establishment of commodity futures markets; (4) developing professional intermediate organizations to cope with new economic conditions such as accounting, auditing and litigation, notarization and arbitration, etc; and (5) setting up chambers of commerce and various other associations based on Western precedent.

Reform of the Banking System

Mainland China's existing banking system is one of the weak links among its economic institutions. The banks lack clearly-defined functions. They are strongly bureaucratic in nature and are insensitive to costs and risks. There are six specialized banks: the Bank of China, the People's Construction Bank, the Agricultural Bank, the China Investment Bank, the Communications Bank, and the Industrial and Commercial Bank. Besides these six specialized banks, the People's Bank of China (PBC)

---

[13]Liao Ye, "Shanghai: Changes in Ownership Structure," *Beijing Review* 37, no. 13 (March 28-April 3, 1994): 17-19.

serves as a central bank. However, in practice, all the banks lack autonomy and fail to perform their assigned functions.[14]

The PBC, the central bank of the country, performs many functions
of a commercial bank by directly providing funds to state enterprises.
The specialized banks concurrently perform dual roles as policy-related
banks and as commercial banks. Together, the six state specialized banks
account for 98 percent of all business transactions, hold 84 percent of
assets and 75 percent of deposits and loans, and enjoy monopoly status.[15]
The lack of competition makes banking one of the most backward features
of the mainland Chinese economy.

The new reform aims to strengthen the role of the PBC as mainland
China's central bank and end its function as provider of capital to various
state enterprises. Instead, it will be responsible for independently implementing monetary policies, regulating and controlling the money supply,
and supervising and maintaining financial order through the monetary
instruments commonly used by most central banks in the world. These
include the adjustment of reserve ratios on deposits, changes of lending
rates, and open market operations.

Three new policy-related banks will be established to issue loans to
enterprises in accordance with state policy. They are the National Development Bank—in charge of capital investment; the Import and Export
Credit Bank—in charge of foreign trade; and the reorganized Agricultural
Bank of China—in charge of agricultural loans.

The four existing specialized banks will be gradually relieved of
their present policy-lending business and will operate as commercial banks
making their own decisions, bearing responsibility for their own profits
and losses.[16]

Reform of the Fiscal and Taxation Systems

Under the current reform, the decision to revamp fiscal and taxation systems has become highly controversial and has engendered strong
local resistance.

Under the previous system, each province, after fulfilling its tax
quotas, could retain surplus tax revenues accruing from a rising tax base.
The system benefitted the prosperous coastal provinces at the expense of

---

[14]"Decision," 20-21.

[15]Kiyoyuki Senguchi, "A Banker's View of the Chinese Economy," *China Newsletter* (New
York), no. 107 (November-December 1993): 10-14. Also Chang Chün-chou, "Basic Con-
ditions for Macro Financial Control," *Ts'ai-mao ching-chi* (Finance and Trade Economics)
(Peking), 1993, no. 12:23-24.

[16]*Ts'ai-mao ching-chi*, 1993, no. 11:6-7.

the central government. By 1992 central government revenues accounted for merely 45 percent of total national revenues, compared with 60 percent in 1978. Half of the central expenditures had to be financed through issuance of state bonds and bank loans.[17] In 1993, national revenues rose by 19.8 percent, with a 35 percent increase for local governments and a 6.3 percent decline for the central government. It is against this backdrop that a new system of sharing tax revenues between the central and local authorities was implemented in early 1994.

Under the new system, tax revenues are allocated to central and local authorities according to tax categories. Taxes closely related to the state's rights and interests or the exercise of macroeconomic control, such as turnover taxes and customs duties, are delineated as central taxes. Taxes closely related to local economic development and suitable for levy and management by local authorities are defined as local taxes; for example, enterprise income taxes, personal income taxes, and business taxes. Taxes directly related to economic development, including value-added taxes (VAT), security exchange taxes, and resource taxes, are delineated as taxes shared between central and local authorities.

Since the major tax resources are now collected by the central authorities, the excess tax revenues are to be returned to the local governments. The goal of the reform is to guarantee that the central government's share of national revenues returns to the 60 percent level of the early 1980s so that it may exercise macroeconomic control.[18]

Apart from the revenue-sharing system, the fiscal reform also includes the following four major aspects:

1. *Unifying the personal income tax:* The amended individual income tax law seeks to eliminate tax differentials on employment income between foreigners and Chinese citizens by establishing one rate table. The minimum monthly wage subject to taxation is 800 *yuan*. The tax rate for wages above the 800 *yuan* ranges between 5 percent and 45 percent according to income earned. As part of an effort to standardize the tax systems, the personal income tax has been revised to include the original personal income tax, a personal income regulatory tax, and an income tax on urban/rural industrial and commercial households.[19]

2. *Reforming the enterprise income tax:* The former practice of applying different tax categories and tax rates to enterprises of different

---

[17]New China News Agency (NCNA), Peking, February 18, 1994.

[18]Li Ning, "China Adopts New Taxation System," *Beijing Review* 37, no. 11 (March 14-20, 1994): 15.

[19]Ibid., 12.

ownership forms will be changed to a uniform income tax for domesti-
cally-funded enterprises. Such enterprises will be subject to a 33 percent
proportional tax rate, a rate identical to that levied on foreign-funded
enterprises and foreign firms. The new law unifies income tax rates for
both domestic and foreign enterprises in the future.[20]

3. *Turnover tax reform:* The original turnover tax consisted of the
value-added, product, and business taxes. Tax rates ranged from 3 percent
to 60 percent. As a result of the reform, the turnover tax is now included
in the general and special double-level regulatory systems and exists simultaneously with the value-added, consumption, and business taxes.

The VAT is levied and collected based on the value added to a good
at each stage of the production cycle, from the initial acquisition of raw
materials by producers to the purchase of finished goods by consumers. At
each stage, the VAT on a sale is collected by the seller and paid to the tax
authorities. The seller can deduct VAT paid at the previous stage from the
output tax he owes and thus pay only the difference to the tax authorities.[21]

Mainland China began introducing the VAT in the early 1980s. At
that time, the levying scope was rather limited and there were too many
different tax rates, rendering tax calculation extremely complicated. In
the current reform, the VAT is regarded as the first large tax category,
and tax rates are thoroughly simplified. The basic tax for most goods is
17 percent; food, water, energy, books, and fertilizers are taxed at 13
percent. It was calculated that government income from the VAT will
reach 200 billion *yuan* in 1994.[22]

4. *Reforming the tax levying and management systems:* Two sets
of tax authorities will be set up. The State Tax Bureau will take charge
of levying central taxes and tax sharing, while the local tax bureaus will
be responsible for collecting local taxes.

Reform of the Investment System

Since capital investment accounts for one-fourth of GNP, the goal
of the reform is to define the main body of investment and its scope of
responsibilities. Thus, accountability for each investment project should
be based on certain standards. The new guidelines include: (1) establishing
risk liabilities for corporate investment and banking credit; (2) competitive
project investment should be decided by the enterprises, which bear any

---

[20]Ibid.

[21]Desmond Yeung, "China's New Individual Income Tax Rates," *China Business Review*,
January-February 1994, 43-44.

[22]Li, "China Adopts New Taxation System," 12-13.

risks that may be involved; (3) a project registration system is to be set up in place of the current systems of administrative examination and approval; (4) construction of infrastructure projects is to be encouraged, and investments from various sources are to be drawn into this work; local governments are to be responsible for construction of infrastructure within their areas; and (5) the capital of major state construction projects is to be furnished by policy related banks, such as the National Development Bank.

Reform of the Planning System

To transform mainland China from the central planning system to a market economy, the nature and role played by the state plan is to be significantly changed: (1) state plans should be based on market conditions and should be guidance-oriented; (2) the tasks of state planning should be (a) to define development strategy; (b) to set objectives of macroeconomic control and industrial policies; (c) to make economic forecasts; (d) to plan major economic structures; (e) to plan distribution of productive forces; and (f) to plan the construction of key projects; (3) planning work should concentrate on the overall situation, strategies, and policies, with emphasis on drafting medium and long-term plans; and (4) a new national economic accounting system should be established, and the macroeconomic monitoring and warning systems should be improved.

In other words, the new planning system is to be suggestive instead of imperative. Like the systems implemented in Taiwan and Japan, it will provide only general guidelines, but not detailed plans.

Reform of the Foreign Trade System

The goals of expediting the reform of the foreign trade system are to accelerate mainland China's opening-up to the outside world, to bring the domestic economy in line with the international economy, and to enhance mainland China's competitiveness in the international market.

The basic requirements for the reform are to unify policies, to liberalize management, to encourage competition, to allow enterprises to assume responsibility for their own profits and losses, to integrate industry with trade, and to promote an agency system.

The main measures to be implemented include: (1) reforming foreign trade enterprises in accordance with the modern enterprise system and developing diversified, transnational trading conglomerates; (2) improving the state's foreign trade management by abolishing mandatory planning for import and export of commodities and standardizing the distribution of import and export quotas through bidding and auctions; (3) lowering the general level of tariffs and optimizing the structure of tariffs; (4) promoting the strategies for gaining greater market share and diversifying markets; and (5) revising the foreign exchange control systems by establishing a market-based floating exchange rate and gradually transforming the *jen-min-pi* into a convertible currency.

Establishing a Rational Income Distribution
System and Social Security System

The guiding principle of income distribution is "to each according to his work," whereby priority is placed on efficiency without jeopardizing fairness. A new mechanism will be established to reward individual labor and break away from egalitarianism. The policy of encouraging prosperity of some localities and people through honest labor and legal operations should be continued. Those who first become wealthy should be encouraged to support those lagging behind. Major measures designed to maintain even distribution of incomes include: (1) introducing regular wage increase mechanisms—the growth rate in the gross payroll of an enterprise should remain below that of its economic return; increases in staffing and the average wage of workers should remain below the rate of increase in labor productivity; (2) state protection of the legitimate incomes and property of all legal entities and residents, encouraging urban and rural residents to deposit their money in banks and to make investments, and permitting the distribution of earnings by capital and other production factors; and (3) establishing a stratified social security system which includes social insurance, social relief, social welfare, special care for the disabled, jobs for demobilized soldiers, and social mutual assistance and security based on accumulation of individual accounts.

The reform program highlighted above represents the most detailed and comprehensive blueprint ever advanced by the CCP Central Committee. A browse through this 55,000-word document reveals several salient features of the new reform program.

First, unlike early reform documents, the new Decision addresses almost every major aspect of economic life in mainland China. It specifically deals with enterprises, markets, money, banking, fiscal systems, taxation, planning, investment, price, foreign exchange, foreign trade, income distribution, and social security. The Decision also discusses scientific, technological and educational systems, legislation, and the legal establishment in terms of their compatibility with a market economy. The document should be considered as the definitive blueprint of mainland China's transformation from a command to a market economy.

Second, the entire program basically takes the Western capitalistic experience as its model. The goal of enterprise reform is to convert state enterprises into shareholding companies. The new banking system, revenue-sharing scheme, the introduction of the VAT and floating exchange rates, and the establishment of the social security system all are borrowed from

Western practices. Implementation of this program will move mainland China closer to a Western-style market economy.

Third, while the document is detailed in content, it fails to provide a timetable for implementation. Nor does it delineate the sequential order for implementation of the various reform plans. The realization of the plan thus depends on the will of the leader with ultimate power in Peking.

The Socioeconomic Consequences

Although the overall reform program has been acclaimed by many economists, initial implementation of portions of the plan has encountered strong resistance from various interest groups and has aggravated many social and economic problems.

Resistance from Local Authorities

One major goal of the reform plan is to curb the economic power of local authorities and reinforce central authority over macroeconomic control. Resistance from local authorities is seemingly inevitable.

The chief target of local resistance is the revenue-sharing system. Prior to the reform, under the "financial responsibility system," local authorities retained most tax revenues arising from local economic development. In 1992, only 20 percent of the total increase in national revenue flowed into central coffers while 80 percent was retained by local governments. With the advent of new revenue-sharing system, 70 percent of revenue increases will go to the central government and only 30 percent to local governments. Local authorities in those prosperous provinces in the coastal regions are particularly resentful of the new system.[23]

The new budget law has also triggered discontent among local administrations because it mandates the balancing of all local budgets. Local governments are not allowed to issue bonds to finance deficits. Since more than half of all counties are still in the red, the new laws adopted by the NPC in March 1994 have been widely criticized as impractical.

Monetary reforms depriving local autonomy in the soliciting of foreign loans have also provoked conflicts between central and local authorities. The friction will intensify as the reform progressively encroaches upon the basic interests of local authorities.

Outbreak of Labor Unrest

Another cardinal goal of the reform is to transform the overstaffed

---

[23]Joyce Peck, Peter Kung, and Khoon-Ming Ho, "Enter the VAT," *China Business Review*, March-April 1994, 40-41.

state firms into modern enterprises responsible for their own financial
well-being. Reduction of superfluous personnel becomes a necessity. In
1993, many state enterprises began to curtail employment. The coal industry alone has dismissed some 300,000 laborers. Under the old system,
the state provided not only jobs but also housing, transport and food
subsides, medical care, and many welfare programs. Unemployed workers
have now become not only jobless but also homeless. The change from
implicit unemployment under the old system to explicit unemployment
under the new system has become the main source of labor unrest in many
cities. In some cases, managers in charge of personnel dismissal were
murdered by laid-off workers. In other cases, the desperate unemployed
set fire to factories and mines.

Bureaucratic Sabotage

Implementation of the reform plan depends on the 27 million government bureaucrats. Although many top leaders and young officials see
the reform as the only hope for the country, a good number of middle-
echelon bureaucrats believe the reform directly threatens their authority
and privileges, and have consequently sought to stall the program. Instead
of explicit resistance, they sabotage the reform. The tactics of the Chinese
bureaucrats are captured by the expression, "When the boss sets a policy,
the subordinates always devise countermeasures." For instance, although
the Enterprise Bankruptcy Law was enacted in December 1986 and went
into effect on November 1, 1988, fewer than 1,000 bankruptcies have
been officially declared to date. As a result, despite the fact that tens of
thousands of state-owned enterprises are losing money, the government
must still pour huge funds into their subsidization.[24]

Bureaucrats not only sabotage the reform but also take advantage of
the relaxation of central control to engage in all kinds of illegal activities.
Corruption has become so widespread that the CCP Central Committee
launched several nationwide anticorruption campaigns, which have been
largely ineffective. Liang Kuo-ch'ing (Liang Guoqing), deputy prosecutor-
general, warned that the number of corruption and bribery cases has risen
rapidly in recent years. The exchange of favors for money is spreading
among some government departments and officials. Liang considers the
control of corruption and graft a precondition of further reform.[25]

Market Disturbance

In implementing reform, the abolition of the irrational price system

---

[24]Li, "China Adopts New Taxation System," 13.
[25]"China Launches Graft Crackdown," *Beijing Review* 36, no. 26 (June 28-July 4, 1993): 6.

was considered a key to the institutional transformation. Although a pattern of stop-and-go cycles was experienced in price reform during the first twelve years, giant strides have been made in the past two years. In September 1992, the State Price Administration announced that it has lifted price controls on 593 types of production materials. The number of production materials whose prices were controlled was, thus, reduced from 737 to 89.[26] A more significant move was adopted in 1993, when the price of grain was decontrolled. The government also relaxed wholesale prices on most steel products and a certain portion of coal subject to the state's unified distribution plan. Agency pricing was introduced for food grain, cotton, paper pulp, and detergent materials. The moves helped to further expand the role of market mechanisms in the formation of prices.

During the process of price reform, the government also raised the prices of railway freight transportation, cotton, and timber, as well as salt, electric power, and a certain amount of crude oil and refined oil. Some localities also increased prices for rents, running water, and public transportation. All these measures, while relieving a burden on basic industries, injected a cost-push inflation into the economy.[27]

The inflation was also fueled by the excessive investments in fixed assets during the past two years. Excessive demand for construction materials created a demand-push inflation. Overall retail prices rose 13 percent in 1993 while living costs in thirty-five large and medium-sized cities rose 24 percent. Toward the end of 1993, as the government considered raising the purchase prices of food grain, cotton, and other farm products in order to raise peasants' incomes, prices for food grain and vegetables soared 40 to 50 percent, triggering panic buying in many cities. In the first quarter of 1994, retail prices rose to a record high of 20.1 percent, and living costs for thirty-five cities increased by 30 percent. The upward price adjustments have created considerable disturbance in the market.

In summary, while the new reform program has boosted hopes about the establishment of a market economy, the road to be traveled promises to be a tortuous one.

Pitfalls and Prospects

Underlying the resistance, corruption, and disturbances are a host of severe hazards of the current reform program.

---

[26]"New Pricing Measure Sets Firms Free," ibid. 35, no. 37 (September 14-20, 1992): 6.

[27]Ling Bin, "1994 Influences on Continued Price Hikes," ibid. 37, no. 5 (January 31-February 6, 1994): 4.

First, one major goal of the economic reform is to transform the 110,000 large and medium-sized enterprises into financially independent, Western-style companies. The main reason for their chronic losses stems from two factors: they are overstaffed, and they have heavy welfare burdens. During the past four decades, the mainland Chinese government has adopted an employment maximization policy. Official sources indicate that at least 14 to 25 percent of the total work force was "latently unemployed." The number of superfluous personnel was approximately 30 million.[28] The annual cost to the state enterprises of supporting persons officially employed but lacking job assignments was estimated at 60 billion *yuan* (US$10.5 billion at the prevailing exchange rate). The existence of extensive, disguised unemployment in the state's economic system hindered any improvement in labor productivity. Moreover, since the country lacks social security for the retired and disabled, the state enterprises are still responsible for the cradle-to-grave services of each employee. The ratio of workers to retirees has fallen to 6 to 1 in recent years. There were 23 million retirees in 1991, and the number is growing yearly.[29] Between 1980 and 1989, profits and taxes of the state enterprises rose by only 87.8 percent, while welfare and pension expenditures rose 4.6 times.[30] Without a substantial reduction of superfluous workers, labor productivity will only continue to decline. Yet, large-scale layoffs will immediately cause social unrest and political crises. Despite the promulgation of laws and decisions to reform the state enterprises, there is still no effective solution to this dilemma.

Second, another major goal of the reform is to build a market economy by reducing government intervention. One precondition to this goal is the separation of the state and the enterprise. This, in turn, requires a thorough reform of the government structure and a radical streamlining of the state personnel system. Unlike the reforms in Russia and Eastern Europe, which started from political reform, mainland China intends to keep the political system intact by continuing the one-party dictatorship and maintaining the world's largest bureaucracy. Government employment has now swelled to more than 27 million, many of whom are in charge of economic affairs. Without a fundamental change of government functions and a substantial reduction of state personnel, the bureaucrats will continue to interfere in the affairs of the state enterprises. Establishment of a genuine market economy will not come easy.

---

[28]*Ching-chi jih-pao* (Economic Daily) (Peking), September 7, 1988, 1.

[29]China News Service, Hong Kong, July 10, 1991.

[30]*Chung-kuo t'ung-chi* (China Statistics) (Peking), November 1991, 9.

Finally, reform implies the transformation of the old system, ideas, and habits. The process inevitably conflicts with the interests of certain social groups. In mainland China, resistance to reform comes not only from the hard-liners but also from tens of millions of common people who resent the profits that some will stand to gain from reform. As more millionaires emanate from the reform, social conflict can be expected to grow. Moreover, reform of the old price system by lifting price controls and eliminating those below-cost pricing will naturally trigger a cost-push inflation. All of these will become sources of social unrest and will challenge the goal of stability.

For all these reasons, the mainland Chinese economic reform will experience a "stop-and-go" effect: two steps forward followed by one step back. However, the reform and opening-up policy carried out in the past fifteen years have expedited the processes of marketization, privatization, and globalization of the mainland Chinese economy. At the end of 1979, the first year of reform, the government still controlled more than 90 percent of commodity prices. By the end of 1992, commodity prices subject to the market mechanism accounted for 93 percent of the total value of retail sales, 81.8 percent of the total sales value of farm produce, and 73.8 percent of the total revenue received from sales of capital goods.[31] The marketization of prices has basically been completed.

In 1979, of total industrial output, state enterprises accounted for 78.5 percent, collective firms accounting for the other 21.5 percent. No private sector existed. By 1993, state enterprises' share dropped to 48 percent. The nonstate sector, including individual, private, foreign-funded, and village industries, accounted for 52 percent. It is expected that by the year 2000, the state enterprises' share of total industrial output will drop to only 25 percent.[32]

In 1978, foreign trade accounted for only 9 percent of mainland China's GNP. In 1993, its share of GNP rose to 37 percent. There are now 170,000 foreign-invested and foreign-owned firms in mainland China. They contribute 11 percent of mainland China's 1993 industrial output and 34 percent of its total foreign trade.[33]

Based on these three sets of statistics, regardless of the tortuous path the mainland Chinese reformers may tread in the years ahead, one thing is quite sure—there will be no returning to the old planned system.

---

[31]See note 27 above.

[32]Liu Kuo-kuang, "Theory and Practice of China's Socialist Market Economy," *Chung-kuo ching-chi wen-t'i* (Problems of Chinese Economy) (Amoy), 1993, no. 1:3.

[33]*People's Daily*, April 27, 1994, 1.

6

Reemergence of Chinese Nonstate Enterprises: Trends, Fluctuation, and Regional Variations

Belton M. Fleisher
Wen Lang Li, and Jian Chen

The purpose of this chapter is to examine the growth of nonstate ownership forms in the manufacturing sector of the mainland Chinese economy and the relationship between ownership structure and economic growth. The mainland Chinese economy is currently undergoing rapid industrialization and by some measures is one of the most dynamic economies in the world. The annual rate of economic growth was more than 10 percent over the last five years. Depending on how one prices total output, the current value of mainland China's gross domestic product (GDP) may place it as the third largest economy in the world.

Sheer size notwithstanding, based on per capita GDP, mainland China is still a Third World country. Despite the uncertainty of economic estimates, mainland China's per capita income currently does not exceed US$500 per year. The low standard of living was mainly caused by political turmoil in China's recent history. Since 1850 China has experienced numerous civil wars and political disasters. The Communist victory in 1949 was a major turning point, signaling an end of international colonialization. Unfortunately, internal political struggles did not cease in 1949. The economic tragedies of the Great Leap Forward movement during 1958-62 and the political tragedies of the Cultural Revolution during 1966-76 severely set back the Chinese economic development process. Orthodox Marxist ideology initiated both movements. The underlying ideological commitment was to collectivize and nationalize the Chinese industrial structure. Previously, the Chinese economy was more or less a privately owned agrarian economy. Marxist social policies considered the private industrialized mode of production as inefficient and outmoded. To the Chinese Communists (following to some extent the example set by the former Soviet Union), modernized industrialization implies a collectivist, large-scale industrial organization. Consequently, the Chinese industrial structure was transformed from individualist to state and collective ownership.

The death of Chairman Mao in 1976 was the beginning of economic liberalization of the mainland Chinese economy. Since then the mainland Chinese economy has undergone a slow process of recovery from central planning, moving toward a market orientation. Teng Hsiaop'ing's (Deng Xiaoping's) economic policy is widely acclaimed to be market oriented. The now famous agricultural reforms introducing the "household responsibility system" have largely privatized the work force in the largest sector of the mainland Chinese economy. In the nonagricultural sector, various forms of ownership have emerged from within the socialist economy. Roughly speaking, mainland China currently has four types of ownership outside of agriculture: state-owned enterprises (SOEs), collective-owned enterprises (COEs), joint government-private ownership ("joint ventures"), and private ownership (*ke-t'i-hu*). Despite its decline in importance, the state-controlled sector is still the largest. The share of SOEs in the total output value of industry peaked in the late 1970s at over 75 percent, and has now declined to slightly less than 50 percent. The fastest growing sector consists of the COEs in rural and small urban areas, called "township and village enterprises" (TVEs) (*hsiang-chen ch'i-yeh*). They engage in nonagricultural projects beyond their original geographic boundaries.

Denationalization implies the relative decline of SOEs and growth of the COEs, joint ventures, and individual household businesses. Only the fourth ownership form, the so-called individual household, is truly a private enterprise controlled by the individual. Severe limitations are imposed on the development of this sector, as it is incompatible with the Marxist ideology. However, the COE form of ownership is viewed by many orthodox leaders as consistent with Chinese socialism. In its TVE form, the clan or village organizes itself into a business enterprise. It then competes with other enterprises of all forms just as a conventional corporation might.

Whether COEs or TVEs should be viewed as employee-controlled firms, some hybrid of state-owned and private enterprises, or as motivated by strictly private, profit-maximizing objectives is open to debate. What is not questioned is their phenomenal economic success (as a group) over the past fifteen years. Martin Weitzman and Chenggang Xu develop an interesting interpretation of TVEs as a product of, and well adapted to, the social structure of mainland China's rural com-

munities.[1] Barry Naughton points out that TVEs are certainly not em-
ployee-owned enterprises; he argues persuasively that as a first approximation TVEs are best viewed as conventional profit-maximizing enterprises
with property rights that are well defined de facto if not de jure.[2] It is
beyond the scope of this chapter to investigate the property rights, control
mechanisms, and incentive structures of TVEs and COEs. For our purposes it is sufficient to assume that they behave as conventional profit-
maximizing firms of standard economic theory, even though a more
thorough analysis would yield interesting hypotheses not proposed or
tested in this chapter.

In the next section, we first examine the change of mainland China's
industrial structure since the 1950s. We then look at the relative size of
the nonstate portion of the Chinese economy. We see that the private
sector was very strong before 1955. It was then reduced to a negligible
proportion of the economy through the 1960s-1970s. Currently it is
regaining its former strength in mainland China. Third, using provincial
data, we examine the association between the change in proportion of
nonstate ownership and employment and output growth in mainland
China's manufacturing sector. Finally, we explore factors associated with
growth of the nonstate sector across provinces and suggest factors that
may have played a causal role. We will pay special attention to economic
changes during the reform period which began in the Teng era.

In the final section, we draw some conclusions about the importance
of the movement away from state ownership for mainland China's economic growth and the likely continuing role of the state sector as an
absorber of excess labor. We also consider some problems involving
mainland China's denationalization process.

The Structural Transformation of Mainland China's Economy

At the time of the 1949 Communist takeover, China was a Third
World society with more than 80 percent of its labor force in agriculture.
However, in the last ten years, mainland China's economy has undergone
a tremendous transition. Its agricultural population has drastically declined to roughly 300 million people, approximately 60 percent of the

---

[1]Martin Weitzman and Chenggang Xu, "Chinese Township Village Enterprises as Vaguely
Defined Cooperatives," Centre for Economic Performance Discussion Paper no. 155 (London, June 1993).

[2]Barry Naughton, "Chinese Institutional Innovation and Privatization from Below," *American
Economic Review* (Papers and Proceedings of the 106th Annual Meeting of the American
Economic Association) 84, no. 2 (May 1994): 266-70.

Figure 6.1
Social Labor Force (Employment) by Type of Industry

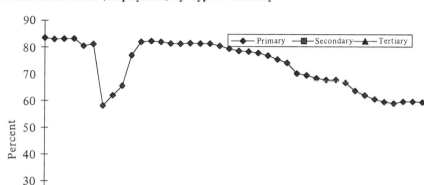

Source: *China Statistical Yearbook, 1992*, 83.

total labor force. Rapid industrialization has created a number of disruptions in China's traditional society.

Figure 6.1 illustrates the change in mainland China's industrial structure since 1952. The period during 1958-62 was an exceptional example of mainland China's industrialization process. It clearly illustrates the dramatic effect of state intervention in mainland China's economic condition. The so-called Great Leap Forward was conceived by Chairman Mao as a means of mobilizing China's abundant agricultural labor force to create a labor-intensive manufacturing sector. Mao viewed this campaign as a means of lifting mainland China from its Third World status and drastically raising labor productivity. Because of its emphasis on steel production, Mao's policy is labeled as *t'u-fa lien-kang* (indigenous approach to steel production). All households in mainland China were forced to join in steel production enterprises. People's backyards were transformed into metal producing furnaces. As shown in figure 6.1, from 1956 to 1957 mainland China's agricultural population was drastically reduced from 82 percent to 58 percent, and the nonagricultural population surged from 22 percent in 1957 to 42 percent in 1958.

Mao's sociological solution to accelerate the industrialization process proved to be an economic disaster. In 1962, mainland China's agricultural labor force rebounded to more than 80 percent. Demographers showed that nearly 20 million people starved to death during the four-year Leap Forward period. The indigenous route to producing metal resulted in useless and low quality products, and the farm population could not produce enough to feed the Chinese population. Famine and starvation prevailed during the drastic social mobilization process. Mainland China learned from this example that state intervention should not be relied upon to produce industrialization artificially.

Mainland China's modern economic growth accelerated with Mao's death in 1976. Currently nearly a quarter of mainland China's labor force is in the industrial sector, and the trend of the past fifteen years shows no sign of abating. While mainland China cannot currently be classified as an industrial society, it seems feasible that in the next decade mainland China will approach the status of a truly industrializing society, with perhaps 60 percent or more of its labor force in the nonagricultural sector.

The Changing Role of the State in the Mainland Chinese Economy

The development of mainland China's economy follows roughly four stages of development: the revolutionary period, 1949-56; the turbulent period, 1957-63; the collectivist period, 1964-77; and finally, the denationalization period, 1978-present.

The Revolutionary Period

In the revolutionary period (1949-56) China's Communist government underwent consolidation. The private sector was initially strong. In fact, more than a third of Chinese workers were employed in individually owned enterprises. Even though the Communists would have liked to eliminate individually owned enterprises, they were not successful until 1956. In the revolutionary period two distinctive trends were visible: (1) the gradual decline of individually owned enterprises (through 1955) and (2) the sudden increase in township (collective) enterprises. Whereas TVEs accounted for only 1 percent of nonagricultural employment in 1952, their employment share had increased to over 20 percent by the end of 1956. It is fair to say that Chinese Communist economic policy was not a drastic elimination of private enterprise, if by private we include the nonstate, collective form of ownership. Rather, there was a gradual transformation from traditional private enterprise to collective ownership.

The Turbulent Period

The turbulent period (1957-63) represented an all-out attack on the nonstate sector of mainland China's economy. The nonstate sector's share of nonagricultural employment fell from 23 percent in 1957 to 15 percent in 1959. However, by 1963 it had recovered to 28 percent. Obviously, the turbulent period was an economic disaster. The attempt to radicalize mainland China's state economy was unsuccessful. We should point out that even amid the political turbulence, individual enterprise was allowed to exist. A minimum of roughly 5 percent of mainland China's nonagricultural employment was accounted for by individual households. Combined with the huge agricultural sector which was predominantly owned by individual farmers, mainland China's economy could hardly have been considered nationalized up until 1964.

The Collectivist Period

The collectivist movement of the mainland Chinese economy reached its climax during the Cultural Revolution (1966-76). The massive agricultural sector was transformed into the people's communes. Nearly 80 percent of China's workers were organized into socialist economic units. Agricultural land was no longer in individuals' hands. Within the nonagricultural sector, township industry was allowed to exist, accounting for roughly 23 percent of mainland China's nonagricultural labor force. However, even vestigial individual ownership was no longer permitted. It was virtually eliminated between 1964 and 1976.

The Denationalization Period

The end of the Cultural Revolution represented the beginning of the reprivatization of the mainland Chinese economy. In contrast to the Soviet Union, mainland China experienced a "truly Communist" economy only for roughly a ten-year period. After the death of Mao, mainland China's economy became rapidly liberalized. Township enterprises began to grow, as did those owned by individual households. Currently, about 25 percent of mainland China's workers are employed by township enterprises and about 5 percent by individual households as shown in figure 6.2. As figure 6.2a shows, these 30 percent of the work force account for over 40 percent of nonagricultural production, and this superiority in nonstate worker productivity is a significant and well-known factor in mainland China's recent explosive economic growth.

It is becoming difficult to characterize today's mainland Chinese economy into three sectors: state, township, and individual. Currently, nearly 1 million Chinese are employed in the mixed private-state ownership (joint ownership) sector. The infusion of foreign capital to mainland China has been an important catalyst for the privatization of mainland China's economy. This fourth mixed type of enterprise has just begun, but it is very dynamic and strong. Joint ownership generally takes two forms. One is a joint venture between some level of government (state,

Figure 6.2
Nonagricultural Social Labor Force (Employment) by Ownership

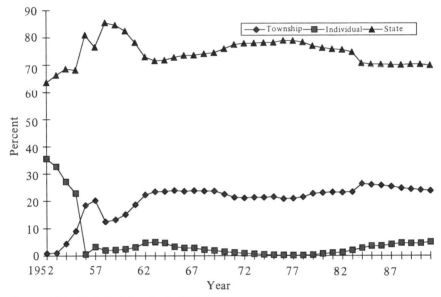

Source: *China Statistical Yearbook, 1992*, 79.

Figure 6.2a
Percentage of Gross Output Value of Manufacturing Sector by Ownership

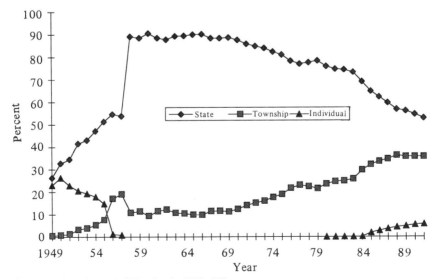

Source: *China Statistical Yearbook, 1992*, 368.

Figure 6.3
Annual Growth Rate of Staff and Workers by Ownership and Industry (1978-91)

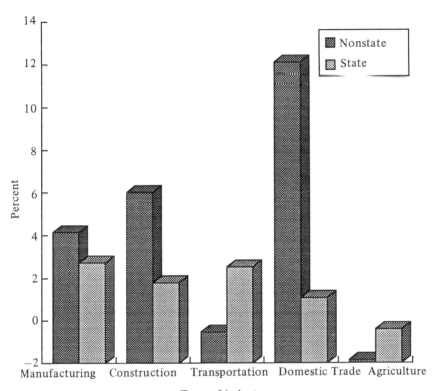

Sources: *China Statistical Yearbook, 1992*, 86, 89.
Note: "Staff and workers" does not include rural laborers and urban individual laborers.

provincial, or municipal) and foreign enterprises, and the other is govern-ment-individual joint ownership. From 1974 to 1991 Chinese workers employed in joint venture enterprises increased drastically from 31,000 to well over 1,000,000.

The increasingly important role of the nonstate sector is illustrated clearly in figure 6.3. Over the period 1978-91, in every major industry group except agriculture and transportation, employment growth in non-state-owned enterprises has outstripped growth in the state sector. In trade, perhaps the flagship industry reflecting the transmission of the benefits of economic growth to the general public, nonstate growth out-stripped the state by a ratio of more than six-to-one.

Problems in Denationalization

Mainland China's economic development strategy has been characterized by a serious conflict between the desire to maintain the vitality and dominance of state enterprises on the one hand, and the drive to increase the autonomy of township enterprises, on the other. These two strategies are obviously difficult to achieve simultaneously. The state enterprises are notoriously inefficient, as is suggested by the much sharper downward trend in the state's output share in figure 6.2a, compared to its employment share in figure 6.2. Nevertheless, the mainland Chinese government is at least nominally committed to guaranteeing the survival of the state enterprises even though it often has to turn to international loans and assistance in order to continue funding them. Even with such enormous effort, many state enterprises fail. Because of such failures (and an apparent willingness to tolerate them in the name of forcing increased efficiency), mainland China is faced with the threat of social disorganization and massive unemployment.

Nonstate Ownership and Economic Growth in the Mainland Chinese Economy

In this section, we present the results of a frankly exploratory statistical investigation of the role of denationalization in mainland China's recent economic growth and of the factors associated with the variation in the size of the nonstate sector within mainland China. Data at our disposal currently limit us to the period through 1989.

In table 6.1 we explore the role of the average level of denationalization on the growth rate of nonagricultural GDP per capita across

Table 6.1

Dependent Variable Percentage Growth of Nonagricultural Real GDP per Nonagricultural Population, by Province, 1978-89 (%)

Constant	Mean nonstate/total manufacturing output ratio (%)	Initial Y (in real 1978 nonagricultural GDP/nonagricultural population	Per capita foreign investment (1989, US$)	Coastal location	Adj. R^2
36.36	0.145	−5.30	0.04	−0.63	0.76
(8.69)	(5.33)	(8.46)	(3.21)	(0.98)	

See text for variable definitions.
Absolute values of *t*-ratios in parentheses.
Source: Tien-tung Hsueh, Qiang Li, and Shucheng Liu, *China's Provincial Statistics 1949-1989* (Boulder, Colo.: Westview Press, 1993).

twenty-nine provinces. (Tibet is excluded.) The variable representing denationalization is the 1978-89 mean proportion of each province's total output value in the manufacturing sector produced in nonstate enterprises, which includes collectives, joint ventures, and urban individual proprietors (*ke-t'i-hu*). The other right-hand variables are selected on the basis of their intuitive appeal as "causes" of economic growth. The initial Y variable is included because it is consistent with well-known models of economic growth which imply *convergence* toward an equilibrium value of GDP over time. It is hypothesized to have a negative regression coefficient.

The adjusted R^2 in table 6.1 is quite high, and the regression coefficients all have signs as expected, except for coastal location. The weak performance of coastal location suggests that the remaining variables capture much of the impetus underlying economic growth associated with the well-known advantages of the coastal provinces. The "effect" of the proportion of a province's nonstate economic sector on economic growth is quite significant, both statistically and substantively. A ten percentage point difference in this ratio (which is well within the sample range) is associated with a higher growth rate of about 1.5 percent per year, which is about one-third of the average growth rate in the sample over the period observed.

The coefficient of initial Y implies that a doubling of initial GDP per capita is associated with a 5.3 percentage point decline in average annual growth. Other things equal, provincial GDP per capita tends to converge to a common equilibrium value. Foreign investment is positively associated with GDP growth, and is highly significant. Its reported range is from virtually zero up to almost US$100 per capita. This implies that economic growth in the province receiving the greatest foreign investment per capita was 4 percent per year greater than the province with no foreign investment, other things equal.

Table 6.2 summarizes our exploratory investigation of factors associated with the size of the nonstate, nonagricultural sector. The rationale for selection of the right-hand variables is as follows. Nonagricultural GDP per nonagricultural population of 1978 is chosen to represent a source of funds to provide initial capital for urban collectives, individuals, and joint venture. It is hypothesized to be positively associated with the size of the nonstate sector. The impact of the share of nonagricultural labor in the total provincial labor force (in 1978) is hypothesized to be negative, because it (inversely) reflects the number for agricultural workers seeking to improve their standard of living. That is, the greater the relative size of agriculture in the economy, the greater is the potential "reserve army of unemployed" available for jobs in collectives or as self-employed workers. Coastal location reflects both access to export markets and ties

Table 6.2

Dependent Variable Mean Nonstate/Total Manufacturing Output Ratio 1978-89, by Province (%)

Constant	Log 1978 nonagricultural GDP per nonagricultural population	1978 nonagricultural labor/total labor (%)	Coastal location	1957 nonstate/total manufacturing output ratio (%)	Adj. R^2
42.36	–1.09	–0.32	16.95	–0.07	0.68
(1.49)	(0.49)	(4.16)	(5.39)	(0.77)	

Absolute values of t-ratios in parentheses.

Source: Hsueh, Li, and Liu, *China's Provincial Statistics 1949-1989.*

to overseas Chinese and thus direct foreign investment. It is therefore expected to be positively associated with the size of the nonstate sector of the economy. Finally, we chose the variable, 1957 size of the province's nonstate/total manufacturing output ratio, to reflect an initial tradition of nonstate enterprise. Its sign is expected to be positive.

The overall "fit" of the regression reported in table 6.2 encourages us to believe that we have identified some factors associated with the size of the nonstate sector in mainland China. Perhaps most surprising is that the size of the nonstate/total manufacturing output ratio in 1957 does not appear to be significantly associated with the size of the nonstate sector in the period of post-Mao economic reform. One explanation for this may be that by 1957 (the earliest year for which we have provincial data) the Communist government of China had already severely curtailed private forms of business, as discussed above. More exploration of the role of provincial tradition in determining the current size of the non-state sector is called for. Another possible explanation for the "poor" performance of the tradition variable is that its influence is reflected in the coastal-location variable. The sign of nonagricultural GDP per capita is negative, contrary to hypothesis. The other two estimated regression co-efficients in table 6.2, reflecting the influences, respectively, of coastal location and the relative size of the nonagricultural labor force in 1978 (representing inversely the importance of the potential "industrial reserve army"), are as hypothesized and are both large and highly significant. A coastal province, other things equal, is estimated to have almost seventeen percentage points of its average 1978-89 manufacturing output produced in nonstate enterprises (slightly more than double the mean and approximately half of the difference between the maximum and minimum of this variable). A province with the maximum proportion of its 1978 labor force in agriculture (85 percent) had, on average, about thirteen percentage points more of its average 1978-89 manufacturing output produced in nonstate enterprises than a province with the minimum proportion of nonagricultural labor force in 1978 (36 percent).

In conclusion, we find that the size of the nonstate sector is positively associated with nonagricultural GDP growth in mainland China, and a principal factor that we have identified as determining the size of the nonstate sector is that it is a critical absorber of mainland China's immense surplus rural population. These observations are broadly consistent with the well-known theory of "economic development with unlimited supplies of labor," stated in modern times by W. Arthur Lewis.[3] That this model applies to the Chinese case is, of course, intuitively appealing. We note that data on wages are also consistent with this view.

Although mainland China has experienced significant economic growth as measured by both GDP and per capita GDP since reform began in the late 1970s, the legendary incomes received by a few taxi drivers and exceptional *ke-t'i-hu* are not reflected in the wages of workers in either the state or collective sectors as illustrated in figure 6.4. Most significantly, the relative growth of the nonstate sector has been maintained without increasing wages relative to the state sector. This is consistent with the model of an "infinite" supply of labor readily flowing from agriculture to nonagricultural jobs as soon as they become available.

Conclusion and Prospects for the Nonstate Sector

Joseph Schumpeter advocated the linkage between entrepreneurship and democratic systems. The theoretical underpinnings lie in the formation of a strong middle class. The rise of the middle class is generally believed to be the fundamental social force for mainland China's future and continuing reform. It is generally believed that a strong middle class is likely to strive for economic privatization and consequently, the rise of political liberalization. If mainland China's nonstate sector grows rapidly in the next few years, the formation of an entrepreneurial class may contribute to mainland China's political democratization.

However, the most important portion of the nonstate sector consists of the COEs, not the so-called individual households, which are likely to be the strongest impetus for democratization. Thus, mainland China's future political development and progress toward a democratic society may be a very slow process. An important reason for the relatively slow

---

[3]W. Arthur Lewis, "Economic Development with Unlimited Supplies of Labour," *The Manchester School of Economic and Social Studies* (1954): 139-99.

Figure 6.4
Annual Wage by Ownership

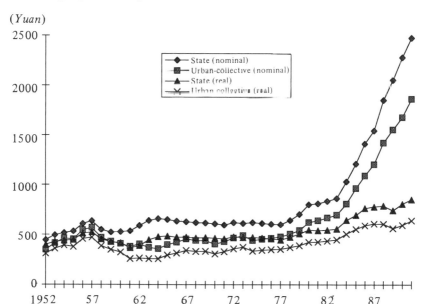

Source: China Statistical Yearbook, 1992, 112, 206.

growth of the *truly* private sector in mainland China is capital constraints. Private entrepreneurs rely on family networks, within mainland China and overseas. They do not in general have equal access to all the forms of investment funds that government-sponsored collectives do. Moreover, they are not allowed to hire a large number of nonfamily employees. Thus, the proportion of individual workers has not yet exceeded 5 percent of mainland China's nonagricultural labor force.

A further constraint of growth of the private sector is that relatively few enterprises are found in manufacturing industries. As figure 6.5 indicates, domestic trade is the most important industry group in which individual proprietors are found. Individual workers encounter enormous difficulties to penetrate the manufacturing sector, both legally and because of capital constraints mentioned above. Foreign capitalists are allowed to penetrate mainland China's secondary industries more readily than are native Chinese. Less than 20 percent of mainland China's urban individual workers are allowed to get into production industries.

Figure 6.6 provides another indicator of the relative unimportance of private ownership in mainland China's nonagricultural industries. Across

Figure 6.5
Percentage of Individual Ownership by Industry

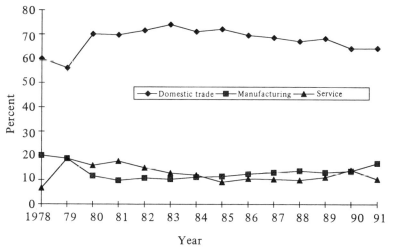

Year

Source: *China Statistical Yearbook, 1992*, 92.
Note: Percentage of individual ownership is measured by the ratio of urban individual laborers in specific sector to total urban individual laborers.

Figure 6.6
Individual Ownership vs. Percentage of Nonagricultural Labor by Provinces (1991)

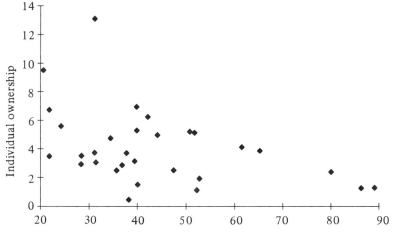

Percentage of nonagricultural labor

Source: *China Statistical Yearbook, 1992*, 84, 95.
Note: Individual ownership is measured by the ratio of urban individual laborers to total nonagricultural labors.

all of mainland China's provinces, there is a pronounced negative cor-
relation between the relative size of the nonagricultural labor force and
individual ownership. It is an interesting curiosity that the most unexpected growth of individual entrepreneurship has been in Tibet, the most
isolated and remote area in China. Tibet apparently was given special
local autonomy for its economic development.

In this chapter we have presented a picture of mainland China's
mixed progress toward denationalization Although the central government occupies a diminishing role in mainland China's economy, provincial,
municipal, and village governments have taken the lead in industrialization
in the post-Mao reform era. Relaxation of laws restricting the role of
private entrepreneurs outside the areas of trade and services and modernization of credit markets are probably both necessary for mainland China's
emerging private sector to continue to prosper and to move heavily into
manufacturing industries. If those conditions emerge, then there will be
greater hope for a growing middle class to propel mainland China into
the ranks of the world's modern industrial democracies.

7

Migration and Politics on the Shanghai Delta

Lynn T. White III*

The largest quick urban immigration in all human history has occurred since the early 1970s in mainland China. Measurement problems and official embarrassment have obscured this cataclysmic shift of people. A United Nations agency estimates the city portion of China's people as 17 percent in 1970, up only to 26 percent in 1990. The World Bank suggests a much more dramatic change: from 18 percent urban in 1970 to 56 percent in 1990.[1] The differences come mostly from diverse definitions

*All mistakes that have migrated into this essay are the faults of the author. He is nonetheless grateful to the following organizations and people for their generous support of his research: He thanks the Institute of International Relations at National Chengchi University and its Director Bih-jaw Lin, as well as the Centre of Asian Studies of the University of Hong Kong and its Director Edward Chen, for unstinting logistic help and library access. He also thanks the financial supporters of his current research on Shanghai's reforms: the Chiang Ching-kuo Foundation for International Scholarly Exchange (USA) and its North American Director Hsing-wei Lee, and Princeton University's Woodrow Wilson School and its Dean Henry Bienen. Superb advice on sources has come from geographer Ronald Skeldon of the University of Hong Kong and this author's colleague and friend Cheng Li of Hamilton College.

[1]The UN figures are from its Department of Economic and Social Information and Policy Analysis, *World Urbanization Prospects: 1992 Revision*, ST/ESA/SER.A/136 (New York: United Nations, 1993), 76-77, table A-1; these are based on PRC censuses in jurisdictions officially designated as "urban"—which can change at administrative whim. The World Bank uses similar figures, "supplemented" by its own adjustments, to estimate the 1991 urban portion of mainland China at 60 percent. This seems a high guess, but perhaps it is useful for international comparisons, because of the many Chinese who live in densely populated green areas that are now largely industrial. See World Bank, *World Development Report, 1993* (New York: Oxford University Press, 1993), 298, table 31, with 56 percent estimated on the same basis for 1990 in the previous year's edition. A Chinese time series, closer to that of the World Bank (somewhat lower, and thus probably more reasonable in terms of most readers' sense that "urban" requires a settlement to look built-up,

of "urban." However this massive influx is exactly gauged, it presents a dilemma to Chinese leaders who want to guide development of all kinds. The state elite of the People's Republic of China (PRC) has mixed interests in such a fast growth of city people. So do many other kinds of actors, including long-term residents of cities, factory managers, youths, and peasants who become workers by becoming urban.

What caused this migration, and to what extent should it be under state control? Data from Shanghai and nearby cities can help to answer such questions here, even though the Shanghai delta in effect began its reform process long before most parts of China. Concepts for such study come from migration theory, which links urban influxes to development in general.

The archetype of modernization is economic, and Nobel economist Arthur Lewis has explained how the capital-accumulating sector grows for a long period before its prosperity begins to help most laborers.[2] Output gains, at an early stage of modern growth, involve the migration of ex-agricultural subsistence-wage labor into industry—and largely into towns. These workers produce industrial output at the traditional low wage (plus a nominal markup) as long as the supply of them lasts. They keep coming to towns even after urban factories are unable to hire them all, because their expected wages exceed what they would receive in farming—even after a major discount for the probability that many of them will not be employed quickly in cities.[3]

Mainland China's subsistence-level population has until recently been overwhelming. Mao's state developed a political constituency of urban workers, for whom the markup that Lewis noted was guaranteed. To gratify the officials' constituency and maximize taxes, the state set up urban residence controls and rural checks against migration. These measures gave the state some support in China's most volatile political cities. But the effectiveness of the system began to decline in the 1970s, and it delayed

---

not just industrialized) has thus far been found only for early years. See State Statistical Bureau, *Chung-kuo she-hui t'ung-chi tzu-liao, 1987* (Chinese social statistics, 1987) (Peking: Chung-kuo t'ung-chi ch'u-pan-she, 1987), 17. The present author is responsible for any mistakes, but he offers great thanks to Dr. Ronald Skeldon, Department of Geography, University of Hong Kong, for help with the "simple" question: How many of the Chinese people are urban? A sufficient answer for purposes here is also simple: Compared to years before 1970, now very many more.

[2] W. Arthur Lewis, "Economic Development with Unlimited Supplies of Labour," *The Manchester School of Economic and Social Studies* (1954): 139-99 (also, Indianapolis: Bobbs-Merrill Reprint E-189).

[3] This follows work by theorist Michael P. Todaro, whose ideas on migration are most succinctly put in his textbook *Economic Development* (New York: Longman, 1994).

the industrial—only partly urban—migration of labor that Lewis describes for early modern growth.

Local Networks as Political Forces

Politics are linked to residential location (including migration), but the reader is hereby given early warning that this essay's definition of "politics" is broad. During reforms, many local power networks whose politics are not usually considered within the scope of political science (including families) have deeply eroded the power of the revolutionary state that was founded in 1949 and reached its zenith of centralization in the mid-1960s. More studies of contemporary China should focus on the cumulative and powerful effects of many local networks that face similar situations and act together, with the result that the state is weakened. If politics and policy are sought only within the institutions of the state, most actual influences on the structure of power in mainland China today will be missed.

The massive country-to-city migration is a major example of politics that the PRC state did not mandate or plan. The Cultural Revolution tended to disable bureaucrats who previously had enforced urban and rural residence rules.[4] Small-town collective entrepreneurs, beginning in the early 1970s, had a large supply of cheap labor and could compete with state factories. The collapse of effective migration controls in the 1970s and 1980s correlated with a quick rise of profits in the "rural" factories of rich, densely populated, green-but-industrializing parts of China—especially plains along the southern coast, of which the Shanghai delta is the largest.

Extent of the Migration

China's largest metropolis and the "green city" surrounding it provide much evidence of these trends.[5] Even more than other cities, Shanghai is a grouping of "sojourners."[6] Shanghai was already a populous trans-

---

[4]For more on residence controls since the 1950s, see Lynn T. White III, *Careers in Shanghai: The Social Guidance of Personal Energies in a Developing Chinese City, 1949-1966* (Berkeley: University of California Press, 1978). On Cultural Revolution aspects, see the same author's *Policies of Chaos* (Princeton: Princeton University Press, 1989), e.g., 227.

[5]The "green city" description of Shanghai's suburbs is detailed in the present author's "Shanghai-Suburb Relations, 1949-1966," in *Shanghai: Revolution and Development in an Asian Metropolis*, ed. Christopher Howe (Cambridge: Cambridge University Press, 1981), 241-68.

[6]See Frederic Wakeman, Jr. and Wen-hsin Yeh, eds., *Shanghai Sojourners* (Berkeley: University of California Institute of East Asian Studies, 1992).

shipment center before the arrival of European settlers in the early 1840s.
Net immigration took off, especially in three waves: (1) refugees fled the
Taiping Rebellion during the late 1850s; (2) another tide came to the International Settlement in 1937 because of Japanese invasion; and (3) the
civil war of the late 1940s saw a further deluge of about 2 million.[7]
    In the next four decades, the flow reversed. From 1950 to 1992, a
cumulative total of 11.2 million people had their household registrations
removed from Shanghai. Fewer, 10.8 million, came legally into the city.
During the years of greatest emigration, from 1955 to 1972 alone, the net
outflow was 2.2 million people. Table 7.1 offers a survey of registered
migration in and out of Shanghai. It suggests the strength of direct policy
efforts to move people out. The long-term limits of that policy would be
more evident, especially from the 1970s onward, if reliable statistics on
unregistered migration could be included; but the table omits migrants
who did not obtain police permission to be in Shanghai. The low net
rates after 1970, especially in the 1990s, show mainly that the state was
somewhat effective in controlling registrations.
    The table can show much about political history.[8] During reforms,
a new pattern of net migration emerged by the early 1970s. In 1973, for
the first time in many years, the net inflow percentage was positive. Its
pattern throughout the reform years (positive but low) was set at that
time. Migration data fly in the face of the usual notion that 1966-76
must be conceived as a single period of Chinese history. A partial exception in the reform pattern was 1979, when greater numbers of rusticated
ex-youths could return to Shanghai (although only a minority took their
parents' jobs, as will be shown below). The 1979 migration ratio was the
highest since 1957. It was historically medium, however, and was caused
by a temporary political allowance to families that had suffered during
the Cultural Revolution—at a time when the state elite was blaming an
earlier state elite for that injustice. After 1972, no year except 1979 showed
a major net immigration of registered residents.[9]

---

[7]Lin You Su, "Urban Migration in China: A Case Study of Three Urban Areas" (Ph.D.
dissertation, Department of Geography, Australian National University, 1992), 71.

[8]A mid-1970s essay, before these statistics were available but with conclusions they support,
is Lynn T. White, "A Political Demography of Shanghai after 1949," in *Proceedings of
the Fifth Sino-American Conference on Mainland China* (Taipei: Institute of International
Relations, 1976), reprinted serially in *Ming Pao* (Hong Kong), November 1976.

[9]The rise of *unregistered* migrants in the 1990s was nonetheless quick. This concerns migration, not population growth. About one-third of China's provinces showed lower growth
rates than Shanghai, even though the metropolis probably had the most severe birth control
in China. Some provinces had net emigration, and Shanghai's age structure was fairly
young. More information about unregistered immigrants is provided below.

Table 7.1
Migration to and from Shanghai*

	pop.	pop. in	% in	p. out	% out	net in	% net
1950	4,978,213	566,951	11.4	623,342	12.5	− 56,391	− 1.1
1951	5,224,621	1,004,032	19.2	566,208	10.8	437,824	8.4
1952	5,624,141	430,039	7.6	352,117	6.3	77,922	1.4
1953	5,939,367	487,806	8.2	255,492	4.3	232,314	3.9
1954	6,339,740	457,576	7.2	296,712	4.7	160,864	2.5
1955	6,429,039	260,430	4.1	847,293	13.2	− 586,863	− 9.1
1956	6,290,196	382,551	6.1	443,326	7.0	− 60,775	− 1.0
1957	6,623,157	418,474	6.3	134,833	2.0	283,641	4.3
1958	7,202,492	193,728	2.7	513,432	7.1	− 319,704	− 4.4
1959	8,895,972	323,163	3.6	322,050	3.6	1,113	0.0
1960	10,423,439	237,697	2.3	265,903	2.6	− 28,206	− 0.3
1961	10,576,449	192,723	1.8	335,522	3.2	− 142,799	− 1.4
1962	10,584,286	213,809	2.0	375,867	3.6	− 162,058	− 1.5
1963	10,657,542	152,565	1.4	238,262	2.2	− 85,697	− 0.8
1964	10,799,301	154,140	1.4	200,999	1.9	− 46,859	− 0.4
1965	10,900,050	161,679	1.5	206,458	1.9	− 44,779	− 0.4
1966	10,948,123	101,005	0.9	178,724	1.6	− 77,719	− 0.7
1967	11,007,744	39,983	0.4	73,385	0.7	− 33,402	− 0.3
1968	11,073,463	94,274	0.9	172,413	1.6	− 78,139	− 0.7
1969	11,014,847	77,488	0.7	352,535	3.2	− 275,047	− 2.5
1970	10,832,725	58,527	0.5	370,955	3.4	− 312,428	− 2.9
1971	10,698,848	126,392	1.2	253,829	2.4	− 127,437	− 1.2
1972	10,654,624	128,718	1.2	188,503	1.8	− 59,785	− 0.6
1973	10,670,592	171,298	1.6	158,909	1.5	12,389	0.1
1974	10,718,962	166,509	1.6	161,670	1.5	4,839	0.0
1975	10,752,502	212,096	2.0	217,199	2.0	− 5,103	0.0
1976	10,790,117	200,180	1.9	202,068	1.9	− 1,888	0.0
1977	10,838,868	196,291	1.8	188,350	1.7	7,941	0.1
1978	10,923,759	248,335	2.3	181,288	1.7	67,047	0.6
1979	11,152,094	598,260	5.4	333,390	3.0	264,870	2.4
1980	11,465,200	287,559	2.5	210,834	1.8	76,725	0.7
1981	11,628,400	236,223	2.0	192,127	1.7	44,096	0.4
1982	11,805,100	234,601	2.0	196,557	1.7	38,044	0.3
1983	11,940,100	226,773	1.9	190,821	1.6	35,952	0.3
1984	12,047,800	196,551	1.6	174,842	1.5	21,079	0.2
1985	12,166,900	182,904	1.5	129,873	1.1	53,031	0.4
1986	12,323,300	197,700	1.6	135,000	1.1	62,700	0.5
1987	12,495,100	221,700	1.8	154,000	1.2	67,700	0.5

Table 7.1 (Continued)

	pop.	pop. in	% in	p. out	% out	net in	% net
1988	12,624,200	221,100	1.8	170,200	1.3	50,900	0.4
1989	12,764,500	210,900	1.7	169,500	1.3	41,400	0.3
1990	12,833,500	188,700	1.5	174,100	1.4	14,600	0.1
1991	12,872,000	167,000	1.3	145,400	1.1	21,600	0.2
1992	12,893,700	175,300	1.4	149,200	1.2	26,100	0.2

*Registered migrants in and out, counting no births or deaths; and ratios to total population in the whole municipality.

Sources: The raw data begin in *Chung-kuo jen-k'ou: Shang-hai fen-ts'e* (China's population: Shanghai volume), ed. Hu Huan-yung et al. (Peking: Chung-kuo ts'ai-cheng ching-chi ch'u-pan-she, 1987), 77. Slightly different figures are in *Shang-hai t'ung-chi nien-chien, 1988* (Shanghai statistical yearbook, 1988), ed. Li Mou-huan et al. (Shanghai: Shang-hai-shih t'ung-chi-chü, 1988), 92, 76. The last dozen years' data are in *Shang-hai t'ung-chi nien-chien, 1990*, 60, 67; *1991*, 60, 68; *1992*, 60, 82; and *1993*, 64, 70. Some of the figures are separately confirmed (with slight differences) in Lin You Su, "Urban Migration in China: A Case Study of Three Urban Areas" (Ph.D. dissertation, Department of Geography, Australian National University, 1992), 72. The first source makes clear that these numbers come from police records on legal permanent and temporary residents. Illegal migrants are thus not counted; and their number was sometimes substantial even before the last seventeen years reported above.

Notes: Percentages are calculated. Most figures after 1979 are rounded in the sources, as prior ones surely should have been. Migrants to and from Shanghai, except in recent years, have generally been registered; but increasingly since the mid-1980s, arrivals not counted here have become numerous. Most migration has involved the urban districts, although this also became less pronounced after the mid-1980s, when many migrants lived in nearby counties.

Administrative changes also compromise the comparability of figures between speci-fiable periods. The population of the ten counties incorporated into Shanghai from Kiangsu (Jiangsu) in the late 1950s (by different decrees) was a noticeable fraction of the munici-pality's total at that time. This jurisdictional change, which mainly affects the first column, means that 1950-59 figures are not quite comparable to later ones. The reliability of reporting also varies over time: The 1958 and 1967-70 migration figures may be wrong by especially sizeable margins, overstating the net outflow; they are republished here from the source only to encourage in the reader a sense of critical humor about such things. Also, the first-column figures through 1987 are average populations during those years; but the best source found for 1988-90 does not specify this, and the increment rate of total population for the last two years may thus be slightly understated. But none of these problems affect the most im-portant trends the table shows.

Comparative Migration:
Genders, Ages, and Settlement Sizes

Comparative theory offers several normal facts about migration, and a review of these can throw much light on the increasing normalcy of residential patterns in China. If migration means movement between settlements, then most migrants in the PRC (56 percent, according to a 1987 study) are women. This is unsurprising in a strongly patrilocal society; but in many other low-income countries, especially in the past, most migrants have been men.[10] Women apparently move more often between villages to marry in China than in other places.

Males predominate among people who move from Chinese rural areas and towns to large cities.[11] The influx to coastal provinces has been greatest, especially to Shanghai, Peking (Beijing), and cities in Hopei (Hebei) and Shantung (Shandong). Most provinces, which are inland, have shown net outflows.[12] In the years 1983-87, over 30 million people moved long distances between different cities, towns, or counties in China. That is about 3 percent of the national population. Such a figure would not be high in an industrialized nation, but it is very high for a developing country.

Migration volumes correlate inversely with the distance that the migrants move. Comparative data from Shanghai, Shaohsing (Shaoxing), and the smaller Chekiang (Zhejiang) city of Hsiashih (Xiashi) all show this phenomenon for the reform years. (Only the Shanghai data do not show it for earlier periods, because of the government's interprovincial, long-distance send-down program then.) Also, young people tend to move farther than older people. Retirees often move within the same county. Migrants who come from larger settlements tend to go farther to their new residences; those from small places travel on average less far. Especially after 1970, most migration to Shanghai delta cities was toward larger settlements there, but an increasing majority of migrations were short-distance.[13] These patterns became more pronounced in China during the reforms, as state efforts to limit urbanization became less potent. In comparative international terms, the picture was increasingly typical.

The sources of immigration to Shanghai have been mostly nearby, but previous send-downs to provinces far away have also brought some people returning. A 1986 survey suggests that seven-tenths of interpro-

---

[10]Migration theorists moot the likelihood of a broad trend in several developing countries toward more female migrants, because women work in light industries that trade internationally.

[11]See Wen Lang Li, "Migration, Urbanization, and Regional Development," in *Forces for Change in Contemporary China*, ed. Bih-jaw Lin and James T. Myers (Taipei: Institute of International Relations, 1992), 153.

[12]See *Chieh-fang jih-pao* (Liberation Daily) (Shanghai), March 16, 1988.

[13]Except as noted, these relationships tend to hold regardless of the size of destination settlement (as shown in the three delta cases of Shanghai, Shaohsing, and Hsiashih). See Lin, "Urban Migration in China," 81-84, 184.

vincial migration to Shanghai came from five other provinces: Kiangsu (Jiangsu), 31 percent; Chckiang, 14 percent; Anhwei (Anhui), 11 percent; Kiangsi (Jiangxi), 8 percent; and distant Heilungkiang (Heilongjiang), 7 percent.[14] These proportions changed somewhat over time. Because of very fast economic growth in southern Kiangsu, which reduced the "push factors" for emigration from Kiangsu more than from inland provinces, only one-fifth of the migrants hailed from Kiangsu in 1986-90.[15] Anhwei exceeded Chekiang then, each still counting for more than one-tenth of the total influx. The majority by that time came from a wide assortment of other provinces, because booming rural industries in southern Kiangsu kept many potential migrants out of Shanghai.

Construction teams (*chien-chu tui*) became very busy at Shanghai especially during 1986-90, when roughly two-thirds of the registered immigrants were men.[16] This pattern is typical of what comparativists call the "construction" phase of migration. Women, more liable to take jobs hawking in Shanghai and less likely to have work units register their residences, may be underrepresented in these figures; but most of the migration to Shanghai was male. This pattern was also not sharply different from what has been seen in booming cities of other developing countries. China has shown some delays of migration to very large cities, but the administrative barriers causing these delays have not been impermeable. To see what the pattern means politically—for the people who move, for established residents, and for national and local leaders—it is useful to look not just at broad trends but also at the motives of individuals and families.

Changing migration patterns can be expressed in terms of conflicts between large forces: the attractive pull of urban and suburban employment, the push of poverty in many inland places that offered few good

---

[14]Peking supplied only 3 percent; Sinkiang, 2 percent; Yunnan, 2 percent; Fukien (Fujian), 3 percent; and Shantung, 4 percent; all other provinces were less. See Chinese Demography Editorial Group, ed., *Chung-kuo 1986 nien 74 ch'eng-chen jen-k'ou ch'ien-i ch'ou-yang tiao-ch'a tzu-liao* (Sample survey materials on 1986 Chinese migration in 74 cities and towns) (Peking: Chung-kuo jen-k'ou k'e-hsüeh pien-chi-pu, 1988), 14.

[15]Kiangsu and Chekiang migrants to Shanghai reportedly tended to have somewhat less difficulty than migrants from elsewhere being registered; but because of proximity, they also could make repeated trips to the city from their previous homes more easily than others could. Most of the basic data, and the sex ratios on immigrants reported later, come through the generosity of Dr. Ronald Skeldon. But the base for the estimated portions comes from figures in table 7.1.

[16]Men were then more than twice as many (213 for each 100 women) from Kiangsu. They were nearly as high a proportion from Chekiang and Anhwei (199 and 181 men per 100 women, respectively). These data were provided by Dr. Ronald Skeldon, who has nationwide statistics on migration in the PRC.

jobs, and the official barriers against moving in both cities and country-side. These broad forces are useful to describe, so long as they do not obscure the motives of individuals affected by migration. The same story can be told, often more vividly, in terms of the personal interests of many kinds of actors. These include ex-agricultural workers who wanted higher incomes, managers and police who could arrange urban household regis-trations, and state leaders needing fiscal revenues and political support.

Ex-Rusticates' Interests:
Residential Justice and Children's Education

Immigration to Shanghai and to smaller cities on the delta cannot be understood separately from the two main factors that have recently im-pelled it: the flow back from coercive rustications in 1955-58 and 1968-71, and the boom of rural industries that deeply affect both the metropolis and its suburbs.

In the 1960s and 1970s throughout mainland China, more than 16 million young people went "up to the mountains and down to the villages" (*shang-shan hsia-hsiang*).[17] In the 1970s, half of these people came back; and by the 1980s, the cumulative portion was two-thirds. In Shanghai alone, roughly half a million (413,000 by 1985 and more later) were of-ficially "returned" from this rustication—out of the approximately 1 million who had been sent down.[18] These were given legal household registrations and jobs. Many others returned to find work on their own.

In 1979, state policy allowed some youths whose families were im-portant but mistreated to come back to the metropolis. But in the same year, many cadres tried to impel youths flowing into Shanghai to return back to rural places. The Nanshih District Office for Educated Youth called a meeting, to which a "consolation team" (*wei-wen t'uan*) from Heilungkiang along with many youths who had returned were "invited."[19] By the time this Heilungkiang team's visit to Shanghai was finished, it

---

[17]With these rusticates went many older people who had been attacked during the Cultural Revolution, although their number has been estimated with so much variance that it is hard to know. See Ch'en Pen-lin et al., *Kai-ke k'ai-fang shen-chou chü-pien* (Great change in the sacred land [China] during reform and opening-up) (Shanghai: Chiao-t'ung ta-hsüeh ch'u-pan-she, 1984), 65-66.

[18]This is based on a rough calculation from figures in *Shang-hai ching-chi, nei-pu pen: 1949-1982* (Shanghai economy, internal [i.e., classified] volume: 1949-82), ed. Shanghai Academy of Social Sciences (Shanghai: Shang-hai she-hui k'e-hsüeh-yüan ch'u-pan-she, 1984), 961.

[19]Nanshih District had this "Chih-shih ch'ing-nien pan-kung-shih." *Wei-wen t'uan* had been common in 1964-65 also. See *Wen-hui pao* (Shanghai), May 20, 1979.

had also held meetings in Nanpu, Puto (Putuo), Ching'an (Jing'an), Hung-kou (Hongkou), and Changning districts, as well as Shanghai County. The names of youths who revolunteered to return north were published in newspapers.[20] Whether they actually went is less certain.[21]

A similar problem existed among graduating university students, who were reluctant to leave the metropolis but in 1979 were still told "unconditionally to obey the state's requirements."[22] Cultural Revolution excesses in work assignments had made enforcement of such mandates difficult. Return to cities in that year was less a state policy than a back-down by the regime from a policy that local power networks could now resist. This immigration was not just inspired by the notion that "city air makes for freedom" (*Stadtluft macht frei,* the proverb says). It was fired also by a sense of injustice among many whom the state had sent to rural places in earlier years. The Party was blaming previous leaders, the Gang of Four, for its own past problems. It could not, at the same time, effectively enforce Maoist migration policies.

Anger not just against the old policies, but also against bureaucrats who had implemented them, ran high among some returning migrants. Occasionally in the early 1980s, "educated youths" back from rural areas went to their old schools in Shanghai and physically attacked their previous "teachers."[23] The targets were school administrators who had assigned them outside Shanghai.

More than 90,000 educated youths were reregistered in Shanghai in 1979. About 20,000 of these received jobs in state units, but 70,000—the vast majority—found work in collectives.[24] The collective sector, which at this time had only 21 percent of Shanghai's labor force, was able to absorb fully 78 percent of the new job-seekers. The state sector, which in 1979 still had four-fifths of the workers, absorbed only one-fifth of the new influx.[25] Often the police were induced to reregister returnees

[20] *Wen-hui pao*, May 29, 1979.

[21] See a 1976 photo by Lynn T. White, reproduced in Thomas Bernstein, *Up to the Mountains and Down to the Villages: The Transfer of Youth from Urban to Rural China* (New Haven, Conn.: Yale University Press, 1977), showing a bulletin board in a Wusih silk factory that differentiated young migrants (offspring of the factory's workers) who had volunteered from those whose registrations had legally been changed, and also from those who had actually gone.

[22] *Wen-hui pao*, May 24, 1979.

[23] *South China Morning Post* (Hong Kong), October 12, 1981, and *Sing Tao Jih Pao* (Hong Kong), October 14, 1981. Reports about this (and a list of other subjects such as strikes) could not be printed in PRC papers, but they appeared in Hong Kong.

[24] *Wen-hui pao*, October 30, 1979.

[25] These portions are calculated from raw data in *Shang-hai t'ung-chi nien-chien, 1986* (Shanghai

in Shanghai. The problem of finding a job was simply left until later.

Many immigrants to Shanghai were the children of rusticated parents who remained outside the metropolis. The evidence for this unusual phenomenon (three-generation families in which the middle generation is absent) can be compiled from various kinds of sources. For example, although Shanghai primary school enrollments increased in the decade beginning 1978 by 3 percent, national enrollments decreased by 16 percent.[26] The reason for this sharp difference was not that Shanghai families went against the national demographic trend toward lower primary enrollments; data show that primary enrollment in Shanghai had already been nearly universal by the early 1970s and remained so thereafter, and birth control in Shanghai was stringent. Both these factors pushed strongly against the rise of enrollments in Shanghai that nonetheless occurred. But other data indicate that two-thirds of permanently registered immigrants to Shanghai were, at the time of their arrival, in young age cohorts, 15 to 29; and many were younger. Fully three-quarters were unmarried.[27] Many Shanghai permanent immigrants were of school age.

Over three-fifths of all migrants registered as temporary in Shanghai in the mid-1980s were either children or, *in more cases*, grandchildren of the household head.[28] The grandchildren were more numerous than the children, especially among grandsons. Many of their parents had apparently been "educated youths," sent down in previous years. These ex-Shanghai parents remained away from Shanghai but returned the youngest generation there in the 1980s. Their children lived in grandparents' households and attended schools in the metropolis.

The state long ago had forced these parents out of their city. In many cases, they were now accustomed to their new places—often marrying there, sometimes becoming "big fish in little ponds." Life had vastly improved for them since the Cultural Revolution, but they wanted a different future for the next generation. Education back in Shanghai was

---

statistical yearbook, 1986), ed. Li Mou-huan et al. (Shanghai: Shang-hai-shih t'ung-chi-chü, 1986), 70. Interviewees report that from the mid-1950s to 1979, new hires to Shanghai state factories were "distributed" there by organizations above or outside the factories.

[26]See *Shang-hai t'ung-chi nien-chien, 1988*, 327, and State Statistical Bureau, ed., *Chung-kuo t'ung-chi chai-yao, 1988* (A statistical survey of China, 1988) (Peking: Chung-kuo t'ung-chi ch'u-pan-she, 1988), 105.

[27]The first datum is based on a survey of long-term immigrants by the Population Research Institute of the Chinese Academy of Social Sciences, and the second reports 1977-86 migrations. To the much smaller Shanghai delta city of Hsiashih, fewer (just below half) of the 1977-86 immigrants were unmarried. See Lin, "Urban Migration in China," 111, 115.

[28]See Alice Goldstein, Sidney Goldstein, and Guo Shenyang, "Temporary Migrants in Shanghai Households, 1986," *Demography* 28 (1991): 275.

the obvious way to obtain it. They had certainly done their bit for the state. They now made their decisions according to the interests of their families.

Ex-Peasant Workers' and Rural Managers' Interests: Better Jobs and Cheap Labor

Mao's colleagues for more than two decades tried to stop people from coming to large cities. By doing this, the state leaders could muster resources to gratify their own political constituencies in crucial urban centers like Shanghai, gathering support for (and preventing opposition to) their rule. Technological pressures on the economics of labor migration, impelling people toward industrial settlements, were long matched by state counterpressures to maintain the government's fiscal and political bases in large cities.

Small and medium-sized settlements on the Shanghai delta were also affected by official efforts to reduce urban populations, but by the 1980s these smaller cities were also expanding. Information is available from two places in northern Chekiang. The smaller is Hsiashih, a county seat containing about 40,000 people inland from the northern shore of Hangchow (Hangzhou) Bay. The larger is Shaohsing, a famous cultural center and prefectural capital with a 1986 population just over 250,000 (see table 7.2). As table 7.2 shows, both these places showed some net out-migration between 1961 and 1970. The county seat in particular had net immigration at other times, especially during the 1980s—when Hsiashih had lower emigration than in either of the earlier periods for which data are available, perhaps because much employment was available in small cities during the reforms.

The Employment Pull

In the late 1960s and early 1970s in a few rich areas of China, new agricultural technologies began to free vast amounts of labor from field work. This "green revolution" came from various kinds of agricultural extension: walking tractors and rice transplanting machines, new seeds for grains with shorter stalks that yielded more edible calories faster, especially when nourished by more inorganic fertilizer and more reliable water (supplied by canals during dry spells, and by tube wells in soggy seasons). Shanghai's suburbs in 1965, for example, were only 17 percent machine-tilled. By 1972, this portion was already 76 percent; and by 1984, 89 percent.[29]

---

[29]Kojima Reeitsu, ed., *Chūgoku no toshika to nōson kensetsu* (Chinese urbanization and rural construction) (Tokyo: Ryūkei shosha, 1978), 293-94, 299.

Table 7.2

Migration to and from Shanghai Delta Cities: Shaohsing and Hsiashih

| | Percentages of population | | | |
	1949-60	1961-70	1971-80	1981-85
Shaohsing				
Immigration	3.3	1.5	1.3	2.7
Emigration	2.1	2.4	1.4	1.6
Net migration	1.2	− 0.9	− 0.1	1.1
Hsiashih				
Immigration	2.5	2.0	3.5	4.4
Emigration	1.4	2.5	2.4	1.8
Net migration	1.1	− 0.5	1.1	2.6

Source: Registration data of the Shaohsing and Hsiashih public security bureaus, 1986, reported in Lin, "Urban Migration in China," 75.

What did the ex-peasants, displaced by these methods, do for incomes? Their local leaderships set up factories, almost always in brigade or team collectives, at first using local labor. Many techniques for making cement, silk, cigarettes, bricks, pumps, and other easily salable products did not require large amounts of capital or high technology. So in the early 1970s local leaders established such factories. Just a few examples may suffice here. In Tangchia Village (Tangjiacun), Feng County, Shanghai, only 7 percent of the gross output value in 1970 was industrial; but by 1974, that portion was up to 59 percent. In Tangchiao (Tangqiao), Soochow (Suzhou) Prefecture, Kiangsu, the average growth of industrial output value from 1971 to 1977 was 154 percent annually (and from 1980 to 1985, slightly less at 143 percent). In Kiangsu as a whole (including much poorer areas in the northern part of the province), this measure of rural industrial growth was 24 percent annually in 1971-77 (as compared to 10 percent in 1980-85).[30]

Such quick rural industrialization—not planned by the national government and disserving its interests—meant that state-run enterprises could no longer commandeer the raw materials to which they had become

---

[30]Calculated from figures in Hsü Yüan-ming and Yeh Ting, T'ang-ch'iao kung-yeh-hua chih lu (The way to industrialization in Tangchiao) (Shanghai: Shang-hai she-hui k'e-hsüeh-yüan ch'u-pan-she, 1987), 61; and Chiang-su hsiang-chen kung-yeh fa-chan-shih (History of the development of Kiangsu rural industry), ed. Mo Yüan-jen (Nanking: Nan-ching kung-hsüeh-yüan ch'u-pan-she, 1987), 321-22, 402.

accustomed at the fixed prices they were budgeted to pay. Inputs were going to rural collective factories, instead. Inflation, bribes for procurement agents, government budget deficits, quick economic growth, and all the other most salient aspects of mainland China's reforms—including a drop of state control over migrants—followed agricultural mechanization and rural industrialization. Green revolution, not state policy, began mainland China's reforms.[31]

In countries undergoing fast economic change, "temporary population movement—circulation—may serve as an alternative means for populations to adjust to changing economic conditions," as a comparative study of Thailand and China shows.[32] Half the migrants to Shanghai suburban towns in the 1980s admitted they came "to change jobs."[33] People left rural China in droves to seek employment, certainly in cities as large as Shanghai if they could. From one county in Honan (Henan), for example, 190,000 people had departed; if the unidentified county was of typical size, this might be roughly two-fifths of its population.[34] Women especially sought jobs in housekeeping; and men, in building. A survey showed that, "After all expenditures are excluded, each person can have an average income of 500 *yuan* per year," i.e., far more than they could earn in the impoverished places they left. A popular saying put it in rhyme, "If you want to get rich, run to Shanghai." A recent rap specified the city's fastest-growing part: "East, west, south, north, center; to find a job, go to Putung."

Most ex-agriculturalists "come to cities because they can make more money and because they are surplus in the countryside. Recently, the development of services and municipal engineering projects provide a lot of employment opportunities. These jobs generally are manual; and urban people, especially youths, are unwilling to do such work. So cities have

---

[31]The author will publish a book entitled *Unstately Power: Local Causes of Chinese Reforms and Reactions after 1970*, with more on the effects of agricultural and rural-industrial policies in Mao's time, arguing that the reforms were unintended effects. On Tangchia Village, a typical part of Shanghai's suburbs, see the work of anthropologist Ishida Hiroshi, *Chûgoku nôson keizai no kiso kôzô: Shanhai kinkô nôson no kôgyôka to kindaika no ayumi* (Rural China in transition: Experiences of rural Shanghai toward industrialization and modernization) (Kyôto: Kôyô shobô, 1991), 151.

[32]See Sidney Goldstein, "Forms of Mobility and Their Policy Implications: Thailand and China Compared," *Social Forces* 65, no. 4 (1987): 915.

[33]Liu Cheng et al., eds., *Chung-kuo yen-hai ti-ch'ü hsiao ch'eng-chen fa-chan yü jen-k'ou ch'ien-i* (Migration and the development of small cities and towns on the China coast) (Peking: Chung-kuo ts'ai-cheng ching-chi ch'u-pan-she, 1989), 195.

[34]Foreign Broadcast Information Service, *Daily Report: China* [hereinafter cited as *FBIS-CHI*]-87-242 (December 17, 1987): 30, radio of December 16, for the quotation below and the number of departing ex-peasants.

to absorb skillful people from the countryside, towns, and small cities."
Many transients also became domestic maids—and this trend was likewise
approved in publications: "In big cities, the family structure is being
transformed . . . so family service workers are popular. . . . It is not an
exaggeration to say that without them cities, especially big cities, would
not operate well. . . . Another stable source of services is contract
workers. They organize themselves voluntarily and contract with the units
or companies that need them."[35]

The organization of these labor hiring systems was "voluntary" only
in the sense that the state could no longer control it. Autonomous labor
bosses flourished, of a sort known in many developing capitalist countries
including China before 1949.[36] Booming rural industries absorbed vast
amounts of labor on the Shanghai delta. Many rural people, not working
in either fields or local factories, "floated" in cities like Ningpo (Ningbo)
and Hangchow. From Chekiang, for example, many also left the province
or moved from poor to rich areas within it. So by the mid-1980s,

> Over 1.3 million [Chekiang] laborers are working in other provinces. . . .
> Chinhua (Jinhua) Prefecture [the province's poorest] "exports" about 200,000
> workers, which is about 25 percent of the total agricultural labor power in that
> prefecture. . . . The local government of Yungchia (Yongjia) County allowed
> 30,000 peasants to work at other places in 1983; this figure was about 15 percent
> of the county's total labor power. These peasants had a total income of 56
> million *yuan* that year, which was about 49 percent of the county's total agri-
> cultural income.[37]

Long-distance migration to rich cities like Shanghai occurred because the supply of rural surplus labor from peasant families long resident
on the delta was by the late 1980s much reduced. A Chinese economist
has calculated the demand for labor in agriculture, its alternative use in
rural industries, and the demand for it in other local activities. He charted
these kinds of employment in rural Wusih (Wuxi) between 1975 and 1985,
at each point deducting from the county's total supply and calling the
residual a surplus. He showed that "rural surplus labor" with Wusih
registration was already down to 55 percent of the work force in 1975,
and just 4 percent in 1985.[38] Long-distance migrants arrived to take jobs,

---

[35]Che Hsiao-yeh, *Ch'eng-shih tsai chuan-che-tien shang* (Cities at a turning point) (Peking: Chung-kuo fu-nü ch'u-pan-she, 1989), 23-29.

[36]On labor contractors in old Shanghai, see many sources including Jean Chesneaux, *The Chinese Labor Movement, 1919-1927*, trans. Hope M. Wright (Stanford, Calif.: Stanford University Press, 1968).

[37]T'ien Fang and Ling Fa-t'ung, eds., *Chung-kuo jen-k'ou ch'ien-i* (Population shifts in China) (Peking: Chih-shih ch'u-pan-she, 1987), 248-59.

[38]This is based on work by Meng Hsin (Meng Xin); see graphs in *China's Rural Industry:*

as local subsistence-wage labor disappeared about 1985.

Although the PRC government has traditionally attempted to prevent the formation of a national labor market, especially by restricting
movement to cities, the official system collapsed in a context of rising
prosperity.[39] Rather than pay higher wages to ordinary workers from the
delta, as surplus labor dried up, entrepreneurs in collectives sometimes
often promoted locals into less arduous jobs or administrative posts—and
imported outsiders to work near subsistence wages in either factories or
fields. During 1985, the origin of Wusih's permanent industrial workers
in rural factories was still reported at more than nine-tenths local—higher
than a comparable county in Anhwei, and much higher than one in Kwangtung (Guangdong) for which data have been gathered—but this does not
report contract labor.

There was major variation according to the administrative level that
licensed a factory. Township (or higher) collective factories largely employed local labor. A 1989 survey near Chiating (Jiading), Shanghai,
indicated that district- and town-run enterprises (i.e., at the levels of
hsiang or *chen*) seldom hired even temporary laborers who came from a
distance at that time. But the pattern was strikingly different for the
nominally collective—de facto private—factories licensed by lower formal
levels. Village-run Chiating firms so often hired outside workers that 90
percent of the labor force in some of their factories came from Anhwei
or Kiangsi.[40] Migrant outsiders, mostly in village-run collectives that employed roughly half the whole work force in rural industries, were subject
to severe labor exploitation.

At least two-thirds of Shanghai's registered "agricultural" peasants
(over 3 million people) by the late 1980s were working in suburban industries and services. Municipal officials also publicly reckoned that the
city then had "several hundred thousand" contract workers.[41] The vagueness of the estimate suggests that nobody had been able to make a reliable
count.

It was relatively easy during the reforms to justify labor exploitation.
As a demographer wrote in 1987,

Structure, Development, and Reform, ed. William A. Byrd and Lin Qingsong (Washington,
D.C.: World Bank, 1990), 300 and 326-27 for the end of the next text paragraph.

[39]See the main argument, showing the same phenomenon for a much earlier period, in White,
Careers in Shanghai.

[40]Interview with anthropologist Lu Fei-yün, who has done field work in the Shanghai delta.
See also Hua Ta-ming, "The Overexploitation of Peasant Workers by Township-Run Factories Calls for Attention," *She-hui* (Society) (Shanghai), 1990, no. 2:12-13.

[41]The exact figure is probably unknown to anyone. See *FBIS-CHI*-87-244 (December 21,
1987): 42, radio of December 18.

Some peasants have contracts with urban units. . . . Generally, the income of those doing temporary work in cities is much higher than of those working in rural areas. When peasants go to cities, they widen their vision, increase their knowledge, and become familiar with life in cities. Especially, they learn what urban people need. Peasants see a lot of new products, which they produce following the city models. . . . Because of growing unofficial markets in cities, many surplus workers get jobs.[42]

The reasons "floaters" came to Shanghai, according to a 1988 survey, were occupational for 68 percent and "social" for 23 percent. Over seven-tenths were men, and at least a quarter of the total came explicitly to work in construction projects. Nearly half (48 percent) of this nonpermanent influx had previously been farmers, and only 15 percent had been workers.[43]

Labor-seekers who came to the metropolis did not remain second-class citizens forever. Three-fifths of the long-term permanent Shanghai immigrants since the regime's early years had, by the mid-1980s, acquired regular blue-collar jobs. More than a quarter had achieved managerial or professional posts. A larger portion of long-term permanent immigrants than previous Shanghai citizens held white-collar jobs. Some of these were political appointees into Shanghai during the PRC's early years, but many were ordinary migrants who had worked hard and done well.

Most newcomers who were registered as nonpermanent did menial tasks. But people who had been in the city for a number of years on average made more money than nonmigrants (those born in Shanghai or living there before mid-century). They put up with hard conditions to establish urban households, but later many were successful. This was true not just in the metropolis, but also to a lesser extent in smaller delta cities.[44] Economic pull is not just a demographic abstraction. From the viewpoint of the individual or the family, statistics show that migration to Shanghai followed by years of work there was, in the long term, a highly rational action.

---

[42] T'ien and Ling, *Chung-kuo jen-k'ou ch'ien-i*, 19-21.

[43] Only 8 percent of the registered floaters were of school age, and 16 percent were retirees. Of the remaining tenth, half reportedly came to Shanghai for adult training and half for other reasons. For these and the following figures, see Li Meng-pai et al., eds., *Liu-tung jen-k'ou tui ta ch'eng-shih fa-chan te ying-hsiang chi tui-ts'e* (Policies on the influence of transient population for the development of large cities) (Peking: Ching-chi jih-pao ch'u-pan-she, 1991), 153, and for the following data, 156.

[44] The main survey, a 1986 effort by the Chinese Academy of Social Sciences, oddly omits to report temporarily registered migrants or illegal migrants. But see Lin, "Urban Migration in China," 96, 98, 103. Long-term migrants to Shanghai were surprisingly like those to the smaller city of Hsiashih in terms of occupations.

Urban Managers' and Police Interests:
The Erosion of Household Controls

Managers who wish to hire migrants have some interests that parallel the migrants' hopes. In Shanghai, each large firm includes public security liaison officers, who generally must approve residence registrations for any new employee of the company, either permanent or temporary. So long as the firm does not incur too many costs for housing, and so long as the number of new employees passes muster with higher officials, this system is supposed to tie legal migration closely to economic work. What it also does is to keep a power, albeit one of declining value, for the managements of state enterprises—during a period when most of their other resources are declining quickly. The result is a great deal of registered "temporary" migration among people who stay in Shanghai on an actually (but not legally) permanent basis.

This is not supposed to happen, according to the official rules. All temporary household approvals were, at least by the mid-1980s, formally subject to police review for renewal or termination after three months. "Numerous officials have indicated, however, that these requirements for temporary registration are not always rigorously enforced, nor is careful attention given to the length of time that an individual has remained at a destination, provided that the individual does not become a burden on the community."[45] Such approvals are very local, and the cadres who control them have scant incentive to report quickly or fully to higher bureaucrats.

Any rural migrant to a city is supposed to have a letter from police in the rural township. Urban police are supposed to require that document (among others) if the migrant applies for temporary or permanent registration in a city. But by no means does every farmer leave a rural area with such a letter, and not every urban immigrant applies for the benefits of registration.

The most important of these benefits, since food rationing and job allocation are now less effectively regulated than before the reforms, is the possibility of having an employer apply for housing space. Little new space is available for the state to distribute, however, because low urban rents discourage residential construction. State enterprises, about half of which are technically bankrupt and fighting for their financial lives, have scant money to build new homes for staff. Housing that has already long been allocated to old employees in Shanghai is often the strongest

---

[45]Goldstein, "Forms of Mobility and Their Policy Implications," 930.

tie between them and the state sector, since for most ordinary people there, residential space is the scarcest resource. But immigrants now get little of this anyway; so they have less incentive to register.

Many migrants apply for permanent (*ch'ang-chu*) registration. If the police do not issue this document, the effect on the newcomer's behavior is usually not great. Since most facilities, other than housing, are now available for money, many who would prefer permanent registration in Shanghai nonetheless stay there without it. Manager-patrons, following their own interests which can differ from those of the state, keep better control both of their budgets and of their worker-clients by arranging less permanent documents.

Nonpermanent household registrations come in two kinds: (1) temporary (*chan-chu*) documents are legally needed by any citizen in Shanghai for more than three days; and (2) seconded (*chi-chu*) registration is for officially sanctioned activities, e.g., in the economy or in government. Application for either kind of registration is supposed to be made within three days of arrival in the city.

Applications to migrate to Shanghai usually go through either of two agencies: the city's Personnel Department for cadres, or the Labor Bureau for most other people. The ordinary criterion for approval is backing from a Shanghai employer. After 1979-80, Shanghai "educated youths" were encouraged to take their parents' jobs if the latter would retire, and practically everyone else was kept out of the system for a while.[46] Professional cadres could, however, move to Shanghai if they were sent by state units (including most companies). The majority of ex-peasant immigrants apparently arrived either under the auspices of a labor contractor, or else without papers to join relatives.

Greater freedom of movement for Chinese citizens within their own country is an aspect of reforms that many writers have neglected.[47] After the internal migration that accompanied the removal of bad labels in

---

[46]The two bureaus are the Lao-tung chü and Jen-shih chü. There is a procedure by which unmarried members of Shanghai families can be reunited in the city. But the conditions are written restrictively: The single member applies to return home, but the application is approved only if older relatives in Shanghai are "severely sick" and have no able-bodied younger family members to care for them (especially if the offspring outside Shanghai is an only child). Practice has been less restrictive than the rule in *Shang-hai shih-min pan-shih chih-nan* (Citizen's practical guide to Shanghai), ed. Shanghai Municipal Government (Shanghai: Shang-hai jen-min ch'u-pan-she, 1989), 2 on the previous paragraph; and here, 91-92.

[47]An exception is Guilhem Fabre, "The Chinese Mirror of Transition," *Communist Economies and Economic Transformation* 4, no. 2 (1992): 263. Foreign travel, as he points out, was still severely restricted.

1979, most Chinese could legally buy a train or bus ticket between cities without having to show many official documents, as had previously been required.[48] Already by the early 1980s, the arthritic Ministry of Railroads was left far behind the demand for passenger transport from newly rich entrepreneurs, foreign tourists, Taiwanese, migrants, and other travelers. Getting tickets and seats was difficult, but citizens could travel.

Ordinary trains to Shanghai from Anhwei, for example, were densely stuffed with people. Anhwei stations would sell tickets to would-be migrants, who might wait for days trying to get inside the slow trains while they stopped (often by climbing through windows). Train 311, on one day, reportedly was so full that eight people could find standing room only in a single car's small toilet. Claustrophobic migrants were reported sometimes to have died, as they jumped out the windows of moving trains on the Anhwei-Shanghai line. A survey on one such train found a high frequency of "mental disorders" because of crowding, and it determined that 86 percent of the passengers were migrants.[49]

Nonetheless, "the large majority did not have official permission to change their registrations from rural to urban."[50] As a late 1980s source said, "The portion of the people who are 'temporarily resident' is getting higher and higher. Although the government has not recognized their urban citizenship, they are playing important roles in economic and social life."[51] Obtaining food and shelter depended less on state documents than it had in Mao's years.

Permanent Residents' Interests:
Against Criminals and For Housekeepers

Urban immigrants called themselves "free people" (or in the old English term, "freemen"), because they broke the bonds cadres had previously placed on them.[52] Established residents in Shanghai, while bene-

---

[48]Not since the brief period of "revolutionary tourism" in the late 1960s had there been such freedom of movement. Red Guard travelers did not need authorizing documents to buy tickets; they did not even need tickets! They declared pilgrimage goals and hopped on trains. For more, see Gordon A. Bennett and Ronald N. Montaperto, *Red Guard: The Political Biography of Dai Hsiao-ai* (Garden City, New York: Doubleday, 1972).

[49]For this from *Liao-wang chou-k'an* (Outlook Weekly), 1993, no. 36:18, and *Hsin-min wan-pao* (New People's Evening News), April 21, 1994. Thanks go to Professor Cheng Li.

[50]Alice Goldstein and Guo Shenyang, "Temporary Migration in Shanghai and Beijing," *Studies in Comparative International Development* 27, no. 2 (Summer 1992): 42, cites three different PRC authors on this point.

[51]See note 35 above.

[52]See Edward Friedman, "Deng vs. the Peasantry: Recollectivization in the Countryside," *Problems of Communism* 40, no. 5 (September-October 1991): 30-49.

fitting from migrants in some ways, often looked down on them—and thought them libertines. Open disdain between subethnic groups in Shanghai, especially toward people from northern Kiangsu, was an old story.[53] During reforms, immigrants as a group became social scapegoats. They often lived in flimsy housing, were thought to compete with long-term residents for jobs, and were numerous among criminals.

Migrant Numbers and Houses

Three-tenths of migrant workers in the Shanghai suburbs, during the mid-1980s, for example, had no fixed dwellings—and half had no fixed jobs.[54] The residences of the nonregistered population, to the extent they could be sampled in urban areas during late 1988, seem to have been approximately as follows: 6 percent very literally floated by living on boats; 16 percent were in "temporary work shacks, agricultural markets, [train and bus] stations, and docks"; 17 percent resided in hospitals or hotels; and 61 percent had places in permanently registered collectives or families. Fully 85 percent of these people in the urban districts hailed from outside Shanghai, not from nearby counties.[55]

A survey on rising immigration to Shanghai showed that in 1984, more than 700,000 people were immigrants without permanent registration; but in the next year, the number had risen to 1,110,000; and it remained about the same in 1986. Over 30 percent stayed in reception houses, hotels, or hospitals; and many of these were in town to do business. Over 20 percent were transport workers. Less than half came into individual or collective households.[56]

The total registered and unregistered floating population of Shanghai has been difficult to estimate, but the police periodically enlist the support of academics to conduct censuses. In 1988, one such survey tried to cover people without fixed abodes: in hotels, markets, boats, and

---

[53]See Emily Honig, *Creating Chinese Ethnicity: Subei People in Shanghai, 1850-1980* (New Haven, Conn.: Yale University Press, 1992).

[54]Their housing and employment problems were not solved in an extensive 1986 survey. See Liu, *Chung-kuo yen-hai ti-ch'ü*, 205.

[55]The "temporary work shacks" were *lin-shih kung-p'eng*. All the portions are calculated from raw data of the sample that could be found by surveyors for Li, *Liu-tung jen-k'ou*, 152.

[56]Data on itinerants' housing are based on a Futan (Fudan) University survey. Only 3 percent were boat people (some of whom may have obtained legal Shanghai residence in earlier campaigns to settle on land, because they could help the state gather economic information). Just 1 percent came officially as rural traders or representatives of rural market fairs. "Reception houses" (*chao-tai-so*) are the most common form of hotel. *Shang-hai t'ung-chi nien-chien, 1988*, 25.

Table 7.3

Transient Populations of PRC Cities in Mid-Reforms (Thousands of Persons)

	Shanghai	Peking	Tientsin	Wuhan	Canton	24 Cities
1978	—	300	—	—	—	—
1985	—	900	—	—	600	—
1986	1,340	—	—	—	880	—
1987	2,000	1,150	860	800	1,000	10,000

Sources: *Ch'eng-shih wen-t'i* (Urban Problems) (Shanghai), March 1988, 64, and (for 1987) *Shang-hai ching-chi* (Shanghai Economy), June 1988, 6. The twenty-four cities were all those with total populations in excess of 1 million.

transport stations. This survey reached the conclusion that on October 20, 1988, only 2 percent of Shanghai's population was floating—which is almost surely a sharp underestimate. Unregistered persons in Shanghai have no incentive to make themselves available when the census-takers arrive. Of the illegal respondents (to the extent the sample is credible), three-fifths had applied for legal temporary or permanent registration in Shanghai.[57]

A further source claimed that by 1988 Shanghai had "the country's biggest floating population."[58] Another suggests that the portion of floaters in the urban districts rose in the mid-1980s, because the 1982 census found only 246,000 transients, which would be only about 4 percent of the population, and later reports are all much higher.[59] At least up to 1987, as table 7.3 suggests, Shanghai had more unauthorized immigrants than any other Chinese city (even Canton [Guangzhou]). Shanghai remained the country's strongest magnet for immigrants.

By 1987, migrants already comprised one-fifth of the population in mainland China's twenty-four largest cities—and probably more than

---

[57]Police census efforts by 1988 were aided by the Statistics Bureau, Futan University, East China Normal University, and the Population Institute of the Social Sciences Academy. The pollsters asked each adult's name, sex, age, education level, former job, and reason for coming to Shanghai. In 1988, they added questions about number of children, method of birth control, and (of women) whether pregnant. For some queries, as for the census as a whole, it would have been hopeful to expect complete coverage. See Chu Tz'u in *Shang-hai liu-tung jen-k'ou* (Shanghai's floating population), ed. Shanghai Statistics Bureau (Shanghai: Chung-kuo t'ung-chi ch'u-pan-she, 1989), 11-16.

[58]Ibid., 11.

[59]Peking had a 3 percent rate as late as 1988, but the report for Canton was so high that different census-taking methods may make such rates incomparable. See Che, *Ch'eng-shih tsai chuan-che-tien shang*, 23-24.

that in the built-up parts of Shanghai.[60] In the urban districts of Shanghai, according to an early 1989 estimate, one of every four persons lacked permanent household registration.[61] Toward the beginning of the 1990s, diverse reports from Shanghai suggest that one-fifth of the people were migrants; but these guesses may be somewhat low by then. Comprehensive and comparable figures from many cities have not yet been found for later years, but Shanghai sources indicate that by 1994 the portion of recent arrivals in the population rose quickly. One 1994 report estimated that Shanghai's "floating population" was 3.3 million.[62] Over one-quarter of Shanghai's actual whole population was migrant by the mid-1990s.

Migrants and Jobs

The portion of migrants who were unregistered—i.e., who had no employers to arrange documents—in most Shanghai delta cities was quickly rising.[63] Working-age persons (ages 15 to 59) in a 1988 census of migrants made up 81 percent. Males were 62 percent. Only 52 percent were in the urban districts; so almost half (practically all from Kiangsu or Chekiang) lived in the suburbs. Illiterates and semi-illiterates comprised 15 percent of the total, but those with middle school educations were 45 percent (and with university educations, 2 percent—higher than in the total legal population). These immigrants, self-reporting their former occupations, were 48 percent farmers, 15 percent workers, 8 percent technicians, 4 percent businesspeople, 3 percent cadres, and 20 percent unemployed. Very many worked in construction and transport. Of the women (at 38 percent, a minority of the total), 51 percent were married. Fully 68 percent were of childbearing age; 24 percent had actually given birth to babies in Shanghai, and another 5 percent were pregnant during this census. At least 14 percent of all the floating population worked as domestics, apparently full-time. One-third of the floaters came from Kiangsu, and a strong majority hailed from either Kiangsu or Chekiang.[64]

Many who were unregistered, or who were supposed to be only temporary in the city, could make satisfactory livings. Some did so illegally.

---

[60]*Ch'eng-shih wen-t'i* (Urban Problems) (Shanghai), March 1988, 64.

[61]*Lao-tung pao* (Labor News) (Shanghai), March 19, 1989.

[62]*Shanghai Star*, March 22 and April 15, 1994, suggested that about one-quarter of the migrants were in construction work, and another quarter were not working. Found by Professor Cheng Li.

[63]For example, in Hangchow, migrants were 11 percent of that city's population in 1985 and had already been 9 percent in 1975, but only 4 percent in both 1965 and 1955. See Li, *Liu-tung jen-k'ou*, 281.

[64]See note 57 above.

A man from Hsinghua (Xinghua) in northern Kiangsu, for example, came to Shanghai and "stole" materials from factory rubbish bins. He could in this way make a very high income of 70 or 80 *yuan* per day. Legal activities were less profitable, but they still paid far more than migrants had previously received as peasants. A twenty-five-year-old legal migrant from Honan to Soochow explained in 1994 why he was so much more productive on the delta: "We used to spend three months doing farm work, one month celebrating the Spring Festival, and eight months in idle time every year." Now he was a restaurant waiter, working fourteen hours each day, seven days a week—but receiving 400 *yuan* (about US$50 per month), which was four times his previous Honan wage. When asked whether he thought he was working too hard, he replied:

> No, it is better than sitting idly by watching people in cities getting rich. The conditions here are not bad at all. Color TV, electric heating, and free meals— these are great. What I like most here is that I can take a shower every day. I was not able to take a bath during the entire winter at home. It would be too cold to do so in the river.[65]

Despite the exploitation of migrants' labor, many working in larger settlements, in service industries, and for firms licensed at the township/street level or above were reasonably content.

By 1994, many had come very recently. A report from the previous year indicated that one of every six people in Shanghai had "recently arrived" from rural areas. This immigrant labor force was said to number 2.5 million, but only three-fifths had reliable jobs. One million had to forego money or else look for a job each day. Most immigrants with steady work came from other places in the Shanghai delta, and many of these had relatives already in the metropolis. As one construction team chief from Kiangsu said, "We hire workers from our hometown and from neighboring towns, so that we can be sure of our credibility."[66] These were the fortunate migrants.

Many others, who came disproportionately from Anhwei, Honan, Kiangsi, and Szechwan (Sichuan), took Shanghai jobs without residence permits and thus broke the law—so they lacked any medical or injury benefits despite the dangerous work many of them had to do. They also lacked recourse to police, if their labor contractors did not pay them. Many of these lived on the edge of the city. Their shacks looked like

---

[65]This interview was by Professor Cheng Li in 1994, and it offers the perspective of individuals and families that contemporary Chinese studies has too often lacked.

[66]See the report by journalist T. S. Rousseau in *Eastern Express* (Hong Kong), February 23, 1994.

storage sheds, made of corrugated metal, with asphalted canvas for roofs, bamboo for pillars to hold the structures up, and cardboard or woven straw mats to separate the "rooms." When they were not hired by construction or stevedore teams, they took up individual work selling food on the streets, repairing shoes or bicycles, or picking rubbish.

Places just on the edge of Shanghai city, such as Chenju (Zhenru) which has a train stop or the suburbs of Wuchiaochang (Wujiaochang) or Wanshanpang (Wanshanbang), became the abodes of many ex-peasant migrants without urban registrations. These newcomers wanted to make money, but as illegal residents they of course could not obtain business licenses. So they set up factories and shops without official blessing. Police, during a 1990 raid at Wanshanpang, found thirty "underground" food processing factories, which baked and catered for people living in Shanghai's more central districts.[67]

Women domestic workers came especially from Anhwei to Shanghai. Already in the 1970s, they had organized a housemaids' union informally called the "Anhwei group." Inland authorities were so perturbed by this exodus, which reduced both economic production and political control in their areas, that they prevailed on the Shanghai government to ship some migrants back to Anhwei by train.[68] Domestic helpers and family relatives, however, were generally welcomed by Shanghai residents, even if bureaucrats could not monitor their goings and comings. About three-fifths of Shanghai's temporary migrants, according to a mid-1980s study, lived in the households of permanent residents. When they were not members of the same family, they were usually in Shanghai to work. But when they were relatives, they frankly told the pollsters they were there to visit or live—even though such activities have no status in state plans.[69]

Many migrants stayed for long periods in the city, often half a year or more, on contract work. Of Shanghai's "floating population" without permanent residence permits, at least one-fifth of the estimated total were in building trades. These formed more than 400 construction teams, a larger work force than the city's legally registered population in that industry. Migrants did a great variety of other jobs, too. "Almost all the tea-egg salesgirls . . . are from northern Jiangsu. . . . Many of them earn 15 to 20 *yuan* a day, about six times a government employee's daily

---

[67]The author's student, Professor Zhou Xiao, reports this information from Huang Wan-wei, *Chung-kuo te yin-hsing ching-chi* (China's hidden economy), a 1993 source from Hopei.

[68]This information on the "Anhwei *pang*" comes from Professor Zhou Xiao, who cites a Shanghai 1991 book entitled *Food Is the Basis of People: Report from Rural China.*

[69]Goldstein, Goldstein, and Guo, "Temporary Migrants in Shanghai Households," 275, gives details on methods in the 1984 Shanghai Temporary Migration Survey.

pay."[70]   Other trades in which illegal and impermanent residents pre-
dominated were furniture repair, quiltmaking, and knife grinding.

Migrants and Law Enforcement

Some migrants became criminals. Since many were already violating
registration laws, it was merely a next step to break others. Young rural
immigrants to Shanghai often could not obtain living space in the crowded
central city. But peasants on the outskirts offered them space—at high
rents, and without the blessings of any authorities. Urban firms were
happy to use such a cheap supply of labor. The lifestyles of these young
people were often unstable; and largely because of their influx, suburban
economic crime soared in 1984, rising by 60 percent above the 1983 rate.[71]

Although only 7 percent of Shanghai crime was committed by nonregistered people in 1983, this portion rose to 11 percent in 1984 and 1985,
18 percent in 1986, 20 percent in 1987, 30 percent in 1988, and 31 percent
in 1989—and this is just the floaters' portion; the total crime rate also
rose rapidly over these years.[72]   At the end of the decade, 3 percent of
floaters had been arrested for crimes; the portion among the permanently
registered residents was 1 percent.

Birth control was practically impossible to enforce among migrant
workers, especially suburban farm workers:

> Recently [1989], many people from Kiangsu, Anhwei, and Shantung have come
> to Shanghai seeking jobs because they were impoverished back home. After
> they got a female baby, they still wanted a male baby. Many had two children
> or more. . . . Some couples came to farm [as migrant laborers], but they
> avoid the local urban government's birth control. Almost all these workers had
> one or more "black" children [unauthorized by the state]. Because the workers
> moved around, it was difficult for leaders on suburban farms to carry out the
> birth control policy among them. Some cadres were aware of this problem and
> wanted to adopt effective methods; but if so, the workers just floated to other
> places. Workers would move repeatedly until they had a male baby.[73]

The Interests of Long-Term Residents and Officials

Permanent residents of Shanghai could disdain such behavior while

---

[70]The Population Institute of Futan University directed a census on October 20, 1988, for
policymakers who wanted to reduce the floating population. See *China Daily* (Peking),
November 25, 1988. Later estimates of the portion of migrants in construction varied but
were not sharply different from one-fifth or one-quarter. Many registered for construction
jobs supplemented their incomes in other activities.

[71]Data from *FBIS-CHI-84-242* (December 14, 1984): 3, radio of December 13.

[72]Li, *Liu-tung jen-k'ou*, 160. A similar and compatible report is *Hsin-min wan-pao*, March
24, 1989.

[73]*Hsin-min wan-pao*, April 7, 1989.

at the same time envying it. The attitudes of established families to immigrants were generally negative but complex. Even beyond the useful maids and construction workers, there was a grudging acceptance of migrants. As one writer put it by 1989, the "floaters . . . do not live in Shanghai temporarily; they are 'actual' Shanghai residents." Older locals obtained some specifiable benefits from migrants. "Now, because a lot of peasants came, Shanghai citizens could sell surplus grain to them. . . . Some outsiders are working for Shanghai residents. They did not want to be paid in cash but in rice."[74]

Local people could sell ration coupons to migrants. The monthly legal grain quota per Shanghai resident had not been lowered since the 1950s (despite nondeliveries in bad times, and despite the greater availability of meat and vegetables since the early 1970s). But because many kinds of meats and vegetables could now be had, Shanghai legal residents could easily forego some of their grain. A newspaper suggested that, "If we reformed this policy, the problem [for official budgets] would be solved."[75] But nothing happened. The matter was politically sensitive. Top socialist administrators apparently thought that until general inflation could be reversed, a reduction of Shanghai residents' traditional food entitlement could stir resentment among workers in state factories. PRC leaders may occasionally remind themselves that workers in cities like Shanghai do not lack revolutionary histories.

Reportedly just 45,000 people were unemployed in Shanghai by the end of 1988—but this underestimate does not capture the concerns of Shanghai's long-established workers. Some state firms were closing at that time, and 96,000 workers had resigned or been dismissed that year. The *Liberation Daily* estimated that on a national basis state-owned enterprises had 20 million "surplus workers" and that another 50 million were "expected to move from the countryside to the city in the early 1990s. . . . These unemployed and surplus laborers pose a serious threat to Shanghai."[76] As the wife of a factory manager in another Chinese city put it, "Everyone is sick of the drifters. . . . They are rascals. They come with hardly any money, are dirty, and don't have any skills. If they don't find work, they start begging or stealing. They are the reason crime is so bad. . . ."[77]

---

[74]The price of rationed rice in April 1989 in Shanghai (.55 *yuan* per *chin*) was 27 percent less than on the free market. So the state subsidy was still heavy—and costly—though many unrationed foods were available. This and the quotation are from the source in the next note.

[75]Sheng Li and Fu Ch'i-p'ing in *Hsin-min wan-pao*, April 18, 1989.

[76]*China Daily*, May 15, 1989.

[77]Tom Hilditch, "The Drifters," *South China Morning Post Magazine*, December 12, 1993, 23.

Conclusion on State Leaders and Residents

A Shanghai author nonetheless claimed that, "We should have a positive attitude toward the current floating population." He admitted that migrants bring big problems. Among Shanghai crimes "in the water area, 72 percent were perpetrated by the transient population. These people were also responsible for 32 percent of the burglaries, 34 percent of frauds, and 22 percent of rapes and homicides. . . . Many women in the floating population gave birth illegally. Among those who did so in Shanghai, 13 percent had two children, and 4 percent had three or more." Despite all this, the migrants were helping to construct a modern metropolis. "Without them, it would be difficult to imagine so many new buildings in today's Shanghai. A quarter million laborers from other places work in the textile industry and in environmental sanitation. . . ."[78] Such a sanguine attitude was not shared by all, but state leaders' interests in immigration were very mixed.

The influx brought cheap labor, and apparently managers supposed it would not directly bring worker unrest. Migrant proletarians, even if they lived under extraordinarily cramped conditions, were often in their own "communities outside the system" (*t'i-chih-wai ch'ün-lo*). One young unmarried man, who had arrived in early 1994 at a "Szechwan village" in the Pengpu area of Shanghai (and lived with five hundred other Szechwan migrants in a 300-square-meter asphalt-roofed shack), expressed some contentment: "I like to stay with my fellow Szechwan people. We take care of each other like brothers. We shoulder our hardships together, just as we share our dreams."[79]

It is as yet unclear whether strong traditional organization among temporary laborers in China—which has certainly caused unrest among contract (perhaps not migrant) laborers in the past—will provide forums through which they make political demands. Comparative research from other cultures, especially on the politics of migrants in Mexico City, Lima, Rio de Janiero, and other fast-developing cities, has suggested that ex-peasant urban villages in Latin America have not become hotbeds of political unrest—at least for the first generation of "urban villagers."[80]

---

[78]The number of such laborers was specified at 240,000. See Mao Chung-wei and Chou Tzu-keng in *Shang-hai liu-tung jen-k'ou*, 47-57.

[79]Professor Cheng Li mentioned the phrase and provided this interview quotation about community.

[80]Latin Americanists reporting the slums of São Paolo, Lima, and Mexico City, have provided the earliest and best material. See works by anthropologist Oscar Lewis on Mexico and sociologist François Borricauld on Perú; by political scientist Wayne Cornelius, espe-

New arrivals to big cities from rural areas, reproducing their conservative form of community separate from the surrounding metropolitan environments, have been politically quiescent. Even when sanitation, water supply, and other urban services for them are minimal—as is currently the case for many migrants in Shanghai—they are not a direct threat to the state order.[81] Indirectly, however, their presence may create such a threat because of the reactions of more established residents.

The migration to cities of millions of unlicensed migratory workers in the 1980s and 1990s has been unpopular with many long-term Shanghai residents, who have permanent household registrations and fear their jobs are endangered by immigrant labor. The state's public policy has thus often called for migrants' expulsion back to the countryside; official sermons with this theme please state-sector workers. But migrants provide low-cost help to many state enterprises with tightly constrained budgets.

Migrants also deliver food to cities and provide many services at low prices, thus fighting inflation. Although migrants often break household control laws, the police since 1989 need as much legitimacy as they can muster—and migrants provide many occasions for police to prove their constabulary worth. Long-term residents readily believe that official coercion has a rightful role at least for keeping vagrants in line. The police can publicize their expulsion of relatively few unregistered migrants—while allowing most to stay, because of the benefits these newcomers bring to state enterprises.[82]

Urban intellectuals in mainland China have long fulminated against "blindly flowing population" (mang-liu jen-k'ou). When a book on the history of Chinese hooliganism was published in 1993, it traced in great detail the state's efforts to control migrants, from before the First Emperor to 1911.[83] Planners who tell citizens where to live suggest that intellectuals

cially "Urbanization and Political Demand Making," *American Political Science Review* 74, no. 4 (December 1980): 1125-46, with data from Mexican barrios; and for theoretical background, the classic "tunnel effect" article by economist Albert Hirschmann on the "Changing Tolerance for Income Inequality in the Course of Economic Development," *World Development* 1, no. 12 (1973): 24-36.

[81] The best student of labor unrest in mainland China has orally suggested that Latin American and African experiences may not be replicated there. Chinese organizational traditions, especially in same-place associations, seem strong. But the present author still supposes the main threat migrants pose to the state is indirect, through their interactions with political networks of older urban residents, rather than direct through their own capacities for political organization. The jury is still out, on this question.

[82] Similar arguments appear in a superb essay about the national situation by Dorothy Solinger, "China's Transients and the State: A Form of Civil Society?" *Politics and Society* 21, no. 1 (March 1993): 19-33.

[83] Ch'en Pao-liang, *Chung-kuo liu-mang shih* (The history of Chinese hooliganism) (Peking: Chung-kuo she-hui k'e-hsüeh ch'u-pan-she, 1993).

linked to the state know how ordinary people should conduct their lives better than the people themselves do. This is not a silly opinion, because there is no surefire way of knowing the general conditions under which small groups' (or individuals') benefits come from collective arrangements— or the general conditions under which they do not. There is some chance the planners may plan sagely and fairly, and the state has promoted any discourse suggesting this possibility. But urban intellectuals with good state jobs tend to live in choice spots. Even if would-be migrants fully obeyed whatever leaders decree, it would be hard for an outside observer to believe that such officials give much weight to the interests of people so different from themselves.

The matter is decided politically, and not just according to the interests of any one size of group. During mainland China's reforms, it may be decided more sensitively, because the once overweening role of the state has decreased. The real liberation of China in the 1970s and 1980s, when many more peasants became workers, threatened not only the patronist state but many intellectuals' ideals of plans in power. Migration is a concomitant of development. Increased income has been so strongly in the interests of so many Chinese, as the economy has soared, that the state lost most of its previous ability to control where people lived.

Part III

Trends in Taiwan

8

Trends in Taiwan:
A Political Perspective

Shelley Rigger

In September 1993, several panelists at the American Political Science Association's annual meeting presented papers on recent ROC elections. Their work was detailed and intricate, employing the most sophisticated quantitative analytical frameworks available to political scientists. What was most striking about the papers was how quickly the ROC has become "just another democracy," amenable to analysis using the same tools we use to study the United States or Britain, Japan or France. This was remarkable because for forty years, most Western scholars dismissed the ROC, labeling it an authoritarian state unworthy of inclusion in studies of electoral democracy. In the mid-1980s Taiwan acquired a new position in the political science literature, this time as a case study in the transition to democracy. Today, I would argue, that transitional period is drawing to a close. Before long we will need to shift our focus from the democratization process to Taiwan's consolidation as a full-fledged democracy.[1]

Of course, the ROC's democratizing project still faces challenges. Above all, the steady stream of threats from across the Taiwan Strait prevents Taiwan from acting freely in its domestic and international relations. The Peking (Beijing) government also stymies Taiwan's full participation in the world community, which complicates the ROC's efforts to reinforce its political and social development with overseas ties. Nonetheless, the progress the ROC has made in recent years toward the peaceful development of a stable democratic political system is by far its most

---

[1]The largest remaining institutional obstacle to Taiwan's recognition as a fully-realized industrial democracy is the lack of a popularly-elected chief executive, and that obstacle will fall within the next two years.

noteworthy characteristic. Indeed, Taiwan's experience of democratization eventually may surpass its economic miracle as a model worthy of emulation by other nations. In considering the current stage of Taiwan's political development, which I would characterize as the final consolidation of democracy, I will emphasize three trends: the normalization of politics, the transformation of the electoral system at the national level, and the marginalization of the conservative elements that dominated ROC politics in the prereform era.

Normalization of Politics

The decision to end the state of war with mainland China was a turning point in the return to normalcy of ROC politics. The abnormality of the period between 1947 and 1991 was expressed best by the title of the legislation under which the ROC was governed in those years: Temporary Provisions Effective During the Period of Mobilization for the Suppression of Communist Rebellion. The Temporary Provisions were repealed in 1991, putting the ROC government back on a normal footing.

But normalization of politics includes more than the end of a state of war. At its most basic level, normalization for the ROC means the establishment of constitutional government. In this sense, it corresponds to the stage in Dr. Sun Yat-sen's model of political development when political tutelage ends and constitutional government begins. Normalization means that formal institutions and practices will change only through established, evolutionary devices such as legislation, judicial decision, and constitutional amendment; it excludes such extra-constitutional mechanisms as presidential decrees, national conferences, and extraordinary legal provisions. Normalization also signals the end of the process of political transition.

The normalization of politics entails behavioral as well as institutional changes. During a democratic transition, issues of political organization, national identity, human and civil rights, and expanding participation dominate the national political agenda. As politics becomes normalized, political debate moves away from these narrow transitional issues to include a broader range of concerns, many of which are not political but economic or social. In short, the demand for reform fades as reform is carried out, and in its place new issues gain prominence. Normalization also alters informal, or behavioral, aspects of political life. It strains existing institutions so that alliances and patterns of behavior that developed in extraordinary times no longer work, and need to be reconstructed.

Constitutional government went into effect in the ROC in 1991, when the Temporary Provisions were lifted; however, many constitutional provisions were in effect even before that formal step was taken. De facto implementation of much of the ROC Constitution anticipated the repeal of the Temporary Provisions by several years. For example, the government gave its tacit approval to organized political opposition when it declined to take action against the Democratic Progressive Party (DPP), which was founded in defiance of martial law in September 1986. The decision to lift martial law in 1987 eliminated some—but not all—remaining impediments to constitutional government. The Supreme Judicial Court's decision to replace senior members of the Legislative Yuan and National Assembly in 1992 and 1991, respectively, represented the culmination of a long process designed to bring the national representative bodies into harmony with the ROC Constitution. In short, normalization of the institutions of government was a gradual process which took place over several years.

Legislative Effectiveness

One consequence of the normalization of Taiwanese politics is the growing effectiveness of elected representatives as policymakers. For four decades, Taiwan's representative bodies were scorned by foreigners and many Taiwanese as rubber stamps for the Kuomintang (KMT, the Nationalist Party of China) leadership. Today, KMT proposals still are virtually assured of passage in the legislature, thanks to the party's discipline and hierarchical organization, but representatives are much more likely to leave their mark on the bills that pass before them. In this respect, the ROC legislature is not unlike the British Parliament or the Japanese Diet under LDP rule. In some important cases, opposition legislators have forced the renegotiation of KMT proposals. For example, the legislature passed three controversial bills on National Security in the session ending in January 1994, but vigorous protests from opposition parties compelled the KMT to submit the bills to the Council of Grand Justices for a procedural review. In another case, legislators of the KMT, DPP, and Chinese New Party (CNP) negotiated a proposal to change interpellation procedures, only to have the agreement rejected by the Cabinet. Legislators also have pressed for—and received—reductions in defense expenditures.

The development of a more effective legislature also can be seen in the committee system. The current legislature reduced the size of committees by more than two-thirds to help them function more efficiently. Another sign of normalization in the legislature is the increase in factionalism among KMT members. This breakdown in party discipline, while distressing for party leaders, is necessary if a broad range of viewpoints are to achieve representation in the legislature. Along with the Legislative Yuan, elected officials at other levels have gained new powers during the reform era. The unsuccessful walkout by Provincial Assembly members of both parties to protest the decision to strip them of their power to elect members of the Control Yuan is a particularly astounding example of elected officials asserting their authority, but it is by no means unique. The Control Yuan itself recently has exhibited increasing independence, even though the president now appoints its members. For example, in February 1994 the Control Yuan responded to problems in Taipei City's mass transit authority (the Department of Rapid Transit Systems, or DORTS) by passing a bill of censure against the Executive Yuan and the Taipei City government. The fact that an appointive body operating in the new climate is more autonomous than an elected body under the old one testifies to the extent of the change.

Party Reform

Implementing constitutional government also has altered Taiwan's party system. Although the ROC Constitution provides for a multiparty democratic state, throughout most of its history the KMT saw itself as a revolutionary party built on Leninist organizational principles and devoted to maintaining single-party rule in the tumultuous civil war era. Thus, the first major step toward normalizing the party system was the ROC government's decision not to interfere with the formation of the DPP in 1986. The following year, tacit approval turned to outright acceptance when the government lifted the forty-year ban on new opposition parties. At its Fourteenth National Congress in 1993, the KMT took its party reforms a step further, declaring its intention to set aside its revolutionary tradition and transform itself into an open political party dedicated to winning elections. Early this year, the KMT registered as a corporate entity, placing itself on an equal legal footing with other organizations in Taiwan's civil society.

The most important change in the ROC party system since 1986 is the defection of KMT members to form the CNP. Since the birth of the DPP, rumors of disunity in the two major parties have been a regular feature of political discourse. Until recently, most speculation about party disintegration focused on the DPP, but few close observers were surprised when the KMT succumbed first. Just before the 1993 party congress, KMT legislators affiliated with the New KMT Alliance (NKA) decided to quit the ruling party and found the CNP. The party's first electoral outing in the November 1993 county and municipal executive elections was disappointing; its candidates won less than 9 percent of the vote. However, the CNP's ranks include some of northern Taiwan's most popular and best-known politicians, including Jaw Shaw-kong, Wang Chien-hsien, and Chou Chuan, none of whom was on the ballot in the 1993 elections.

Civil Rights

If political normalization means the implementation of constitutional government, then it also entails respecting civil rights enshrined in the Constitution, especially freedom of speech and participation. Indeed, some of the ROC's earliest political reforms involved lifting restrictions on civil rights, a process Huntington calls liberalization. In his view, liberalization "is the partial opening of an authoritarian system short of choosing governmental leaders through freely competitive elections."[2] In Taiwan, the government gradually reduced censorship and deregulated the mass media. In 1987, it lifted the ban on new newspapers. The market was quickly flooded with new publications, many of which did not survive the tough competition for readers and advertising revenues. One survival strategy was to print what others dared not print, so that by 1990, virtually any topic was fair game. Even conservative publications were forced by competitive pressures to begin reporting on opposition activities. Broadcast media were slower to open up; in fact, this still is an area in which many Taiwanese are dissatisfied with the pace of reform. Television broadcasts still are limited to the three officially-run stations, all of which have close connections to the party-state. That is not to say, however, that reform has fizzled out in this area. Before the end of 1994 the ROC government will make FM radio frequencies between 88 and 98 megahertz available to broadcasters. Even television is liberalizing, thanks to satellite transmissions from abroad and the legalization of cable TV stations.[3]

Political Behavior

The normalization of politics extends beyond the implementation of constitutional government to include changes in informal behavior. One important dimension of the normalization of ROC political practices was the demise of the "strong man" ruling style that characterized Taiwanese politics under presidents Chiang Kai-shek and Chiang Ching-kuo. It may seem paradoxical that institutionalizing the ROC political system has meant more informal bargaining and negotiation than before. But the grandstanding and horse-trading that have emerged in the postreform era are hallmarks of precisely the sort of republican government the ROC Con-

---

[2]Samuel P. Huntington, *The Third Wave: Democratization in the Late Twentieth Century* (Norman: University of Oklahoma Press, 1991), 9.

[3]Even before new TV and radio stations were legalized, widespread pirate broadcasting had effectively destroyed the government's monopoly on the mass media. At least four underground radio stations—with names like "The Voice of Taiwan" and "Treasure Island"—were operating by 1994. Some of the so-called Fourth Stations, or unlicensed cable TV networks, broadcast pro-opposition programming. A number of nonpolitical underground cable networks also operated.

stitution was designed to create. The days of orderly, patrician government are over in Taiwan, and the era of democratic politics has arrived,
carrying a suitcase full of confrontation, mudslinging, and campaign stunts.

Interest Group Politics

Politics as usual in a democracy means a political life dominated
by interest groups, and here, too, Taiwan is showing its political maturity.
The fact that business interests play a leading role in both major political
parties bodes well for those parties' survival and political relevance. Interest group politics makes many Taiwanese uncomfortable, and with good
reason. Well-financed special interests can do great violence to public
policy, especially when the citizen associations which might serve to check
their power are still in their infancy. Every democracy must be vigilant
against the danger of placing particularistic interests ahead of public welfare. But however worrisome it may be, the proliferation of interest groups
in the ROC demonstrates a widespread acceptance of a normal, institutionalized policymaking process. Lobbying the Legislative Yuan makes
sense only if groups believe the legislature is capable of enacting laws that
will be enforced. Thus, the existence of interest group lobbying reinforces
the perception that the Legislative Yuan is no longer a rubber stamp.

Corruption and Fraud

Another issue that worries many Taiwanese is corruption. When
Justice Minister Ma Ying-jeou launched his crusade against vote buying
in the wake of the 1994 county and municipal council chair elections he
exposed a deeply-rooted infection in Taiwan's political life. However, the
infection has been raging for many years; what is new is his determination
to fight it. Attacking and exposing corruption is far preferable to toler-
ating it, which was the policy of previous governments. As early as the
1960s, students of ROC politics reported widespread corruption in public
contracting, land use planning, and elections.[4] By the 1970s, corruption
in local government was institutionalized in the system of clientelistic exchanges through which the KMT maintained its electoral support. Local

---

[4]See, for example, Bernard Gallin, *Hsin Hsing, Taiwan: A Chinese Village in Change*
(Berkeley: University of California Press, 1966); J. Bruce Jacobs, *Local Politics in a Rural
Chinese Cultural Setting: A Field Study of Mazu Township, Taiwan* (Canberra: Contem-
porary China Centre, Research School of Pacific Studies, Australian National University,
1980); Arthur Lerman, *Taiwan's Politics: The Provincial Assemblyman's World* (Washington,
D.C.: University Press of America, 1978); and Ma Ch'i-hua, *Tang-ch'ien cheng-chih
wen-t'i yen-chiu* (Research on contemporary political problems) (Taipei: Li-ming Cultural
Publishing Co., 1991).

factions, the key to KMT electoral mobilization, were rewarded for their loyalty and assistance to the party with public offices and lucrative contracts. However painful it may be to cure the disease of corruption, Taiwan's body politic will be better off in the long term for having endured the treatment. The solution to corruption is a combination of firm legal action against the perpetrators and institutional reform to eliminate opportunities for corruption. Ma's showdown with the county and municipal council members exemplifies the former (as does DPP Chairman Shih Ming-te's purge of bribe-takers in his party); the decision to take the selection of Control Yuan members out of the hands of the Provincial Assembly illustrates the latter.

Electoral fraud is similar to corruption: well-publicized prosecutions create the impression that a problem has appeared recently. In fact, however, what is new is the determination to address the problem, not the problem itself. Non-KMT politicians have complained of fraud for decades, but in the past accusations rarely led to prosecution or even investigation. For example, in 1989 opposition supporters in Tainan County rioted to protest suspected fraud in the county executive election. The case never was resolved to the satisfaction of DPP supporters; the only person convicted of an offense was the DPP county executive candidate, accused of inciting the riot. In contrast, the courts overturned the results of the 1992 legislative election in Hualien County after finding opponents of DPP candidate Huang Hsin-chieh guilty of stuffing ballot boxes. Prosecuting fraud cases vigorously increases the credibility and legitimacy of the electoral process; it encourages voters to take elections seriously. In the long run, a few well-handled fraud cases are a sign of political health.

New Issues

Yet another indication of the normalization of ROC politics is the shift in issue concerns from "transitional issues" such as human rights, increased political participation and representation, restrictions on free speech and assembly, and national identity to the kinds of issues that dominate political discourse in established democracies: social welfare, economic performance, and international relations. The most divisive issue in ROC politics during the transition to democracy was the question of national identity, known in Mandarin as the *t'ung-tu* (unification-independence) problem. For many opposition activists, this question is a central motive for their participation in the opposition movement. Their firm conviction that Taiwan must establish itself as an independent national entity defined by a unique Taiwanese historical experience and cultural identity undergirds their positions on a whole range of issues. At the same time, prounification conservatives have staked out the alternative view.

Neither position in its extreme formulation had broad popular support; still, the national identity issue and related questions (such as laws against speaking out in favor of independence) defined the two ends of the political spectrum throughout the transition period.[5] In the 1990s, however, the leading parties' positions on the issue have converged. Both parties now assert that a declaration of independence is unnecessary, since Taiwan is an autonomous political unit already. Likewise, the KMT has adopted the DPP's position advocating participation in the United Nations. While the parties still are debating what name to use, the DPP has agreed not to interfere with the KMT's efforts to enter international organizations under the "ROC" label.

Since 1991, posttransitional issues have increased in importance, relative to the unification-independence debate and other fundamental questions. For example, during the transition, student protests tended to focus on noneducational issues such as the Constitution, Taiwan independence, and human rights. But recent student demonstrations have been decidedly more ordinary, dealing with issues of tuition, campus security, and academic pressure. Professor Chu Yun-han of National Taiwan University documented the shift toward a posttransitional issue agenda in a paper he presented at the George Washington University in Washington, D.C. in April 1994. According to Chu, "after the convocation of founding elections and a thorough Taiwanization of the KMT leadership, the appeal to democratic ideals and Taiwanese identity has exhausted its electoral utility."[6] In place of these issues, the DPP has redirected its attention to social welfare issues and concern about money politics.

One factor in the leveling out of attitudes on the independence-unification question has been the elimination of restrictions on travel to mainland China. While it is reasonable to expect increased contacts across the Taiwan Strait to promote a feeling of goodwill toward the mainland and increasing prounification sentiment, the actual results of cross-Strait travel are ambiguous. According to Ma Ying-jeou, by the end of 1991, "Taiwan residents had made more than 2.4 million trips to the mainland."[7] Meanwhile, Taiwanese have poured more than US$10 billion into mainland

---

[5]For a complete discussion of the national identity question in Taiwan's democratization process, see Alan M. Wachman, *Taiwan: National Identity and Democratization* (Armonk, N.Y.: M. E. Sharpe, forthcoming).

[6]Chu Yun-han, "Electoral Competition, Social Cleavages, and the Evolving Party System" (Paper delivered at a conference sponsored by the Gaston Sigur Center for East Asian Studies, George Washington University and the Institute for National Policy Research, Washington, D.C., April 8-9, 1994), 9.

[7]Ma Ying-jeou, "The Republic of China's Policy Toward the Chinese Mainland," *Issues & Studies* 28, no. 2 (February 1992): 2.

investments, making Taiwan the second largest investor in the PRC, after Hong Kong.[8]

Not all Taiwanese who visit the mainland return with an enhanced feeling of kinship with their mainland cousins. At the least, Taiwanese return home with a new appreciation of the standard of living they enjoy on the island of Taiwan. More worrisome are concerns about lawlessness on the mainland. A series of hijackings of commercial flights from the mainland to Taiwan raised questions about the willingness and ability of PRC authorities to control crime. But the horrendous tragedy of the Chientao (Qiandao) Lake incident in March 1994 brought Taiwanese anxieties about violent crime in mainland China to new heights. Published reports alleged PRC police and military involvement and accused mainland officials of deliberately covering up the truth.

In response to the Chientao Lake incident the ROC government imposed a travel boycott and suspended cultural and educational exchanges. The incident also affected business relations. The National Federation of Industries and the General Chamber of Commerce encouraged business people to stay away from mainland China as long as questions remained about the incident. According to a public opinion survey conducted April 14-15 by Gallup Taiwan, the percentage of Taiwanese who believed hostility between Taiwan and mainland China was high in the aftermath of the incident exceeded the percentage who believed so in the wake of the Tienanmen (Tiananmen) massacre of 1989. According to the same survey, support for Taiwan independence reached an all-time high after the Chientao Lake incident, while sentiment favoring unification fell to its lowest point ever.[9]

The Chientao Lake incident may boost the ROC government's campaign to encourage businesses to look beyond the PRC for investment opportunities. Premier Lien Chan and President Lee Teng-hui launched the government's so-called Southern Investment Strategy with "vacation diplomacy" tours of Southeast Asia in late 1993 and early 1994. State-run enterprises and KMT-owned businesses took the lead in redirecting investment toward Indonesia, Malaysia, Thailand, and Singapore, with the hope of enticing other Taiwan firms to follow. The strategy is rooted in the concern that heavy Taiwanese investments in the mainland might give the PRC government leverage to pressure Taipei politically. Meanwhile, some Taiwanese firms are finding that the profitability of mainland operations is not unlimited, thanks to the mainland's underdeveloped infrastructure,

---

[8]Osman Tseng, "Risky Business," *Free China Review* 44, no. 1 (January 1994): 34.
[9]*Free China Journal*, April 22, 1994, 2.

shortage of management personnel, lack of legal protection, and arbitrary government fees.[10] In short, Taiwanese enthusiasm for the mainland is more restrained than at any time since the ROC lifted travel restrictions in 1987, excepting the weeks immediately following the Chientao Lake incident.

This is not to say, however, that Taiwanese are taking a strongly pro-independence position today. If anything, major political actors seem unwilling to commit to *either* position, proindependence or prounification. Since 1991, the DPP party platform has included a plank calling for independence; however, DPP electoral campaigns give the issue less and less attention with each successive election. In June of 1994, DPP legislator Parris Chang told foreign scholars that Taiwan's foreign policy would not change if the opposition party were to come to power. According to Tien, many DPP leaders worry that identifying the party too closely with the independence movement "would scare off many potential party members and voters."[11] Given the apparent popular satisfaction with the status quo—de facto separation from the PRC without an official declaration of independence which might invite aggression—the DPP seems willing to soft-pedal the issue, at least for now.[12]

Meanwhile, the KMT has softened its position on unification as well. In ending the state of war in 1991, President Lee relinquished the ROC's claim to be the sole existing government of China. Since then, the administration's official position has been that there is only one Chinese nation, but there are in fact two Chinese governments. This formulation acknowledges that the ROC's power does not extend to mainland China any more than Peking's power extends to Taiwan. Throughout the 1990s, the call for urgent unification has become steadily more feeble, as residents of Taiwan overwhelmingly reject the notion that they soon might be absorbed into their enormous, chaotic neighbor soon. In sum, the national identity issue that was so important during the transition stage no longer pushes all other issues off the agenda. The search for a long-term solution to the *t'ung-tu* problem cannot be abandoned, but its focus has shifted from an ideological confrontation to an argument over how the status quo can best be preserved without limiting Taiwan's options for the future too

---

[10]Jim Hwang, "Sunset, Sunrise," *Free China Review* 44, no. 1 (January 1994): 4-15.

[11]Hung-mao Tien, *The Great Transition: Political and Social Change in the Republic of China* (Stanford, Calif.: Hoover Institution Press, 1989), 101.

[12]This is not to say that there are no longer any politicians who take a strongly proindependence line. Of course, some DPP and independent candidates continue to make national identity a centerpiece of their campaigns. However, as a party, the DPP is deemphasizing the independence issue, as are most of its candidates.

much. Meanwhile, a set of issues more appropriate to Taiwan's post-transition political life has taken center stage.

The normalization of politics does not mean political stagnation; the ROC political system continues to evolve. One example of a maturing consensus is in the area of constitutional reform. After several years of vigorous scholarly and political debate, Taiwan appears committed to developing a presidential system of government. The KMT recently released its proposals for constitutional reform in this year's National Assembly, which included a plan for the direct election of the president.

From the perspective of democratic theory, direct election of the president is a crucial step in the consolidation of democracy in Taiwan. Huntington defines democracy as a system in which the "most powerful collective decision makers are selected through fair, honest, and periodic elections in which virtually all the adult population is eligible to vote."[13] As recently as 1991, the KMT refused to endorse direct presidential elections in its party platform, yet today this step is virtually certain. The ruling party's draft constitutional reform also included a provision aimed at limiting the power of the premier, which will strengthen the presidential system further. Despite arguments by some scholars that a parliamentary system would be more conducive to stability and representative government, political considerations make the presidential system attractive to both major parties, thereby assuring its passage.[14]

Transformation of Electoral Politics
at the National Level

A second trend, which is less advanced than the first, is the gradual transformation of electoral behavior from a clientelistic model to a less particularistic style. This trend is most pronounced in elections for national offices (Legislative Yuan and National Assembly) and in urban areas,

---

[13]Huntington, *The Third Wave*, 7. Some scholars argue that indirect election of the president by the National Assembly is a fully democratic process analogous to the U.S. electoral college system. Regardless of the theoretical merit of their argument, however, the broad popular desire for direct presidential elections suggests that the Taiwanese people will not be satisfied with anything less.

[14]For a summary of scholarly opinion on the KMT's constitutional reform proposal, see Chen Chien-hsün, "Even the Chefs Can't Say for Sure How the Constitutional Amendments Will Taste," *Hsin hsin-wen* (The Journalist) (Taipei), no. 372 (April 24-30, 1994): 32-33, 35-37. On the KMT side, President Lee favors a presidential system in part because it maximizes his own autonomy of action. For the DPP, a presidential system offers the best chance of becoming the ruling party quickly, since it would be much easier to win a presidential election than to carve out a parliamentary majority.

while clientelistic motivations remain strong in local elections and rural regions. Under KMT single-party domination, the ROC electoral system was based on a mobilizational, clientelistic model. Clientelistic politics is one way electoral competition may be organized in a democracy, and many democracies pass through a stage in their development when clientelism plays a major role. However, Western experience suggests that democracies can outgrow this "machine politics" phase, in which interests and preferences tend to be constructed in terms of personal gain and individual connections. In place of clientelistic motivations, voters in mature democracies tend to make decisions based on party identification, issue preferences, and evaluations of candidates' qualifications for office. As clientelistic motivations recede in the minds of Taiwanese voters, these considerations are likely to play a larger role.

The importance of machine politics in Taiwan is attributable largely to institutional factors.[15] The KMT could have suspended elections along with other aspects of the Constitution during the period of civil war. But given the tension between the mainlander-dominated regime and the native Taiwanese after 1947, maintaining the regime's legitimacy was a critical objective. One solution was to hold local elections to give Taiwanese citizens and local leaders a feeling of participation in and commitment to the ROC state. But by limiting electoral competition to offices at the provincial level and below, the KMT ensured that party loyalists in the central bureaucracy and national legislative bodies would monopolize positions of real power in the government. Through its system of bureaucratic domination, parallel administration, and freezing elected central government officials in office, the party leadership was able to dominate decision-making at all levels of government, while coopting participatory urges among Taiwanese.

From the 1950s on, the KMT used local elections to cultivate a loyal native elite capable of maintaining grassroots support for the regime. Local politicians enjoyed high social status in their communities as a result of their electoral victories. Perhaps an even greater incentive to cooperate with the regime was provided by the material benefits available to local politicians and their associates. Networks of politicians, their business associates and supporters developed into local factions. Each faction was responsible for mobilizing voters in its sphere of influence (usually a geo-

---

[15]For a full account of the relationship between institutional reform and electoral behavior, see Shelley Rigger, "The Impact of Institutional Reform on Electoral Behavior in Taiwan" (Paper prepared for the American Political Science Association Annual Meeting, Washington, D.C., September 1-4, 1993).

graphical region) on behalf of the ruling party. The KMT rewarded factions that cooperated with the party's electoral strategy by nominating their members for local offices, ensuring the factions' access to political spoils such as public works contracts, patronage positions, and public monopolies (for example, intercity bus routes).

As a result, by the 1980s, all but a handful of Taiwan's twenty-three municipalities (counties and cities) were dominated by two or three major factions. These factions were not connected to factions within the national KMT leadership; their influence ended at their municipal boundaries. The reason for the limited size of KMT factions was the electoral opportunities available to them: until the late 1960s, the highest level of government chosen by popular election was the Provincial Assembly. There were no national contests which might have inspired candidates to reach across municipal borders. After 1969, when the first supplementary elections for the Legislative Yuan were held, elections for national offices became more and more numerous. However, these still were not truly national elections, since the electoral districts were drawn according to municipal boundaries. And under the ROC's single, nontransferable vote system, politicians were able to win any election just by winning within a single county or city. There was no reason for local factions to extend their mobilizational reach across municipal boundaries, for efficiently-used resources within the locality would be sufficient to win any election. As a result, local factions continued to be the primary structures for electoral mobilization even after the political reforms began opening national offices to popular election.

In short, Taiwan was a textbook case of machine politics (and in most local elections, it still is). As in other machine systems, voters chose candidates based on personal advantage, either because they had a connection to one of the candidates or because the candidate offered a particularistic incentive (special service, gift, or bribe) in exchange for the vote. Candidates for higher offices, whose districts are too large to allow for personal relations with voters, approached voters through intermediaries, known in Taiwanese as *t'iao-a-k'a*. The *t'iao-a-k'a* in turn cultivated personal ties with voters. They mobilized "their" voters behind particular politicians on the expectation that the candidate, once in office, would repay their loyalty with benefits for themselves and for the community. Often the relationships between *t'iao-a-k'a* and politicians were embedded in local factional networks. Given the nature of the vote-getting system, it is not surprising that Taiwan's local factions and politicians became masters of the art of distributing pork barrel projects and exploiting personal relationships with voters. Nor is it surprising that the expression used to describe the process by which local vote brokers mobilized support is "pulling votes" (*la p'iao*).

Ideally, a political machine is fueled by the personal ties and obligations among its members. However, vote brokers often reinforce these ties with gifts designed to demonstrate their esteem for the voter. This arrangement can easily degenerate into vote buying. As long as the personal connections among candidates, vote brokers, and voters are strong, vote buying is as much a courtesy among friends as a cold-hearted transaction; brokers can keep their "gifts" small if they are dealing with a reliable group of voters. It is when these connections become attenuated that candidates are forced to give away more and more money to secure a winning share of votes.

Although reports of gift-giving in exchange for votes go back at least to the 1960s, vote buying came to dominate news coverage of elections only in the late 1980s, after the political reforms were well under way. This was partly a consequence of lifting restrictions on the media that had suppressed coverage of such embarrassing realities, but the astronomical sums of money involved also attracted media attention. Political reform made elections more competitive and undercut traditional mobilizing strategies, driving the "return rate" on vote buying down to only 20 to 30 percent.[16] Candidates were forced to buy more votes, and to pay more for each one. Thus, mounting concern about vote buying is as both a symptom and a result of important changes in Taiwan's political system.

Democratization set off an explosion of political competition that gummed up the KMT's political machine. Local factions and politicians were accustomed to a system in which the important decisions were made in closed-door meetings between party officials and faction leaders; they were used to winning virtually every seat they contested. But after 1986, local factions found themselves facing organized opposition. It was no longer enough to win the party nomination; the possibility of losing general elections loomed. Candidates who previously would have been assured of victory had they cooperated with the party headquarters felt vulnerable. Their reaction was to "poach" in fellow candidates' "responsibility areas"; in effect, to steal votes from other KMT candidates. In some cases, including the 1991 National Assembly election, the KMT was able to keep its strategy intact; in others, such as the 1992 legislative race, the party's carefully-constructed strategy crumbled in the face of fierce competition among KMT, DPP, and independent candidates (see table 8.1). A local faction member quoted in *Tzu-li tsao-pao* (Independence Morning Post) on October 2, 1989 summarized this situation:

---

[16]This estimate emerged from more than eighty interviews with KMT and DPP political activists and candidates conducted in Taiwan in 1991.

Table 8.1
Success Rate for KMT and Non-KMT Candidates

Election	KMT				DPP			
	won/ nom'd	rate (%)	won/ total	rate (%)	won/ nom'd	rate (%)	won/ total	rate (%)
1989 Provincial Assembly	41/50	82	50/90	55	13/35	43	18/41	39
1989 Legislative Yuan	45/54	90	55/107	51	17/43	40	18/49	37
1991 National Assembly	164/183	89	176/212	83	41/94	44	41/95	43
1992 Legislative Yuan	59/94	63	75/153	49	37/57	65	37/65	57

Note: "Nom'd" means officially-nominated candidates only; "total" means all candidates who were party members. Includes geographical districts only.
Sources: *Shih-chieh jih-pao* (World Journal), December 3, 1989; *Tzu-li tsao-pao* (Independence Morning Post), December 22, 1991; *Shih-chieh jih-pao*, December 20, 1992.

> In the past, the two sides [local factions and the KMT] had something like a father-son relationship. After martial law was lifted, both sides wanted to equalize the relationship, to make it more like the relationship between friends. But only after going through this primary election have the two sides discovered that their relationship actually most resembles a business contact. Therefore, it's all "in business, talk business" (*tsai-shang yen-shang*).

Political factions suffered another blow with the introduction of party primaries as a method of selecting KMT nominees in 1989. Party primaries upset the traditional bargaining relationship between the party headquarters and local factions. In the past, nominations for office were negotiated among local KMT officials and leaders of various local factions. Since 1989, however, the party has been experimenting with formulas to collect input directly from party members and local cadres. Although the results of party primaries are not decisive, they have complicated the relationship between factions and the party leadership nonetheless. Primary results tend to overemphasize the preferences of well-organized constituencies within the party. The result has been lists of candidates whose popularity with KMT conservatives far exceeds their popularity with the general electorate. (Likewise, some DPP primaries have produced slates that overrepresented the party's more extreme tendencies.) The party headquarters has little choice but to overrule these primaries, but it does so at the risk of undermining their legitimacy altogether. In any case, the process itself undercuts the role of local factions in the nominating process.

The loss of the CNP and its supporters promises to exacerbate the damage to the KMT's electoral mobilization efforts already wrought by increased competition. The party traditionally relied on certain staunchly supportive populations (military personnel, retired servicemen) to maximize its performance. These constituencies, known as "iron ballots," were allocated to marginal candidates in multi-member races. Because iron ballot constituencies were extremely loyal and well-organized, the party could deploy their votes where they would be most effective. However, many of the iron ballot voters supported KMT politicians who have moved to the CNP; no one knows where their loyalty lies today. Thus, the KMT will face new difficulties when it attempts to allocate votes in the next legislative election.

As the reliability of clientelism as a vote-getting technique in national elections declined, other, less obvious, changes appeared. For example, politicians are no longer a breed of their own. Increasingly, entrepreneurs are becoming politicians, and politicians are behaving more like entrepreneurs. The growing importance of money in politics has made it difficult for those without independent wealth to compete. As a result, candidates for the 1992 legislative elections included a number of prominent business people. According to a report in the November 12, 1992 *Far Eastern Economic Review*, these men believed their interests would be better served if they were to participate in the legislature in person, rather than endorsing a particular candidate or faction and expecting those individuals to defend their interests in the legislature. Politicians who lack personal fortunes must find other ways to build their support bases, since factions and *t'iao-a-k'a* no longer can guarantee victory. The rising cost of vote buying, too, favors politicians capable of raising vast sums of money.

Changes in the rules governing electoral competition also played a major role in transforming electoral behavior in Taiwan. For example, under the Election and Recall Law Effective During the Period of Mobilization for the Suppression of Communist Rebellion, candidate speech was curtailed. Certain topics, most importantly the independence-unification debate, were taboo. Even candidates' positions on noncontroversial subjects received limited publicity, since the law restricted their access to mass media. The length of political campaigns was limited to two weeks or less (it is true that in practice many candidates ignored this restriction; however, to do so put them in danger of sanction by the Electoral Commission);

the number and content of speech meetings was limited; and newspaper and broadcast advertising was curtailed. Candidates' limited access to the tools of mass communication forced them to rely on personal contacts with voters through *t'iao-a-k'a*. With candidates forbidden to air their views and opinions fully, issues were bound to play a less important role in voters' decision-making process than they might otherwise have done.

Since 1989, however, the Central Election Commission has gradually relaxed the restrictions on campaign activities. The only major constraint remaining is the ban on individual television advertising. And it is not clear that television advertising would be an efficient use of resources in Taiwanese elections, anyway, given the small size of districts relative to the broadcast range of Taiwan's three TV stations.[17] In short, Taiwanese voters today have access to far more information about candidates' ideology and qualifications than ever before. In contrast to the prereform era, voters who wish to select candidates on some basis other than clientelistic relationships should have little difficulty finding the information they need to make an informed choice.

Marginalization of Conservatives

In his discussion of the democratization process, Huntington identifies four actors: regime reformers, regime standpatters, opposition moderates, and opposition extremists. Given the hard-line stance of ROC conservatives just a few years ago, one of the most unexpected trends in Taiwanese politics today is the speed with which the influence of those conservative elements has waned. Standpatters are those individuals within an authoritarian regime who believe that its essential characteristics can and should be defended against those demanding democratic reform. In Taiwan, the so-called non-mainstream faction best fills this role in Huntington's schema. The clearest signs of the standpatters' dwindling powers were the lifting of restrictions on independence advocacy, General Hau Pei-tsun's replacement as premier by Lee Teng-hui's protégé Lien Chan, and the KMT's split in 1993.

From 1945 to 1991, the ROC regime rested its legitimacy on its claim to represent all of China. It used this argument to justify a wide range of repressive policies, including the institution of the Temporary Provisions, the decision to keep the "senior legislators" in office from 1947 until 1992, and the suspension of constitutional rights. As recently as 1991,

---

[17]New cable television regulations will create fifty-five regional cable markets. This arrangement promises to make political advertising on television a more cost-effective proposition.

statements in support of Taiwan independence were censored out of candidates' campaign statements in the official election bulletin. Yet in 1992, legislative candidates were informed that favoring a policy of "one China, one Taiwan" was "only a political idea" which did "not involve the instigation of anti-government acts."[18] This decision, although remarkable in light of Taiwan's recent history, served merely to recognize a reality that had been in place for some time.

Relinquishing the independence taboo is but the starkest example of the conservatives' waning influence. More subtle—but perhaps ultimately more significant—is the conservatives' declining political power. President Lee's first victory over the conservatives came when he eased aside his non-mainstream rival Lee Huan. Next, Lee used selective retirements and promotions to undermine Premier Hau Pei-tsun's military base. At the same time, he allowed Hau's poor public image to marginalize him politically. Finally, Hau resigned. Lee's appointment of Lien Chan to succeed Hau as premier cemented the president's control over the executive branch, ending speculation as to which half of the dual executive was the stronger.[19]

Another important sign of the marginalization of conservatives in the ROC is the split in the KMT. The founders of the CNP, including legislators Jaw Shaw-kong and Wang Chien-hsien, are mostly mainlanders who support unification, although they, too, must downplay this issue for political reasons.[20] Before they left the party, their New KMT Alliance often cooperated with the non-mainstream faction in challenging President Lee, whom they believe caters too much to local bosses and factions. Their decision to leave the KMT decimated the party's anti-Lee forces, further strengthening the mainstream faction.

Some CNP leaders are extremely popular, but the party has had difficulty receiving public affirmation. The CNP's appearance on the scene still shows little sign of threatening Taiwan's fledgling two-party

---

[18]*Free China Journal*, November 10, 1992.

[19]Another showdown between President Lee and the non-mainstream faction is likely before the 1996 presidential election. Lin Yang-kang, one of the best-known non-mainstream politicians, has announced his intention to challenge Lee for the KMT nomination.

[20]Chen I-hsin and Wu Wen-cheng, "A New Party Digs in for the Race," *Free China Review* 44, no. 3 (March 1994): 10. According to its supporters, the CNP does not deserve its reputation as a mainlander party that supports unification. They argue that the party includes Taiwanese as well as mainlanders, and that it does not support immediate unification with mainland China. The party's recent statements corroborate this claim. However, the CNP's public reputation is not entirely unfounded, either; it is based on party leaders' behavior during their years in the KMT's conservative wing. Establishing a new political image has proven very difficult.

system beyond the borders of the Taipei municipal area. The KMT and DPP together won 88 percent of the county and municipal executive vote in November 1993, and 78 percent and 89 percent of the town council and local mayoral contests in Taiwan Province, respectively, in January 1994. The KMT mainstream and DPP are closer to each other on some issues than they are to the CNP, which adds to the impression that the political space available to the CNP is limited. The most revealing test of the CNP's strength will be the Taipei City mayoral election in December 1994. The party's most popular leader, Jaw Shaw-kong, will be pitted against incumbent mayor Huang Ta-chou and a popular DPP legislator Chen Shui-bian. Even if Jaw loses, it will be interesting to note which of the other two parties suffers most from his presence in the race.

The Republic of China is built on two cornerstones: Dr. Sun Yat-sen's Three Principles of the People and the idea of a unified China. For decades, these ideas were embodied in the KMT. Until the 1980s, the idea that Taiwan might choose a direction other than those suggested by these two principles was literally unspeakable. Thus it is important to note how both principles have been rendered negotiable as a result of the political reform process. The KMT is preparing to substantially amend the Five-Power Constitution to allow for direct election of the president. At the same time, it is gradually reducing its resistance to the idea of an autonomous identity for Taiwan. This is not to say that KMT leaders are no longer devoted to the Three Principles of the People; indeed, a strong case can be made that what is happening in Taiwan today is the fulfillment of Dr. Sun's dream of a Chinese republic. Nonetheless, it is difficult to overstate the degree to which traditional conservative views of Taiwan's historical destiny have lost their power over Taiwanese public opinion and political thought. While, of course, these issues are hotly debated, the very existence of debate is noteworthy, given the long years when discussion itself was impossible.

Conclusion

This essay identifies three broad trends in Taiwanese politics. In conclusion, I would like to suggest some implications of these trends. To use the vocabulary of democratization theory, Taiwan is moving out of the transition phase and into the phase of democratic consolidation. There are few major reforms left to complete before Taiwan can claim the title of a fully democratic polity. The search for a posttransition political agenda is now under way; political parties, especially the DPP, must come up with alternative visions of economic, social, and political development that go beyond the implementation of constitutional government. Defining those new issues will require creativity and insight. One important task which still is not complete is that of training Taiwanese voters to use their democratic rights and privileges well. It is not surprising that institutional reforms which progressed as quickly as Taiwan's outpaced popular attitudes, but the long-term health of Taiwan's democracy depends on the voters' willingness to demand representation, not red envelopes.

Taiwan's political success reinforced the tremendous self-confidence sparked by the economic miracle of an earlier era. This self-confidence is evident in the number of Taiwanese students returning from abroad after completing degree programs. It is evident in the "It's Very Well Made in Taiwan" marketing campaign that seeks to establish international recognition for Taiwan's high-quality manufactures. It is evident in the island's flourishing cultural life; in its burgeoning fine arts, dance, and literary communities; in the Academia Sinica's new emphasis on Taiwan history; in the international prizes awarded to films about Taiwan's history and culture.

There is no question that this self-confidence is beneficial to Taiwan; however, there is a danger in it, too. The Peking government has responded to Taiwan's success with jealous disapproval. As Taiwan grows more self-confident, the Peking authorities may become even more determined to keep Taiwan from expanding its domestic successes into the international realm. Convincing Peking that it has nothing to lose—and much to gain—from allowing Taiwan to take its place in the international community may make the transition to democracy look easy.

9

Trends in Taiwan: An Economic Perspective

Cal Clark

The post-Cold War period of the early 1990s has several distinguishing characteristics: the end of East-West ideological confrontation, the growing saliency of economic competition among advanced industrial nations, and growing instability in many parts of the Third World. An assessment of the position of the Republic of China (ROC) on Taiwan in this new environment is somewhat tricky because the post-Cold War era was "both early and late" in arriving on the island.[1] It was early in the sense that economic frictions between Taiwan and the United States heated up in the mid-1980s, well before the collapse of Communism in Europe. It was late, however, in that the "unfinished civil war"[2] between mainland China and Taiwan constitutes an ongoing legacy of Cold War conflict and hostility.

The advent of the post-Cold War era has obvious implications for Taiwan's geopolitical position and strategic problems; and the "China question" has assumed an important role in the domestic political debate. Yet, the relevance of the changed international environment for economic trends in Taiwan, the subject of this chapter, is more controversial. On the one hand, the ROC's dynamic economy rests on evolutionary trends that can be traced throughout the postwar period. On the other hand, several of the challenges that are now arising to maintaining this dynamism were clearly exacerbated by post-Cold War phenomena—in particular, increased American economic pressure hastened the obsolescence of the

---

[1]Cal Clark, "Post-Cold War Relations between the U.S. and Taiwan: Both Early and Late in Arrival," in *Post-Cold War Policy: Economic and International Trade*, ed. William Crotty (Chicago: Nelson-Hall, forthcoming).

[2]Ralph N. Clough, *Island China* (Cambridge, Mass.: Harvard University Press, 1978).

island's assembly industries which led to their relocation on the Chinese mainland. This economic interdependence, in turn, has ambiguous implications at present both for surmounting Cold War tensions in Asia and for Taiwan's further successful development. On the one hand, it could promote a "Chinese community," thereby overcoming the Cold War rivalry across the Taiwan Strait, but on the other, it could also make Taipei increasingly vulnerable to pressure from its Cold War rival.

Taiwan has long been characterized as presenting an "economic miracle" that has produced an extremely rare combination of "growth with equity." The economy has been marked by sustained rapid growth throughout the postwar era and by what, at least in retrospect, appears easy structural transitions as the ROC climbed upward along the "international product cycle." Thus far, Taiwan's economic performance during the post-Cold War period of the early 1990s appears to continue these successful economic trends. Overall growth remains in the 5-7 percent range, only down slightly from the previous several decades; the country passed the mark of US$10,000 in per capita gross national product (GNP) at the beginning of 1993; the labor market remains quite tight in what must be the envy of America and Europe; and Taiwan has become a significant actor in the global and especially regional economy.

At a more interpretive level, the ROC's economic success rests upon three broader trends in its political economy. The first has been an almost astounding ability to upgrade from one economic activity to another, continually moving ahead into more sophisticated and higher value-added production. Second, economic and social development trajectories have reinforced each other in a "virtuous cycle" of positive feedback. Finally, the roles of the public and private sectors have generally meshed together quite well, although this effect probably was far from intentional.

This chapter, hence, considers how each of these trends may be affected in the post-Cold War era on the assumption that such "macro" phenomena are vital for determining "micro" economic outcomes. The first section provides an overview of Taiwan's economic performance during the postwar period. The next three sections then discuss respectively how structural upgrading, reciprocity of economic and social development, and complementarity between public sector and private sector economic activities facilitated past development and how each appears to be evolving at present. As will be argued, there is some reason to suppose that these positive forces will continue to work; but challenges to each are also on the horizon.

The Taiwan Economic Miracle: Growth with Equity

Taiwan's record in the economic realm since the early 1950s has been phenomenal by almost any standard as indicated by the data in table 9.1.

Table 9.1

Indicators of Economic Development Level

	1952	1958	1962	1968	1973	1978	1983	1988	1990
Population (million)	8.1	10.0	11.5	13.7	15.6	17.1	18.7	19.9	20.4
GNP per capita (NT$1,000)	2.0	4.3	6.5	12.2	26.6	58.3	113.1	181.2	215.0
GNP per capita (US$)	153	173	162	304	695	1,577	2,823	6,333	7,997
Manufacturing % GDP	12.9	16.8	20.0	26.5	36.8	35.6	36.0	37.8	34.1
Agriculture % GDP	32.2	26.8	25.0	19.0	12.1	9.4	7.3	5.0	4.2
Agriculture % Employment	56.1	51.1	49.7	40.8	30.5	24.9	18.6	13.7	12.9
Export % GDP	8.5	8.6	11.3	18.6	41.6	47.4	48.5	50.5	41.4
% Industrial exports	8.1	14.0	50.5	68.4	84.6	89.2	93.1	94.5	95.5
Trade balance (US$ mil.)	-71	-70	-86	-114	691	1,660	4,836	10,994	12,498
% Exports to U.S.	3.5	6.2	24.4	35.3	37.4	39.5	45.1	38.7	32.4
Foreign reserve (US$ bil.)	—	—	0.1	0.3	1.0	1.4	11.9	79.0	—
Inflation (%)	18.8*	1.3	2.3	7.9	8.2	5.8	1.4	1.3	4.1
Savings % GNP	9.2	9.9	12.4	22.1	34.6	34.9	32.1	34.4	29.7
Investment % GNP	15.3	16.6	17.8	25.1	29.1	28.2	23.5	23.3	22.2
U.S. aid % Investment	45.5	37.3	20.2	0.6	0.0	0.0	0.0	0.0	0.0
Foreign investment % Investment	0.5	0.8	1.5	8.4	7.9	2.8	3.5	4.2	6.6
Unemployment rate (%)	4.6	4.0	4.3	1.8	1.3	1.7	2.7	1.7	1.7

*One year later.

Sources: Steve Chan and Cal Clark, *Flexibility, Foresight, and Fortuna in Taiwan's Development: Navigating between Scylla and Charybdis* (London: Routledge, 1992), Appendices; Council for Economic Planning and Development (CEPD), *Taiwan Statistical Data Book, 1991* (Taipei: CEPD, 1991).

For the last forty years, real GNP growth has averaged approximately 9 percent, one of the highest in the world, demonstrating sustained development. GNP per capita has risen well over fifty-fold from US$150 in 1952 to US$1,500 in 1978, to US$6,000 in 1988, and to US$10,000 at the beginning of 1993. Concomitantly, the economy was transformed from a dominantly rural one in which agriculture composed over half of employment, a third of national product, and three quarters of exports (mostly sugar and rice) in the early 1950s to a predominantly industrial one. At the beginning of the 1990s, for example, manufacturing accounted for 34 percent of gross domestic product (GDP), nearly three times its 1952 share.

This economic drive began in the early 1950s with a radical land reform program which stimulated increased output that was used to finance industrialization and that also greatly altered the economic, political, and social relations in the countryside by destroying the socioeconomic and political power of the traditional landlord class. The land reform was quickly followed by an import-substitution industrialization program based on strong protectionist controls. Import substitution produced a spurt of light industrial growth, but by the early 1960s the domestic market was becoming saturated. Taiwan then made the fateful decision to radically change its economic strategy by liberalizing trade and by emphasizing labor-intensive export industries. This new strategy proved extremely successful. Real GNP grew at an annual rate of 11 percent between 1963 and 1973; and the period from the early 1960s to the early 1970s saw major improvements in most of the indicators of economic performance in table 9.1.

By the mid-1970s, however, rising labor costs and growing international protectionism were beginning to undermine the island's niche in the global economy; and these problems were brought to a head by the oil price explosion of 1973-74. In response, the government slapped on stringent fiscal controls to combat inflation but also made a big push by investing in large-scale infrastructure projects to help revive the economy and by moving into heavy industry (e.g., steel and petrochemicals) primarily based on state corporations. Then in the 1980s, a new structural transformation toward high-tech production began as the island's small-scale private electronics industry became competitive in more high-tech industries. The continued rapid growth of the economy in the early 1990s is all the more impressive because the ROC clearly began to leave many labor-intensive industries behind. This resulted in a tremendous outflow of capital first to Southeast Asia and then, ironically from a political perspective, to the People's Republic of China (PRC) as many Taiwan businessmen moved their production offshore to economies with cheap labor.[3]

---

[3]See Steve Chan and Cal Clark, *Flexibility, Foresight, and Fortuna in Taiwan's Develop-*

Returning to the summary data in table 9.1, the export-led nature of Taiwan's development after the early 1960s[4] is also quite clear as exports have constituted almost half of GNP and been overwhelmingly industrial in composition since the early 1970s. Moreover, the composition of industrial exports has increasingly moved up the product cycle into more sophisticated and higher value-added products (e.g., from textiles and shoes to assembly electronics to more high-tech goods and machine tools). This surge in exports was accompanied by a dramatic change in the nation's balance of trade from the deficits during the 1950s and 1960s to the current huge (and, for U.S. trade, politically embarrassing) surplus. By the late 1980s the ROC had accumulated the world's second largest amount of foreign reserves; and it even moved past Japan into first place, at least momentarily, after the Japanese paid their contribution to the Gulf War in 1991. For a small island with a per capita GNP of US$100 in 1950, this export and foreign reserves boom was certainly quite an accomplishment.

---

ment: Navigating between Scylla and Charybdis (London: Routledge, 1992); Cal Clark, *Taiwan's Development: Implications for Contending Political Economy Paradigms* (Westport, Conn.: Greenwood, 1989); Walter Galenson, ed., *Economic Growth and Structural Change in Taiwan: The Postwar Experience of the Republic of China* (Ithaca, N.Y.: Cornell University Press, 1979); Thomas B. Gold, *State and Society in the Taiwan Miracle* (Armonk, N.Y.: M. E. Sharpe, 1986); Stephan Haggard, *Pathways from the Periphery: The Politics of Growth in the Newly Industrializing Countries* (Ithaca, N.Y.: Cornell University Press, 1990); Samuel P. S. Ho, *Economic Development in Taiwan, 1860-1970* (New Haven, Conn.: Yale University Press, 1978); Shirley W. Y. Kuo, *The Taiwan Economy in Transition* (Boulder, Colo.: Westview, 1983); Shirley W. Y. Kuo, Gustav Ranis, and John C. H. Fei, *The Taiwan Success Story: Rapid Growth with Improved Income Distribution in the Republic of China* (Boulder, Colo.: Westview, 1981); Danny K. K. Lam, "Explaining Economic Development: A Case Study of State Policies Towards the Computer and Electronics Industry in Taiwan (1960-80)" (Ph.D. diss., Carleton University, Ottawa, 1992); K. T. Li, *The Evolution of Policy Behind Taiwan's Development Success* (New Haven, Conn.: Yale University Press, 1988); Ching-yuan Lin, *Industrialization in Taiwan, 1946-1972: Trade and Import Substitution Policies for Developing Countries* (New York: Praeger, 1973); Ramon H. Myers, "The Economic Transformation of the Republic of China on Taiwan," *China Quarterly*, no. 99 (September 1984): 500-528; Gustav Ranis, ed., *Taiwan: From Developing to Mature Economy* (Boulder, Colo.: Westview, 1992); Robert Wade, *Governing the Market: Economic Theory and the Role of Government in East Asian Industrialization* (Princeton, N.J.: Princeton University Press, 1990); Edwin A. Winckler and Susan Greenhalgh, eds., *Contending Approaches to the Political Economy of Taiwan* (Armonk, N.Y.: M. E. Sharpe, 1988); and Yuan-li Wu, *Becoming an Industrialized Nation: ROC's Development on Taiwan* (New York: Praeger, 1985).

[4]Shirley W. Y. Kuo and John C. H. Fei, "Causes and Roles of Export Expansion in the Republic of China," in *Foreign Trade and Investment: Economic Development in the Newly Industrializing Asian Countries*, ed. Walter Galenson (Madison, Wis.: University of Wisconsin Press, 1985), 54-84; Chi Schive, "Trade Patterns and Trends of Taiwan," in *Trade and Structural Change in Pacific Asia*, ed. Colin I. Bradford, Jr. and William H. Branson (Chicago: University of Chicago Press, 1987), 307-31; Maurice Scott, "Foreign Trade," in Galenson, *Economic Growth and Structural Change in Taiwan*, 308-83.

Taiwan's excellent overall economic performance was based on the regime's ability, rare among developing nations, to control inflation. The hyperinflation of the late 1940s that had been imported from the Chinese mainland was brought under control fairly quickly by a combination of high interest rates and conservative fiscal policy;[5] and since the late 1950s inflation has remained well under 10 percent except for the two price surges induced by the energy crises of 1973-74 and 1979-80. A major reason for Taiwan's very successful inflation record has been its conservative monetary policy. For example, except during the oil-induced inflationary surges, money supply has generally not expanded much faster than the overall economy. In addition, until the huge Six-Year National Development Plan in the early 1990s, government budgets almost always ran surpluses. However, the huge export surpluses and foreign reserves have generated growing inflationary pressures since the late 1980s, especially in the forms of skyrocketing land and housing prices and of an extremely volatile stock market.

The high interest rates that resulted from the ROC's conservative monetary policies helped stimulate savings and investment, a key factor for promoting economic growth. Sustained investment is seen by many as a prerequisite for economic growth, and an amount of 12 percent of GNP has been suggested as a threshold necessary for economic "takeoff."[6] In Taiwan massive American aid, which accounted for almost 40 percent of total investment,[7] kept the investment rate well above the "takeoff threshold." The reason that dependence on a foreign power brought aid rather than exploitation almost certainly lay in the nature of America's basic goal regarding Taiwan—the strategic one of maintaining a Cold War client which made the United States willing to subsidize Taipei.[8]

Once growth began to accelerate in the 1960s, the savings and investment rates became extremely high, averaging about 30 percent of GDP during the 1970s and 1980s, as domestic savings replaced and then surpassed the U.S. aid that had largely financed the initial stages of the island's development drive. This allowed massive capital accumulation without much foreign borrowing or deficit spending by the government.

---

[5]See Kuo, *The Taiwan Economy in Transition*, and Li, *The Evolution of Policy Behind Taiwan's Development Success.*

[6]W. W. Rostow, *The Stages of Economic Growth: A Non-Communist Manifesto* (Cambridge: Cambridge University Press, 1960).

[7]Neil H. Jacoby, *U.S. Aid to Taiwan: A Study of Foreign Aid, Self-Help, and Development* (New York: Praeger, 1966).

[8]Chan and Clark, *Flexibility, Foresight, and Fortuna in Taiwan's Development*; Clark, *Taiwan's Development*; and Clough, *Island China.*

Foreign capital for its part has never dominated the economy nor even reached 10 percent of total annual investment; however, it was very important in the key electronics sector in the 1960s and 1970s and is still seen as playing a vital role for the country's push into high-tech industries.[9]

Rapid growth in Taiwan, finally, created a steadily expanding job market. Consequently, the unemployment rate has generally been quite low, averaging 4 percent during the 1950s and early 1960s. It then fell to 2 percent or less in the 1970s, rose back to about 3 percent in the mid-1980s, before dropping under 2 percent again at the end of the decade. Low unemployment, furthermore, has stimulated steadily rising wages throughout much of the postwar period. For example, real manufacturing wages, after stagnating from the mid-1950s to the mid-1960s, grew by 5 percent a year during 1965-72, 10 percent a year for 1975-79 (after falling 4 percent a year in the 1973-74 recession), 6 percent a year during 1980-86, and a strong 9.5 percent annually in 1987-88 as the tight labor market at a time of economic expansion pushed up salary levels.[10]

Similarly, Taiwan's record is impressive indeed, for example, on income inequality which tends to be grossly exacerbated during the early stages of industrialization before dropping again according to Kuznets' "inverted-U" curve.[11] In the ROC in sharp contrast, rapid growth brought an immediate narrowing of income differentials, as indicated by the data on social outcomes in table 9.2. The ratio of the income of the richest fifth of the population to the poorest fifth dropped dramatically from 20.47 in 1953 to 11.56 in 1961 to 5.28 in 1968—a level comparable to that found in advanced industrial societies. Much of the initial rapid drop in income inequality can be attributed to the effects of the land reform. After the mid-1960s, the rapid growth of export-oriented industries created nearly full employment which resulted in rising real wages for unskilled and semiskilled labor.[12] While income inequality rose some-

---

[9]Stephan Haggard and Tun-jen Cheng, "State and Foreign Capital in the East Asian NICs," in *The Political Economy of the New Asian Industrialism*, ed. Fredric C. Deyo (Ithaca, N.Y.: Cornell University Press, 1987), 84-135; Chi Huang, "The State and Foreign Investment: The Cases of Taiwan and Singapore," *Comparative Political Studies* 22, no. 1 (April 1989): 93-121; Gustav Ranis and Chi Schive, "Direct Foreign Investment in Taiwan's Development," in Galenson, *Foreign Trade and Investment*, 85-137; Chi Schive, *The Foreign Factor: The Multinational Corporation's Contribution to the Economic Modernization of the Republic of China* (Stanford, Calif.: Hoover Institution Press, 1990).

[10]Chan and Clark, *Flexibility, Foresight, and Fortuna in Taiwan's Development*, 160-61.

[11]Simon Kuznets, "Economic Growth and Income Inequality," *American Economic Review* 45, no. 1 (1955): 1-28.

[12]John C. H. Fei, Gustav Ranis, and Shirley W. Y. Kuo, *Growth with Equity: The Taiwan Case* (New York: Oxford University Press, 1979); Susan Greenhalgh, "Supranational Proc-

Table 9.2
Indicators of Social Outcomes

	1952	1958	1962	1968	1973	1978	1983	1988	1990
Income ratio**	20.47*	—	—	5.28	4.49*	4.18	4.36	4.85	4.94*
Literacy rate (%)	57.9	69.1	75.2	83.6	86.2	88.8	90.9	92.6	93.2
Infant mortality (per 1,000 live birth)	44.7	41.0	31.4	20.7	14.1	9.9	7.6	5.3	—
Life expectancy (years)	60.3	66.0	66.4	67.0	70.2	71.6	72.4	73.5	—
Calories (day)	2,078	2,359	2,317	2,545	2,754	2,822	2,721	3,017	2,931*
Proteins (day)	49.0	56.9	57.8	64.9	73.7	77.0	77.0	89.5	89.8*
Communicable disease rate (per 100,000 people)	14.1	22.7	8.3	6.3	1.3	0.5	1.7	1.2	1.4
Food % Household spending	62.0	59.2	57.8	53.6	49.0	47.1	39.3	32.4*	—

*One year earlier or later.
**Ratio of the income of the richest fifth of the population to that of the poorest fifth.
Sources: Same as table 9.1.

what in the 1980s, it still remained very low by international standards. Consequently, rapid growth on Taiwan brought a rising popular standard of living.[13]

Table 9.2 shows that the popular standard of living rose considerably, although at somewhat different rates in specific areas. Central measures of the standard of living are provided by the three components (literacy, infant mortality, and life expectancy) of the physical quality of life index (PQLI) developed by Morris.[14] On these scores, Taiwan has surely "come a long way." Between 1950 and 1988, its literacy jumped from 56.0 percent to 92.6 percent, its infant mortality rate declined from 35.16 deaths to 5.34 deaths per 1,000 live births, and its people's average life expectancy increased from 55.57 years to 73.51 years. This caused the island's PQLI rating to rise from 63 to 95, with 100 being a hypothetically "perfect score," about equal to that of the United States in 1979.[15] Taiwan's dramatic improvements in standard of living are also reflected in other basic indicators of popular welfare. The quantity and quality of food consumption, as measured by caloric and protein consumption respectively, rose by 50 percent or more during the postwar period. Furthermore, the rate of communicable disease fell from about 15-20 to 1 per 100,000 people between the 1950s and the 1980s; and the proportion of household earnings spent on food, beverages, and tobacco—a central indicator of disposable income—was nearly halved from 62 percent to 32.4 percent between 1952 and 1988. This is not to say, of course, that growth in Taiwan produced universal blessings since many farmers and unskilled workers were left behind to only "get by";[16] and a deteriorating environ-

esses of Income Distribution," in Winckler and Greenhalgh, *Contending Approaches to the Political Economy of Taiwan*, 67-100.

[13]Gary S. Fields, "Living Standards, Labor Markets, and Human Resources in Taiwan," in Ranis, *Taiwan: From Developing to Mature Economy*, 395-433; Wen Lang Li, "Social Development in the Republic of China, 1949-1981," in *China: Seventy Years After the 1911 Hsin-hai Revolution*, ed. Hungdah Chiu and Shao-chuan Leng (Charlottesville, Va.: University of Virginia Press, 1984), 478-99; David C. Shack, "Socioeconomic Mobility and the Urban Poor in Taiwan," *Modern China* 15, no. 3 (July 1989): 346-73; Wen-hui Tsai, "Taiwan's Social Development," in *Survey of Recent Developments in China (Mainland and Taiwan), 1985-1986*, ed. Hungdah Chiu (Baltimore: University of Maryland School of Law, 1987), 125-38; Charlotte Shiang-Yun Wang, "Social Mobility in Taiwan," in *Contemporary Republic of China: The Taiwan Experience, 1950-1980*, ed. James C. Hsiung et al. (New York: Praeger, 1981), 246-57; Yung Wei, "Taiwan: A Modernizing Chinese Society," in *Taiwan in Modern Times*, ed. Paul K. T. Sih (New York: St. John's University Press, 1973), 435-505.

[14]Morris David Morris, *Measuring the Condition of the World's Poor: The Physical Quality of Life Index* (New York: Pergamon, 1979).

[15]Ibid.

[16]Fredric C. Deyo, *Beneath the Miracle: Labor Subordination in the New Asian Industrialism*

ment is undoubtedly exacerbating many health problems.

Rapid Economic Upgrading

The idea of the international product cycle has modified the traditional view of a nation's "comparative advantage" in the international economy.[17] Conventionally, comparative advantage in particular economic activities was seen as deriving from such permanent factors of production as land, labor, and capital; thus, it remained fairly immutable over long periods of time. The product cycle perspective conceives the international economy as much more dynamic. Highly sophisticated production is concentrated in the most advanced countries, but the production of many standardized and labor-intensive products is diffused to countries with low wages, allowing developing countries to "get their foot in the door" in the industrialization process. This explains how "newly industrializing countries" (NICs), such as Taiwan, started their developmental drives. The implications of product cycle theory are not entirely pleasant for the NICs, though. To the extent that they succeed in stimulating rapid development, growing prosperity leads to rising wages which pushes them out of their hard won niche in the worldwide industrial division of labor. Thus, development requires not just amassing enough resources for "economic takeoff," but making periodic structural transformations to increasingly sophisticated types of production. These are difficult, not only because of the new resources and skills required, but just as importantly because entrenched economic and political interests may resist change as a threat to their power and perquisites.

From this perspective, Taiwan's economic success has rested upon its ability to make regular "structural adjustments" in the face of economic challenge. In particular, four such periods can be discerned: (1) the 1950s, when the transformation away from an agricultural economy was consolidated; (2) the early 1960s to the early 1970s, when the "export boom" revolutionized the economy and set off significant social changes as well; (3) the mid-1970s to the mid-1980s, when substantial industrial upgrading occurred first in heavy industry and then in high-tech produc-

---

(Berkeley: University of California Press, 1989); Hill Gates, *Chinese Working-Class Lives: Getting By in Taiwan* (Ithaca, N.Y.: Cornell University Press, 1987); Huang Shu-min, *Agricultural Degradation: Changing Community Systems in Rural Taiwan* (Lanham, Md.: University Press of America, 1981).

[17]Robert G. Gilpin, Jr., *The Political Economy of International Relations* (Princeton, N.J.: Princeton University Press, 1987), and Raymond Vernon, "International Investment and International Trade in the Product Cycle," *Quarterly Journal of Economics* 80 (1966): 190-207.

tion; and (4) the late 1980s and early 1990s, when the ROC's high-tech industries developed apace but were accompanied by a massive move of assembly operations offshore, particularly to the PRC, in what has been called the "mainland revolution" in Taiwan's economy.

Taiwan's success in rapid economic upgrading is readily apparent in the data presented in table 9.1 charting the transition from an agricultural economy to an industrial one. Between 1952 and 1970, for example, agriculture's share of GDP fell by almost two-thirds from 32 percent to 12 percent, while manufacturing's almost tripled from 13 percent to 36 percent. The change was even more dramatic in the ROC's export mix as the share of industrial goods skyrockets more than tenfold during these two decades from 8 percent to 85 percent. Clearly, Taiwan's "economic takeoff" really took off.

There was more to Taiwan's development than simply the replacement of agricultural by industrial production. The nature of the dominant industry rapidly changed as well from food processing in the 1950s and early 1960s to textiles in the late 1960s and 1970s to electronics and heavy industry by the mid-1980s.[18] Table 9.3 shows that upgrading was even faster and more pronounced in the export sector of the ROC's most competitive products. Within the burgeoning electronics field there was also substantial upgrading as well from low-tech assembly dominated by foreign corporations in the 1960s to much more high-tech production in which indigenous firms played a more prominent role.[19]

The structural change that commenced in the mid-1980s contained a new element, however. This was that it involved not just the movement upward to new economic activities, but the need to "shed" many of the old labor-intensive businesses that were being priced out of their niche in the global economy by rapidly rising wages in Taiwan. Thus, a tremendous outflow of capital occurred as businessmen who could not upgrade their production facilities moved their factories to countries where low-cost labor was still plentiful, first to Southeast Asia and then the Chinese mainland after Taipei permitted "indirect" economic relations in the late 1980s.

---

[18]Please see Howard Pack, "New Perspectives on Industrial Growth in Taiwan," in Ranis, *Taiwan: From Developing to Mature Economy*, 87, table 3.4.

[19]Sung Gul Hong, "Paths of Glory: Semiconductor Leapfrogging in Taiwan and South Korea," *Pacific Focus* 7 (1992): 59-88; Cheng-Tian Kuo, *Institutions and Global Competitiveness: Industrial Growth in Taiwan and the Philippines* (Pittsburgh: University of Pittsburgh Press, 1994); Lam, "Explaining Economic Development"; Danny K. K. Lam and Ian Lee, "Guerrilla Capitalism and the Limits of Statist Theory," in *The Evolving Pacific Basin in the Global Political Economy: Domestic and International Linkages*, ed. Cal Clark and Steve Chan (Boulder, Colo.: Lynne Rienner, 1992), 107-24; and N. T. Wang, ed., *Taiwan's Enterprises in Global Perspective* (Armonk, N.Y.: M. E. Sharpe, 1992).

Table 9.3
Composition of Exports

Unit: %

	1952	1960	1970	1980	1990
Agricultural products	9	9	9	3	1
Minerals	3	2	1	0	0
Nonmetallic minerals	0	2	3	2	2
Subtotal	12%	13%	13%	5%	3%
Food products	83	57	13	7	3
Textiles, wood products	1	17	42	31	21
Subtotal	84%	74%	55%	38%	24%
Chemicals, pharmaceuticals	3	5	2	4	4
Basic metals	1	6	4	2	2
Metal products	0	1	2	4	6
Machinery	0	0	3	4	6
Electrical machinery	0	0	12	18	27
Transport equipment	0	0	1	3	5
Subtotal	4%	12%	24%	35%	50%
Others	0%	1%	8%	22%	23%
Total	100%	100%	100%	100%	100%

Source: CEPD, *Taiwan Statistical Data Book, 1991.*

International product cycle theory implies that this movement away from labor-intensive assembly was inevitable because the ROC's growing prosperity would have priced it out of the niche of the global economy reserved for low-wage countries sooner or later.[20] It is clear, though, that growing economic strains between Taiwan and America over the second half of the 1980s made this transition sooner and more abrupt than it otherwise might have been. Beginning in the mid-1980s, the United States exerted substantial pressure on Taiwan to reduce its huge trade surplus which had become second to only Japan's in size. While many of the most contentious issues concerning market-opening measures and intellectual property rights probably have had only marginal relevance for Taiwan's

[20]Gilpin, *The Political Economy of International Relations.*

economic performance, the controversy over exchange rates clearly was consequential. Under intense American pressure, the New Taiwan (NT) dollar was appreciated almost 50 percent against the U.S. dollar in the late 1980s, with predictably disastrous consequences for many small businesses operating on thin margins.[21] Thus, the post-Cold War switch to economic competition among Cold War allies clearly affected the economic evolution of the ROC.

Consequently, a tremendous growth in trade and investment across the Taiwan Strait occurred in the late 1980s and early 1990s. Investment in mainland China by Taiwan businessmen was negligible until 1987 but then took off rapidly, helping to stimulate a trade explosion. The nature of this foreign investment became more permanent as well. Taiwan investors moved from joint ventures to solely owned enterprises and began to build their own factories. The nature of these ventures was also upgraded from simple assembly to "upstream" heavy and more capital-intensive or high-tech production. Trade relations between Taiwan and the mainland were fairly low until the mid-1980s, when commercial relations across the Taiwan Strait began to skyrocket with the ROC maintaining a huge trade surplus.[22]

In fact, by the early 1990s, there even appeared to be something of a movement toward economic integration between Taiwan and southern coastal China, especially Fukien (Fujian) Province which many Taiwanese "Islanders" (i.e., those who dominate the small business sector) regard as their homeland. Thus, trade and especially investment across the Taiwan Strait reflect a complementarity between the two economies. Mainland China needs investment and entrepreneurial know-how, while Taiwan's businessmen in labor-intensive assembly activities (e.g., textiles, shoes, and low-tech electronics) need a production base with much lower labor costs than Taiwan. The Chinese mainland appeared as a very enticing

---

[21] Yujen Chou, "Economic Dependence and Changes in Taiwan's Trade Policy, 1984-89," *Issues & Studies* 28, no. 1 (January 1992): 96-118; Cal Clark, "The Limits of Hegemonic Predation as a Response to Competitiveness Problems: A U.S.-Taiwan Case Study," in *American Competitiveness and the World Economy*, ed. David P. Rapkin and William P. Avery (Boulder, Colo.: Lynne Rienner, forthcoming); Szu-yin Ho, "The Republic of China's Policy Toward the United States," in *The Foreign Policy of the Republic of China on Taiwan: An Unorthodox Approach*, ed. Yu San Wang (New York: Praeger, 1990), 29-44.

[22] Chu-yuan Cheng, "Trade and Investment Across the Taiwan Strait: Economic Consequences and Prospects," *Strategic Studies Series* (Montclair, Calif.: The Claremont Institute, 1992); Cal Clark, "ROC-PRC Relations: Resource Disparity, Interdependence, and Conflict Impetus," *Business and the Contemporary World* 5 (1993): 30-47; Ai Wei, "The Development and Limitations of Taiwan-Mainland Economic and Trade Relations," *Issues & Studies* 27, no. 5 (May 1991): 43-60; Yen Tzung-ta, "Taiwan Investment in Mainland China and Its Impact on Taiwan's Industries," ibid., 10-42.

target for their commercial expansion for several important reasons. Mainland China has unlimited low-cost labor; language and cultural ties are very strong; and pragmatic provincial leaders offer substantial incentives to invest in export industries. Thus, ironically from an ideological standpoint, Taiwanese capitalists played a major role in Communist China's export drive in the early 1990s which resulted in the PRC moving past Taiwan into second place for the largest trade surplus with America in 1991.[23]

The nature of this complementarity is indicated by the data in table 9.4 on the commodity composition of Taiwan's 1992 trade with Hong Kong which can serve as a rough surrogate for ROC-PRC commercial relations. These data list all the commodity classes for which Hong Kong constituted 20 percent or more of Taiwan's total exports by either value or volume (e.g., number of units). When the volume percentage is much higher than the value one, this indicates that Hong Kong and mainland China are buying the cheapest (and lowest quality) goods in the particular product mix.

Table 9.4 shows that mainland China seems to be buying two principal types of products from Taiwan. First, there is an export concentration in intermediate products which are almost certainly used in the factories being established by Taiwan businessmen and in machinery destined for these factories. Good examples of these are polymers, textile products like fibers and fabrics (as opposed to finished clothing), machine tools, some types of machinery, electrical capacitors and circuits, cathode tubes, integrated circuits, and parts for cassette players and VCRs. For all these products, the value and volume percentages are approximately equal, indicating that Taiwan is sending an average quality of output to mainland China. In short, these data show that Taiwan businessmen have moved their labor-intensive assembly operations "offshore" to the Chinese mainland to take advantage of the PRC's very cheap labor. Second, mainland China also serves as an outlet for some of Taiwan's cheapest finished goods. For example, while 98 percent of Taiwan's exports in cassette recorders and VCRs go to Hong Kong, they only constitute 11 percent of the value of total export sales, indicating that a small

---

[23]Clark, "ROC-PRC Relations"; Dennis Van Vranken Hickey, "Will Inter-China Trade Change Taiwan or the Mainland?" *Orbis* 35, no. 4 (Fall 1991): 517-31; N. T. Wang, "Taiwan's Economic Relations with Mainland China," in Wang, *Taiwan's Enterprises in Global Perspective*, 53-80; Yu-Shan Wu, "The Political Economy of Taiwan-Mainland Economic Relations," in *Inherited Rivalry: Conflicts Across the Taiwan Strait*, ed. Tun-jen Cheng, Chi Huang, and Samuel Shiouh Guang Wu (Boulder, Colo.: Lynne Rienner, forthcoming).

Table 9.4

Importance of ROC-Hong Kong Trade by Commodity, January-May 1992

	Hong Kong % Total Volume	Hong Kong % Total Value
Plastic fabrics	77	75
Polymers products	64	58
Woven fabrics, synthetic yarn	53	54
Electrical capacitors	53	52
Cassette, VCR parts	52	45
Nonreturned synthetic fibers	38	42
Synthetic yarn	40	41
Knit fabrics	39	39
Other machinery/machine tools	43	39
Synthetic woven fabrics	40	38
Synthetic fibers	35	36
Electrical wire	43	36
Plywood	27	28
Cotton woven fabrics	23	27
Machine tools	23	26
Cameras	83	26
Cathode tubes, ICs, etc.	29	23
Electrical motors/generators	25	20
Electrical circuits	27	20
Plastic materials	22	17
Telephone/telegraph arts	21	12
Lamps	20	12
Cassette players, VCRs, etc.	98	11
Sewing machines	26	7
Calculating machines	20	7
Office machinery	58	6
Auto data processing machines	33	3

Source: Ministry of Finance, Department of Statistics, *Monthly Statistics of Exports and Imports, Taiwan Area, Republic of China* (Taipei), May 1992.

number of high quality goods are being sold elsewhere (primarily the United States). Other goods in this category include office machinery, automatic data processing equipment, telephones, and cameras. Both types of trade, therefore, imply a growing complementarity between the more developed Taiwan and the less developed mainland China.

The growth of this complementarity, therefore, again demonstrates Taiwan's ability to respond rapidly and effectively to the signals of the international marketplace. However, unlike the earlier structural adjustments, this situation is not without problems. In the economic realm there is some fear that the outflow of capital will undercut domestic economic dynamism, despite the momentary spur to trade. One sophisticated econometric calculation, for example, concluded that capital outflow caused more investment and employment loss than increased ROC-PRC trade stimulated increased production in nineteen out of twenty major industries (all except iron and steel) with textiles suffering the greatest losses.[24] More broadly, the growing dependence of many of Taiwan's businesses on the mainland market raises the specter that the PRC may be able to pressure the ROC in the future by holding these economic relations hostage, although how much leverage either side has upon the other remains uncertain.[25]

The Intertwining of Economic and Social Development

Describing why Taiwan has been so effective and flexible in responding to market signals and economic opportunities, of course, does not really explain why Taiwan has been much more successful than most developing countries in this regard. A major reason would appear to be that social and economic development trajectories reinforced each other from the 1950s through the 1980s in an escalating "virtuous cycle." In particular, the provision of universal primary education created the "human capital" of labor and entrepreneurs who were vital in the industrialization drive.[26] The resulting economic growth, in turn, created an ever broader middle class who became increasingly productive economically, as well as generating the popular pressure for the democratization reforms of the late 1980s and early 1990s.[27]

---

[24]See Yen, "Taiwan Investment in Mainland China," 37, table 6.

[25]Clark, "ROC-PRC Relations"; Hickey, "Will Inter-China Trade Change Taiwan or the Mainland?"; James C. Hsiung, "China in the Twenty-first Century Global Balance: Challenge and Policy Response," in Clark and Chan, *The Evolving Pacific Basin*, 67-82; Wang, "Taiwan's Economic Relations with Mainland China."

[26]Ching-hui Chang, "Public Finance," in Ranis, *Taiwan: From Developing to Mature Economy*, 223-52; Ping-huang Huang, "Modernization of Education in the Republic of China Since 1949," in *Chinese Modernization*, ed. Yu-ming Shaw (San Francisco: Chinese Materials Center Publications, 1984), 171-91.

[27]Tun-jen Cheng, "Democratizing the Quasi-Leninist Regime in Taiwan," *World Politics* 41, no. 4 (July 1989): 471-99; Tun-jen Cheng and Stephan Haggard, eds., *Political Change in Taiwan* (Boulder, Colo.: Lynne Rienner, 1992); John F. Copper, *A Quiet Revolution: Political Development in the Republic of China* (Washington, D.C.: Ethics and Public Policy Center, 1988); Peter R. Moody, *Political Change on Taiwan: A Study of Ruling Party Adaptability* (New York: Praeger, 1992); Ramon H. Myers, "Political Theory and the Recent Political Developments in the Republic of China," *Asian Survey* 27, no. 9 (September 1987): 1003-22; Hung-mao Tien, *The Great Transformation: Political and Social Change in the Republic of China* (Stanford, Calif.: Hoover Institution Press, 1989).

Table 9.5 presents a variety of indicators concerning social development in the ROC. Collectively, they illustrate the growth of Taiwan's middle-class society. The "demographic transition" did not really occur until the mid-1960s but once it started, the population growth rate fell by a half in just a decade. The educational data are very impressive. Taiwan's high literacy rate was noted above. Beyond the bare requirements of literacy and a primary schooling, the educational achievements of Taiwan's population expanded rapidly during the postwar period, especially after the mid-1960s. The proportion of the population with a secondary education, for example, only rose from 10 percent to 22 percent over the 1950s and 1960s, but then jumped quickly to 41 percent at the end of the 1970s and 54 percent at the end of the 1980s. Opportunities for college education also expanded greatly; and there was a significant shift in the nature of college coursework from the traditional humanities to science and engineering. The data on home ownership, the average space in each apartment, and how widely the various types of amenities (electricity, running water, refrigerators, washing machines, air conditioners, color televisions, and VCRs) were available, indicate the emergence of a widespread middle-class lifestyle by the mid-1980s.

Another indicator of the increasing size of the middle class is provided by the data on the proportion of households with incomes under NT$100,000, NT$200,000, and NT$300,000.[28] While Taiwan did not have an official poverty line, the cutoff for public assistance was a family income of under NT$36,000. Thus, a family income of NT$100,000 probably represents a level of not quite extreme poverty; NT$200,000 comfortable but less than middle class; and NT$300,000 a middle-class lifestyle. These data show that harsh poverty was probably quite limited as only about 5 percent of the population had incomes of under NT$100,000 (in constant prices) during the 1980s. If incomes under NT$200,000 are assumed to indicate the "near poor," the rapid economic growth of the 1980s reduced this group considerably from a third to a fifth of the population. Conversely, the proportion of the population with probable middle-class incomes jumped from a third in 1982 to half in 1987—certainly a dramatic improvement.

There can be no doubt then that the bulk of the population benefitted from Taiwan's "economic miracle" or that the image of "growth with equity" has considerable merit. The development of a middle-class society, in turn, helped create the conditions permitting continued eco-

---

[28]See Fields, "Living Standards, Labor Markets, and Human Resources in Taiwan," 397, table 10.2.

Table 9.5
Indicators of Social Development

	1952	1958	1962	1968	1973	1978	1985	1988	1990
Population growth (%)	3.3	3.6	3.3	2.7	1.8	1.9	1.5	1.2	1.3
People per family	—	—	5.6*	—	5.2*	5.0	4.5	4.1	—
Literacy rate (%)	57.9	69.1	75.2	83.6	86.2	88.8	90.9	92.6	93.2
% Population with secondary education	10.2	13.0	15.7	22.1	32.2	41.0	48.4	54.3	—
% Primary graduates to junior high school	34.9	51.1	55.1	74.2	83.7	94.1	98.0	99.1	99.1
College students % population	0.1	0.3	0.4	1.2	1.7	1.8	2.1	2.5	—
% College students in humanities	22	—	21*	12*	14*	12*	9*	9*	—
% College students in science and engineering	33	—	29*	30*	35*	30*	39*	41*	—
Real expenditure/primary student (1981 NT$)	3,296	2,784	3,501	4,781	7,861	13,002	13,327	20,224	—
% Homes self-owned	—	—	—	—	67*	70	75	78	—
Average space per home (p'ing**)	—	—	—	—	23*	24	29	32	—
% Population with electricity	—	—	77	94	98	99	99	99	99
% Population with tap water	29	29	31	41	46	62	75	82	—
% Homes with refrigerator	—	—	—	—	74*	86	95	98	—
% Homes with washing machine	—	—	—	—	39*	54	74	84	—
% Homes with air conditioning	—	—	—	—	4*	9	20	34	—
% Homes with color TV	—	—	—	—	23*	47	88	97	—
% Homes with VCR	—	—	—	—	0	0	9	51	—

*One year earlier or later.

**One *p'ing* equals approximately 36 square feet.

Sources: See sources cited in table 9.1 and Paul K. C. Liu, "Science, Technology, and Human Capital Formation," in *Taiwan: From Developing to Mature Economy*, ed. Gustav Ranis (Boulder, Colo.: Westview, 1992), 372.

nomic dynamism. Intuitively, this linkage is obvious. Climbing the ladder of industrial sophistication as Taiwan did so rapidly requires an increasingly skilled work force and an ever growing number of professionals and entrepreneurs. Moreover, workers and managers cannot stand still and rely on their current skills and expertise. Instead, the rapid evolution of economic activities requires a constant change and upgrading in personal duties. Only an educational performance such as that manifested by the data in table 9.5 can supply the necessary human capital. This logic is also supported by empirical econometrics. One study, for example, decomposed the sources of the growth of GDP in the ROC between 1953 and 1979 into three components: capital accumulation (18 percent), labor growth (27 percent), and technological improvement (54 percent). Since much of technological improvement is usually attributed to changes in education and human capital, this confirms the supposition that an expanding middle class reinforced and further stimulated economic growth in Taiwan.[29]

A virtuous cycle, such as the one between social and economic development in the ROC, creates a very rosy scenario. Simultaneous growth should continue into the indefinite future because the two factors are interdependent and mutually reinforcing. However, Taiwan's economic and social development trajectories were beginning to throw off some negative spinoffs at each other by the beginning of the 1990s. On the one hand, cumulative industrialization had produced a pollution crisis that threatened the amenities of middle-class living. Moreover, Taiwan's very success led to skyrocketing land and housing prices that pushed middle-class home ownership beyond the means of many in the younger generation, just as is occurring in Japan and part of the United States.

Conversely, a nation with middle-class expectations may actually be at a disadvantage in responding to the pushing of its basic industries offshore because this creates a significant amount of downward social mobility. Additionally, the growth of the middle class certainly contributed to the welcome political liberalization of the late 1980s and early 1990s.[30] Yet, democratization has had some worrisome side-effects itself.

---

[29]Chang, "Public Finance."

[30]Cheng, "Democratizing the Quasi-Leninist Regime in Taiwan"; Cheng and Haggard, *Political Change in Taiwan*; Moody, *Political Change on Taiwan*; Myers, "Political Theory and the Recent Political Developments in the Republic of China"; Hsin-huang Michael Hsiao, "The Changing State-Society Relations in the ROC: Economic Change, the Transformation of Class Structure, and the Rise of Social Movements," in *Two Societies in Opposition: The Republic of China and the People's Republic of China After Forty Years*, ed. Ramon H. Myers (Stanford, Calif.: Hoover Institution Press, 1991), 127-40.

"Money politics" allows rich businessmen to buy political influence that is used to distort the economy for personal rent-seeking; raucous politics has led to gridlock and policy stagnation; and the relative power of technocrats has been undercut.[31]

Complementarity of State and Private Business

A central debate in development turns on whether state or market should play the leading role in stimulating industrialization. On the one hand, neoclassicalists argue that the free market provides optimum results and that political interference in the market inevitably creates inefficiency. On the other hand, statists retort that only governments can mobilize resources and lead major economic transitions in the Third World where private business is relatively weak. From the perspective of this debate, the ROC on Taiwan is quite interesting because both sides cite it to "prove" their arguments! On the one hand, many economists point to Taiwan's superlative performance in the international marketplace as confirmation that all a nation has to do for calling up the magic of the marketplace is to "get the prices right."[32] On the other hand, sociologists and political scientists point to the strong role of the government in Taiwan's economy as validating the statist model.[33] That scholars can look at the same case and reach diametrically opposed conclusions suggests that each side probably contains both important insights and oversights. Thus, deciphering how state and market have interacted to promote development on Taiwan appears a far more promising analytic tack than making a forced choice between them.[34]

One does not have to look very far to find a considerable govern-

---

[31]Chan and Clark, *Flexibility, Foresight, and Fortuna in Taiwan's Development.*

[32]Bela Balassa, *The Newly Industrialized Countries in the World Economy* (New York: Pergamon, 1981); John C. H. Fei, "A Historical Perspective on Economic Modernization in the ROC," in Myers, *Two Societies in Opposition*, 97-110; Li, *The Evolution of Policy Behind Taiwan's Development Success.*

[33]M. Shahid Alam, *Governments and Markets in Economic Development Strategies: Lessons from Korea, Taiwan, and Japan* (New York: Praeger, 1989); Alice H. Amsden, "The State and Taiwan's Economic Development," in *Bringing the State Back In*, ed. Peter B. Evans, Dietrich Rueschemeyer, and Theda Skocpol (New York: Cambridge University Press, 1985), 78-104; Yun-han Chu, "State Structure and Economic Adjustment of the East Asian Newly Industrializing Countries" *International Organization* 43, no. 4 (Autumn 1989): 647-72; Gold, *State and Society in the Taiwan Miracle*; Haggard, *Pathways from the Periphery*; Robert Wade, "State Intervention in 'Outward-Looking' Development: Neoclassical Theory and Taiwanese Practice," in *Developmental States in East Asia*, ed. Gordon White (London: Macmillan, 1988), 30-67; Wade, *Governing the Market.*

[34]Chan and Clark, *Flexibility, Foresight, and Fortuna in Taiwan's Development.*

Table 9.6
Indicators of State's Economic Role

	1952	1958	1962	1968	1973	1978	1983	1988	1990
Government expenditure % GDP	—	23.8	20.0	19.5	19.5	22.9	24.0	24.0	27.2
Government employees % Work force	—	—	6.1	6.3	6.2	6.3	6.6	6.4	—
State % Industrial production	56.6	50.0	46.2	31.1	21.1	21.5	19.8	18.1	19.0
State % Investment	55.7	62.6	46.8	36.6	34.7	45.0	48.9	34.6	49.5
Defense spending % GNP	—	—	9.4	10.5	8.1	7.5	8.0	4.6*	—
% Government employees civil service examination	—	—	10.8	18.7	27.6	33.9	38.6	45.3	—
% Government employees college education	—	—	—	—	37.6	55.5	58.0*	—	—
Direct taxes % Taxes	24.4*	22.8	21.6	21.4	26.2	30.8	37.8	45.1	56.8
Social welfare % Budget	6.0*	6.9	7.2	7.8	10.8	10.8	15.2	17.5	17.3

*One or two years earlier or later.
Sources: Same as table 9.1.

mental impact on Taiwan's economy, although the state's role varies considerably across sectors as indicated by the data on governmental activities in table 9.6. Taiwan has always had a fairly "small state" in terms of the government budget's share of GNP which has stayed relatively constant at about 20-25 percent despite the normal tendency for development to lead to larger government. Likewise, public employees have averaged an almost constant 6.5 percent of the work force over the last thirty years.

In contrast, state corporations (initially based on confiscated Japanese assets) have been very important in the economy, accounting for half of industrial production until the early 1960s. However, the export-led industrialization drive of the 1960s and 1970s was primarily based on new private industries, so that the state's share in industrial production fell dramatically to 20 percent in the early 1970s where it has stayed since (the creation of new private industry was counterbalanced by the growth of state utilities and by the development of state corporations in heavy industry). This is equivalent to about 9 percent of GNP which places Taiwan within but at the lower end of the 7-15 percent range that Jones and Mason consider the "normal" level of state entrepreneurship in developing countries.[35]

---

[35]Leroy P. Jones and Edward S. Mason, "The Role of Economic Factors in Determining the Size and Structure of the Public-Enterprise Sector in Less-Developed Countries with Mixed Economies," in *Public Enterprise in Less-Developed Countries*, ed. Leroy P. Jones (New York: Cambridge University Press, 1982), 17-47.

The state (both the government and public corporations) has also played a major role in investment (data not presented because there are no temporal trends), although its investment rate has been quite cyclical ranging from 30 percent to 60 percent of gross domestic capital formation (GDCF) depending on economic circumstances. In general, state investment was highest during the 1950s and, subsequently, during periods of economic downturn when it was used to substitute for private resources, suggesting that state investment (and state spending in general) have been used in a countercyclical fashion.[36] On the other hand, the state has imposed a heavy defense burden on the economy for almost the entire postwar period which makes the nation's economic record all the more remarkable.[37]

State capacity or the ability to implement policy is obviously of the utmost importance to a developmental state. In terms of its personnel, Taiwan has upgraded its professionalism quite a bit over the last forty years, creating a highly competent group of technocrats.[38] This is illustrated by the data in table 9.6 on the proportion of government employees having a college education and passing the civil service examinations. A similar picture emerges about the government's financial capabilities. The ratio of direct taxes to total revenue is often used to measure a government's capacity to extract resources from society. Weaker governments tend to depend more on indirect taxes such as customs duties and license fees which are easier to collect than direct taxes based on personal income.[39] Taiwan's proportion of direct taxes remained fairly low at about 25 percent until the mid-1970s, when it commenced a fairly sharp rise to 57 percent in 1990. Thus, the regime appears to have significantly increased its economic and redistributive capacities at a time when the island is facing the challenge of fundamental economic and political transformation. Not so coincidentally, perhaps, despite its image for a "hands off" approach to social welfare, the regime has manifested a growing commitment in this area. For example, the share of social welfare and social security spending in the total budget jumped from 11 percent in 1980 to 17 percent in 1988 and 1990 after growing slowly from 6 percent in 1954 to 8 percent in 1964 to 10 percent in 1971.

---

[36]Chan and Clark, *Flexibility, Foresight, and Fortuna in Taiwan's Development.*

[37]Steve Chan, "Defense Burden and Economic Growth: Unraveling the Taiwanese 'Enigma'," *American Political Science Review* 82, no. 3 (September 1988): 913-20, uses time series analysis to show that defense spending has not acted to slow down the ROC's growth.

[38]Samuel P. S. Ho, "Economics, Economic Bureaucracy, and Taiwan's Economic Development," *Pacific Affairs* 60, no. 2 (Summer 1987): 226-47; Wade, *Governing the Market.*

[39]Lewis W. Snider, "Identifying the Elements of State Power: Where Do We Begin?" *Comparative Political Studies* 20, no. 3 (October 1987): 314-56.

Thus, the state has made several signal contributions to the island's development. Its monetary and fiscal policies have controlled inflation, the scourge of the Kuomintang (KMT, the Nationalist Party of China) in the late 1940s, and provided countercyclical adjustment; its ability to negotiate with more powerful trading partners and to regulate foreign capital on the island were instrumental in maximizing Taiwan's economic potential;[40] and the state's investment in education both developed human capital and helped to promote social and political change. More broadly, while not pursuing the extent of government intervention and industrial targeting that Japan did,[41] the state acted to create conducive environments for specific economic activities (for example, small-scale agricultural production, the beginnings of light industry behind protectionist walls, the export of labor-intensive products and, more recently, the upgrading to heavy industry and high-tech goods) in what in retrospect must be regarded as a well-chosen developmental sequence. Several of these state-guided economic transformations, such as the land reform program and the period of import-substitution industrialization, it should also be noted, involved blatant interference in the market and private property rights and also came at the expense of "dominant" economic classes.[42]

The ROC, then, seems to qualify as a successful "developmental state" whose policies or "statecraft" stimulated economic development. Despite the undoubted role of state activity and leadership, however, much occurred that was independent of the state. In Taiwan, the most dynamic parts of the economy have generally been small and medium-

---

[40]David B. Bobrow and Steve Chan, "Assets, Liabilities, and Strategic Conduct: Status Management by Japan, Taiwan, and South Korea," *Pacific Focus* 1 (1986): 23-55; David B. Bobrow and Steve Chan, "Understanding Anomalous Successes: Japan, Taiwan, and South Korea," in *New Directions in the Comparative Study of Foreign Policy*, ed. Charles F. Hermann, Charles W. Kegley, Jr., and James N. Rosenau (Boston: Allen & Unwin, 1987), 111-30; Steve Chan, "The Mouse That Roared: Taiwan's Management of Trade Relations with the United States," *Comparative Political Studies* 20, no. 3 (October 1987): 251-92; David B. Yoffie, *Power and Protectionism: Strategies of the Newly Industrializing Countries* (New York: Columbia University Press, 1983).

[41]Chu, "State Structure and Economic Adjustment."

[42]Alam, *Governments and Markets in Economic Development Strategies*; Amsden, "The State and Taiwan's Economic Development"; Chan and Clark, *Flexibility, Foresight, and Fortuna in Taiwan's Development*; Chu, "State Structure and Economic Adjustment"; Clark, *Taiwan's Development*; Bruce Cumings, "The Origins and Development of the Northeast Asian Political Economy: Industrial Sectors, Product Cycles, and Political Consequences," *International Organization* 38, no. 1 (Winter 1984): 1-40; Gold, *State and Society in the Taiwan Miracle*; Haggard, *Pathways from the Periphery*; Chien-kuo Pang, "The State and Socioeconomic Development in Taiwan Since 1949," *Issues & Studies* 26, no. 5 (May 1990): 11-36; Wade, *Governing the Market* and "State Intervention in 'Outward-Looking' Development."

sized enterprises (SMEs) which have few direct linkages with the state. SMEs played a surprisingly strong role in the overall economy, accounting for almost half of the manufacturing sector and over three-quarters of the commercial one from the mid-1970s to the mid-1980s. In particular, small firms are generally credited with being the backbone of the crucial export sector (e.g., they accounted for about two-thirds of total exports during 1978-85) and, thereby, with setting the overall tone of the economy.[43]

The importance of small businesses for Taiwan's economy is also implied by the data on the average number of employees in firms broken down by industrial sector. According to Howard Pack, "by international standards the typical size of firm in each sector is remarkably small."[44] Furthermore, small enterprises were not sectorally concentrated. Rather, they spread to a very broad array of industries. In addition, the number of firms grew substantially in most sectors between the mid-1960s and the mid-1980s. Thus, despite Taiwan's rapid climb up the international product cycle into more sophisticated industrial activities during this time (which is usually associated with a declining niche for small business), opportunities for small firms evidently remained quite vibrant.

Consequently, recent discussions of Taiwan's "economic miracle" have turned to the great flexibility and dynamism of this sector. The SMEs in Taiwan pursue highly entrepreneurial strategies termed "guerrilla capitalism" by Danny Lam.[45] Guerrilla capitalism includes extreme flexibility in rapidly filling even small orders, attention to quality and design, audacious bidding, participation in complex networks of subcontracting, and only partial observation at best of government regulations and international laws, such as those regarding intellectual property rights. The SMEs have also demonstrated a remarkable capacity to innovate and upgrade their operations. Thus, while guerrilla capitalism took off in the textile and shoe industries in the 1960s, such entrepreneurs moved into low-tech electronics assembly in the 1970s; and some were able to upgrade into more sophisticated high-tech production in the 1980s.[46]

---

[43]Wu Hui-lin, "A Future for Small and Medium Enterprises?" *Free China Review* 38, no. 11 (November 1988): 7-8, presents these data. Also see Karl J. Fields, *Developmental Capitalism and Industrial Organization: Business Groups and the State in Korea and Taiwan* (Ithaca, N.Y.: Cornell University Press, 1994); Hong, "Paths of Glory"; Lam, "Explaining Economic Development"; Kuo, *Institutions and Global Competitiveness*; and Myers, "The Economic Transformation of the Republic of China on Taiwan."

[44]Pack, "New Perspectives on Industrial Growth in Taiwan," 104.

[45]Lam, "Explaining Economic Development."

[46]Danny K. K. Lam, "Independent Economic Sectors and Economic Growth in Hong Kong and Taiwan," *International Studies Notes* 15 (1990): 28-34; Lam, "Explaining Economic

The SMEs, furthermore, have operated quite independently from the government. The gap between the government and the guerrilla capitalists was exacerbated by ethnic relations—that is, the social distance between the majority Taiwanese or "Islanders" and the minority "Mainlanders" who came to Taiwan with Chiang Kai-shek in 1949 and who monopolized state power until quite recently through the ruling KMT.[47] This social and political distance discouraged collusion between entrepreneurs and the state and tended to preempt the rent-seeking behavior characteristic of traditional China and the mainland years of the KMT. Small firms also remained relatively invisible in dealing with an alien and potentially hostile state. Thus, the relationship between the state and SMEs in Taiwan is generally regarded as "cool and distant."[48]

While the guerrilla capitalists were quite independent of the state, governmental policy did, in fact, set and at times radically change the parameters within which they operated. Thus, the state did adopt policies and incentives that guided the economy through several important structural transformations, each one leading to greater productivity, generally through more sophisticated and higher value-added production—(1) the momentous land reform in the early 1950s, (2) import-substitution light industrialization in the 1950s, (3) exporting labor-intensive goods in the 1960s and 1970s, (4) heavy industrialization in the 1970s, and (5) high-tech production in the 1980s. Each of these stages, moreover, redefined the relationship between the state and society on Taiwan in ways that created varying types of complementarity between the public and private sectors.

The 1950s witnessed two such policy transformations, land reform and import-substitution industrialization, which had very different implications for complementarity (or the absence of it) between the state and society. The emerging industrial economy was dominated by state

Development"; and Lam and Lee, "Guerrilla Capitalism and the Limits of Statist Theory." See also Susan Greenhalgh, "Networks and Their Nodes: Urban Society in Taiwan," *China Quarterly*, no. 99 (September 1984): 529-52; Susan Greenhalgh, "Families and Networks in Taiwan's Economic Development," in Winckler and Greenhalgh, *Contending Approaches to the Political Economy of Taiwan*, 224-45; Stevan Harrell, "Why Do the Chinese Work So Hard? Reflections on an Entrepreneurial Ethic," *Modern China* 11, no. 2 (April 1985): 203-26; Kuo, *Institutions and Global Competitiveness*; Wen Lang Li, "Entrepreneurial Roles and Societal Development in Taiwan," *Journal of Chinese Studies* 3, no. 1 (January 1986): 77-96; Ian Skoggard, "Local Forms of East Asian Capitalism" (Paper presented at the Annual Meeting of the Association for Asian Studies, Boston, 1994); Wong Siu-lun, "Modernization and Chinese Culture in Hong Kong," *China Quarterly*, no. 106 (June 1986): 306-25; Wong Siu-lun, *Emigrant Entrepreneurs: Shanghai Industrialists in Hong Kong* (Hong Kong: Oxford University Press, 1988).

[47]Gold, *State and Society in the Taiwan Miracle*; Tien, *The Great Transformation*.

[48]See Chu, "State Structure and Economic Adjustment."

corporations and a few large capitalists with *kuan-hsi* (personal connections) with the KMT, leaving little room for private initiative.[49] Land reform, however, was instrumental in creating a system of small-holder agriculture that became very productive, thereby making a considerable contribution to accumulating the resources necessary for industrialization.[50] In short, complementarity could be seen in one important sector (agriculture) but not another (industry).

The export boom of the 1960s radically changed this situation, as small enterprises took a leading role in producing labor-intensive exports and rapidly multiplied, thus establishing a complementarity between the independent and somewhat antagonistic sectors of government and private enterprise. The move toward heavy industrialization in the 1970s provided mixed blessings for the guerrilla capitalists. On the one hand, they received more government "services" in the form of infrastructure and educated workers; on the other, the control over upstream inputs by not particularly efficient state corporations almost certainly increased the production costs in many industries. By the late 1980s and early 1990s, the guerrilla capitalists were undergoing a fundamental differentiation. Some were successfully upgrading into high-tech industries which often brought them into cooperative linkages with state laboratories; others moved their production offshore—ironically, in many cases to the PRC.[51]

The last transition, therefore, has been a mixed blessing for maintaining the balance and complementarity between public and private economic activities. On the positive side, some aspects of the high-tech industry are promoting interactions between the state and the most innovative entrepreneurs which can only benefit industrial upgrading and national competitiveness. On the other side, a much more nefarious interaction has arisen through growing political corruption and "money politics" which threatens to distort both public policy and private entrepreneurship. Moreover, the massive movement of capital offshore, especially to the hostile PRC, threatens to upset the "balance" that existed between the government and the independent guerrilla capitalists in either of two deleterious ways. On the one hand, capital outflow may simply

---

[49]See Gold, *State and Society in the Taiwan Miracle.*
[50]See Ho, *Economic Development in Taiwan.*
[51]Chan and Clark, *Flexibility, Foresight, and Fortuna in Taiwan's Development*; Gold, *State and Society in the Taiwan Miracle*; Kuo, *Institutions and Global Competitiveness*; Lam, "Explaining Economic Development"; Robert H. Silin, *Leadership and Values: The Organization of Large-Scale Taiwanese Enterprises* (Cambridge, Mass.: Harvard University Press, 1976); Winckler and Greenhalgh, *Contending Approaches to the Political Economy of Taiwan.*

lead to a complete divorce between the government and "offshore" businessmen which would detract from the ability of both to contribute to the well-being of Taiwan. On the other hand, wealthy business interests with large investments in the PRC could use "money politics" to pressure Taipei on behalf of the Communist regime on the mainland.

Implications

The basic trends in the ROC's "economic miracle" can be summarized succinctly as "growth with equity." Three broader trends in Taiwan's political economy can be viewed as underlying this superb set of statistics: (1) a remarkable ability of flexible and rapid response to changes in the economic environment; (2) a virtuous cycle of positive reinforcing impacts between social and economic development; and (3) generally balanced and complementary (although not usually integrated) economic roles for the public and private sectors. As the ROC moves into the post-Cold War era, all three of these macro trends retain significant strength, yet all are challenged by current economic, social, and political changes. It is far too soon to decipher whether the positive or negative forces will predominate. However, state and society, the public and private sectors will have to mesh better than they appear at present if the negative trends are to be controlled.

The central problem is to renew a complementary relationship between the state and the business community which will solve, rather than exacerbate, the emerging problems noted in the three previous sections. The previous pattern of a "cool and distant" independence is probably not viable any longer. The state will almost of necessity have to take the lead in moving toward a new equilibrium. However, if it does so, policymakers must keep in mind the vital fact that what worked in the past was not really direct state control or leadership of the economy. Rather, the genius of Taiwan's developmental state (which may well have been more fortuitous than intended) was to have government create a policy environment in which business and society were free to apply their talents. If this "success" is kept in mind, Taiwan may well "reinvent its government"[52] and political economy once more. If it is not, the ROC will almost inevitably fall victim to one or both of the dual dangers of the stifling of business by the bureaucracy or the cooperation of businessmen and politicians to reap joint monopoly rents from the middle-class citizenry.

---

[52]David Osborne and Ted Gaebler, *Reinventing Government: How the Entrepreneurial Spirit Is Transforming the Public Sector* (New York: Penguin, 1992).

Part IV

Mainland China's Military and Security Policy

10

The PRC's National Security Objectives in the Post-Cold War Era and the Role of the PLA

Ralph A. Cossa

To date, the end of the Cold War has had little if any significant impact on the Asian geopolitical landscape. Unlike Europe, no new states have emerged, no boundaries have shifted, and no new alliances or political alignments have been formed.[1] The changes that have occurred in Asia since the beginning of this decade have largely been evolutionary rather than revolutionary. The most significant changes—the emergence of greater democracy in South Korea and Taiwan, the move of the United States out of the Philippines and (on a considerably smaller scale) into Singapore, the establishment of diplomatic relations between the People's Republic of China (PRC) and South Korea, and the slow but steady readmission of Vietnam into the Southeast Asian community of nations—arguably would have occurred even if the Cold War had not ended. And, the region's most unpredictable player, North Korea, seems unaware that the Cold War is over.

This does not imply, however, that the strategic landscape has been left unchanged. In truth, the Asia-Pacific strategic environment has been altered significantly by the end of the Cold War and the subsequent collapse of the Soviet Union, and by the impetus these two events provided to the twin phenomena of worldwide economic and political reform. The

---

[1] The one exception that could be cited is the emergence of the newly-independent Central Asian republics of the former Soviet Union, but this region seldom if ever falls within the classic definition of Asia proper. Nonetheless, as will be discussed shortly, the emergence of these states has had a significant impact on Asia's, or more specifically, mainland China's strategic environment.

process of change—albeit slow and deliberate—continues throughout Asia today.

Nowhere in Asia has this change been more dynamic and more potentially destabilizing—or potentially stabilizing—than in the PRC. There are a great many questions to be answered when we survey the Chinese landscape in the post-Cold War era. What are the PRC's strategic objectives and priorities? How are they tied to economic development and reform? And, how does all this relate to the PRC's ongoing military modernization efforts? The question of succession also looms large. Who will lead the PRC when Teng Hsiao-p'ing (Deng Xiaoping) and the other "long marchers" finally go to meet Marx? Will this new generation of Chinese leaders continue to pursue Teng's economic and strategic game plan? What are the consequences of all this for the United States? . . . for Taiwan? . . . for the PRC's other neighbors?[2]

This chapter will only begin to scratch at the surface of these questions, as it surveys the current strategic environment and speculates on the PRC's overall national security objectives and the role of the People's Liberation Army (PLA) in achieving those objectives. It will close with some recommendations on how the PRC can go about achieving its national security objectives in a manner that will not appear overly threatening to its neighbors but, instead, will help promote the regional peace and stability Peking (Beijing) professes to seek.

Strategic Environment

The post-Cold War security environment has been a mixed blessing for the PRC. On balance, however—as most Chinese officials and security specialists are quick to admit—it has been largely favorable to Peking. In terms of its national security, China finds itself, for the first time in over a hundred years, without a significant external threat. As Colonel Hsü Hsiao-chün (Xu Xiaojun) from the PRC's Academy of Military Science points out:

> China enjoys the best security environment since 1949. It is not facing any real military threats. There is no obvious danger of a major attack by any adversary. And the eruption of a world war or a major regional conflict which

---

[2]Questions abound in other parts of Asia as well. However, in few instances will the answers have as profound an impact—not just on the nation involved but on regional, if not global security—as with these questions regarding the PRC. For the author's views on the broader Asian security environment, see Ralph A. Cossa, "Asia-Pacific Security Issues," Asia-Pacific Senior Seminar Proceedings, "Toward New Dimensions in Security: Forging a Strategic Balance in East Asia," East-West Center/Pacific Forum CSIS, December 1993.

might threaten China's security is a far-away possibility. At present, there is not a single country in its neighboring or surrounding areas which China should define as an antagonist.[3]

This has provided the PRC with the secure international environment essential to pursue its ambitious domestic programs. It should come as no surprise then that maintaining this stable international environment is frequently cited as one of the PRC's primary security goals.

One of the most dramatic and far-reaching changes in the PRC's strategic environment has been the disappearance of the Soviet Union, not only as an all-encompassing threat, but also as a rival model for Marxist-based reform. Clearly, Teng Hsiao-p'ing's "socialism with Chinese characteristics," which emphasizes "economic reform with political stability" (i.e., without political reform), has prevailed over Mikhail Gorbachev's *perestroika* model which called for political reform (*glasnost*) concurrent with, if not in advance of, economic restructuring.

The irony is not lost on the PRC. Not too many years ago, its leaders were being admonished (particularly by American officials) to follow the Gorbachev model. They elected instead to stay with the "Asian model"—economic reform first, followed by political reform later—that had worked so successfully in South Korea and Taiwan. Economic strategists like William Overholt in early 1990 accurately foretold what was to come:

> As this is written, China's reform is in some difficulty, and Gorbachev's efforts are receiving rave reviews. But Deng Xiaoping has institutionalized reform to an extent Gorbachev has not. Deng's reforms are likely to overcome their current problems, whereas Gorbachev's are likely to be defeated by similar problems.[4]

Many challenges remain before Teng's economic program can be labeled a complete success and there is still considerable debate over when, if ever, meaningful political liberalization will follow. Yet, the PRC can now "sell" its model of economic development and reform. As Boston College China specialist Robert Ross points out, "In a reversal of the 1950s pattern, Chinese are now going to Russia as experts in capitalism, bringing entrepreneurial skills necessary to exploit Russian resources and

---

[3]Xu Xiaojun, "China's Grand Strategy for the 21st Century" (Paper presented at the National Defense University's 1994 Pacific Symposium on "Asia in the 21st Century: Evolving Strategic Priorities," February 15-16, 1994), 7.

[4]William Overholt, "Strategic Consequences of Pacific Asian Growth," in *Asia-Pacific Strategy Development Workshop: Proceedings*, ed. Ralph A. Cossa (Washington, D.C.: National Defense University, May 1990), 11.

provide consumer goods and services to the Russian Far East."[5] The PRC's continuing economic miracle adds to the credibility of Teng's programs at home and abroad and, by extension, to the PRC's image (and place) in the world at large.

Even more significant has been the greater sense of security that the PRC feels as it looks around its periphery, now that the Soviet Empire has crumbled. No doubt the PRC still harbors some concerns that nationalist sentiments in Kazakhstan, Kyrgyzstan, and Tajikistan may spread over into its remote, ethnically diverse regions. But more significant in terms of national security is the realization that these three new Central Asian republics now represent buffer zones (if not potential allies), rather than staging bases, in any potential future conflict with the Russian army. PRC Premier Li P'eng's (Li Peng's) April 1994 visit to several of the Central Asian republics, complete with promises of economic cooperation and assistance, underscores Peking's efforts to expand its influence in this region.[6]

Another very important buffer zone was created in the north following Mongolia's exit from the Kremlin's camp. One of Peking's primary objectives in its earlier rapprochement with Gorbachev was to obtain the withdrawal of then-Soviet forces from Mongolia; a goal now fully accomplished.[7] In short—and unlike the view from Japan, where the boundaries with Russia are unchanged—along broad sections of the Chinese border, Russia is not nearly as close or as threatening as the Soviet Union once was.

In addition, there has been a partial demilitarization along the PRC's remaining borders with Russia itself. As a result of a memorandum of understanding signed during Russian President Boris Yeltsin's visit to Peking in December of 1992, details are reportedly being finalized for the establishment of a demilitarized zone for 100 kilometers on either side of the common frontier.[8] Mr. Yeltsin, for his own very valid reasons, is

---

[5]Robert Ross, "China's Response to Emerging Multipolarity and the Implications for Stability in Northeast Asia" (Draft paper presented during the Pacific Forum CSIS seminar on "China and Northeast Asia: Looking Toward the 21st Century," Waikoloa, Hawaii, January 7-8, 1994), 3.

[6]For details of Li P'eng's visit, see Ahmed Rashid, "Chinese Challenges," *Far Eastern Economic Review*, May 12, 1994, 30.

[7]On the other hand, tiny Mongolia—which no longer resides under Moscow's security umbrella—increasingly fears being absorbed by the PRC. Over the long term, the PRC's willingness to coexist with—and resist the temptation to engulf—Mongolia will serve as a major signal of the PRC's long-term intent to be a responsible member of the Northeast Asian family of nations.

[8]"China Adopts a New Stance," *Jane's Defence Weekly*, February 26, 1994, 19.

even more anxious than the leadership in Peking to ensure that a stable security environment is maintained along the Russo-Chinese border.

These positive developments notwithstanding, the Chinese cannot ιotally dismiss Russia as a potential threat. Although Russia is largely benign today, the potential for a reversal of governments and attitudes in the Kremlin remains. There is no guarantee that a less cooperative (or even openly antagonistic), ultra-nationalistic hard-line government may one day return to power in the Kremlin.[9]

Even under the current democratic leadership a new Russian military assertiveness is reemerging. Russian Defense Minister Pavel Grachev announced in November 1993 that Russia was abandoning the old Soviet nuclear "no first use" policy, and that Russia's new military doctrine sanctions both the use of troops beyond Russia's borders to protect national interests, and their use at home to quash civil conflict or terrorism.[10]

Such pronouncements are sobering, since, regardless of who reigns in Moscow, the Russian Republic will still control one of the world's largest armed forces and a strategic nuclear capability and arsenal second to none. Given the size (and new assertiveness) of the Russian military, and a national history of expansionism that predates the Bolshevik Revolution by several centuries, to say that the Russians no longer pose a *potential* threat to China is to deny both history and reality.

The Chinese recognize that troubled times might lie ahead: "In view of the fact that Russia is still . . . the country with the largest territory, richest resources, and greatest number of nuclear weapons, its general mood of expansionism and national chauvinism mirrored in the current elections will naturally arouse the vigilance of various countries throughout the world."[11]

Nonetheless, the PRC sees Russia today as weak and vulnerable. More importantly, the PRC appears ready and able to exploit Russia's desire for cordial relations and its need for hard currency and economic investment and assistance. As a result, relations continue to improve despite the rocky start prompted by Peking's barely-disguised approval of the 1991 Kremlin coup attempt that was foiled by Mr. Yeltsin. Chinese security specialists, when speaking off-the-record, acknowledge that they

---

[9]The strong showing of Vladimir Zhirinovsky and his ultra-nationalist Liberal Democratic Party during Russia's first multiparty parliamentary election in December 1993 makes this possibility more than just an idle concern.

[10]Fred Hiatt, "Russia Shifts Doctrine on Military Use," *Washington Post*, November 4, 1993, 1. Military modernization, including production of new ICBMs, also continues in Russia.

[11]Ross, "China's Response to Emerging Multipolarity," 4, citing Chung-kuo t'ung-hsün-she, December 16, 1993.

remain concerned over Russian instability (although less concerned, they say, than their Western counterparts). They also seem resigned to the fact that Russia will eventually regain its "big power mentality" and become a force to be reckoned with, even if the current wave of ultra-nationalism is held in check.[12] In the near term, however, the PRC feels it has little to fear and appears to have the upper hand in the relationship.

Not all the changes in the PRC's strategic environment vis-à-vis Russia have been positive, however. One potential downside emerging from the collapse of the Soviet Empire, in Peking's eyes, has been the boost that the resultant emergence of democracy in Russia has given to democracy movements already under way in mainland China and elsewhere in Asia. Remember, for example, that the 1989 pro-democracy demonstrations coincided with Mikhail Gorbachev's historic visit to Peking.

Today, the PRC appears at least as concerned—and perhaps even more concerned—about democracy movements beyond its current span of control than it is about cries for greater democracy on the mainland proper. I refer, of course, to the democracy movement on Taiwan and, to a lesser extent, the push toward greater democracy in Hong Kong. To the extent these movements challenge the "one-China" principle, they will be seen in Peking as significant potential threats. Should the "one-China" principle become a future casualty of the end of the Cold War, the Asian strategic landscape would be significantly altered, to the PRC's perceived detriment and at great risk to regional stability.

To the south, the downfall of the Soviet Union has improved the strategic picture for Peking, as Vietnam and India are no longer viewed primarily in terms of being threatening links in the Kremlin's attempt to encircle and contain the PRC. India, in particular, seems considerably less threatening than when it enjoyed its "special relationship" with Moscow.[13]

---

[12]This assessment is derived from "not-for-attribution" discussions with senior Chinese military leaders and defense specialists. Discussions with their Russian counterparts indicate that the Russians are less concerned about the potential Chinese threat and, while somewhat cautious about such events as Chinese migration into their Far Eastern provinces, welcome the immediate benefits the Chinese bring. Moscow tends to see mainland China primarily as a source of much needed investment and hard currency, the latter to be provided in significant measure through the sale of advanced Russian weapons systems. For more information on Chinese and Russian attitudes, see Ralph A. Cossa, "China and Northeast Asia: What Lies Ahead?" Pacific Forum CSIS Policy Report Series, February 1994.

[13]This special relationship began to dissolve under Gorbachev due to his need to promote more harmonious relations with Peking. India's tacit endorsement of the 1991 coup attempt against Gorbachev (and, by extension, Yeltsin) and its bitterness over Yeltsin's backing out of the cryogenic engine deal (following U.S. pressure) have helped ensure that the special relationship will not be revitalized.

India is more accommodating toward the PRC today—even if still intensely distrustful—given Mr. Yeltsin's apparent lack of interest in anything other than a "normal" relationship with New Delhi (and India's lack of confidence in the prospects of a strategic relationship emerging with the United States). As a result, India and the PRC signed a memorandum of understanding in September 1993 aimed at reducing troop levels along their common border and have introduced other confidence building measures aimed at reducing tensions.[14]

The PRC's relations with Vietnam have also improved, although historical animosities compounded by overlapping territorial claims in the South China Sea help ensure that relations will remain less than fully cordial. Largely gone are the PRC's concerns about Vietnam serving as a Southeast Asian foothold for the Kremlin's naval and air force power projection forces. (Russia's residual token presence at Cam Ranh Bay hardly appears threatening today.) On the horizon, however—in the wake of Vietnam's exit from Cambodia and its subsequent normalization of relations with the member states of the Association of Southeast Asian Nations (ASEAN) (and ultimately, one assumes, with the United States)— is one potential concern; namely, that Vietnam may one day become a new ASEAN or U.S. "card" to be played against the PRC, especially as regards the Spratlys, where all have a common concern about Peking's pronouncements and intentions.

To the northeast, relations between the PRC and South Korea have shown dramatic improvement over the past decade, driven by factors that had little to do with the Cold War's ending. Both sides benefit politically as well as economically from this expanded relationship and it is likely to continue to improve. Meanwhile, relations with North Korea have become strained for a variety of reasons, not the least of which is the PRC's improved relations with Seoul. Nonetheless, given the dismal state of North Korea's relations with virtually everyone else, relatively speaking, the PRC remains one of North Korea's closest and most important friends. One can question just how much leverage the PRC has over North Korea, or if Peking has been totally forthcoming in using whatever leverage it has. Still, no one in Northeast Asia (perhaps in the world) has more influence over North Korea than the PRC. The PRC has in common with its Northeast Asian neighbors (and the United States) a vested interest in a stable, nonhostile, nonnuclear Korean Peninsula.

Current relations with Japan fall into the "good news, bad news"

---

[14]See note 8 above. Disagreements still exist over boundary demarcation and the relationship remains strained, despite the toned down rhetoric.

category. In the economic realm, Japan is emerging in the post-Cold War
era both as a vital near-term partner and as a potential long-term rival.
Of particular concern is the possibility of greater economic competition
between the PRC and Japan, with Asians taking sides and de facto spheres
of influence perhaps being carved out. Some fear that such lines are
already being drawn.[15] Although a division of Asia into Japanese and
Chinese spheres of influence or semiexclusive economic zones is not likely,
increased competition between the two—with political overtones—is inevitable, even under the most benign scenarios.

In the security realm, the Chinese are also sending mixed signals as
to whether or not they believe Japan constitutes a future (or perhaps even
a near-term) military threat. The desire for closer relations (and continued Japanese economic investment and assistance) has prompted Peking
to tone down its warnings about Japanese militarism in general and its
criticism about Japanese participation in peacekeeping operations in particular. However, privately (and on occasion publicly) the Chinese still
remind Tokyo's neighbors about Japan's unrepentant past and raise doubts
about future Japanese military capabilities and intentions.[16]

On balance, however, Sino-Japanese relations are at least as good
as, and perhaps even better today than, at any point in their long history.
During the Cold War, the United States served as a catalyst and facil-
itator for improved Sino-Japanese relations, with impetus provided by
the common Soviet enemy. The challenge today is to prevent post-Cold
War tensions between the United States and the PRC from driving a
wedge between either U.S.-Japan or Japan-PRC relations.

This leads to the most obvious downside to the end of the Cold
War, in the context of Peking's strategic environment; namely, the PRC's
reduced leverage with the United States. This became especially true when
the PRC added in the self-inflicted wound administered at Tienanmen
(Tiananmen).[17] The Tienanmen incident prompted a harsh, overly an-

---

[15]This was a subject of some debate during the aforementioned Pacific Forum seminar on
"China and Northeast Asia," as noted in my "China and Northeast Asia: What Lies
Ahead?" Policy Report.

[16]The Japanese seem inept at helping their own cause in this regard. Statements by Prime
Minister Hata and former Prime Minister Hosokawa acknowledging past sins quickly become overshadowed by the cavalier attitude of other Japanese officials and bureaucrats;
witness the latest "crisis" over now-deposed Justice Minister Shigeto Nagano's ill-conceived
comments about the "Rape of Nanking" being a hoax.

[17]As poorly as the Chinese military handled themselves at Tienanmen, their performance
pales in comparison to the abysmal manner in which Chinese political leaders handled the
aftermath. Tienanmen was not the first time that military forces called in to quell civil
disturbances failed to handle the situation; witness the Kent State tragedy during the Viet-

tagonistic, and perhaps even premature review of the strategic rationale for continued close ties between Washington and Peking. It also made it extremely difficult (at least in the United States) for rational assessments to emerge.

It is impossible to define either the nature or the future of U.S.-PRC relations in a few short paragraphs. Suffice it to say that this relationship appears quite fragile today. I would argue that U.S.-PRC relations are at a historic crossroad. Debates appear under way in both capitals as to how much one side can or should trust and cooperate with the other. Should either side conclude that the other is its next enemy, this forecast could easily become a self-fulfilling prophesy. Neither side, nor anyone else in Asia, would benefit from such an occurrence.

While cooler heads seem to be prevailing today, it is not beyond the capability of the current or next generation of leaders in mainland China—or in the United States—to turn current tensions and ill feelings into genuine animosity, given Chinese xenophobia and the American tendency to focus on single issues (such as human rights) to the detriment of an overall coherent policy.

As a result, while the PRC still feels relatively secure and unthreatened today, we have begun to see hints that post-Tienanmen sanctions and continued U.S. "interference in the PRC's internal affairs" in areas such as democracy and human rights—especially when combined with recent sales of advanced weapons to Taiwan by the United States and others—are reinforcing traditional xenophobia and may be creating a perception among some Chinese leaders—particularly, but not exclusively within military circles—that an attempt to "surround" or "isolate" the PRC is once again under way by a coalition of hostile powers intent on ensuring China's continued weakness. As one Chinese analyst put it:

> The new world order advocated by the United States and other Western powers is nothing more than a revised expression of power politics made to fit the new situation. In fact, what's behind it is the leadership of the United States, European powers, and Japan; . . . the ultimate goal is a world completely dominated by capitalist countries.[18]

---

nam War era when U.S. national guardsmen opened fire on a crowd of antiwar protestors who were taunting and stoning them. What makes Kent State a tragedy and Tienanmen a massacre, at least in part, is the way the respective governments handled the aftermath.

[18]Xu Xin [Hsü Hsin], "Changing Chinese Security Perceptions," North Pacific Cooperative Security Dialogue Working Paper No. 27, April 1993, citing Du Gong [Tu Kung], "Some Perceptions of a Changing Pattern of International Relationship," *International Studies*, October 1991, 5.

Finally, in a strictly Asian context, the biggest change in the PRC's security environment is mainland China's increasingly important place in it, given its continuing economic development and the level of integration, especially in economic terms, that the PRC already enjoys with its neighbors. As the world's most populous nation, with the world's largest military and fastest growing economy, the PRC will play a major role in defining the Northeast Asian security environment for the indefinite future. Add in on the diplomatic side its United Nations Security Council veto, and on the military side its pivotal ability to be either part of the solution or part of the problem as regards global and regional nonproliferation efforts, and on the economic side the vast potential markets a prosperous (consumer-oriented) PRC would provide, and mainland China's prominent place on the strategic landscape of Asia becomes clear. And, it is equally clear that the PRC recognizes, seeks, and will increasingly demand its destiny as a major regional and global power.

The question for the PRC—and for those who will be most affected by the outcome—is: What path will Peking take in pursuing its national objectives in the coming years, in light of the current strategic environment it currently finds itself in and how, in the process, will this strategic environment be changed as a result?

The Chinese, for their part, say little about their overall national security strategy or national security objectives beyond citing their preoccupation with the development of their national economy and their desire for peace and stability in Asia. Typical is this commentary from Senior Colonel Ting Pang-ch'üan (Ding Bangquan) during a presentation on the PRC's strategic outlook:

> Although China is of great importance in the world affairs, it is still a regional power. And I doubt if it has a formal regional security strategy at all, as Beijing has been concentrating itself on the economic development at home. However, because China has adopted an open-door policy since the latter part of the 1970s, it has devoted itself to creating a peaceful and stable regional environment. Against this background, one can draw some ideas about China's strategic concepts for the Asia-Pacific security.[19]

The PRC's National Security Objectives

Since the Chinese appear reticent to explicitly spell out their national security objectives, let me postulate the following, based on Chinese pro-

---

[19]Ding Bangquan, "China's Strategic Concepts for the Asia-Pacific Security" (Paper presented at the National Defense University's 1994 Pacific Symposium on "Asia in the 21st Century: Evolving Strategic Priorities," February 15-16, 1994), 1.

nouncements and actions, and in keeping with the earlier description of today's strategic environment: (1) maintenance of internal stability and control; (2) preservation of regional stability; (3) development of the national economy; (4) reunification with Hong Kong and Taiwan; (5) international respect and recognition; and (6) development of a modern military.

These objectives, and the steps the PRC is taking to achieve them, frequently overlap. Each affects, and is affected by, the others. Each also affects, and is affected by (or impacts upon), the role of the PLA in Chinese society in the post-Cold War era.

In the section that follows, I will briefly discuss how the Chinese will likely pursue each of these objectives, with particular attention to the role of the PLA. I will begin with the last stated objective, the development of a modern military, since this objective represents not only an end in itself, but also a means to achieving the other stated objectives.

Development of a Modern Military

While military modernization was originally the lowest priority among the "four modernizations" outlined in the 1980s by Teng Hsiao-p'ing and is reputed to remain in fourth place, it has received greater emphasis in recent years. By Peking's own figures, defense spending has increased by two-thirds since 1991 and by 21 percent this year alone: 1991: 32.5 billion *yuan*; 1992: 37.78 billion *yuan*; 1993: 42.5 billion *yuan*; and 1994: 54.0 billion *yuan*.[20]

Few believe that the numbers being cited by Peking are an accurate accounting of the actual dollars spent on defense. When hidden costs such as defense research, special weapons projects, and costs associated with militia, reserve, and paramilitary People's Armed Police (PAP) forces, among other costs, are added in, most analysts estimate that the actual budget is double the stated amount.[21] Nonetheless, the Chinese figures document a steadily upward trend in defense spending, even as the immediate challenges to the PRC's security (and all other major powers' military budgets) are diminishing.

Many reasons have been offered for this increase in defense outlays. The Chinese explain it away by citing a variety of reasons: the need to

---

[20]Ibid., 15, and "Balancing the Books," *Far Eastern Economic Review*, February 19, 1994, 35. As the latter points out, the Chinese can actually claim a reduction in defense spending if measured in U.S. dollars, since a 33 percent reduction in currency value in the beginning of 1994 equates to a drop in spending in 1994 (US$6.21 billion) when compared with 1993 (US$7.45 billion) based, in each instance, on prevailing exchange rates.

[21]"Balancing the Books," 35.

raise military standards of living; increased pay and benefits, necessary to compensate the troops for recent legislation limiting their involvement in private enterprises; an attempt to keep up with inflation; and the need to modernize a sorely outdated military force after several years of neglect. They also point out that PRC military spending pales in comparison with the United States and most of China's neighbors, both in absolute terms and, even more dramatically, when considered on a per capita basis.[22]

Others speculate that it involves "payback" to the PLA for its role in putting down student demonstrations in Tienanmen and elsewhere, or that it was prompted by the "wake-up call" regarding the value of hi-tech weaponry provided by the U.S. performance in the Gulf War; the latter leading to the realization that quantity was not as effective a counter to quality as the Chinese traditionally believed. Still others point to the combination of increased PRC revenues and bargain prices in the current "buyer's market." Critics also cite Peking's desire to intimidate its neighbors, which requires the ability to project power beyond its shores.[23] There is probably an element of truth in all of these answers.

The Chinese make no apologies regarding their defense modernization effort, noting that it is their sovereign right—and their obligation to the Chinese people—to ensure that the PRC possesses a modern conventional military capable of reacting to potential threats or defending Chinese territory against any hostile powers. This includes the continued building and preserving of the PRC's modest nuclear deterrence capability, in addition to the upgrading of its conventional arsenal. When asked why the PRC is devoting precious resources to military modernization if the threat to China's security is lower today than at any time since the PRC was created, Chinese military strategists respond with a litany of potential threats:[24]

1. Three powerful neighbors (the United States, Russia, and Japan), all with the ability to project power against China;
2. A complicated situation on the Korean Peninsula that could degenerate into warfare;

---

[22]Ding, "China's Strategic Concepts for the Asia-Pacific Security," 15-16. Also see Chen Xiaogong [Ch'en Hsiao-kung], "'China Threat' Is Absolutely Groundless" (Background paper presented to the author in Chinese and translated by Wang Jian-wei, East-West Center visiting fellow).

[23]Lin Chong-pin, "The Stealthy Advance of China's People's Liberation Army," *The American Enterprise*, January/February 1994. For a more comprehensive review of PRC military developments, also see Lloyd R. Vasey, "China's Growing Military Power and Implications for East Asia," Pacific Forum CSIS Policy Report Series, August 1993.

[24]Cossa, "China and Northeast Asia: What Lies Ahead?" 14.

3. Taiwan's growing independence movement and the fact that Taipei's military already has some air and sea superiority over the mainland's forces;
4. Possible social unrest in Hong Kong, supported by "foreign forces" (British and "others");
5. Lingering territorial disputes, especially the Spratlys;
6. India's development of nuclear weapons and long-range delivery systems; and
7. Nationalism in Inner Mongolia, Tibet, and elsewhere in China, which represents a potential internal security challenge.

Some of these no doubt represent genuine security concerns (at least over the long term); others appear to be simply excuses. Nonetheless, all contribute to the rationale for developing the military force that the PRC seems intent on possessing in order to adequately provide for its own defense and to underscore its position as a major Asian (if not global) power. Ironically, despite their ability to see threats all around themselves, the Chinese seem indignant and almost surprised when their neighbors express concern about the nature and intent of the PRC's military modernization program. According to PRC spokesmen, China's neighbors should not feel threatened since the PRC supports peaceful settlement of disputes and has no hegemonic intentions.

Such assurances notwithstanding, the PRC's ongoing acquisition of extended-range aircraft and other pieces of state-of-the-art Russian military hardware, and speculation about Peking's intention to develop a true blue-water navy have the PRC's neighbors nervous. Of particular concern was the acquisition, in 1991, of twenty-four to twenty-six SU-27 fighter aircraft from Russia. Although primarily used as interceptors, there are indications that these potent airframes may be adapted for ground attack role as well. These aircraft are nearing operational status and there are reports that the sale of another twenty-four is currently being negotiated. The Russians also sold the Chinese one hundred RD-33 jet engines (used in the supersonic Russian MiG-29) for use in upgrading mainland China's indigenously-produced fighters.[25]

The Chinese have also introduced a new generation of warships into their fleet since the beginning of this decade. The Lühu-class destroyer and Jiangwei-class frigate represent marked improvements over earlier-generation naval vessels and signal the beginning of a true blue-water force. Rumors also abound about Peking's intentions to purchase Russian

---

[25]"Chasing the 20th Century," *Jane's Defence Weekly*, February 19, 1994, 26-27.

Kilo-class submarines and to either purchase, or more likely, construct their own mid-sized aircraft carrier.[26] This would give them a most dramatic power projection capability.

These actual and suspected acquisitions, when combined with unyielding official statements and parliamentary legislation reinforcing island claims, have increased regional apprehensions. This has been exacerbated by the lack of transparency regarding the PRC's military budgets, inventory, strategy, tactics, and future acquisition or development plans. As a result, even some of Peking's closest friends in Asia have begun to sound alarms. Singapore's Defense Minister Yeo Ning Hong recently warned that Peking's assertiveness "has aroused distrust and suspicion," especially among other Spratly claimants, and that "countries in the region may still be uncertain about how an economically stronger China will behave in the longer term."[27]

While the Chinese are eager to avoid being painted as the next "threat" in Asia or globally, the current lack of transparency seems to be by design. I would argue that it suits Peking's needs and strategy, as well as its xenophobic nature. The PRC today wants to appear more powerful and capable than it actually is, since this improves its international stature and bargaining position and causes its neighbors to be more deferential to Peking's wishes or demands. From the PRC's perspective, a little apprehension on the part of its neighbors is not necessarily a bad thing. An enhanced or even highly inflated view of the capabilities of the PLA, and a certain amount of ambiguity about Peking's intentions, makes the PLA a more effective instrument in support of the attainment of the PRC's other national security objectives.

Maintenance of Internal Stability and Control

"In the early period of establishing a socialist market economic structure, it is of strategic importance to maintain social stability," said recently Premier Li P'eng.[28]

The Chinese leadership attaches the highest priority to the maintenance of internal stability and control. In the words of senior leader Teng Hsiao-p'ing, "Without a stable social and political environment, it will be impossible to carry out reforms and construction."[29] Teng has

---

[26]Ibid.

[27]As reported by Nicholas Kristof, "China Builds Its Military Muscle, Making Some Neighbors Nervous," *New York Times*, January 11, 1994, 1.

[28]As cited in "China Urges Calm as 5th Anniversary of Massacre Nears," *International Herald Tribune*, May 21, 1994, 5.

[29]Ibid.

witnessed what happened in the former Soviet Union and to some of his closest comrades in Eastern Europe, and he remains fully cognizant of turbulent eras of the PRC's not-too-distant past. He also remembers what happened the last time he tried to loosen the reins of control; namely, the protests in Tienanmen (and elsewhere) that proved impossible to control without resorting to force.

The Chinese leadership will, therefore, take all steps necessary to prevent the reoccurrence of another Tienanmen incident. If they err, it will be on the side of increased caution. This would be true under even the most ideal circumstances—and today the circumstances are far from ideal, with Teng's long march nearing its end and the leadership succession issue far from settled.

There is a great deal of debate and uncertainty about mainland China after Teng. Forecasters seem to agree on only one point—Teng will eventually die. Predictions as to who will emerge as the next paramount leader—or as first among equals in a collective leadership—vary, as do assessments of the prospects for either short- or long-term stability in the post-Teng era.

I remain optimistic that, at least in the short term, there will be a period of relative stability, despite inevitable behind-the-scenes jockeying for power. This optimism stems from the fact that (except for the very top) the next generation of leaders and bureaucrats is already in place, the foundations of reform have been largely institutionalized, and the divergence of views among the various rivals for power is not that extreme (especially when compared to the Teng versus "gang of four" post-Mao era).

In addition, the PLA leadership appears ideally situated to play a stabilizing role. As the Chinese Communist Party (CCP) becomes more discredited and less influential, the PLA has emerged as a more independent power base. While the debate over whether the Party controls the gun or the gun controls the Party continues, the PLA exercises considerable power today and all aspiring Teng successors will likely be vying for PLA support. In the words of a recent U.S. Congressional Research Service (CRS) report, the PLA "could provide the key political margin in the event of a serious political struggle for power among civilian leaders in Beijing."[30] For its part, the PLA leadership understands the need for, and will thus help ensure, an orderly political transition.

This stabilizing force may well be needed, since no one with the

---

[30]Robert Sutter, Shirley Kan, and Kerry Dumbaugh, "China in Transition: Changing Conditions and Implications for U.S. Interests" (CRS Report to Congress, December 20, 1993), 3.

credentials or depth of support of Mao or Teng appears to be waiting in the wings, nor is such a paramount leader likely to emerge soon. This lack of stand-alone credentials makes it all the more essential for leadership aspirants to have the backing of the PLA. The Chinese military thus appears destined to play a "kingmaker" role during the leadership transition period, first in helping to select and promote the next ruling elite and second, in giving them the political and, if necessary, military backing to consolidate and exercise their power.

The PLA will also continue to play an important domestic security role. As the enforcement arm of the CCP, the PLA has always had an internal security role, but it had seldom been as publicly tested as it was during Tienanmen, when the army was called in to deal with an unfamiliar phenomenon—a massive crowd of protestors. Prior to this (admittedly limited) experiment in political liberalization, a crowd of this magnitude would never have been permitted to gather in the first place. More importantly, the Chinese leadership previously would not have allowed extensive international media coverage of the event.[31] The results are well known. Peking is still suffering the international political fallout resulting from the explosion in Tienanmen five years ago.

Since 1989, the PLA has taken a reduced role in civilian crowd control and a somewhat lower profile in domestic security affairs. Instead, the Chinese leadership has reinvigorated the paramilitary PAP to serve as the lead internal population control mechanism. Modeled after the very successful riot control forces of Japan and South Korea, the PAP has the primary responsibility for the day-to-day policing role, although the PLA still provides essential backup and would no doubt be called upon once again to curb widespread civil unrest; it could also feel compelled to initiate action in this regard, whether called upon or not. As the CRS report states,

> The People's Liberation Army (PLA) remains the ultimate instrument of central control over society and an important potential lever to be used by central authorities to impose their policies on possibly resisting localities. At the same time, the PLA remains important as a possible arbiter should central, civilian policymakers reach an impasse on sensitive decision points involving domestic or foreign policies.[32]

---

[31] As noted earlier, the international media was not there to cover Tienanmen but to cover the visit to Peking of then-Soviet President Gorbachev. The Tienanmen protestors capitalized on Gorbachev's visit and the presence of the press, and the government obviously underestimated its ability to keep it all under control. Having once been burned, the Chinese are now twice as shy about permitting demonstrations, and understandably so (from their point of view).

[32] Sutter, Kan, and Dumbaugh, "China in Transition," 13.

Just recently, during a rare public reference to the June 4 incident, President Chiang Tse-min (Jiang Zemin) noted that without the PLA's "resolute action" at Tienanmen, mainland China "would not be enjoying its current stability."[33] This is a clear signal that the current leadership is prepared to use all available means, to include the return of the PLA to the streets, to ensure domestic stability.

Preservation of Regional Stability

The preservation of regional stability is another prerequisite for continued economic development. This requires friendly, or at least not hostile, relations between the PRC and its neighbors and, most importantly, with Japan and the United States. It also entails either the deferral or the peaceful (favorable) resolution of outstanding border/territorial disputes.

The PRC's improving relations with its neighbors were chronicled in the first section of this chapter and require little amplification here. As regards the broader topic of nonhostile relations with both the United States and Japan, for better or worse, the security environment of the twenty-first century will be shaped in large part by the interrelationship among these three great powers. This is not to imply that other challenges will not arise; some capable of severely disrupting regional harmony (war on the Korean Peninsula, for example). But, to the extent that the PRC, Japan, and the United States can cooperate, at least there will be a generally secure environment in which to deal with these challenges. Conversely, tensions among the three will have an unsettling effect regionwide, and will make it extremely difficult, if not impossible, to deal with potentially destabilizing regional crises.

Improving international relations is, of course, the job of diplomats and politicians, not soldiers, and the military instrument does not play a lead role in this endeavor. Nonetheless, the PLA has an important supporting role since it provides the PRC—one of the world's five acknowledged nuclear weapons states—with the sense of security that allows Peking to deal with the United States and Japan essentially on equal terms.

The PLA has also proven to be the beneficiary of improved relations with Russia. As observed earlier, the fact that the Russians have an even greater need and desire for harmonious ties with Peking than vice versa has put the PRC in an advantageous position. The PLA has benefitted from this in several ways. First, the reduced threat has allowed Peking to reduce the size of its military by about one million troops—an

---

[33]See note 28 above.

effort that began prior to the demise of the Soviet Union—and to focus instead on developing a more streamlined, modernized, capable, professional military force. Second, Russia's desperate need for hard currency has permitted the PLA to speed up its modernization timetable through the purchase, at bargain prices, of top-of-the-line Russian military hardware.[34] This, in turn, enhances Peking's bargaining power when dealing with its other neighbors. The more modern hardware the PRC purchases (especially weapons systems with power projection capability), the less likely is it that neighboring states will challenge Peking's territorial claims.

Finding peaceful solutions to outstanding territorial claims and the successful avoidance of confrontation over these claims is primarily a political/diplomatic rather than a military task, but the military has a role to play here as well, by convincing others not to dare challenge Chinese claims in the first place. This employment of the threat of force as a political instrument plays a prominent role in Chinese diplomacy and political maneuvering.

Take, for example, the Chinese legislature's harsh statements last year regarding its unyielding claims to the Spratlys and Tiaoyütai (Senkaku) Islands and its right to use military force to enforce these claims. This sabre-rattling seemed aimed, at least in part, at preventing any other claimant from taking action that Peking would feel compelled to react to. True, it is not an uncommon bargaining tactic to forcefully stake out an unyielding position to keep your opponents off balance and thus more willing to compromise—especially if you are considerably more powerful than those with whom you are compelled to bargain. But the primary purpose, in my view, was to discourage others from calling Peking's hand, especially in the Spratlys, where its ability to enforce the most distant of its claims is suspect today.

The PRC understands the need to avoid conflict in the Spratlys and elsewhere. But, it also has no intention of allowing other nations to "violate its sovereign territory." If another nation should challenge its claims, the PRC would find itself in a lose-lose situation—initiate military action and suffer the consequences (in terms of international censure and economic, if not military, reprisals) or, by failing to react, de facto give up territory and be seen as a paper tiger (not to mention setting a poten-

---

[34]It seems appropriate to remind the Russians of Lenin's prophesy that "the capitalists will sell us [the communists] the rope we need to hang them with." What Lenin did not foresee was that the capitalists would be in the Kremlin, while the "us" would be the Chinese, who are eagerly buying up as much rope as the Russians are willing to sell, and at bargain prices to boot.

tially dangerous precedent). As a result, they have chosen to use the threat of force as a deterrent, to discourage actions by others that would force them to have to select between two bad choices.

Development of the National Economy

> The centerpiece of China's grand strategy for the first half of the [twenty-first] century as well as this century's remaining years has been set forth as early as [the] late [1970s], that is, the development of national economy. . . . [This] requires a peaceful international context and a stable domestic situation.[35]

Continued development of the national economy is also essential to the attainment of the PRC's other objectives (and vice versa). Economic reform lies at the base of this effort and significant challenges lie ahead, even as Peking is taking steps to combat many of the ills and potential pitfalls associated with rapid economic growth.[36] It remains to be seen if they will be successful, since efforts to slow down an overheated economy do not win favor with regional and local leaders (including military officials) who may feel that they have not yet received their fair share of the benefits.

The PLA has been a major beneficiary of the economic boom, both in terms of increased spending for defense modernization and, more personally, in terms of extensive involvement in many industries and private ventures, which is making individual PLA members and units wealthy. As the *Far Eastern Economic Review* points out, more than 10,000 companies have already been officially registered by PLA units, running the gauntlet from textile factories to night clubs.[37] The central government also benefits. When arms exports are added to the army's other money-making ventures, the PLA becomes the third largest foreign exchange earner in mainland China, with a large portion being turned over to the central government or used to defray the costs of maintaining the PLA.[38]

Nonetheless, this extensive PLA involvement in the economic sector is becoming an increasing cause for concern in Peking. In addition to the most obvious reasons (graft, corruption, and the possible stifling of

---

[35]Xu, "China's Grand Strategy for the 21st Century," 6.

[36]See Cossa, "China and Northeast Asia: What Lies Ahead?" for details on mainland China's economic (to include environmental) challenges and steps being taken to address them.

[37]Frank Ching, "China Makes Concessions," *Far Eastern Economic Review*, April 21, 1994, 40.

[38]Lu Yu-shan, "CPC Prohibits Armed Forces from Engaging in Business," *Tang-tai yüeh-k'an* (Contemporary Monthly) (Hong Kong), February 15, 1994, no. 35:14-15, as reported in Foreign Broadcast Information Service, *Daily Report: China*-94-025 (February 7, 1994): 23.

legitimate private enterprise) is a more fundamental concern; namely, that military units are becoming so involved in economic activities that they are forgetting their primary mission of training to defend the nation.

As China-watcher Frank Ching points out, "So involved has the military become in business ventures that there is concern in both military and government circles regarding the maintenance of professional army standards."[39] In fact, two of the PRC's most senior military men, Central Military Commission vice chairmen Liu Hua-ch'ing (Liu Huaqing) and Chang Chen (Zhang Zhen), have cautioned against the military "wallowing in luxury and pleasure," noting that "many armies in China and abroad have lost their fighting capability and been defeated by peace or by themselves."[40] There is also concern that the military's entrepreneurial activities are providing the PLA with an independent financial base that will decrease its reliance on (and thus promote greater independence from) the Party and central leadership.

As a result, dramatic steps are now under way to restrict the PLA's ability to participate in economic ventures. The central leadership has decided to "again focus the efforts of the armed forces on national defense construction by adopting some orderly steps." More specifically, in remarks directly and jointly attributed to Chiang Tse-min and Li P'eng, it was stated that "the central leadership has decided to stop the production and business activities undertaken by the armed forces, and transfer all the enterprises run by military units to local civilian institutions."[41]

Three measures will reportedly be taken to bring about this transformation. First, businesses originally run by the PLA will be converted into state-owned enterprises run by "demobilized soldiers" whose gains and interests will be protected by the state. Second, military salaries (to include military retirement pay) will be substantially increased (especially for officers) and military living conditions will be improved. Finally, a concerted effort will be made to solicit the endorsement and support of senior military leaders. Reportedly, Liu Hua-ch'ing and Chang Chen have already agreed in principle to support this effort, although both cautioned that it "must be handled prudently and properly."[42]

Attempts to get the deeply-entrenched military out of the market-

---

[39]See note 37 above.

[40]Gerald Segal, "China Changes Shape: Regionalism and Foreign Policy," *Adelphi Paper*, no. 287 (March 1994): 26, citing *People's Daily*, July 26, 1993.

[41]Lu, "CPC Prohibits Armed Forces from Engaging in Business," 23-24.

[42]Ibid.

place and back into the barracks could prove to be a difficult task. As the *Asian Wall Street Journal* points out:

> In China's new, free-for-all market economy, it's often difficult to determine exactly what entity owns or otherwise controls many companies. . . . Ambiguous identities are even more of a problem when dealing with companies run by the People's Liberation Army. Operating as a virtual state within a state, the army has flourished in business, setting up joint ventures and companies that even the Chinese government finds difficult to monitor.[43]

Given the extent of the PLA's involvement in the private sector, and the need for Peking's political aspirants to curry the PLA's favor, one can question just how fast or far-reaching (or successful) the effort to move the PLA back into the barracks will be—or even how wise it might be to tackle such an ambitious and potentially explosive task at this time. Vigorous pursuit of this effort could underscore just how concerned the leadership is about the PLA's growing strength and independent financial power base.

Reunification with Taiwan[44]

Reunification remains a long-term goal to which all current and future aspiring leaders must remain fully committed. While the mainlanders have not attached a timetable for reunification and seem prepared to wait a long time (perhaps forever) for attainment of this goal, it is extremely unlikely that this objective will be abandoned. No Chinese leader could survive being seen as the leader who "lost Taiwan."

The PLA plays an important role in this drama, given the PRC's refusal to give up the right to use force, if necessary, to solve the reunification problem. This refusal, in part, involves the issue of sovereignty. To pledge not to use force to settle "an internal Chinese security matter" constitutes, to Peking, an abrogation of its sovereign rights. More important is the fear that removal of the military threat might provide additional impetus or otherwise embolden the independence movement on Taiwan. Once again, the threat to use force—or more accurately in the case of Taiwan, the refusal to rule out that possibility—is aimed at discouraging an action on the part of Taipei that would place Peking in another lose-lose situation.

---

[43]Kathy Chen, "Limiting Sanctions May Be Tricky," *Asian Wall Street Journal*, May 19, 1994, 1, 20.

[44]For the purposes of this chapter, I will assume that the first step in this process, the reversion of Hong Kong in 1997, is essentially on track. A breakdown in this process would have a dramatic effect not only on the reunification question but on the complexion of the overall strategic environment.

The PRC's military modernization effort ties directly to this. As Robert Ross notes, "China seeks sufficient military power to dissuade the Taiwan leadership from risking a declaration of independence and to coerce Taiwan to retract such a declaration should deterrence fail."[45]

This is not to imply that the threat to use force is an idle one. Should Taiwan declare independence, the PRC would feel compelled to take all measures possible to undo this act; this could very well include the use of force in some fashion, despite the negative consequences for Peking and the region (and for the citizens of Taiwan).

In this regard, the U.S. decision to sell F-16s to Taiwan represents a multidimensional challenge to Peking. It increases Taiwan's defense capability, thereby making Taipei less susceptible to PRC threats. It also could serve to embolden independence activists. In the event of an independence declaration, it could limit Peking's options toward applying pressure on Taipei, especially if Peking's complaint that "Taipei's military already has some air and sea superiority over the mainland's forces" proves true—and I suspect it is. Most importantly, Peking is concerned that such arms sales, especially when combined with vocal expressions of support for Taiwan's democracy and independence movements, may signal an abandonment on the part of the United States of its commitment to a "one-China" policy.

I strongly believe that any shift away from the "one-China" position, especially in the context of a unilateral Taiwanese declaration to the contrary, would be viewed as highly threatening by Peking in a most fundamental way and thus would be immediately destabilizing. At best it would cause severe political turmoil (with significant economic implications). At worst (and not entirely unlikely), it could plunge the region into war. Continued adherence to the "one-China" policy, therefore, appears to be in everyone's political, economic, and security interest.[46]

International Respect and Recognition

> Many believe that China's goals in building up its military include gaining regional dominance, in the sense that China would have influence or control over developments in Asia. . . .

---

[45]Ross, "China and the Security of Northeast Asia" (Draft paper, to be included in forthcoming CSIS Significant Issues Series volume, *China and Northeast Asia: Looking Toward the 21st Century*), 16.

[46]I believe the PRC sees Taipei's ongoing attempt to gain separate representation in the United Nations as part of the independence movement that threatens China's national sovereignty. In response, Peking has been increasingly flexing its considerable economic and political muscle and appears less willing to enter into bilateral and multilateral dialogue with Taiwan, even at the nongovernmental level.

> Adhering to a balance of power perspective on world politics, many Chinese leaders see building China's military capability as necessary to check Russian, Japanese, and U.S. influence in Asia. . . .
>
> According to this view, China can be expected to use military power (including upgraded nuclear capability) to back its political claims to world power status and to help to check U.S. global influence when it conflicts with Chinese aspirations.[47]

Last but not least is the PRC's quest for its "historical place" as the dominant power in Asia and as a major, respected player on the international stage. Many Chinese believe this is not possible without a first-rate military force capable of countering (or matching) the power projection capabilities of the PRC's "three powerful neighbors." In particular, Peking is wary of Japan's technological edge and its military potential (and history). This traditional rivalry for predominance in Asia, fueled by Peking's recollection of the exploitation that accompanied periods of inferiority, shows little sign of abating.

As the PRC has come of age economically and diplomatically, there has been a corresponding growth in national pride and a desire for respect and acknowledgment of Peking's status as a great regional power capable of independently protecting its interests. This ambition provides powerful incentive behind the drive for expanded military budgets and defense modernization. A great deal of homage is currently being paid to the role of economics as the future source of international power and the PRC is surely committed to becoming a world economic power. However, Peking also realizes that without a credible military capability (with more than just a preponderance of numbers), it cannot take its "rightful place" on the world scene as a major, respected (or feared) international power.

I would only partially agree with the assessment of Robert Ross, among others, that today, "Chinese military power is insufficient to reach this objective; Chinese leaders cannot be sure that China's military in the foreseeable future will afford it either an independent security policy or a major role in region-wide issues."[48] This is valid vis-à-vis the United States, Russia, and perhaps even Japan. But the PLA's overwhelming size and potential already ensure that any nation, large or small, who attempts to ignore the PRC will be doing so at great peril.

Ironically, the PRC's heavy-handed attempts to use the threat of force to achieve its political and security objectives, and its reluctance to

---

[47]Robert G. Sutter and Shirley Kan, "China as a Security Concern in Asia: Perceptions, Assessment, and U.S. Options" (CRS Report for Congress, January 5, 1994), 12.

[48]Ross, "China and the Security of Northeast Asia," 6.

make the PLA more transparent, while perhaps helping to achieve individual objectives, have added to regional suspicions and mistrust over the nature of the PRC's future intentions and its professed commitment to regional peace, stability, and harmony.

Conclusion

It is too soon to say where pursuit of these national security objectives will take the PRC. One hopes that, by the turn of the century, the PRC will have become a prosperous, stable, responsible member of the community of nations, fully committed to political, economic, and security cooperation with its neighbors. It could, however, just as easily become a sprawling, amorphous, undisciplined, perhaps even somewhat fragmented giant, troubling to its neighbors and a real challenge to the rest of the world. More likely, it will fall somewhere in between, and the key question will be, "Toward which of these two directions is it heading?"

Those who will be most responsible for charting the PRC's future course have yet to be fully ordained. But, regardless of who will steer the Chinese ship of state, the PLA will have one hand on the rudder. PLA actions, and the manner in which the central leadership chooses to employ the military instrument of power, will have a great deal of influence on how the PRC is ultimately perceived, and treated, by its neighbors.

If the PRC is genuinely intent on becoming a responsible member of the international community, there are certain things it should do—or, in some cases, stop doing—to enhance both its own image and the prospects for stability.

In the economic realm, the PRC must vigorously pursue reform programs already on the books and further develop and then implement strict enforcement measures to see them through. The good news is that the Chinese leadership appears aware of many of the pitfalls that lie ahead and is attempting to develop and refine programs to deal with them. But serious challenges remain, especially if Peking cannot control the growing corruption that inevitably seems to come with rapid economic growth. Many new laws are required, dealing with bank and tax reform, and with economic and political standards of behavior; then, they must be enforced!

Peking must also continue its efforts to ease the PLA out of the marketplace and into the barracks, but on a measured timetable that causes the least disruption to the economy and to the military's morale and standard of living. A military with a vested interest in economic liberalization can be a positive force over time.

To allay its neighbors' concerns, the PLA must increase the transparency of its military budgets, inventory, strategy, tactics, and specific weapon system acquisition or developmental plans—publishing a White Paper would be a useful beginning. Otherwise, there is a growing risk that increased Chinese military expenditures will prompt or fuel an arms race in Asia, as Peking's neighbors see the need to strengthen their own military capabilities in the face of a perceived expanded PLA threat.

Greater military-to-military dialogue and other confidence building measures are needed, not only between the PRC and the United States, but between the PRC and each of its neighbors, in order to help promote greater understanding of one another's capabilities, intentions, and concerns.

The PRC should also take a more proactive role in offering solutions to the problems on the Korean Peninsula and elsewhere in the region, rather than remaining content to have others always take the lead. If it wants to be respected, it must take a responsible leadership role commensurate with its membership among the permanent five of the United Nations Security Council.[49]

Finally, more bilateral and multilateral dialogue is needed across the political, economic, and security spectrum to create greater regional confidence and awareness. There are a growing number of mechanisms in existence (official and nongovernmental) to support such dialogue. The PRC should take greater advantage of these opportunities, and other nations should take the steps necessary to facilitate its doing so. At the nongovernmental level, the recently-formed Council for Security Cooperation in the Asia-Pacific (CSCAP) can play a major role in this regard, especially if it can bring both the PRC and Taiwan (plus Russia, North Korea, Mongolia, and others) into the unofficial dialogue. Peking should recognize the wisdom of increased dialogue, on security as well as economic issues, with its brothers on Taiwan. More inclusive dialogue is needed, along with a greater willingness by all concerned to candidly and dispassionately address the sensitive, potentially divisive issues that can threaten regional stability; nongovernmental organizations best provide this type venue.

As a sovereign nation with a proud history and a promising future, the PRC has every right to pursue the national security objectives out-

---

[49]The PRC also needs to demonstrate greater adherence to the United Nations Universal Declaration of Human Rights. If it wants other countries to respect its own path toward democratization, it should stop hiding behind such excuses as "Asian values" and "noninterference in domestic affairs" when denying its people fundamental rights that it has pledged to assure. As a great power that demands equal and fair treatment from others, the PRC is obligated to hold itself to a higher standard than is currently being evidenced.

lined in this chapter. The achievement of these objectives need not be threatening; it can serve the interests of both the PRC and the rest of Asia—provided it is done in a nonthreatening manner that recognizes the valid security concerns of Peking's neighbors and the emerging geopolitical realities in post-Cold War Asia.

11

The PRC's Military and Security Policy in the Post-Cold War Era

Harlan W. Jencks

The PRC's Global and Regional Power

The international security and military policy of the People's Republic of China (PRC) has four major goals. In order of priority these are: (1) maintenance of internal political stability; (2) maintenance of external security against invasion or encroachment; (3) achievement of "hegemony" over China's near neighbors; and (4) achievement of "great power" status. The Chinese Communist Party (CCP) elite seeks to assure the internal security of the existing party-state primarily by fostering economic growth, and with police power. Internal legitimacy, as well as external security, "hegemony," and great power status are also served by various diplomatic initiatives, and by the expanding military capability of the People's Liberation Army (PLA).

The PRC's neighbors, who implicitly used to depend on the Soviet Army to tie down most of the PLA, feel much more vulnerable since the collapse of the Soviet Union. Backed by the perception of increased PLA power, PRC diplomats have maintained their relationships with old friends and mended fences with former antagonists. The June 1989 Tienanmen (Tiananmen) incident did not significantly damage the PRC's relations with any of its regional neighbors. Many Asian governments have "human rights problems" of their own, and were not interested in joining Western-sponsored sanctions against the PRC. The Persian Gulf crisis (August 1990-February 1991) allowed the PRC to escape its post-Tienanmen diplomatic isolation.[1]

---

[1] Ellis Joffe, *China After the Gulf War,* SCPS Paper (Kaohsiung, Taiwan: Sun Yat-sen Center for Policy Studies, National Sun Yat-sen University, May 1991).

Mainland Chinese officials and scholars unanimously reject the notion of a new "unipolar" world order. They insist that the bipolar era has given way to a multipolar order dominated by the PRC, the United States, Japan, Russia, Western Europe, and emerging regional powers like India.[2]

In two studies written in 1992 and 1993, I examined the PRC's military and security developments.[3] In mid-1994, I find that military policy and modernization continue with little visible change. However, PRC diplomacy has taken strong new initiatives, significantly increasing Peking's (Beijing's) influence in neighboring capitals, notably in Burma (Myanmar) and the new republics of Central Asia. The PLA elite publicly supports these initiatives.[4]

The PRC's Security Concerns

Economic development calls for internal and external stability. This consideration strongly moderates Chinese foreign policy behavior. However, a leading external/internal goal of the Peking leadership, tied to the legitimacy of the regime, is the reunification of China. Hong Kong will revert to PRC control in July 1997. Its fate is closely tied to the more complex issue of Taiwan. PRC irredentism in the South China Sea involves regime legitimacy, as well as great power status and access to natural resources.

Speaking off the record, official and unofficial Chinese say that Japan is the most significant middle- and long-term military threat to China. This accounts for some of the Chinese ambivalence about the Japanese-American security alignment and about American military presence in the East Asia-Pacific (EAP) region. The U.S. presence is seen in China—indeed everywhere in Asia—as a constraint upon possible Japanese military

---

[2]Foreign Minister Ch'ien Ch'i-ch'en's Speech to the UN General Assembly on September 29, 1993, New China News Agency (NCNA) Domestic Service, September 29, 1993, trans. in Foreign Broadcast Information Service (FBIS), *Daily Report: China* [hereinafter cited as *FBIS-CHI*]-93-188 (September 30, 1993): 1 [hereinafter cited as Ch'ien Ch'i-ch'en's UN Speech]; and Liu Hua-ch'ing, "Unswervingly Advance Along the Road of Building a Modern Army with Chinese Characteristics," *Chiu-shih* (Seeking Facts) (Peking), 1993, no. 15, reprinted in *Chieh-fang-chün pao* (Liberation Army News), August 6, 1993, 1, 2, trans. in *FBIS-CHI*-93-158 (August 18, 1993): 16.

[3]Harlan W. Jencks, "China and the Security Environment in Southeast Asia in the 1990s" (A study prepared for the Southeast Asian Security Environment Project of the National Bureau of Asian Research, Seattle, Washington, 1992-93); and Harlan W. Jencks, "China's Defense Buildup: A Threat to the Region?" in *China's Military: The PLA in 1992/1993*, ed. Richard H. Yang (Taipei: Chinese Council for Advanced Policy Studies [distributed in the United States by Westview Press], 1993), 95-120.

[4]*Cheng Ming* (Hong Kong), no. 192 (October 1993): 8-9, trans. in *FBIS-CHI*-93-191 (October 5, 1993): 68-69; and *Ching Pao* (Hong Kong), October 5, 1993, cited in *Asia-Pacific Defence Review* (Kuala Lumpur), January/February 1994, 48.

adventurousness; but it also tends to hinder PRC efforts to achieve regional hegemony. The American military presence is at least implicitly anti-PRC. Recent U.S. Navy exercises with Southeast Asian navies "casting China as the potential troublemaker" have reinforced this perception.[5] Peking's foreign policy toward the United States, however, is primarily focused on maintaining economic ties.

The PRC's Objectives

PRC spokesmen constantly reiterate that there is no such thing as a "China threat," and denounce those who entertain such a notion. It is certainly true that PRC leaders hope to avoid armed conflict, and will go to some lengths to achieve their objectives bloodlessly. Peking's declaratory policy constantly denounces "hegemonism" (*pa-ch'üan chu-i*) as a crime perpetuated primarily by American "self-appointed international cops."[6] Nevertheless, some mainland Chinese leaders seem to assume that the PRC is the rightful "hegemon" in Asia. That is to say, Peking should have freedom of action in the region without constraint by any countervailing power, while no Asian government should take any action contrary to Chinese interests. To maximize its freedom of action, Peking appears to be trying to prevent the formation of new Asian military blocs. In particular, an enlarged Association of Southeast Asian Nations (ASEAN) which included the Indochinese states would not be in Peking's perceived interest.

The PRC's maximum goal is "hegemony," but not at the cost of its minimum goal, which is stability. Chinese leaders wish to preserve stability in the EAP and—more important—internally. The latter, in fact, is the PRC's primary security problem. The gravest threat the PRC poses to Asia—indeed to the world—is its own internal breakup.

The post-Mao reforms have caused a general loss of political discipline, cohesion, and central control. A good example is the involvement of PLA units and personnel in illegal or nonsanctioned activities like smuggling. In the late 1990s, it is conceivable that the PLA, and with it the PRC, could actually break up into warring factions.[7] If the unraveling of central authority continues beyond a certain point, and the PRC actually begins to come apart, the security implications for the rest of Asia could

---

[5]Nayan Chanda, "Distant Thunder," *Far Eastern Economic Review* (*FEER*), November 19, 1992, 16.

[6]Ch'ien Ch'i-ch'en UN Speech, 3.

[7]On the possibility of internal breakup in the PRC, see Harlan W. Jencks, "Civil-Military Relations in China: Tiananmen and After," *Problems of Communism* 40, no. 3 (May-June 1991): 27-29.

become extremely serious.[8] Because it is impossible to predict the details of a "breakup scenario," this study stipulates the assumption that, for the remainder of the 1990s, PRC foreign policy will continue to be decided in Peking—albeit disrupted somewhat by regional leaders, businessmen, criminals, and even PLA officers, who will sometimes work at cross-purposes with Peking. This study further—and crucially—assumes that the PLA will remain under the centralized control of the CCP's Central Military Commission (CMC), albeit with increasing corruption and in-discipline in the ranks.

Central leaders are vitally concerned to maintain political and economic discipline against the rising internal forces of regional and provincial autonomy. This has direct implications for the PRC's external security policy, especially in Southeast Asia. Political and economic leaders in the southern provinces strongly favor further expanded trade and investment links with Southeast Asia. In the past several years the official press has increasingly depicted the South China Sea as a source of vital resources. This dubious assertion may be a calculated appeal to economically minded southeastern Chinese, who may not be particularly interested in irredentist claims to the South China Sea. Nor may they care much about political reunification, as long as they can maintain open trade and investment ties with Taiwan. The preference of local leaders for trade rather than conflict is generally true throughout China. Although far less developed in the north and west than along the southern coast, border trade everywhere is expanding rapidly.

The Arms Trade

PRC trade with Asia has expanded rapidly. Breaking into the Asian arms market, however, has been difficult. Arms sales to Burma (see below) seem to be as much politically as economically motivated. The symbolism of Chinese weapons transfers to Southeast Asia unquestionably has been a primary PRC motive. However, the PRC is also commercially interested in the lucrative Asian arms market, where military budgets are increasing.[9]

Contacts between the PRC and Thai armed forces began about 1984. In 1986-87, the Chinese provided heavy artillery, tanks, antiaircraft guns, and armored personnel carriers at "friendship" prices.[10] The Thai Navy

---

[8]See Jencks, "China's Defense Buildup."

[9]"Options for Defence," *Jane's Defence Weekly* (*JDW*), December 22, 1992, 293.

[10]"Thai Army in Chinese Tank Deal," ibid., March 21, 1987, 467; and "Thai Army to Buy 400 Chinese APCs," ibid., April 4, 1987, 575.

has purchased four modified Jianghu-class frigates since 1990.[11] The Thai Air Force has also ordered nine Chinese Z-9A helicopters (license-built French SA-365N Dauphin).[12] Military delegations routinely exchange visits.

The United States and various other governments have expressed concern about the PRC as a source of nuclear, missile, and conventional weapons proliferation. Yet, oddly, only India, among the PRC's neighbors, seems to be alarmed at Chinese willingness to sell military technology to virtually anyone willing to pay.

"Limited and Regional Wars"

By the mid-1980s, Peking had managed to convince most Southeast Asian governments that it had severed its links with Communist insurgents in the region. Malaysia and Indonesia still profess concern with this "Chinese threat," though their domestic Communist movements are practically nonexistent. Since the late 1980s, however, China's neighbors have become far more concerned about the development of Chinese naval and air forces, and the new PRC strategic doctrine of "limited and regional wars."

In early 1986, the CMC decreed that global nuclear war was no longer inevitable. For the foreseeable future, the world scene would be characterized by "limited and regional wars" (*yu-hsien chü-pu chan-cheng*).[13] The military press immediately took up the problem of "limited wars" and called for the formation of "rapid reaction units" (RRUs). RRUs would have two missions: to react to internal disturbances beyond the capability of the People's Armed Police (PAP) and to deploy to scenes of border fighting.

Mainland Chinese theorists emphasize that a grave danger in "limited war" is becoming bogged down in a protracted blood-letting, as Iran and Iraq did in the 1980s. "Avoiding at all cost protracted wars" is a major reason for providing RRUs and other "small war" forces with over-

---

[11]Pictured in Joris Janssen Lok, "Blue Water Navies: Flagship Fleets of Asia/Pacific," ibid., April 11, 1992, 624.

[12]Ibid., March 28, 1992, 508.

[13]Teng Hsiao-p'ing's speech on April 24, 1986, in *People's Daily*, quoted in *Hung-ch'i* (Red Flag), July 1, 1986, no. 13:20-26, trans. in *FBIS-CHI*-86-144 (July 28, 1986): A5-A14, esp. A11 and A14; An T'ien, *Hsien-tai yu-hsien chan-cheng te li-lun yü chan-lüeh* (The theory and strategy of modern limited war), National Defense and the Future Series (Peking: Liberation Army Press, 1986); and Huang Yu-ch'ang, ed., *Chü-pu chan-cheng te tso-t'ien, chin-t'ien, ming-t'ien* (Limited war: Yesterday, today, and tomorrow) (Peking: National Defense University Press, 1987).

whelming firepower.[14] This helps explain PLA interest in tactical nuclear weapons[15]—an interest that has not gone unnoticed among China's
neighbors.[16]

The instability of the post-Cold War world has reinforced "limited
and regional war" thinking. The Chinese expect instability and conflict
to provoke a buildup in high-technology weapons among various developing states, causing frequent limited regional warfare.[17] "Desert Storm"
(January-February 1991) strengthened the hand of PLA advocates of
"limited and regional war" and of elite, highly trained troops equipped
with high-technology weapons.[18]

The primary RRUs are 15th Airborne Army, stationed in the Wuhan
area, and the Naval Infantry. There are supposedly at least two brigades
of the latter, which are still developing doctrine, training, and deployment.
Six division-sized RRUs or "fist units" (ch'üan-t'ou pu-tui) supposedly
exist in the Chengtu (Chengdu), Canton (Guangzhou), Lanchow (Lanzhou),
and Tsinan (Jinan) military regions.[19] On paper, each of the twenty-four
group armies has a battalion or regiment designated as its RRU. This
does not mean that all of these units can really react rapidly or effectively.
However, such developments do contribute to a nascent force projection
capability which concerns China's neighbors, particularly in Southeast Asia.

The Air and Naval Buildup

PLA rapid reaction units need reliable, modern, and flexible logistics,
communications, weapons, and equipment; the troops must be very well
trained. This has proven to be so expensive that the rest of the PLA's
modernization has suffered commensurately. In fact, after nuclear forces,
RRUs, some naval and air units, and the PAP have taken their share, the
rest of the PLA has not benefitted much from the increased military budget.

---

[14]Zhang Lin with Zang Shiming, "Let Us Pursue the Study of Operations Theory in Greater
Depth," Kuo-fang ta-hsüeh hsüeh-pao (National Defense University Journal), December
1987, no. 12:27-31, trans. in Joint Publications Research Service—China [JPRS-CAR]-88-044
(August 5, 1988): 72.

[15]Gao Runqiang, "Effects of High-Tech Weapons on Local Wars," Chieh-fang-chün pao,
January 23, 1987, 3.

[16]Harlan W. Jencks, "China's Nuclear Strategy," Asia Pacific Review 1, no. 1 (Spring
1989): 73-98.

[17]Chieh-fang-chün pao, January 4 and 11, 1991.

[18]Harlan W. Jencks, "Chinese Evaluations of 'Desert Storm': Implications for PRC Security,"
Journal of East Asian Affairs (Seoul) 6, no. 2 (Summer/Fall 1992): 447-77.

[19]"Chasing the 20th Century," JDW, February 19, 1994, 27.

Trends in PRC military spending are clear in the officially announced budgets. However, published CIA estimates of actual defense spending are more than double the official figures. The official 1994 defense budget is 52 billion *yuan*, plus shares of science and technology, education, and capital construction funds[20] (see table 11.1).

Over the past fifteen years, the PRC military industrial system has introduced a variety of new weapons systems and equipment drawing upon Soviet and, more recently, Western technologies. While the main effort has been to develop arms for export, the PLA has received some improved equipment, although it is still an obsolescent force on many counts. According to most recent reports, the priorities in PLA equipment development are air defense, electronic warfare, and antisubmarine warfare.

The Sino-Russian arms connection has been restored, and is playing a major role in the modernization of PRC military industry. The Russians seem willing to sell almost anything at bargain prices. A "senior Russian Defence Ministry official" told *Far Eastern Economic Review*'s Tai Ming Cheung that over 1,000 Russian military "scientists and technicians have traveled to China since 1991 on defence-industrial exchanges."[21] Some 300 more work permanently with PRC defense organizations, while 300-400 Chinese work in Russia. "This does not include the scores of Russian defence scientists who have been quietly recruited by the Chinese government." The PRC has reportedly become Russia's most important arms customer, buying US$1.8 billion worth in 1992.

The PLA Air Force is trying to build a modern air defense system, extend its reach, and improve its command, control, communications, and intelligence (C^3I) capabilities. The PLA Air Force is trying to acquire "force multiplier" systems. The latter—maritime surveillance, airborne early warning (AEW), and in-flight refueling—are especially relevant to the military balance in the South China Sea.[22] A disturbing possibility is that the Russians might sell the PRC the Tu-22M Backfire bomber, which has a 4,000-kilometer combat radius.[23] Equipped for long-range anti-shipping strikes, a Chinese Backfire force would drastically alter the military situation in the entire EAP.

Twenty-six SU-27 Flanker fighters were delivered in 1991-93, along

---

[20]"Balancing the Books," ibid., 35; and Lincoln Kaye, "Pre-Emptive Cringe," *FEER*, March 24, 1994, 48.

[21]This paragraph, including all quotations, is drawn from Tai Ming Cheung, "China's Buying Spree," *FEER*, July 8, 1993, 24.

[22]Zhang Changzhi, "What Do Changes in Modern Aeronautical Weapons Indicate?" *Chieh-fang-chün pao*, July 6, 1990, 3, trans. in *FBIS-CHI*-90-150 (August 3, 1990): 25-27.

[23]"'Backfire' Bomber for Export Soon," *JDW*, October 17, 1992, 19.

Table 11.1
Official PRC Defense Budgets[1]

(Billion *yuan*)

Year	Announced budget	Actual expenditures	Percentage change
1979		22.27	
		(Vietnam War)	
1980	19.33		
1981	16.8		
1986	20.08		
1987	20.96[2]		
1988	21.53[3]		
1989	25.1		
1990	28.97[4]		+ 15.2%
1991	32.5[5]		+ 12%
1992	37[6]	37.8	+ 13.9%
1993	42.5[7]	43.2	+ 12%
1994	52.0[8]		+ 22%

[1]As announced by Finance Minister to the National People's Congress, unless otherwise noted. While the trends in PRC military spending are clear in the officially announced budgets, American CIA estimates of actual defense spending are more than double the official figures. In 1986, for example, the CIA estimated 45 billion *yuan*, while the Chinese announced 20 billion *yuan*. Central Intelligence Agency, *China: Economic Policy and Performance in 1987* (Report submitted to the Subcommittee on National Security Economics of the Joint Economic Committee, U.S. Congress, April 21, 1988), 17-18.

[2]*Jane's Defence Weekly* (*JDW*), April 30, 1988, 819; New China News Agency (NCNA), June 26, 1988, trans. in Foreign Broadcast Information Service (FBIS), *Daily Report: China*-88-123 (June 27, 1988): 32-33.

[3]Ibid.

[4]This was 11.4 percent of the total national budget. There was an overall increase of only 4.8 percent in government spending. Tai Ming Cheung, "Political Payoff," *Far Eastern Economic Review* (*FEER*), April 5, 1990, 23-29. Also see *Ming-pao yüeh-k'an* (Ming Pao Monthly) (Hong Kong), no. 286 (October 1989): 3-15, trans. in Joint Publications Research Service—*China* [*JPRS-CAR*]-90-005 (January 22, 1990): 1-17; and *Wen Wei Po* (Hong Kong), March 22, 1990, 2.

[5]This 12 percent gain, compared to an overall national budget increase of 5 percent. Tai Ming Cheung, "Short on Solutions," *FEER*, April 4, 1991, 8-9.

[6]The military also got part of the approximately 62 million *yuan* earmarked for science and technology, education, and capital construction. Lincoln Kaye, "Business as Usual," ibid., April 2, 1992, 64.

[7]Lincoln Kaye, "Bottomless Pockets," ibid., March 25, 1993, 68.

[8]Lincoln Kaye, "Pre-Emptive Cringe," ibid., March 24, 1994, 48. Somewhat higher figures are reported in "Balancing the Books," *JDW*, February 19, 1994, 35.

with at least four batteries of S-300 (SA-10 Grumble) air defense missiles, and one hundred RD-33 jet engines. The latter, which power the Russian MiG-29 Fulcrum, reportedly will be used to upgrade export versions of the Chinese F-7 Fishbed fighter. Recent negotiations for an additional SU-27 buy reportedly have bogged down over Chinese insistence upon technology transfer.[24]

In late 1989, the PLA Navy completed a force development study entitled *Balanced Development of the Navy in the Year 2000*, which called for a strategy of "active offshore defense." To enhance its power projection capability, the PLA Navy has created a significant Naval Infantry force, and introduced new classes of resupply, amphibious assault, and intelligence-gathering ships. It has begun to approach credible "blue-water" capability. So far, the new ships have mainly appeared in the East Sea and South Sea fleets.[25] The PLA Navy probably will not attempt to put an aircraft carrier into service in the near future, since it would be prohibitively expensive. However, they might buy a used one as a "training aid."[26]

Since the mid-1980s, the Navy has imported an impressive list of Western systems to try to bring some vessels up to international standards. Of particular note are coproduction of the PR/SEMT Pielstick marine diesel engine, the SRBOC Mark 33 chaff dispenser, Mark 32 and PRC/Honeywell Mark 46 mod 2 antisubmarine warfare (ASW) torpedoes, Whitehead ASW torpedo, the Sea Crotale surface-to-air missile (SAM), the General Electric LM-2500 naval gas turbine engine, and Z-9A helicopter coproduction. Results include the significantly modernized Lühu-class destroyer, Jiangwei-class air defense frigates, and at least two new large patrol craft classes.[27]

The PLA Navy has over one hundred diesel-electric submarines, but many are inoperable and all are obsolete. In the mid-1980s, Chinese submarine builders reportedly sought bids in Western Europe for modern submarine technology, production management, and training systems.[28] In addition to upgrading their Romeos, they also reportedly intend to develop new diesel-electric and nuclear attack submarines.[29] The PLA

---

[24]"'Flanker' Sale Stalls as China Seeks New Deal," ibid., January 22, 1994, 3; "Chasing the 20th Century," 26; and "Making a Modern Industry," *JDW*, February 19, 1994, 28.

[25]Robert Karniol, "China's New Navy Takes Shape," *JDW*, June 6, 1992, 958; and Gordon Jacobs, "New Ships for the PLAN," ibid., January 18, 1992, 88-89.

[26]"Chasing the 20th Century," 26-27.

[27]Ibid.; Lok, "Blue Water Navies," 622-24; and Informant.

[28]*JDW*, February 28, 1987, 343.

[29]Ibid., May 16, 1987, 945; and "China's Project E5SG Submarine," ibid., May 9, 1987, 912.

Navy may acquire several Russian Kilo-class conventional submarines. The Kilo has a range of 9,650 kilometers and can stay at sea without replenishment for up to forty-five days. It would be a giant step beyond the obsolescent Romeo, particularly if the Chinese acquired additional units, or the technology to build it themselves.[30] A private informant claims that the Russians have transferred nuclear submarine propulsion and sonar signal suppression technologies to the PRC.

The PRC and Its Neighbors

China is essentially free from external threat for the first time in two centuries. It has improved relations with virtually all of its neighbors.[31]

Russia

The PRC's relationship with the Russian Federation is friendly, if somewhat ambivalent. The border had been "extremely quiet" since 1989.[32] During President Boris Yeltsin's December 1992 visit to Peking, a memorandum of understanding was signed to establish a 100-kilometer demilitarized frontier zone—a measure the Soviet Union resisted for decades. Details are scheduled to be finalized by the end of 1994.[33]

The Chinese are concerned that the Russian Republic might further unravel, especially the Russian Far East.[34] PRC news coverage of the October 1993 parliamentary revolt in Moscow was extensive but noncommittal.[35]

The Chinese have strategic reasons to improve their security relationship with the Russians, to counterbalance the United States.[36] The Russians have high-quality products to sell and a desperate need for foreign exchange, while the Chinese have money and consumer goods to exchange for the weapons they need.[37] Though only a few military agreements have

---

[30]Cheung, "China's Buying Spree," 26; and Robert Karniol, "'Kilo' Goes Hunting for East Asian Exports," *JDW*, February 12, 1994, 3.

[31]Gary Klintworth, "Asia-Pacific: More Security, Less Uncertainty, New Opportunities," *Pacific Review* 5, no. 3 (1992): 222.

[32]NCNA, May 22, 1991, in *FBIS-CHI*-91-100 (May 23, 1991): 11.

[33]"China Adopts a New Stance," *JDW*, February 26, 1994, 19.

[34]Jeffrey Lilley, "Far Eastern Satraps," *FEER*, January 13, 1994, 21; and Sophie Quinn-Judge, "Hobbled by Old Habits," ibid., March 12, 1992, 16-18.

[35]See typical reports from NCNA, October 4, 1993, trans. in *FBIS-CHI*-93-190 (October 4, 1993): 14-15.

[36]Lowell Dittmer, *Sino-Soviet Normalization and Its International Implications: 1945-1990* (Seattle: University of Washington Press, 1992), 244-45.

[37]"Russia and China Talk about Talks," *JDW*, March 14, 1992, 425; and "Soviet Republics' Exports Are Falling," ibid., February 1, 1992, 144.

been announced, both sides have every incentive for further cooperation.

A succession of Russian and Chinese delegations has negotiated various aspects of military cooperation, including technology and hardware transfers. Ships of the Russian Pacific Fleet called at Tsingtao (Qingdao) in August 1993,[38] and the PLA Navy called at Vladivostok in May 1994. When the PLA Chief of General Staff Chang Wan-nien (Zhang Wannian) visited Moscow in August 1993, Defense Minister Pavel Grachev told him that developing relations with China was a major direction of Russia's foreign policy.[39] China and Russia are currently building railroad lines to connect from Chita to eastern Mongolia, Liaoning, the Tumen delta, northeastern Korea, and Vladivostok.[40]

Mongolia

Chinese influence is increasing in Mongolia. The Chinese reopened the Ulan Bator to Tientsin (Tianjin) Railway in 1992.[41] In April 1994, Premier Li P'eng (Li Peng) visited Ulan Bator, signing a number of economic agreements, as well as a new "Treaty of Friendship and Cooperation" to replace the treaty of 1960.[42] In part, the new treaty is intended to preclude reassertion of Russian influence in Mongolia. It provides that "neither party shall join any military or political alliances targeted against the other or sign with any third country any treaties that infringe on the other side's sovereignty and security," or permit a "third country" to use its territory to "hurt the other side's sovereignty and security."[43]

Peking wants to assure that Mongolia is not a base for subversion in the Inner Mongolian Autonomous Region of the PRC. In summer 1991, two Mongolian nationalists were arrested and accused of being in contact with nationalists from the Mongolian Republic. Peking was openly displeased at the enthusiastic welcome given the Dalai Lama when he visited Mongolia later that year. Lamaist Buddhism is reemerging in Mongolia, making it a potential source of subversion not only in Inner Mongolia, but in Tibet as well. With an army of only 20,000 poorly equipped troops, the Mongols are in no position to resist the PRC militarily, should the issue ever arise.[44]

---

[38]Tsinan Shantung Radio, August 23, 1993, trans. in *FBIS-CHI*-93-163 (August 25, 1993): 3.

[39]NCNA in English, August 17, 1993, in *FBIS-CHI*-93-158 (August 18, 1993): 5.

[40]Peking Radio, August 21, 1993, trans. in *FBIS-CHI*-93-163 (August 25, 1993): 3.

[41]Lincoln Kaye, "Faltering Steppes," *FEER*, April 9, 1992, 17-18.

[42]"PRC Premier's Central Asian Trip Promotes Expanded Ties," *FBIS Trends*, FB TM 94-19 (May 11, 1994): 4-5.

[43]NCNA, April 29, 1994.

[44]James L. Tyson, "Chinese Officials Aim to Limit Spread of Unrest over Borders," *Christian Science Monitor* (*CSM*), August 27, 1991, 5.

Central Asia

Because the Chinese are concerned about ethnic and religious unrest in Central Asia, their relationships with the former Soviet republics of Central Asia (Kazakhstan, Kyrgyzstan, Tajikistan, Turkmenistan, and Uzbekistan) are crucial. Two possible outcomes of Central Asian turmoil would spell trouble for the PRC. The republics might define themselves in terms of some sort of pan-Turkic nationalism that would surely extend its appeal to the Turkic peoples of Sinkiang (Xinjiang). Worse, Central Asian peoples might come to define themselves in terms of militant Islam. Ethnic, religious, and nationalistic tensions already appear to have "spilled" across the borders into Sinkiang. Since 1989, the PLA and PAP have been "confronted with the new situation of collaboration between domestic separatists and international hostile forces in an attempt to split the Motherland."[45] Since at least April 1990, violent incidents have occurred repeatedly.[46]

There were two serious incidents in southern Sinkiang in May 1993 "supported and instigated by international reactionary forces," which were quelled by large-scale PAP actions.[47] A PLA officer was quoted by Hong Kong's *Ming Pao* as saying that since that "Uygur riot," Han people were "afraid to enter this region." He also said that while local police have cracked down on extremist nationalists, the PLA thus far has not become involved. He also revealed that there are about 50,000 minority people on the former Soviet side of the border; "Uygurs and Kazakhs who fled China in the mid-1960s but who now want to return to Xinjiang."[48] In September 1993, the Sinkiang Military District moved to improve morale and political reliability among minority soldiers by inaugurating the Uygur-language *Jen-min chün-tui pao* (People's Army News)—the first PLA newspaper to be published in a national minority language.[49]

Perhaps the most likely threat to the PRC would be if the various peoples of the Central Asian republics fell to warring among themselves.

---

[45] *Hsin-chiang jih-pao* (Sinkiang Daily) (Urumqi), June 13, 1990, 1, trans. in *FBIS-CHI*-90-142 (July 24, 1990): 39.

[46] Agence France Presse (AFP), Hong Kong, July 24, 1990, in *FBIS-CHI*-90-143 (July 25, 1990): 64; Lincoln Kaye, "China Feels the Chill," *FEER*, January 9, 1992, 14; and *CSM*, August 26, 1991, 3.

[47] Urumqi Sinkiang Television Network, August 2, 1993, trans. in *FBIS-CHI*-93-146 (August 2, 1993): 26.

[48] *Ming Pao* (Hong Kong), September 28, 1993, A16, trans. in *FBIS-CHI*-93-190 (October 4, 1993): 42-43.

[49] Urumqi Sinkiang Television Network, September 24, 1993, trans. in *FBIS-CHI*-93-189 (October 1, 1993): 27. The newspaper's title, curiously, is in Chinese.

Eventually, they would start searching for support, allies, and sanctuary on the PRC side of the sometimes ill-defined frontier. A situation or situations might arise that provoked Chinese intervention or preemption. That could draw the PLA into ethnic or nationalist or religious conflicts that originated outside the PRC. All of this makes the PLA's "limited and regional war" doctrine even more appropriate than it was when it was first voiced in 1986. Much of the current doctrinal, equipment, and force development for limited and regional war seems to be pointed toward China's Inner-Asian borders.

Even before the final breakup of the Soviet Union, Peking was attempting to improve its relationship with Central Asian governments. In 1993, a delegation of the National People's Congress visited Tajikistan following a visit to mainland China by the head of the Tajik Supreme Soviet.[50] On July 19, Peking announced a joint plan between the Sinkiang Autonomous Region and Kazakhstan to establish a Sino-Kazakh Joint Development Zone on their border "to unfold close cooperation . . . and provide preferential investment conditions for third countries."[51]

Reuters reports that the PRC, rather than Iran or Turkey, is challenging Russia's influence in the region. On April 18-28, 1994, Premier Li P'eng toured Central Asia. He signed a border treaty with Kazakhstan,[52] provided trade credits to four of the five states, and struck a number of trade deals. In Turkmenistan, he signed a memorandum of understanding on what he called "the project of the century"—a gas pipeline from Turkmenistan across Central Asia and China to the Pacific.[53]

Taken together, Peking's diplomatic initiatives in Central Asia not only bolster internal security in Sinkiang, but also may serve to increase PRC access to Central Asian resources. The PRC and all five Central Asian governments, in effect, have formed a latter-day "holy alliance" to maintain the political status quo—preventing ethnic and religious separatism anywhere in the region. Premier Li said Moscow, too, has a role to play in Central Asia, saying that Peking "has no interest" in filling the "so-called vacuum" left by the breakup of the Soviet Union.[54] Russia

---

[50]NCNA Domestic Service, July 24, 1993, trans. in *FBIS-CHI*-93-144 (July 29, 1993): 2.

[51]Chung-kuo hsin-wen-she (China News Service), July 19, 1993, trans. in *FBIS-CHI*-93-147 (August 3, 1993): 5.

[52]ITAR-TASS, April 27, 1994.

[53]This and the following are drawn from "PRC Premier's Central Asian Trip Promotes Expanded Ties," 1-5; and James Kynge, Reuters, April 28, 1994, via Executive News Service, April 29, 1994. Turkmenistan has also held pipeline talks with Pakistan, Iran, and Turkey. See Ahmed Rashid, "Finding an Exit," *FEER*, February 24, 1994, 71.

[54]NCNA, April 7, 1994, reported in *FBIS Trends*, FB TM 94-19 (May 11, 1994): 4.

is also a member of the de facto "holy alliance." Ironically, the PRC press now sympathetically portrays Russian military efforts to guard the Tajik-Afghan border against the same Islamic guerrillas the PRC supported only a few years ago.[55]

Li P'eng won public assurance of support from all of the region's leaders for China's internal struggle against separatists in Sinkiang. He was particularly well received by Uzbek President Islam Karimov. Echoing the leaders of Turkmenistan and Kyrgyzstan, Karimov declared, "We cannot overemphasize the role which China plays in this particular region in preventing separatist feelings and establishing peace and stability." Even in Kazakhstan, a Chinese spokesman quoted President Nazarbayev as giving a similar pledge, though Nazarbayev himself did not mention the issue publicly. Since several groups supporting independence in Sinkiang have been operating with more-or-less official sanction in Kazakhstan, moving too strongly against them might present internal political problems for Nazarbayev. It is not clear whether he intends to limit their activities in the future. China is Kazakhstan's second-biggest trading partner, after Russia. Total trade was US$433 million in 1992, but fell to US$205 million in 1993.[56]

Peking is concerned about ex-Soviet nuclear weapons in Kazakhstan. In the spring of 1992, Nazarbayev indicated that, for complete destruction of all nuclear weapons on his territory, Kazakhstan needed security guarantees from the United States.[57]

PRC nuclear testing in Sinkiang also is a contentious issue between Peking and the Central Asian governments.

The PRC, Japan, and the United States

Almost everyone in Asia hopes the United States-Japanese alliance, and with it the U.S. military presence in Asia, will continue. ". . . Any expansion of Japanese military activities to compensate for the withdrawal of U.S. bases from the Western Pacific would be particularly unsettling to the states in the region."[58]

The PRC will probably remain the primary justification for continuing the United States-Japanese Mutual Security Treaty. Sometime

---

[55]NCNA in English, in *FBIS-CHI*-93-147 (August 3, 1993): 6.

[56]ITAR-TASS, April 27, 1994; and NCNA, April 27, 1994. Both are reported in *FBIS Trends*, FB TM 94-19 (May 11, 1994): 4.

[57]Quoted by Daniel Sneider, "Kazakhstan Seeks U.S. Pact for Further Nuclear Cuts," *CSM*, April 27, 1992, 2.

[58]James A. Winnefeld et al., *A New Strategy and Fewer Forces: The Pacific Dimension*, R-4089/1-USDP (exec. summary) (RAND, 1992): 18-19.

early in the next century, we may see a strong and confident PRC turn to a more assertive regional role. That would certainly provide a renewed rationale for the Japanese-American alliance and for an American military presence. On the other hand, if the PRC should founder or begin to break up, its weakness would also have major consequences for regional security. "Americans should consider how the United States would cope with an Asia over the next 20 years to 30 years in which China either stagnates or . . . falls further behind, leaving Japan in a completely dominant position."[59]

Avoiding a Sino-Japanese arms race is an excellent reason for the United States to maintain a credible military presence in the EAP. PRC leaders, generally speaking, would rather deal with U.S. forces in the EAP than with hypothetical Japanese forces. Since 1989, Southeast Asian governments have openly expressed their preference for the U.S. military to remain in the region. They fear a Sino-Japanese arms race because "when elephants fight, the grass gets trampled."

Since the end of the Cold War, the Japanese government has been under increasing domestic pressure for deep military budget cuts. Japanese Self-Defense Forces spending, still guided by a 1976 "defense program outline," emphasizes naval and air defense of the home islands against the erstwhile Russian threat. The 1994 defense budget "is set to rise by 0.9% over a year ago, the smallest increase in 33 years and equivalent to a real cut of at least 1%. This marks a sharp reversal from the years when defence was one of the fastest-rising items in the budget." After a pay raise for service personnel and the Japanese subsidy to U.S. forces stationed in Japan, ". . . spending on almost all other items will continue to fall. . . ."[60] Despite cuts, some Japanese defense acquisitions are likely to continue, as indeed will defense spending throughout the EAP. Japan's equipment acquisitions, however, are motivated primarily by political pressure from the United States to equalize the foreign trade balance—not by military threat. That irritates Peking as well as Tokyo.[61]

Japan has one territorial conflict with the PRC—their rival claims to the Tiaoyütai (Senkaku) Islands. Japan officially protested when the PRC passed a law claiming sovereignty over these islands in February 1992. In an interview with Japanese correspondents in April, however, Chiang Tse-min (Jiang Zemin) reiterated the previous PRC policy that Peking

---

[59]Richard J. Ellings and Edward A. Olsen, "Asia's Challenge to American Security," *NBR Analysis Monograph*, no. 3 (June 1992): 12.

[60]Charles Smith, "Tomorrow's Strategy," *FEER*, March 17, 1994, 23.

[61]"ASEAN Special Report: Options for Defence," *JDW*, February 22, 1992, 293.

has "shelved" its territorial claim and wants "a settlement through talks over the island issue." Japanese officials say they regard the February 1992 law as a restatement of longstanding PRC policy—not an escalation of the dispute.[62]

The Chinese have been outspoken in their view that Japanese Self-Defense Forces should neither expand nor participate in overseas deployments—even UN-sponsored peacekeeping operations. For public consumption at least, the Chinese evince an almost pathological fear of Japanese military power, particularly naval power. Even in private, PLA Navy officers say they regard Japan as a major and growing threat.

The Chinese attitude was nicely illustrated during Japanese Prime Minister Morihiro Hosokawa's visit to Peking in March 1994, when he asked his hosts to explain the big increases in PRC military spending. "He was brushed off with the assertion that the 22% hike in defence appropriations in the latest budget amounted to no real increase in light of inflation and currency depreciation. Besides, Hosokawa was reminded, China's total defence outlays, in dollar terms, stood at just one eighth of Japan's."[63] The Chinese assertion is true—"in dollar terms." The U.S. dollar is so weak against the yen that dollar figures give a much exaggerated notion of how much military defense the Japanese are actually buying. Moreover, because Japan does not export weapons, unit costs of Japanese-made weapons are extraordinarily high, even compared to other Japanese products. The Chinese assertion further rests upon their own seriously understated official defense budget.

The Koreas

PRC relations with the Republic of Korea (ROK) have been warming for a decade, paced by a rapidly expanding economic relationship. The two governments concluded formal diplomatic relations in the fall of 1992. Naturally, the Democratic People's Republic of Korea (DPRK) is incensed, but the Chinese are not about to abandon the lucrative relationship with Seoul simply to maintain solidarity with the moribund regime in Pyongyang. North Korea's only real value to the PRC is as a military and ideological buffer. The Chinese leadership wants the DPRK to survive, but may prefer that it remain isolated and backward.

Although ROK forces are oriented northward, the ROK Navy has been receiving most of the funding in the past year or so. Seoul has purchased six German 209-class diesel-electric submarines with the latest

---

[62]Kyodo, February 27 and April 1, 1992.
[63]Lincoln Kaye, "'No Great Success'," *FEER*, March 31, 1994, 21.

electronics and weapons systems. The South Koreans also are license-producing eight new P3C ASW patrol aircraft. The "KDX" program, which seems to be on track, will result in ROK construction of about nineteen modern destroyers.[64] This naval hardware does not seem particularly appropriate for resisting a North Korean invasion. It may reflect ROK concern about growing Japanese and/or PRC naval power.

Peking is exerting behind-the-scenes pressure to get the North Koreans to behave themselves internationally, particularly regarding nuclear weapons. In November 1991, the PRC supported, for the first time, the idea of a nuclear-free zone (NFZ) in Korea. Following removal of American nuclear weapons from the ROK, Foreign Minister Ch'ien Ch'i-ch'en (Qian Qichen) stated that nuclear weapons on the Korean Peninsula would not be in China's interest.[65] In April 1994, Ch'ien flatly stated that "China, for its part, insists that the Korean Peninsula should be denuclearized."[66]

With Chinese prodding, the North Koreans agreed to sign a mutual nonaggression pact with the ROK on December 13, 1991, and on December 31 the two Koreas agreed to an NFZ on the peninsula. In April 1992, while PRC President Yang Shang-k'un (Yang Shangkun) was visiting Pyongyang, the DPRK Supreme People's Assembly finally ratified an agreement with the International Atomic Energy Agency (IAEA) to open North Korean nuclear facilities to inspection.[67] Unfortunately, Iraq had demonstrated that a clandestine nuclear weapons program could go undetected by then-existing IAEA inspection procedures.[68]

The North Koreans were surprised at the technical effectiveness of the IAEA inspections. Almost immediately, the IAEA caught them lying about how much and how often they had extracted "experimental" plutonium. Pyongyang repeatedly refused to allow inspectors access to two suspicious sites at its Yongbyon nuclear complex; so the IAEA, for the first time in its history, demanded a "special inspection." Pyongyang refused, denouncing the IAEA as a tool of U.S. espionage.[69] Meanwhile,

---

[64]Robert Karniol, "South Korea Plays a Waiting Game on Unifying with the North," *JDW*, April 30, 1994, 22; ibid., April 4, 1992, 572; ibid., January 4, 1992, 11; and ibid. January 18, 1992, 72.

[65]George D. Moffett and Peter Grier, "Persuading NK Not to Build the Bomb," *CSM*, April 29, 1992, 3; and *Pacific Research*, February 1992, 26.

[66]Quoted by *Yomiuri Shimbun* (Tokyo), April 14, 1994, 3. Also note NCNA, June 9, 1994, in *FBIS-CHI*-94-111 (June 9, 1994): 1.

[67]*FEER*, April 23, 1992, 14.

[68]*Pacific Research*, August 1991, 20.

[69]Pyongyang Radio, August 31, 1993, trans. in *JPRS Report: Proliferation Activities* [*JPRS-TND*]-93-029 (September 17, 1993): 13.

the North-South Korean talks on mutual nuclear inspection quickly broke down. On February 25, 1993, the IAEA demanded access to Yongbyon by March 25. While the ROK and the United States proceeded with the "Team Spirit" 1993 military exercise, Peking quietly tried to persuade the North Koreans to relent. On March 11, however, Pyongyang gave the required thirty-day's notice that it would withdraw from the Nuclear Non-proliferation Treaty (NPT) as of June 12, 1993.[70]

On June 11, 1993, Pyongyang announced "suspension" of its withdrawal, one day before it was to take effect. Pyongyang, in effect, has reserved the right to withdraw from its obligation not to develop nuclear weapons on 24 hours' notice, and now claims "special status" for itself with regard the NPT.[71] IAEA inspections ceased, and the weapons program, in all probability, proceeded.

The stakes are greater than just the possibility of North Korea becoming a nuclear weapons state. Such a development might well prompt both Japan and the ROK to develop nuclear weapons of their own—which the Chinese desperately wish to avert. Moreover, the precedent of a signatory government withdrawing from the NPT could endanger the entire global nuclear nonproliferation effort on the eve of the NPT Review Conference scheduled for 1995. Peking clearly hopes to forestall a North Korean nuclear bomb and to preserve the NPT.

Peking has a great deal at stake, and appears to be sincerely and persistently counseling moderation and compromise from all sides. Until 1994, the PRC publicly opposed even the threat of sanctions against Pyongyang, and carefully preserved its relatively friendly relations with the North Korean government and army.[72] The Chinese believe (correctly) that quiet behind-the-scenes diplomacy will probably fail to halt Pyongyang's efforts to build nuclear weapons; but that confrontation, threat, and sanctions are absolutely certain to fail. Pyongyang is not likely to respond to public pleas or threats from outside.

The Chinese are concerned that North Korea, if driven into a corner, might launch a war, or simply collapse—sending floods of refugees into northeastern China in either case.[73] Moreover, economic sanctions would depend almost entirely upon Chinese enforcement, since mainland China

---

[70]Andrew Mack, "The Nuclear Crisis on the Korean Peninsula," *Asian Survey* 33, no. 4 (April 1993): 339-59.

[71]Kyodo, Tokyo, June 4, 1994, in *FBIS-CHI*-94-108 (June 6, 1994): 8.

[72]On a PLA delegation to Pyongyang meeting with Defense Minister O Chin-u, see Peking Radio, October 3, 1993, trans. in *FBIS-CHI*-93-190 (October 4, 1993): 28.

[73]*Yomiuri Shimbun*, February 3, 1994, 4.

is the source of most of North Korea's oil and almost all of its imported food. It is not at all certain whether Peking *could* enforce an embargo upon enterprising Chinese and Korean smugglers and corrupt Chinese officials.[74] Failure of the blockade would embarrass Peking internationally.

In February 1994, reportedly under PRC pressure, Pyongyang agreed to resumed IAEA inspections. The Chinese also suggested the intriguing possibility that Pyongyang's bomb program is stalled. According to Shih Chin-k'un (Shi Jinkun), a former PLA officer now at the China Institute for International Strategic Studies, the North Koreans approached the Chinese in summer 1993, asking for technical assistance with the trigger for a plutonium bomb, and were turned down cold. According to Shih, Pyongyang refuses to allow inspections precisely because "it will be known they don't have a bomb." That revelation would erase the world's only reason to take North Korea seriously.[75] Such a strategy of ambiguity is entirely plausible; Koreans read Sun Tzu just as carefully as Chinese do.

By late March 1994, Chinese patience with North Korea seems to have been wearing thin. Moreover, the situation provided Peking an opportunity to appear helpful—even indispensable—as the Clinton administration contemplated renewal of the PRC's most-favored-nation (MFN) trading status. PRC leaders were no longer saying they would "oppose" sanctions against Pyongyang, but that they would "not approve" them.[76] In April, the Chinese extracted a promise from the North Koreans not to escalate their confrontation with the IAEA. They reportedly told the North Koreans that the PRC would abstain from (i.e., not veto) a UN sanctions vote if the Koreans refueled their 25-megawatt reactor at Yongbyon without IAEA safeguards. The North Koreans promised to allow IAEA access to the irradiated fuel.[77]

In April 1994, the PRC insisted on downgrading a UN Security Council resolution calling on Pyongyang to comply with IAEA inspections, to a nonbinding "statement." Chinese participation in the Security Council

---

[74]The existence of a smuggling problem was implied by the unusual publicity accorded "regular" Sino-DPRK meetings on border security and railroads in August-September 1993. See *Liao-ning jih-pao* (Liaoning Daily) (Shenyang), September 13 and 17, 1993, trans. in *FBIS-CHI*-93-190 (October 4, 1993): 29.

[75]Peter Copeland (Scripps Howard) in *The Monterey County Herald*, February 25, 1994, 2A.

[76]Li P'eng first used the "will not approve" formulation in a January 1994 meeting with Japan's foreign minister, and again at a news conference on March 22. See *Yomiuri Shimbun*, March 25, 1994, 4. Ch'ien Ch'i-ch'en repeated it in talks with ROK Foreign Minister Han Sung-ju in early June. See AFP, Hong Kong, June 9, 1994, in *FBIS-CHI*-94-111 (June 9, 1994): 1.

[77]This and the following are drawn from Mark Hibbs, "Threat by China Led North Korea to Call on Carter to Mediate," *Nucleonics Week*, June 30, 1994, 8-9.

debate, including its suggestion of compromise language, disappointed Western diplomats, but was more assertive than Peking previously had been on the Korean nuclear issue.[78] As two specific steps in resolving the impasse, the PRC recommended permanent cancellation of "Team Spirit" exercises and resumption of routine IAEA inspections in North Korea.

In mid-May the North Koreans broke their promise to Peking. They hurriedly began refueling the 25-MW reactor, "preventing the IAEA from tagging and/or sampling a selected cross-section of irradiated fuel, in effect preventing the IAEA from verifying the DPRK's fissile inventory declaration." That procedure probably would have clarified whether or not there is a DPRK nuclear weapons program. The Chinese were infuriated that Kim Il-sung had lied to them, and told him they would likely abstain from the sanctions vote which was expected about June 21.[79]

On June 3, Peking intensified pressure on Pyongyang with a six-column article in *Ta Kung Pao*, the leading PRC-controlled newspaper in Hong Kong. It bluntly stated, "If the United Nations decides to impose economic sanctions, China will stop supplying food and oil to North Korea together with border trade involving all other commodity goods."[80] Chinese pressure may well have forced Pyongyang to relent. On June 4, Chu Chang-chun, the North Korean ambassador to Peking, called for renewed talks with the United States.[81]

Through early June, the Chinese offered to take "a bigger role" in resolving the crisis, while continuing to urge restraint. They reiterated their opposition to UN involvement and especially to "sanctions and threats." PRC Vice Foreign Minister T'ang Chia-hsüan (Tang Jiaxuan) told Japanese visitors, "The most important thing is not to force North Korea out of the NPT."[82] Although Chinese diplomats and press criticized the IAEA's June 10 decision to cancel technical assistance to North Korea,[83] the PRC, in fact, abstained from that IAEA vote.[84]

---

[78]Susumu Awanohara and Shim Jae Hoon, "No Compromise," *FEER*, April 14, 1994, 17.

[79]See note 77 above; Kyodo, Tokyo, in English, May 16, 1994, in *FBIS-CHI*-94-095 (May 17, 1994): 1-2; Peter Grier, "N. Korea Crosses a Nuclear Line," *CSM*, June 3, 1994, 1, 4.

[80]"Situation on Korean Peninsula Becomes Tense Again," *Ta Kung Pao* (Hong Kong), June 3, 1994, quoted by Yonhap, Seoul, in English, June 3, 1994, in *FBIS-CHI*-94-107 (June 3, 1994): 7.

[81]Kyodo, Tokyo, June 4, 1994, in *FBIS-CHI*-94-108 (June 6, 1994): 8.

[82]Quoted in Kyodo, Tokyo, June 14, 1994, in *FBIS-CHI*-94-114 (June 14, 1994): 1.

[83]"Imposing Sanctions on DPRK Is Not a Good Method," *Ta Kung Pao*, June 8, 1994, trans. in *FBIS-CHI*-94-111 (June 9, 1994): 11; NCNA, June 9, 1994; and AFP, Hong Kong, June 9, 1994. The latter two are in *FBIS-CHI*-94-111:1.

[84]AFP, Hong Kong, June 16, 1994, in *FBIS-CHI*-94-116 (June 16, 1994): 1.

It was in this context that Kim Il-sung invited former U.S. President Jimmy Carter to visit Pyongyang. On June 18, Kim promised Carter that "as long as the U.S. and the DPRK are engaged in . . . bilateral talks, the DPRK will not load the Yongbyon reactor with fresh uranium fuel, will not operate an adjacent reprocessing plant, and will allow IAEA inspectors continued access to the . . . fuel just removed from the reactor."[85] This defused the situation for the moment. With Kim Il-sung's sudden death in early July, the situation, at this writing, is on hold.

Southeast Asia

General: The PRC, along with the other leading powers, has extricated itself from the situation in Cambodia (Kampuchea), having achieved essentially all its goals there.[86] The major remaining international security issue involving the PRC in Southeast Asia is its rival claim against Taiwan and four Southeast Asian states (Brunei, Malaysia, the Philippines, and Vietnam) to islands in the South China Sea. Many Southeast Asians would add two other security issues: the relationship of the CCP with Southeast Asian Communist parties, and the relationship of both the Peking and Taipei governments with the ethnic Chinese populations of the region.

Overcoming Southeast Asian fear and suspicion continues to be difficult. Nevertheless, PRC trade with the member states of ASEAN has markedly increased since the mid-1980s. In 1992, Malaysian Defense Minister Tun Haji Abdul Razak Najib made an official visit to Peking, which PRC Defense Minister Ch'ih Hao-t'ien (Chi Haotian) reciprocated in May 1993. General Ch'ih assured his hosts that "the 'Chinese threat' preached by Westerners is baseless. China does not want to threat [*sic*] anyone or to fill a 'power vacuum' in the region."[87]

In Peking's view, it is not the PRC, but Japan and the United States, that pose the military and economic threat to Southeast Asia. This is in line with the PRC's policy of identifying itself globally with the economic and political "South." Peking applauds Malaysian Prime Minister Mahathir Mohamad's criticism of "hegemony by democratic powers," and approvingly quotes his attacks on "proponents of democracy [who] are not averse to international dictatorships."[88]

---

[85]See note 77 above.

[86]See Jencks, "China and the Security Environment in Southeast Asia in the 1990s."

[87]NCNA in English, May 25, 1993.

[88]See, for example, Chinese press coverage of Mahathir's address to the UN General Assembly in September 1991.

The PRC's security relationships in the region gradually improved over the past decade, as Peking cooperated with ASEAN and the United States against the Vietnamese occupation of Cambodia. Peking also has cooperated with various Southeast Asian states and with the United States concerning such issues of mutual concern as drug smuggling and the spread of AIDS. With respect to both drugs and AIDS, however, the Peking government has been thwarted to some degree by its own officials and criminal elements, particularly in Yunnan Province, where some local officials, police, and soldiers have been colluding with smugglers.

Burma: Peking's policy toward Burma is ambivalent. On the one hand, Peking is trying to cement a close government-to-government relationship. Peking is likely to veto any UN move to impose sanctions on Burma for its human rights violations.[89] Since 1989, Peking reportedly has sold US$750 million worth of weapons to Burma. On the other hand, the Rangoon regime is heavily involved in drug trafficking. Peking is sincerely concerned about drug smuggling and the spread of AIDS across southern China to Hong Kong, to say nothing of rising corruption among its own officials.[90] It is not clear how or whether some corrupt local authorities in southern China are distorting Peking's intent for their own nefarious purposes. Currently, southern Yunnan may be the most extreme case of a Chinese region beyond central control.

To facilitate arms deliveries and other trade, the Chinese are upgrading the port of Hainggyi on the Bay of Bengal, building roads and bridges into northern Burma, and reportedly have promised more, including a possible hydroelectric power station in Kachin state. Bertil Lintner of the *Far Eastern Economic Review* cites a "conservative" estimate that Sino-Burmese trade is now US$1 billion a year, not counting the drug trade. In return, Peking now wields enormous influence in Rangoon.[91] The Indians reportedly are trying to increase their diplomatic and trade influence to counterbalance the Chinese.[92] The port facilities at Hainggyi probably are not specifically military. There are conflicting reports as to whether or not the Chinese are building an electronic monitoring station on Burma's Great Coco Island.[93] In June 1994, the PRC Foreign Ministry

---

[89]Susumu Awanohara and Irene Wu, "Hard Line, Soft Target," *FEER*, March 31, 1994, 31.

[90]Na Jiahua and Li Yirong, "Plug the Sources and Stop the Flow—Peng Jianfei on Drug Enforcement in Yunnan," Chung-kuo hsin-wen-she, June 24, 1994, trans. in *FBIS-CHI-94-124* (June 28, 1994): 79; and Bertil Lintner, "Plague Without Borders," *FEER*, July 21, 1994, 26.

[91]Bertil Lintner, "Rangoon's Rubicon," *FEER*, February 11, 1993, 28.

[92]"Worried Neighbour," ibid., April 1, 1993, 9.

[93]Hamish McDonald reports there is no evidence of this in "Mutual Benefits," ibid., February

denounced the allegation that China was building "*a naval base* on the islands" as a "sheer fabrication."[94]

The PRC, Vietnam, and Cambodia: The Agreement on a Comprehensive Political Settlement of the Cambodian Conflict, signed in Paris in October 1991, allowed Peking "to claim victory in Indochina, and thus enter into a new era in which it develops cooperative relations with its southern neighbors in the context of both peace in Cambodia and uncontested Chinese regional authority."[95] Peking seems satisfied to have Balkanized Indochina and to have it free from Soviet control. From April 1992 to February 1993, the PRC's first-ever UN peacekeeping force—a 400-man PLA Engineer Battalion—worked on roads in Cambodia.[96]

Recent moves by the Vietnamese to accept PRC hegemony and to reduce their own military burden indicate that Hanoi has decided to meet Chinese intimidation with appeasement rather than defiance. They resumed formal diplomatic relations in November 1991. Sino-Vietnamese border trade (much of it illegal) increased from US$2.7 million in 1988 to US$20 million in the first half of 1992.[97] PLA units have reportedly cleared over 60,000 land mines from the Vietnamese border since mid-1993; the remainder are scheduled for removal this year.[98] Even the two armies have resumed formal relations.[99]

Peking seems interested in extracting concessions from Hanoi on their outstanding border disputes, as well as their conflicting claims for islands in the South China Sea. The Vietnamese make little secret of their uneasiness with their giant neighbor,[100] but have little choice since their erstwhile Russian protectors are all but gone.

Peking also may be trying to encourage Vietnamese dependence on mainland China's economically dynamic southeast. Hanoi appears to be concerned about this possibility, and has been opening up to trade from

---

3, 1994, 14. Robert Karniol reports the opposite in "Chinese Puzzle over Burma's SIGINT Base," *JDW*, January 29, 1994, 14.

[94]NCNA, June 30, 1994, in *FBIS-CHI*-94-126 (June 30, 1994): 1. Emphasis added.

[95]This and the following are from Robert S. Ross, "China and the Cambodian Peace Process," *Asian Survey* 31, no. 12 (December 1991): 1185.

[96]*Hsien-tai chün-shih* (Conmilit) (Hong Kong), no. 191 (December 1992): 97; NCNA, March 8, 1993, in *FBIS-CHI*-93-044 (March 9, 1993): 23; and "China 'UN' in Cambodia," *Chieh-fang-chün hua-pao* (Liberation Army Pictorial), May 1993, no. 5:26-28.

[97]This and the following are drawn from James L. Tyson, *CSM*, November 13, 1991, 3; and Ann Scott Tyson, ibid., November 5, 1991, 3.

[98]"Chinese Clear Mines," *JDW*, March 19, 1994, 8.

[99]NCNA, June 28 and 29, 1994, in *FBIS-CHI*-94-126 (June 30, 1994): 17 and 13, respectively.

[100]Sheila Tefft, "Chinese, Vietnamese Ease Tensions Along Border," *CSM*, January 31, 1992, 6.

all over Asia, partly to prevent any one trading partner from gaining too much economic or political influence. This is an important reason why the Socialist Republic of Vietnam (SRV) is trying to achieve full diplomatic and economic ties with the United States. Conversely, Peking quietly opposes U.S. recognition or ASEAN membership for Vietnam. It is hardly surprising that the strongest advocates of ASEAN membership for Hanoi are Malaysia and Indonesia—the most consistently anti-Chinese members of ASEAN.

The South China Sea dispute: The PRC claims the Paracel (Hsisha) Islands, which are also claimed by Vietnam; and the Spratly (Nansha, Truong Sa, Kalayaan) Group, which also is claimed wholly or in part by Vietnam, Taiwan, Malaysia, the Philippines, and Brunei.

Oil is much on the minds of most claimants. Some authorities expect the PRC to become a net importer of oil by A.D. 2000.[101] The Philippines and Vietnam have both been almost totally dependent on imports until quite recently, when they began modest offshore production. Taiwan remains almost completely dependent on imported energy.[102] In 1992, *Chung-kuo ch'ing-nien pao* (Chinese Youth News) claimed that the South China Sea "holds [oil] reserves worth US$1 trillion." It further asserted that once the oil fields of Sinkiang had been fully developed, the South China Sea would be the only remaining source of petroleum for China.[103] However, David Findley, an oil expert at the East-West Center, contends that a military grab for "one potentially minor oil field" in the Spratlys does not make economic sense.[104]

The PLA, specifically the Navy, is particularly aggressive in asserting Chinese sovereignty in the South China Sea. PLA Navy institutional interests in bigger budgets and force modernization are well served by the argument that the Sea and its islands are future sources of lebensraum (*sheng-ts'un k'ung-chien*, literally "survival space") and "vital resources" for China. As early as August 1984, then-PLA Navy Commander Liu Hua-ch'ing (Liu Huaqing) emphasized the Navy's mission to assert PRC sovereignty over the "vast resources" of the South China Sea.[105] Today, PLA Navy influence is at an all-time high. Liu is now the PRC's senior uniformed military man. Moreover, for the first time ever, there are two

---

[101]Larry Chuen-how Chow, "The Changing Role of Oil in Chinese Exports, 1974-89," *China Quarterly*, no. 131 (September 1992): 751.

[102]"Treacherous Shoals," *FEER*, August 13, 1992, 15.

[103]*Chung-kuo ch'ing-nien pao*, n.d., quoted in "Treacherous Shoals," 15-16.

[104]Ibid., 16.

[105]John W. Garver, "China's Push Through the South China Sea: The Interaction of Bureaucratic and National Interests," *China Quarterly*, no. 132 (December 1992): 1022-23.

deputy chiefs of the PLA General Staff who are career naval officers.

The PRC's declared position has long been that these territorial disputes are a problem "left over by history" and that "the problem of sovereignty [should be] pushed aside for a certain period of time."[106] Teng Hsiao-p'ing (Deng Xiaoping) himself has suggested that "countries can start first with joint development in settling territorial disputes. In tackling economic Issues of common interest, it might be easier to find a mutually acceptable solution to such disputes."[107] The PRC already has such an arrangement with Japan over the disputed Tiaoyütai Islands. In July 1990, during a Southeast Asian tour, Premier Li P'eng for the first time extended the same policy to Vietnam. Accordingly, the November 1991 Sino-Vietnamese agreement included a provision that the island dispute would be resolved peacefully. During a visit to Peking in November 1993, presidents Le Duc Anh and Chiang Tse-min reportedly agreed verbally to shelve the Spratlys issue.[108]

Peking's fundamental policy in the South China Sea, however, has not changed. The PRC National People's Congress Standing Committee passed a law on territorial waters in February 1992 stipulating PRC sovereignty over the South China Sea islands—and over the sea itself—authorizing the use of force to keep foreign naval and research vessels away. In an April 1992 interview, PLA Navy Deputy Commander Admiral Chang Hsü-san (Zhang Xusan) stated that China has "three million square kilometers of territorial sea" and called for intensified exploitation of its resources. The PRC government "maintains that China possesses sovereignty over the South China Sea [sic], but is ready to cooperate with 'the countries concerned' to jointly exploit petroleum and gas."[109]

In effect, the PRC insists that "the other claimants first recognize its sovereignty before joint development can begin."[110] Nearly every Southeast Asian government protested the 1992 sovereignty legislation; many were alarmed at Admiral Chang's comments. The action seemed at odds with the conciliatory Chinese policy of 1991, when PRC delegates at a conference

---

[106]Ji Guoxing, "Current Security Issues in Southeast Asia," *Asian Survey* 26, no. 9 (September 1986): 981. Also see "China's Indisputable Sovereignty over the Xisha and Nansha Islands," *Beijing Review* 23, no. 7 (February 18, 1980): 15-24.

[107]Quoted by Wang Chunyuan and Wu Ximing, "Deng Xiaoping on Peace and War," *Beijing Review* 32, no. 14 (April 3-9, 1989): 22.

[108]See note 33 above.

[109]Gao Anming, "Navy to Participate in Economic Reform Drive" [An interview with PLA Navy Deputy Commander Zhang Xusan], *China Daily*, April 6, 1992, 4. Also see *FEER*, April 16, 1992, 14.

[110]Mark J. Valencia, "Spratly Solution," *FEER*, March 31, 1994, 30.

in Hong Kong agreed with all parties present that no one should take unilateral action with respect to the islands. Some observers speculated that the Chinese were just trying to reinforce their claims to the area while drawing out the legal and negotiating strategies of others.[111]

The PLA Navy, however, is interpreting the law literally and acting accordingly—implementing its new doctrine of "active offshore defense." This has meant, inter alia, much more aggressive enforcement of maximum PRC Exclusive Economic Zones and territorial claims. In July 1993, a major Canton Military Region maneuver included a large-scale amphibious landing exercise, implicitly threatening the other claimants to the Spratlys as well as Taiwan.[112] As noted above, PLA officers say they are developing a long-range air force and blue-water navy to meet a future threat from Japan. Southeast Asians, however, see these military developments as more relevant to Chinese territorial claims.

As the PLA Navy builds up its bases and logistical staying-power in the area, the military situation steadily worsens for the other claimants. Moreover, the PLA Navy outnumbers the other navies, especially in larger combatants. While most Chinese warships are obsolescent by world standards, Vietnamese vessels are even worse. The Vietnamese could harass, but not seriously oppose, the PLA Navy. The relatively small but modern armed forces of Taiwan, Malaysia, and Brunei might pose more serious opposition. However, they all lack the staying power and logistical capacity needed for extended offshore operations.

The new high-performance PLA airfield on Woody Island (Lin Tao) in the Paracels extends the theoretical reach of Chinese air power far south. From there, SU-27s theoretically could range 1,500 kilometers, covering the entire group.[113] Since Woody Island has only about 1.8 square kilometers, however, it will serve as a forward operating base for units from Hainan, not as a permanent air base. (It is worth mentioning that the PLA's SU-27s are currently in the Nanking [Nanjing] area, and that none has ever flown over the South China Sea.)

Peking's and Taipei's policies and claims in the South China Sea are essentially identical. The largest island in the Spratly Group is Itu Aba Island (Taiping Tao), garrisoned by ROC forces. In June 1992, the ROC Legislative Yuan introduced legislation parallel to the PRC's law

---

[111]"Testing the Waters," ibid., March 12, 1992, 8-9. For a recent detailed explication of PRC policy, see Ji Guoxing, *The Spratlys Disputes and Prospects for Settlement* (Kuala Lumpur: Institute of Strategic and International Studies, 1992), 121.

[112]"China Adopts a New Stance," 21.

[113]"Treacherous Shoals," 16; and *Jane's All the World's Aircraft, 1987-88*, ed. John W. R. Taylor (London: Jane's Publishing Co., 1987).

on territorial waters of the previous February.[114]   On December 3, 1992, an ROC inter-Cabinet committee passed a draft "South China Sea Policy Outline" that claimed "indisputable" Chinese sovereignty over the archipelagoes in the South China Sea since ancient times. It also called for peaceful cooperation among claimants in developing the sea's resources, settling claims, and preserving the environment. The only significant difference from the PRC policy appears to be that there is no specific authorization to use force to protect Chinese sovereignty.[115]

There has been some semiofficial coordination of PRC and ROC negotiating positions vis-à-vis the other claimants. It has even been hinted that in the event of warfare with a non-Chinese claimant, the "two Chinas" might cooperate militarily.[116]   In May 1991, scholars from both PRC and ROC government think-tanks gathered in Hong Kong to share data, legal strategies, etc.[117]

PRC strategy in the South China Sea, at least the strategy of the PLA Navy leaders who are making the moves, may be understood in terms of the East Asian board game called *go* in Japanese and *wei-ch'i* in Chinese. In *wei-ch'i*, it is not necessary to occupy all the spaces to control the board. Rather, the object is to establish an unassailable position while reducing one's opponent to a helpless one. This is done by placing counters on empty points, not by attacking the opponent's counters directly. That essentially describes what the PRC has been doing in the Spratlys since 1988.

Until now, actual PRC attacks in the Spratlys have been entirely at the expense of Vietnam. Some PLA leaders believe "other claimants are unlikely, on the basis of past form, to react strongly against occasional displays of Chinese firepower."[118]   An important reason is that the SRV is still, to some degree, an international pariah. Hanoi, however, is breaking its isolation. Vietnam's admission into ASEAN would curtail PRC aggressiveness. Equally important, American recognition of the SRV would help stabilize the area by inhibiting the PRC's creeping conquest of the Spratlys.

Thailand and Singapore still see the PRC as a useful counterweight to "residual Vietnamese hegemonic ambitions" in Indochina. On the other hand, if the SRV does join ASEAN, its regionalist and strongly anti-Chinese

---

[114]*JDW*, June 13, 1992, 1022.

[115]Tammy C. Peng, "ROC Sovereign over Spratlys," *Free China Journal*, December 8, 1992, 1.

[116]*FEER*, May 5, 1988, 26.

[117]The Hong Kong conference, entitled "Asia-Pacific Maritime Economic Cooperation: Conditions and Prospects of the South China Sea," was organized by Lingnan College's Asia-Pacific Research Center.

[118]"Treacherous Shoals," 15.

orientation will reinforce the similar orientations of Malaysia and Indonesia.[119] The PRC hopes to prevent ASEAN from becoming an anti-
Chinese bloc. It is doing what it can to drive wedges between ASEAN
and Vietnam, and to convince Southeast Asian governments that the
potential "hegemonists" they have to fear are the United States and,
especially, Japan.

The PRC will probably continue to push in the South China Sea.
However, the Chinese do not want to endanger their trade or political
relations with ASEAN or the United States. They will continue the pattern
they have established—taking another unoccupied island or two as frequently
as they dare, then speaking softly while ASEAN and the United States
cool off, before the PLA Navy takes another "bite."[120]

The latest series of Chinese moves began with the May 1992 announcement of a PRC contract with the Crestone Energy Corporation of
the United States to explore for oil in a block contiguous to an offshore
Vietnamese oil field. The president of Crestone publicly claimed that the
PLA Navy would protect his operation. In July 1992, the PLA Navy
landed troops on a reef claimed by the SRV and set up a "sovereignty
post." Also in July, at the ASEAN Foreign Ministers' meeting in Manila,
Ch'ien Ch'i-ch'en repeated the offer of "shelving the sovereignty issue"[121]
but disregarded SRV Foreign Minister Nguyen Man Cam's urging to cancel
the Crestone contract.

Peking sent four representatives to Jogjakarta, Indonesia, from June
29 to July 3, 1992, for a workshop on managing conflict in the South
China Sea. The day after the workshop, PLA Navy forces landed on
another reef. An influential Malaysian scholar, E. A. Humzah, editorialized
in the *Far Eastern Economic Review* that it is "hard to believe that China's
actions . . . are not coordinated." Humzah wrote that Chinese actions
were only providing the Japanese with an excuse to rearm. He called on
Peking to base its relationships with Southeast Asia on "predictability,
goodwill, and reciprocity." Otherwise, he threatened "the possibility of
a reversion by some countries to a two-China policy which may have the
effect of embarrassing China by embracing Taiwan."[122]

Professor Chi Kuo-hsing (Ji Guoxing) of the Shanghai Institute for

---

[119]Sheldon W. Simon, *The Regionalization of Defense in Southeast Asia*, National Bureau
of Asian Research, Analysis Series 3, no. 1 (1992): 7.

[120]Tai Ming Cheung, "Fangs of the Dragon," *FEER*, August 13, 1992, 19.

[121]"Treacherous Shoals," 15.

[122]E. A. Humzah, "China's Strategy," *FEER*, August 13, 1992, 22. Humzah was then
assistant director-general of the Institute of Strategic and International Studies (Malaysia),
and is now director of the Malaysian Institute of Maritime Affairs.

International Studies has a different explanation for the PLA landings on July 4, 1992, which is as credible as Humzah's—and even more disturbing in its implications.[123] According to Chi, the PLA action—Humzah's doubts notwithstanding—really was a "failure of coordination." The PLA had not been informed about Peking's diplomatic initiative in Jogjakarta. Chi denies that the PLA Navy is consciously pursuing its own aggressive policy in opposition to the Foreign Ministry's. Rather, in the absence of co-ordinated guidance from Peking, the Navy is literally and assertively in-terpreting the official policy that the islands are sovereign Chinese territory. Chi's explanation is entirely plausible, in light of other recent events. Lack of coordination probably will continue to contribute an element of un-predictability to PRC foreign affairs, just as it does on China's domestic scene. Humzah's call for PRC "predictability" is entirely reasonable, and exactly to the point.

There is another, more generalized, sort of "unpredictability." In 1993-94, PLA Navy and PAP vessels have been firing on foreign vessels, or even stopping them, in PRC waters, the high seas, or even in Taiwan and Hong Kong waters, confiscating their cargoes, and essentially holding their crews for ransom ("bail").[124] While some of these incidents are part of a Peking-directed campaign to intimidate Vietnamese and Hong Kong authorities, some are plain piracy. In either case, it does nothing to build confidence in Hong Kong's future, or to reassure China's neighbors.

The July 1992 ASEAN Foreign Ministers' meeting in Manila gave the South China Sea Islands issue "top priority," and, "with uncharacteristic frankness," called for a continued American military presence in the region. Without naming the PRC, the ASEAN declaration emphasized the need to resolve sovereignty and jurisdictional issues "by peaceful means, without resort to force." Vietnam announced its full support of the declaration, as did Japan and the Western "dialogue partners."[125]

Peking expressed its support only for the declaration's principles. In an earlier statement, however, the PRC warned against "outside powers' involvement in the South China Sea"—apparently referring to the United States and Japan. Peking's negotiating strategy emphasizes regional con-fidence building measures and functional cooperation on specific issues like environmental protection, aid to navigation, and suppression of illegal immigration and piracy. This is in keeping with Peking's oft-repeated policy

---

[123] Ji Guoxing, Seminar at the Naval Postgraduate School and private discussions, Monterey, California, April 7, 1993.

[124] *South China Morning Post* (Hong Kong), June 28, 1993, 1.

[125] "Treacherous Shoals," 17.

of "setting aside for the time being" the knotty issue of sovereignty.[126]

The Indian Subcontinent

Since the 1960s, Peking has had a simmering, sometimes violent, border dispute with India and a close military alignment with Pakistan. In 1991, the PRC and India agreed to settle incidents and disputes peacefully. Moreover, the Indians seem to have obliged the Chinese by restricting the activities of the Tibetan government in exile.[127] In September 1993, the PRC and India signed a memorandum of understanding aimed at reducing troop levels and tension along the "line of actual control." In view of the political weakness of the Indian government and the emotional nature of the border issue, this is the nearest thing we are soon likely to see to a final boundary settlement. Troop reduction talks in early 1994 have been inconclusive, but reporting in both the Indian and PRC presses has been remarkably upbeat.[128]

Peking's relations with Pakistan are stronger than ever. In 1990, the U.S. Congress cut off US$573 million in military aid to Pakistan because of its nuclear weapons program, pushing Islamabad still closer to Peking. The PRC continues to value Pakistan as its window to the Moslem world. The PRC has been a leading source of weapons to Pakistan for three decades. In July 1991, the PRC Embassy in Washington confirmed that Peking had provided Pakistan with "very small quantities" of M-11 surface-to-surface missiles.[129] In April 1994, former Army Commander Gen. Mirza Aslam Beg published a list of Pakistani nuclear delivery systems, which included "M11s which we are now getting from China."[130]

The PRC is a major factor in the nuclear situation in the subcontinent; Pakistani nuclear weapons are intended to deter Indian nuclear weapons that originally were intended to deter the PRC. Moreover, Peking is widely suspected of assisting the Pakistani nuclear program.[131] In February 1992, Foreign Secretary Shahryar Khan admitted, in a *Washington Post* interview, that Pakistan has "elements which, if put together, would become

---

[126]Ji Guoxing, *Maritime Security Mechanisms for the Asian-Pacific Region* (Center for International Security and Arms Control, Stanford University, February 1994).

[127]James L. Tyson, "China Seeks a Buffer in a Friendly India," *CSM*, December 13, 1991, 7.

[128]*ISI Diplomatic Information Service*, April 25, 1994; NCNA, April 28, 1994; and AFP, April 25, 1994—all reported in *FBIS Trends*, May 4, 1994, 16-17. Also see "Border Talks Concluded," *JDW*, February 26, 1994, 14, and "China Adopts a New Stance," 19.

[129]Wei Guoqiang, "Chinese Embassy in the United States Refutes Lies Spread by a U.S. Newspaper," NCNA, July 15, 1991, in *FBIS-CHI*-91-136 (July 16, 1991): 7-8.

[130]Ahmed Rashid, "Bare All and Be Damned," *FEER*, May 5, 1994, 23.

[131]*Pacific Research*, August 1991, 21-22.

a [nuclear explosive] device."[132]

Peking is clearly interested in maintaining peace between India and Pakistan. India may not feel a direct threat from the PRC, but quite reasonably regards PRC military assistance to Pakistan as threatening. This three-way relationship has existed for decades, however, and seems less tense than in the past. Since late 1991, Peking has joined with the United States, Pakistan, and Russia in calling for a five-nation conference, with a view to creating a South Asian nuclear-free zone. India has long resisted this proposal, but might be somewhat reassured by the PRC's 1992 accession to the NPT and possible Chinese willingness to come to some sort of nuclear nonaggression agreement with India.[133] At this writing, the United States is promoting expanded talks of the five declared nuclear powers, plus India, Pakistan, Japan, and Germany, with the immediate objectives of banning further fissile material production and a global halt to nuclear testing.[134]

Arms Control and Disarmament

In the aftermath of the Gulf War, the United Nations acted with uncharacteristic speed and unanimity to facilitate arms control and nonproliferation activities. One step was establishment, in December 1991, of the United Nations Register of Conventional Armaments. The Chinese representative participated actively in developing the details of the Register. Simultaneously, in early 1992, the PRC joined the other permanent members of the UN Security Council in the Arms Control in Middle East (ACME, or "Perm 5") talks. These talks broke down by mid-May 1992. In both the ACME talks and the Arms Register negotiations, the Chinese successfully maneuvered to prevent SAMs from being distinguished from the general category of "missiles." That rendered the Register's missile accounting meaningless, and concealed significant Chinese transactions. On the other hand, they tried unsuccessfully to include electronic warfare and reconnaissance items in the Register.[135]

The PRC was one of seventy-nine governments submitting reports for 1992, the first full year of the Conventional Arms Register. Their

---

[132]"Pakistan 'Able to Build Bomb'," *JDW*, February 15, 1992, 213.

[133]*Pacific Research*, August 1991, 20. For an excellent discussion of India-China-Soviet relations, see John W. Garver, "The Indian Factor in Recent Sino-Soviet Relations," *China Quarterly*, no. 125 (March 1991): 55-85.

[134]Hamish McDonald and Ahmed Rashid, "Half a Deal," *FEER*, April 21, 1994, 22-23.

[135]Private informant close to the UN Conventional Arms Register.

report fully complied with requirements, though it was no more detailed than required. Significantly, Peking reported exporting 106 large-caliber artillery pieces to Iran, a transaction which no foreign agency had publicly noted.[136]

In the aftermath of "Desert Storm," the number of states adhering to the Missile Technology Control Regime (MTCR) nearly doubled. In early 1992, Peking agreed to observe the "parameters and guidelines" of the Regime,[137] though it had been a vocal opponent of the MTCR until then, and had sold missile technology to a number of regimes in the Middle East, including Iran, Iraq, and Pakistan. How scrupulously Peking has observed MTCR restrictions has become a contentious issue.[138]

The Chinese have long made a distinction between international arms control initiatives that apply equally to all states (e.g., the Chemical Warfare Convention [CWC]) and those that are suppliers' cartels of the rich and powerful (e.g., MTCR and NPT).

In September 1992, in retaliation for the American F-16 sale to Taiwan, the PRC withdrew from the ACME talks. They also intimated that they might withdraw, at least temporarily, from the CWC, which they had earlier announced they would sign. (In the event, the PRC did sign as a CWC charter member in January 1993.) Additionally, the New China News Agency (NCNA) announced that an Iranian military team had visited Peking to discuss arms purchases, without saying just *when* the Iranian visit took place. Most disturbing was Peking's threat to reconsider its MTCR compliance in view of the United States' violation of the August 1982 joint communiqué on arms sales to Taiwan.[139]

As the ACME talks got more specific, PRC participation had become increasingly reluctant. By May 1992, they had reached an impasse. The consensus among Western participants was that the Chinese were looking for an excuse to suspend their participation. The F-16 sale provided the excuse. While Peking did announce that it would not be restrained in its

---

[136]Edward J. Laurance and Herbert Wulf, "An Evaluation of the First Year of Reporting to the United Nations Register of Conventional Arms," *Research Report*, Monterey Institute of International Studies Program for Nonproliferation Studies, October 1993.

[137]*Pacific Research*, February 1992, 27; and *FEER*, March 5, 1992, 14.

[138]The PRC has made promises about restricting missile exports before, and then evaded them by such subterfuges as capricious definitions of missile categories. See Timothy V. McCarthy, *A Chronology of PRC Missile Trade and Developments*, International Missile Proliferation Project, Monterey Institute of International Studies, Monterey, California, February 1992.

[139]David Silverberg, "Amid Arms Flurry, Nations Pursue Arms Curbs," *Defense News*, October 5-11, 1992, 4, 5, 44; and Paul Lewis, "Chinese Ire at U.S. Could Prompt More Arms Sales to Iran," ibid., September 14-20, 1992, 19.

arms sales to the Middle East in light of U.S. sales to Taiwan, Peking has neither renounced the MTCR nor said it would disregard MTCR guidelines. There is still little open-source evidence of proscribed PRC sales. Chinese spokesmen have been insistent that Peking is not selling missiles, but evasive when asked about missile technology.

Unofficial PRC spokesmen insist that Peking will continue to adhere to MTCR guidelines. They claim that foreign trade has become so important to mainland China that it cannot afford to let a few billion dollars' worth of arms sales upset overall trade—for example, by causing loss of MFN trading status with the United States. According to this argument, the PRC's days as a major missile proliferator are probably over because of the success of its civilian export economy.[140]

Americans tend to mistrust the Chinese in arms control matters. The F-16 sale heightened Chinese mistrust of the United States, as well. In 1993, the U.S. government accused Peking of violating the MTCR by selling additional M-11 components and technology to Pakistan. The United States claims that the M-11 exceeds MTCR guidelines (that is, is capable of delivering a 500-kilogram warhead over a range of at least 300 kilometers). The Chinese denied that they had violated MTCR, perhaps basing their claim on the M-11 having a range of only 160 kilometers (with an unspecified warhead size). On August 25, 1993, the United States announced sanctions against the Chinese Ministry of Aerospace and a number of other PRC and Pakistani entities, in retaliation for the alleged MTCR violations. The Chinese continue to protest their innocence and to cite the sanctions as a brazen example of the United States' propensity to cast itself as the world's policeman and moral arbiter.[141]

In July 1993, the United States alleged that the ship *Yinhe* had sailed from China with chemical weapon "precursor chemicals" for Iran. The PRC denied this and, after an extended period at sea and much recrimination in the international press, allowed Saudi Arabian inspectors and

---

[140] Jin Gan (Foreign Affairs Subcommittee of the National Committee of the Chinese People's Political Consultative Conference) interview at the Monterey Institute of International Studies, November 1993; and Hua Di, "China's Arms Proliferation in Perspective: Prospects for Change Due to Economic Reforms," in *The Proliferation of Advanced Weaponry: Technology, Motivations, and Responses*, ed. W. Thomas Wander and Eric H. Arnett (American Association for the Advancement of Science, 1992), 123-34.

[141] Editorial, "China Refutes U.S. Decision on Sanctions," *Ta Kung Pao*, August 27, 1993, 2, trans. in *FBIS-CHI-93-165* (August 27, 1993): 2-4; Peking Radio, August 27, 1993, trans. in *FBIS-CHI-93-165*:4-5; NCNA, Washington, August 26, 1993, in *FBIS-CHI-93-165*:1; NCNA, Peking, August 27, 1993, in *FBIS-CHI-93-165*:1-2. For a nonpolemical PRC view, see Chen Yanping, "The Need for a Greater Chinese Role in Missile Nonproliferation Issues," *The Nonproliferation Review*, Spring-Summer 1994, 66-70.

American technical advisors aboard in a Saudi port on August 26. No illegal chemicals were found. The PRC has made much of the incident, as another example of American heavy-handed self-righteousness, and as an example of how the United States bases its interference in other countries upon faulty intelligence.[142]

PRC authorities are becoming more sensitive to proliferation issues, and at least want to appear to be acting responsibly. However, they are as susceptible to the "If we don't sell it, someone else will" syndrome as other arms dealers. The PRC government is particularly sensitive to issues of sovereignty and equality, and has long accused the West (particularly the United States) of having a double standard in international affairs. American harping about nonproliferation while selling F-16s to Taiwan strikes Peking as a blatant example of that double standard.

Four times since May 1992, the PRC has broken an informal international moratorium on nuclear test explosions. Although this is not a violation of the NPT, to which Peking acceded in April 1992, testing has caused Peking considerable international opprobrium, notably in the United Nations, and complicated its relationships with the Central Asian states.[143] In a September 1993 speech to the UN General Assembly, Foreign Minister Ch'ien Ch'i-ch'en emphasized that Peking strongly favors nonproliferation agreements and a Comprehensive Test Ban Treaty (CTBT). He pointed out that Peking has "exercised great restraint in nuclear testing," conducting far fewer tests than any other nuclear power. Nevertheless, other Chinese spokesmen have made it clear that as long as there is no CTBT, the PRC intends to continue testing until approximately 1996. By then, they have implied, they will have done enough testing to participate in a CTBT. To help deflect some of the criticism, the Chinese are countering with the demand that the other nuclear powers follow Peking's example by unilaterally pledging not to be the first to use nuclear weapons nor to use or threaten to use them against any nonnuclear state or in any nuclear-weapons-free zone.[144]

Conclusion

Economic development and internal security are the considerations

---

[142]Liu Yegang, "The Whole Story of the *Yinhe* Incident," NCNA Domestic Service, September 5, 1993, trans. in *JPRS-TND*-93-029 (September 17, 1993): 3-6. The official PRC Foreign Ministry communiqué on the incident is NCNA in English, September 4, 1993, in *JPRS-TND*-93-029:6-8.

[143]The PRC government statement on its nuclear test is in NCNA Domestic Service, October 5, 1993, in *FBIS-CHI*-93-191 (October 5, 1993): 17.

[144]Ibid.; and Ch'ien Ch'i-ch'en's UN Speech, 3.

that dominate the PRC's foreign, security, and military policies. Beyond these immediate concerns, the Chinese are determined to achieve the international status and influence of a "great power." To achieve that, they are building "great power" armed forces.

PRC leaders are not consciously aggressive, but their actions often seem that way to their neighbors. Much of this behavior stems from fundamental assumptions about China's special status in Asia. PRC leaders assume, for example, that the South China Sea islands really are "indisputably Chinese." They regard the other claimants simply as unreasonable, and tend to treat them like selfish children who patiently must be taught the error of their ways. It is an open question whether the PRC would ever be willing to compromise its maximum claims in order to get a comprehensive settlement.

Peking sincerely wants to be friendly and cooperative in the EAP, just as the United States sincerely wants to be friendly and cooperative in Latin America. The Chinese assume that they should be the dominant regional power, and that other powers, including the United States, should recognize and defer to their regional interests. More than the Americans (who are, after all, outsiders) they resent and fear the Japanese, the only strong rival for regional hegemony.

At the logical extreme of the PRC's hegemonist aspiration is a willingness to intervene militarily if a neighbor's behavior goes "out of bounds," or if it gets too close to an outside power. In 1978-79, Peking denounced Vietnam as the "Cuba of the East," and has treated Hanoi much as Washington has treated Havana. The April 1994 Treaty of Friendship and Cooperation with Mongolia echoes American agreements in Latin America, and implies a similar readiness to intervene militarily if hegemonic interests are challenged.

Naturally, the Chinese deny all this, just as the Soviet Union denied exercising hegemony in Eastern Europe and Mongolia, just as postwar Americans have denied it in Latin America.

Part V

Mainland China's Foreign Policy and Foreign Relations

12

Mainland China in a Changing Asia-Pacific Regional Order

Samuel S. Kim

The People's Republic of China's (PRC's) international conduct in a rapidly changing world poses a puzzle. The progressive removal of the Soviet threat from mainland China's expansive regional security parameters from Southeast Asia, through South Asia and Central Asia, to Northeast Asia, has brought perhaps the deepest international peace that China has ever experienced this century. What is remarkable about Sino-Russian relations in the wake of the collapse of the Soviet Union is not that there has been a roller coaster of so many abrupt shifts and U-turns, but that the relationship has survived the domestic upheavals in both countries becoming at least over the short-to-medium term a mutually profitable "partnership" of sorts with neither side viewing the other as a security threat. And yet Peking (Beijing) today acts as if it were faced with the greatest external security challenge busily beefing up its military power projection capabilities with the real military spending increasing at double-digit rates even as global military spending began to fall sharply since 1992.[1]

What accounts for the paradox of the PRC's post-Cold War international relations? Part of the answer—or part of the problem—has to

---

[1] In his political report to the Chinese Communist Party's (CCP's) Fourteenth National Congress, Chiang Tse-min offers such an upbeat assessment of the external security environment as having "never been more satisfactory since the founding of the Republic" coupled with a rationale for strengthening the military. See the full text of the report in Foreign Broadcast Information Service (FBIS), *Daily Report: China* [hereinafter cited as *FBIS-CHI*]-92-204 (October 21, 1992): 1-21, esp. at 15-16 [hereinafter cited as Chiang's Political Report]. See also Chen Qimao, "New Approaches in China's Foreign Policy: The Post-Cold War Era," *Asian Survey* 33, no. 3 (March 1993): 237-51, esp. at 239, and Stockholm International Peace Research Institute (SIPRI), *SIPRI Yearbook 1993: World Armaments and Disarmament* (New York: Oxford University Press, 1993), 10.

do with the profound structural uncertainties in the transition from the Cold War to a post-Cold War world order. Part of the problem has also to do with the wrenching national identity difficulties that practically all major powers confront in trying to adjust to a rapidly changing world order. The post-Cold War world seems increasingly like a turbulent multi-centric one faltering at a crossroads where contradictory forces—globalism, regionalism, unilateralism, and ethnonationalism—are vying for primacy. History has not ended, as Francis Fukuyama would have us believe,[2] it has been accelerating, even overheating. Of course, at a time of such a rapid and unpredictable change, it is easy to succumb to the fallacy of premature optimism and pessimism on the changing relationship between the future of China(s) and the future of the Asia-Pacific regional and world orders.

To fully comprehend and explain how Peking is coping with the multiple challenges of post-Cold War and post-Soviet world, we need to erase the boundary between domestic and external as deeply encoded in the classical realist tradition of international relations. Domestic and foreign policies—and policy consequences—are so thoroughly intermeshed as to constitute mutually interdependent and interpenetrable domains of a single political chessboard that encompasses state and nonstate actors engaged in competition for loyalties and resources. The fusion of domestic and foreign policy came most dramatically to the fore during and after June 4, 1989. To improve on the Maoist saying, Peking's foreign policy may be said to be walking or dancing on three legs—domestic, external, and inter-China—all in the pursuit of three central foreign policy objectives: modernization, reunification, and anti-hegemonism.[3]

With the clarity and simplicity of East-West conflict gone the foreign policies of most states, including the United States, Russia, Japan, and South Korea, have increasingly become mired in and symptomatic of domestic politics. The demise of East-West conflict makes it easier for external factors to influence a state's domestic politics even as domestic special interest groups intervene more aggressively in the shaping of state foreign policy. The 1920s slogan—"Business of America is Business"—seemed to have become the lodestar of post-Cold War U.S. foreign policy as domestic politics is and becomes foreign policy. The post-Cold War

---

[2]See Francis Fukuyama, "The End of History?" *National Interest*, no. 16 (Summer 1989): 3-18, and *The End of History and the Last Man* (New York: Free Press, 1992).

[3]Notice, for example, the interdependence of domestic and external factors in environmental protection. Since environmental pollution does not respect state sovereignty, what Peking does, or does not do, regarding its own environment will surely affect the regional and global ecosystems—and the PRC's foreign relations.

era is an age of mercantile diplomacy, we are told at least in the United States, and that the new game of international relations is profit-driven geo-Monopoly. The irony here is that the Leninist notion—as expounded in *Imperialism: The Highest Stage of Capitalism*—that the main motive force driving U.S. foreign policy are monopoly capitalists in the global search for ever-higher profits abroad is becoming increasingly credible with substantial help from Chinese "market Leninism." President Clinton's decision to delink principles (human rights) from profits (trade) may well end the cacophonous (Stravinsky-like) annual "Rite of Spring" in American domestic politics, but it also signals the extent to which America's China policy has been domesticated and marketized.[4] Peking's foreign policy is no exception to this post-Cold War phenomenon of profit-driven mercantilist international relations.[5] The flip side of domestic/external fusion is the ease with which Peking can intervene in American domestic politics in a lavish lobbying effort for the most-favored-nation (MFN) renewal[6]— and alas, without anybody complaining about Chinese violation of American state sovereignty!

One thing seems obvious in the particular case of post-Tienanmen (Tiananmen) China. An inordinate demand is placed on diplomacy to seek China-specific exemption and China-specific entitlement as a way of shoring up sagging domestic legitimation. A dramatic—and disastrous— example of the quest for international legitimation is the extraordinary politicization of Peking's much-publicized bid in 1992-93 to host the summer Olympics in the year 2000. The PRC's top leaders decided at a July 1, 1992 meeting in Chungnanhai that "2000—Beijing" should be promoted as "the cornerstone of an overall strategy" for establishing China's place in the world.[7] For the study of Chinese foreign policy, this means that

---

[4]If more evidence of Clinton's mercantile diplomacy is needed, one should read Anthony Lake's single major foreign policy speech, in which he used the word "market" forty-two times! I owe to Richard Falk who has brought this point to my attention.

[5]As Peking's Foreign Minister Ch'ien Ch'i-ch'en would put, foreign policy "is the extension of China's domestic policies." Likewise, a leading Chinese international relations scholar argues that the blurring of domestic and external decision is one of the defining features of international relations in the post-Cold War era. See "Qian Qichen on the World Situation," *Beijing Review* 33, no. 3 (January 15-21, 1990): 16, and Sung I-min, "The West's Second Thoughts on the Post-Cold War World and Some New Characteristics of the Current International Situation," *Kuo-chi wen-t'i yen-chiu* (International Studies) (Peking), July 1993, no. 3:1-8, esp. at 1.

[6]See Ann Scott Tyson, "China Uses U.S. Firms to Lobby," *Christian Science Monitor*, May 9, 1994, 4.

[7]See Lucian W. Pye, "China's Self-Image as Projected in World Affairs," in *Sino-American Relations at a Time of Change*, ed. Gerrit W. Gong and Bih-jaw Lin (Washington, D.C.: The Center for Strategic and International Studies, 1994), 169-70.

we have to pay greater attention to the question of what really constitutes a strong or weak state in the post-Cold War era as well as to the question of how Chinese leaders' domestic politics and self-image shape Peking's definition of and response to the changing international situation.

There is also a need to reconceptualize Chinese foreign policy as a multidimensional and multilayered structure (iceberg) adrift in the sea of turbulent domestic and world politics with the most visible and flexible levels at the top and the most invisible and invariant ones at the base. Thanks to the post-Mao turn outward, during the past fifteen years mainland China has, in quite unprecedented fashion, opened itself to almost every actor and every issue area of world politics. Notice the extent to which Peking had to expend its precious diplomatic capital and global time in its human rights diplomacy in recent years. Today what we see from one level of analysis or in one issue area is no longer, if it ever was, what we get in Chinese foreign policy.

Global Bipolarity Versus Regional Multipolarity

The PRC's Asian regionalism has remained deeply ambivalent. Although most of the country's external relations pivot around the Asia-Pacific region, Peking seldom articulated any coherent definition of its place in Asian international relations. During the long Cold War years, none of China's multiple identities and role playing had much to do with Asian regionalism, bespeaking of a vast gap between being and becoming in China's international status drive. The antinomy between regional status that comes with the territory and global aspirations beyond actual reach has introduced a fundamental paradox in the prioritization of China's multiple national identities and role conceptions. The PRC's quest for an appropriate niche in a changing international order can be seen as an ongoing struggle to enhance physical and psychological well-being, in the course of which the Self attempts to secure an identity as a global power that others do not bestow, while others attempt to bestow an identity as a regional power that the Self does not appropriate.

The difficulty of accurately assessing the PRC's emerging role in the Asia-Pacific region is greatly compounded by the fact that the perception of what constitutes "power" has changed significantly in the wake of the demise of the socialist superpower and the multipolarizing process in East Asia. Even the North-South or Center-Periphery divide is more blurred in East Asia than in any other region of the world. As a result, the geopolitical and geoeconomic realities of the region are now amenable to contending interpretations, even as a maverick group of international relations scholars is finally shifting its attention toward East Asia. For Aaron Friedberg, the dominant trend in world politics is toward regionalization rather than globalization, toward fragmentation and "multi-multipolarity" rather than global interdependence and integration, whereas for Richard Betts global unipolarity now coexists with regional multipolarity as "the worldwide structure of power no longer governs the regional structure of power, as it did in the Cold War." According to James Rosenau, the post-World War II structural transformation of world politics has come about through the replacement of the state system with a dual system in which a new multicentric world competes with the old state-centric world. Rosenau rejects the term "nonstate actor," as it "creates a residual category for all collectivities other than states, implying that they occupy subordinate statuses in the ranks of postinternational politics."[8]

Of particular concern and threat to mainland China today as a multinational state is that local and regional ethnonational conflicts, previously overshadowed and repressed by the global superpower contention, are breaking out in many parts of the world. Very few of the eighty-two armed conflicts in the four-year period 1989-92 were classic interstate conflicts befitting the traditional definition of "war." The overwhelming majority of armed conflicts are "internal conflicts" and "state-formation conflicts."[9] Wars of national identity mobilization have emerged as the primary species of regional conflict in the post-Cold War setting.

Since 1983 multipolarity (to-chi-hua) entered the Chinese definitions of the international situation. There still remained more confusion than consistency in Chinese assessments of the multipolarizing (power diffusion) process because of disagreement about the implications for mainland China in a rapidly changing world. A multipolarizing world was seen by many Chinese strategic analysts as one bereft of the much-coveted balancing third force—the vaunted China card—in global triangular geopolitics. It was, after all, bipolarity that had served Chinese global politics in the 1970s and 1980s, enabling Peking to exploit superpower rivalry to gain its own strategic leverage, economic and trade benefits, and global weight. The structural reality of what the Chinese call "the Yalta system" is an answer to the puzzle of how a regional power managed to be treated as a

---

[8]Aaron L. Friedberg, "Ripe for Rivalry: Prospects for Peace in a Multipolar Asia," *International Security* 18, no. 3 (Winter 1993-94): 5-33; Richard K. Betts, "Wealth, Power, and Instability: East Asia and the United States After the Cold War," ibid., 41; and James N. Rosenau, *Turbulence in World Politics: A Theory of Change and Continuity* (Princeton, N.J.: Princeton University Press, 1990), 36. For an alternative interpretation, see Samuel S. Kim, "Superpower Cooperation in Northeast Asia," in *The Cold War as Cooperation: Superpower Cooperation in Regional Conflict Management*, ed. Roger E. Kanet and Edward A. Kolodziej (London: Macmillan, 1991), 367-401.

[9]Peter Wallensteen and Karin Axell, "Armed Conflict at the End of the Cold War, 1989-92," *Journal of Peace Research* 30, no. 3 (1993): 331-46.

global power—without first having acquired the reach or the requisite normative and material resources of a global power. As late as early 1990, one publicist insisted that bipolarity, though somewhat weakened, would continue for a long time. Yet only three months later, his assessment of the world structure, influenced by the collapse of the bipolarized system and the demise of the Warsaw Pact, had taken on a more pessimistic tone. A multipolar world of indeterminate form and direction was replacing the bipolar world order.[10] That a multipolar world is moving too fast and too far away from the comfort and safety of the Chinese realpolitik turf is suggested by another reassessment of the emerging world structure:

> The current world presents neither a U.S. unipolar structure, nor one with three poles of the United States, Europe and Japan, nor a joint dominance by the "club of the seven industrialized nations," *nor a multipolar pattern.*
> Although the world is in the transitional period and a new pattern has not yet taken shape, there is a rough structure in international relations, in which one superpower and several powers depend on and struggle against each other.[11]

The habitual and ritualized assault on "power politics" notwithstanding, Peking, in the end, has come to define the changing international situation primarily in realpolitik balance-of-power terms even if the center of gravity shifted from the global arena to the Asia-Pacific region. While the long Cold War helped the PRC project power well beyond the Asia-Pacific region, the allure of the China market has more recently become the new China card in the post-Cold War balance-of-power game in the Asia-Pacific region and beyond. "No major economic power can afford to lose China's big market with its great potential," writes mainland China's leading international relations scholar, "if they wish to gain a strong position in the competition."[12]

The most recent and authoritative Party line that bipolarity is gone for good and that the international system is heading toward multipolarity may well signal an official closure to the cost-benefit debate about polarity versus multipolarity.[13] Increasingly, multipolarity, or more accurately multipolarization as a power diffusion process, is being framed in new

---

[10]Wang Lin, "Looking Toward the 1990s," *Kuo-chi wen-t'i yen-chiu*, January 1990, no. 1:1-4, 9; Wang Lin, "The World Situation in the Process of Profound Change," ibid., April 1990, no. 2:1-3.

[11]Chen Xiaogong, "The World in Transition," *Beijing Review* 35, nos. 5-6 (February 3-16, 1992): 15; emphasis added.

[12]Chen, "New Approaches in China's Foreign Policy," 239.

[13]Chiang's Political Report, 16.

light as giving Peking more leverage opportunities and more behavioral space than could be realistically considered if the predominant definition of the world situation was bipolar:

> *Multipolarization in which Peking is a major player offers more genuine freedom to be and act as a Group of One in world politics and more diversification options to counter U.S. hegemony or "peaceful evolution" (*ho-p'ing yen-pien*) than bipolarity in which Peking had more limited alignment options;
>
> *Multipolarization, especially a floating kind, is preferred to both tight bipolar conflict and tight bipolar collusion since as one of those newly emerging poles the PRC by self-definition becomes a key player in global high politics; and
>
> *Multipolarization naturally opens up the new pathway of improving Sino-Russian relations as part of a strategy of diversification, which might also allow Peking to play any residual effects of a Russian card in Sino-U.S. relations, an option more credible now than ever before with the demise of a Soviet/Russian military threat.

The new foreign policy line may be characterized as the "comprehensive national strength" (*tsung-ho kuo-li* or CNS) line. In Peking's view, a multipolarizing world is seen as giving rise to new geopolitical alignments in the Asia-Pacific region and, concomitantly, intensified rivalry for power politics in a new regional setting. The consequence of such a multipolar conception of the international situation has been to accelerate the strategic decision made in 1985 to delink local and regional conflicts from global superpower rivalry. In the wake of the Gulf War the CNS line seems to have received another major military shot in the arms as the military has since been called on to take up a new mission possible and desirable: limited war to achieve a quick, decisive *high-tech military victory* in a matter of days. The broader point is that the CNS interpretation of the world situation comes much closer to a realist-nationalist rather than a Marxist interpretation of uneven development and international conflict formation.

The recent Chinese debate on world order, triggered by what Peking perceived as a clear and present danger of a unipolar/hegemonic world order, draws distinctions between *world* order, on the one hand, and *regional* or *international* orders, on the other. Whereas a world order is basically a set of world regulations—hence a potential threat to state sovereignty—an international order is a more benign notion, embodying certain statist norms needed to facilitate transactions in the absence of a supranational Leviathan. Although theoretically a new world order and new regional orders may develop in tandem, the former is dismissed as a wish list of idealpolitik values, while the latter have become more concrete, realistic, and feasible. In actuality, the major powers are said to have concentrated their efforts on the establishment of new regional orders. At the same time, global debate on the new world order is said to be symptomatic of the emerging neo-Darwinian contest for an all-out struggle for power in which every major state actor jockeys for a favorable position during the process of tumultuous change. Indeed, the most basic characteristic of post-Tienanmen Chinese foreign relations is the supremacy of state sovereignty: *no state sovereignty, no world order nor regional order.*[14]

From a post-Tienanmen perspective, the collapse of the Soviet Union and the prospects of U.S. military disengagement in East Asia represent a newer *danger* in the form of the rise of an unbridled Japan as an assertive regional and global power seeking to transform its enormous economic power into military and political power, as well as an *opportunity* for Peking to prevent this from happening by preemptively filling the power vacuum. Once again, Peking has demonstrated a remarkable capacity to redefine the international situation in a self-serving realpolitik terms. The world military pattern is said to be shifting from global military threats to regional military threats, giving rise to "strategic no-man's-lands of various sizes in certain regions."[15]

Apparently, the rise of power vacuums is not a danger to be avoided or managed through regional or global conflict-management mechanisms but an opportunity to be unilaterally exploited. As if to legitimize Peking's gunboat diplomacy in the South China Sea, it is claimed that all countries have taken the capabilities of coping with regional conflicts as the major objective of military modernization. The 1985 strategic decision requiring the People's Liberation Army (PLA) to redirect its military thinking and policy from the preparation for general war to the preparation for more probable local and regional wars around mainland China's expansive regional security zone has now become a more credible and feasible tableau. Peking today regards the disputed but oil-rich Paracel and Spratly islands in the South China Sea in terms all too reminiscent of the Third Reich's lebensraum imperial policy.[16]

---

[14]For extended analysis, see Samuel S. Kim, *China In and Out of the Changing World Order* (Princeton, N.J.: Center of International Studies, Princeton University, 1991).

[15]For a comprehensive Chinese description and analysis of the changing global military order, see five-part articles by Li Ch'in-kung in *Chieh-fang-chün pao* (Liberation Army Daily) and translated in *FBIS-CHI*-92-095 (May 15, 1992): 20-22; 92-103 (May 28, 1992): 30-32; 92-118 (June 18, 1992): 26-27; 92-142 (July 23, 1992): 32-34; and 92-153 (August 7, 1992): 20-22; quote at 92-095 (May 15, 1992): 20.

[16]A recent internal Chinese document states that these island groups, some of them situated

Although one cold war has ended, we are told, two new cold wars have already started—the confrontations among the imperialist powers of Japan, the United States, and Western Europe and the confrontations among imperialist states, Third World countries, and socialist countries that survived the fall of Soviet Communism. The central challenge of post-Cold War Chinese foreign policy is said to be three-fold: "We must especially take advantage of confrontations among Western nations, strengthen ourselves, and consolidate the neighboring region by giving priority to our maneuvers in Asia and the Pacific region."[17] At the same time, the military "should enhance combat strength in an all-around way; should more successfully shoulder the lofty mission of defending the country's territorial sovereignty over the land and in the air, as well as its rights and interests on the sea; and should safeguard the unification and security of the motherland."[18]

Regional Fend-Mending or Fence-Straddling?

Having lost the vaunted China card in the strategic triangle to magnify its leverage in world politics, Peking has been active in mending fences with its regional neighbors. It may be recalled that all the turning points in Peking's foreign policy during the Cold War, though instantly reverberating throughout the entire region, concerned primarily the United States and/or the Soviet Union. Consider, for instance, how Peking justified its war against Vietnam in 1979 in terms of *global* security imperatives—alas, even as Peking's surrogate function of UN peacekeeping—not as a matter of *bilateral* or even *regional* conflict. The quest for a proper national identity and role in global terms led Steven Levine to conclude that "China is outgrowing Asia and trying the world on for size" and that "China has been a regional power without a regional policy."[19] Although Peking's

---

nearly 1,000 kilometers south of China's Hainan island province and most of them subject to conflicting jurisdictional claims, could provide lebensraum (*sheng-ts'un k'ung-chien*—literally, "survival space") for the Chinese people. See the cover story, "South China Sea: Treacherous Shoals," *Far Eastern Economic Review* [hereinafter cited as *FEER*], August 13, 1992, 14-20, and John W. Garver, "China's Push Through the South China Sea: The Interaction of Bureaucratic and National Interests," *China Quarterly*, no. 132 (December 1992): 999-1028.

[17]See Kyodo in English, Tokyo, in *FBIS-CHI*-92-039 (February 27, 1992): 24-25; see also Nicholas D. Kristof, "As China Looks at World Order, It Detects New Struggles Emerging," *New York Times*, April 21, 1992, A1, A10.

[18]See Chiang's Political Report, 15-16.

[19]Steven I. Levine, "China in Asia: The PRC as a Regional Power," in *China's Foreign Relations in the 1980s*, ed. Harry Harding (New Haven, Conn.: Yale University Press, 1984), 107.

"regional" policy is no longer an extension of its superpower policy, still the United States as the lone superpower—and as mainland China's single largest export market—looms over the whole spectrum of Peking's variegated, omnidirectional, and Janus-faced policy.

To a significant extent and in most areas, Peking still does not have a regional policy. Instead, Peking's policy in most domains seems to be propelled by unilateralism in bilateral clothing with little Asian multilateral regionalism. The absence of a multilateral regional policy at the level of public policy pronouncements does not mean an absence of Peking's desire and will to fill the power vacuum left with the dissolution of superpower rivalry in the region. As well it is another testimonial to Peking's differentiated policy of pursuing good-neighbor diplomacy on one track while at the same time seeking regional domination on another track (albeit more in Southeast Asia than in Northeast Asia).

There is also a sense in which China's stunted regional identity reflects and effects the general situation of the Asia-Pacific region as a whole dominated by the twin pressures of globalism and nationalism with little if any of pan-Asian regionalism to speak of. It makes little sense to talk about Asia as an international regional system. The idea of international regional system has been closely keyed to the idea of an association of states linked together not only by a condition of geographical proximity but also by shared features of history, climate, and culture. Asia is only a vague geographical notion with no shared cultures, ideologies, and identities as it is overlaid by four or five major cultures, three or four major religions, hundreds of languages, and myriad ethnic cleavages and widely varying climatic conditions. Of all the major regions of the world, Asian regionalism is perhaps the weakest. It is true that one version of multipolarization envisions a world of three large regional economic blocs of the European Community, the North American Free Trade Area (NAFTA), and East Asia. It is also true that intra-East Asian trade has been rapidly growing in recent years. Yet the notion of an East Asian trading bloc is an idea whose time has been lagging behind the General Agreement on Tariffs and Trade/World Trade Organization (GATT/WTO).

At the official diplomatic level, the PRC today enjoys cordial relations with its regional neighbors. Instead of being further isolated and marginalized by the twin blows of the Tienanmen carnage and the collapse of transnational Communism, post-Tienanmen China has actually managed to establish or renormalize its official diplomatic relations with all Asian neighbors including Indonesia, Singapore, India, Vietnam, South Korea, and newly minted Central Asian states of Uzbekistan, Turkmenistan, Kyrgyzstan, and Kazakhstan. The past several years have seen substantial progress in its ties with Russia, India, and South Korea. The number of states recognizing the PRC has increased by 26, from 132 in 1989 to 158 by the end of 1993. Apparently, Peking's unusually swift recognition in December 1991 of twelve newly independent states in the wake of the collapse of the Soviet multinational empire was prompted by fear that Taiwan would jump the gun in the game of competitive legitimation and delegitimation. The greatest leverage Peking had in this connection was its veto power in the UN Security Council and the threat to use it in blocking the entry of any of these newly formed states into the world organization.

In actuality, however, the overall appearance of Peking's foreign policy in the region at this level of analysis can be quite misleading as Peking is trying to realize its foreign policy objectives with differentiated policies in different issue areas toward different states. Northeast Asia, Central Asia, South Asia, and Southeast Asia have varying degrees of importance in post-Tienanmen China's foreign relations.

Northeast Asia

The geostrategic and geoeconomic importance of Northeast Asia for Chinese foreign policy cannot be gainsaid. For this is the only region or subregion where four of the world's five recognized centers of power—the United States, Russia, China, and Japan—uneasily meet and interact; it is the only region where such a mixture of two-power, three-power, and four-power games are played out on multiple chessboards with all their enormous complexities and shifting configurations. It is as well the only region where the Cold War has ended only partially contrary to the more synchronized rhythms and expanding virtuous circle of great-power co-operation elsewhere. Above all, it is in Northeast Asia, not in Europe or any other region in the world, where both the United States and the former Soviet Union were first made aware of the multipolarizing trends and the limits of their power.

Sino-Japanese relationship is one of the keys to understanding the shape of an Asia-Pacific regional order to come. Today almost everyone on the Chinese side presents the uniformly upbeat assessment of the current state of Sino-Japanese relations. Sino-Japanese economic relations registered three "firsts" in 1993: (1) Sino-Japanese trade increased by 35 percent between 1992 and 1993 to reach US$39 billion elevating Japan for the first time in years as mainland China's biggest trading partner (and mainland China as Japan's second biggest trading partner); (2) Japan's technology exports to mainland China constituted the largest portion of mainland China's technology imports; and (3) Japanese enterprises led the rest of the world in investing capital in mainland China.[20]

---

[20]New China News Agency (NCNA), March 21, 1994, in *FBIS-CHI*-94-055 (March 22, 1994): 6.

Yet Sino-Japanese relations have evolved toward a two-level relationship, consisting of the visible diplomatic and economic and deeper national identity levels. To a significant degree, China's ambivalent Asian identity is a mirror image of Japan's Asian identity. As one of a few true "nation-states" where a state's jurisdiction coincides perfectly with its own nation (homogeneous people), Japan should have had no identity problems that have afflicted so many old and new multinational states. Yet by a more comprehensive and synthetic definition of national identity,[21] the state defines and differentiates itself not only behaviorally by what it does but also essentially by what it is. National identity is thus embedded in the national symbol system which the Japanese refer to as the *kokutai* (national essence). Asia and the West—and since the end of World War II the United States—constituted two opposite poles with the former standing for barbarism and backwardness and the latter for civilization and modernity (power and plenty) in the making of modern Japanese national identity.

Even today, the West, in Japanese eyes, represents peace, democracy, and prosperity while Asia is a temptation to trigger its predatory chauvinism and attitudinal conceit bespeaking of a curious mixture of inferiority complex toward the West and superiority complex toward Asia. Across the ideological spectrum, as Masaru Tamamoto writes, there still exists abiding self-doubt about Japan's ability to control itself in assuming East Asian leadership.[22] At the same time, the widely shared perception in East Asia that Japan is *in* Asia, but not *of* Asia and thus unfit to be a new successor leader or hegemon has a lot to do with pendulum swings in Japan's Asian identity, so to speak, rotating between escaping and conquering Asia. On the diplomatic level, Japan's ambivalent image of China is expressed in stylized diplomatic language of apologies ("apology diplomacy") and ever more expensive official aid packages, while at the deeper emotional level there is growing resentment and refusal to make long-time foreign direct investment (FDI) commitments.[23]

On the Chinese side there is the greater abiding tension between two contradictory sets of images and perceptions. One set is encompassed and overlaid by the shadows of the past, widely prevailing negative perceptions

---

[21]For the reconceptualization of national identity along this line, see Lowell Dittmer and Samuel S. Kim, "In Search of a Theory of National Identity," in *China's Quest for National Identity*, ed. Lowell Dittmer and Samuel S. Kim (Ithaca, N.Y.: Cornell University Press, 1993), 1-31.

[22]See Masaru Tamamoto, "Japan's Uncertain Role," *World Policy Journal* 8, no. 4 (Fall 1991): 579-97.

[23]Hidenori Ijiri, "Sino-Japanese Controversy Since the 1972 Diplomatic Normalization," *China Quarterly*, no. 124 (December 1990): 639-61.

of Japan as a ruthless historical enemy and predator, and the real, if un-spoken, assumption that a past enemy remains an enemy today beyond repentance. The other set of images is encompassed and overlaid by the shadows of the future—positive perceptions of Japanese as a developmental model and rising expectations of what Japan as an economic superpower could do for China's modernization drive. The antinomies between hostile imagery and pragmatic self interest, never fully or satisfactorily resolved, seem to wane or wax in a situation-specific way in Peking's Japan policy.[24]

Central to Japanese worries about the PRC's role in the post-Cold War Asia-Pacific regional order is the growing perception that the PRC is not a normal state or a satisfied status quo power but a highly nationalistic power seeking primacy as the regional hegemon in the creation of a "Greater Sinocentric East Asian Order." While the diplomatic surface is calm, in Tokyo's view, there are any number of troublesome conflicts lurking around and below Peking's CNS drive ready to explode: the unilateral legislative strike in 1992 to claim sovereignty over the disputed Tiaoyütai (Senkaku) Islands; gunboat diplomacy in the South China Sea; a rapidly expanding role in the global arms trade both as buyer and seller at a time when Tokyo has been pushing the idea of a UN arms registry and has been the leading regional voice in support of greater restraint and transparency in global arms trade, perfidious behavior on a host of arms control and disarmament issues including nuclear test and proliferation; a problematic role in the resolution of the nuclear crisis on the Korean Peninsula; and human rights and environmental conditions in mainland China. In its 1993 annual review of diplomatic and security developments, the Japanese Foreign Ministry for the first time expressed its concern over Peking's military modernization program, especially over the PRC's naval buildup and its claims to the Spratly Islands.[25]

At the same time, the upbeat Chinese assessment of current Sino-Japanese relations should not be accepted as the transformation of Peking's basic attitudes and policy toward Japan. Some carefully calculated steps that the Peking government has taken in the past two years need to be understood as part of a deliberate maxi-mini strategy to further the mod-ernization (Japan) and anti-hegemonic (the United States) goals in what some Chinese now consider a new Peking-Tokyo-Washington axis in the Asia-Pacific region.

---

[24]Allen S. Whiting, *China Eyes Japan* (Berkeley: University of California Press, 1989). For acknowledgment of the double-bind historical legacy of Sino-Japanese relations, see also *People's Daily* (Overseas edition), September 29, 1992, 1.

[25]*Asia 1994 Yearbook* (Hong Kong: Review Publishing Co., 1994), 19.

In December 1993 Peking and Tokyo started first-ever bilateral security talks, at Tokyo's initiative, even as Peking for the first time hinted, tantalizingly, its possible future support ("when the time is ripe") of Japan's quest for a permanent membership in the Security Council, presumably in order to dilute American hegemony. More revealingly, hundreds of elderly Chinese activists (in their 60s and 70s) peacefully demonstrating and demanding war compensation from Japan were preemptively detained by the Chinese security forces on the eve of Japanese Prime Minister Horihiro Hosokawa's official state visit in March 1994. The Chinese government decided that Japanese investment and soft loans were more important than seeking justice and compensation for its own citizens (members of the unofficial Victims of Japanese War Crimes Reparation Committee). Yet Hosokawa's China state visit left both sides dissatisfied. Peking failed to get the more concrete details it sought on the next round of Japanese development aid packages (i.e., firm figures for the amount and timing) after the current five-year aid package of US$7.6 billion runs out in 1995, while Tokyo failed to enlist any specific promise from Peking in getting North Korea come clean on the nuclear issue and in establishing greater transparency on Chinese military spending and arms trade.

Peking's Korea policy in the post-Mao era has been a balancing act adjusting to the logic of the changing domestic, regional, and global situations. By fits and starts, it has evolved through several phases, shifting first from the familiar one-Korea policy to a one-Korea de jure/two-Korea de facto policy, and then again to a two-Korea de facto and de jure policy. Peking's Korea policy seems to have been guided by the realist interest-driven strategy of enhancing its own drive for modernization and international legitimation. In the pursuit of such interest-driven policy toward the Korean Peninsula, Peking has adopted a multitasking approach of emphasizing different but mutually complementary priorities in different issue areas. Despite the inauguration of formal diplomatic relations with Seoul, Peking still takes a dual-track approach of strengthening its traditional geostrategic ties with North Korea, even as it actively promotes new geoeconomic ties with South Korea.

It is clear that Peking's policy took a new turn when in 1991 Peking withdrew its former support to Pyongyang's increasingly problematic pursuit of absolute international legitimation (i.e., one-Korea stand). It is reported that after numerous secret meetings, Peking finally persuaded Kim Il-sung to shift to a "two countries, two systems" strategy and jump on the UN bandwagon supporting Seoul's UN membership bid. If Peking was somewhat forced to play a reluctant second fiddle to the Korean UN membership issue, the same cannot be said about the decision to formally recognize and establish full diplomatic relations with Seoul as of August 24, 1992. Obviously, Peking's decision came as a major triumph of Seoul's

Nordpolitik and as such a major loss in Pyongyang's quest for absolute legitimation. It should be noted, however, that the August 1992 decision was merely the culmination of a carefully designed series of small steps suddenly gaining tempo. Unlike the Russians, the Chinese delivered their blows to Pyongyang not all at once, but by installments. The timing of Peking's decision seemed closely keyed to and triggered by Taiwan's victory in winning recognition from Niger in June 1992.

Peking's decision to recognize Seoul (reportedly made by Teng Hsiao-p'ing [Deng Xiaoping] himself) underscores a balance-of-power strategy in Chinese foreign policy thinking and behavior. Foreign Minister Ch'ien Ch'i-ch'en (Qian Qichen) is reported to have used the metaphor of "downing four birds with one stone" in favor of full normalization with Seoul in his secret report to the Chinese Communist Party's (CCP's) foreign affairs group. Such a preemptive strike would (1) increase Taiwan's diplomatic isolation, (2) strengthen Peking's growing economic cooperation with Seoul, (3) diminish Pyongyang's seemingly endless requests for more economic aid, and (4) give more leverage to defuse the mounting "Super 301" pressure from the United States on unfair trade practices.[26] According to South Korean officials, Chinese leaders have also promised support in the denuclearization of the Korean Peninsula as part of the diplomatic deal. Above all, the Seoul connection is another way of demonstrating the indispensability of the China factor in the reshaping of a new regional order in Northeast Asia.

Two other major considerations which were not mentioned in Ch'ien's secret report, were the Gorbachev and Japan factors. The greatest impact of Gorbachev's Pacific overture can be seen in divided Korea. The 1988 Seoul Olympiad was a watershed in accelerating cross-bloc functional cooperation between Seoul and Moscow, as it has been between Seoul and Peking. The Soviet interest in Korea shifted from a passive desire to avoid an unwanted confrontation with the United States to a more active solicitation of South Korean support in Soviet Far Eastern development, and greater integration of the Soviet economy with that of the dynamic East Asian newly industrializing countries (NICs). For various reasons, including the supersensitive China factor, Taiwan, Hong Kong, and Singapore do not offer Moscow much room to maneuver, leaving South Korea as the most promising option. Peking followed the Moscow example, but proceeded in a more careful way. "In recent years," as two PRC scholars

---

[26]Lo Ping and Lai Chi-king, "Secret Talks Between Chinese, Vietnamese Communist Parties and Between Chinese, Korean Communist Parties," *Cheng Ming* (Hong Kong), no. 166 (August 1991): 12-13, in *FBIS-CHI*-91-148 (August 1, 1991): 1-2.

put it, "it has been China's practice to let Moscow take the lead in approaching Seoul while it avoided lagging too far behind."[27] What Moscow does in a sweeping single-blow fashion, Peking attempts to do in a more measured and incremental manner.

The rapid progress in Moscow-Seoul relations, coupled with the equally rapid decompression of Moscow-Pyongyang relations, has taken the sting out of the longstanding ideological and geopolitical Sino-Soviet rivalry over North Korea. However, the ending of Cold War bipolarity means that Pyongyang's leverage in Moscow and Peking has considerably weakened, although North Korea still possesses a certain measure of geopolitical leverage in the form of nuisance value by demonstrating its unreliability and unpredictability. The post-Cold War developments forced Pyongyang into a corner where the only way to draw the attention of Washington, Peking, and Moscow is to demonstrate that it still retains the negative power to disrupt the peace and stability of this trouble spot—the military powderkeg—in the Asia-Pacific region.

Apart from the Moscow factor, it may also be safely assumed that Peking looks upon South Korea as a potential ally against Japanese hegemony. While anti-Japanese demonstrations are frequent in South Korean society, the Japanese government seems chronically unable or unwilling to put an end to old historical enmities. At the same time, Peking uses the Seoul card to fuel ROK-Japanese rivalry in the competitive slicing of the China market as a cost-effective way of attracting more Japanese investment and technology transfer.

Of the four birds mentioned in Ch'ien's secret report, three are concerned with the promotion of mainland China's economic interests. Sino-ROK trade, starting slowly from a zero base (about US$40,000 in 1978), increased to US$461.6 million in 1985, and, after the 1986 Asian Games in Seoul, to US$1.49 billion in 1986 (about 80 percent of Seoul's total trade volume with all socialist countries at the time), to US$3 billion in 1989, to US$3.8 billion in 1990, US$5.8 billion in 1991 (nearly ten times the value of China's trade with North Korea), US$8.22 billion in 1992, and about US$9 billion in 1993. The volume of Sino-ROK trade in 1992 at US$8.22 billion was over eight times that of Sino-African trade (US$1 billion) and nearly three times that of Sino-Latin American trade (US$3 billion). By the end of 1993, mainland China became the third biggest export market for South Korea, and South Korea mainland China's sixth biggest export market.

Moreover, the composition of Sino-ROK trade also defies the typical

---

[27] Jia Hao and Zhuang Qubing, "China's Policy Toward the Korean Peninsula," *Asian Survey* 32, no. 12 (December 1992): 1140.

Sino-Third World pattern, with mainland China exporting coal, minerals, raw materials, and agricultural products and importing steel, industrial products, petrochemical items, advanced machinery, and electronic parts and technology. In a sense, South Korea (along with Hong Kong and Taiwan) has been drawn in as another key player in the implementation of Peking's coastal developmental strategy. South Korea is well poised to transform Shantung (Shandong) Province, which lies across the Yellow Sea from the Korean Peninsula, as another export-launching platform, as much of the Korean investment and trade is concentrated on this nearby province. FDI is flowing into Shantung from South Korea, as mainland China's plentiful supply of cheap labor is attractive to South Korean entrepreneurs who face rising production costs in their own country. One of the hidden factors driving Seoul's China policy is a new partnership of sorts against growing protectionism in the United States. South Korea's new strategy is to accelerate the shift in its manufacturing sector away from labor-intensive products to high-value exports such as cars, petrochemicals, specialty steel products, and semiconductors on the one hand, while at the same time changing the pattern and direction of its exports away from the overdependence on U.S. and Japanese markets to Chinese, Vietnamese, and Russian markets. Indeed, in this dual strategy of structural adjustment and diversification, mainland China is emerging as a huge new market for South Korean goods and overseas investment. Mainland China has already become the third most popular place for South Korean overseas investment after Thailand and Indonesia. From Peking's standpoint, the Sino-ROK economic relations are part of its new strategy of diversification designed to overcome mainland China's overdependence on the American market, which currently represents well over one-third of mainland China's global exports.

While, from the Chinese viewpoint, the South Korean economy represents opportunities to be more fully exploited, the North Korean economy poses a continuing burden to be progressively lessened, although without causing any catastrophic crash landing. By the 1980s, it became increasingly obvious that the official ideology of *Juche* (self-reliance) could no longer perform its multiple legitimizing functions. Pyongyang received a major diplomatic blow when Seoul, in return for Moscow's full diplomatic recognition, together with the implied support for Seoul's bid for UN membership, pledged US$3 billion in foreign aid. Furthermore, Moscow served notice that Pyongyang would have to start servicing its debt to Moscow (estimated at about US$4.6 billion), and shifted from barter trade to trading in hard currency as of January 1, 1991. The change in Soviet policy could not have come at a worse time, as North Korea's gross national product (GNP) for 1989 stood at where it was in 1984. Before 1991, the Soviet Union was North Korea's largest trading partner (about 57 percent of total trade as late as 1990), but already in the first six months of 1991, two-way trade dropped to 1.2 percent of the volume in the same period in 1990.

The PRC has, *faute de mieux*, become the main trading partner of North Korea, although in 1991, Sino-North Korean trade represented still less than one-tenth of Sino-South Korean trade. In less than a decade (1985-91), mainland China's exports to North Korea more than doubled, while imports from North Korea virtually disappeared. Moreover, following the breakup of trade talks between Peking and Pyongyang in November 1992, Peking decided to follow the Moscow lead in demanding for cash payment in trade effective as of January 1, 1993. Since the beginning of 1993, Peking has stopped supplying crude oil to North Korea in barter trade, while in the recent past, it annually supplied about 1.2 million tons of crude oil to North Korea, of which 650,000 tons in the form of barter trade and the remaining 550,000 tons on credit.

However, the euphoria of 1990-92 engendered by Sino-ROK and Soviet-ROK normalization was greatly overshadowed, if not completely belied, by the Korean nuclear crisis in 1993-94. Contrary to what is widely believed, Peking is unlikely to play the role of mediator between North Korea and the United Nations. Clearly, the Korean nuclear issue has confronted Peking with a danger and an opportunity. As already mentioned, Peking had promised Seoul to assist in the denuclearization of the Korean Peninsula. Peking does little to dampen the rising expectations in Washington, if not in Tokyo, that as the last remaining ally and major economic patron of a diplomatically isolated and economically crippled North Korea, Peking remains the gateway to Pyongyang. As in the Gulf crisis, Peking has once again succeeded in making the Clinton administration an overly anxious supplicant for Chinese help. As one senior government official put it in late April 1993, "The consensus [within the Clinton administration] is that China is the key to solving the North Korea crisis."[28] When the annual MFN deadline approached, the Clinton administration announced that it would extend the PRC's MFN status for another year without any conditions, but that its future renewal would be tied solely to human rights. Thus, the Clinton administration decided to turn a blind eye to Peking's own violations of the nonproliferation norms, based on the dubious assumption that the Korean crisis could only be dealt with support from Peking. The major policy reversal of May 26, 1994, too, was based on the indispensable China factor in pressing North Korea to abandon its nuclear weapons program.

---

[28]Quoted in Douglas Jehl, "U.S. Agrees to Discuss Arms Directly with North Korea," *New York Times*, April 23, 1993, A10.

However, the notion that Peking is able and willing to play a decisive role in controlling Pyongyang's nuclear behavior stands on shaky historical and behavioral ground for at least several closely related reasons. First, Peking's own perfidious behavior in the field of ballistic missile technology and nuclear war-making equipment belied its own nonproliferation policy pronouncements. The evidence shows that between 1966 and 1976, at a time when Peking was publicly supporting proliferation as a means of breaking the superpower nuclear duopoly, Peking in practice provided little nuclear assistance to other countries (except training North Korean scientists in nuclear technology in the late 1950s and much of the 1960s). In the 1980s, however, Peking's nuclear proliferation principle and policy have moved on two divergent tracks. While making repeated nonproliferation pledges and pronouncements, Peking in the post-Mao era, either directly or indirectly, has helped jump-start ballistic missile and nuclear weapons programs in Algeria, Argentina, Brazil, Iran, Iraq, Pakistan, India (heavy water), North Korea, Saudi Arabia, and Syria by providing expertise and technology, gaining the dubious distinction as the "single most cynical and remorseless superweapon proliferator."[29] Although there is no hard evidence that Peking is assisting North Korea in its current nuclear weapons program, Peking is reported to have helped North Korea in the development of missiles and even provided technology for the North Korean reprocessing plant.[30] Thus, Peking cannot be expected to capture the high moral ground on the Korean nuclear issue. Nor does it command any credibility to lecture, let alone control, Pyongyang on the nuclear issue.

Second, while giving rhetorical support to the idea of a nuclear-free Korean Peninsula (who doesn't?), Peking has repeatedly denied any role or responsibility as the Korean nuclear issue is said to be directly and exclusively a dispute between the Democratic People's Republic of Korea (DPRK) on the one hand, and the United States, the International Atomic Energy Agency (IAEA), and the ROK on the other. In other words, it is none of Peking's business. At the same time, Foreign Minister Ch'ien Ch'i-ch'en made it clear on many occasions that his government is not only opposed to economic sanctions but also against bringing up the issue

---

[29]For thoroughgoing analysis and documentation, see Jag Mohan Malik, "Chinese National Security and Nuclear Arms Control" (Ph.D. diss., Department of International Relations, Australian National University, 1990), esp. chap. 4, and William E. Burrows and Robert Windrem, *Critical Mass: The Dangerous Race for Superweapons in a Fragmenting World* (New York: Simon & Schuster, 1994), esp. chap. 12, 378-402; quote on *Critical Mass*, 380.

[30]Larry A. Niksch, "North Korea's Nuclear Weapons Program," *CRS Issue Brief* (Washington, D.C.: Congressional Research Service, the Library of Congress, 1992), 3.

at all in the IAEA and the Security Council.[31]

When push comes to shove, Peking would issue a thinly veiled threat to cast its veto on any "hard" resolution. Because the PRC alone among the Big Five had taken such a hard line, the Security Council first had to delay and then dilute the text of the draft resolution so as to make it more acceptable to Peking. On May 11, 1993, the Security Council adopted a resolution by a vote of 13 to 0 with only the PRC and Pakistan abstaining, merely calling upon North Korea to reconsider its announced withdrawal from the Nonproliferation Treaty (NPT). It was against this backdrop that the issue was taken out of the Security Council and became a subject of U.S.-DPRK bilateral negotiations in New York between June 2 and 11, 1993. On March 28, 1994, Peking brushed aside demands for a rather mild Security Council draft resolution, insisting successfully instead on a still milder "presidential statement." On May 29, 1994, the Security Council, in diluted diplomatic language once again aimed at appeasing Peking, tried to send another statement that "further Security Council consideration will take place" to achieve Pyongyang's full compliance.

Third, Peking is more committed to maintaining stability on the Korean Peninsula than to the long-term objective of denuclearizing the Korean Peninsula. Peking seems determined enough not to have another socialist regime collapsing on its vital northern strategic cordon sanitaire nor a chaos or war with the ominous implications that would have for its domestic and regional stability (including a flood of refugees joining its already uncontrollable floating population within its porous borders). The establishment of PRC-ROK diplomatic relations has had no discernible impact on PRC-DPRK military and strategic ties, as PRC-DPRK military delegation visits continue unabated, and the 1961 PRC-DPRK alliance pact remains intact. Geographically, North Korea remains the PRC's indispensable strategic shield. Strategically, too, Pyongyang's value to Peking stems from its being an unstable and unpredictable actor just as Peking's influence stems from its having good relations with both Koreas. To abandon Pyongyang is to lose whatever leverage Peking may still have on the politics of divided Korea.

---

[31]In his annual speech before the plenary session of the General Assembly on September 29, 1993—and this comes close to being the PRC's annual state of the world message— Ch'ien made it clear where his government stood on the question of economic sanctions, nuclear proliferation, and U.S. hegemony: "China is opposed to the all too frequent arbitrary use of sanctions by one country to bring pressure to bear on another under the pretext of controlling arms transfers while engaging in massive arms sales of one's own which jeopardize the sovereignty and security of the country concerned." For the full text of Ch'ien's speech, see *FBIS-CHI*-93-188 (September 30, 1993): 1-4; quote at 3.

And finally, there is very little that Peking can actually accomplish in reshaping Pyongyang's national security thinking and behavior. From Pyongyang's vantage point, developing nuclear weapons program is perhaps a cost-effective nuclear deterrent and "strategic equalizer" in its competition with the South.[32] The diminution of Russian support for the North and de facto removal of the Russian nuclear umbrella seemed to have made the nuclear option a matter of necessity, not choice. That Pyongyang would be forced to go nuclear as a cost-effective substitution strategy was made evident in a memorandum issued by the DPRK Foreign Ministry in September 1990, stating that if Moscow-Seoul diplomatic relations were established, the Soviet-North Korean alliance pact would cease to exist and the North would have "no other choice but to take measures to provide for ourselves *some weapons* for which we have so far relied on the alliance."[33] "Some weapons" in this context can only mean nuclear weapons. Peking's recognition of the Seoul government in 1992, coupled with its imposition of a new cash payment system of trade, provided a further incentive for Pyongyang to go nuclear. Pyongyang cannot be assumed to be ignorant of the real, if unstated, code of conduct for threshold states, namely that going nuclear is the shortest way of being taken seriously in regional and global geopolitics. Capitalizing on all the uncertainties and ever-shifting goalposts in Washington, Seoul, and Tokyo about what is now widely conceded as a virtually impossible goal of certifying that North Korea does not possess a single nuclear bomb, Pyongyang has skillfully played a now-yes, now-no cat-and-mouse game constantly changing the rules of entry and the rules of play in this strange mind-guessing game.

The PRC today commands a rather unique position as the only major power that maintains a good relationship with both Koreas. Russia's sudden and decisive tilt to Seoul, combined with Tokyo's and Washington's refusal to recognize Pyongyang, have transformed the great-power equation on the Korean Peninsula. All the same, maintaining a close strategic relationship with North Korea remains one of Peking's central security concerns. Such a balance-of-power approach is likely to be maintained, not only because it directly serves the PRC's geostrategic interests, but also because it gives Peking greater leverage in its regional and global diplomacy. As a result of its participatory experience in the global strategic triangular power politics in the 1970s and 1980s, Peking has become a firm believer

---

[32]For a cogent analysis along this line, see Andrew Mack, "The Nuclear Crisis on the Korean Peninsula," *Asian Survey* 33, no. 4 (April 1993): 339-59.

[33]Quoted in ibid, 342; emphasis added.

in, and a skilled practitioner of, national security as a function not only of pure muscle power, but more importantly, of cognitive power of cultivating expectations that Peking has both the capability and will to play a balancing role in any great-power rivalry.

For the first time in decades, it is now possible to speak of a truly normal relationship between Peking and Moscow. Soviet President Mikhail Gorbachev's Pacific overtures in 1986-88 for a comprehensive security system for the entire Asia-Pacific region were countermanded and scaled back to the bilateral negotiating level in order to pressure the Soviets to meet Peking's three security demands (the so-called Three Obstacles) as the price for renormalizing Sino-Soviet relations. The May 1989 summit was the culmination of a slow but steady rapprochement process that started in 1982 but gained big momentum with Gorbachev's Vladivostok Speech of July 28, 1986. From the May 1989 summit to the collapse of the Soviet Union in December 1991 the relationship evolved through several stages of jagged development buffeted by a series of abrupt shifts and reversals, given the profound domestic upheavals in both countries. Remarkably, the relationship has been able to survive and even transformed itself into a partnership despite the widening ideological chasm. The former Sino-Soviet border has been divided among four newly minted sovereign states, but the remaining 3,605-kilometer Sino-Russian border, still the longest in the world, has been turned into a mutually beneficial commercial artery.

Once again, Peking has demonstrated its capacity to adjust its policy following the Palmerstonian maxim—there are no perennial friends nor perennial enemies, only perennial national interests.[34] Peking seems to have recovered rather quickly from the reality shock of the collapse of Soviet Communism turning Russia into a wholesale arms bazaar for advanced weapons systems (e.g., Peking bought US$1.8 billion of weaponry from Russia in 1992, including twenty-six advanced SU-27 long-range jet fighters). All the same mutual economic needs—and Peking's economic cooptation strategy—are gradually turning a once hostile and highly militarized borderland into a bustling barter trade zone. Paradoxical as it may seem, Communist China and anti-Communist Russia are now poised to form a profitable symbiosis with the dynamism of the East Asian political economy as a way toward securing a long peace in this part of the world. In December 1992, Russian President Boris Yeltsin visited Peking and signed a long list of accords with his Chinese counterpart, including an agreement

---

[34]"With the exception of eternal interests," we are told, "there are neither eternal enemies nor eternal friends." See *Chieh-fang-chün pao*, July 17, 1987, 3.

to partially demilitarize the Sino-Russian border. One of the agreements would establish a 100-km demilitarized strip of land on either side of the border. The Sino-Russian border is no longer a flashpoint. The former Soviet Union and Russia have been steadily cutting down troop levels in the strategic area abutting North China with troop levels reduced from more than 500,000 to roughly 200,000. In June 1992 the last remaining combat troops were withdrawn from Outer Mongolia (which hosted some 65,000 troops in the 1960s). Since March 1990, the PRC has also pulled from its border with Russia almost twenty-five divisions, leaving another twenty-five, less than one-sixth the number during the heyday of Sino-Soviet conflict (and saving some 7 billion *yuan* a year in military expenditure).

While Sino-Russian border trade dropped considerably in the first quarter of 1994 owing to a host of reasons including Russia's new visa regulations, the military cooperation continues unabated. With an attractive package of high salaries, free housing, and paid annual home vacations, the Peking government is reported to have successfully recruited several hundred senior scientists from the former Soviet Union to work on new military research and development and weapons systems.[35] In November 1993 Peking and Moscow signed a five-year, renewable military cooperation agreement providing for detailed annual military cooperation plans in such areas as logistics, personnel exchanges, training, intelligence information, and joint military exercises to be drawn up bilaterally each December. It has recently been reported that another squadron of SU-27, with Chinese markings already painted on, is waiting in Russia while the two sides are working out payment details before delivery. According to a secret report from the Central Military Commission (CMC), a strong military cooperation with Russia and other former Soviet republics is said to be a prerequisite for breaking the Western embargo on military technology.[36]

For the first time since 1949, a trio of Chinese warships made a port call at Vladivostok in May 1994 even as Vladimir Lukin, Moscow's former ambassador to the United States who now chairs the Russian Parliament's Foreign Affairs Committee, publicly touts about Russia's "dynamically developing" military relationship with Peking, even though "not everybody likes it."[37] It may be recalled in this connection that even during the heyday of the Sino-Soviet alliance in the 1950s Peking was constantly testing

---

[35]Guocang Huan, "The New Relationship with the Former Soviet Union," *Current History* 91, no. 566 (September 1992): 254.

[36]Kyodo in English, December 16, 1992, in *FBIS-CHI*-92-242 (December 16, 1992): 9.

[37]See *FEER*, May 26, 1994, 24.

the twin alliance dilemmas of abandonment and entrapment while at the same time rejecting Soviet proposals (1958) for joint military exercises.

In late May 1994, Russian Prime Minister Viktor Chernomyrdin arrived in Peking to discuss bilateral trade, scientific, financial, security, and border issues. Both Moscow and Peking seemed eager to transform barter trade to a hard-currency trade system involving major state and private corporations. The trade is expected to rise soon to US$10 billion a year from last year's US$7.68 billion. Among many other trade agreements, such as furthering scientific and technological cooperation, and banking and financial arrangements, Chernomyrdin's visit was also expected to result in agreements on redeveloping factories and plants built in mainland China by the former Soviet Union.

One parsimonious explanation of this remarkable and somewhat unexpected transformation of Sino-Russian relationship in the post-Cold War era is functional theory—an incremental "peace by pieces" approach. As Lowell Dittmer argues, the demise of the strategic triangle is necessary but insufficient to fully account for "the current cordiality of the relationship. The sufficient cause is the strategy of diplomatic bridge building by small steps, an approach inaugurated by the resumption of normalization talks in 1982."[38]

The conservative and anti-American turn in the PRC's domestic politics offers an alternative explanation. In April 1993, Adm. Liu Hua-ch'ing (Liu Huaqing), a Standing Committee member of the Politburo, was reported to have mobilized top fifty military officers to send an anti-U.S. petition in which the military "strongly oppose bartering away [China's] principled criteria for state-to-state relations in exchange for bilateral trade."[39] In a little book entitled, *Can the Chinese Army Win the Next War?* that mysteriously found its way to a bookstore in Peking but quickly banned and recalled, the United States was clearly singled out as the principal military adversary in the PRC's future war scenarios, underscoring the extent to which Peking's military leaders have begun to challenge the civilian leaders over the strategic and military policy making. In a meeting with President Chiang Tse-min (Jiang Zemin) on September 8, 1993, according to a Hong Kong journal with close ties with Peking, eight senior generals led by Defense Minister Ch'ih Hao-t'ien (Chi Haotian) were said to have presented Chiang with a petition signed

---

[38]Lowell Dittmer, "China and Russia: New Beginnings," in *China and the World: Chinese Foreign Relations in the Post-Cold War Era*, ed. Samuel S. Kim (Boulder, Colo.: Westview Press, 1994), 110.

[39]Quoted in Lincoln Kaye, "China: Role Reversal," *FEER*, May 27, 1993, 11.

by 180 high-ranking officers demanding that Peking "take a solemn and just stand" against the United States.[40] In early September 1993, two top-secret documents, based on two policy analysis and recommendation reports prepared by the CCP Central Policy Research Center and CMC Research Office, were relayed to Politburo members, Secretariat secretaries, CMC members, and Party committees of all armed services of the PLA, military regions, provinces, municipalities, and autonomous regions, stressing the importance of building a new type of relations with Russia as "a new strategic move to prevent U.S. hegemonism from subverting China and intervening in the internal affairs of other Asian countries."[41]

Central Asia

In the wake of the collapse of the Soviet Union came five newly established states in Central Asia with three of them—Kazakhstan, Kyrgyzstan, and Tajikistan—abutting volatile Muslim Sinkiang (Xinjiang). Contrary to the initial expectations, it is China, not Turkey or Iran with extensive ethnic, cultural, and historical links with the region, that is emerging as the main challenger to Moscow's eroding but still substantial influence in the region. The PRC has already become the second largest trading partner for most of Central Asian states. In April 1994 Premier Li P'eng (Li Peng), while on a twelve-day official visit to Uzbekistan, Turkmenistan, Kyrgyzstan, Kazakhstan, and Mongolia, pronounced Peking's good-neighbor Central Asia policy based on the Five Principles of Peaceful Coexistence. The open-door policy is now extended to Central Asia as Peking is now "willing to work to build a new Silk Road."[42] The PRC and these Central Asian republics seem to be forging a marriage of convenience in promoting "market Leninism"—economic reform without loss of any political control. The New Silk Road diplomacy is a kind of "peaceful evolution" cooperative strategy to deepen economic interdependence between Central Asian states and Western China as a way of arresting the tide of Islamic fundamentalism that threatens to infect its own restive Muslims in Sinkiang with the separatist virus and as such threatens the integrity of the Chinese multinational state.

---

[40]See Patrick E. Tyler, "China's Military Regards U.S. as Main Enemy in the Future," *New York Times*, November 16, 1993, A5.

[41]*Cheng Ming*, no. 193 (November 1993): 20-21, in *FBIS-CHI*-93-214 (November 5, 1993): 1-2.

[42]"China's Basic Policy Towards Central Asia," *Beijing Review* 37, no. 18 (May 2-8, 1994): 18-19.

South Asia and Southeast Asia

As we move from Northeast and Central Asia to South Asia and Southeast Asia, Peking's differentiated role playing on the diplomatic, human rights, and military domains comes to the fore. At the level of official state-to-state relations, Peking's fence-mending diplomacy has garnered substantial progress in the past four years. The restoration of diplomatic relations with Indonesia on August 8, 1990 opened a new chapter in Sino-ASEAN (Association of Southeast Asian Nations) relationship as Singapore followed suit on October 3, 1990 and Brunei on October 1, 1991. Thus, Peking has established formal relations with all of the ASEAN countries.

Some progress has also been made in Peking's relations with India and Vietnam. In the first state visit to Peking in decades, Indian Prime Minister P. V. Narasimha Rao and his Chinese counterpart, Li P'eng, managed to agree to disagree on border questions—sticking to their sides of the "line of actual control." It should be noted in this connection that a major obstacle to India's and hence Pakistan's accession to the NPT has been and still is Peking's unwillingness to forgo use of its nuclear capability in the South Asian region. Peking is also turning away from the Khmer Rouge in Cambodia (Kampuchea) to Myanmar (Burma) as a major political and military client state in the region. Peking is reported to have helped the Myanmar military dictatorship with an estimated US$1 billion in military equipment in 1992 and agreed to support an expansion of its military from 300,000 to 400,000 in return for building naval facilities on two adjacent islands in the Indian Ocean.[43] The dispute over the Sino-Vietnamese land border seemed resolved in the course of Vietnamese Vice Foreign Minister Vu Khoan's official visit to Peking in August 1993 even as the two sides remained further apart than ever before on the contested and volatile Spratly Islands.

It is in the domain of human rights politics, more than any other issue area, that draws the PRC and ASEAN in a partnership of common misery in post-Cold War global politics. The most basic, recurring theme in Chinese human rights thinking is that communities come before individuals, duties and obligations before rights and privileges; hence, human rights inhere not so much in individuals as in collectivities. Even the much touted "right to development," one of the central themes in post-Mao China's human rights diplomacy, inheres solely in the state, not in the individual. This theme of collective human rights-cum-state rights—and

---

[43]Reuters, February 8, 1993.

the theory of cultural and economic relativism—was somewhat tempered in the 1980s as Peking began to participate in UN human rights politics only to come back with greater shrill in post-Tienanmen foreign relations. If a nation within a state demands independence or self-government, according to leading Chinese international law scholars, this is also a matter of domestic jurisdiction of that *state* and the principle of *national* self-determination is not applicable in such a case.[44]

In the wake of the publication of an official "White Paper" on human rights in late 1991—which signaled an acknowledgment that the best defense is a good offense—Peking has positioned itself as the Third World's most vociferous (anti-) human rights "champion" in global normative politics. It has adopted a *regional* approach as part and parcel of a "divide and demolish" strategy in the United Nations. The logic of Peking's "divide and demolish" strategy is to slice up the concept of *universal* human rights little by little, region to region, to the point where there is little left of the UN human rights monitoring and implementation regime. Peking has led the way on behalf of some of the most oppressive Third World countries to keep the UN human rights regime small, fragmented (regionalized), and ineffective. The efforts to alter the structure and terms of reference of a World Conference on Human Rights (WCHR '93) to be held in Vienna in June 1993 to conform with its own minimalist view received little support.[45] However, Peking pressed successfully for the General Assembly to include the relationship between development and human rights as one of the priority topics at the WCHR '93 as well as to hold preparatory regional conferences.

As a result, Asia's first regional human rights conference was held in Bangkok in late March 1993, attended by governmental delegates from forty countries stretching from the Middle East to the South Pacific. The 30-point Bangkok Declaration that emerged from the conference is full of contradictions and ambiguities papering over some serious intraregional cleavages among several groups of countries. That the chief delegates from the PRC, Myanmar, and Iran, three notorious human rights offenders, made up the drafting committee speaks volumes about Peking's "leadership" role in this first-ever Asian human rights conference. The Declaration, sharply challenged by nearly 250 representatives of 110 Asian nongovernmental organizations (NGOs) in their "Bangkok NGO Declara-

---

[44]Wei Min et al., eds., *Kuo-chi-fa kai-lun* (Introduction to international law) (Peking: Kuang-ming jih-pao ch'u-pan-she, 1986), 247.

[45]This is the first global conference on human rights in twenty-five years. The General Assembly decided to convene such a conference via its Resolution 45/155 of December 18, 1990.

tion" for the governments' transparent attempt to avoid accountability for their failures to protect human rights, urged that states be allowed to set up their own human rights mechanisms and discouraged Western countries from making progress on human rights a conditionality for extending development aid. Much to its credit, Japan—and South Korea—voiced serious reservations about the content of the Bangkok Declaration, restating its stand that expressions of concern about human rights violations do not constitute interference in a nation's internal affairs. The Declaration was adopted by "consensus" thanks largely to the support from ASEAN.[46]

On the eve of the WCHR '93, Peking led a pack of worst Third World offenders to attack the core principle of *universal* human rights. As a self-styled Third World champion, Peking had issued a threat that the drafting of the final document of the WCHR '93 should be based on the Bangkok, Tunisia, and San Jose declarations of the three regional preparatory meetings with emphasis on state sovereignty, territorial integrity, and noninterference in the internal affairs of states rather than on the working paper proposed by the Secretariat with emphasis on the strengthening of the global human rights regime. Peking's demands to ostracize Tibet's spiritual leader, the Dalai Lama, eventually collapsed in the face of rising opposition from host country, Austria, the United States, other Western delegations, and human rights NGOs. Still, Peking was successful in having its "either us or them" ultimatum accepted. Much to ASEAN's delight, the Conference expelled all NGOs' representatives from the committee charged with drafting the final WCHR Declaration. In the end, however, the final Declaration rejected the Chinese cultural relativist line: "The international community must treat human rights globally in a fair and equal manner, on the same footing and with the same emphasis."

The Sino-ASEAN partnership in common human rights misery is a temporary political alliance with no positive functional spillovers. The allure of Peking's cultural relativist line—that human rights should be applied differently where cultures and levels of development vary—is quite obvious for any authoritarian or repressive state in search of a fig leaf. But cultural relativism theory is deeply flawed as it proceeds from the dubious premise and mistaken logic that what is being done in various countries in varying cultural and developmental conditions should be accepted as international norms and standards. To accept varying human rights conditions and practices throughout the world as empirical reality (the "is") is one thing but to accept multiple culture-specific (governmental) practices as normative reality (the "ought") is something else—to have no

[46]Gordon Fairclough, "Standing Firm," *FEER*, April 15, 1993, 22.

international standards. Besides, no country has to reach a certain higher cultural and developmental stage to be able to respect the first generation of civil and political rights (as encoded in the International Covenant on Civil and Political Rights and Its Optional Protocol), as they constitute "negative rights," which merely require the state *not* to kill, torture, or repress its own citizens. On the other hand, it is the second generation of economic, social, and cultural rights ("positive rights")—as encoded in the International Covenant on Economic, Social, and Cultural Rights which to be achieved had to be demanded of the state. Indeed, the Vienna Declaration reaffirms the right to development—rightly so—but condemns using this as a justification for human rights abuses. Even in terms of cultural relativism theory, the PRC is far behind in terms of some of the development rights claimed (e.g., the PRC lands in 101st place with 0.566 in global "human development ranking").[47]

That Peking has managed to piggyback on the Third World's power of numbers to wriggle off the hit list of the UN Human Rights Commission since 1990 has a lot to do with the new Sino-Third World partnership of human rights misery against the Western linkage politics in international institutions—linking multilateral aid to democratization and environmental protection. The bottom line of Peking's "right to development as an inalienable human right" seems simple enough: "If one really intends to promote and protect human rights . . . then the first thing for him to do is to help remove obstacles to the development of developing countries, lessen their external debt burden, provide them with unconditional assistance. . . ."[48] It is precisely this proposition of unconditional aid that is sweet music to the ASEAN states even if Peking has always received special treatment in getting the lion's share of bilateral and multilateral aid with virtually no strings attached (i.e., the world's third largest economy is the world's largest recipient of Japan's bilateral aid and the World Bank's multilateral aid!).

In global human rights politics, the chief divide is no longer, if ever was, between the states of North and South but between states, more particularly authoritarian South and Southeast Asian states such as Singapore, Pakistan, Malaysia, Indonesia, and Myanmar and their human rights NGOs. Even in the post-Cold War world as in the long Cold War, when the issue is framed as a contest between state and human rights, collective

---

[47]Paul Lewis, "New U.N. Index Measures Nations' Quality of Life," *New York Times*, May 23, 1993, 14.
[48]"The Right to Development: An Inalienable Human Right," *Beijing Review* 35, no. 51 (December 21-27, 1992): 13.

international (read: interstate) response still tends to close ranks in defense of the sanctity and inviolability of state sovereignty. As shown at the WCHR '93 and more dramatically in President Clinton's unconditional surrender to Corporate America on the MFN issue, there is still no contest between Chinese state interests and Chinese human rights. In a joint statement, NGOs described the Vienna Declaration as a flawed document that confirms many basic rights, but also reflects "attempts by governments to shirk their human-rights obligations." Of all the regional NGO declarations, the Bangkok NGO Declaration was the most unequivocal in its support for *universal* human rights. The most organized and unified group of NGOs at the WCHR '93 were those from the Asia-Pacific region including the Human Rights in China (HRIC), an external Chinese NGO alliance based in Hong Kong, the United States, Europe, and Taiwan. The Peking government won ASEAN (governmental) gratitude for the vigor with which it pursued the "divide and demolish" strategy especially in excluding NGOs from the drafting committee of the WCHR '93.

Sino-ASEAN relationship appears in new light when we turn from the diplomatic and human rights to military and strategic domains. It is in this region—and on the military/strategic domain—that we begin to hear about the so-called "China threat theory" (*Chung-kuo wei-hsieh lun*). It is in this region as well that the question of an East Asian collective security has been frequently raised. What gave rise to the growing perception of a rising dragon rampant in the post-Tienanmen and post-Cold War era is Peking's assertive unilateralism in bilateral clothing made manifest in a combination of unilateral legislative preemptive strike, gunboat diplomacy, fastest growing military budget, and major naval and air buildup with power projection capabilities including aerial refueling technology. Despite repeated public denials, the PRC leadership approved in principle the acquisition of an aircraft carrier. That the PRC is Asia's least satisfied power would not loom as large as it does in this region of the world if Peking did not have so many territorial disputes with its South Asian and Southeast Asian neighbors. The demonstration of an assertive China so readily engaged in gunboat diplomacy in the South China Sea became a matter of acute security concern in Taipei (and Tokyo). In its first-ever *National Defense White Paper* released on February 17, 1992, Taipei now prognosticates seven, not three, plausible scenarios of a possible PRC military invasion.[49]

On February 25, 1992, the National People's Congress adopted "The

---

[49]The Ministry of Defense, *Kuo-fang pao-kao-shu* (National defense white paper) (Taipei: Li-ming wen-hua shih-yeh ku-fen yu-hsien kung-szu, 1992), 42.

Law of the People's Republic of China on Its Territorial Waters and Contiguous Areas," "in order to enable the People's Republic of China to exercise its sovereignty over its territorial waters and its rights to exercise control over their adjacent areas, and to safeguard state security as well as its maritime rights and interests" (Article 1). The new law stipulates China's territorial sovereignty as including "the mainland and its offshore islands, Taiwan and the various affiliated islands including Diaoyu [Senkaku] Islands, Penghu Islands, Dongsha [Pratas] Islands, Xisha [Paracel] Islands, Nansha [Spratly] Islands, and *other islands* that belong to the PRC" (Article 2). Furthermore, it claimed the right to "adopt all necessary measures to prevent and stop the harmful passage of vessels through its territorial waters" (Article 8). It empowers "PRC military ships or military air carriers . . . to chase" violators out to the open sea (Article 14).[50] It was the first time Peking claimed direct sovereignty in such unilateral legislative sleight of hand.

On the question of a collective security system in the Asia-Pacific region, the Peking leadership has expressed a strong preference for a unilateral approach in bilateral clothing. The dogged determination to define national identity in terms of state sovereignty, state status, and state security stands in the way of responding positively to any proposal for a regional collective security system. Peking quashed Australian, Canadian, and Japanese proposals for a multilateral Asia-Pacific security conference—a sort of Conference on Security and Cooperation in Asia (CSCA). Likewise, Peking categorically rejected any international conference, let alone the establishment of a multilateral regime for handling territorial disputes, maintaining instead that disputes should be resolved by the countries directly involved on a *bilateral* basis.[51] The general silence and passivity on regional arms control and disarmament (ACD) issues, in contrast to its activism on global ACD issues in the United Nations, seem to reflect Peking's acute concern that the establishment of an Asia-Pacific ACD regime would impinge too closely on its expansive regional security zone for comfort.[52]

---

[50]NCNA, February 25, 1992, in *FBIS-CHI*-92-040 (February 28, 1992): 2; emphasis added.

[51]As Li Luye, director-general of the China Center for International Studies, put it: "Any attempt to copy Europe's model of collective security or to duplicate the pattern of integration of the two Germanies in Northeast Asia is not realistic and could by no means bring peace and stability to this area. It would be desirable to start establishing a security mechanism in the Asia-Pacific region, including Northeast Asia, on a bilateral basis." Li Luye, "The Current Situation in Northeast Asia: A Chinese View," *Journal of Northeast Asian Studies* 10, no. 1 (Spring 1991): 78-81; quote at 80.

[52]Alastair I. Johnston, "China and Arms Control in the Asia-Pacific Region," in *Superpower*

The multinational conflict over the Paracel and Spratly island groups in the South China Sea underlines the dialectics of Chinese conflict-making and conflict-coping behavior. While Chinese diplomats often talk about international cooperation for the pacific settlement of disputes, Chinese strategists reject the proposition that the seabed resources of disputed areas in the South China Sea should be jointly developed, while shelving the issue of sovereignty. The Spratly and Paracel islands also straddle sea lanes vital to East Asian states, including Japan, adding a geostrategic dimension to the simmering conflict. Mainland China, Taiwan, and Japan are also locked in dispute over the Tiaoyütai Islands farther north in the East China Sea. To possess the Tiaoyütai Islands, which comprise five islands some 166 kilometers northeast of Taiwan, is to have legal jurisdiction over about 21,645 square kilometers of the continental shelf that is believed to be one of the last unexplored hydrocarbon resource areas in the world—possibly up to 100 billion barrels of oil.

Ironically, Peking's gunboat diplomacy has injected new life into the ASEAN as a regional organization, just when the UN-brokered peace settlement in Cambodia seemed to have removed Vietnam as a common thread that held the six member states together. At the July 1992 meeting, all six member states gave top priority to the South China Sea conflict, calling openly for the first time on the United States to maintain a military presence in the region. A separate declaration on the peaceful resolution of the South China Sea conflict was obviously addressed to Peking as a rallying point for ASEAN to have its common security act together in this unsettling post-Cold War transitional setting.

Whatever its real motivations and intentions, Peking rather quickly backed off when it looked as if the new maritime law might jeopardize its chances for a visit from the Japanese emperor in the latter half of 1992. The visit was viewed by the Chinese as a litmus test of Sino-Japanese relations and was threatened by right-wing opposition the new maritime law had generated in Japan. Rather than risk giving such groups ammunition, Peking retreated from the aggressive posture of the law. Instead, an official of the Ministry of Foreign Affairs softened its impact, stating that the passage of the law is a "normal domestic legislative process" and that despite its passage, "it doesn't mean any change in China's policy of 'leaving aside the controversy and jointly developing the islands with countries involved in the dispute'."[53] The official also claimed that a law addressing China's

Maritime Strategy in the Pacific, ed. Frank C. Langdon and Doulgas A. Ross (London: Routledge, 1990), 173-204.

[53]"Legislation Doesn't Mean Policy Change," _Beijing Review_ 35, no. 13 (March 30-April 5, 1992): 10.

territorial claims had been in the works for ten years, and that the timing was not meant to be offensive. Rather, it was simply meant as a clarifier: "China's position on the islands issue and its policy of settling it by peaceful means will not change . . . since the law simply reiterates its long-standing position." To further reassure the Japanese, President Chiang Tse-min reconfirmed the shelving of the issue on April 1, 1992, as a precursor to his own scheduled trip to Japan. Peking's reactions to Tokyo's passage of the so-called peacekeeping operation (PKO) bill in mid-1992 were remarkably restrained, as *Reference Materials*, a daily internal news digest for senior Party leaders, recommended that "public comment should be restrained in view of China's need for Japanese aid."[54]

While the desire to host the emperor was part of Peking's motivation in softening its maritime policy, a further factor was the desire not to create too many enemies at one time. The new maritime law had already outraged many of the PRC's Southeast Asian neighbors, who also claimed many of the other islands Peking had included in its proclamation, and reports of Chinese aggressive militarization were sparking anti-Chinese rhetoric ("China threat theory") in the region. Thus a relaxation of its line with Japan would prevent the PRC from being encircled by doubters, as well as undermine any efforts by the Japanese right wing to use the dispute to justify Japanese remilitarization.

Despite, perhaps because of, Peking's unilateralist-cum-bilateralist stand, the ASEAN effort to engage Peking in multilateral security dialogue on the Spratlys continued apace. Indeed, Peking's military and economic expedition in the cauldron of the South China Sea has become a primary catalyst for the inauguration of the ASEAN Regional Forum (ARF) on political and security matters at the ASEAN Post-Ministerial Conference in Singapore in July 1993, a first major step toward the CSCA. The ARF would include eighteen states as well as the PRC and Russia as a way of forming the broadest possible regional united front to deal with security issues in a regional multilateral framework. The ASEAN interest in a multilateral regional security framework is to influence Chinese policy away from the idea of the PRC's role as a regional cop which would entail ASEAN's subordination. Without external support, ASEAN would face Peking alone and the pressure to surrender to the PRC over the South China Sea dispute would be overwhelming.

The PRC was a special guest of the 25th Annual Ministerial Meeting (AMM) held in Manila in July 1992. At the initiative of the Philippines the AMM came out with a Spratly Declaration emphasizing restraint and

---

[54]Nayan Chanda, "Japan: Why They Worry," *FEER*, June 25, 1992, 18.

joint development of the area without prejudicing the sovereignty of the claimants. True to form, Peking's response was ambiguous, saying only that it "appreciated some of the basic principles" and that it was ready to enter formal negotiations with others "when the conditions are right." Indonesia has sponsored four informal workshops bringing together the claimants to the South China Sea, the last was held in Surabaya in August 1993. When Ali Alatas proposed to move from informal discussions to a formal government to government dialogue over the issue, the Chinese refused. Peking has also opposed the Philippine proposal, raised by Foreign Affairs Undersecretary Rodolfo Severino, for an international conference over the South China Sea, stating that the discussions should be kept to the claimants. Peking does not favor holding an international conference as mooted by the Philippines and the formalization of the dialogue process on the South China Sea conflicts as favored by Vietnam and some ASEAN members. Since the Paracel and Spratly islands have been Chinese territory since ancient times, the issue cannot and should not be "internationalized." To Peking, the *internationalization* (multilateralization) of the issue greatly weakens the leverage it would enjoy in bilateral negotiations.

For Peking, there seems little room for compromise on the Spratly dispute, if not on the Tiaoyütai dispute, largely because of the synergy of sovereignty, security, status, and "lateral pressure." The Party line is clear enough: "When it comes to issues involving national interests and state sovereignty, China will never concede to outside pressure."[55] It should be noted in this connection that ASEAN hardly requires a mention in terms of the scale and scope of the PRC's expanding foreign economic relations. Sino-ASEAN economic relationship is more competitive than complementary. Although Sino-ASEAN trade increased from US$1.85 billion in 1980 to US$6.6 billion in 1989, it is still modest (about 4-6 percent of the global total and about 10 percent of the Asian trade), marked more by competition than by complementarity, as both parties are more concerned with the major developed economies than they are with each other. For the first time in years, ASEAN's confidence in Japan as a benevolent economic superpower began to flag as Japanese companies climb on the global gold rush to the China market by massively diverting their FDI away from Southeast Asia to mainland China.[56]

The conflation of national economic interests and state sovereignty in the vortex of the South China Sea means Peking's rush to establish an

---

[55]Chiang's Political Report, 16.
[56]Michael Richardson, "Southeast Asia Loses Faith in Japan 'Supermen'," *International Herald Tribune*, April 7, 1994, 1, 7.

overwhelming military presence in the area that cannot be challenged by any combination of Southeast Asian military forces. Peking will probably continue to harass, and possibly to attack the weakest link in the area, Vietnam, since Hanoi, weak and friendless, could do nothing about Peking's de facto territorial grab. Peking's carefully orchestrated southward gunboat diplomacy may have been spurred by the belief that other claimants as well as the global community, on the basis of past behavior, are unlikely to react strongly against Chinese coercive diplomacy given the putative indispensability of the China factor in the resolution of the Korean nuclear crisis. Equally significant is the fact that the post-Cold War strategic environment in this contested zone presents a timely challenge and opportunity for the Chinese military to strengthen its blue-water naval power and for the Chinese government to enact a new national role as the dominant military power in the region.[57]

The PRC Multipolarizing or Fragmenting?

Nothing is irreversible in Chinese politics. Nothing is preprogrammed for the future of China. Yet more than ever before in its checkered history, the party-state is incrementally losing authority, legitimacy, and control. Paradoxically, post-Tienanmen China is at one and the same time a growing regional military power abroad and a decaying weak state at home. To reformulate and reverse Lucian Pye's image of China as "a civilization pretending to be a state,"[58] the PRC today is *a weak state pretending to be a strong state*. The defining and differentiating feature of a weak state is the lack of a unifying value system *and* system effectiveness and the correspondingly high level of internal threats to state security. The changing external situation is defined and acted upon in terms of how it affects internal state security. The People's Armed Police (PAP) has recently enjoyed unprecedented growth in manpower, equipment, and training as a way of coping with growing internal security threats even as the PLA is forging for itself a new identity as protector of mainland China's expanding economic and political interests in the South China Sea and other disputed areas. Irrespective of the amount of violence power at its command, such a repressive state is ipso facto a weak state. No state, certainly not huge

---

[57]The PLA, according to Chiang's political report, "should more successfully shoulder the lofty mission of defending the country's territorial sovereignty over the land and in the air, as well as its rights and interests on the seas; and should safeguard the unification and security of the motherland." Chiang's Political Report, 15.

[58]Lucian W. Pye, "China: Erratic State, Frustrated Society," *Foreign Affairs* 69, no. 4 (Fall 1990): 58.

multinational state, can be held together for too long without a legitimizing democratic system.

To be sure, legitimacy is a relative, not an absolute, concept, as there is no government that commands absolute compatibility of the values of those who rule and those who are ruled. Obviously, the crisis of legitimacy alone cannot account for the existence of so many illegitimate authoritarian regimes. The mutual interdependence of state legitimacy and state effectiveness is of particular relevance for the strong versus weak state debate because the presence or absence of one can contribute to the growth or decay of the other. The stability of a regime is closely keyed to the dynamics of legitimacy and effectiveness. The stability of a regime faced with an effectiveness crisis (e.g., economic depression) depends on the degree of legitimacy that it enjoys among its people, on the one hand, while the stability of a regime faced with a legitimacy crisis depends on the degree of performance effectiveness that it actually commands in governance, on the other.[59] Despite some remarkable diplomatic achievements abroad, the party-state today confronts the dual crises of legitimacy and effectiveness. Indeed, post-Tienanmen China suffers from a megacrisis at home—that is, multiple and mutually interrelated crises of authority, identity, legitimacy, and effectiveness. The megacrisis of the weak state suggests that the domestic order of multinational China is coming undone. Indirect signs of normative and structural decay are already manifest in at least five interrelated areas.

First of all, *the state is losing its identity and legitimacy*. The Tienanmen bloodletting at home (*nei-luan*) and the collapse of transnational Communism in the second (socialist) world (*wai-huan*) coming together as they almost did reflected and effected a profound identity-cum-legitimacy crisis. "Market Leninism" is said to be the answer to the crisis of legitimation and identity—the only way to protect the inviolability of one-party, Communist rule by improving the people's social and economic welfare.[60] Lacking Mao's charisma or any "rational-legal" claim to legitimacy (in the Weberian sense), Teng Hsiao-p'ing began to shift his "theoretical" gears from ideology-based legitimacy to performance-based legitimacy. Teng's theory of building socialism with Chinese characteristics calls for intensifying

---

[59]For extensive discussion on the dynamics of legitimacy and effectiveness, see Seymour M. Lipset, *Political Man: The Social Basis of Politics* (New York: Doubleday, 1959), and Mattei Dogan, "Conceptions of Legitimacy," in *Encyclopedia of Government and Politics,* ed. Mary Hawkesworth and Maurice Kogan, vol. I (London and New York: Routledge, 1992), 116-26.

[60]Nicholas D. Kristof, "China Sees 'Market-Leninism' as Way to Future," *New York Times,* September 6, 1993, 1, 5.

economic growth and prosperity as the only way to maintain one-party dictatorship. In short, the stability of an illegitimate regime now rests more than ever before on its effectiveness in economic performance.

It seems on the diplomatic and economic surface that Teng's Leninist/ capitalist strategy has worked. Yet appearance is deceptive. The collapse of transnational Communism at its epicenter is bad enough for China's official identity as the People's Republic of China "under the leadership of the Communist Party of China and the guidance of Marxism-Leninism and Mao Zedong [Mao Tse-tung] Thought" (as embodied in the preamble to the present [1982] constitution). The transformation of Mongolia from a one-party Communist state into a democratic country is another ideological blow. More dubious is the argument that strongman politics and bureau-cratic-authoritarian state-led developmental model are particularly relevant in the East Asian Confucian civilizational zone. Putting aside the anom-alous cases of Hong Kong and Singapore as "city-states," the remarkable transformation of South Korea and Taiwan from highly authoritarian to newly democratizing countries (NDCs) punctures the myth that East Asian people are less interested in or concerned about human rights and democratic governance. The failure of Taiwan's quest for international legitimation required it to replenish its supply of legitimacy by first seeking performance-based legitimacy and then deeper legitimation via democrati-zation. For the first time in more than half century, Taiwan is demolishing— and with considerable help from Peking's often self-delegitimating be-havior—the myth that Chinese political culture is irredeemably encoded in the authoritarian Confucian past.

Perhaps nothing underscores as much as corruption the degree of legitimacy and effectiveness. Historically, the level of corruption is accepted as one of the best proven symptoms of the extent to which the state has lost its legitimacy. Corruption in post-Mao China has been increasing so rampantly and multifariously as to make it a single measuring stick for state legitimacy and state effectiveness (capacity). Harry Harding ad-vances a three-eyed view of corruption as symptomatic of political decay in post-Mao China: (1) the abuse of public power for private gain; (2) the decline in the capability of the state; and (3) the decline in the legitimacy of the political system such that the state can no longer evoke popular compliance.[61]

Money worship—the Tengist axiom, "getting rich is glorious"—has become a substitution ideology, to replace the carcass of Communism, that

---

[61]Harry Harding, "China at the Crossroads: Conservatism, Reform or Decay?" *Adelphi Paper*, no. 275 (London: The International Institute for Strategic Studies, March 1993), 44.

keeps the Leninist capitalist system running and that set in motion several successive tidal waves of corruption among Chinese officialdom, each worse than the preceding one. The first wave occurred around the late 1970s and early 1980s on the crest of mercantile tide in the form of abuse of power for monetary gain; the second wave in the mid-1980s saw rampant official speculation; and the third wave began in 1992 and took almost every possible form as to threaten the very foundation of the party-state.[62]

Just as the mercantilist spirit percolates mainland China's opening-up to the capitalist world system, the mercenary spirit has radiated downward in the Chinese state with about one-third of the 103 million government officials have gone into business on the side. The two-tier pricing system is made to order for licensed corruption by government and Party officials as they engage in what Marxists call "an exchange of unequal values" (i.e., exploitation) by first buying cheap at subsidized prices and then selling dear at market prices. Another favorite form of official corruption is the use of public funds on banquets and overseas travel in the tune of about 100 billion *yuan* annually. Some high-ranking cadres are reported to be selling highly confidential documents they spirited out of the country for huge sums of money.

The contradictions in China's self-proclaimed identity as a socialist and proletarian state—the post-Mao phenomenon of deepening "socialist" alienation—are everywhere for everyone to see. "The system of exploitation of man by man has been eliminated," states the preamble to the present PRC constitution, "and the socialist system established." And yet by shifting from the "iron rice bowl system" to the market, the state has effectively deprived workers of welfare state protection against abuses by their born-again capitalist employers. Hong Kong entrepreneurs are openly boasting that their total labor costs are only US$30 a month because officials have waived company obligations to cover such costs as pensions, health care, and other benefits even as many employers find it more profitable to carry out the antisocialist personnel policy on the shop floor: "Hire

---

[62]In his February 28, 1994 speech at the third plenary session of the Central Commission for Discipline Inspection on Planning for Anticorruption Work, Chiang Tse-min warned: "Corruption has spread to many sectors of social life, especially to cadres in CPC party and government organs. Power abuse, embezzlement, fraud, stealing impounded goods, obstruction of justice, bribery, and graft have reached alarming proportions. The danger of the party and the country being toppled if we are not determined to fight this tough battle against corruption is real enough. . . . We will be toppled if we do not handle the economy well. But—suppose the economy is doing well—we will still be toppled if corruption spreads, graft and bribery run amok, and the party is divorced from the people." Quoted in Jen Hui-wen, "Why Has Corruption Within the CPC Worsened?" *Hsin Pao* (Hong Kong), May 6, 1994, in *FBIS-CHI-94-090* (May 10, 1994): 14.

the children, but fire their mothers.'' In foreign policy, too, there is today only one kind of ''socialist'' China, the one that is becoming a proletarian state in a new way by vigorously peddling its cheap labor—including prison and child labor—as a comparative advantage in the global marketplace. Thanks to post-Mao China's U-turn away from socialist paternalism to the commodification of labor, a large section of the Chinese working class remains alienated from the so-called reform program. In the post-Mao era, China's socialist identity in practice, if not in theory, suffered steady burnout just when China's working class itself was rapidly expanding owing to the growing enmeshment in the capitalist world system.[63]

Second, *the state is losing control over the peripheries and restive population.* The habitual invocation of state sovereignty in the PRC's international comportment cannot belie the fact that the center no longer controls the peripheries, restive peasants, and workers, and that Chinese state sovereignty is a highly perforated paper tiger. With the growing globalization of the Chinese political economy, the devolution of power at home, and the fragmentation of authority and decision-making structures at the apex during the post-Mao era, the center has been forced to make a series of decentralizing compromises enabling the party-state's central planners to maintain the appearance that they were still controlling the economic reforms and opening-up to the outside world. In effect, the center has allowed the camel's nose of market-based competition to enter the tent of central planning, releasing enormous entrepreneurial energies of sovereignty-free actors (mostly ethnic Chinese entrepreneurs from Hong Kong, Taiwan, Macao, and Southeast Asia) that transformed the process of economic development with their own pace, logic, and direction. Nor does the state have macroeconomic monetary and fiscal levers and discipline by which other capitalist countries regulate investment and credit circulation. Ironically, the center relaxed its control to cause such an unprecedented economic growth only to lose, by installments, its sovereign power over the economy. At the same time, the implications of mainland China's growing regionalism, especially ''regional protectionism,'' extend far beyond domestic politics as more provinces are trading more with the outside world than with domestic counterparts both in real terms and as a percentage of a province's total trade.[64] Here is another example of the extent to which

---

[63]For a more detailed discussion about symbolic deconstruction and reconstruction of China's national identity in the post-Mao era, see Samuel S. Kim and Lowell Dittmer, ''Whither China's Quest for National Identity?'' in Dittmer and Kim, *China's Quest for National Identity*, 237-90.

[64]See Gerald Segal, ''China's Changing Shape,'' *Foreign Affairs* 73, no. 3 (May-June 1994): 43-58.

foreign policy is and becomes domestic policy.

The state is not only losing control over the increasingly autonomous peripheries but also over the increasingly restive population. With many of the traditional levers of control rusting away, the state increasingly depends for control on the gun power of three coercive institutions—the PAP, the Ministry of Public Security, and the PLA. The rise of China chorus—and China's new "first world" economic status as the world's third largest economy—seems like a half-truth that tends to obscure rather than clarify the decaying underpinnings of the Chinese state. The PPP-based confirmation of China's new "first world" economic status obscures the rise of a two-tier economy that is rapidly widening the gap between rich coastal China and poor interior China. With income disparities and class differences between coastal China and interior China rising rapidly—per capita income in the former is already sixteen times that of the latter—many Chinese refer to the latter (four-fifths of the country) as "China's third world." As well, the rise of China thesis skates over the shining surface of mainland China's bubble economy ready to burst.[65]

The post-Mao phenomenon of growing distributive injustice and deepening "socialist" alienation has given rise to an unprecedented degree of "relative deprivation." Relative deprivation—social actors' perceived discrepancy between their expectations and capabilities—is generally accepted as constituting the necessary precondition for violent civil conflict but its likelihood and magnitude of resulting in overt civil violence depend on the availability of mediating societal and institutional mechanisms.[66] Lacking assertive civil society and mediating social and political institutions, the number and type of civil violence in the cities and rural areas, triggered by growing relative deprivation, have increased by the day. Symptoms of deepening "socialist" alienation, rising social unrest, widening omnipresent money-worshipping, and mounting lawlessness—and eroding state control—are manifest everywhere for everyone to see.

The problem of controlling the outlying peripheries is greatly compounded by the presence of restive national minority peoples in "autonomous" regions, including Sinkiang, Tibet, Tsinghai (Qinghai), Inner Mongolia, and Ningsia (Ningxia) which together comprise almost exactly half of China's current territory. The image of sovereign Kazahks, Kyrgyzcs, Uzbeks, Tajiks, and Mongols in the post-Cold War setting of substate

---

[65]Richard Hornik, "Bursting China's Bubble," ibid., 28-42.

[66]See Ted Gurr, "Psychological Factors in Civil Violence," in *The War System: An Interdisciplinary Approach*, ed. Richard A. Falk and Samuel S. Kim (Boulder, Colo.: Westview Press, 1980), 248-81.

fragmentation and rising ethnonationalism could prove too inspiring for the non-Han peoples in Sinkiang, Inner Mongolia, and Tibet to put up with their second-class citizenship. Ethnonationalism is spreading from the newly minted Central Asian states to China's 20 million Muslims. Reports of demonstrations and riots in the strategically important Muslim areas (China's nuclear test site, Lop Nor, is in Sinkiang) have reached the outside world almost continuously in recent years. Here is another example of a seemingly domestic issue waiting to be exploded onto the world stage and into the PRC's international relations. Clearly, Peking confronts here a "too little, too much" double-sided dilemma in its domestic/foreign policy.

Third, *the state is losing control over environmental deficit financing.* Mainland China's seeming economic boom, resting on decades of anti-ecological policies and practices, has proceeded apace as if there are no limits to environmental deficit financing. At stake is the ecological underpinnings of Chinese state and society. Already some 15 percent of mainland China's GNP is being lost due to environmental degradation and damage. The National Environmental Protection Agency (NEPA) has an annual budget of 10 million *yuan,* equivalent one *yuan* for about every 8,600 that are lost annually due to environmental damage. A study by World Bank scientists in 1992 warned that "the increasing pressure on this limited resource base to feed, house and meet the energy needs" of the Chinese was rapidly destroying "whole ecosystems" and threatening to put the brakes on mainland China's current economic boom.[67]

The greatest threat of all for Chinese leaders today in maintaining political and social stability at home is therefore not Western imperialism or hegemonism but the progressive decaying of life-supporting ecosystems with the colossal social, economic, and political implications for the future of the Chinese state. Many of the floating population are "environmental refugees" pushed out of their denuded and desertified villages in search of work in cities or coastal provinces. Even under the best of circumstances, the environmental challenge is more often met in promise than in performance as "whatever posterity has ever done for me?" is the unstated norm everywhere including democratic societies. For Chinese gerontocracy with a serious legitimation crisis preoccupied with the question of its political survival, these social and ecodevelopmental challenges are daunting, to say the least.

From the perspective of sustainable development, between now and 2010 it will be possible only to modify mainland China's decline, with virtually no chance of halting or reversing it. The projections of major

---

[67]*New York Times,* November 7, 1993, 17.

indicators of environmental change in mainland China suggest that there is no realistic hope for a reversal of China's environmental degradation during the coming two decades (1990-2010): a 25 percent decline in per capita availability of arable land; a 30 percent decrease in forest reserves; a 40 percent higher demand for water; and a 50 percent higher need for commercial energy; such increases in pollution rates as a nearly triple release of wastewater; and a 50 percent rise in SO_2 emissions. And these projected changes will have profoundly unsettling effects on the course and success of the modernization drive, but more significantly, some scholars and policymakers suggest that mainland China has already crossed critical thresholds of environmental sustainability, presaging new local, regional, and even international conflicts of seriousness unprecedented in recent history.[68]

Fourth, *as dramatized by the Tienanmen tragedy in global prime time, the state is losing its control over information.* China is *in*, if not *of*, the global village. The contemporary global information/transparency revolution is under way in mainland China, even in the remote hinterlands as it breaks down in its pathway the monopoly that the state once enjoyed. Economics, ecology, communications, technology, and human rights, thanks to the global transparency revolution, do not respect state sovereignty. With the price of acquiring information steadily declining, this information/ transparency revolution reflects the globalization of increasingly intertwined political, economic, social, and normative structures and values and as well fosters the rapid mobilization of people's needs, demands, frustration, and intolerance—indeed, the second "revolution of people power." Information so easily acquired offers more options for and pathways of popular empowerment. In a sense, Peking has lost its sovereign control over global human rights politics. With increasing PRC participation in global human rights politics, the shrinkage of social and geographical distances, the emergence of global human rights standards and norms, and the proliferation of human rights NGOs providing a steady flow of information on human rights violations, it is becoming increasingly more difficult for Peking to maintain a policy of "do as I say, not as I do." In short, the significant challenge to state control has not only come from below and within but also from

---

[68]See He Bochuan, *China on the Edge: The Crisis of Ecology and Development* (San Francisco: China Books and Periodicals, 1991); Vaclav Smil, *China's Environmental Crisis: An Inquiry into the Limits of National Development* (Armonk, N.Y.: M. E. Sharpe, 1993); Vaclav Smil, "Environmental Change as a Source of Conflict and Economic Losses in China," and Jack A. Goldstone, "Imminent Political Conflict Arising from China's Environmental Crises," in *Occasional Paper Series of the Project on Environmental Change and Acute Conflict*, no. 2 (December 1992) (International Security Studies Program, American Academy of Arts and Sciences, Cambridge, Mass.); and Shanti R. Conly and Sharon L. Camp, *China's Family Planning Program: Challenging the Myths*, Country Study Series no. 1 (Washington, D.C.: The Population Crisis Committee, 1992).

above and without—many thanks to the global information/transparency revolution.

And finally, *the state is faced with a leadership/succession crisis.* All of the domestic vulnerabilities and weaknesses listed above would not separately and individually do the party-state system in. However, when combined with the impending leadership crisis manifest in the progressive degrading of the level of coherence of the state itself and in the conflicting foreign policy signals, these vulnerabilities of a weak state assume greater significance. Peking's third-generation leaders in the post-Teng era will not be able to steer the ship of the state as Mao did and, to a lesser extent, Teng has done. Lacking the most crucial power resources, authority, and legitimacy, the new leadership will not be in a position to cope effectively with multiple threats at home and multiple foreign policy challenges abroad. Nor will the leadership be in a position to manage the rising tension between nationalism and internationalism or to make the necessary compromises on issues of state sovereignty relating to Hong Kong, Taiwan, Tibet, Sinkiang, Spratlys, Tiaoyütai, and the remaining irredentist claims to territory held by many of China's sixteen neighboring countries.[69] Thus, the absence of an all-powerful leader leaves domestic/foreign policy open to greater contention than ever before. An internal (*nei-pu*) policy analysis by two Yale-educated Chinese for circulation among senior officials points to growing "regionalism" and the loss of state control as a harbinger of an unravelling China: "If a 'political strongman' dies, it is possible that a situation like post-Tito Yugoslavia will emerge. In years, at the soonest a few and at the latest between ten and twenty, the country will move from economic collapse to political break-up, ending with its disintegration."[70]

The sound and fury of state sovereignty in Chinese diplomacy cannot paper over the unpleasant reality on the ground that the PRC today is a weak, Balkanizing state. Herein lies the great irony of all—that today the main danger to the stability of the Asia-Pacific region stems primarily from the PRC's domestic weaknesses, even as the success of Peking's foreign policy inevitably rests on domestic stability. Clearly, this weak, reactive, insecure, and fragmented China is more unpredictable and dangerous than a strong, confident, and cohesive China posing a major challenge to the establishment of a more peaceful regional and global order in the years to come. All things considered, then, I cannot conclude with any confident prognostication of the future of the Chinese ship of state charting its way clear to the promised land.

---

[69]See David Bachman, "The Limits to Leadership in China," *NBR Analysis* 3, no. 3 (August 1992): 23-35.

[70]Quoted in *The Economist* (London), September 25, 1993, 14.

13

How Flexible Is Peking's Foreign Policy?

Chih-yu Shih

At the 1990 American Political Science Association annual meeting held in San Francisco, Chinese-American scholar Chao Ch'üan-sheng (Zhao Quansheng) gave a presentation on Peking's (Beijing's) foreign policy, arguing that Peking was rigid on issues involving principles but flexible otherwise.[1] Asked how one was able to judge if there was an issue of principle, Chao encouraged the audience to observe to what extent Peking's behavior appeared rigid. He did not appreciate the subsequent questions which challenged his seemingly tautological explanation. For Chao, I believe, there was no tautology. It is the situation and the atmosphere that determine if an issue would become a matter of principle. What situation and atmosphere, then, generate a sense of principle?

Four years before that conference, British Japan expert Ronald Dore titled one of his books, *Flexible Rigidities*, noting a style of political economy not all that familiar to his colleagues.[2] The Japanese appear to enjoy a kind of mind-set which allows a complete, collective shift of position after a prolonged internal negotiation: rigid in any period of time, flexible in the long run. It is claimed by some others that this reflects a unique battlefield philosophy.[3] The locus of the battlefield identifies the enemy, not vice versa, but the locus may shift as the context changes. Why, then,

---

[1]Zhao Quansheng, "Achieving Maximum Advantage: Rigidity and Flexibility in Chinese Foreign Policy" (Paper presented at the American Political Science Association Annual Meeting, San Francisco, September 1, 1990).

[2]Ronald Dore, *Flexible Rigidities: Industrial Policy and Structural Adjustment in the Japanese Economy, 1970-80* (Stanford, Calif.: Stanford University Press, 1986).

[3]Jun-ichi Kyogoku, *The Political Dynamics of Japan*, translated by Nobutaka Ike (Tokyo: University of Tokyo Press, 1987).

does any specific context come into being?

It is useful to reflect on what Louis Hartz called "natural liberalism" in 1955. American liberalism is natural, according to Hartz, because it developed not as a response to tyranny or as a war of one principle against another as it did in Europe, where tyranny had been a part of life. Consequently, what is not liberal is not natural to the Americans. Therein is derived the American absolutism against Communism and authoritarianism.[4] Natural liberals would probably fail to tolerate natural authoritarianism even in its most moderate form. Where, then, is the demarcation between naturalism and absolutism?

One can recall countless philosophers caught, though in different ways, in similar dilemmas: that Leviathan must sway supreme sovereignty over subjects, who voluntarily submit the mandate in order to avoid the state of nature but at the expense of their own free will;[5] that the Prince must necessarily wield wits to deceive without moral constraint and protect from the City of God his citizens who submerge without individuality;[6] that the General Will must prevail with no check as long as it acquires the consent of the ruled first.[7] Who, then, is to separate the external anarchical realm of flexible sovereign deed and the internal orderly domain of rigid sovereign governing?[8]

It would almost seem that flexibility and rigidity are both antithetic and symbiotic. The same is true of Peking's foreign policy. Peking's foreign policy loses flexibility when principles are disputed. Previously trivial things may become matters of principle. What is meant by principles from Peking's perspective? Principles are those statements with which the Chinese are historically and customarily comfortable in using to differentiate themselves from others. In essence, this is an argument of identity.[9] If identities are about principles which, in turn, are about behavioral rigidities, then there must be periods of flexibility, in contrast to which rigidities, and thus identities, are meaningful.

---

[4] Louis Hartz, "The Concept of a Liberal Society," in Louis Hartz, *The Liberal Tradition in America* (Boston: Harcourt Brace Jovanovich, 1955).

[5] Cornelia Navari, "Hobbies and the Hobbesian Tradition in International Thought," *Millennium* 11, no. 3 (1982): 202-22.

[6] Mark Hulliung, *Citizen Machiavelli* (Princeton, N.J.: Princeton University Press, 1983).

[7] In a sense, the general will dictates functionalism instead of free will. See the feminist critique in Susan Moller Okin, *Women in Western Political Thought* (Princeton: Princeton University Press, 1979), 106-39.

[8] This is a point made by the postmodern critic R. B. J. Walker in his *Inside/Outside: International Relations as Political Theory* (Cambridge: Cambridge University Press, 1993).

[9] For a good summary of different perspectives, see Lowell Dittmer and Samuel S. Kim, eds., *China's Quest for National Identity* (Ithaca, N.Y.: Cornell University Press, 1993).

I will use Richard Nixon's visit to mainland China and the Peking-London dispute over Hong Kong as two cases of interest to illustrate my own confusion over the flexibility-rigidity dialectics.

The Sino-U.S. Rapprochement in the Early 1970s

Strategic Flexibility

The Strategic Flexibility Argument. Generally speaking, the Shanghai Communiqué of 1972 signified a dramatic shift in Peking's foreign policy position. Western as well as Chinese scholars conceive the breakthrough of Sino-U.S. relations as a typical show of flexibility, especially Chou En-lai's (Zhou Enlai's) ability to explore new possibilities in a changing world. The flexibility demonstrated here is said to have shocked the world. In fact, the shock had started earlier when Mao decided to invite the U.S. national table tennis team for a tour in Peking, and when U.S. national security advisor Henry Kissinger made two subsequent visits to establish a mutual understanding and arrange an ensuing trip for President Richard Nixon. From the legacy of total confrontation, suddenly the two countries were ready to deal with each other in a peaceful tone.

Peking's willingness to explore a sociable relationship with the United States indeed developed in a short time period. The flexibility argument could easily be made based on Peking's capacity to accommodate the recent change in the Washington-Moscow-Peking strategic triangle. Scholars have convincingly demonstrated how the Soviet invasion of Czechoslovakia in 1968 launched a series of trilateral signaling which finally led to a switch of alliance in the triangle on February 28, 1972, the date the Shanghai Communiqué was signed.[10] Meanwhile, the People's Republic of China (PRC) and the Soviet Union fought over the Chenpao Island twice on March 2 and 15, 1969 and along China's western borders during following summer. In November, the Soviet Union sent Aleksey Kosygin to Peking for peace talks, which were basically successful.

In fact, Mao personally noted as early as 1967 that Nixon's vision of an Asia after the Vietnam War would include a place for mainland China.[11] Consistent with the flexibility argument, on November 25, 1968, the PRC sent a message through its Polish office that Peking was willing

---

[10]Richard Wich, *Sino-Soviet Crisis Politics* (Cambridge, Mass.: Harvard University Press, 1980).

[11]Kung Li, *K'ua-yüeh hung-kou: 1969-1979-nien Chung-Mei kuan-hsi te yen-pien* (Crossing the grand ditch: The evolution of Sino-U.S. relationship, 1969-79) (Honan: Honan People's Press, 1992), 39-40.

to reopen the bilateral talks at an ambassadorial level. Research efforts also took place in mainland China. Chou En-lai had Ch'en I (Chen Yi) lead a group of top officials to study the world situation. They concluded in March 1969 that the Soviet Union was unlikely to intensify the war with the PRC, but Peking should still consider attempting to relieve tensions between the United States and itself.[12] In July, Chou En-lai was personally involved in the decision to free two American sailors who were rescued in Chinese sea space. The Chinese side meant this as a message of goodwill.[13]

Scholars may debate about the earliest moment of the Sino-Soviet dispute, but they would probably agree on its culmination in the border war. The impression is that Peking's decision to try rapprochement with the United States reflected its primary concern for a potential Soviet threat. The Shanghai Communiqué not only revealed a long extant (and known) problem in the relationship between Peking and Moscow, but also generated a brand new scene, unperceived at that time by most world watchers. For them, therefore, Peking's move to fulfill its fresh roles required by the new juxtaposition in the loose bipolar system can only be interpreted as a high degree of flexibility.[14] In short, Peking alone could not have begot a systemic level transformation, so hence the significance should have lied in its quick adjustment to forces outside its sphere of influence. Perceptual sensitivity and behavioral conformity gave birth to a new impression of flexibility, representing the departure from an entirely different image of the China as a potential source of world revolution.

I suggest that the China of flexibility observed in the process leading up to the signing of the Shanghai Communiqué does not represent flexibility without qualification, nor can it be easily separated from a China of rigid principle. At least two questions deserve attention. One may wonder why Peking decided to receive Kissinger at that particular moment, and not right after the border war, nor before Kosygin's reconciliation tour. Secondly, one may wonder how is it that Peking could not reach the process of normalization in a more incremental way. The abrupt style itself is a point of interest.

Peking's Timing. First of all, one should recall that the proposal to reopen the bilateral talks in Poland was withdrawn upon the U.S. de-

---

[12] *Yeh Chien-ying chuan-lüeh* (A brief biography of Yeh Chien-ying) (Peking: Military Science Press, 1987), 217.

[13] Kung, *K'ua-yüeh hung-kou*, 42.

[14] For a typical systemic analysis, see Michael Ng-Quinn, "Effects of Bipolarity on Chinese Foreign Policy," *Survey* 26, no. 2 (1982): 102-30.

cision to extend asylum to a Chinese defector in the Netherlands.[15] Also, Chou's decision to release two American intruders was in response to the U.S. decision to ease restrictions on trade with and tours to mainland China, and thus was not an initiative.

It goes without saying that the first public move had to be made by the United States. Nixon, in his inauguration speech on January 20, 1969, sent the message that the United States was ready to deal with all countries, a message that Peking heard with interest and a message which Mao decided should be in newspapers to inform the Chinese public.[16] Most importantly, Kosygin's China tour produced significant results. We now know that Chou and Kosygin reached four agreements in the November meeting, the contents of which focused mainly on how to meet the mutually recognized need to avoid armed conflict over the disputed areas.[17]

It was after this meeting that the dramatic anecdote of U.S. Polish Ambassador Walter Stoessel chasing after Chinese Attache Lei Yang in a social party came to fore. This was December 3, 1969. Lei successfully avoided a face-to-face encounter with Stoessel, but nonetheless some kind of message was received. On December 6, Peking released another two American civilian intruders. On December 11, Stoessel arrived at the Chinese embassy upon Lei's invitation. On December 18, Kissinger announced that the United States was ready to dialogue with any country regardless of that country's domestic ideology. On January 8, Lei returned the visit and in that meeting, the two sides agreed to resume ambassadorial-level talks. They met formally on January 20 and again on February 20. Stoessel inquired about the possibility of the U.S. sending a representative to Peking and Lei responded positively but demanded that China's sovereignty claim over Taiwan be respected before the Sino-U.S. relationship could fundamentally improve.[18] The series of exchanges stopped as a result of the U.S. military action in Cambodia.[19]

Shortly thereafter, a second round of talks was initiated by the U.S. side. On Capitol Hill on June 4, Congress removed its opposition to the PRC's participation in the United Nations. On July 10, Nixon was quoted as saying that he thought that the United States should recognize the

---

[15]Kung, K'ua-yüeh hung-kou, 40.

[16]Ibid.

[17]Chou En-lai wai-chiao wen-hsüan (Selected works of Chou En-lai on diplomacy) (Peking: Central Literature Press, 1990), 462-63; also in Kung, K'ua-yüeh hung-kou, 44-45.

[18]This is based on the CCP Central Committee Politburo's report on the Sino-U.S. talks cited by Kung Li, in K'ua-yüeh hung-kou, 50-51.

[19]See People's Daily, May 19, 1970, 6.

People's Republic.[20] On the same date, Peking released an American intelligence agent arrested in 1958. On October 1, National Day, Mao received Edgar Snow on top of Tienanmen (Tiananmen), letting him know privately that Nixon would be welcome if he chose to come. The amicable atmosphere was then destroyed by U.S. military action in Laos in February 1971.

But in March, the table tennis teams from the two countries met in Tokyo. The American team expressed a wish to visit mainland China on March 30. Peking's Foreign Ministry discussed the matter and felt it premature for the U.S. team to come to mainland China.[21] On March 4, the two teams had a direct encounter which was subsequently reported in the highly restricted circulation *Ts'an-kao hsiao-hsi* (Reference News) in mainland China. On the same day, the PRC was elected to vice chairmanship of the relevant world table tennis association, with U.S. cooperation and compliments. There were warm congratulatory remarks from the U.S. team after the election.[22] On March 7, Mao personally extended an invitation to visit mainland China to the U.S. team, together with four other teams.[23] The Chinese dropped at the same time a firm stand that Peking opposed the "two Chinas" or "one China, one Taiwan" policy.[24] Although the players might not have understood the political implication, when they met Chou En-lai on March 14, their government removed the twenty-one-year-old trade embargo on mainland China. On the other hand, Nixon announced normalization of the Sino-U.S. relationship to be his top priority. From then on, the two sides worked through a Pakistani channel in preparation for Kissinger's clandestine visit to Peking.

Obviously, Nixon's way to mainland China was not without obstacles. Negotiations over the terms of the visit and preparation for the draft statement showed signs of struggle. On Kissinger's second visit on October 20, 1971, however, he returned with an impression that Chou did not like to bargain over trifles for Chou readily agreed to drop those sentences Kissinger thought humiliating to the U.S. side.[25] Chou's conciliatory move

---

[20]Peking heard Nixon's message loud and clear. See Li Ch'ang-chiu and Shih Lu-chia, eds., *Chung-Mei kuan-hsi liang-pai-nien* (Two-hundred years of Sino-U.S. relations) (Peking: Hsinhua Press, 1984), 214-15.

[21]Kung, *K'ua-yüeh hung-kou*, 79.

[22]See Chi Hung-sheng, *Wu-shih-nien Chung-Mei kuan-hsi* (Fifty years of Sino-U.S. relations) (Shanghai: Pai-chia Press, 1993).

[23]See Ch'ien Chiang, *P'ing-p'ang wai-chiao shih-mo* (The entirety of table tennis diplomacy) (Shanghai: Oriental Press, 1987), 137.

[24]*Ts'an-k'ao hsiao-hsi* (Reference News), April 7, 1971, quoted in Kung, *K'ua-yüeh hung-kou*, 83.

[25]Kissinger's appreciation was noted by the Chinese. See Kung, *K'ua-yüeh hung-kou*, 149.

did not occur without a context, though. Precisely during Kissinger's second visit, the PRC staged a fight to replace the Republic of China in the United Nations. In fact, victory could be anticipated. Since Peking had defeated the United States in the United Nations, a few sentences of anti-imperialism lost their significance. Chou could afford generosity, having his cake and eating it too.

The Abrupt Style. The second point of interest is that the Chinese style of normalization is abrupt rather than incremental. It was abrupt in the sense that except for the top leaders, everyone else in the country had to be prepared to redefine imperialism in a very short time period. The failure to engage in normalization incrementally suggests that the flexibility argument is indeed with qualification. The abrupt style implies that there must have been rigidity in the first place. Lei Yang's case is an example. Chou later remarked that Stoessel's chase after him almost caused him a heart attack. Although Chou might have been joking, Lei would have certainly failed to appreciate the joke in Poland. Given the context of the Cultural Revolution, it was unlikely that a Chinese foreign representative would attempt any creative move or respond to one initiated by an imperialist.[26]

In actuality, the abrupt style probably reveals more continuity than change in the Chinese revolutionary drama. If Mao had believed that the Cultural Revolution had gone too far and had to bring in troops to curtail its absurdity, Mao must have also had to consider a substitute for a domestic revolutionary target in order for his appeal of permanent revolution to survive. The Soviet Union served this purpose best because it was permanent, social imperialistic, and seemingly imminently threatening. The task left was to portray the Soviet Union as the most formidable enemy of the cultural revolutionaries so that domestic unity could be resumed and consolidated at the same time. For this reason alone, Peking could not possibly treat U.S. imperialism as the target of the revolutionary united front. Some adjustment was, thus, imperative in the light of the domestic political need.[27]

In other words, Peking's rapprochement with the United States was a domestic derivative. Peking's reappraisal of the world situation reflected *both* the opportunity available in the world *and* the political motivation inside. Peking's flexible gesture toward the United States was therefore short of an intrinsically independent logic. If the Cultural Revolution

---

[26]Ibid., 48.

[27]See Jonathan Adelman and Chih-yu Shih, *Symbolic War: The Chinese Use of Force, 1840-1980* (Taipei: Institute of International Relations, 1993), 210-20.

was ended without a good explanation, the legitimacy of the regime would have been seriously jeopardized. Similarly, if U.S. imperialism could become a friend, the legitimacy of the regime might also be challenged. In comparison, however, the external shift of position was obviously a lesser evil. In reality, the Sino-U.S. rapprochement might actually serve as a perfect drama to cast the Soviet Union in the role of the world's leading evil.[28] Such an abrupt change in foreign policy position had, to a large extent, preserved the revolutionary pretension in domestic politics, hence a show of rigidity, not flexibility.

It appeared that there had been no time for Mao to come up with another revolutionary target. Everything pointed to the Soviet Union. Experiences could suggest that domestic revolutionary appeal might result in efforts to overthrow himself. The 1967 revolutionary climax reminded him of that possibility and the Lin Piao (Lin Biao) incident of 1971 reconfirmed this potential. Although anti-imperialist rhetoric had to continue, imperialism could not be allowed to match the evil of the Soviet Union lest this would distract the revolutionary unity. The internal political concern deprived the leaders of the incremental option. The abrupt show of Mao's and Chou's bold policy was the result. When external flexibility reflects only a demand of internal rigidity, the flexibility argument can no longer be sustained.

Tactical Flexibility

The Tactical Flexibility Argument. Even if one acknowledges that flexible adjustment of external relations primarily reflects an internal logic, the flexibility argument still follows in the sense that diplomats effectively adjusted in a brief period of time. That is to say, if Chinese diplomats were never flexible in manipulating triangular relationships according to international power calculus, their leaders were at least capable of flexibly and tactically executing the adjustment when internal interests required.

Since the shift of the revolutionary target toward the Kremlin redefined the U.S. role, Peking was able to utilize those negligible signs (genuine as well as imagined) of friendship coming from the United States and acted upon them whenever they appeared. Sometimes, it was also necessary to fix a few clues for the U.S. side to make the first move. The use of table tennis diplomacy was illustrative. The leaders themselves were in full control. For example, Chou En-lai was personally in charge

---

[28]On the role of the United States in Sino-Soviet relations, see Chih-yu Shih, *China's Just World: The Morality of Chinese Foreign Policy* (Boulder, Colo.: Lynne Rienner, 1993), 79-81.

of all the news releases during the table tennis match to make sure that the messages were correctly worded.[29] Another clue was Mao's willingness to receive Nixon secretly despite the lack of glory that provided as compared with a public visit.[30] Chou was also quick to remove anti-American slogans from Kissinger's sight during his second visit and from the joint statement of the two countries.

Doubtlessly, there was suspicion in Peking about the wisdom of the rapprochement. On May 26, 1971, the Politburo responded point by point, which well exemplifies the flexibility argument concerning diplomatic tactics. In response to concern that the rapprochement would destroy the American people's determination in opposing imperialism, the Politburo believed that the rapprochement could achieve exactly the opposite by linking it with the U.S. withdrawal from Vietnam and Taiwan. The same logic applied to Vietnamese people's determination against imperialism, hence no damage would occur in the long run. In response to uneasiness that Washington was using the rapprochement to score on its "two Chinas" goal, the Politburo maintained that this would expose U.S. imperialism sooner and better and contribute to the Chinese people's long-term devotion to anti-imperialism. Furthermore, the Politburo reminded those reluctant members that a successful rapprochement may have exacerbated the confrontation between the two hegemonies.[31]

In retrospect, China scholars may find this exchange of words somewhat amusing for they are all clothed in revolutionary rhetoric. However, the rapprochement gained its legitimacy specifically because the leaders were amenable to camouflaging their flexibility with a rigid appearance. This paved the way for Chou En-lai's unique approach to the rapprochement. Chou explained in detail to Kissinger the necessity that the two sides be honest about their differences in public.[32] This eventually led to the "agree to disagree" formula in the Shanghai Communiqué. Chou focused on the atmosphere of the rapprochement, not any specific contents, and conditioned the friendly atmosphere upon the U.S. withdrawal from Asia. This way, neither the PRC nor the United States needed to make

---

[29]Kung, *K'ua-yüeh hung-kou*, 90.

[30]Mao was quoted as having said to Snow: ". . . pass on the message, tell him to take on a plane in secret, not in public and come. Our talks can be vain but they can also be effective. Don't just hold there." See ibid., 62.

[31]Politburo's report cited in ibid., 102-6.

[32]See Wang Li and Ch'iu Sheng-yün, "Historic Accomplishment—Chou En-lai in the Process of Opening the Door of Sino-U.S. Relations," in *Yen-chiu Chou En-lai wai-chiao ssu-hsiang yü shih-chien* (Studying Chou En-lai's diplomatic thought and practices), ed. P'ei Chien-chang (Peking: World Knowledge Press, 1989), 208.

any concessions, but together shocked the world by simply shaking hands.

Multiple Principles. In a deeper sense, however, tactical flexibility is premised on the availability of multiple principles in Peking's foreign policy. Flexibility results not simply from manipulation of words or appearance, but from political necessity which is delineated by the seeming coexistence of anti-imperialism, anti-social imperialism (later anti-hegemonism), peaceful coexistence, etc. These principles evolved gradually as the PRC struggled to justify its foreign policy to the domestic audience at different points in time. Consequently, there developed a group of principles which Peking claimed had internal consistency, though others thought them mutually incompatible. Maintaining consistency became a burden: instead of Peking using principles flexibly to suit ulterior purposes, these principles began to occupy the leadership, which became short and busy justifying itself on all principles.

It was indeed unlikely that Peking could satisfy these principles all at once in any given time period. A move on the anti-social imperialist front would render the appearance that Peking was about to jettison anti-imperialism. When leaders rescued anti-imperialism, the world would think that Peking cared no more about peaceful coexistence. One tiny move toward peace incurred the image that Peking was just giving lip service to anti-social imperialism. The process of rapprochement illustrates this. Following the Soviet invasion into Czechoslovakia, anti-social imperialism had supremacy. The ensuing sequence of rapprochement once made Washington surmise that Peking was ready to give up anti-imperialism. Peking stopped to resume criticism amidst the escalating U.S. involvement in Indochina, but then caught the opportunity at the world table tennis tournament to renew the peace pose.

Multiple principles disallowed Peking from targeting only one country and, thereby, encouraged Peking to make moves that could be interpreted as containing multiple signals. The decision to release the American agent on July 10, 1970 was aimed both at balancing the recent reopening of Sino-Soviet border negotiations and at responding to the American decision to partially lift its trade embargo on mainland China.[33] In this sense, flexibility loses meaning. The notion of flexibility is deconstructed because flexibility is the product of political necessity to satisfy several rigid principles. Since one could hardly satisfy all principles simultaneously, one could not help working on them alternatively, giving the appearance of inconsistency or flexibility.

The Chinese revolutionary experience before 1949 had actually pre-

---

[33]See *People's Daily*, July 11, 1970, 2.

pared the PRC in this style. (Not mentioning Lucian Pye's argument that the Chinese culture breeds a mind-set comfortable with inconsistency,[34] or Arthur Schlesinger's similar argument that there has been periodical shifting between two sets of values in American diplomatic history.[35]) Mao's united front strategy precisely asked the masses to tolerate enemies in one's own camp for the short-run sake of the struggle. The united front tactic reminded everyone that enemies remain enemies, though perhaps temporarily on one's side, en route to a long-term revolutionary goal of a socialist utopia.[36] It could never be a fundamental mistake (in the language of united front) to cooperate with enemies under special circumstances. Tactical errors possible? Yes, but never irrevocable. Whether correcting tactical errors or executing accurate united front adjustments, policy must, by definition, display flexibility, a definition premised upon multiple enemies and multiple principles. Principles identify enemies; enemies dramatize principles.

Forced Flexibility. It would take too much semantic discussion to deny that the Sino-U.S. rapprochement represents flexibility in Peking's foreign policy, but the enormous effort spent to explain away the undesired political connotations of the rapprochement indicates that the flexibility argument itself is a matter of semantic presentation. Foreign policy leaders in Peking constantly worried about their image during the normalization process. They struggled to prepare their fellow citizens to accept the imperialist connection. For example, Mao deliberately instructed that the *People's Daily* print Nixon's inauguration speech. On May 31, 1971, all basic-level Party divisions received the notes on Mao's remarks with Snow on December 18 of the previous year which included an invitation to Nixon.[37] In fact, Snow's appearance at Tienanmen during his visit was already an effective harbinger for those more sensitive watchers. Between June 4 and 14, 1971, over two hundred central cadres gathered to study and discuss the expected opening of the Sino-U.S. normalization process.[38]

The Politburo prepared at the same time. Members reached eight conclusions on May 26, 1971 in preparation for Kissinger's secret visit scheduled for the following month (later postponed to July 9). All eight

---

[34]Lucian Pye wrote a whole book based on this theory. See *The Mandarin and the Cadre* (Ann Arbor: The University of Michigan Center for Chinese Studies, 1988).

[35]Arthur Schlesinger, *Cycles in American History* (New York: Free Press, 1986).

[36]For a good reference, see Kuo Chih-ming and Jen T'ao, eds., *Mao Tse-tung lun t'ung-i chan-hsien* (Mao Tse-tung on united front) (Peking: Chinese Literature and History Press, 1987).

[37]Kung, *K'ua-yüeh hung-kou*, 108.

[38]Ibid.

concerned principles: that the Americans should withdraw from Taiwan; that Taiwan was a part of China; that Peking would work on a peaceful solution on the Taiwan issue; that the PRC, as the sole legitimate government of China, resolutely opposed the idea of "two Chinas" or "one China, one Taiwan"; that the PRC and the United States could not set up any diplomatic relationship without the U.S. first confirming the above principles; that Peking would not raise the issue of the PRC's participation in the United Nations with Kissinger; that Peking would not raise the issue of bilateral trade; and that U.S. troops should withdraw from the Far East.[39]

Moral pretension continued during this preparation period. Perhaps, the leaders themselves were unsure of the wisdom of the rapprochement. Any ideologically antagonistic move on the U.S. side could have thus revoked normalization. In actuality, Peking had to call off the process every time the United States escalated involvement in Cambodia and Laos. The *People's Daily* did not cease its anti-imperialist accusations or its calls for world revolution.[40] Only those most observant and involved watchers, like Kissinger, could recognize (or imagine) that there had been fewer personal charges against American leaders.[41] When he visited Peking the second time on October 20, 1971, he was still surprised by the prevalence of anti-American posters. More awaited him in his guest room where he encountered an English pamphlet which invited the readers to bring down the American imperialist and running dogs.

These were possibly not just pretensions, especially at the time when the Americans thought they had been. Peking consistently presented its principled positions since the first confrontation in Poland between Lei and Stoessel. The people, time, and place all had changed, but two of the Chinese messages did not: Taiwan being a part of China and the U.S. evacuating the Far East (including Indochina). Peking's stand against the Soviet Union, in contrast, came and went in these meetings, although the Shanghai Communiqué did incorporate Peking's most favored anti-Soviet code word, "not seeking hegemony."

The flexibility argument looks particularly hypocritical as one examines Chou's unique approach to maintaining differences while seeking common ground. In fact, it was almost imperative for the Chinese leaders to epitomize their differences with the United States in order to demonstrate that they were not compromising principles. The Shanghai Communiqué

---

[39]Ibid., 103-4.
[40]For one good example, see *People's Daily*, May 21, 1970.
[41]Kung, *K'ua-yüeh hung-kou*, 58-59.

dramatizes this attitude best by claiming that countries with different systems should talk with each other peacefully. Hence, Peking enacted principles by preserving them in word and flexibility by the pure act of talking. With Mao's advance knowledge, Chou En-lai explained:

> Between China and the United States, there exist serious discords in ideology, social systems, and positions on important international issues. Twenty years of misunderstanding cannot be expected to evaporate over night. Under that circumstance, it would be discouraging if the two sides choose to sign a document of nonsense which tells no truth and guarantees no observance. Any act to cover up these discords would give the people of the two countries and the world an illusion which would disappoint and be harmful to the relationship between the two countries.[42]

Mao and Chou were most likely worried that the Chinese people would be disappointed and the rapprochement harmful to Mao's leadership. In any case, Peking had to demonstrate that it had made no concession, nor compromise, but had at the same time displayed flexibility. Flexibility attends to the mode of expression, rigidity relates to attitude. As long as both sides held the right attitude, they did not have to fight; if they continued to disagree, Chou proclaimed that Peking could wait.[43] What flexibility!

Whose Flexibility

Whether or not the Sino-U.S. rapprochement represents flexibility in Peking's foreign policy is a matter of perspective. If we take the perspective of the Republic of China on Taiwan, Peking was not flexible at all for it made no adjustment in its Taiwan policy.[44] In fact, since the 1950s, Peking had decided that the peaceful resolution of the Taiwan issue depended on the American attitude. The less the international involvement, the more likely the resolution would be peaceful. This continues to be Peking's official position in the 1990s. Interestingly, Peking always also claims that Peking is not flexible on the issues involving principles.[45]

For a scholar of balance-of-power theory,[46] Peking's foreign policy

---

[42]See note 32 above.

[43]Chou's remark quoted in the *New York Times*, August 9, 1971 and copied in *Ts'an-k'ao hsiao-hsi*, August 15, 1971. See Kung, *K'ua-yüeh hung-kou*, 133.

[44]For example, see Huang Kun-huei, *Kuo-t'ung kang-ling yü liang-an kuan-hsi* (The Guidelines for National Reunification and cross-Strait relations) (Taipei: Mainland Affairs Council, 1992), 6.

[45]On the Hong Kong issue, for example, see *Kwangming Daily*, November 18, 1992, 4, and *People's Daily*, November 24, 1992, 1.

[46]For example, see Harvey W. Nelsen, *Power and Insecurity: Beijing, Moscow, and Washington, 1949-1988* (Boulder, Colo.: Lynne Rienner, 1989).

was highly flexible for it seemed to have fulfilled its systemic roles as the triangular relationship shifted after the 1960s. It began to explore the American option after the Prague Spring and correctly perceived and acted upon the developments in Indochina which necessitated the ultimate American withdrawal. Peking was also flexible in executing its strategic shift, always patiently waiting out each U.S. escalation in Indochina, both as a precaution for itself and as a test of U.S. intentions.

For some Chinese scholars, it may be true that the Taiwan issue was secondary to the Indochina issue during the negotiation of the Shanghai Communiqué, but from Peking's point of view, this was a gesture at most. Chou, in his interview with the *New York Times* published on August 15, 1971, highlighted the Indochina war. And Mao, when speaking with Nixon on February 21, 1972, stressed the relative importance of international issues. They did this because they wanted to preserve the Taiwan issue as a purely domestic question.[47] Nonetheless, the willingness to concentrate on other issues can only be interpreted as flexibility.

In contrast to the argument that Mao and Chou deliberately bypassed the Taiwan issue in the Shanghai Communiqué, opinion from the Chinese diplomatic circle contended that the most important issue between the two countries at that time had precisely been the Taiwan issue: the Shanghai Communiqué was the first public statement made by the United States that there was only one China.[48] For them, the rapprochement meant a significant shift of U.S. China policy. Accordingly, Peking's firm stand on that position continued to arouse celebration even in 1990. A diplomacy textbook author writes:

> China correctly and resolutely supported the people of the three Indochinese countries in their resistance of the United States in their struggle to save their own countries. Their efforts significantly weakened the hegemonic status of the U.S. imperialist, and made obsolete the postwar imperialist influence advanced by (1) the American imperialist's anachronistic policy of invasion first of the intermediate areas, primarily Asian and previously African colonial and semicolonial nations and their peoples, and (2) Cold War policy against the Soviet Union.[49]

However, having written that, the author drifted away from the applauded firm stand of principle:

---

[47]Kung Li is the representative here. See Kung, *K'ua-yüeh hung-kou*, 165, 168.

[48]Hsieh I-hsien, *Che-ch'ung yü kung-ch'u: Hsin Chung-kuo tui-wai kuan-hsi ssu-shih-nien* (Conflict resolution and coexistence: New China's forty-year foreign relations) (Honan: Honan People's Press, 1990), 165.

[49]Ibid., 166.

China correctly anticipated that the Soviet Union would begin to execute hegemonist policy and, to China, there existed simultaneous military threats from the United States and the Soviet Union. Under these circumstances, China correctly and resolutely adjusted its policy, improved its relationship with most countries, and changed the earlier abnormal situation in diplomacy corrupted by the world revolution conception. This practice had significant implications to the correct making of foreign policy in later periods. . . . Having received the message sent by the American leaders expressing willingness to ameliorate its relationship with China, China firmly invited the U.S. president to visit China. This opened the process of normalization and moved international relations into a brand new period.[50]

The Sino-U.K. Talks on Hong Kong

Peking's Sovereignty Sensitivity

In contrast with the Sino-U.S. normalization, the Sino-U.K. talks on Hong Kong have been the most contemporary demonstration of rigidity in Peking's foreign policy. Peking and London began their talks in 1982 and, in the following year, the United Kingdom agreed to hand over Hong Kong in 1997. In return, Peking promised to practice "one country, two systems" for no less than fifty years after reversion, thus preserving Hong Kong's current capitalist convention.[51] In 1984, the two sides signed a joint statement documenting the above agreement and concurred that they should together prepare a smooth transition in 1997. The subsequent negotiations had to do with detailed arrangement of Hong Kong's transition and, most importantly, Hong Kong's political institution after 1997.

In all the negotiations between Peking and London, Peking refused to permit the participation of Hong Kong representatives because of the island's colonial status.[52] The people of Hong Kong nonetheless strived to enhance their participation through China's domestic channels, which Peking had set up exactly to enlist their support. On the other hand, London struggled to design a sort of representative government and an electoral system, hoping Peking would take the whole package after 1997. From the British point of view, it might be necessary to make such arrangements so that the United Kingdom could create a legacy of

---

[50]Ibid.

[51]Wu Hsüeh-ch'ien, "Report to the Standing Committee of the National People's Congress on Processing the Review of Document Concerning the Sino-U.K. Agreement on the Issue of Hong Kong," in *Hsiang-kang wen-t'i hsüan-chi* (Selected essays on the Hong Kong issue) (Peking: People's Press, 1985), 16-17.

[52]Hsü Chia-t'un, *Hsü Chia-t'un hui-i-lu* (Memoirs of Hsü Chia-t'un) (Taipei: Linking Publishing Company, 1993), 96, 123.

crown rule after independence in Hong Kong as it had done in all its previous colonies.[53] Since Hong Kong was not going to be independent after the British withdrawal, it created a tasking job for Westminster. An honorable retreat would include two elements: a U.K.-style political system and continued opportunities for British business.

Both elements were contrary to Peking's principles of sovereignty and anti-imperialism (or anti-colonialism).[54] For Peking, Hong Kong never had representative government under colonial rule. The U.K. proposal to institute an electoral system was obviously targeted at Peking. This became particularly poignant when Peking felt increasingly uneasy about the Western attempt to transform mainland China (i.e., peaceful evolution) after the collapse of the Eastern Bloc and, above all, the June 4 Tienanmen massacre. After the June 4 incident, the United Kingdom not only took part in the international sanctions on the PRC for its oppression of the movement, but also deepened its connection with those in Hong Kong who favored a more democratic system after 1997. Nonetheless, Peking passed the Hong Kong Basic Law in April 1990, combining direct election and indirect election in a representative system.

The newest, and last, governor, Christopher Patten, arrived in Hong Kong in 1992. He appealed for international (the United States, Canada, Australia, etc.) and internal support, later nicknamed the international and the democracy cards.[55] The international card heightened Peking's alertness to imperialism; the democracy card to a more intense peaceful evolution strategy. Patten played the democracy card by insisting on enlarging the scope of direct election and wedging in a check-and-balance design to make the legislative branch more independent.[56] Concomitant with the polemic over Patten's proposal was the renewed dispute over the financial arrangement for the construction of a new airport. Peking's public charges were twofold: that the United Kingdom breached its promise made in the joint statement and subsequent exchange of letters and that the United Kingdom never consulted with Peking before it announced

---

[53]"Lee Kuan Yew on the Sino-U.K. Controversy," *Wen Wei Po* (Hong Kong), December 18, 1992, 6.

[54]Teng Hsiao-p'ing insisted that Peking could not allow any drifting on the sovereignty issue. See *Teng Hsiao-p'ing wen-hsüan* (Selected works of Teng Hsiao-p'ing), vol. 3 (Peking: People's Press, 1993), 12.

[55]Concerning the internationalization card, see *Ming Pao* (Hong Kong), November 20, 1992, 36; concerning the democracy card, see *Chung-kuo shih-pao* (China Times) (Taipei), February 5, 1993, 16 and *People's Daily*, February 3, 1993, 4.

[56]Christopher Patten, *Our Next Five Years: The Agenda for Hong Kong*, Address at the Opening of the 1992/93 Session of the Legislative Council, October 7, 1992 (Hong Kong: Government Printer, 1992).

all the intended new arrangements. In short, Peking was first deceived, then bypassed.

The Chinese claim was simple: Hong Kong is a part of China.[57] Accordingly, any arrangement affecting the situation of Hong Kong after 1997 was a matter of China's sovereignty and the United Kingdom must consult China. In the subsequent polemics, Peking insisted that this notion of "togetherness" was the key of the joint statement. Peking would not accept anything, reasonable or not, which did not go through Peking. The fact that Peking was always the last to know each of Patten's new moves confirmed the perception that the United Kingdom did not have China's sovereignty in mind at all. This led to the talk of Peking being ready to "build a new stove" (*ling-ch'i lu-tsao*, meaning completely abandoning the U.K. system and starting all over again in 1997).[58] In the Chinese media, the charges, now much more intense, recalled the history of the allied invasion of Peking in 1900 (colonialism) and provoked apprehension of hegemonism and imperialism.

Patten challenged Peking to be more positive by at least responding to his proposal.[59] Peking declined for fear of being tied to false ground.[60] Peking's inaction demonstrated Patten's ultimate constraint: he would have to leave Hong Kong after 1997 no matter what. This weakness, however, could be an asset, for Patten seemed determined to have his way and then simply watch and invite the world to watch the PRC destroy Hong Kong. This was the strategy of "burning the jade with the stone" (*yü-shih chü-fen*, a counterpart of the Western saying of throwing out the baby of Hong Kong with the bath water of the British legacy).[61] Patten chose not to give in, and Peking ordered that no official should meet with him or even visit Hong Kong. In spring 1994, the negotiations completely broke down. Like every previous breakdown, the Hong Kong stock market plummeted, taking with it the PRC's own massive investments in Hong Kong.[62]

Peking's Adherence to Principle

Sovereignty is such an abstract concept that Peking would almost have to decide case by case if a certain issue involved the principle of sovereignty. There is no guarantee, however, that an issue previously not

---

[57]This is unambiguously a sovereignty argument. See Editorial, *Wen Wei Po*, December 17, 1992, 2.

[58]*People's Daily*, December 17, 1992, 4.

[59]*Chung-yang jih-pao* (Central Daily News) (Taipei), December 1, 1992, 7.

[60]*People's Daily*, December 3, 1992, 4.

[61]See *Ming Pao*, December 23, 1992, 2.

[62]*Chung-kuo shih-pao*, December 1, 1992, 7.

considered to have involved sovereignty concerns, will not have sovereignty implications the next time. It would appear that the essence of sovereignty is itself a flexible matter. Patten's push on the direct election front was not without precedent. In negotiating with Peking about the contents of the Basic Law, London had consciously enlisted the democracy card and achieved success by catching the Chinese by surprise.[63] This was in 1985. In Patten's case, the timing was wrong. Patten's proposal of October 1992 came after the Tienanmen incident of June 4, 1989, the collapse of the Eastern Bloc,[64] the passing of the Hong Kong Act by the U.S. Congress in August 1992 despite Peking's protests, and Washington's decision in September to sell F-16 fighters to Taiwan.[65]

Patten's proposal to enlarge the scope of direct elections would possibly not have infuriated Peking to the extent it actually did without this context. As the Basic Law had already acknowledged direct election as a legitimate system, Peking could not have opposed it in principle. Peking's reason this time was sovereignty. The Basic Law could accommodate direct election because Peking had agreed, willingly or not. Patten's new proposal to enlarge its application in 1995 was never agreed to by Peking. Furthermore, Peking denounced the proposal for violating the understanding established in the exchange of letters between the two governments which embodied a spirit of sharing, but which Patten now claimed was not a part of the bilateral agreement. In the proposal Peking would agree to allow the Hong Kong system of 1995 to continue beyond 1997. If Peking were to endorse Patten's proposal in this way, that would mean that the United Kingdom could unilaterally determine, partially at least, Hong Kong's system after 1997.

Peking then decided to bypass Patten as he had bypassed Peking. Peking forbid officials from visiting Hong Kong. On the other hand, Chinese officials still flew to London. Patten was personally attacked in the Chinese media, suggesting that Peking carefully avoided confrontation at the governmental level.[66] This type of flexibility was evident elsewhere. For instance, while Peking insisted that only Peking could legitimately represent the people of Hong Kong and, thus, refuse to permit them to sit at the table with the PRC and the United Kingdom, Chinese officials

---

[63]Hsü, *Hsü Chia-t'un hui-i-lu*, 85-192.

[64]Peking was conscious of the implications for the Hong Kong Issue. *People's Daily*, January 29, 1993, 4.

[65]Allen Whiting draws the linkage between the F-16 sale and the Hong Kong issue. See *Chung-kuo shih-pao*, December 25, 1992, 17.

[66]For example, see *Lien-ho pao* (United Daily News) (Taipei), January 29, 1993, 10.

received Hong Kong delegates from all sources as long as they entered without their official title. Needless to say, if these people did not occupy their current positions, Chinese officials would not have even noticed them. It was as if they had to show cards with official titles to get known and then substitute other cards without titles to be accepted.

This sovereignty pretension footnoted Peking's vehement opposition to Patten's proposal. One implication of Patten's attempt to enlarge the scope of direct election and outfit a more independent legislature was that the Hong Kong people were better than Peking in taking care of themselves.[67] Worse was the further implication that the British governor, who had had no need of democracy during his rule, took care of the Hong Kong people better than they themselves could do.[68] Peking ranked at the bottom. Having once endured this disgracing implication in the Basic Law, Peking was determined not to allow this to happen again.

As a result, all other arrangements in preparation for Hong Kong beyond 1997 were contaminated. One example was the construction of the platform for the new airport. Both sides had agreed that it was necessary to build a new airport. Peking's initial concern was how much financial burden Hong Kong would be carrying in 1997, and how much would be left in its treasury.[69] Nonetheless, Peking thought it was all right to contract out the construction of the platform even before reaching a resolution. The United Kingdom disagreed. The memorandum that the two governments cosigned in September 1991 did not totally soothe the dispute. Peking continued to suspect that London intended to use up Hong Kong's financial resources before leaving and to possibly reserve most of those construction contracts for British firms. When Patten decided to contract out the construction of the platform in 1992, reversing his previous position, Peking took that as an offense of China's sovereignty. Peking claimed that Patten did not consult with Chinese officials ahead of time. From that, Peking also perceived a strategy by Patten of using the financial burden of the new airport construction to impede mainland China's economic development.[70]

The way Peking extensively defined sovereignty issues was not a new

---

[67]According to Patten, a democratized Hong Kong would not be easily mismanaged. See Patten, *Our Next Five Years*, 30.

[68]It may seem that London has extended its distrust toward newly independent colonies to Peking. See *Sing Tao Jih Pao* (Hong Kong), November 22, 1992, 20.

[69]Ho Hsiao, "The Entirety of the Sino-U.K. Talks Regarding the New Airport in Hong Kong," in *Shen-mi chih men: Kung-ho-kuo wai-chiao shih-lu* (A secret door: Notes on the PRC diplomacy), ed. Ts'ao Ying (Peking: Unity Press, 1993), 264-79.

[70]Regarding the Chinese perspective, see *People's Daily*, November 15, 1992, 4 and November 16, 1992, 4.

phenomenon. Back in 1985, Teng Hsiao-p'ing (Deng Xiaoping) publicly denounced two top officials for their casual remarks on Peking not stationing troops in Hong Kong after 1997. Here, Peking interpreted the right to station troops as the same as the stationing of troops in actuality. This caused great anxiety in Hong Kong.[71] Later, over a million Hong Kong people signed a petition to persuade Peking from building a nuclear Plant in Daya Bay, which borders Hong Kong. Teng decided that this had become a political issue, so Peking could not afford a feeble gesture lest the Hong Kong people learn to use the same trick on other issues regarding sovereignty.[72] An issue initially unrelated to sovereignty thus developed into one of sovereignty concerns.

Informal charges escalated to the ideological level toward the end of 1992. Peking wielded its influence in the media to expose Patten's "conspiracy": to divide the Hong Kong people into a pro-U.K. and a nationalist group, and a bourgeois class and a working class. The whole idea, it was said, was to retain colonial forces in many different disguises.[73] This, Peking affirmed, would contradict the principle of "smooth transition" professed in the joint statement. Chinese officials worried that the United Kingdom was installing a strategy of "thirteen years of change, fifty years of no change."[74] Since Teng had promised not to change the Hong Kong status quo for fifty years, the Chinese perceived that the United Kingdom intended to change as much as possible in the remaining thirteen years before 1997. Patten's proposal squarely confirmed these suspicions. The atmosphere was filled with anti-imperialism and the sovereignty apprehension defiled the whole scenario.

What Sovereignty

The lesson from Hong Kong is that Peking typically did not have a standard to separate issues of sovereignty from others. The principle of sovereignty is often initially irrelevant on concrete issues. Normally, rhetorical respect for the principle of sovereignty would satisfy Peking's need for dignity and sense of independence. However, as the international atmosphere changes, concrete issues begin to acquire sovereignty implications. Still, Peking's initially sloppy style of conceptualizing concrete matters may have been mistaken as an indication of weakness. If the opponent pushes on those concrete fronts with the wrong international

---

[71]Hsü, *Hsü Chia-t'un hui-i-lu*, 107-11.

[72]Ibid., 205-6.

[73]*Ta Kung Pao* (Hong Kong), December 19, 1992, 11.

[74]Hsü, *Hsü Chia-t'un hui-i-lu*, 172.

timing (sometimes a calculated timing), these moves would incur serious counterattacks. This is especially true if Peking is not sure of what has been going on and may want to wait and see the true intention of the other side more clearly. In such case, the other side most likely misinterprets that Peking intends to back out and responds by acting more aggressively. Suddenly, everything is linked to sovereignty for the Chinese.[75]

In other words, what is sovereignty-related is itself flexible. Peking's obsession with sovereignty compels its negotiators to concentrate on highly abstract principles and statements to make sure that the intention of the other side is proper. But, this leads to a seeming lack of attention to short-term, tangible problems. Subsequent compromises on those concrete matters are not compromises in the sense that they are not expected to impinge on the principle of sovereignty. This flexible attitude on the tactical front makes the later revocation unusually dramatic when the principle is thought to be violated. The impression that Peking is rigid in principle is actually a product of its flexible position on the scope the principle can govern.

The Hong Kong experience warns Peking's opponents of the potential for the extensive use of principle when Peking feels vulnerable. A typical news column describes the kind of atmosphere that had overstretched the principle of sovereignty:

> . . . China's ten-year reform has made eminent achievements and attracted the inflow of enormous wondering capital; in contrast, the economies of Europe and America stagnate where investors lack interest. In the situation of their own decline and our growth out here, the Western governments experience pressure. In order to strike at, or even drag down, China's economic development, the two grand camps of Europe and America have finally discovered an opening in Hong Kong. The U.K. government thus sent Patten to be governor of Hong Kong and prepared a three-revoking proposal [author: revoking the Basic Law, joint statement, and exchange of letters], using the pretext of the "public opinion card" and "international card" to ruin Hong Kong's prosperity and smooth transition. This profoundly affects the confidence of Hong Kong and international investors, destroying Hong Kong as [China's] window facing the South China Sea and slowing down the economic development of the Pearl River delta.[76]

Conclusion

The most difficult part of this essay has been reached—drawing a

[75]At one point, a pro-Peking writer invites Patten to watch carefully the PRC's national flags flying on top of most Hong Kong buildings. See Kao Yün-ts'ai, "The Inside Story of the Sino-U.K. Great War over Hong Kong," in Ts'ao, *Shen-mi chih men*, 290.

[76]Huang Ch'iang, "Hong Kong Has Become the Leakage Which Western Countries Utilize to Strike China's Development," *Ta Kung Pao*, November 25, 1992, 7.

conclusion out of an inconclusive discussion. The Sino-U.S. normalization could be the archetypical example of flexibility in Peking's foreign policy. Peking was effective in responding even to minor signs of goodwill from the United States, during the most rigid, political period of the Cultural Revolution. The Sino-U.K. talks on Hong Kong's transition in 1997, in contrast, explicated that Peking could be rigid about principles notwithstanding the very loose political atmosphere of reform. Rigidity in domestic politics witnessed flexibility in external relations; flexibility on internal issues accompanied rigidity in foreign affairs.

Furthermore, the seeming flexibility in the Sino-U.S. rapprochement was actually mixed with messages and moves which affirmed that the principles and, indeed, the result of the rapprochement contained nothing contradictory to the principles which Peking had held for over twenty years. The flexibility argument holds only if the claim of flexibility is juxtaposed with the reiteration of principles. Similarly, a rigid stand on the principle of sovereignty and the justification of this principle by the principle of anti-imperialism in the Hong Kong case were not all that rigid in practice. Chinese officials were willing to create opportunities for the United Kingdom to adjust its policy and for the Hong Kong people to express their opinions. Besides, what was regarded as principles was itself a matter subject to flexible interpretation and contingent upon the atmosphere of the greater environment.

Finally, the Chinese themselves are not always cognizant of the distinction between rigidity and flexibility. If they are, they may not care about consistency. They celebrate their own firm stand on principles probably to divert attention away from their flexible practice; and they claim flexibility often with the purpose of shunning responsibility of breakdown due to their insistence on a certain principle. Chao Ch'üan-sheng's aforementioned analysis is doubtlessly tautological, but he is right, not in the sense of his analysis, but to the extent that he spoke from his intuition. His analysis is not necessarily helpful to strangers to his culture in understanding Peking's foreign policy, for his remarks are themselves a subject of study for the students of Peking's foreign policy. One can learn from him, if not from his argument.

Again, this essay fails to answer meaningfully the question of how flexible Peking's foreign policy is. It seems that the task which was to be tackled in this essay is embarrassingly the source of frustration. The question is itself problematic, for it assumes that flexibility and rigidity are phenomena of two different worlds. Perhaps, this essay achieves one thing: it challenges us to consider whether or not flexibility in Peking's foreign policy is a worthwhile topic for research. What a minor and insignificant achievement!

14

Peking's Post-Tienanmen Foreign Policy: The Human Rights Factor *

John F. Copper

After the June 1989 massacre of Democracy Movement students in Tienanmen (Tiananmen) Square, the matter of mainland China's human rights record, or, more accurately, foreign criticism of mainland China's human rights abuses, became a major issue in Peking's (Beijing's) foreign policy construction for the first time. The importance of the human rights topic since 1989 has been reflected in both foreign policy statements emanating from Peking and in the People's Republic of China's (PRC's) relations with other countries. As well it often appears and is a salient issue in the media in mainland China and in Peking's statements and positions in various international organizations.

This was not always so. Before 1989, the PRC had an "edge" in terms of its human rights abuses.[1] The Western media did not scrutinize mainland China's record or its problems in this area. For a variety of reasons, including the fact that it was a leftist regime and that its human rights violations did not involve people of the white or black race, the media did not say much about the PRC in this realm. Of course, access to information about human rights abuses in mainland China was also a problem. In any event, human rights violations in mainland China did

---

[1] See Roberta Cohen, *The People's Republic of China: The Human Rights Exception* (Baltimore: University of Maryland School of Law, 1988), for further details. It is interesting to note that Teng Hsiao-p'ing is reported to have said, also about the late Mao period: "Even I had no rights; why didn't the Americans raise the human rights issue then?" This quote is from Wang Jen-chih, *Tang-tai* (Contemporary) (Hong Kong), July 15, 1992, cited in James D. Seymour, "Human Rights in Chinese Foreign Relations," in *China and the World: Chinese Foreign Relations in the Post-Cold War Era*, ed. Samuel S. Kim (Boulder, Colo.: Westview Press, 1994), 206.

not attract much attention and thus the issue of human rights criticism was not a matter that affected Peking's policymakers very much.

Why the change? In the spring of 1989, expectations were high that the PRC was evolving into a democracy. The PRC, for more than a decade, had had intense commercial and diplomatic relations with the West. Meanwhile, the world was undergoing a historic transition, from the "old world order" of bipolarity and deterrence based on threats with weapons of mass destruction, to a "new world order" that was supposed to be universal and peaceful. For both reasons mainland China was perceived to be at a crossroads. With the media giving the PRC attention it had never had before and with confidence high in the government of *Time* magazine's twice "Man of the Year" Teng Hsiao-p'ing (Deng Xiaoping), it was expected that historic change was in the offing and that mainland China would contribute in a significant way to the tide of global democracy. Instead, Teng called on the troops—who killed a large number of students and other protesters in Tienanmen, thus dashing hopes for democracy in mainland China and for the PRC becoming a part of the global community of civilized nations.

Western countries, and the Western media in particular, could not forgive mainland China's leaders for this. The rest of the world to a considerable extent agreed, or at least went along.[2] The reaction was negative and it was deep. And it was persistent.

The PRC was hurt. It was disgraced. It became a pariah nation. Trade and investment were affected. This had an impact on the mainland Chinese economy. The PRC was isolated.[3]

PRC leaders had to respond. They felt compelled to quickly adopt new policies to cope with this situation; these policies were understandably ad hoc and inconsistent. Nevertheless, three different sets of responses are observable. Peking at times responded with a tough line: pressing the argument that human rights abuses in mainland China are a matter of

---

[2]There were, of course, some nations that did not; also there were considerable differences among nations in their condemnation of the PRC. Western countries were the most hostile toward Peking, France being the most unfriendly while taking more actions in response. See David Shambaugh, "China and Europe," *The Annals* 519 (January 1992): 109-12. African countries generally took a wait-and-see position. See Gerald Segal, "China and Africa," ibid., 123. Middle East countries did not condemn Peking very much and in the next few months trade increased. See Yitzhak Shichor, "China and the Middle East Since Tiananmen," ibid., 89, 91. Still the PRC felt isolated and condemned.

[3]See Chu-yuan Cheng, *Behind the Tiananmen Massacre: Social, Political, and Economic Ferment in China* (Boulder, Colo.: Westview Press, 1990), chap. 7, and James D. Seymour, "The International Response to the 1989 Massacre," *The Fletcher Forum of World Affairs* 14, no. 1 (Winter 1990): 55-61.

domestic concern only and not the business of other countries, based on the concept of sovereignty fundamental to the Westphalian system, and it was not the business of other countries. Furthermore, expressing concern by other nations was not welcomed and would be dealt with in an unfriendly manner.

Second, and on the other hand, Peking made concessions. Mainland Chinese leaders, at times, made statements and even policy pronouncements to placate or please the critics and promised (and at times followed this up with specific actions) a better human rights record. In short, Peking responded in a conciliatory or positive (in the Western view) way to outside pressure.

Third, Peking sought to promote its own position on human rights, which it said other Asian and Third World countries also espoused, while criticizing Western countries for their human rights records.

Peking's human rights (foreign) policy may thus be said to be a mixture of: (1) adopting a hostile defensive posture, (2) responding to pressure and making concessions, and (3) taking the offensive by promoting Peking's own view on human rights. Which of these approaches Peking took (or will take in the future) at any given time or in reaction to any specific situation, to a considerable degree, depended on the vagaries of Chinese politics and/or the perceptions or aims of the leadership at the moment. Peking's top leaders have been in disagreement about many issues and clearly human rights has been one of them; in fact, differences of views about this issue have been more acute than about most others.[4] This, indeed, explains in part why Peking's human rights policies have changed frequently and have appeared contradictory and inconsistent. The success, or perceived success, of one policy choice has also affected its selection of one policy alternative or another. So, too, the world's reactions to Peking's human rights policies.

In the pages below, the author will delineate Peking's different responses and different policies vis-à-vis human rights criticisms. He will also attempt to explain why there have been different policies and what one can expect in the future in terms of the human rights issue in Peking's foreign policy.

---

[4]See Ta-ling Lee and John F. Copper, *Failure of the Democracy Movement: Human Rights in the People's Republic of China, 1988/90* (Baltimore: University of Maryland School of Law, 1991), chap. 4; John F. Copper and Ta-ling Lee, *Tiananmen Aftermath: Human Rights in the People's Republic of China, 1990* (Baltimore: University of Maryland School of Law, 1992), chaps. 1 and 2; and Ta-ling Lee and John F. Copper, *The Bamboo Gulag: Human Rights in the People's Republic of China, 1991-1992* (Baltimore: University of Maryland School of Law, 1994), chap. 2.

Peking's Hard-line Response

Early on after June 1989, the responses of mainland Chinese leaders to the storm of foreign criticism of the Tienanmen massacre were clearly mostly defensive and hard-line. This style of reaction remained a frequently used policy option, though as time has passed it has diminished in frequency and has more and more been blended with concessions and/or an offensive policy.

The reasons for a defensive, hard-line reaction stems mainly from fear on the part of mainland Chinese leaders that the Democracy Movement and changes in the world that this movement mirrored, threatened the very survival of the Chinese Communist Party (CCP) and the government. Teng Hsiao-p'ing, on June 9, just days after the massacre, said in a public speech: "If we had not stopped them, they would have brought about our collapse."[5] At his first press conference after he became CCP general secretary, Chiang Tse-min (Jiang Zemin) described the massacre as a "counterrevolutionary rebellion aimed at opposing the leadership of the Communist Party of China and overthrowing the socialist system."[6]

Peking's leaders might have moved away from this hard-line response after a short time had it not been for events elsewhere that were perceived as life-threatening.[7] In the fall of 1989, Communism collapsed in Eastern Europe underscored by the tearing down of the Berlin Wall. In December, the Communist regime in Romania was overthrown with the assassination (with the help or acquiescence of the army) of General Secretary Ceausescu. Romania, and especially Ceausescu, had long been a close friend of Peking's; in fact, Peking had only recently pledged "militant unity" with Ceausescu to resist the anti-Communist tide elsewhere in the region.[8]

---

[5]See "'Us-or-Them' Talk by Deng Reported," *San Francisco Chronicle,* June 17, 1989, A12. This was later reported in *Beijing Review* for international consumption. The former quoted Teng as saying to troops: "I myself, and all of you commanding officers present, would have been shoved under the guillotine."

[6]"Top Party Leaders Answer Questions at Press Conference," *Beijing Review* 32, no. 40 (October 2-8, 1989): 15.

[7]Four months after the massacre at Tienanmen Square, Teng told Richard Nixon, with reporters present, that Peking would never tolerate interference in mainland China's internal affairs. Teng also said that the Chinese people would never forgive their leaders for apologizing to another nation. Yet the former president also noted that Teng told him that differences between mainland China and the United States could be bridged by discussions behind the scenes. See Richard M. Nixon, *Beyond Peace* (New York: Random House, 1994), 132.

[8]For details, see Foreign Broadcast Information Service (FBIS), *Daily Report: China* [hereinafter cited as *FBIS-CHI*]-89-224 (November 22, 1989): 17. It is also worth noting that Politburo member Ch'iao Shih (Qiao Shi) had just been sent to Bucharest to attend a congress of the Romanian Communist Party to discuss unity and preserving Communism.

In early 1990, Premier Li P'eng (Li Peng), in the context of discussing relations with the Soviet Union (which were improving) and the United States (which were strained due to the "events" of 1989), said that normal relations between states must be on an equal footing.[9] What Premier Li meant, obviously, was that the PRC would not accept criticism from other nations about its human rights situation. Just days later, Peking detained and canceled the visas of a foreign delegation that had arrived to express concern about political prisoners in mainland China.[10] Subsequently, Li announced that the decision to end martial law was in no way influenced by international pressure or economic or military sanctions.[11]

A month later, the Peking government sent a strong protest to U.S. Ambassador James Lilley in response to a Senate vote (even though it allowed President Bush to waive enforcement) on sanctions against the PRC. Peking also voiced a loud objection to the Department of State following publication of its annual survey of nations' human rights, which gave mainland China a bad (though certainly not unfair) evaluation.[12]

At almost the same time, Peking responded in a very hostile fashion to United Nations criticism of mainland China's human rights abuses. Peking's spokespersons responded that the West was trying to overthrow China's socialist system.[13] *Beijing Review* said it was the PRC's policy to "oppose harmful Western ideas."[14] Subsequently, Peking reportedly put the United States on a list of "enemies."[15] And when the French government granted asylum to dissidents Ch'ai Ling (Chai Ling) and Feng Ts'ung-te (Feng Congde), the Peking government issued an official protest saying that this action was an "interference in China's internal affairs."[16] Peking used similar words when Vice President Dan Quayle subsequently met Ch'ai Ling.

In ensuing months Peking's hard-line protests were heard with somewhat less frequency and were less strident. At year's end, however, Peking

---

[9]See "Quarterly Chronicle and Documentation," *China Quarterly*, no. 122 (June 1990): 350.

[10]"Pro-Democracy Movement Leaders Sentenced," *Asian Bulletin* 16, no. 3 (March 1991): 90.

[11]Tai Ming Cheung, "Cosmetic Change," *Far Eastern Economic Review* [hereinafter cited as *FEER*], January 25, 1990, 8-9.

[12]"Hard-line Reaction to U.S. Human Rights Report," *Asian Bulletin* 15, no. 4 (April 1990): 78.

[13]Ibid., 80.

[14]Reported by CBS News on March 13 and cited in ibid.

[15]"Hard-line Stance Reaffirmed, World Democracy Movement Denounced," *Asian Bulletin* 15, no. 5 (May 1990): 81.

[16]"Affirming and Strengthening Communist Ideology: Human Rights Abuses Acknowledged," ibid., no. 6 (June 1990): 73.

accused the United States of practicing "dollar diplomacy" in its human rights policies and said that Washington was "trying to be guardians of human rights" while practicing hypocrisy and subversion.[17] Almost paralleling this statement, a Communist Party publication warned that the United States had "hegemonic aims" in its "human rights diplomacy" and this kind of diplomacy is "more effective and duplicitous than directly dispatching troops."[18]

In early 1991, in response to the U.S. Department of State's human rights report, the PRC's Ministry of Foreign Affairs condemned the report, saying that it was "entirely unacceptable" and constituted an "unscrupulous interference in the internal affairs of many countries on the pretext of human rights." It also said that it "cites false rumors to distort and attack China" and is "ridiculous" for mentioning population policy, state treasury purchases, water conservancy works, etc.[19]

A few weeks later Peking complained in the UN Human Rights Commission about countries (obviously meaning the United States) that "attempt to peddle ideology . . . in the name of human rights." Peking's delegate also spoke of countries that "use human rights to practice power politics, interfere in other countries' internal affairs and exert pressure on weak and small countries." These practices, he said, have "hampered international relations."[20]

A specific issue that evoked very harsh Chinese criticism at this time was Tibet. In March, when the Dalai Lama went on a foreign trip, and while in England, Peking arrested a Tibetan for spying for the Dalai Lama and gave the case unusual publicity.[21] When the Dalai Lama was in the United States, Vice Foreign Minister Liu Hua-ch'iu (Liu Huaqiu) delivered a strong message of protest to the U.S. Embassy.[22] Meanwhile, PRC missions in the United States warned various colleges and universities not to arrange speeches for the Dalai Lama.[23]

---

[17]"Human Rights Issue Raised; CCP Convenes Central Committee Meeting," ibid. 16, no. 2 (February 1991): 97.

[18]Ku Chao-chi (Gu Zhaoji) and Chang Chün (Zhang Jun), "The Answer to the Human Rights Question Is Doubtful and Disputable," *Hsüeh-hsi yü yen-chiu* (Study and Research), November 5, 1990, 18-21, cited in Seymour, "Human Rights in Chinese Foreign Relations," 210.

[19]New China News Agency (NCNA), February 7, 1991, cited in *FBIS-CHI*-91-026 (February 7, 1991): 1.

[20]"Quarterly Chronicle and Documentation," *China Quarterly,* no. 126 (June 1991): 436.

[21]"Tibetan God-King Visits U.K.," *Asian Bulletin* 16, no. 5 (May 1991): 107.

[22]"Bush-Dalai Lama Meeting Protested," *Beijing Review* 34, no. 17 (April 29-May 5, 1991): 11.

[23]"Quarterly Chronicle and Documentation," *China Quarterly,* no. 127 (September 1991): 681.

Subsequently, when the issue of the U.S. granting the PRC most-favored-nation (MFN) trade status came up again, Peking again took a hard position. The Ministry of Foreign Affairs said that Peking would never accept the attachment of conditions. A spokesman then said that if the United States cancels MFN, "China is ready for it."[24] Mainland Chinese leaders exhibited a similar tough line when discussions about Radio Free Asia (an organization similar to Radio Free Europe) were launched in the United States. Chu Ch'i-chen (Zhu Qizhen), Peking's ambassador to the United States, said that he did not recognize the authority of the commission that was considering the proposal and the PRC would not grant its members visas to visit mainland China.[25]

In early 1992, when another U.S. Department of State's human rights report was published, a state-owned radio station reported that it "interfered in China's internal affairs." Subsequently, the *People's Daily* reported that Premier Li P'eng had "set the West straight" on the issue of human rights during a recent trip abroad.[26] Later, when the U.S. Senate debated attaching conditions to MFN trade status for mainland China, Chinese officials said the bill violated "principles of mutual benefit and bilateral trade."[27] It is worthy of note, however, that these criticisms were milder than those heard earlier; also Peking criticized the United States more indirectly, meaning through the media rather than directly via official channels.

In April, when the Japanese government criticized Peking on the human rights issue, Chiang Tse-min replied that the "right of survival of China's population is more important than political rights." He also said that such criticism "constitutes interference in domestic affairs, which China will not accept."[28] This rather tough reply seemed to indicate Chinese leaders were not accustomed to Japanese comments about human rights abuses in mainland China or were less patient in hearing it.

A month later the Peking government detained *Washington Post* correspondent Lena Sun, when she was found in possession of confidential documents, which Chinese police said she had obtained illegally. This, however, probably did not reflect a harder line toward the United States,

---

[24]"China Ready for Worse Ties with U.S.," *Journal of Commerce,* May 10, 1991, 3A.

[25]John M. Goshko, "U.S. Radio Panel Cancels Planned Visit to Beijing," *Washington Post,* June 8, 1991, A17.

[26]"Reformers Gather Strength for Economic Overhaul; Human Rights Still an Issue of Contention," *Asian Bulletin* 17, no. 4 (April 1992): 72.

[27]Ibid., 73.

[28]Sam Jameson, "Japan Raises Rights Issue with China During Party Chief's Visit," *Los Angeles,* April 7, 1992, A4.

but rather a specific or isolated "serious" case, which was probably blown out of proportion at the behest of the PRC's security officials and leftist hard-liners in the Chinese leadership.[29] The same may be said about the detention of foreign reporters and the beating of a Japanese media representative in June on the anniversary of the Tienanmen massacre when they attempted to stage a protest demonstration.[30]

The exception to the trend of the government lessening its hostile attitude and/or leaving criticism of the United States to the media came in the fall when President Bush granted amnesty to approximately 70,000 Chinese students and their families in the United States. The Ministry of Foreign Affairs derided the decision and called it "unacceptable."[31] The explanation for Peking's tough language seems to be that this was a sensitive and divisive issue in the Peking leadership.

Peking continued to take a hard line on Tibet. This, in fact, was the one issue regarding which Peking did not noticeably take a softer position. In March 1993, the Peking government refused talks with the Dalai Lama, saying that he was trying to "undermine the unity of China."[32] Peking's leaders apparently calculated that they could not soften their stance because that would be seen as making a concession on a territorial issue which would have repercussions elsewhere. Alternatively they perceived that Asian and Third World countries supported them on this issue because it centered on the right of sovereignty. Peking took this position notwithstanding U.S. pressure and in April even criticized President Clinton for playing host to the Dalai Lama.[33]

When the issue of the U.S. granting MFN to mainland China arose again with summer 1993, Peking said it firmly opposed Washington setting any conditions. Chiang Tse-min warned that terminating MFN would hurt both nations and would mean a loss of 100,000 jobs in the United States. But these were not tough statements and were noticeably milder than in the previous three years when the issue came up. When MFN was approved, while linking it with an improvement in mainland China's human rights, Peking said that it "seriously impaired" Washington-Peking relations. But Peking did not threaten retaliation in any way; thus the

---

[29]See various issues of the *Washington Post*. The details of this matter are summarized in "U.S. Human Rights Policy Criticized; Foreign Reporter Detained," *Asian Bulletin* 17, no. 7 (July 1992): 92.

[30]See "Third Tiananmen Anniversary Passes Quietly; Teng's Reforms Receive Further Boost," ibid., no. 8 (August 1992): 71.

[31]"Dissident Shen Tong [Shen T'ung] Released, Deported," ibid., no. 12 (December 1992): 90.

[32]"Tibetan Pro-Independence Protesters Arrested," ibid. 18, no. 5 (May 1993): 79.

[33]"U.S. Urges Peking to Revive Talks on Tibet," ibid., no. 6 (June 1993): 82.

reaction seemed only pro forma.[34]

In November, when President Clinton and General Secretary Chiang Tse-min met in Seattle at the Asia-Pacific Economic Cooperation (APEC) meeting, Chiang told Clinton, in response to demands on human rights, that it was "important" not to interfere in the "affairs of other countries." He also said it was Peking's practice "not to approve of the practice of linking things which have nothing to do with trade issues."[35] Again the rebuke was not a strong one and seemed to suggest Asian differences on the issue of human rights rather than a hostile policy.

In March 1994, however, when Secretary of State Warren Christopher visited Peking and brought up the issues of human rights, he got a quick and stiff rebuff. Christopher took a message from President Clinton saying that the PRC had to improve its human rights performance or face the cutoff of MFN. Peking's leaders reportedly told Christopher that Peking would "never accept U.S. dictates on how to behave toward their own citizens." Foreign Minister Ch'ien Ch'i-ch'en (Qian Qichen) also accused Christopher of disrespect. And Premier Li P'eng said Peking "flatly rejected Clinton's conditions" and asserted that "China will never accept the United States' human rights concepts." He also reportedly said that history "has proven it futile to apply pressure against China."[36]

The hard Chinese response can probably be explained in terms of their perception that Peking had leverage due to the North Korean nuclear weapons problem and/or because they saw Clinton's foreign policy as weak and vacillating. President Clinton clearly did not want to face accusations of ruining relations with Peking at this time. Also Peking was aware of the strong support in the U.S. business community for not linking trade and human rights policies. Peking's response to Christopher, on the other hand, did not constitute, looking at Peking's human rights policy overall at the time or what happened later, a regression back to a hard-line stance. Also, as will be noted below, Peking responded to Christopher's demands with approaches number two and three.

Making Concessions

While a tough or hard-line response to criticism of its human rights

---

[34]"U.S. Renews Most-Favored-Nation Status," ibid., no. 7 (July 1993): 72-73.

[35]"CCP Central Committee Announces Blueprint to Step Up Economic Reforms," ibid. 19, no. 1 (January 1994): 23.

[36]"Leaders Reject U.S. Views on Human Rights; Dissidents Detained," ibid., no. 5 (May 1994): 25.

in the wake of the Tienanmen massacre was Peking's initial response and such a policy has remained in use since then, mainland Chinese leaders have also espoused a soft line at times making concessions and bending to foreign and international pressure.

A soft-line policy was advocated shortly after the Tienanmen massacre cautiously by some Chinese leaders who argued it was helpful to improve mainland China's image abroad and win it support form the international community.[37] It also sought to keep economic growth, and to a lesser extent political modernization, on track, by preserving foreign trade and investment. This was a policy favored by rightist reformists, though even they generally agreed with the leftist hard-liners that Peking had to maintain a "hard-line inside and a soft-line outside" policy.

During the several months after the massacre in Tienanmen Square, Peking made only a few concessions and any indication of an evolving soft-line policy on human rights was barely visible. Where mainland Chinese leaders did exhibit a more moderate stance was in the realm of economic policies. Reformist leaders wanted to prevent a regression to the self-reliance and the radical egalitarian policies of Mao's time that had so patently impeded mainland China's economic growth.

The record of the rightist reformists on economic growth was so good that they were able to defend their policies quite easily and relate domestic economic policies to their "open door" foreign policy. But other factors also favored the reformers. The precipitous decline in international aid, foreign investment, trade, and tourism as a result of the Tienanmen massacre had an immediate impact. So did the left's policies of trying to reverse privatization in mainland China while attempting to outlaw many private businesses. The results were a slowdown in economic growth and opposition to leftist economic policies by the provinces and the Chinese masses.[38]

While no concessions of any consequence were made during 1989, except exhortations by reformist leaders not to close mainland China and promises to foreign countries that this would not happen, Peking leaders did take some actions in early 1990 to please the foreign community, especially the United States. Most of these concessions can be tied to efforts to keep commercial ties on track—ties that were needed to sustain mainland China's economic development.

Coinciding with a visit to Peking in early 1990 by Japanese Minister

---

[37]See Copper and Lee, *Tiananmen Aftermath*, chap. 2.

[38]For details on the economic impact of the massacre as it relates to this point, see Lee and Copper, *Failure of the Democracy Movement*, 67-72.

of Finance Hashimoto (who went there to discuss Japan's aid to and investment in mainland China), martial law was ended in Peking and troops were withdrawn. Within days lenient sentences were handed down to some that were arrested in June 1989. Premier Li P'eng was careful to note that the decision to end martial law was not influenced by international pressure; yet the timing suggests it was.[39]

In May, Peking lifted martial law in Tibet. At the same time, over two hundred people jailed after the Tienanmen massacre were released. Both seemed timed to influence discussions in the United States on whether to continue MFN trade status for the PRC.[40] After the decision was made to renew mainland China's favored trade status, Peking released more people arrested in mid-1989. Then, on June 25, the government announced that renowned dissident Fang Li-chih (Fang Lizhi) and his wife, both of whom had taken refuge in the American Embassy, would be allowed to go to the United States "for medical treatment."[41] Peking seemed to be rewarding the United States and/or sending a message of support to the Bush administration.

In August, the PRC made a major move to improve its image abroad when Premier Li P'eng "clarified" Peking's policy toward Cambodia (Kampuchea)—which helped in bringing a tentative peace to that long-troubled Southeast Asian nation. Two months later Peking's Foreign Minister Ch'ien Ch'i-ch'en visited Washington for high-level talks. These diplomatic actions—concessions or a soft line in the context of Peking's otherwise hard posture—helped improve the PRC's international image considerably. Peking made even more points with the U.S. government, though this had less influence on its public image, when it acted in concert with the United States (though it abstained rather than voting with the United States in the United Nations) on condemning Iraq's invasion of Kuwait.

In early 1991, U.S. Ambassador to the PRC James Lilley reported that he had received a positive response on the issue of political prisoners when talking to the Chinese government.[42] In May, in the context of the now annual debate on granting MFN status on trade to the PRC, a Foreign

---

[39]See note 11 above. It is relevant in this connection to note that Japan at this time was mainland China's most important source of foreign investment and Hashimoto promised to resume economic aid while asking for a change in mainland China's human rights situation.

[40]See "Leaders Make Conciliatory Remarks as Washington Extends Most Favored Trade Status," *Asian Bulletin* 15, no. 7 (July 1990): 86.

[41]"Washington Ties Improved as Fang Li-chih Released," ibid., no. 8 (August 1990): 65.

[42]Susumu Awanohara and Tai Ming Cheung, "Abusive Treatment," *FEER,* January 3, 1991, 8.

Ministry official explained, regarding the charge that mainland China was selling products made by prison labor in the United States, that this might have happened through "management oversight." He pointed to trade enterprises as having considerable autonomy and that it was not Peking's policy or intent to export prison-made products.[43] Not long after, Peking made a major concession on arms sales, accepting an invitation to discuss limiting its sales of weapons to Middle East countries.[44] Peking similarly informed the United States that it was "actively considering" joining the Nuclear Nonproliferation Treaty (NPT) and the Missile Technology Control Regime (MTCR). Peking also allowed unprecedented interviews to American reporters with political prisoners in mainland China, including its most famous dissident Wei Ching-sheng (Wei Jingsheng), while encouraging think tanks and university professors to discuss human rights issues. This, in fact, seemed to constitute a major policy shift.[45]

In August, when Japanese Prime Minister Kaifu visited Peking (the first by a head-of-state from a developed nation since the Tienanmen massacre), Peking announced, on the forty-sixth anniversary of the dropping of the atomic bombs on Japan, that Peking would "in principle" sign the NPT. Peking won kudos from a number of nations, including the United States, for this announcement.[46] Peking also "made a commitment" not to sell certain kinds of missiles to Syria, Pakistan, and some other countries. And Peking promised to account for eight hundred dissidents when U.S. Secretary of State James Baker visited Peking at the end of the year. However, the latter may have been a very cheap concession, since Peking made only vague promises and got the United States to break its ban on high-level official visits to mainland China.[47]

In March 1992, Peking applauded President Bush's veto of a Senate bill linking MFN to an accounting of people arrested during and after the Tienanmen massacre and announced that the PRC was acceding to the NPT.[48] In May, Peking gave reporter Lena Sun a warning rather than

---

[43]P. T. Bangsberg, "China Shifts Stance on Prison Labor," *Journal of Commerce,* May 10, 1991, 5A.

[44]John E. Yang, "China Agrees to Confer on Mideast Arms Sales," *Washington Post,* June 8, 1991, A17.

[45]See Lena Sun, "China Signals Change in Human Rights Approach," ibid., July 9, 1991, A12.

[46]Sheryl WuDunn, "China Backs Pact on Nuclear Spread," *New York Times,* August 11, 1991, A1.

[47]Thomas L. Friedman, "Baker's China Trip Fails to Produce Pledge on Rights," ibid., November 18, 1991, A1.

[48]See "Reformers Score Major Victory Under Teng Hsiao-p'ing," *Asian Bulletin* 17, no. 5 (May 1992): 74.

expelling her (see section above) and released three Catholic priests that had been in prison for many years for professing loyalty to the Vatican and not to the "Patriotic Church" in mainland China.[49] Not long after, Peking approved the choice of a Tibetan "Living Buddha"—the first since the PRC launched "democratic reform" in Tibet in 1959—indicating a change in policy on this issue.[50] In August, Peking opened Tibet again to the outside world.

In November, Peking released dissident Pao Tsun-hsin (Bao Zunxin), the most famous of the Democracy Movement participants to be released early. The action seemed to stem from U.S. pressure.[51] In December, for the first time mainland Chinese leaders welcomed a delegation of U.S. Senators to discuss the issue of Tibet—apparently as a friendly gesture to president-elect Clinton.[52]

In February 1993, Peking released a number of prominent political prisoners, including two who were imprisoned for their political views, one that had been on the most-wanted list, and a Catholic priest. The releases were interpreted as an amicable act toward President Clinton, who had just assumed office, and/or an effort to improve Peking's chances of hosting the Summer Olympic Games in 2000.[53]

In May 1993, the Peking government released Hsü Wen-li (Xu Wenli), one of the longest held political prisoners—apparently hoping to please the United States in the context of debate in Washington on extending MFN to mainland China.[54] In July, Peking announced that it was extending for eighteen months a ban on nuclear testing. In September, Peking released several more political prisoners—including the most prominent one, Wei Ching-sheng. This was done probably to abet the PRC's efforts for a bid to hold the Olympic Games in Peking.[55]

In January 1994, during talks between U.S. Secretary of State Christopher and PRC Foreign Minister Ch'ien, Ch'ien promised to discuss the status of a list of 235 political prisoners the United States had earlier presented to Chinese leaders. Subsequently a number on this list were

---

[49]Lincoln Kaye, "Earning Credit," *FEER*, June 4, 1992, 17.

[50]"Chinese Leaders OK Choice of Tibetan 'Living Buddha'," *Washington Times*, June 29, 1992, A8.

[51]"Teng Further Consolidates Power with Military Reshuffle," *Asian Bulletin* 18, no. 1 (January 1993): 78.

[52]See "Ten Jailed over Tibet Protest," ibid., no. 2 (February 1993): 74.

[53]See "Pro-Democracy Activists Released," ibid., no. 4 (April 1993): 70-71.

[54]See note 34 above.

[55]"Cargo Ship Incident Dampens U.S. Ties; Olympic Bid Fails Despite Release of Dissidents," *Asian Bulletin* 18, no. 11 (November 1993): 75.

released.[56] After his visit, Christopher cited a number of concessions Chinese leaders made on human rights: codifying earlier understandings on the rights of the United States to inspect Chinese prisons suspected of exporting prison-made goods, providing a detailed accounting of the 235 political prisoners earlier mentioned by the United States plus 106 in Tibet, confirming Peking's support for the UN Universal Declaration on Human Rights, and proposing talks with the Red Cross allowing visits to prisons.[57]

Taking the Offensive

Peking's third category of responses vis-à-vis foreign criticism of the PRC because of the Tienanmen massacre specifically and human rights abuses in general, is an offensive policy. This consists of promoting Peking's own view of human rights (previously called the Communist perspective) that emphasizes economic rights as opposed to political rights, group rights as opposed to individual rights, and the obligations of citizens to the state. This view may now be said to constitute also the Third World view and/or the Asian view, or at least this is Peking's perspective. Peking's offensive response also consists of attacking Western countries for their "narrow" human rights perspective as well as their own problems. Together one might call these responses the PRC's "human rights diplomacy." As time has passed, this style response has become more and more popular in Peking.

Since mainland Chinese leaders were not well prepared for the Tienanmen massacre and its fallout, they found it difficult in mid-1989 to adopt quickly an offensive policy to parry the intense foreign criticism of the PRC's human rights abuses. This also explains why Peking's reactions (not to mention the fact that there were serious differences between two factions in the leadership about the Democracy Movement) were disparate, disconnected, and in many ways dysfunctional at first, and as time has passed Peking has developed a more cogent, rational policy to deal with human rights criticism.

Peking's initial response that may fit in the category of an offensive strategy was to deny that anything important had happened or that many people were killed or injured.[58] This reaction was clearly a knee-jerk one.

---

[56]"U.S. Officials Visit, Hold Talks on Human Rights, Trade, and Nuclear Arms," ibid. 19, no. 3 (March 1994): 22.

[57]"Leaders Reject U.S. Views on Human Rights," 26.

[58]Lee and Copper, *Failure of the Democracy Movement,* 15-16. A Chinese official later told this writer: "You have cited twenty million or more people in labor camps and many

Different organs of the government and the media did not even coordinate their data. They published figures on the number of people killed and injured that contradicted each other and even reports published by the same organization a few days earlier.[59]

Subsequently the government published a book that may be viewed as its version of the events of May and June 1989. This publication, which includes graphic pictures of soldiers who had been beaten, set on fire, lynched, and castrated by the protesters in Tienanmen Square before June 4, suggests the reason for the government's brutal response was that the demonstrators engaged in violence. It also says that the "turmoil" happened because of a "very small number of political careerists." Finally, it argued that the military showed restraint after soldiers had been killed.[60] As with the case of its denials, this policy was not effective.

Peking's next tack (remember that the hard-line left is now in the ascendancy) was to blame the "turmoil' on economic factors. Mainland Chinese leaders said that the reformist economic growth model had caused the economy to overheat and widened income differences. They mentioned greed that was engendered by privatization and the fact that the "trickle down" economic policy did not work.[61] They seemed to understand the liberal bent of the Western media and human rights groups and sought to persuade them that capitalism was to blame for what happened rather than fears by the leaders that they might be overthrown by the Democracy Movement or the tide of history.

Some mainland Chinese leaders also sought to appeal to fears in nearby countries that chaos in mainland China might spread across its borders. They even warned Western countries and international organizations about the possibility of turmoil in mainland China creating millions of refugees.[62]

Later, in September 1990, the Ministry of Foreign Affairs invited former Secretary of State Henry Kissinger to Peking. Kissinger was the first

---

millions killed in China under Mao. I am not saying that is true, but if it is, why are you concerned about a few hundred or even a few thousand that were allegedly killed in Tiananmen Square in June?"

[59]For an assessment of the different figures released, see ibid., 15-17.

[60]*The Truth About the Beijing Turmoil* (Peking: Peking Publishing House, 1989). See especially the preface.

[61]See Nina P. Halpern, "The Impact of Tiananmen on the Political Climate of Economic Reform," in *The Aftermath of the 1989 Tiananmen Crisis in Mainland China,* ed. Bih-jaw Lin (Boulder, Colo.: Westview Press, 1992), 256-73.

[62]Mainland Chinese leaders have used this tack many times before and it has influenced leaders particularly in border countries in Southeast Asia. It, however, has also been taken seriously; clearly, international organizations concerned with refugees have taken notice.

prominent American to visit Peking after the Tienanmen massacre. In Peking he met Premier Li P'eng and Yang Shang-k'un (Yang Shangkun)—the two leaders that were notorious for ordering the massacre. Kissinger made public comments to the effect that Washington-Peking relations should be based on the national interest of the two countries. The Peking government and media gave this big play since it confirmed their view about human rights and their effort to change world opinion on this matter.[63]

In the spring of 1991, the PRC took another and different step in applying its offensive strategy: Foreign Minister Ch'ien Ch'i-ch'en announced that Peking was willing to discuss human rights in an international context, but would not be singled out for criticism. In other words, the PRC had to be treated as a part of a bloc of nations—meaning Third World and/or Asian nations. In the same announcement he accused the United States of hypocrisy for not ratifying some important human rights conventions because they conflicted with U.S. law.[64] Coinciding with his statement, the *People's Daily* said the United States was guilty of denying economic, social, and political rights and committing apartheid, racial discrimination, torture, and sex discrimination in violation of UN documents.[65] This followed a story carried by the *People's Daily* about President Bush having a double with him during a trip to Argentina because of his concern about an assassination attempt there, asking about American respect for the human rights of this person.[66]

In November 1991, Peking formalized its "third option" policy when the Information Office of the State Council issued a "White Paper" called "Human Rights in China."[67] This sixty-two-page booklet was translated into English, French, German, Japanese, and Spanish. It was subsequently published in the *People's Daily,* and through other avenues, given widespread dissemination. The document contained an explanation of mainland China's domestic policies and its political system and in that context argued that the issue of human rights is a domestic matter and other countries do not have the right to interfere and described such interference as "engaging in power politics." Yet by virtue of publishing such a document the PRC appeared to give legitimacy to international human rights standards and

---

[63]"Peking Seeing to Improve Ties with Moscow, New Delhi, Washington," *Asian Bulletin* 15, no. 11 (November 1990): 83.

[64]"Mending Foreign Relations: Defending Human Rights Accord," ibid. 16, no. 6 (June 1991): 108.

[65]Ibid., 103.

[66]Sung Chih-chien, "Commentary on Human Rights, Bush's Double," *People's Daily,* January 27, 1991, cited in *FBIS-CHI*-91-027 (February 8, 1991): 5.

[67]*Beijing Review* 34, no. 44 (November 4-10, 1991): 8-45.

concerns; thus it represented an effort by Peking to push its own views of human rights rather than simply opposing any and all foreign criticism.

More specifically, the "White Paper" set forth Peking's definition of human rights, which emphasizes economic rights and stresses the right to work and the equality of citizens "irrespective of their money and property status" and denied that the PRC practiced censorship or had any political prisoners. It promised free speech and free press and a number of other rights. It also discussed mainland China's population problem and rationalized population control policies.

The publication of this document was clearly aimed at taking the initiative on the human rights as best Peking could. While the document did not stand up well to the criticism of the Western media or human rights experts, it did provide Peking's foreign policy makers with a document to quote and a policy to try to implement in the course of carrying on foreign relations. Most important, it put forward a position taken by other Communist nations in the past and a stance similar to the views of many Third World countries.[68]

In early 1992, Premier Li P'eng visited New York for a UN summit meeting. There Li asserted that the PRC had been consistent in abiding by the purpose and principles of the United Nations Charter. He also asserted that human rights matters essentially fall under the sovereignty of each nation. He went on to say that it is "not appropriate or workable" to demand that all countries measure up to the human rights criteria of one or a small number of countries.[69] Again Peking seemed to be seeking to promote a Third World view of human rights while associating such a view with its own. And the PRC seemed to make some progress in this effort: Not many weeks later, Peking succeeded in rallying support of Third World countries against a UN Human Rights Commission censure motion on mainland China's human rights abuses in Tibet.[70]

In the fall of 1992, the State Council issued a second report entitled "Criminal Reform in China." It detailed progress made in the PRC's penal system after 1949. Its authors also denied that prisoners in mainland China were ill-treated. This report, especially its denials of bad prison conditions in mainland China, did not find many believers, especially in view of the fact that a book was published in the United States at this

---

[68]For a criticism of the document, see Frank Ching, "Peking's Flawed White Paper," *China News* (Taipei), November 10, 1991, reprinted in *Asian Bulletin* 17, no. 1 (January 1992): 13-14.

[69]For details, see note 26 above.

[70]Ibid.

time by a former political prisoner who carefully detailed prison conditions in mainland China.[71]

In March 1993, representatives of Asian countries met in Bangkok to discuss a UN General Assembly resolution that called for a world conference on human rights. The document that came out of this meeting was called the "Bangkok Declaration" and reflected to a considerable degree Peking's thinking on human rights. Using this document Peking was able to plug its view that its policies on human rights coincide or agree with other Asian countries, and moreover, need to be considered when discussing mainland China's or any other Asian country's human rights situation.

The main points in the document were: (1) the promotion of human rights must be done in the context of international cooperation; (2) the current codification of human rights stresses only one category of human rights; (3) the principles of sovereignty and noninterference in the internal affairs of states must be observed when discussing human rights; (4) double stands and the politicization of human rights issues must be avoided; (5) the right of development must be considered an essential human right; (6) international human rights norms must coincide with the development of a just and fair world order; (7) economic and social progress facilitates the growth of democracy and the promotion of human rights; and (8) education and training are important in improving human rights.[72]

The document recommended, among other things, that human rights not be made a condition for development assistance; that human rights not be used as an instrument of political pressure; that national and regional particularities and historical, cultural, and religious backgrounds be considered when assessing a nation's human rights condition; that economic, social, cultural and civil rights be seen as interdependent; that poverty be seen as an obstacle to the enjoyment of human rights; and that regional arrangements be established to promote human rights.[73]

After this document was published, Peking cited it often in human rights discussions and took the position that provisions in the document— which generally supports its view—should be given serious consideration when speaking of mainland China's human rights problems. Mainland Chinese leaders seemed to perceive that they can in this way redirect the

---

[71] This book was Harry Hongda Wu, *Laogai—The Chinese Gulag* (Boulder, Colo.: Westview Press, 1992).

[72] See "Bangkok Declaration," *Beijing Review* 36, no. 22 (May 31-June 6, 1993): 9-11.

[73] Ibid.

debate on human rights.[74]

In June, when Malaysian Prime Minister Mahathir Mohamad visited Peking, Premier Li P'eng stated, with Mahathir's concurrence, that "each country must define its own concept of human rights." He went on to say that democracy "is not an end but a means."[75]

At the World Conference on Human Rights held in Vienna, Peking again found an opportunity to promote its—and what it assumed to be the Asian—view of human rights. The *People's Daily* said that some "Western nations, under the banner of protecting human rights, interfere in other nations . . . trying to impose their own ideology and version of democracy. . . ."[76] The Ministry of Foreign Affairs echoed this view when a spokesman said that "individuals must put the states' rights before their own."[77]

Peking, over the last two years, has also spoken more openly about improvements in the standard of living in mainland China and Peking's successes in eradicating poverty. This accords with mainland China's emphasis (on which Asian and Third World countries agree) on improving the economic conditions of its citizens, which affect life span, educational standards, and much more.[78] Chinese leaders have also used this as the basis of an argument that mainland China is different from other countries because it is poor and that improving the standard of living will result in a better human rights record and that the passing of time will see big improvements in mainland China's human rights.[79]

When U.S. Secretary of State Christopher visited Peking in early

---

[74]See, for example, "Asia's Major Human Rights Concerns," ibid., no. 16 (April 19-25, 1993): 10-11; this article was published before the Bangkok Declaration. Also see "China's View on the Final Document," ibid., no. 22 (May 31-June 6, 1993): 8-9; "Proposals for Human Rights Protection and Promotion," ibid., no. 26 (June 28-July 4, 1993): 8-11; and Dong Yunhu, "Fine Traditions of Human Rights in Asia," ibid., 11-12.

[75]"Tiananmen Quiet as Rural Peasants Revolt over Inequalities," *Asian Bulletin* 18, no. 8 (August 1993): 74.

[76]"Peking Assails Universal Human Rights; Tibet Remains Tense," ibid., 77.

[77]Ibid.

[78]See, for example, Jin Ling, "Comfortable Life Coming Soon to Cities," *Beijing Review* 36, nos. 3-4 (January 18-31, 1993): 4. Mainland China's representatives to the 49th session of the UN Human Rights Commission and the regional meeting in Asia for the World Conference on Human Rights emphasized the importance of "subsistence rights" above others. See Liu Fenzhi, "Right to Subsistence Should Be Given Priority," ibid., no. 25 (June 21-27, 1993): 9-10.

[79]See, for example, General Secretary Chiang Tse-min's interview with Mortimer Zuckerman, editor-in-chief of the *U.S. News & World Report,* reproduced in *Beijing Review* 36, no. 12 (March 22-28, 1993): 8. Also see "Standpoint on Human Rights Aired," ibid. 37, no. 2 (January 10-16, 1994): 6-7.

1994 and criticized the PRC for human rights abuses, Chinese leaders replied that it is not fair to impose the human rights standards of a developed country on a developing country. They also announced that Peking was working hard on wiping out poverty in mainland China by the year 2000 (two major tenets in the Bangkok Declaration). Foreign Minister Ch'ien Ch'i-ch'en added that the United States uses a free emigration policy in judging the human rights situation in mainland China, yet does not give visas to Chinese who want to go to the United States. He also cited the United States for exporting goods made with prison labor (referring to the double standard problems cited in the Bangkok Declaration).[80]

Meanwhile, Peking leaders, citing the "Bangkok position," defeated a Western-sponsored motion to censure the PRC in the UN Human Rights Commission in Geneva, Switzerland.[81] Peking's tack in promoting its and the Asian view of human rights seemed to be working.

Conclusions

The PRC has exhibited three different kinds of responses, or has adopted three different policy lines, to deal with the wave of foreign criticism and hostility expressed toward Peking after the Tienanmen massacre. All three of these responses were adopted early on and are still part of what may be called the PRC's "human rights foreign policy." The frequency of use of each, however, has varied over the last five years.

Mainland Chinese leaders clearly did not expect such a potent or visceral reaction to what Peking termed "dealing with the counterrevolutionary rebellion." Their first response, thus, was more reactive than a well-thought out or calculated. For this reason, a hard-line policy was dominant in the months immediately after the Tienanmen massacre. The political shift to the left favoring hard-liners in May and June 1989 was also a significant factor governing human rights policies. As time passed, however, Peking increasingly favored granting concessions and/or taking an offensive stance.

Which mode of reaction Peking took later at any given time or in response to any specific criticism or complaint, depended, and still depends, to some degree on the complaint and who made it. If the criticism was of the type that appeared to be blatantly interfering in mainland China's internal affairs, a hard-line response was favored. Also if Tibet were mentioned. In contrast, general kinds of criticism or citing mainland China

---

[80]See Frank Ching, "Inching Forward on Rights," *FEER,* April 7, 1994, 34.
[81]See note 36 above.

in a way that did not threaten the leadership or political stability in main-land China, were more likely to be met with concessions or an offensive reply.

The choice among the three policies cited above was, and is, also a matter of the factional struggles in the Party or government line at the moment. Teng's decision to order troops into Tienanmen and crush the Democracy Movement was motivated by a combination of fear that the protest would lead to anarchy and a deep apprehension that events were playing into the hands of Teng's opponents and that he had to compromise or preempt them. Teng probably did not want to make such a decision as he did. Clearly, he understood better than others in Peking that there would be negative consequences in term of his relations with the West and especially the United States. It seems improbable that he anticipated the degree of hostility that he got.

As Teng recovered and as his rightist reforms were put back on track, concessions or an offensive strategy became the policy choice used with greater frequency. Teng and the reformists were not always in a position to make many or major concessions given the fact that the left was quick to criticize such actions. Nor did they always want to. Yet it is apparent that Peking used a hard-line response less often after Teng strengthened the position of the rightist reformers. This was particularly noticeable after Teng purged many leftists and successfully attacked leftist policies in 1992.

As time passed, foreign criticism of Peking became more muted and less energized and, as a consequence, Chinese leaders needed to respond less often with anger or take a hard-line position. Hence, the revival of the rightist reformers and the weakening of foreign complaints happened simultaneously and are hard to separate in terms of which had the greatest influence.

U.S. President Bill Clinton is another factor. President Clinton took a hard position on human rights abuses in mainland China during the campaign—speaking of "dictators from Baghdad to Beijing." When he became president, mainland Chinese leaders, it seems, were prepared to make concessions and did. But due to Clinton's lack of concern about foreign affairs that many perceived reflected a U.S. withdrawal or isola-tionist policy, and the new administration's ineptness in dealing with foreign policy issues, not to mention its lack of concern about Asia (the APEC meeting notwithstanding), Peking was encouraged to use a hard-line, tough policy more often. Peking also perceived, and no doubt this was reasonable, it had more leverage with the United States in the context of the North Korean "nuclear crisis"; this was another reason for an unyielding stance on human rights.

This does not mean that Peking has recently regressed to favor a hard-line policy. Rather, it reflects special circumstances. Peking's foreign policy vis-à-vis human rights criticism is still evolving and appears to be favoring the offensive tenet of its human rights policy. On the other hand, one should bear in mind the PRC's preoccupation with its sovereign rights and its leaders' world view is not an international one in which the rights of the nation-state diminishes in importance to make global human rights standards possible. Furthermore, Peking, given the makeup of its political leadership, cannot budge on issues such as Tibet and Taiwan as this will mean that it will in the future stick to a hard-line approach to these and related human rights charges.

It is, however, necessary to note that throughout the period under discussion, Peking did not want to anger the Western countries, in particular the United States. Good relations were needed to keep economic growth on track. And PRC leaders perceived that they could get what it wanted from the United States and other Western countries by making some not too important concessions and they could maintain a tough stance at home. If releasing some political prisoners and promising to agree to Western standards on human rights did not hurt the leadership's credibility at home, why not?

Last but not least, Peking's offensive policy on human rights has been successful—both from an objective perspective and from the Chinese point of view. Moreover, its good prospects rationalize making concessions, especially if these concessions can be viewed as less than meaningful or temporary. In fact, Peking may in the future more often adopt an offensive policy vis-à-vis human rights complaints. The perspective in Peking appears to be that mainland China can win the human rights debate because Asia is the center of the world's economic development and because other Asian as well as Third World countries generally agree with Peking on the definition of human rights.

Part VI

Cross-Strait Relations

15

Cross-Strait Relations and Their Implications for the United States

Robert G. Sutter

U.S. Involvement in Cross-Strait Relations

The United States has remained deeply involved in relations between the People's Republic of China (PRC) government on mainland China and the Nationalist Chinese government on Taiwan since the outbreak of the Korean War.[1] U.S. involvement has experienced three general stages.

1. The first stage: At the start of the Korean War, President Truman ordered the U.S. Seventh Fleet to intervene in the Chinese civil war and to block an expected Communist assault on Taiwan.[2] Two decades of U.S. containment of the PRC saw the United States side with the Nationalists, protecting them in their civil conflict with the PRC.

2. The second stage: This period gave way to the American opening to Peking (Beijing) in the 1970s. U.S. policy struck an ambiguous but effective balance between the contending Chinese regimes in Peking and Taipei. In 1979, the United States switched formal diplomatic relations from Taipei to Peking and established a legal framework under the Taiwan Relations Act (TRA) to govern extensive, albeit unofficial, U.S. ties with

---

[1]For background see, among others, Ralph N. Clough, *Island China* (Cambridge, Mass.: Harvard University Press, 1978); Thomas B. Gold, *State and Society in the Taiwan Miracle* (Armonk, N.Y.: M. E. Sharpe, 1986); Hung-mao Tien, *The Great Transition: Political and Social Change in the Republic of China* (Stanford, Calif.: Hoover Institution Press, 1989); and Ralph N. Clough, *Reaching Across the Taiwan Strait* (Boulder, Colo.: Westview Press, 1993).

[2]The intervention also effectively blocked any possible Nationalist assault on the mainland from Taiwan.

the people and administration on Taiwan. Maintaining an appropriate balance in U.S. policy toward mainland China and Taiwan was difficult as leaders in Peking and Taipei saw U.S. policy as central to their respective strategies against each other. Peking and Taipei repeatedly pressed for advantage in relations with the United States that would support their position against their adversary.

3. The third stage: In the late 1980s, the U.S.-PRC-Taiwan triangular relationship began to change in important ways. In particular, the Nationalist administration on Taiwan began to allow large-scale contacts and exchanges between Taiwan and mainland China. Trade, tourism, and investment from Taiwan to the mainland grew rapidly and tensions along the Taiwan Strait eased greatly. Peking and Taipei continued to compete for international standing and influence, especially in relations with the United States, but the burgeoning contacts had the effect of easing the heretofore zero-sum game quality of U.S. relations with mainland China and Taiwan. No longer did Peking always assume that improved U.S.-Taiwan relations came at its expense, nor did Taipei necessarily conclude that improved U.S.-PRC relations were against its interests. Up to the present, growing mainland-Taiwan contacts have occupied leaders in Peking and Taipei, who have worked out strategies to deal with the new situation that have placed somewhat less immediate importance on the role of the United States.

U.S. policymakers have welcomed this new situation. The mainland China-Taiwan contacts have reduced the respective pressures that those governments have applied on the United States, thereby increasing the room for maneuver the United States has as it pursues American interests in relations with both sides of the Taiwan Strait. Nevertheless, the increased cross-Strait contacts add another element of change and uncertainty to a U.S. China policy already attempting to deal with several other new elements, notably:

> *The collapse of nascent political reform in the PRC after the June 1989 Tienanmen (Tiananmen) crackdown and the concurrent sharp negative shift in U.S. attitudes toward the PRC;
> *The collapse of the Soviet empire and the decline of the previous U.S. need for good relations with Peking as a strategic asset against Moscow;
> *The continued democratization and economic progress on Taiwan—a trend giving increased stature to the regime in the United States and elsewhere;
> *Amid worldwide movements pressing for national or ethnic independence, the emergence of a vocal opposition group in Taiwan calling for formal independence of the island (Peking has said it

will use force to prevent Taiwan independence);

*The increasing economic integration of Taiwan and Hong Kong with nearby PRC coastal provinces, raising issues for a possibly distinct U.S. policy toward this area, sometimes called "greater China"; and

*The uncertainty surrounding leadership situations in Peking and Taipei—leadership shifts could result in possible shifts in policies affecting U.S. interests in mainland-Taiwan relations.

Background: Taiwan-Mainland Relations Since the Korean War

The rivalry between the Chinese Communist government in Peking and the Nationalist administration in Taiwan has deep roots in the civil conflict that marked the history of China during much of the first half of the twentieth century. The Communists won the civil war on the mainland and established the PRC in 1949; the Nationalists under Chiang Kai-shek retreated in disarray to Taiwan.[3] It appeared that it would be only a matter of months before the PRC attacked and conquered Taiwan, but the outbreak of the Korean War in June 1950 prompted the United States to intervene, sending the Seventh Fleet to block the expected invasion. By October, PRC forces had entered Korea to throw back the allied march north after the defeat of North Korean forces following General Douglas MacArthur's dramatic landing at Inchon. Three years of bitter U.S.-PRC warfare followed.

For the next two decades, U.S. strategy in Asia centered on forward deployed military forces, alliance relations, and foreign assistance programs in Asia designed to "contain" the suspected expansionism of the PRC and its associates in the region. As part of this approach, the United States sided firmly with Chiang Kai-shek's Nationalists in Taiwan, provided billions of dollars in military and economic aid, and encouraged Taiwan's economic development through advice, favorable trade and aid policies, and other programs. The United States continued to recognize the Nationalists' government as the sole legal government of China, and supported its continued occupation of the China seat on the U.N. Security

---

[3]Taiwan had been under Japanese colonial rule for fifty years but had been returned to Chinese rule at the end of World War II. The Nationalist authorities were often resented as new colonial masters by people in Taiwan, especially after the so-called February 28, 1947, incident which saw the arrest and murder of thousands of Taiwan residents suspected by Nationalist authorities. See Clough, *Island China*, 37-42; and Tien, *The Great Transition*, 36-37.

Council. The United States joined with Taiwan forces in defending approaches to Taiwan in the face of PRC military attacks in 1954-55 and 1958. In 1954, the United States signed a formal defense treaty with Taipei.

Chiang Kai-shek's Nationalist government often chafed under the constraints imposed by the United States (e.g., the United States repeatedly discouraged large-scale Nationalist military action against the mainland). But the United States provided needed aid, defense support, and international political support. Taipei was well aware of its dependency on the United States and adjusted its actions accordingly.

Throughout this period, Peking faced a hostile rival regime in Taipei that claimed to be the legitimate government of China, was backed firmly by the United States, and enjoyed widespread international standing. Employing both hard and soft tactics, the PRC leaders in the 1950s repeatedly used force in the Taiwan Strait in an effort to demonstrate PRC resolve not to accept the status quo and ultimately to "liberate" Taiwan, as well as diplomatic initiatives designed to probe for openings in the U.S.-Taiwan relationship. Taiwan policy received less attention in the 1960s as PRC leaders wrestled with massive, disastrous economic, social, and political consequences of the Great Leap Forward and the Cultural Revolution. In foreign affairs, the PRC isolated itself from most sources of world support and stood in confrontation to both the United States and the Soviet Union.[4]

U.S.-PRC Rapprochement

In the late 1960s, a convergence of strategic needs drove Peking and Washington closer together, leading to the Sino-American rapprochement seen during President Nixon's 1972 visit to mainland China. The United States needed a means to sustain a favorable balance of power in Asia while withdrawing over 600,000 troops from Indochina and elsewhere in Asia under terms of the Nixon Doctrine, and a means to balance the growing power and assertiveness of the Soviet Union. The PRC faced a new and growing Soviet military threat along its northern border and needed the relationship with Washington to counter Soviet threats and intimidation.[5]

In the interests of solidifying U.S. relations with Peking in the so-

---

[4]For background on the PRC policy see, among others, A. Doak Barnett, *China and the Major Powers in East Asia* (Washington, D.C.: The Brookings Institution, 1977).

[5]The early years of the rapprochement are reviewed in Barnett, *China and the Great Powers.* The more recent years are reviewed in Harry Harding, *A Fragile Relationship: The United States and China Since 1972* (Washington, D.C.: The Brookings Institution, 1991).

called great-power triangular relationship (i.e., U.S.-PRC-USSR), U.S. leaders increasingly accommodated Peking's demands regarding U.S. policy in the U.S.-PRC-Taiwan triangular relationship. Throughout the 1970s, the United States gradually cut back its military presence in Taiwan and in 1979 it ended official relations, including the U.S.-Taiwan defense treaty, in order to establish formal relations with Peking as the sole, legal government of China.[6] The U.S. shift was accompanied by a massive decline in Taiwan's international standing as scores of countries switched to Peking and Taiwan withdrew or was excluded from the United Nations and other international organizations.

Peking endeavored to capitalize on its enhanced stature and Taipei's growing international political (but not economic) isolation. It followed a carrot and stick policy of concurrent gestures and pressures designed to bring Taipei into formal negotiations on reunification. "Carrots" included ceasing the largely symbolic PRC artillery barrages against the Nationalist-held offshore islands of Kinmen (Quemoy) and Matsu, launching a series of official statements underlining Peking's flexibility regarding conditions for Taiwan's return to the mainland, and gestures designed to encourage the so-called three communications (i.e., direct mail, trade, and transportation) between Taiwan and the mainland.[7]

The PRC's success in negotiating an agreement with Great Britain in 1984 calling for Hong Kong's return to the mainland in 1997 prompted Teng Hsiao-p'ing (Deng Xiaoping) and other senior PRC leaders to hold up the "one country, two systems" approach used in that accord as a model for Taiwan's reunification. Teng and others promised that not only would the political, economic, and social systems in Taiwan be guaranteed, as in the case of Hong Kong, but Taiwan would be able to maintain its separate defense forces.

The PRC "stick" took various forms. Taipei leaders were warned— sometimes with allusions to possible PRC use of force—against undue delay, with PRC leaders repeatedly asserting that the so-called Taiwan issue must be settled in the 1980s. America and others with unofficial

---

[6]In the process, the United States put aside its stance of the 1950s and 1960s that Taiwan's official status remained to be determined, in favor of a position that did not quarrel with the stance of Chinese on both sides of the Taiwan Strait that Taiwan was part of China. The most important U.S. positions included those taken in the Shanghai Communiqué of February 28, 1972, and statements at the time of U.S.-PRC diplomatic normalization in December 1978. See Harding, *A Fragile Relationship,* 23-87.

[7]Peking's approach is reviewed in Harding, *A Fragile Relationship,* 82-87, 108-19, 154-62; Qingguo Jia, "Changing Relations Across the Taiwan Strait: Beijing's Perceptions," *Asian Survey* 32, no. 3 (March 1992): 277-89; and Hung-mao Tien, "The PRC Approach Toward Taiwan" (Conference Paper, Pennsylvania State University, July 16-18, 1991).

contacts with Taiwan were repeatedly pressed to cut back those ties in sensitive areas, especially the sale of weapons. They were also warned against efforts to boost Taiwan's international standing through membership in international governmental organizations.

The Challenge to Taipei's Legitimacy and Taipei's Response

These developments posed the most serious challenge for the Nationalist administration in Taiwan since the retreat from the mainland in 1949.[8] Taipei officials were loath to enter talks with Peking on reunification. In part, this reflected their sense that they would be the decidedly weaker party in the talks and that Peking would likely use the negotiations to further undermine U.S. and other backing for Taiwan as a separate entity,[9] thereby leaving little alternative other than acceptance of PRC terms. In part, it reflected Taipei's awareness that the vast majority of people in Taiwan had little attachment to the mainland regime. They might interpret Nationalist-Communist talks on reunification as a thinly disguised effort by Nationalist officials to "sell out" local interests for the sake of their personal gain. They might take to the streets to register their opposition.

At the same time, the international developments undercut the main political rationale for the Nationalist administration on Taiwan. The government of the Republic of China (ROC) in Taipei was dominated at senior levels by refugees from the mainland—"mainlanders"—who represented only about 15 percent of Taiwan's total population. It was an authoritarian, one-party state that gave little voice at the national level to the 85 percent of the population whose roots in Taiwan went back centuries before 1949 and whose identity with the mainland was blurred—"Taiwanese."[10] Nevertheless, all in Taiwan paid taxes, military service, and other means to support the Nationalist government. The fact that Chiang Kai-shek was able to point to U.S., UN, and other international recognition of the ROC as the legitimate government of China helped to justify his demands that citizens of Taiwan support the regime. As U.S.

---

[8]Reviewed in, among others, Robert G. Sutter, *Taiwan: Entering the 21st Century* (New York: Asia Society, 1988).

[9]Most notably after derecognition of Taipei, the United States in 1979 passed the Taiwan Relations Act, which gave a legal framework for continued U.S. "unofficial" relations, including arms sales and other sensitive exchanges, with Taiwan as an entity separate from PRC control.

[10]In the minds of many Taiwanese, the Nationalist rule was a pseudo-colonial rule of the island following fifty years of Japanese colonial rule. See Tien, *The Great Transition*, 90-103.

and other world backing declined rapidly, Taipei had to find new sources of political legitimacy.

Under the leadership of Chiang Kai-shek's son, Chiang Ching-kuo, who ruled as premier prior to the elder Chiang's death in 1975 and then served as president from 1978 until his death in 1988, the Nationalist administration adopted a multifaceted reform program designed to build a strong political base of support for the regime on the island. Critical elements included:

*The government fostered rapid economic development and modernization of Taiwan in the 1970s and 1980s—development accomplished with a relatively egalitarian distribution of wealth and social-educational benefits throughout the society;[11]

*A major affirmative action program designed to bring native Taiwanese into the ruling Nationalist Party (or the Kuomintang, KMT) and into the national government, including the military, at senior as well as other levels; and

*A gradual political liberalization encouraging local, provincial, and national elections which selected some top decision-makers in government and served as indirect referenda on the state of Nationalist Party rule.

By the 1980s, the Nationalist regime under the leadership of Chiang Ching-kuo and his successor, Lee Teng-hui (a Taiwanese), had initiated a series of reforms that put the government's legitimacy more firmly into the hands of the people on Taiwan and reflected more closely the interests of the people there. In particular: (1) martial law was lifted; (2) opposition parties were allowed to organize and their candidates to run for elections; (3) censorship and sedition regulations were eased; and (4) political prisoners were released.

In the 1990s, President Lee and the Nationalist leadership undertook major reforms of national government bodies. By December 1991, all legislators and National Assembly members elected on the mainland over forty years earlier were retired.[12] A newly elected National Assembly rep-

---

[11]This growth was especially favorable to the indigenous Taiwanese who tended to dominate the economy of the island.

[12]Many such legislators had died in the forty-year period, posing a challenge for the government which remained interested in showing some representation from regions throughout China.

resenting predominantly people from Taiwan undertook to amend the Constitution; an election to make the Legislative Yuan (national legislature) predominantly representative of the people in Taiwan was held in late 1992, and an election of a new president under terms of the revised Constitution was slated for 1996.[13]

Loosened governmental control and greater concern for popular opinion in Taiwan meant that Nationalist leaders could no longer block Taiwanese from traveling to or doing business with the mainland. Although few in Taiwan showed any interest in accommodating with the PRC politically, business interests backed by press and popular opinion showed great interest in economic opportunities on the mainland where labor, land, and other costs were often much lower than in Taiwan.

The economic attractiveness of the mainland grew as Taiwan entrepreneurs sought to link up closely with the rapidly growing mainland Chinese economy at a time when other markets were seeing lackluster growth. At first, representatives of Taiwan's so-called "sunset" industries located on the mainland. Increasingly, business representatives of more advanced corporations moved into the mainland, seeing operations there as critical to Taiwan's longer-term growth and ambition to become a hub for investment, services, and other business interaction with East Asia.

Meanwhile, many in Taiwan wished to visit long-separated family members or to travel around the mainland as tourists. PRC leaders strove to facilitate such trade, travel, and other exchanges.[14]

Faced with popular pressure to increase contacts with the PRC, the Nationalists took a series of measures to regulate the strong flow of contacts and control their policy implications. President Lee Teng-hui convened a National Unification Council (NUC) in October 1990, to advise on these matters, and later that year, a Mainland Affairs Council (MAC) was set up under the premier to direct cabinet-level policy on Taiwan-mainland relations. As part of his political reform program, President Lee in May 1991 ended the state of civil war with the PRC and opened the way to official contacts under the "one country, two governments" formula—a

---

[13]In the past, the National Assembly generally served to amend the Constitution and to act as an electoral college in choosing the President. The Legislative Yuan was the main lawmaking body. The National Assembly broadened its responsibilities in passing constitutional amendments in 1992. See *Free China Journal*, June 23, 1992.

[14]See, among others, Dennis Van Vranken Hickey, "Will Inter-China Trade Change Taiwan or the Mainland?" *Orbis* 35, no. 4 (Fall 1991): 517-31, and Natale Bellocchi, "U.S. Perceptions of Taiwan's Democratization and Reunification" (Conference Paper, Pennsylvania State University, July 16-18, 1991).

formula known to be unacceptable to Peking.[15] To deal with the many practical issues that arise given extensive exchanges across the Strait, an ostensibly unofficial body, the Straits Exchange Foundation (SEF), was established in February 1991 and after some uncertainty proved able to deal with important practical issues. The PRC set up a counterpart body, known as the Association for Relations Across the Taiwan Straits (ARATS), in December 1991. Representatives of the two offices have talks on practical issues in cross-Strait relations and other matters on a regular basis. Taiwan passed a law, on July 16, 1992, to govern the growing exchanges with the mainland.[16] (See appendix 15.1 for major organizations in Taiwan and the mainland that deal with Taiwan-mainland relations.)

The main opposition party in Taiwan, the Democratic Progressive Party (DPP), viewed the progress in mainland-Taiwan relations with some concern. Party leaders were careful not to stand against the popular support for greater Taiwan trade, investment, and other unofficial exchanges with the mainland; but they opposed the Nationalists' repeated calls for eventual reunification, and argued that a plebiscite should be held in Taiwan to determine Taiwan's future status. DPP calls for self-determination were followed by calls for independence[17] and sometimes prompted harsh warnings from Peking that it would resort to force to prevent moves toward formal separation of Taiwan from the mainland. In elections during late 1991, Nationalist leaders were effective in referring to the PRC "threat" to encourage voters in Taiwan to steer away from "radical" DPP candidates and support the Nationalists and the status quo. At the same time, DPP leaders capitalized on Peking's relentless diplomatic competition against Taipei to argue that Taiwan would be better off internationally as a de jure separate state than in its current claimed status as the government, or at least one government, in China. In response to this challenge, Nationalist leaders have pursued more pragmatic diplomacy. In particular, Taipei has been willing in recent years to establish official relations with countries, even though they may also have relations with Peking. It similarly seeks representation in the United Nations and other official international

---

[15]Taiwan officials have sometimes used formulas other than "one country, two governments" to describe their position. The law governing relations with the mainland, passed July 16, 1992, referred to "one country, two areas." See *Free China Journal*, July 21, 1992. PRC officials have refused to endorse formulas which give official status to Taipei as an independent political entity.

[16]For background, see Robert G. Sutter, *Taiwan: Recent Developments and U.S. Policy Choices,* CRS Issue Brief 92038 (regularly updated).

[17]Supporters of a plebescite for self-determination often assumed it would lead to results favoring independence.

organizations. Peking rejects this "one China, two governments" formula. Its formal objections have included an official PRC "white paper" on Taiwan, issued on August 31, 1993, and strongly critical reaction to the MAC's release of a "white paper" on Taiwan on July 5, 1994. Up to now, Taipei's efforts, backed by a generous foreign aid program, have won diplomatic recognition from a handful of small states. More important results have been achieved through Taipei's efforts to upgrade ostensibly unofficial representative offices in a number of important developed and developing countries.[18]

Current Status of Taiwan-Mainland Exchanges[19]

Taipei's new openness to contacts with the mainland has resulted in remarkable progress in some areas—mainly economic and other unofficial contacts. There has been a good deal of activity as well on the political side of the relationship, but Taipei's complicated three-stage approach leading to talks on reunification with the mainland (see appendix 15.1) is widely seen as an indirect but effective tactic to slow any movement toward formal mainland-Taiwan talks on reunification which Taipei sees as adverse to its interests. Meanwhile, the critical figures on mainland-Taiwan contacts since 1987 include: (1) over five million visits of Taiwan residents to the mainland—but only 50,000 mainland visitors went to Taiwan; (2) trade, mainly conducted via Hong Kong, grew to US$14.3 billion in 1993 and was heavily in Taiwan's favor; it was expected to top US$20 billion in 1994; (3) total Taiwan investment, mainly in Fukien (Fujian) Province and other coastal areas, amounted to over US$3 billion in over 9,000 enterprises in 1993 alone—Taiwan is now the second largest outside investor on the mainland, after Hong Kong.[20]

The crucial role of Hong Kong as a conduit for Taiwan trade and investment in the mainland also has prompted Taipei to put aside its formal refusal to recognize the legitimacy of the PRC-British accord returning Hong Kong to PRC sovereignty in 1997, and to make preparations to deal with the new situation. Taiwan already has 2,500 companies doing business in Hong Kong; the Taipei Trade Center Hong Kong and other quasi-official representative offices in Hong Kong have been assisting Taiwan investors

---

[18]For background, see note 16 above and Robert G. Sutter, *Taiwan's National Assembly Elections, 1991,* CRS Report 92-62F (January 10, 1992).

[19]Recent coverage of this subject appears in *Far Eastern Economic Review* and Foreign Broadcast Information Service (FBIS), *Daily Report: China* [hereinafter cited as *FBIS-CHI*]. This section also relies on the author's interviews with officials in mainland China and Taiwan, 1992-94.

[20]Ibid. See also FBIS, *Pacific Rim Economic Review,* January 26, 1994, 30.

to establish operations there.[21] In February 1994, Taiwan's MAC completed a draft law governing relations with Hong Kong after 1997.[22]

Politically, both Peking and Taipei have generated numerous proposals (see appendix 15.1) and employed varied forums to get their respective messages across, but their basic positions remain far apart.

The core of Peking's approach calls for Taiwan's reunification with the mainland under a "one country, two systems" formula, whereby Taiwan would revert to Chinese (Peking's) control but would be guaranteed a great deal of autonomy by Peking for a long period of time. PRC leaders stress an approach of "peaceful reunification" through party-to-party talks between representatives of the ruling Communist Party on the mainland and the ruling Nationalist Party on Taiwan. They acknowledge that the opposition DPP in Taiwan may also be a participant in such talks. To build mutual interest and trust between the mainland and Taiwan, Peking encourages the so-called three communications—direct mail, trade, and transportation. Peking also facilitates Taiwanese investment throughout the mainland, but especially in nearby regions, notably Fukien Province. Peking refuses to rule out the possibility that it would be compelled to resort to the threat or the use of force to prevent Taiwan from declaring independence, developing nuclear weapons, aligning with a hostile power, or unduly delaying the reunification process.

For its part, Taipei used to stick firmly to the position that there could be only one legitimate government of China, i.e., the ROC in Taipei. The collapse of its official international standing, the passing of "old guard" leaders loyal to Chiang Kai-shek's legacy, and popular, media, and business pressure on Taiwan to open ties with the mainland resulted in Taipei's shift to a position ending the official state of civil war and accepting a stance of "one China, two governments." In effect, Taipei now argues that there are two political entities in China and that reunification of China must take them into account. Taipei also argues that whatever unification takes place should be peaceful and democratic, suggesting changes will be required in Peking's stance on the use of force and its Communist-dominated political system. Finally, Taiwan officials are frank in noting they seek a "gradual" process in three phases and that uppermost in their minds will be the need to respect the rights and interests of the people in the Taiwan area. The three-phase process, which is only now entering phase one, involves first a phase of "exchanges and reciprocity,"

---

[21]On Taiwan's approach to Hong Kong, see *Free China Journal,* March 24, 1992, 7.
[22]Ibid., February 25, 1994, 2.

then a phase of "mutual trust and cooperation," and finally, a phase of "consultations and unification" (see appendix 15.1).

Interests and Policy Approaches of Mainland China, Taiwan, and the United States

Mainland China

Although PRC leaders were unsuccessful in their stated effort of using Peking's international advantage and Taiwan's isolation in order to achieve Chinese reunification in the 1980s, they remain determined to pursue reunification on terms favored by the PRC. In general, their current approach to Taiwan is based on what they see as the mixed results of recent trends regarding mainland-Taiwan relations.[23]

On the positive side, mainland Chinese officials point to several notable accomplishments in recent years:

> *Markedly reduced military-political tension in the Taiwan Strait area;
> *Greater economic integration of Taiwan and the mainland, replacing the economic separation that prevailed until recently. One result has been to add to the booming south China economy;
> *Increasing contacts, especially by people from Taiwan traveling to the mainland; and
> *The breakdown of Taipei's previous policy of the "three nos"—no contacts, no negotiations, and no compromise. At present, there is a consensus on both sides of the Taiwan Strait that exchanges and contacts are good, even though Taipei insists that its restrictions on "official" contacts, negotiations, and compromise have not been breached.

The positive trends are balanced by mainland Chinese officials' frustrations over what they see as the slow pace of change, and by their anxiety over other trends affecting mainland-Taiwan ties:

> *The exchanges with Taiwan are still indirect (e.g., much goes through Hong Kong); one-way (over five million Taiwanese visits to the mainland,[24] but only 50,000 mainland visitors allowed to visit

---

[23]A review is provided in Jia, "Changing Relations Across the Taiwan Strait." This section also relies on interviews conducted in mainland China in May-June 1992, April 1993, and April 1994.

[24]It is important to note that since many from Taiwan are repeat visitors to the mainland, far less than five million residents from Taiwan have traveled to the mainland.

Taiwan); nonofficial (Taipei refuses official contacts unless Peking recognizes Taiwan's official status, which Peking refuses to do); and developing only gradually in the political area;
*Internal politics in Taiwan concern the PRC on several points:
(a) The DPP, with its stance favoring Taiwan independence, may continue to grow in stature;
(b) The Nationalist Party is divided among mainlander old guard and indigenous Taiwanese. Peking is concerned, on the one hand, that the Nationalists will not be able to sustain a firm stance against Taiwan independence if Taiwanese in the Nationalist Party align with the DPP on the issue. On the other hand, it also worries that even Nationalist Party mainlanders are pursuing a deliberately slow policy on reunification in anticipation that the Communist system on the mainland will succumb to pressures felt by other Communist regimes and collapse or change more gradually into a more democratic, free market state more compatible with Taiwan's interests;
*The United States and other countries seem prepared to give more support to Taiwan. The end of the Cold War has reduced PRC influence among developed countries, whereas Taiwan's prosperity and democratization have attracted favorable attention. High-level visitors, formal agreements, and even the sales or transfers of new weapons systems have worried PRC officials.

Against this backdrop, Peking continues to follow its carrot and stick approach of the past designed ultimately to achieve reunification along the lines of the "one country, two systems" formula. There is little optimism among PRC observers that the big breakthrough in relations called for in the 1980s will be achieved any time soon, but mainland Chinese officials continue to voice optimism about the longer-term trends. Sometimes, they also repeat old warnings to Taipei that if reunification is delayed too long the "forces of history" ultimately will "crush" those who stand in the way of Chinese reunification.[25]

On the positive side, Peking continues to offer attractive economic incentives for greater Taiwan trade and investment in the mainland; it attempts to accommodate Taiwan concerns in order to facilitate cultural, academic, business, and other exchanges; and it generally expresses patience with Taipei's slow approach regarding political contacts. Mainland Chinese officials also are well aware that their smooth handling of the transfer of Hong Kong to PRC sovereignty and control in 1997 will have a major

---

[25]Interview with PRC officials responsible for Taiwan affairs, Peking, May 23, 1992.

impact on how people in Taiwan will perceive possible reunification with the mainland. Some in mainland China also judge that smoothly handling Chinese economic reform and renewing significant political reform on the mainland would reduce mainland-Taiwan differences and enhance prospects for reunification.

On the other hand, Peking continues to believe that pressures in various forms also must be applied in order to prod Taipei to the negotiating table. Thus, the warnings against Taiwan independence or undue delay on reunification are repeated occasionally and backed by PRC military activities, including a continued buildup in Peking's naval and air forces. Mainland Chinese diplomats work assiduously to keep Taiwan as isolated as possible in the official world community—a trend made more difficult by recently growing international interest in including representatives of Taiwan's vibrant economy in international deliberations. Some officials on the mainland also judge that in the near future the mainland will develop economically to such a degree that it will be able to challenge and undermine Taiwan economically; in order to survive, Taiwan businesses will have to link up with mainland enterprises. By manipulating the China market, these officials judge, Peking will gain considerable leverage over Taiwan and prod Taipei toward reunification talks."[26]

Variables affecting the PRC approach in the future relate to events in Taiwan, international support for Taiwan, and possible changes in the PRC. Western analysts often focus on how these developments could challenge and force a change in the PRC approach. Notable challenges would be posed by an accelerated trend toward Taiwan independence; markedly higher U.S., Western, and other international support for Taiwan; or a leadership succession struggle in the PRC where nationalistic issues like policy toward Taiwan figured prominently. An alternative view stresses the common economic interests of Taiwan, the mainland coastal provinces, and Hong Kong. It argues that this rapidly growing economic area—called "greater China" by many—will become increasingly integrated economically and that the economic integration will break down barriers and foster an unstoppable trend toward greater political cooperation and eventual reunification.[27] This view sometimes also judges that the PRC leadership that succeeds the current "old guard" will likely be more flexible in dealing

---

[26]Interview with PRC officials responsible for Taiwan affairs, Peking, May 22, 1992.

[27]Reunification under these terms might be more compatible with Taipei's current stance than with Peking's as it appears to assume such major economic and perhaps related political change on the mainland that it remains uncertain that the Communist system there as we know it today would continue to exist.

with issues like Taiwan than the current PRC leadership.[28]

Taiwan[29]

Taiwan leaders' approach to the mainland reflects many of the same international trends and developments in mainland China and Taiwan seen in the PRC leaders' approach. But Taiwan's posture also reflects the ongoing political debate on the island regarding its future identity and relationship with the mainland. Under the authoritarian rule of Chang Kai-shek and Chiang Ching-kuo, the Nationalist Party was generally able to sustain unity on this issue and to impose its views on the sometimes unsympathetic Taiwanese populace. Growing democratization in Taiwan has meant that the government's view and that of the DPP opposition now must take into account the often competing interests and perspectives of business, media, intellectual, and other groups. In general, there are two major poles of opinion reflecting Taiwan's current approach to the mainland, one centered on the ruling Nationalist Party and the other on the opposition DPP.

Within the Nationalist Party, there is a wide spectrum of views ranging from old guard mainlanders who place reunification very high on their preferred list of national priorities, to Taiwanese politicians who merely go through the motions in expressing an interest in reunification as they focus on issues relating to Taiwan's development and prosperity. Nevertheless, the party has come to agreement on major points reflected in the government's current basic approach to the PRC. In particular:

> *They favor some economic exchanges with the mainland, but wish to place some limits on trade and investment in order to avoid making the Taiwan economy heavily dependent on the mainland;
> *They prefer to wait—or at least to go slow—on significant political exchanges. At bottom, it is judged that the time is not right for significant political exchanges with Teng Hsiao-p'ing and Peking's old guard, who will die soon. Any understandings reached could easily fall victim to the expected leadership succession struggle in

---

[28]See, among others, Tien, "The PRC Approach to Taiwan."

[29]This section relies on such sources as Ying-jeou Ma, "The Republic of China's Policy Toward the Chinese Mainland," *Issues & Studies* 28, no. 2 (February 1992): 1-10; Thomas Ching-peng Peng, "President Lee's Rise to Power and His Reform Program," ibid., no. 6 (June 1992): 59-69; Hungdah Chiu, "Constitutional and Political Reform in the ROC and Relations Across the Taiwan Strait" (Conference Paper, Center for Strategic and International Studies, Washington, D.C., May 13, 1991); and deliberations at a Library of Congress symposium on Taiwan, April 3, 1992.

Peking. It is better to wait for a more stable successor leadership to emerge. Moreover, waiting could play to Taiwan's advantage as the Communist system in the mainland may be subject to pressures for reform that might lead to rapid or more gradual political change that could make reunification more acceptable to Taiwan.

In the meantime, Taiwan has stressed the importance of maintaining a strong national defense. It has endeavored to upgrade its armed forces through transfers from the United States, its chief supplier, indigenous development, and increased contacts with other suppliers, notably France. The Taipei administration has decided to deal pragmatically with the consequences of Hong Kong's reversion to PRC control, despite the fact that it refuses officially to recognize the PRC-British agreement. The Nationalist leaders have also attempted to deal pragmatically with the consequences of Taiwan's international isolation by practicing flexible diplomacy (i.e., establishing relations with states which already have official ties with Peking); attempting to return in some capacity to official international bodies from which Taiwan has been excluded (e.g., the United Nations, the General Agreement on Tariffs and Trade [GATT]); and upgrading the important "substantive" relations and exchanges Taiwan has on an ostensibly unofficial basis with many developed and important developing countries.

Within the opposition party, the DPP, there are also major divisions on the reunification/independence debate, with one wing of the party calling for rapid movement toward independence and another favoring a more low-keyed approach that would avoid antagonizing the ruling Nationalist leaders or the PRC by flaunting the independence banner. Nevertheless, the party has agreed on some common points regarding Taiwan-mainland relations, including:

*The DPP endorses Taiwan-mainland economic exchanges;
*The DPP expresses concern over Nationalist Party intentions, especially on the part of Nationalist mainlanders who are suspected to be seeking some way to achieve a reunification agreement that the DPP would see as a "sell out" of Taiwanese interests;
*The DPP hammers away at the Nationalist government's lack of great success in improving Taiwan's official international isolation, with some DPP leaders arguing that an independent Taiwan would enjoy much more world support than the current ROC government which claims to be the government of China;
*Like the Nationalists, the DPP also wants to wait before undertaking significant political talks with the mainland. In large measure, they want to wait at least until the completion of Taiwan's planned

political reform over the next few years which they judge should give the party greater influence in the government and provide an atmosphere more conducive to the DPP's stance of national self-determination and independence.

Variables important in determining Taiwan's future approach continue to center on PRC actions; actions by the United States and to a lesser degree other nations; and the extent of unanimity or discord in Taiwan over these issues. Regarding the PRC, for example, it seems logical to assume that if the PRC reforms markedly in both economic and political ways, it will become more like Taiwan and reunification under these conditions would be easier for Taiwan to consider than it is today.[30] If the PRC leaders fall into a chaotic struggle for power that undermines the current economic reforms and prolongs political repression, this trend logically would seem to prod Taiwan leaders to move away from the mainland and toward a more independent posture. If the PRC leadership transition is prolonged and the outcome unclear, this may cause Taiwan leaders to grow impatient with their current approach. Under these circumstances, advocates of self-determination and independence could become more outspoken, especially as mainlander old guard Nationalists in Taiwan pass away.

The United States[31]

In considerable measure because of its unique role in protecting, nurturing, and interacting closely with Taiwan's development since 1950, and its continued position as the most powerful military force along the rim of East Asia, the United States remains by far the most important international actor in the mainland-Taiwan relationship. In general, U.S. policy follows a "have your cake and eat it too" approach designed pragmatically to obtain maximum U.S. benefit from U.S. interaction with both the mainland and Taiwan. Features of the U.S. approach include:

*Efforts to trade, invest, and conduct other economic exchanges with the mainland and Taiwan;

---

[30]Some envisage a loosely defined "commonwealth" as providing a framework for eventual reunification along these lines.

[31]For background see, among others, Robert G. Sutter and William R. Johnson, eds., *Taiwan's Role in World Affairs* (Boulder, Colo.: Westview Press, 1994); Bellocchi, "U.S. Perceptions of Taiwan's Democratization and Reunification"; James Lilley, "A Formula for Relations Between China and Taiwan," *Asian Wall Street Journal Weekly,* September 30, 1991; and David M. Lampton, "America's China Policy: Developing a Fifth Strategy," *Proceedings of the Academy of Political Science* 38, no. 2 (1989): 149-63.

*U.S. refusal to get directly involved in promoting negotiations between the mainland and Taiwan, but emphasizing U.S. interest in the peaceful settlement of mainland-Taiwan differences;

*The changes in U.S. foreign policy brought about by the end of the Cold War, the collapse of Communist regimes in various parts of the world, and U.S. antipathy against Peking over the Tienanmen massacre and other issues prompted the United States to downgrade the importance it places on the PRC. Concurrent economic prosperity and democratization in Taiwan prompted a somewhat more positive U.S. approach to Taiwan;

*Nevertheless, few in the United States want to take a radical step, such as restoring official relations with Taiwan, that in the judgment of many would endanger peace in the Taiwan Strait and strongly alienate the United States from the PRC for a long time.

Role of Congress: In the recent past, Congress and the Administration at times have been at odds over policy in this area, with Congress adopting a stance more supportive of U.S. interests in Taiwan than the Administration preferred. For example, at the time of the Carter Administration's decision to normalize relations with Peking and break ties with Taiwan, many in Congress judged that the Administration had provided insufficient safeguards for U.S. interests in Taiwan. They set about to heavily amend the draft Taiwan Relations Act that was to provide the legal basis for continued U.S. ties with Taiwan. In the end, the Act (P.L. 96-8) clearly implied that the United States would continue to support the people of Taiwan from pressure from the mainland—a stance that appeared to some U.S. observers and to the PRC government to be in implicit contradiction with the Administration's normalization communiqué with Peking, which they saw as implying that the United States expected Taiwan to be reunified with the mainland.[32]

More recently, the antipathy in Congress toward the PRC and Congress' generally favorable view of Taiwan have prompted some in Congress

---

[32]Peking leaders were quick to point to the seeming contradiction but U.S. officials have generally preferred to adopt a policy that supports both the communiqué and the Taiwan Relations Act. Not all American experts see such a contradiction, or an implication that the normalization communiqué seemed to move U.S. policy in a direction of Taiwan's reunification with the mainland. Some judge that a careful reading of the English-language text of the normalization communiqué supports their contention, though they acknowledge that the Chinese-language text seems to imply support for reunification. They are careful to note that the United States recognizes the English-language text as the official text. Interview, Washington, D.C., July 29, 1992.

to go beyond the features of current U.S. policy noted above. In one case, this has seen some Members pushing the Administration to provide greater political, economic, and military support for the Nationalist Party-dominated government through supporting initiatives to allow Taiwan to enter the GATT before the PRC, to provide the Taiwan armed forces with advanced U.S. jet fighters, or other steps. Another trend has seen Members long associated with the DPP and groups of Taiwanese-Americans who back the party come out in favor of Taiwan self determination.

Prospects

The mix of the PRC, Taiwan, and U.S. approaches with the range of international and internal factors affecting mainland-Taiwan relations leads to several general conclusions about the prospects of mainland-Taiwan relations.

Economic contacts are likely to continue and probably to expand substantially. The comparative economic advantage of Taiwan entrepreneurs investing in and trading with the mainland appears to be likely to remain strong. The PRC authorities encourage this trend and the Taiwan authorities do not seem prepared to bear the serious domestic political costs of trying to cut back or severely limit such exchanges.

Cultural, social, intellectual, and even political exchanges will also grow. Both sides will emphasize their willingness to engage in dialogue, build trust, and promote mutual understanding. But no breakthrough regarding talks over reunification appears likely. As in the past, Taiwan continues to keep its foot on the brake in this area, fearing that entering talks on reunification under current circumstances would put it in a weak and disadvantageous position. At minimum, there seems to be agreement in Taiwan that meaningful talks must await the passing of Peking's old guard Communists and the establishment of a stable successor government. Understanding reached with Peking now runs the risk of being overturned in a political succession struggle. This posture has the added benefit for Taiwan in that it buys time to wait to see if economic reform will continue on the mainland and perhaps lead to political reforms and moderation that will make a future Peking government easier to deal with. The passage of time might also allow Taiwan leaders to work toward a more unified posture on dealing with the mainland than has been seen in Taiwan in recent years. In any event, the DPP leaders are currently in agreement with the Nationalists that talks with the mainland should be delayed if only because they want to wait for the completion of political reforms in Taiwan over the next few years that would presumably make government institutions there more representative of their interests.

Critical variables likely to affect the pace and direction of future mainland-Taiwan relations that bear watching by U.S. policymakers include: (1) the PRC leadership succession; (2) Taiwan leadership, especially its ability to handle the sensitive question of self-determination and independence; (3) Hong Kong's transition to PRC rule; (4) the success of economic integration among Hong Kong-Taiwan-coastal China—the so-called "greater China"; (5) international actions, especially actions by the United States; and (6) relative change—through acquisition of advanced military equipment or other means—in the military balance in the Taiwan Strait.

U.S. Policy Options

U.S. policymakers in Congress and the Administration currently face two general policy options. One option, advocated by some in Congress, argues for a more assertive U.S. effort to support perceived American interests in Taiwan, and on the Taiwan side of the mainland-Taiwan equation. The other favors a continuation of the status quo, maintaining the current balance in U.S. policy toward the mainland and Taiwan. These two general options and the specific steps associated with them are examined below.

Other U.S. policy approaches are possible. For example, the United States could adopt a more active role in attempting to mediate mainland-Taiwan differences. In the past, this was seen as a high risk strategy which was tried twice by the United States in the 1940s and ended in disaster. Over the past decade, Taiwan has particularly objected to it out of fear that Peking would be able to encourage the United States to press Taipei into peace talks where Taiwan would appear as the weaker party subject to Peking's domination and manipulation.[33] A case can be made, however, that the situation has changed. U.S. officials may have learned from history, and Taipei may be less likely to see Washington biased against it given the current state of U.S.-PRC relations. Some also argue in support of U.S. intervention and mediation on grounds that the alternative to the U.S. keeping hands off mainland-Taiwan negotiations could be a military conflict in the Taiwan Strait contrary to U.S. interests.

---

[33]Taipei has been reassured by U.S. promises made since 1982 and known as the "six assurances." They involve U.S. promises not to: (1) set a date for ending arms sales to Taiwan; (2) hold prior consultation with Peking on U.S. arms sales to Taiwan; (3) play any mediation role between Peking and Taipei; (4) revise the Taiwan Relations Act; (5) alter the U.S. position regarding sovereignty over Taiwan; and (6) exert pressure on Taiwan to enter into negotiations with the PRC.

Option One: Greater Support for Taiwan

This approach judges that recent developments give the United States greater leeway and more opportunity to readjust the balance in U.S. policy toward mainland-Taiwan relations. There is less U.S. strategic need for the PRC; a less favorable U.S. view of the PRC; a more favorable U.S. view of Taiwan; and considerable economic advantage from accommodating Taiwan's interests. Specific steps advocated by many of this persuasion would see the United States allow senior-level officials to visit Taiwan to secure for economic contracts; strong U.S. lobbying to allow Taiwan entry into the GATT and other international governmental organizations from which it is now excluded because of PRC objections;[34] and upgrade U.S. defense cooperation with Taiwan.

A different set of steps is suggested by other Americans in Congress who use the same arguments regarding U.S. leeway in this policy area to argue that the United States should now more forthrightly support Taiwanese self-determination. Of course, such a step would invite a more strenuous PRC response (Peking has said it would use force to prevent Taiwan independence and it views Congressional calls for self-determination as disguised efforts to support independence). But advocates maintain that the current situation precludes precipitous PRC action adverse to American interests.[35]

Option Two: Support the Status Quo

This approach argues that the United States has a good situation in developing economic and other advantageous relations with both sides of the Taiwan Strait, and proponents see no advantage for U.S. policy in changing the current situation. In particular, advocates argue that a decided tilt toward Taiwan could seriously alienate the PRC and lead to confrontation and possible tensions in the Taiwan Strait. Greater U.S. support for Taiwan also could be misinterpreted by political groups there. Thus, support for the Nationalist requests for high-level exchanges and advanced weapons might prompt authorities in power in Taipei to use this tangible show of U.S. support to their advantage against political opponents pressing for democratic political reform. Or, U.S. support for Taiwan self-determination might encourage pro-independence advocates

---

[34.] It is assumed by some that for Taiwan to gain entry, it would have to be flexible about terminology, and would not receive strong U.S. support if it were to insist on entry as the "Republic of China."

[35] They aver, for instance, that the end of the Cold War has reduced the PRC's leverage over the United States, while Peking dependence on the U.S. market has grown markedly.

to take formal action that could prompt a PRC show of force that would seriously complicate U.S. security interests in the Taiwan Strait. U.S. supporters of the status quo also maintain that the United States has important economic and other interests in the mainland as well as Taiwan, and should avoid taking action at the expense of one over the other, or adopting steps that would lead to tensions and confrontation detrimental to economic and other interests on both sides of the Taiwan Strait.

Specific steps in this approach include maintaining existing relationships with both sides of the Taiwan Strait, and avoiding policy actions, not forced by circumstances, that run the risk of upsetting the current seemingly advantageous situation. Admittedly U.S. policy is ambiguous, with the Taiwan Relations Act promising strong support for Taiwan against mainland pressure and the U.S.-PRC communiqués seen by some as accepting that Taiwan will revert to China. But the argument is made that this ambiguity has worked well for U.S. policy interests for over a decade and should be continued until better or more clear-cut conditions develop for a change in American policy. Thus, for example, some Americans of this persuasion strongly believe that the economic development and integration currently under way in coastal China, Hong Kong, and Taiwan will invariably lead to better prospects for reunification, led by the Chinese parties concerned, that will naturally elicit a change in U.S. policy more supportive of reunification.

Appendix 15.1

Taiwan: Major Organizations Concerned with Relations with the Mainland[a]

1. The **National Unification Council** is a task force headed by the President with the Vice President, the Premier, and a senior presidential advisor as deputies and comprised of leaders of various segments of the society, functioning as an advisory organ and providing the President with guidelines, suggestions, and research findings for setting the fundamental guidelines on national unification.

2. The Executive Yuan's (cabinet's) **Mainland Affairs Council,** a formal administrative agency under the supervision of the Premier, is in charge of the overall study, planning, deliberation, coordination, and partial implementation of the mainland policy and related work. It also is responsible to the Legislative Yuan

---

[a]See, among others, Ying-jeou Ma, "The Republic of China's Policy Toward the Chinese Mainland," *Issues & Studies* 28, no. 2 (February 1992): 1-10, and Huang Kun-huei, *The Key Points and Contents of the Guidelines for National Unification* (Taipei: Mainland Affairs Council, December 1991).

(parliament), as stipulated in the ROC Constitution. Members of the Council include all ministers and related commission chairmen.

3. The ministries and commissions of the Executive Yuan, according to their official functions, are involved in individual research, planning, and implementation of policy and operations concerning the mainland. In addition, the Nationalist Party has a Department of Mainland Affairs and the DPP has specialists who focus on mainland policy.

4. The **Straits Exchange Foundation**, entrusted by the Executive Yuan's Mainland Affairs Council, handles matters of a technical nature of people-to-people exchanges across the Strait that may involve the ROC government's authority, but are not appropriate for the government to handle directly under current policy.

Taiwan's Official Stance on Reunification

Excerpts from *Guidelines for National Unification,* approved by the Executive Yuan (cabinet) in Taiwan, March 1991.

I. Foreword

The unification of China . . . is the common wish of Chinese people. . . . After an appropriate period of forthright exchange, cooperation, and consultation conducted under the principles of reason, peace, parity, and reciprocity, the two sides of the Taiwan Strait should foster a consensus of democracy, freedom, and equal prosperity, and together build anew a unified China.

II. Goal

To establish a democratic, free, and equitably prosperous China.

III. Principles

. . . The timing and manner of China's unification should first respect the rights and interests of the people in the Taiwan area, and protect their security and welfare. It should be achieved in gradual phases under the principles of reason, peace, parity, and reciprocity.

IV. Process

1. Short Term: A phase of exchanges and reciprocity.

(1) To enhance understanding through exchanges, eliminate hostility through reciprocity, establish a mutually benign relationship by not endangering each other's security and stability, . . . and not denying the other's existence as a political entity.

(2) To set up an order for exchanges across the Strait, to draw up regulations for such exchanges, and to establish intermediary organizations . . . ; to gradually ease various restrictions and expand people-to-people contacts so as to promote the social prosperity of both sides.

(3) . . . in the mainland area economic reform should be carried out forthrightly, the expression of public opinion there should gradually be allowed, and both democracy and the rule of law should be implemented. . . . .

(4) The two sides . . . should end the state of hostility and respect, not reject, each other in the international community.

2. Medium Term: A phase of mutual trust and cooperation.

(1) Both sides of the Strait should establish official communication channels on equal footing.

(2) Direct postal, transport, and commercial links should be allowed, and both sides should jointly develop the southeastern coastal area of the Chinese mainland and then gradually extend this development to other areas of the mainland in order to narrow the gap in living standards between the two sides.

(3) Both sides of the Strait should work together and assist each other in taking part in international organizations and activities.

(4) Mutual visits by high-ranking officials on both sides should be promoted to create favorable conditions for consultation and unification.

3. Long Term: A phase of consultation and unification.

A consultative organization for unification should be established through which both sides, in accordance with the will of the people in both the mainland and Taiwan areas, and while adhering to the goals of democracy, economic freedom, social justice, and nationalization of the armed forces, jointly discuss the grand task of unification and map out a constitutional system to establish a democratic, free, and equitably prosperous China.

The PRC's Institutions Concerned with Taiwan Affairs[b]

Central Leadership Group on Taiwan Work. This is the highest decision-making body in the formal institutional structure concerning Taiwan affairs. Members of this group—reportedly a unit of the Chinese Communist Party (CCP)—have been drawn from leaders who speak for the CCP, the PRC government (i.e., foreign, security, trade, and other ministries) and the military units. Since 1979, Teng Hsiao-p'ing (Deng Xiaoping) has undoubtedly held the highest authority on matters related to Taiwan, but the formal institutional leadership belongs to President Chiang Tse-min (Jiang Zemin). The CCP also has an office on Taiwan work, namely the Central Committee Office on Taiwan Work.

CCP United Front Work Department. Traditionally, this is the CCP's institutional unit that supervises and coordinates activities concerning the satellite "democratic parties," affairs of the racial minorities and religious groups, the overseas Chinese (in Taiwan, Hong Kong, and other areas), and mass organizations. The department has placed emphasis on mobilizing support for the unification campaigns. Under its supervision are the following groups: Chinese

---

[b]See, among others, Hung-mao Tien, "The PRC Approach Toward Taiwan" (Conference Paper, Pennsylvania State University, July 16-18, 1991).

People's Political Consultative Conference's Work Team for Unification, KMT Revolutionary Committee, Alliance for Taiwan Democracy and Autonomy, Association of Taiwanese Compatriots, Association for Unification of China, Taiwan Studies Association, and Association of Whampoa Classmates.

Government Offices. The Taiwan Affairs Office of the State Council (cabinet) coordinates with various government activities concerning Taiwan. Taiwan affairs offices or divisions are established in the ministries of Foreign Affairs, Foreign Economic Relations and Trade, State Security, and Radio, Film and Television, and other ministries and agencies as well as provincial and municipal governments. The Chinese Academy of Social Sciences also has a policy-oriented Taiwan Research Institute. The Overseas Chinese Affairs Office deals with overseas Chinese who have Taiwan connections. Taiwan research institutes are established in several leading universities. The New China News Agency in Hong Kong, Peking's main official presence in the territory, also has a Taiwan affairs office.

The Military. The military continues to be heavily involved in matters related to Taiwan. PRC leaders still emphasize armed liberation against Taiwan as an option should all efforts at peaceful unification fail. Key figures in the CCP Central Military Commission are members of the decision-making Leadership Group.

Association for Relations Across the Taiwan Straits. An ostensibly unofficial body, set up in December 1991, to interact with Taiwan's Straits Exchange Foundation.

The PRC's Guidelines for Unification

The current generation of PRC leaders headed by Teng Hsiao-p'ing have made several statements proposing formulas for unification. The most important include:

1. "A Message to Compatriots in Taiwan," issued by the Standing Committee of the National People's Congress on January 1, 1979, proposed the establishment of "three communications" (mail, trade, and transportation services) and "four exchanges" (relatives and tourists, academic groups, cultural groups, and sport teams) between the mainland and Taiwan.

2. A nine-point proposal by Yeh Chien-ying (Ye Jianying) on September 30, 1981, reiterated the earlier call for establishing three communications and four exchanges, and urged KMT-CCP direct negotiations for unification that would allow Taiwan to preserve its separate socioeconomic system as a local autonomous district of the PRC.

3. A six-point supplement to Yeh's nine-point proposal put forth by Teng Hsiao-p'ing on June 26, 1983, during a conversation with Winston Yang, a visiting Chinese-American scholar. Teng promised, following unification, judicial independence and separate armed forces for Taiwan. In addition, Taiwan would be permitted to administer its own party, government, and military systems. Peking would not dispatch its personnel to be stationed in Taiwan, and would set aside

certain central government posts in Peking for Taiwan leaders. He defined Taiwan's status as having a limited, but not complete, autonomy.

PRC proposals center on two famous slogans, "peaceful unification" and "one country, two systems." The ultimate goal is to amalgamate Taiwan with the mainland and place it under the PRC's central authority. The goal is to be achieved step-by-step through CCP-KMT negotiations. Once united, the Nationalist authorities could maintain a local administration and armed forces along with Taiwan's different social, economic, and political systems. As in the case of provisions governing Hong Kong's status in the 1984 PRC-British agreement on Hong Kong, such separate and autonomous systems are envisioned to exist for at least half a century before a complete integration with the mainland system becomes enforced.

16

Cross-Strait Economic Relations and Their Implications for Taiwan

Ramon H. Myers and Linda Chao

The last five years of rapid, expanding investment by Taiwan business interests in mainland China are unique in the history of international trade and finance. Typically, if one country's entrepreneurs locate in another country to produce goods and services for the domestic and export markets, that foreign investment and trade will serve to integrate the product and factor markets of the two countries. Yet, such market integration still has not characterized the expanding economic relationship between Taiwan and the mainland.

Ever since mid-1989, when Taiwanese entrepreneurs began to establish their factories in the southeastern coastal provinces, Taiwanese investment in mainland China has increased by leaps and bounds. That investment has been associated with the transfer of substantial amounts of technology, financial and physical capital, and consumer goods from Taiwan to the mainland. Taiwanese entrepreneurs have also settled in this very different Chinese society.

Although mainland China's exports to Taiwan increased slightly during the five-year period, its share of Taiwan's total imports remained minuscule, around 2 percent of total imports. To this day there still is no direct shipment of products and raw materials from the mainland to Taiwan. Taiwan's exports through third countries to the mainland accelerated, however, and by October 1993 had reached almost 9 percent of Taiwan's exports. We do not know the exact amount of remitted earnings to Taiwan by its enterprises in the mainland, but it seems to have been very small. In other words, the flow of financial, material, and human resources has been primarily one-way: from Taiwan to the mainland. Can this economic pattern of activity continue?

Our aim is to describe some new pull forces that have come into play during the last two years and will draw ever-greater human, material, and financial resources from Taiwan to the mainland but might facilitate a greater remittance of investment earnings back to Taiwan than previously has been the case. As Taiwanese investment in the mainland expands, there will be costs that Taiwan must bear. We examine these costs and explain why they pose a new challenge for Taiwan's democratic polity.

A New Pattern of
Taiwanese Business Activities in Mainland China

Whether the figures are correct, they are striking. The amount of Taiwanese investment in the mainland has apparently grown from US$3.5 billion in 1991 to US$6.4 billion in 1992 and to US$16.8 billion in September 1993.[1] The number of items that could be produced and/or distributed as a result of Taiwanese investments increased from 3,967 in 1992 to over 18,000 in late 1993.[2] In late 1992, over 7,500 Taiwanese enterprises were doing business in the mainland, and that number is now even larger. The leap in Taiwanese investment between the end of 1992 and 1993 was huge, and if the figures are valid, direct investment by Taiwan in the mainland now greatly exceeds its investment in the rest of the world.[3] In 1993, for example, Taiwanese entrepreneurs invested US$2.4 billion abroad; Taiwanese investment in the mainland for that same year amounted to US$10 billion.[4]

---

[1]For information related to 1992 and before, see Huang T'ien-chung and Chang Wu-ch'iu, eds., *Liang-an kuan-hsi yü ta-lu cheng-ts'e* (Cross-Strait relations and mainland policy) (Taipei: Wu-nan t'u-shu ch'u-pan yu-hsien kung-szu, 1993), 247. For information related to 1993, see Sung K'o-han, "A Major Event That Will Stimulate Economic and Trade Relations Between Taiwan and the Mainland," *Ching Pao* (The Mirror) (Hong Kong), no. 201 (April 1994): 80.

[2]In 1991, approved outward Taiwanese investment equalled US$1.6 billion, less than half the alleged Taiwanese investment in the mainland.

[3]Council for Economic Planning and Development (CEPD), *Taiwan Statistical Data Book 1992* (Taipei: CEPD, 1992), 248.

[4]Allen Pun, "Outward Investment in a Surge," *Free China Journal*, April 1, 1994, 3. The discrepancy between Taiwanese outbound investment and those Taiwanese investments in the mainland each year is great. It is not at all clear what these figures precisely mean or if they are exclusive of each other. Another ROC government report, however, states that between January and October 1993 the ROC approved US$4.56 billion worth of foreign investment, with US$3.038 billion going to the mainland. See "Majority of Taipei's Foreign Investment Goes to PRC," Foreign Broadcast Information Service (FBIS), *Daily Report: China* [hereinafter cited as *FBIS-CHI*]-94-041 (March 2, 1994): 62. This report states that Taiwan's export reliance on mainland China reached 8.84 percent by October 1993, a 14.5 percent increase over 1992. But on March 11, 1994, Vincent Siew, chairman of the CEPD,

By 1992, the siren call of higher profits earned by factories in the mainland had proved irresistible for Taiwanese enterprises. Cheap labor, low-cost materials, and convenient export through Hong Kong and other coastal ports induced Taiwanese entrepreneurs to move some of their machinery, equipment, and staff to the mainland and manufacture as they had done at home. A common language and culture made it easy for the people on the two sides of the Taiwan Strait to strike deals and resolve those legal and bureaucratic obstacles that typically discouraged other foreign investors.

We contend that the year 1992 marked a critical turning point in cross-Strait economic relations. Teng Hsiao-p'ing (Deng Xiaoping) visited the southeastern provinces in January-February of that year and made important statements urging that economic development be accelerated even more.[5] His remarks at the Chinese Communist Party's (CCP's) Fourteenth National Congress in October signaled a major policy shift within the Party. Party leaders decided to build a socialist economic marketplace within the next few decades in order for the country to achieve economic modernity. The concept of a socialist economic marketplace became the subject of immense debate inside and outside the CCP. Over the next eighteen months, the State Council and the National People's Congress (NPC) approved new policies and laws, creating the most favorable economic conditions for foreign investors since 1949.[6] "These steps greatly opened the internal market [of the mainland] and expanded the role for services."[7]

Prior to 1992, Taiwanese investments in the mainland mainly produced electrical products, vehicle parts, shoes, and plastic products; service-oriented investments were concentrated in hotels, restaurants, entertainment, etc.[8] Roughly four-fifths of all Taiwanese business investments were concentrated in Fukien (Fujian) and Kwangtung (Guangdong) provinces and their principal cities of Amoy (Xiamen), Shenzhen, and Canton (Guangzhou). Between April 1991 and August 1992, Taiwanese enterprises reportedly set up 387 new factories representing total investments

---

said that Taiwan's export balance with mainland China reached 14.9 percent at the end of 1993. See *FBIS-CHI*-94-050 (March 15, 1994): 66.

[5]"Gist of Deng's Southern Tour Speeches," Joint Publications Research Service, *JPRS Report: China*, February 24, 1994, 7-14.

[6]These new laws and policies are discussed in Chen Te-sheng, "Mainland China's Economic Situation in 1993," *Chung-kuo ta-lu yen-chiu* (Mainland China Studies) (Taipei) 37, no. 2 (February 1994): 15-26.

[7]Huang and Chang, *Liang-an kuan-hsi yü ta-lu cheng-ts'e*, 263.

[8]Ibid., 287.

equalling US$2.8 billion.[9] But these circumstances began to change after 1992 because of the mainland's new economic policies that took place in the country's interior provinces.

The New Policies

In recent years, eager to catch up with the booming coastal provinces, high-ranking officials in the interior provinces have tried to attract more foreign investors, particularly from Taiwan. In 1993, Governor Hsiao Yang (Xiao Yang) of Szechwan (Sichuan) Province declared that "this will be the year to attract business and capital to our province."[10] Chengtu (Chengdu), a major city of Szechwan, also made special efforts to attract Taiwanese investors, who by late 1993 already were ranked just behind Hong Kong investors there.[11] Similarly, Governor Ch'en Hsiehneng (Chen Xieneng) of Kweichow (Guizhou) Province appealed to foreign investors to come to his province to develop energy, tourism, and agricultural resources.[12]

Other cities like Tientsin (Tianjin), Shenyang, and Hankou also offered enterprises special arrangements to establish department stores and use vacant floors of large buildings to sell their products.[13] In Changsha city, local officials induced Kennex Corporation to manufacture and sell its sporting goods in the city.[14] Nanking (Nanjing) city also had attracted more than one thousand Taiwan business enterprises to locate there by early 1993.[15] Wuhan city of Hupeh (Hubei) Province encouraged Yü-lung Motor Company of Taiwan to set up a plant there.[16] In Tsinan (Jinan) city of Shantung (Shandong) Province, a special high-tech zone was established in December 1993 to attract foreign investors.[17]

The interior provinces also copied the pattern already well developed in the coastal cities: they set aside a special zone for foreign investors to

---

[9]Ibid.

[10]See Lo Jih-lan, "Aiming at the Internal Market: The New Strategy to Attract Business Persons and Capitalists by Szechwan Province," *Chung-kuo shih-pao chou-k'an* (China Times Weekly) (Taipei), no. 71 (May 9-15, 1993): 3.

[11]Ibid., 15.

[12]Fu An, "Kweichow Opens a Great Mountain Door to Attract Foreign Investment," ibid., 3.

[13]Ku Pi-lung, "Mainland Consumer Product Markets Attract Foreign Businesses," ibid., 50.

[14]Ibid.

[15]Cheng Han-liang, "Nanking's Complete Open-Door Policy," ibid., 58.

[16]Chan Ch'ung-te, "Foreign Investment Expands in Wuhan and Three Policies Encourage Foreign Investment," ibid., no. 74 (May 30-June 5, 1993): 54.

[17]Ching Hsin, "The Many Advantages of Tsinan's Development Zone," ibid., no. 76 (June 13-19, 1993): 62.

locate and establish their factories to carry out the manufacturing or processing activities. These special development zones (*k'ai-fa-ch'ü*) adopted the same practices long used by the special economic zones (SEZs) along the coast. Officials authorized these areas to grant low rents and low tax rates for three- to five-year periods.[18] Foreign firms in the special development zones also enjoyed customs duties exemption on all the importation of machines, building materials, and equipment.[19] In 1993-94, these development zones began to emerge in all large cities of the interior provinces.[20]

The following examples show the economic incentives used to court Taiwanese and other foreign investors. In Changsha, officials arranged for the Kuangnan Group, a business group based in Taiwan, to use floors of the city's Friendship Store and the Chungshan Commercial Building to display and sell their products such as underwear, leather goods, stationery, cosmetics, and jewelry.[21] This unusual opportunity provoked one Taiwanese businessman to say that "whoever intends to set up business in mainland China and gain access to the local market ahead of others will be the winner and the leader in the market."[22] For many years, "the dream of every Taiwan business people has been to go into the [mainland's] consumer market."[23] In 1993-94, that dream began to come true for many Taiwan business people.

In Nanking, local officials offered cheap land rents and provided easy access to hire the city's many university graduates in science, technology, and business administration.[24] Wang Yung-ping (Wang Yongbing), mayor of Nanking, optimistically reminded Taiwanese business people that "as Sun Yat-sen once said, the future development of Nanking is without limits."[25] In Wuhan, local officials offered Taiwanese investors a 15 percent break on their local income taxes upon beginning to make a profit and a much lower income tax rate for the first three to five years of operation.[26] Foreign firms were also exempted from paying customs duties on imported machinery, materials, and equipment.[27] Similar tax

---

[18]See note 16 above.

[19]Sung, "A Major Event," 81.

[20]Ibid.

[21]Ku, "Mainland Consumer Product Markets Attract Foreign Businesses," 51.

[22]Ibid.

[23]Ibid., 52.

[24]Cheng, "Nanking's Complete Open-Door Policy," 59.

[25]Ibid.

[26]See note 16 above.

[27]Ibid.

breaks were granted to Taiwanese investment in Tsinan's high-tech park.[28]
Their income taxes were further deducted if they produced primarily
for export and reinvested their profits in Tsinan's development zone.
In Lüshun (Port Arthur), not far from Dairen (Dalian) in northeast
China, a 500-square-mile zone has been set up to welcome Hong Kong and
Taiwanese investors.[29] The city also planned to auction off its zoo facilities and lease that land to developers for promoting tourism. Officials
of Kweichow Province promised foreign investors they could use local
currency to buy and export the mainland-made goods to earn foreign currency.[30] They also exempted Taiwanese businessmen from paying the
local income taxes for ten years and provided other tax exemptions on
purchases of real estate, vehicles, etc.

New state economic reforms were also put in place to supplement
the above-mentioned policies. More than a half decade ago, in July 1988,
Peking's (Beijing's) State Council had passed a draft law to regulate
Taiwanese business investment on the mainland (Regulations Encouraging
Taiwan Compatriots to Invest in the Mainland—the 22 Articles). These
regulations, however, were too vague and difficult to enforce, and Taiwanese business people did not derive great benefit from them. In November
1993, realizing the limitations of the law, mainland China drew up a new
law which was approved by the NPC Standing Committee in the following
December. On March 5, 1994, the NPC Standing Committee finally approved a fifteen-article law, Taiwanese Investment Protection Law, making
it easier for Taiwanese businessmen to transfer their property rights on
the mainland and to be duly compensated.[31] The law also stipulates how
Taiwanese investors can remit their after-tax profits to Taiwan.

The People's Bank of China and the government also announced
that after January 1, 1994, there would be a new foreign exchange rate
system.[32] The new rate was set at US$1.00 equal to 8.7 *yuan*, which repre-
sented a 50 percent devaluation compared with the former rate (US$1.00 =
5.8 *yuan*). Equally significant, the foreign exchange note (*wai-hui-ch'üan*),
long issued only to foreigners, was abolished. All foreign currencies, even
the American dollar, were forbidden in market exchange throughout the

---

[28]Ching, "The Many Advantages of Tsinan's Development Zone," 63.

[29]"The City of Lüshun Welcomes Business for the First Time," *Chung-kuo shih-pao chou-
k'an*, no. 78 (June 27-July 3, 1993): 61.

[30]See note 12 above.

[31]Sung, "A Major Event," 81.

[32]Yüan Ming-jen, "What You Must Know about Mainland Investment in 1994," *Chung-kuo
shih-pao chou-k'an*, nos. 109-110 (January 30-February 12, 1994): 72.

country. This reform benefits Taiwanese investors in two ways. First, they now can exchange their business earnings in local currency for foreign currency at the local banks according to a fixed exchange rate and remit any amount they want. Second, the new, devalued exchange rate gives new foreign investors greater purchasing power in the local market. Those investors already doing business and holding large reserves of the devalued local currency, of course, suffered a loss at the current exchange rate if they immediately exchanged for foreign currency.

The state also reformed the tax code. The complex commercial unified tax, production tax, and income tax were abolished and replaced by a new value-added tax, a consumption tax, and an enterprise tax.[33] This tax reform supposedly simplified enterprise tax payments and official collections. Whether that is true still remains to be seen.

A New Pattern of Taiwanese Investment

In 1993 and 1994, Taiwanese investments began moving into the interior provinces, especially into the large cities of roughly one million or more population. Some of the investments were similar to those in the SEZs along the southeast coast: the production of electrical products, textiles, shoes, machinery, equipment, vehicle parts, and sportswear for export. But there were now new Taiwanese investments associated with high-technology-related products. The Formosa Plastics Group, a petrochemical giant in Taiwan, announced that it would lead "three Taiwan downstream manufacturers in establishing PVC pipe factories in Shandong, Anhui [Anhwei], and Fujian provinces."[34]

Some investments, however, went into wholesaling and retailing and other service sectors. Many large Taiwan department store operators began to establish branch enterprises in Shanghai and many inland cities in order to take advantage of a new consumerism that has been sweeping across the country.

In the past five years, real per capita income in mainland China rapidly increased in spite of inflationary price surges. Most urban dwellers had satisfied their basic consumer needs, and they now wanted to purchase more high-quality, high-value consumer products.[35] A fever of conspicuous consumption broke out, especially among the young. Consumers began to mob the stores seeking discounts and new products. For example,

---

[33]Ibid., 73.

[34]Deborah Shen, "Formosa Plastics to Build PVC Plants in Mainland," *Free China Journal*, April 1, 1994, 3.

[35]See Lin Fan, "The Mainland Consumer Goods Market Will Open and Prosper," *Chung-kuo shih-pao chou-k'an*, nos. 56-57 (January 24-February 6, 1993): 70.

recently when department stores in Shenzhen and Hangchow (Hangzhou) began to sell a new brand of T-shirt that is popular in Hong Kong, many policemen had to be stationed to regulate consumers' entry into the stores at five- to ten-minute intervals in order to avoid injury to life and property.[36]

In mid-1993, supermarkets and high-class consumer commodity stores or boutiques rapidly mushroomed in Shanghai.[37] These stores sprang up everywhere in this city of over 11 million population. They carried the brand-name products well known in Taiwan, Japan, North America, and Western Europe, including Nike shoes from Taiwan, Ace clothing from the United States, Mexx clothing from Holland, and Pierre Cardin from France. Consumers paid with their credit cards; on the streets people used cellular phones to discuss their recent purchases.

This great consumer boom did not escape the notice of Taiwanese business people. In that same year they began to set up wholesale and retail stores in Shanghai. Their large department stores were eye-catching, including the Hua-tung pei-erh-tun, the Mou-shih-ta Commercial Building, and the Shanghai Pacific Department Store.[38] A Taiwan-based large food chain store, Wei-Chuan Foods Corporation, already has a large store in Chengtu.[39] The Taiwan Kuangnan Group, established by the Kennex Company, produces sports equipment, shoes, and clothing in Tientsin, Shenyang, Hankou, and other cities. In Changsha, this same company alone earned over 500 million *yuan* from its sales.[40] Taiwan companies are now selling Taiwan-brand consumer products to mainland Chinese. This represents a major shift in business investment activity to a market that presently seems limitless.

The Integration of Mainland and Taiwan Markets

Although the flow of human, physical, and material resources from Taiwan to mainland China accelerated in 1993 and 1994, in the mainland, imports from Taiwan through third countries or remittances of Taiwanese investor earnings to Taiwan still did not increase greatly. Even so, there

---

[36]Ibid.

[37]Yang Shih, "A Special Name-Brand Boutique Competes and Spreads Throughout Shanghai City," ibid., no. 74 (May 30-June 5, 1993): 57.

[38]Ta Ti, "Taiwan Merchants Have Their Eyes on Shanghai Retail Stores," ibid., no. 115 (March 13-19, 1994): 47.

[39]Lo, "Aiming at the Internal Market," 15.

[40]See note 13 above.

seem to have been three major ways in which Taiwanese investors in the mainland transferred their earnings back home. First, they used an accounting procedure to report a lower-than-actual value of their exports and a higher-than-actual value of their imports. This gave the illusion that they earned less profit than was the actual case. The value difference represented the company funds transferred abroad.[41] Prior to January 1994, Taiwanese business people purchased the foreign exchange notes used by foreigners in the mainland, then sold to foreign investors and tourists, and converted their earnings into the foreign exchange they wanted to remit.[42] Finally, they might loan funds to a new Taiwanese business person in local currency to establish a factory or store, and request that the loan be repaid to the lender's bank in Taiwan in New Taiwan dollar.[43]

We do not know how well these methods facilitated the flow of remitted earnings by Taiwanese investors in the mainland to Taiwan or third countries. Nor do we know the precise amount of their annual remitted earnings, or whether those amounts varied over time. We conjecture that these remitted earnings were small before 1993 but increased thereafter. All existing evidence points to the bulk of Taiwan-invested earnings being reinvested in the mainland. Even so, mainland China's new tax and foreign exchange reforms of January 1994 might have significantly improved the remittance picture and increased the flow of investor earnings back to Taiwan. If indeed that is the case, the capital markets of the two economies are becoming more integrated. Meanwhile, as Taiwan's exports to mainland China grow more than 10 percent annually and mainland China's imports expand, the product markets of the two economies will slowly become more integrated. Since 1993-94, a modest speeding-up of market integration between the two Chinese nation-states has been taking place.

What is the likelihood that the above-mentioned Taiwanese investment patterns and market integration will continue? We postulate that the rapid evolution toward a socialist market economy cannot be reversed by the CCP. Moreover, in view of the trend toward greater marketization, privatization, and integration with the world economy, these two economies will slowly become more integrated. The evidence is that a complex and serious debate has been raging in mainland China for the past two years over how to evaluate, organize, and regulate this emerging socialist

---

[41]Wu Ling-lang, "The Problem of Factory Merchants Remitting Money and Their Financial Investments in Mainland China," *Liang-an ching-mao yüeh-k'an* (Cross-Strait Economic and Trade Monthly) (Taipei), no. 14 (February 10, 1993): 3.

[42]Ibid.

[43]Ibid.

market economy. As long as this debate continues and produces some consensus on key issues, mainland China's economic policies should be sufficiently innovative to modulate the development of a marketplace comprising new economic organizations, consumers, and economic institutions. The key issues of this ongoing debate and the indications that consensus might be forming are as follows.

1. New economic criteria have been proposed to judge whether a new socialist type of market economy is performing satisfactorily.[44] Some of these standards, such as avoiding extremely unequal distribution of income and increasing productivity, have won acceptance.

2. There has been vigorous disagreement on the desirable mix of property rights for the socialist type of market economy.[45] Eve so, some diversity of property rights is now accepted.

3. There is still debate about what kind of system of organizations and laws should replace state enterprises to compete with cooperative/collective enterprises, hybrid organizations, and private proprietorships.[46] Different forms of management are now accepted along with the idea that ownership and management can be separated.

4. There is also discussion about how certain prices might have to be regulated to minimize economic fluctuation in the new socialist type of economic marketplace so that it will perform according to appropriate

---

[44]The literature on this theme is large. For example, see He Hui, "New Understanding of the Essence of a Socialist Society," in *JPRS-CAR*-93-084 (November 23, 1993): 1-7, and Zhang Qinde, "Standards for Distinguishing Between Social Systems," *JPRS-CAR*-93-090 (December 22, 1993): 1-4.

[45]See Hu Deqiao, "Positive Progress in Reform of Property Rights System," *FBIS-CHI*-94-053 (March 18, 1994): 53; "The Necessity of Straightening Out Property Rights," *Inside China Mainland* (Taipei) 16, no. 2 (February 1994): 27-30; Liu Runwei, "Clarifying the Concept of 'Owner Mentality'," *JPRS-CAR*-93-079 (October 29, 1993): 10-11; Bao Yueyang, "Survey of Privately Owned Enterprises in Fifteen Provinces Reveals New Features in Developing China's Private Economy," *JPRS-CAR*-93-085 (November 30, 1993): 28-29; and "Symposiums Discuss Ownership Reform," *JPRS-CAR*-94-006 (January 21, 1994): 13-15.

[46]The literature on ownership reform is extremely large, and we cite only a few items: Zhang Xiaowen, "Survey Report on Shandong's and Zhejiang's Implementation of 'The Regulations'," *JPRS-CAR*-93-083 (November 17, 1993): 7-16; "Liu Guoguang on Modern Enterprise System," *JPRS-CAR*-94-005 (January 19, 1994): 3-6; "Gao Shangquan Views Decision on Socialist Market," ibid., 6-13; Wu Jinglien et al., "Basic Ideas About the Establishment of a New System for Macroeconomic Regulation and Control and Management of State-Owned Assets," *JPRS-CAR*-94-003 (January 10, 1994): 4-13; Zuo Taihang and Fu Shan, "Heavy State-Owned Enterprise Burdens—Summary Findings of a Nationwide Sample Survey," *JPRS-CAR*-93-075 (October 12, 1993): 11; Fang Xiangdang, "Enterprise Reform Under the Existing Economic Pattern," *JPRS-CAR*-93-069 (September 17, 1993): 1-8; and "Studying the Reorganization of China's Large Enterprises as Stock Companies," *JPRS-CAR*-93-071 (September 23, 1993): 4-9.

economic standards, provide a fair distribution of income, avoid economic fluctuations, improve productivity, and achieve steady and sustained economic growth without destroying the physical and human environments.[47] There is general agreement that prices must be market-driven but not allowed to fluctuate in the extreme.

5. There is much debate on what kind of monetary and fiscal institutions should be used to guide this socialist economic marketplace.[48] The fiscal system must be designed to prevent tax cheating and guarantee fairness.

How soon these debates will be resolved and new policies adopted, we do not know. But there is no doubt that economic reform will continue, barring unforeseen events. How these reforms are to be sequenced is also part of this ongoing debate. Our purpose here is not to explicate this complex debate, except to say that the mainland Chinese elite, the academy, and the intellectuals are seriously discussing the pace and character of economic reforms. As long as that debate continues and appropriate reform policies follow, the mainland Chinese economy should continue to evolve according to the patterns described above for 1993-94. For these reasons, then, the development of a socialist economic market system can only mean a gradual integration of the Taiwan and mainland economies in the near future.

The Implications for Taiwan of Greater Mainland-Taiwan Economic Integration

Greater economic integration between the economies of Taiwan and mainland China will tend to equilibrate factor and product market prices, expand employment and output, and increase economic welfare. Both economies will benefit. On the one hand, Taiwanese enterprises may exploit the cheaper resources in the mainland to earn profits. They transfer

---

[47]See Zhang Zhuoyuan, "On Nurturing and Developing a Unified, Open, Competitive, and Orderly Market System," *JPRS-CAR*-94-007 (January 27, 1994): 19-23, and Zhou Wen, "Problems in Public Order Under the Market Economy, and Policies to Deal with Them," *JPRS-CAR*-93-072 (September 23, 1993): 34.

[48]See Lou Jiwei and Li Keping, "Basic Approach for Building a New Macroeconomic Regulation and Control, and a State-Owned Assets Management System," *JPRS-CAR*-93-091 (December 29, 1993): 10-20, and "Symposium on Guiding Peasants to Market Economy," *JPRS-CAR*-93-073 (September 30, 1993): 26-27. There are numerous articles on the issue of tax fraud and how the government might extract more tax revenues. For how the Communist Party hoped to establish a socialist market economic structure, see Zou Aiguo and Zheng Qingdong, "Magnificent Program of Action That Marches Toward the New Century— Birth of 'Decision of CPC Central Committee on Some Issues Concerning Establishment of a Socialist Market Economic Structure'," *JPRS-CAR*-94-014 (March 2, 1994): 1-5.

resources to the mainland to produce greater income and wealth. On the other hand, Taiwanese firms may remit some of the income they earned in the mainland to Taiwan, thereby benefitting that economy.

As economic integration increases between Taiwan and mainland China, however, Taiwan stands to incur new costs. First, there are social costs, difficult to measure but easy to describe, especially those relevant to the national identity issue. This refers to the intensity of feeling that Taiwanese people possess when they perceive themselves as being either Taiwanese and Chinese or only Taiwanese. Any shift in popular perceptions from the former to the latter means that more individuals and groups are likely to increase their political demands to elect leaders favoring the restructuring of the ROC polity, including the constitution, the flag, and the national anthem.

Some observers have mentioned the negative social influences on family stability and harmony of Taiwanese businessmen operating on the mainland. Contrary to the behavior of Taiwanese entrepreneurs who have invested and operated in other countries for many decades, it seems that far more Taiwanese businessmen in the mainland have become entangled in extramarital relations.[49] Their illicit relationships have severely strained family ties back home and often produced tragedy and trauma for kin and children alike. Is this a serious social problem, as some critics claim? We do not know. We do know that it has become a much-reported social problem which has taken many in the Taiwan society by surprise and caused grave concern for social stability and harmony. As a social problem it cannot but influence in some small way the attitudes of ordinary people toward the mainland and the desirability of closer cooperation between these two Chinese societies.

Still another sociolegal factor closely connected with expanding economic integration influences the national identity issue: the trend for more Taiwan residents to travel to the mainland as tourists or on business. The lawlessness growing throughout mainland China gives ROC citizens little guarantee of protection and compensation for their property and life. A recent tragedy underscores this point.

On March 31, 1994, twenty-four Taiwanese tourists lost their lives in a strange boating accident on Chientao (Qiandao) Lake in Chekiang (Zhejiang) Province where their boat reportedly caught fire and all of them perished.[50] The events surrounding the fire were exceedingly strange, and

---

[49]For a good discussion of this problem, see Ming Hua, "To Go to the Mainland to Find a Bride: It Is Cheaper Than Seeking a Prostitute in Taiwan," *Chiu-shih nien-tai yüeh-k'an* (The Nineties Monthly) (Hong Kong), no. 277 (February 1993): 54.

[50]See Patricia Kuo, "Taiwan-China Detente at Risk," *San Francisco Chronicle*, April 13,

it seems neither crew nor tourists escaped. Mainland officials immediately tried to cover up the incident. To make matters worse, local officials were extremely uncooperative with Taiwanese relatives, who soon arrived on the scene seeking information and demanding the return of their beloved kin. The bungling manner in which the mainland officials handled this incident so enraged the Taiwan authorities that they immediately halted all cultural and educational exchange between the two sides. The press in Taiwan also excoriated the Peking government for its cover up and unwillingness to be held accountable for the tragedy.

Until the Peking government can enforce its laws, ROC citizens are at enormous risk while traveling and working in the mainland. Why is this the case? Peking does not recognize the sovereignty of the ROC government or its right to protect its citizens. Peking does not always extend the same guarantees of protection and accountability to ROC citizens as it does to other foreign citizens living or traveling in the country. The ROC elite and ordinary people recognize this unfairness, and more tragedies like the Chientao Lake incident only exacerbate the national identity problem within Taiwan. A Gallup opinion poll conducted in Taiwan after the incident showed that popular feeling in support of an independent nation (Taiwan) shot up to its highest level—27 percent, exceeding the high of 23.7 percent in 1991.[51]

Finally, there are the rising transaction costs for the ROC government to manage the cross-Strait economic relations. These costs can be broken down into three components: costs to monitor, regulate, and prevent smuggling and illegal entry of mainland labor into Taiwan; costs to manage the incidences of aircraft hijacked by mainland Chinese to Taiwan; and the costs to deal with the mainland dissidents seeking asylum in Taiwan.[52] These three costs have dramatically increased in the past two years and produced greater demands on Taiwan to deal with those people wanting to come to Taiwan illegally.

The above transaction costs originate from the rising demand of more people on the mainland to escape their misery. Their actions invite

---

1994, A12; Jeremy Mark, "Taiwan Curtails Trade with China in Tourist Deaths," *Wall Street Journal*, April 13, 1994, A10; Julian Baum, "Cross-Strait Purposes: Little Action on Cooperation with China," *Far Eastern Economic Review*, April 14, 1994, 18; and "Secrecy Veils Deaths in Mainland Boat Fire," *Free China Journal*, April 9, 1994, 1.

[51]"A Gallup Poll Shows That the Voice of Taiwan Independence Has Clearly Increased," *Chung-kuo shih-pao* (China Times) (Taipei), April 18, 1994, 2.

[52]For a good account of Taiwan's difficulties and costs of granting asylum to the mainland dissidents, see Julian Baum, "No Refuge: Taipei Reluctant to Offer Asylum to Mainland Dissidents," *Far Eastern Economic Review*, March 31, 1994, 22-23.

different groups inside and outside Taiwan to assist them in relocating to Taiwan or moving to third countries. These actions become political demands that not only impose great costs on the ROC public sector agencies and officials but become issues that political parties use to criticize each other.

In conclusion, mainland China's economic reform and rapid economic growth will elicit more Taiwan's economic resources to flow to the mainland economy, thus expanding economic integration between the two Chinese economic systems, as occurred in the past two years. There are bound to be fluctuations in the flow of Taiwan's resources to the mainland, but if current conditions on the mainland prevail, gradual integration of the two economies is inevitable.[53]

There are social, legal, and transaction costs associated with this expanding economic integration, and these costs are bound to increase as more economic integration takes place. Peking's leaders are committed to isolating Taiwan from the international community. Unwilling to treat the ROC leaders and people as belonging to a separate and sovereign political regime, the Peking government remains intent on forcing Taiwan to enter into a subordinate relationship with mainland China that would jeopardize Taiwan's democracy and political life as it now exists. Naturally, the ROC leadership avoids direct negotiations with Peking and will not agree to forging any direct links between the two Chinese societies until Peking alters its position.

Under these circumstances, the invisible hand of expanding market integration will become associated with rising social, legal, and transaction costs in Taiwan to manage the cross-Strait exchange relationship. Those increasing costs are very likely to become translated into greater political demands that can only produce greater tension in the ROC polity. The tensions, in turn, will invariably influence the national identity issue. If these influences conflate to shift national popular perception in the direction of "greater Taiwanese identity," the democratic process of elections, the passage of new laws, and constitutional reform can only move Taiwan further from the orbit of Chinese culture and political interests. This would not only threaten Taiwan's growing democracy but also endanger the security of its people.

---

[53] An account published in July 1994 states that Taiwanese investment in the mainland for the first five months of 1994 fell "45 percent from a year earlier, to $32.7 billion from $58.76 billion." See Edward A. Gargan, "For Taiwanese Investors, the Mainland Loses Lustre," *New York Times*, July 5, 1994, C1, C3.

17

Mainland China's Economic Policy Toward Taiwan: Economic Needs or Unification Scheme?

Yu-Shan Wu

Since the late 1980s, Taiwan has become more and more economically dependent on mainland China. The main reason is that Peking (Beijing) provides strong incentives to encourage investment from the cash-rich island, and the success of its policy is witnessed by the phenomenal growth of Taiwan's investment on the mainland and the exponential rise of investment-driven trade across the Taiwan Strait. Taiwan's growing economic dependency on its Communist neighbor arouses fear among those who consider Peking's policy politically motivated, i.e., designed to deepen economic integration of the two entities and to create bargaining chips that can be used when the Communist leadership decides to push for unification. The economic explanation for Peking's policy, on the other hand, emphasizes the mainland's economic needs and maintains that Taiwan's investment is courted because it serves the Communist government's desire to develop an export industry, earn badly-needed foreign exchange, pay off foreign debt, and import technology and consumer goods. The two explanations differ in the presumed policy goal of the Communist leadership: unification on the one hand, and economic reform on the other, two of the three "great missions" designated by Teng Hsiao-p'ing (Deng Xiaoping) in 1980.[1]

---

[1]Another way of looking at the same issue is to characterize Peking's economic policy toward Taiwan as either exceptional or general. If the policy is geared toward unification, it is exceptional. If it is designed to meet the needs arising from the mainland's economic reform, then it is general. This author is grateful to Professor Brantly Womack for bringing up this alternative perspective.

This chapter is a preliminary examination of the strength of the two arguments, and its purpose is to ascertain the determinants of Peking's economic policy toward Taiwan. It is reasonable to assume that an economically motivated policy will fluctuate with the changing economic situation in which the policymakers find themselves, which means, for example, that Peking's motivation to court Taiwan's investment will be dampened when direct foreign investment is not considered beneficial to the mainland's economy, or when Taiwan's investors fail to channel funds to targeted industries. A policy that is designed to promote unification, however, will not change when Taiwan's investment loses its economic significance. By the same token, a unification-based policy may fluctuate when the Communist leaders consider it necessary to change their political gesturing toward Taipei, for example, because of a different reading of Taiwan's domestic politics. A purely economically based policy, on the other hand, will not be sensitive to changes in the political situation. Thus, for example, one should not expect Peking to change its attitude toward Taiwan business on the mainland simply because Taipei achieved a diplomatic breakthrough and Peking wants to play hard ball. If we can determine the nature of the mainland's economic policy toward Taiwan, we will then know which set of variables, political or economic, are our best referents for understanding and predicting Peking's behavior.

Although it may be true that both political and economic factors contribute to Peking's attitude toward Taipei, for reasons mentioned above, it is still important to see which is dominant. The most difficult task, however, is to determine whether the roles of the two factors might change over time, for when push comes to shove, a policy that was originally based on economic considerations may turn out to be a wieldy instrument for unification, and begin to fluctuate to the political tempo. This being said, our investigation will shed light on the track record of Peking's policy, and help us understand future shifts, for our analysis is based on the nature of the mainland's past policy, and not on the intuitive speculation that both economic and political factors are inherently involved and intertwined in the decision-making of the Communist leadership.

In a nutshell, our dependent variable is mainland China's economic policy toward Taiwan, and our independent variables are the economic needs of reform and the political goal of unification. I am not satisfied to assume that both sets of independent variables are equally relevant or that they are inseparable, and in this chapter I attempt to gauge their relative importance by first presenting the economic reform case, then raising the unification argument against it, to see whether purely economic factors can adequately explain Peking's attitude on cross-Strait economic relations.

The Economic Reform Argument

One explanation of the mainland's economic policy toward Taiwan is the economic reform argument. According to this theory, the post-Mao Communist leadership was clearly aware of the regime's legitimacy crisis, and economic reform was their main strategy for the Chinese Communist Party's (CCP's) survival. The form that the mainland's economic reform took, however, caused "soft budget constraint," investment hunger, and import cycles. This gave rise to the need to accumulate foreign exchange, and a shift in mainland China's open-door policy from importing Western technology to export expansion based on labor-intensive production. Hence the need to court Taiwan capital. The major policy shift in 1988 was accompanied by several structural economic factors (such as the difference in labor and land costs) and Taiwan's decision to liberalize its mainland policy. The results were surging investment by Taiwan on the mainland and phenomenal growth of investment-driven trade across the Taiwan Strait. In short, it is claimed that the mainland's economic policy toward Taiwan and the resultant investment and trade can be sufficiently explained in terms of the needs derived from the particular form of the mainland's economic reform, and there is no need to invoke a noneconomic explanation.

After the traumatizing events of the Three Red Banners and the Cultural Revolution, the CCP, in desperation, resorted to radical economic reform. Teng Hsiao-p'ing was acutely aware of the regime's legitimacy crisis and hoped that raising people's living standards could save the CCP's rule.[2] The collapse of Communist rule in the Soviet Union and Eastern Europe further intensified Teng's conviction that economic reform was linked with the CCP's survival and should be assigned top priority. Since the purpose of Teng's economic reform is to sustain the CCP's monopoly on political power, it is independent of political reform.[3]

Teng's prescription coincides with a growing literature that deplores the miseries that Mikhail Gorbachev's political reform brought to the Soviet Union and extols the CCP's decision to push for economic restructuring without loosening the Party's political grip on society.[4] They argue

---

[2]Wu Kuo-kuang and Wang Chao-chun, *Teng Hsiao-p'ing chih-hou te Chung-kuo: Chieh-hsi shih-ke sheng-szu yu-kuan te wen-t'i* (China after the death of Teng Hsiao-p'ing: Analyzing ten critical questions) (Taipei: Shih-chieh shu-chü, 1994), 101.

[3]Teng Hsiao-p'ing, "The Main Points of Comrade Teng Hsiao-p'ing's Talks in Wuchang, Shenzhen, Zhuhai, and Shanghai," in *I-chiu-chiu-erh nien ch'un: Teng Hsiao-p'ing yü Shenzhen* (Spring 1992: Teng Hsiao-p'ing and Shenzhen), ed. Propaganda Department of the CCP Shenzhen City Committee (Shenzhen: Hai-t'ien ch'u-pan-she, 1992).

[4]See Susan L. Shirk, *The Political Logic of Economic Reform in China* (Berkeley: University of California Press, 1993).

that the political systems of socialist countries cannot be reformed, but
that their economic systems can and that liberalization and democratization
will inevitably lead to the demise of Communist rule, creating populist
immobilism that may hinder economic reform to a greater degree than
obstruction by the Communist bureaucracy.[5] To push for economic reform without political reform, on the other hand, would have a much
better chance of achieving concrete economic progress and raising living
standards. The Chinese scenario is thus preferred to the Soviet one, even
though it is recognized that Gorbachev may not have had the option of
pure economic reform open to him when he launched the *glasnost* campaign, because the situation in the Soviet Union was not as clear cut as
in mainland China[6] and the Soviet central bureaucracies were much more
entrenched and resistant to reform than their Chinese counterparts.[7] From
the point of view of regime's stability, Teng was correct in reforming mainland China's economic system without tinkering with political reform.[8]

Teng's reform recipe is tailored for an ideologically exhausted population. The key point is rapid economic progress as reflected in growing
availability and affordability of necessities and consumer goods. Teng
is obsessed with double-digit growth, which pits him against the more
stability-concerned Ch'en Yün (Chen Yun) and the moderate reformers
led by him.[9] Since reform began in the late 1970s, the mainland's economy
alternated between a high-growth phase and a retrenchment phase. There
are two explanations for these wide swings. The first emphasizes the
features of mainland China's partial reform and what Janos Kornai calls
"soft budget constraint." The second explanation links economic cycles
with factional politics in the CCP.

According to the first theory, what reform brought to the mainland's
economy was not a pure market, but "indirect bureaucratic control," i.e.,
the state retaining powerful levers (prices, tax rates, grants, etc.) to manip-
ulate enterprise managers who are sensitive to profit as their success

---

[5]For a dissenting opinion, see Yu-Shan Wu, "Economic Reform under Different Political
Contexts: Poland and the PRC" (Paper presented at the annual meeting of the International
Studies Association, Washington, D.C., March 28-April 1, 1994).

[6]Andrew J. Nathan, *China's Crisis: Dilemmas of Reform and Prospects for Democracy*
(New York: Columbia University Press, 1990), 200.

[7]Shirk, *The Political Logic of Economic Reform in China*, 12-13.

[8]Yu-Shan Wu, "The Collapse of the Soviet Union: A Crises and Sequences Approach,"
Political Science Review, no. 4 (December 1992): 179-224.

[9]Lowell Dittmer and Yu-Shan Wu, "The Political Leadership in Reform China: Macro and
Micro Informal Politics Linkage" (Paper presented at the 1993 annual meeting of the Association for Asian Studies, Los Angeles, March 25-28, 1993).

indicator.[10] Under this partially reformed system, enterprises are sensitized to profit, unlike under the traditional command economy where only gross output counts. However, because the regime cannot bear the social and political costs that unemployment entails, state enterprises can always count on the government to bail them out when they are running at a loss. There is thus no genuine threat of bankruptcy. Managers are turned into profit-maximizers, but they can achieve more profit by bargaining with the bureaucrats who control the economic levers, than by attending to the market. At the same time, they are not disciplined by bankruptcy. In short, they take the benefits but not the losses. Their budgets are thus "soft."[11]

Not constrained by a real budget, state enterprise managers are likely to make insatiable demands for investment. This is the case because energy and materials are usually priced low, funds are either free or in the form of bank loans not requiring collateral and with low interest rates, expansion can bring managers power and prestige, and central planning has been traditionally much weaker in mainland China than in other command economies, thus giving enterprises more leeway to make investment decisions. Not only is there investment hunger, but also extravagant wage increases and bonuses, resulting from the same soft budget constraint. Accompanying this phenomenon is the loose monetary policy pursued by local authorities and local bank branches, which serves to amplify the enterprises' demands. As aggregate demand rises, bottlenecks develop, projects fail, and prices skyrocket. The state then slashes investment and freezes wages. However, since the structure of the system remains the same, expansionary pressure inevitably builds up,[12] which leads to another cycle of expansion and contraction.[13]

The second explanation takes a political economy approach. During the post-Mao period one finds cyclical development of mainland China's economy. There are two kinds of cycles: the business cycle and the re-

---

[10]Yu-Shan Wu, "Reforming the Revolution: Industrial Policy in China," *Pacific Review* 3, no. 3 (September 1990): 243-56.

[11]Janos Kornai, *Contradictions and Dilemmas* (Cambridge, Mass.: MIT Press, 1986).

[12]With the nonstate sector rapidly growing to about the same size as the state sector in industry, it seems that the "soft budget constraint" argument may lose some strength, as this theory primarily applies to state enterprises and cannot explain the behaviors of the nonstate businesses. This is more apparent than real, however, as state enterprises accounted for 67 percent of investment in fixed assets in 1992. Thus investment hunger and an investment cycle based on "soft budget constraint" of the state sector are still prominent phenomena of the economy.

[13]Yu-Shan Wu, *Comparative Economic Transformations: Mainland China, Hungary, the Soviet Union, and Taiwan* (Stanford, Calif.: Stanford University Press, 1994), chap. 2.

form cycle. The business cycle consists of two distinctive phases: boom and bust.[14] The reform cycle likewise has two phases: economic expansion and retrenchment. These two cycles need not operate synchronously, nor are they inseparable. For example, Hua Kuo-feng's (Hua Guofeng's) Ten-Year Plan was a pro-growth strategy unaccompanied by economic reform. However, the business and reform cycles were synchronized after Hua's defeat in 1982, primarily because the economic reformers need high growth to legitimize their policies. Thus economic expansion was accompanied by reformist measures, and contraction or slower growth by retrenchment. This renders the reformers led by Teng Hsiao-p'ing vulnerable when the economy overheats, and conservatives led by Ch'en Yün become subject to criticism when growth is sluggish. A policy shift thus occurs at the critical juncture, i.e., when the economy is overheated or stalled, and the cycle begins to move in the opposite direction until it hits a point where another shift is required.[15] Where the "soft budget constraint" explanation emphasizes the system's structural bias toward expansion, the political-economy model emphasizes the importance of factional politics at the center and the incentives for managers to attune their investment behavior to the current Party line.

Whatever explanation one takes, it is undeniable that investment cycles are a prominent phenomenon in the post-Mao era.[16] Since one of the major strategies of the mainland's economic reform is to introduce advanced Western technology and raise productivity, investment hunger is easily translated into insatiable demand for imported producer goods. Investment cycles thus turn into import cycles as imports first surge to satisfy the investment demand and then fall as the regime takes austerity measures under the pressure of balance-of-payments problems.

At least four cycles can be discerned since the late 1970s.[17] Imports first went up under Hua Kuo-feng's Ten-Year Plan. They were then slashed by Teng Hsiao-p'ing and Ch'en Yün in 1982-83, which resulted in trade surpluses during these two years. In 1984 serious industrial reform began, and imports, together with the trade deficit, surged again.

---

[14]Lowell Dittmer, "Patterns of Elite Strife and Succession in Chinese Politics," *China Quarterly*, no. 123 (September 1990): 420.

[15]See Dittmer and Wu, "The Political Leadership in Reform China."

[16]For a discussion of the cycles in mainland China, see Dittmer and Wu, "The Political Leadership in Reform China"; Lin Chong-pin, "China: The Coming Changes," *The American Enterprise* 2, no. 2 (March/April 1991): 18-25; and Chen Te-sheng, *Chung-nan-hai cheng-ching tung-hsiang* (Peking's recent political and economic trends) (Taipei: Lifework Press, 1992), 218-21.

[17]See Lin, "China: The Coming Changes," and Wu, "Reforming the Revolution."

In 1986 dramatic measures were taken to curb investment and imports. The third cycle appeared in 1987, leading to the austerity measures of fall 1988, and the recession of 1989. As in 1982-83, the regime was able to balance its foreign trade, and the mainland registered a trade surplus in 1990, the first time since 1983.

In 1988, the mainland successfully shifted to a strategy of export expansion, which it had failed to do in the early 1980s. This was the single most important reason that saved Peking from its worst economic crisis since the reform started, and as a result, a trade surplus was registered for three consecutive years (1990-92). After that, the cyclical pattern set in again, and in 1993, mainland China accumulated a trade deficit of US$12.2 billion. This development demonstrates that investment hunger is such a rampant phenomenon that it can no longer be contained by even a very successful export drive.

Investment and import hunger brought about a desperate need for foreign exchange. In 1988, after five consecutive years of trade deficit, a critical decision was made to shift the focus of the mainland's open-door policy from introducing Western technology to earning badly-needed foreign exchange through exporting labor-intensive products, a strategy based on mainland China's comparative advantage. Following Wang Chien's (Wang Jian's) "grand international circulation" theory, Premier Chao Tzu-yang (Zhao Ziyang) decided to plunge China's east coast into the world market.[18] The mainland's economy was oriented toward export expansion, just as East Asia's newly industrializing countries (NICs) had been several decades before.

This is where Taiwan's investment fits in. Labor-intensive and oriented toward the international market, Taiwan's export industry is a perfect source of direct foreign investment for mainland China at this critical juncture. Following good economic logic, the PRC's State Council promulgated the "Regulations Encouraging Taiwan Compatriots to Invest on the Mainland" (the 22 Articles).[19] Provinces then competed in offering privileges to Taiwan investors, including tax holidays, duty-free imports,

---

[18]Sah Kung-ch'iang, *Chung-kung shih-nien ching-kai te li-lun yü shih-chien* (The theory and practice of the decade-old economic reform in mainland China) (Taipei: Institute of International Relations, National Chengchi University, 1991), 101-2.

[19]Before the 22 Articles, there were several documents directing the mainland's economic policy toward Taiwan. For example, there were "The Temporary Regulations on Expanding Trade with Taiwan Area" (May 1979), "Supplementary Rules on Purchasing Products Made in Taiwan" (April 1980), "Preferences for Taiwan Compatriots Investing in Special Economic Zones" (April 1983), and "The Temporary Regulations on Centralizing Control of Trade with Taiwan Province" (July 1987). None of these, however, is as comprehensive, consistent, and influential as the 22 Articles.

land-use rights, permission to purchase bonds, and special areas exclusively for Taiwan investment.[20] Besides these favorable policies, other "pull" factors include geographical proximity, cultural similarities, great market potential, and much lower production costs. On the "push" side, there is a surging New Taiwan (NT) dollar, rising labor and land costs, pressure from the environmentalists against industrial pollution, and increasing competition from other Asian countries based on low wages.

As a result, Taiwan's investment on the mainland grew by leaps and bounds. It started in 1987 with 80 investment projects worth US$100 million. In the following year it grew to 430 projects worth US$600 million. The investment surge was not affected by the Tienanmen (Tiananmen) incident at all, as witnessed by the fact that at the end of 1989 Taiwan investors had launched 1,000 projects involving US$1 billion. This trend steamed ahead into the 1990s. In 1993, Taiwan investment hit the US$10 billion mark, making Taiwan the second largest foreign investor in the Chinese mainland, behind Hong Kong and Macao.[21] According to a conservative official estimate, mainland China was the main outlet for Taiwan's overseas investment, accounting for 65.61 percent of the total in 1993.[22] The same trend can be said of investment-driven trade, which grew from a low of US$1.5 billion in 1987 and exceeded US$10 billion by 1992.[23] Cross-Strait trade became the main source of Taiwan's overall trade

---

[20] *Ta-lu t'ou-tzu chih-nan* (Guide to investing on the mainland) (Taipei: Chung-Hua Institution for Economic Research, 1991), 112-13.

[21] In 1993, the Ministry of Economic Affairs approved 9,329 projects involving US$3.2 billion for investment on the mainland. These figures are widely considered below the actual numbers.

[22] According to *Liang-an ching-chi t'ung-chi yüeh-pao* (Monthly Statistical Report on Cross-Strait Economic Relations) (March 1994) issued by the Mainland Affairs Council, in 1993 the government permitted US$3.17 billion investment on the mainland, which accounted for 65.61 percent of Taiwan's total overseas investment during that period. The second largest receiver of Taiwan's overseas investment in 1993 was the United States which accounted for US$529 million, or 10.96 percent of the total. In other words, Taiwan's investment in mainland China was six times as large as its investment in the United States, a distant second outlet for Taiwan's outflowing capital. In 1993, Taiwan invested a total of US$275 million in Southeast Asia (Singapore, the Philippines, Indonesia, and Malaysia), which only accounted for 5.71 percent of Taiwan's total overseas investment for the year.

[23] Cross-Strait trade is always underestimated for two reasons. First, researchers usually rely on the statistics provided by the Hong Kong government, but Hong Kong is by no means the only entrepôt for cross-Strait trade. Second, only reexport trade is calculated in the Hong Kong government's statistics, leaving out transhipment trade and triangular trade. It is estimated that cross-Strait trade reached US$14.8 billion in 1992 (the official number is US$7.4 billion) if transhipment and triangular trade of that year are included. See Chien Tse-yüan, "An Analysis of the Intermediary Role of Hong Kong in the Economic Exchanges Between the Two Sides of the Taiwan Strait," *Chung-kuo ta-lu yen-chiu* (Mainland China Studies) (Taipei) 36, no. 11 (November 1993): 69-81.

Table 17.1

Taiwan's Trade Surplus Dependency on Mainland China (1990-93)

Unit: US$ million

Year	Taiwan's total foreign trade surplus (A)	Taiwan's trade surplus with mainland China (B)	Surplus with mainland China as a percentage of the total trade surplus [(A)/(B)]
1990	12,495.2	2,512.9	20.11%
1991	13,299.1	3,541.2	26.63%
1992	9,479.3	5,169.0	54.53%
1993	7,869.8	6,481.9	82.36%

Source: *Liang-an ching-chi t'ung-chi yüeh-pao* (Monthly Statistical Report on Cross-Strait Economic Relations) (Taipei), May 1994, 50.

surplus (see table 17.1).[24] With Taiwan's trade surplus against the United States declining steadily, and its trade deficit with Japan rising at an even higher rate, cross-Strait trade became the main factor preventing Taiwan from developing an overall trade deficit. In 1993, Taiwan's trade dependency on mainland China was 9.3 percent. Its export dependency was 16.5 percent. It was further estimated that by 1996 mainland China will surpass the United States and become Taiwan's largest trading partner.[25]

Up to this point, the economic reform argument seems able to account for the mainland's economic policy toward Taiwan and the exponential growth of investment and trade across the Taiwan Strait. However, the proponents of the unification argument maintain that there are abnormalcies in the economic relations between the two sides of the Taiwan Strait that cannot be understood without taking into consideration the political motive behind Peking's economic policy toward Taiwan.

---

[24] In 1993, out of the US$7.9 billion trade surplus that Taiwan accumulated, US$6.5 billion, or 82 percent of total surplus, was from cross-Strait trade. If cross-Strait trade that did not go through the Hong Kong Customs is included, Taiwan's trade surplus with the mainland is 1.64 times its total trade surplus for 1993.

[25] In May 1994, Taiwan's export to Hong Kong amounted to US$2.06 billion, only US$60 million less than Taiwan's export to the United States, traditionally Taiwan's largest trading partner. In terms of percentage, Taiwan's export to Hong Kong was 24.2 percent of total export. The corresponding figure for Taiwan's export to the United States was 24.9 percent. It is estimated that Taiwan's export dependency on Hong Kong will surpass its dependency on the United States in the latter half of 1994.

The Unification Argument

The thrust of the unification argument is that Peking's economic policy toward Taiwan is primarily part of the Communist leadership's strategy to unify China through economic integration. Modern integration theories propose that economic exchanges are the optimal starting point to produce integrative momentum that may "spill over" into the political realm and achieve political integration.[26] These theories were produced in the political context of the post-World War II movement for European unity.[27] The policy prescriptions of the integrationists have been carefully followed by the major organizations for European unity—the European Community and its successor, the European Union.

Briefly stated, economic interaction is usually beneficial to all the contracting parties and are less threatening to national sovereignty than any direct attempt at political integration. However, the very nature of economic interaction is such that nations are drawn into increasing interdependence. The "spill-over" effect will then force the mutually dependent countries to coordinate their policies and produce institutional mechanisms to regularize such coordination. If the trend of economic integration continues, states may find it reasonable to give up their monopoly over certain domestic policies and to abide by collective decisions reached through a supranational organization in which the country concerned is but a member. The transfer of sovereignty to the supranational entity may ultimately result in the creation of an enlarged political community, under which member states are subsumed.

Political integration through economic interaction does not have to be a voluntary process as suggested by the integration theorists of the postwar era. Adolf Hitler's strategy of creating a group of East European satellites through monopolies and monopsonies in the 1930s serves as a good example of how political dominance can be achieved through economic manipulation. The Prussia-led Zollverein is another case of political integration (the creation of the 1871 German Empire) achieved through economic mechanisms (the customs union). In both these instances, the pattern of dominance established by the economic relations between interacting units is reflected in the emerging political order. Economic power

---

[26]Robert O. Keohane and Joseph S. Nye, "International Interdependence and Integration," in *International Politics*, vol. 8 of *Handbook of Political Science*, ed. Nelson W. Polsby (Menlo Park, Calif.: Addison-Wesley, 1975), 364, 396.

[27]Ernst B. Haas, *The Uniting of Europe: Political, Social, and Economic Forces, 1950-1957* (Stanford, Calif.: Stanford University Press, 1958).

is translated into political power. This reasoning is certainly close to the heart of Marxists who appreciate the economic root of political power more than anyone else. Not surprisingly, this strand of integration theory is endorsed by the Chinese Communist leaders in their dealings with Taiwan.

Proofs abound. At the mainland's 1990 National Working Conference on Taiwan, for example, policy statements such as "to promote political integration through economic exchanges," "to raise popular pressure on the government [of Taiwan]," and "to lead to unification of the motherland" were openly made regarding cross-Strait economic relations.[28] The commitment of the CCP leadership to national unification is unquestionable, as witnessed by Teng Hsiao-p'ing's statements in 1980 (when he announced the "three national missions" for the 1980s), 1983 (when he met Professor Winston L. Y. Yang), 1989 (when he talked with Mikhail Gorbachev), and 1990 (when he received Kuo He-nien),[29] as well as by the categorical assertions on national sovereignty in a White Paper issued in 1993.[30] As cross-Strait economic relations have developed into the most important link between Taiwan and the mainland, it seems only natural that Peking will play economic cards with Taipei to promote unification. However, one cannot know just how much weight this political goal carried in the formulation of economic policies unless sufficient proofs can be found to demonstrate that there are abnormalcies in cross-Strait economic relations that cannot be explained in economic terms.

Two such abnormalcies can be pointed out.[31] The first is that mainland China tolerated an unusually large trade deficit with Taiwan. The second is that investment from Taiwan usually involves saturated production technology, outdated equipment, and high pollution and low added-value products. Why on earth would the mainland welcome such investment? The obvious answer is that noneconomic factors are at work. The CCP leadership must be sufficiently interested in attracting Taiwan

---

[28]The Taiwan policy set at the 1990 conference was issued by the Party's Central Committee in *Chung-fa* (1991) No. 3. For the document, see Chen Te-sheng, *Liang-an cheng-ching hu-tung: Cheng-ts'e chieh-tu yü yün-tso fen-hsi* (Political and economic interaction across the Taiwan Strait: Policy interpretation and implementation) (Taipei: Lifework Press, 1994), 213-21.

[29]See Teng Hsiao-p'ing, *Teng Hsiao-p'ing wen-hsüan* (Selected works of Teng Hsiao-p'ing), vol. 3 (Peking: Jen-min ch'u-pan-she, 1993), 30, 295, 362; and Wu and Wang, *Teng Hsiaoping chih-hou te Chung-kuo*, 284-85.

[30]For the White Paper, see "The Taiwan Question and Reunification of China," *Beijing Review* 36, no. 36 (September 6-12, 1993): i-viii.

[31]Lin Li-chien, "A Veteran Researcher's Reflections on Mainland China Studies," Forum on Mainland China Studies Lecture Series, National Taiwan University, May 3, 1994.

Table 17.2
Cross-Strait Trade Through Hong Kong (1979-93)

Unit: US$ million; %

Year	Total trade		Taiwan's export to the mainland		Taiwan's import from the mainland		Taiwan's trade dependency on the mainland
	Volume	Growth rate	Volume	Growth rate	Volume	Growth rate	
1979	77.76	—	21.47	—	56.29	—	0.25
1980	311.18	300.18	234.97	994.41	76.21	35.39	0.79
1981	459.33	47.61	384.15	63.49	75.18	−1.35	1.05
1982	278.47	−39.37	194.45	−49.38	84.02	11.76	0.68
1983	247.69	−11.05	157.84	−18.83	89.85	6.94	0.55
1984	553.20	123.34	425.45	169.55	127.75	42.18	1.06
1985	1,102.73	99.34	986.83	131.95	115.90	−9.28	2.17
1986	955.55	−13.35	811.33	−17.78	144.22	24.43	1.49
1987	1,515.47	58.60	1,226.53	51.18	288.94	100.35	1.38
1988	2,720.91	79.54	2,242.22	82.81	478.69	65.67	2.47
1989	3,483.39	28.02	2,896.49	29.18	586.90	22.61	2.94
1990	4,043.62	16.08	3,278.26	13.18	765.36	30.41	3.32
1991	5,793.11	43.26	4,667.15	42.36	1,125.95	47.11	4.16
1992	7,406.90	27.86	6,287.93	34.73	1,118.97	−0.62	4.83
1993	8,688.98	17.31	7,585.42	20.63	1,103.56	−1.38	5.36

Source: *Liang-an ching-chi t'ung-chi yüeh-pao*, May 1994, 30.

capital to create the spill-over effect into the political realm that they are willing to pay the economic price of trade deficit and preferential treatment to Taiwan investors.

The Abnormalcies

If one takes a look at the trade balances between Taiwan and mainland China between 1987 and 1993, one unmistakable fact immediately stands out: Taiwan enjoys an increasingly large trade surplus. In 1987, when Peking's economic incentives were not yet in full play, Taiwan exported US$1.23 billion worth of goods to the mainland, while imported US$289 million worth of products from there, giving the island a trade surplus of US$938 million. In 1988, Taiwan's cross-Strait exports jumped to US$2.24 billion, while imports rose to US$479 million, giving Taiwan a surplus of US$1.76 billion. This trend continued into the 1990s, with Taiwan enjoying a surplus of US$2.5 billion in 1990, US$3.5 billion in 1991, US$5.2 billion in 1992, and US$6.5 billion in 1993 (see table 17.2).[32]

---

[32]If cross-Strait trade that did not go through the Hong Kong Customs is included, Taiwan's

Not only was there a steadily rising trade surplus in Taiwan's favor, but the island's export dependency on the mainland market (as calculated by the mainland's share in Taiwan's overall exports) also increased over the years. In 1987, mainland China accounted for 2.29 percent of Taiwan's exports. That figure rose to 8.9 percent in 1993 (or 16.5 percent if transhipment trade, and so forth, are included). The same can be said of the mainland's import dependency on Taiwan. In 1987, Taiwan supplied 2.84 percent of the mainland's overall imports. In 1993, Taiwan's share rose to 8.1 percent (or 13.5 percent if transhipment trade, and so forth, are included). The flow of Taiwan's products to the mainland market was not, however, matched by trade in the opposite direction. Mainland China's exports to Taiwan grew roughly at the same rate as its overall exports, slightly increasing export dependency on the Taiwan market over the years (0.7 percent in 1987, 1.2 percent in 1990, and 1.2 percent in 1993). Taiwan's import dependency on the mainland correspondingly showed a slight increase (0.83 percent in 1987, 1.4 percent in 1990, and 1.4 percent in 1993). In short, over the years, Taiwan's exports to the mainland have grown into a very significant portion of Taiwan's overall exports and of the mainland's overall imports, while mainland China's exports to Taiwan remained a minor phenomenon for both sides (see figures 17.1 and 17.2). In 1993, mainland China and Taiwan were each other's fourth largest trading partner.[33] A full 85 percent of this booming economic relationship, however, is accounted for by Taiwan's exports to mainland China. This can be considered abnormal (see figure 17.3).[34]

If one compares the track record of cross-Strait trade with the overall trade pattern of mainland China, the abnormalcy becomes even clearer. One typical example is the immediate post-Tienanmen development. In the six years between 1984 and 1989, the mainland consistently registered a trade deficit, and foreign debt reached US$41.3 billion at the end of 1989. The brutal suppression of the Tienanmen pro-democracy movement invited international sanctions against mainland China, which added to the economic recession that the mainland had been experiencing since the *chih-li cheng-tun* (countering inflation and combating profiteering) policy was adopted in fall 1988. Foreign exchange reserves dropped to

trade surplus with mainland China in 1993 was US$12.9 billion, which is larger than the mainland's overall trade deficit for the year (US$12.2 billion).

[33]Lee Ch'ing-p'ing, "Cross-Strait Economic Relations and Important Items for Investing on the Chinese Mainland" (Speech to the Taiwan Chamber of Commerce, Vancouver, November 7, 1993; in Chinese).

[34]No comparable imbalance can be found in the mainland's trade with any major countries.

Figure 17.1
Taiwan's Indirect Trade Dependency on the Mainland (1979-93)

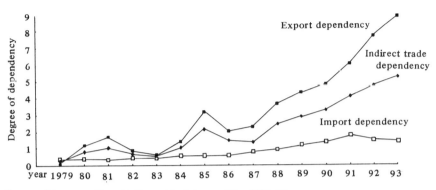

Source: *Liang-an ching-chi t'ung-chi yüeh-pao*, May 1994, 34.

Figure 17.2
Mainland China's Indirect Trade Dependency on Taiwan (1979-93)

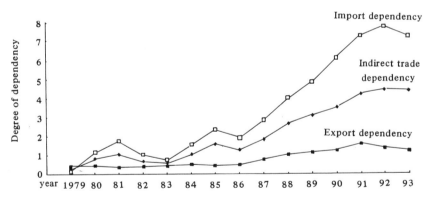

Source: Same as figure 17.1.

their 1987 level. Obviously a policy of contraction was in order, and indeed it was adopted with a vengeance. In 1990, Peking slashed overall imports by 9.8 percent, which greatly contributed to the country's resumption of a surplus position that year. However, in that same year, the mainland's imports from Taiwan increased by 13.2 percent, clearly against the general trade pattern of the mainland and the current phase of the import cycle (in 1990, the mainland's imports from the United States dropped by 16 percent, that from Japan by 28 percent), indicating the influence of noneconomic factors.

Figure 17.3
Cross-Strait Trade Through Hong Kong (1979-93)

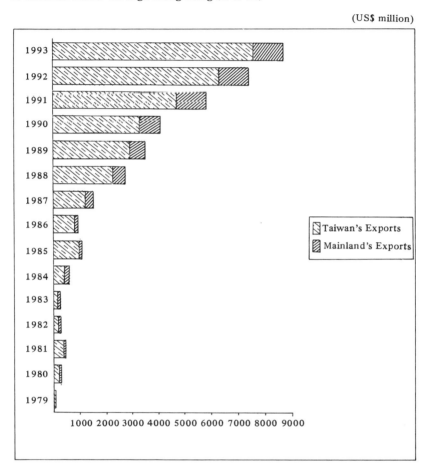

(US$ million)

Source: *Liang-an ching-chi t'ung-chi yüeh-pao*, March 1994, 26.

Another abnormalcy is the lack of advantage to mainland China of the bulk of Taiwan's investment on the mainland, which features: saturated production technology, outdated equipment, high pollution, and low added-value. Typical Taiwan investors are entrepreneurs from small and medium-sized businesses who go to the mainland to seek cheap labor and land. They establish production bases for labor-intensive processing or assembling and they often bring half-depreciated equipment to the mainland. Constrained by limited capital and a short time-frame, these enterprises are seldom in a position to conduct research and development, nor are they willing or capable of taking precautions against environmental pollution. The negative externalities of Taiwan's investment seem enormous, and yet the mainland authorities still offer strong incentives to Taiwan investors. Here again, noneconomic considerations seem dominant.

In Defense of the Economic Argument

The abnormalcies in cross-Strait economic relations—the mainland's increasingly large trade deficit and Taiwan's unsavory investments—can actually be explained in terms of the economic reform argument. The crux of the matter is the nature of Taiwan's investment and its conjunction with the mainland's economic reform.

The economic argument asserts that mainland China needs Taiwan's capital for one particular purpose—to earn foreign exchange. Investment from Taiwan is welcomed because it is export-oriented and has access to the international market. Taiwan-funded enterprises usually receive orders in Taiwan, process imported materials or semifinished products on the mainland, and export through Hong Kong to international markets.[35] In this way, Taiwan investors skillfully mobilize the production factor in which the mainland has a comparative advantage—abundant labor that has been recently released from agriculture—and geared it toward export production. This is indeed what was meant by *liang-t'ou tsai-wai* (receive inputs from outside and sell products to the world market) and is perfectly in tune with the "grand international circulation" strategy. This being the case, it is only rational for the mainland authorities to tolerate the low technological content and negative externalities of Taiwan's investment.

Timing is also an important factor. "Mainland fever" (*ta-lu-je*) hit Taiwan in the late 1980s, primarily because of changes in Taiwan's political situation. Tremendous economic opportunities had been suppressed in past decades for political reasons and the overdue "thaw" understandably brought about a surge in economic activity. Initially investment was small, but both investment and trade grew rapidly. Then came the Tienanmen incident and international sanctions. Many foreign companies withdrew their investments from the mainland. Many more held back or reconsidered their projects. Approved direct foreign investment dropped by half from the third quarter of 1989 to the first quarter of 1990. At this critical juncture, it was quite understandable that Peking would do its

---

[35]Ai Wei, "The Development and Limitations of Taiwan-Mainland Economic and Trade Relations," *Issues & Studies* (Taipei) 27, no. 5 (May 1991): 51.

very best to court investment from Taiwan for purely economic reasons. As it turned out, the pent-up momentum unleashed by the thaw of the late 1980s was strong enough to sustain the shock of the Tienanmen incident, and Taiwan capital poured in at a time when everyone else was withdrawing. In 1990, investment by *T'ai-shang* (Taiwan businessmen) on the Chinese mainland grew by an annual rate of 49 percent. A further development along this line was the "Regulations on Indirect Investment and Technological Cooperation on the Mainland," issued on October 6, 1990 by the ROC's Ministry of Economic Affairs that officially sanctioned *T'ai-shang*'s investment activities across the Taiwan Strait.[36] Timing thus played an important role in intensifying the mainland's need for Taiwan investment, despite its saturated technology and negative externalities.

The economic argument can also explain the persistent and increasingly large trade deficit that the mainland has with Taiwan. Cross-Strait trade is investment-driven; i.e., it is to a great extent to support the investment activities of Taiwan's businessmen on the mainland.[37] This feature can clearly be seen by taking a look at the content of Taiwan's exports to the mainland which constitute the bulk of the cross-Strait trade. From 1988 to 1993, SITC sections 6 and 7 products (materials, parts and accessories, and machinery equipment) averaged around 70 percent of Taiwan's exports to mainland China. A large portion of these producer goods were imported by Taiwan-funded enterprises on the mainland. It is estimated that 54 percent of the materials, and 75 percent of the machinery and equipment needed by *T'ai-shang* were imported from Taiwan, for they were required to provide their own materials and semifinished products, so as not to disturb the mainland's domestic market. As Taiwan's exports to the mainland are predominantly factors of production needed by the mainland's own export drive, it is only reasonable to expect a rising flow of goods from Taiwan to mainland China as the latter's export industry booms.

Based on this theory, the rise in Taiwan's exports to the mainland in 1990 against the background of general import reduction was not an abnormalcy. In order to tide over the unprecedented economic crisis the Communist regime was facing at the time, it was necessary not just to cut imports, but to expand exports. In 1990, SITC sections 6 and 7 commodities constituted 76.7 percent of the mainland's imports from Taiwan. These were producer goods utilized by Taiwan-funded and other mainland-

---

[36]Yen Tzung-ta, "Taiwan Investment in Mainland China and Its Impact on Taiwan's Industries," ibid., 22.

[37]See note 33 above.

based enterprises for export-based production for the international market. Small wonder that cross-Strait trade ran against the general pattern of the time and that economic difficulties gave an additional boost to Taiwan-mainland trade relations.[38]

Other factors are at work to keep the mainland's deficit with Taiwan constantly growing, which are primarily to do with Taiwan's own political considerations. It has been considered prudent for Taiwan not to allow mainland investment on the island. The argument that capital endowment determines the flow of investment and that there is no economic incentive for mainland capital to come to Taiwan is untenable. The major reason for the absence of mainland investment on Taiwan is a political one. This being the case, it would be impossible to expect any investment-driven exports from mainland China to Taiwan. The other obstacle to increasing imports from the mainland is the limits that Taiwan's government sets on the permitted import items. Mainland-produced consumer goods are prohibited from entering the Taiwan market altogether. Agricultural and industrial materials and semifinished products are regulated by a list of permitted items.[39] To import any products beyond these specified items is illegal. On the mainland side, limited transportation capacity and growing domestic needs for materials and semifinished products also restrict products available for export to the Taiwan market. It is only natural that exports from mainland China have grown modestly compared with the huge growth of Taiwan's exports to the mainland. Hence the increasing trade imbalance.

Conclusion

The economic argument asserts that the mainland's economic policy toward Taiwan and resultant cross-Strait economic relations are explainable in terms of the needs derived from the mainland's economic reform. The unification argument challenges this position by pointing out abnormalcies in the relationship—the increasingly large trade deficit in Taiwan's favor and the unsavory nature of investment made by Taiwan on the Chinese

---

[38]Before the investment boom of the late 1980s, cross-Strait trade conformed to the mainland's general trade pattern. Thus, one saw a decline in Taiwan's export to the mainland in 1982 (-49.4 percent), 1983 (-18.8 percent), and 1986 (-17.8 percent), perfectly in tune with the mainland's import cycles. These fluctuations in trade were not to reappear in 1987-93, a period characterized by uninterrupted growth. See Chien, "An Analysis of the Intermediary Role of Hong Kong," 72.

[39]At the end of 1993, 1,500 items were on the government list. They were allowed to enter Taiwan's market to cut the production costs of local manufacturers.

mainland. The economic reform argument replies that since Taiwan's investment is geared to export, and economic reform on the mainland has created a strong need for foreign exchange, the privileges granted to Taiwan investors producing labor-intensive products are reasonable. The availability of Taiwan capital immediately after the Tienanmen incident also makes granting preferences to *T'ai-shang* a reasonable decision. As to cross-Strait trade, since it is investment-driven, and is mainly composed of producer goods exported from Taiwan to mainland China, one should expect it to grow together with the mainland's booming export industry. Since the political considerations on Taiwan's side have excluded the possibility of rapidly increasing the mainland's exports to the island, the current trade imbalance will continue. All the "abnormalcies" thus can be readily explained in terms of needs derived from the mainland's economic reform. Invoking the unification argument is unnecessary to understand the track record of cross-Strait economic relations.

The assumptions of the economic reform argument are sound. The argument asserts that economic reform has assumed paramount importance on the CCP's policy agenda; that the survival of the Communist regime hinges on the success of the reform program; and that from Peking's point of view, the cross-Strait economic relationship has its most important purpose in serving the needs of the mainland's economic development. Based on these assumptions, one may conclude that Peking's economic policy toward Taiwan will vary with the mainland's economic needs.

The most recent developments bear out this deduction. The Standing Committee of the PRC's Eighth National People's Congress passed the "Law on Protection of Investment Made by Taiwan Compatriots" in March 1994, upgrading the legal status of the rules protecting the interests of Taiwan investors on the mainland. Furthermore, from April 11 to 15, the unprecedented "National Economic Working Conference on Taiwan" was held that brought together no lesser figures than Chiang Tse-min (Jiang Zemin), Li P'eng (Li Peng), Ch'iao Shih (Qiao Shi), Hu Chin-t'ao (Hu Jintao), Li Lan-ch'ing (Li Lanqing), Tsou Chia-hua (Zou Jiahua), Ch'ien Ch'i-ch'en (Qian Qichen), Lo Kan (Luo Gan), and Wang Chao-kuo (Wang Zhaoguo). All interested ministries and commissions of the State Council were represented. Also attending the meeting were high economic officials from the provinces, cities, and autonomous regions, heads of local planning agencies and economic-trade commissions, as well as directors of Taiwan affairs offices. Attendance was unprecedented.

The tone of this conference was strikingly different from that of the previous working conferences on Taiwan held in December 1990, March 1992, and November 1993, when the high politics of unification dominated the agenda, military and united front personnel were prominent, and officials promoted "one country, two systems," and denounced Taiwan independence. This time, the main agenda of the economic working conference was to identify parallel economic interests between Taiwan and mainland China, and to encourage large-scale investment on the mainland by Taiwan's major business conglomerates. A blueprint was drawn up in which the mainland and Taiwan joined hands to explore international market opportunities. A "Central Group for Coordinating Economic and Trade Relations with Taiwan" was formed, headed by vice premier Li Lan-ch'ing, the top trade official in the government. From the meeting's participants, organizational initiatives, and policy statements made by national leaders, one can safely conclude that economic considerations are uppermost when the Communist leadership makes decisions on cross-Strait relations.[40] It is true that the goal of unification was still stressed, but the concrete measures taken are clearly for the benefit of the mainland's economic reform. This observation does not exclude the possibility that economic ties may someday be used by Peking when push comes to shove and unification becomes the immediate goal of the Communist regime. It does, however, point out that current decisions regarding cross-Strait relations are made primarily on economic grounds, and that one should take a careful look at the economic needs of the mainland's reform program when trying to explain Peking's economic policies toward Taiwan.

---

[40]Sung Kuo-cheng, "Peking's Taiwan Policy and Cross-Strait Relations in 1993," *Issues & Studies* 30, no. 3 (March 1994): 1-14.

Contributors

Linda Chao is a Research Fellow at the Hoover Institution, Stanford, California and the author of many articles on the democratization of the Republic of China on Taiwan.

Jian Chen was born in Fukien (Fujian) Province and graduated from Amoy (Xiamen) University. He is a Ph.D. candidate (Economics) at the Ohio State University.

Chu-yuan Cheng is Professor of Economics and Chairman of the Asian Studies Committee at Ball State University, Muncie, Indiana, and the author of more than twenty books, including *Behind the Tiananmen Massacre: Social, Political, and Economic Ferment in China* (1990).

Cal Clark is Professor and Head of the Department of Political Science at Auburn University, Alabama. He is the author of *Taiwan's Development: Implications for Contending Political Paradigms*, coauthor of *Flexibility, Foresight, and Fortuna in Taiwan's Development* and *Women in Taiwan Politics*, and coeditor of *North/South Relations, State and Development*, and *The Evolving Pacific Basin*.

John F. Copper is the Stanley J. Buckman Distinguished Professor of International Studies at Rhodes College in Memphis, Tennessee. He is the author of sixteen books on China, Taiwan, and Asian affairs. His most recent books are *Taiwan: Nation-State or Province?* (1990), *China Diplomacy: The Washington-Taipei-Beijing Triangle* (1992), and *Taiwan's 1991 and 1992 Non-Supplemental Elections: Reaching a Higher State of Democracy* (1994).

Ralph A. Cossa is Executive Director of Pacific Forum CSIS, a Honolulu-based, policy-oriented Asia-Pacific research institute affiliated with the Center for Strategic and International Studies in Washington, D.C. He is a member of the Steering Committee of the Council for Security Cooperation in the Asia-Pacific (CSCAP) and also serves as Executive Director of the U.S. Committee of CSCAP.

Belton M. Fleisher is Professor of Economics at the Ohio State University.

Harlan W. Jencks is a Research Associate of the Center for Chinese Studies at the University of California, Berkeley and an Analyst at the University of California's Lawrence Livermore National Laboratory. He has written extensively on international security affairs in Asia, especially concerning China. He is coeditor of *The International Missile Bazaar: The New Suppliers' Network* (1994).

Samuel S. Kim is Senior Research Scholar at the East Asian Institute of Columbia University. He is the author or editor of over a dozen books on East Asian international relations, Chinese foreign policy, and world politics, most recently *China and the World: Chinese Foreign Relations in the Post-Cold War Era* (1994).

Wen Lang Li is Professor of Sociology and Agricultural Economics and Sociology at the Ohio State University.

Ramon H. Myers is Senior Fellow and Curator-Scholar of the East Asian Collection, Hoover Institution, Stanford, California. His most recent publication is *Selected Writings of Sun Yat-sen* (editor, 1994).

Jan S. Prybyla is Professor of Economics at the Pennsylvania State University, University Park, Pennsylvania. He is the author of, among others, *The Political Economy of Communist China* (1970), *Issues in Socialist Economic Modernization* (1980), *The Chinese Economy: Problems and Policies* (1981), and *Market and Plan Under Socialism: The Bird in the Cage* (1987).

Shelley Rigger is the Brown Assistant Professor of East Asian Politics at Davidson College, Davidson, North Carolina. She received her Ph.D. from the Department of Government at Harvard University in June 1994. Her dissertation is "Machine Politics in the New Taiwan: Institutional Reform and Electoral Strategy in the Republic of China."

Chih-yu Shih, Associate Professor of Political Science at National Taiwan University, is the author of *The Spirit of Chinese Foreign Policy: A Psychocultural View* (1990), *Contending Dramas: A Cognitive Approach to International Organization* (with Martha Cottam, 1992), *China's Just World: The Morality of Chinese Foreign Policy* (1993), and *Symbolic War: The Chinese Use of Force, 1840-1980* (with Jonathan R. Adelman, 1993).

Robert G. Sutter has specialized in Asian and Pacific affairs and U.S. foreign policy with the Congressional Research Service (CRS) of the

Library of Congress since 1977. He currently is a Senior Specialist in International Policy with the CRS. Dr. Sutter received a Ph.D. in history and East Asian languages from Harvard University, and teaches regularly at Washington area universities.

Lynn T. White III is Professor at Princeton University, in the Woodrow Wilson School, Politics Department, and East Asian Studies Program. He is the author of *Careers in Shanghai* (1978), *Policies of Chaos* (1989), and *Unstately Power: Local Causes of Chinese Reforms and Reactions after 1970* (forthcoming).

Brantly Womack is Professor of Government and Foreign Affairs and Director of the East Asia Center at the University of Virginia. He is the author of *Foundations of Mao Zedong's Political Thought* (1982), coauthor (with James Townsend) of *Politics in China* (1986), and editor of *Contemporary Chinese Politics in Historical Perspective* (1991). He is currently writing a book on relations between mainland China and Vietnam.

An-chia Wu is Deputy Director of the Institute of International Relations, National Chengchi University. He is the author and editor of numerous articles and books on mainland Chinese politics, the latest one being *Chung-kung cheng-chih fa-chan* (Political development in mainland China) (1994).

Yu-Shan Wu received his Ph.D. in Political Science from the University of California at Berkeley. He is currently an Associate Professor of Political Science at National Taiwan University, is the author of *Comparative Economic Transformations: Mainland China, Hungary, the Soviet Union, and Taiwan* (1994), and has contributed numerous articles to various academic journals.

Suisheng Zhao is an Assistant Professor of Government at Colby College, Maine and Editor of the *Journal of Contemporary China*. He has published broadly on mainland Chinese politics and foreign policy and is coeditor of *The Decision Process in Deng's China* (1994).

INDEX

Agreement on a Comprehensive Political Settlement of the Cambodian Conflict, 247
Agriculture, PRC. *See* Economy, PRC
Arms trade, 228–29, 231, 339
Ash, Robert F., 70n
Asia-Pacific Economic Cooperation (APEC) meeting, 336
Association for Relations Across the Taiwan Straits, 361, 377
Association of Southeast Asian Nations (ASEAN), 205, 227, 246, 251–52, 253, 288–97passim

Bachman, David, 42n
Baker, James, 339
Bangkok Declaration (1993), 289–90, 345
Beijing Review, 332
Betts, Richard, 267
Brunei, 245
Bulgaria, 16
Bureaucrats, 51n
Burma, 228, 246–47
Byrd, William A., 66n, 67n

Cambodia, 245, 247–48, 288, 338
Carter, Jimmy, 245
Ceausescu, Nicolae, 331
Central Committee (CPC), , 42–44, 43t
Central Leadership Group on Taiwan Work, 376
Central Military Commission, CPC, 228
Ch'ai Ling, 332

Chang, Parris, 158
Chang Chen, 218
Changsha, 382, 383
Chao Tzu-yang, 7, 23–24, 399
Chekiang, 131
Cheng-ch'üan chih-shih (Knowledge about negotiable securities), 37
Cheng Ming, 12
Chengtu, Szechwan, 382
Ch'en I, 309
Chenpao Island, 308
Chen shui-bian, 167
Ch'en Yün, 4, 396
Chernomyrdin, Viktor, 286
Chiang Ching-kuo, 359
Chiang Tse-min
    as Teng's successor, 38–39
    and economic reforms, 24, 32
    on external security, 263n
    on human rights, 334, 336
    on MFN, 335
    on PLA, 215
    on Teng thought, 28, 29, 38
    on Tiaoyütai Island, 239
    on Tienanmen incident, 331
Ch'iao-Shih, 27–28, 28–29, 31
Ch'ien Ch'i-ch'en, 37, 265n, 336, 338, 347
Chientao Lake incident (1994), 157, 390–91
Ch'ih Hao-t'ien, 286
Chi Kuo-hsing, 252–53
Chinese New Party (CNP), 151, 152, 164, 166–67
Ching, Frank, 218
Ch'i-shih nien-tai, 12

Chou Chuan, 152
Chou En-lai, 7, 308, 309, 310, 311–
     12, 313, 314, 318
Christopher, Warren, 336, 346–47
Chu Ch'i-chen, 334
Chung-kuo wang-lu (The leftist
     disaster in China), 25
Chu Yun-han, 156
Clinton, Bill, 265, 336, 340, 348
Commodity economy, 22, 23
Communist Party of China (CPC)
     declining influence of, 213
     division in by date of joining, 46
     fear of economic reform, 25–26
     impact of socialist market
          economy, 30
     lack of Party controllers, 53
     leadership and career paths of
          members, 46–51
     opposition to peaceful evolution,
          26
     rationale for its monopoly, 63
Confucius, 7
Crestone Energy Corporation, 252
"Criminal Reform in China," 344–
     45
Cross-Strait relations, economic
     abnormalicies in, 404–8
     balance of trade, 401t, 404t,
          404–8
     legal protection issues, 390–91
     PRC policy as economic need,
          395–401, 408–10
     PRC policy as political integra-
          tion, 402–4
     PRC policy evaluated, 410–12
     social costs, 390
     trade through Hong Kong, 404t,
          407t

transaction costs, 391–92
     See also Economy, PRC;
          Economy, ROC
Cross-Strait relations, political
     1990's strategy of, 362–64
     PRC's viewpoint, 364–66
     prospects for, 371–72
     and reunification, 363
     ROC's official dealing with,
          360–61
     ROC's viewpoint, 367–69
     US options, 372–74
     and US-PRC rapprochement,
          356–58
     US role, 353–55, 355–56, 369–
          71
Cultural Revolution. *See* Great
     Proletarian Cultural Revolution
Czechoslovakia, 308

Dalai Lama, 333, 335
"Decision on Some Issues Concern-
     ing the Establishment of a
     Socialist Market Economic
     Structure," 85
Defense spending, 209–12
Democracy Movement, 331
Democratic People's Republic of
     Korea (DPRK), 205, 240–45,
     279–84
Democratic Progressive Party
     (DPP), 151, 156, 158, 167, 361
Democratic transition, 15
Deng Xiaoping. *See* Teng
     Hsiao-p'ing
Dilemmas of Reform in China
     (Fewsmith), 10–11
Ding Guangen. *See* Ting Kuan-ken
Dittmer, Lowell, 286

EAP, 239
Economy, PRC
  agricultural policy, 52–53
  agriculture technologies, 128–29
  as a mixed system, 72–74
  assessment of, 82–84
  balanced growth, 74–75
  business cycles in, 396–99
  commodity vs. planned, 22
  effect of Tienanmen incident,
    87–88, 337
  employment structure, 105t,
    108t, 109t
  foreign trade, 75–76, 95–96,
    182–83, 278–79, 280
  growth rate, 73, 102
  historical account of, 106–10
  income distribution, 80–82, 114t
  inflation, 99
  investment, 76–77, 87, 94–95,
    204n
  labor unrest, 97–98
  land reform, 74
  market system, 91, 385–86
  market vs. burearcratic coordi-
    nation, 61
  Most Favored Nation status
    (MFN), 334, 335, 338, 339,
    340
  need to learn from capitalism, 27
  ownership structure, 102–4,
    108t, 109t
  price and employment stability,
    77–80
  price structure, 64–67, 72, 86–
    87, 98–99
  reforms of, 57–60, 86, 96
  reforms of assessed, 88–89
  reforms of, consequences, 63n

resistance to reform, 97
revenue distribution, 87, 92–93,
  97
ROC investment in, 382–85
role of state planning, 95
rural property rights, 69
shareholding system, 33
shift from agriculture, 75
size of agriculture sector, 104–5
socialism as an economic entity,
  61–63
status of banking, 91–92
status of private sector, 68, 73,
  110–14, 115t, 116
status of state-owned sector, 32,
  67–68, 69, 90–91
tax reforms, 93–94
See also Cross-Strait relations,
  economic; Shanghai; Socialist
  market economy
Economy, ROC
  character of, 71–72
  decline of labor-intensive
    businesses, 179–81
  exports, 173, 180t
  GNP growth, 73, 172
  growth of, 171t
  growth of middle class, 184–85,
    187
  income inequaltiy decline, 175,
    177
  inflation, 174
  investment in PRC, 181–82,
    380–81, 385, 399–401
  investment patterns, 157–58,
    174–75, 181, 190
  level of state role, 189t
  post–Cold War assessment, 169–
    70

price and employment stability,
    77–80
prospect for integration with
    PRC markets, 386–89
public vs. private sectors, 188–95
remitting of earnings from PRC,
    387
savings, 174–75
social outcomes, 176t
standard of living, 177–78
state-owned share, 73n
structural changes in, 178–79
trade with Hong Kong, 183t
trade with PRC, 182–83
unemployment rate, 175
See also Cross-Strait relations,
    economic
Education, PRC, 82
Exchange rates, 65, 384-85

Fang Li-chih, 338
Fang- "tso" peiwang-lu (Memoran-
    dum on guarding against
    "leftism"), 25
Feng Ts'ung-te, 332
Fewsmith, Joseph, 10–11
Field, Robert Michael, 72n
Formosa Plastics Group, 385
Fourteenth Party Congress, 43

Gorbachev, Mikhail, 201, 204n
Grachev, Pavel, 203
Great Leap Forward, 58, 105, 106–7
Great Proletarian Cultural Revolu-
    tion, 18, 58, 312–13
Guidelines for National Unification,
    ROC, 375–76
Guidelines for Unification, PRC,
    377–78

Hankou, 382
Hartz, Louis, 307
Hegemonism, 227
Hong Kong, 14, 183t, 226, 299,
    320-326, 362, 404t, 407t
Hong Kong Basic Law, 321
Housing, 134–35
Howe, Neil, 44
Hsiashih, Chekiang, 128
Hsü Hsiao-chün, 200
Hsü Wen-li, 340
Hua Kuo-feng, 44
Huang Ta-chou, 167
Human rights, 14, 288–92, 328,
    332–33, 341, 343–47, 348–49
"Human Rights in China," 343–44
Hungary, 16
Huntington, Samuel P., 153, 159, 165
Hu Yanchou, 62n

India, 204–5, 229, 254–55, 288
Indonesia, 229
Inner Mongolian Autonomous
    Region, 235
Institutional pluralism, 47, 50
International Atomic Energy
    Agency (IAEA), 241–42, 243
International product cycle theory,
    178, 180
Iraq, 338

Japan
    image of PRC, 275
    military spending, 239, 240
    national identity, 274
    perceived as threat to PRC, 221,
        226, 240
    and PRC's human rights stand,
        334

relations with PRC, 205–6, 238–
40, 294–95
seen as threat to East Asia, 245,
270
trade with PRC, 273
Japanese Self-Defense Forces, 239,
240
Jaw Shaw-kong, 152, 167
Jiang Zemin. *See* Chiang Tse-min

Kazakhstan, 202, 236, 237, 238, 287
Kennex Corporation, 382, 386
Kiangsu, 129
Kissinger, Henry, 309, 311, 317,
342–43
Kornai, Janos, 62n, 396
Kosygin, Aleksey, 308, 310
Kuangnan Group, 383, 386
Kuomintang (KMT), 156, 167
effect of democratization on,
162–65
electoral system under, 160–62
factionalism in, 151
lessening control over legisla-
tion, 151
position on unification, 158
vote-buying under, 162
Ku-p'iao ju-men (The ABC of
stocks), 37
Kuwait, 338
Kweichow Province, 382, 384
Kyrgyzstan, 202, 236, 287

Lee Teng-hui, 166, 360
Lei Yang, 310, 312
Lenin, Vladimir, 27
Levine, Steven, 271
Lewis, Arthur, 118
Li, K.T., 70n

Liberalization, 5, 16–17
Lieberthal, Kenneth, 42n
Lilley, James, 332, 338
Lin Piao, 7, 313
Lintner, Bertil, 246
Li P-eng, 343
and Central Asia, 202, 237–38
and economic reforms, 4, 63,
212
and human rights, 332, 334, 338,
344, 346
Li-shih te ch'ao-liu (The trend of
history), 25
Lithuania, 16
Liu Hua-ch'ing, 46, 218, 286
Liu Hua-ch'iu, 333
Lüshun, 384

Mainland Affairs Council (MAC),
360, 363, 374
"The Main Points of Propaganda
Work in 1993," 27
Malaysia, 229, 245
Maoist orthodoxy, 6–7
Mao Tse-tung, 59, 308
Mao Tse-tung Thought, 4, 29
Ma Ying-jeou, 154
Mills, William de B., 48n
Missile Technology Control Regime
(MTCR), 256, 339
Mohamad, Mahathir, 346
Mongolia, 16, 202, 235, 287, 299
Most Favored Nation status (MFN),
334, 335, 338, 339, 340
Myanmar, 288
Nanking, 382, 383
National Defense White Paper,
ROC, 292–93
National Environmental Protection

Agency (NEPA), PRC, 303
National Unification Council, 360,
    374
National Working Conference on
    Taiwan, 403
Naughton, Barry, 104
New KMT Alliance (NKA), 152
Ni Chih-fu, 44
Nixon, Richard M., 310, 311
Nixon doctrine, 356
Ni Zhifu. *See* Ni Chih-fu
Nuclear-free zone (NFZ), 241
Nuclear Nonproliferation Treaty,
    339

Oksenberg, Michel, 8, 42n
Olympic Games (2000), 340
Olympic Games, Seoul (1988), 277
"One China, two governments"
    formula, 362
One China policy, 204, 219–20, 319
"One country, two governments"
    formula, 360–61
"One country, two systems"
    formula, 363
Overholt, William, 201

Pakistan, 254–55
Pao Tsun-hsin, 340
Paracel Island group, 248, 294
Patten, Christohper, 14, 321
Peaceful evolution, 26
P'eng Chen, 10
People's Armed Police (PAP), 297
People's Bank of China, 384
People's Daily, 316, 317, 334, 343
People's Liberation Army (PLA),
    215, 227, 270
    and Central Asia, 236
    domestic role, 214

and economic reforms, 37, 217–
    19, 222
increased influence, 213–14
and the South China Sea, 248,
    250, 252, 253, 297
People's Republic of China (PRC)
    arms control and disarmament
        policies, 255–58
    assessment of national security
        objectives, 222–24
    bipolarism vs. multipolarism,
        266–71
    and Burma, 246–47
    and Central Asia, 202, 236, 236–
        38, 287
    central vs. local governments,
        33–37
    declining control over popula-
        tion, 301–3
    democracy movements, 204
    desire for international respect
        and influence, 220–22
    doctrine of limited and regional
        wars, 229–30
    environmental degradation,
        303–4
    external discourse, 5, 12, 14
    fear of political restructuring,
        18–19
    foreign/domestic policy fusion,
        263–66
    government revenue shares, 36t
    human rights issues, 14, 288–92,
        328, 332–33, 341, 343–47,
        348–49
    image of Japan, 274–75
    image of US, 286–87
    inhibitions to reform, 99–101
    institutional pluralism, 50–51
    internal stability, 212–15

issue of democratic transition,
  15–16
issue of sovereignty, 322–26
lose of control over information,
  304–5
military buildup, 209–12, 230–
  34, 231, 232t, 263
and Mongolia, 202, 235
one China policy, 219–20, 310
opinions of party leadership, 18t
policy discourse in, 10–11
political discourse in, 5, 9–10
possibility of internal breakup,
  227–28
pragmatic orthodoxy, 7–9
private discourse in, 5, 11
problem of systemic alienation,
  17
public opinion, 13t
regional issues, 215–17, 227–28,
  271–73
relations with DPRK, 205, 240–
  45, 280–82, 282–84
relations with India, 204–5,
  254–55
relations with Japan, 205–6,
  238–40, 275–76, 294–95
relations with Pakistan, 254–55
relations with ROK, 205, 240–
  45, 276–79
relations with Russia, 202–4,
  234–35, 284–87
relations with US, 206–7
relations with Vietnam, 205
and reversion of Hong Kong,
  320–26
role in South East Asia, 245–46
role of local networks, 119
sabotage of reform, 98
security concerns, 226–27

and the South China Sea, 248,
  250, 252, 253, 297
South China Sea dispute, 228,
  245, 248–54, 270, 296
statistical deficiency, 58n
succession issue, 305
table-tennis diplomacy, 311,
  313–14
and the UN, 310, 312
threats to its legitimacy, 298-301
urban growth, 117–18
See also Cross-Strait relations,
  economic; Cross-Strait relations,
  political
Perkins, Dwight, 67n
Persian Gulf crisis, 225
Philippines, 245, 295–96
Poland, 15, 16
"Policy of Readjustment, Consolidation, Filling-Out and Raising
  Standards," 58
Politburo (CPC)
  career patterns, 48–51, 49t
  change in membership, 44, 46
  education of members, 45t
  lack of inland representation,
    53–54
  lack of rural specialists, 52–53
  specialist groups within, 51
Political alienation, 17
Political orthodoxy, 20<n.21
Pomfret, Richard, 77n
Pragmatic orthodoxy, 7–9, 20
Pragmatism, 3
Privatization, 33
Property rights, 90
Przeworski, Adam, 15
Pye, Lucian, 316

Qian Qichen. See Ch'ien Ch'i-ch'en

Qiao Shi. *See* Ch'iao-Shih
Quayle, Dan, 332

Radio Free Asia, 334
Rapid reaction units (RRUs), 229,
    230
"Regulations Encouraging Taiwan
    Compatriots to Invest on the
    Mainland," 399
Republic of China (ROC), 150–51,
    299
    attack on corruption, 154–55
    coming of presidential elections,
        159
    declining influence of conserva-
        tives, 165–67
    democratization of electoral
        process, 162–65
    efforts to strengthen legitimacy,
        358–60
    government reforms, 359–60
    growing legislative effective-
        ness, 151–52
    growth of TV stations, 153
    independence issue, 158, 220
    influence of special interest
        groups, 154
    liberalization of civil rights, 152–53
    multiparty politics, 152
    national identity, 155–56, 158
    permits travel to PRC, 156–57,
        360
    PRC claim of sovereignty, 310
    reunification issue, 362, 363,
        375–76
    and Sino-US rapprochement,
        318–19
    social development, 186t
    and student protests, 156

and the South China Sea, 248,
    250–51
Republic of Korea (ROK), 205,
    240–45, 278–79, 299
Revisionism, 6–7, 9
Romania, 16–17
Rosenau, James, 267
Ross, Robert, 201, 220, 221
Russia, 16
    military sales to PRC, 202–4,
        231
    relations with PRC, 234–35,
        284–87
    relations with ROK, 277–78
    See also Union of Soviet
        Socialist Repbulics

Schlesinger, Arthur, 316
Schumpeter, Joseph, 113
Seeking truth from facts, 3, 21, 28
Shanghai, 386
    agricultural technologies, 128–29
    attitudes and responses to
        migrants, 142–46
    causes of migration to, 130–31,
        131–32
    criminal activity of migrants, 142
    employment patterns of
        migrants, 139–42
    housing for labor, 134–35
    housing for migrants, 137
    immigration patterns, 123–25,
        125–28
    labor hiring practices, 132–33
    migration structure, 122–25
    number of migrants, 137–39, 138t
    patterns of migration, 129t
    population growth, 119–20,
        121–22t

profile of migrants, 139
rules controlling labor, 134–36
Shanghai communiqué, 308, 309,
    314, 317–18
Shaohsing, Ckekiang, 128
Shenyang, 382
Shih Ming-te, 155
Shirk, Susan, 41n
Singapore, 251, 299
Sinkiang, 236
Sino-US rapprochement
    abruptness of, 312–13
    as flexibility in PRC policy,
        308–9, 313–18
    timing of, 309–12
Skiling, Gordon, 42n
Snow, Edgar, 311, 316
Socialism, 7–8
Socialist market economy, 88
    background, 22–25
    consequences of, 30
    evaluation of, 38–40, 387–89
    impact on PLA, 37
    legal implications, 30–32
    likened to a capitalist
        economy, 26
    requires reform of bureau-
        cracy, 32
    and the world economy, 37
South China Sea dispute, 228, 245,
    248–54, 270, 296
Spratly Island group, 216, 248, 250,
    251, 294
Steel production, 105–6
Stoessel, Walter, 310, 312
Straits Exchange Foundation, 361,
    375
Strauss, William, 44
Sun, Lena, 334, 339–40

Szechwan Province, 382

Table-tennis diplomacy, 311, 313–
    14
Tactical nuclear weapons, 230
Taipei Trade Center, Hong Kong,
    362
Taiwan Affairs Office, 377
Taiwanese Investment Protection
    Law, 384
Taiwan Relations Act, 353, 370
Tajikistan, 202, 236, 287
Tamamoto, Masaru, 274
Tangchia, Feng County, 129
Tangchiao, Kiangsu, 129
Tax reform, 34–36, 385
Technocrats, defined, 51n
Temporary Provisions Effective
    During the Period of Mobiliza-
    tion for the Suppression of
    Communist Rebellion, 150
Teng Hsiao-p'ing, 403
    as authority, 3–4
    as Time's "Man of the Year," 329
    career, 47–48
    and economic reform, 395–96
    on capitalsim and socialism, 61–
        62
    on collective leadership, 43, 50
    and the idealogues, 53
    on internal stability, 212–13
    on leftism and rightism, 25
    on market economy, 24
    on regime legitimacy, 298–99
    on territorial disputes, 249
    on Tienanmen incident, 331
    pragmatic orthodoxy of, 3, 7–9, 11
    socialism with Chinese charac-
        teristics, 27–28

South China talks, 85, 88
southern tour, 381
Teng Hsiao-p'ing Thought, 29
Thailand, 228–29, 251
Thirteenth Party Congress, 43
Tiaoyutai Islands, 216, 239–40, 294
Tibet, 235, 333, 335, 338, 340
Tienanmen incident, 213, 214, 225
  assessment of PRC response,
    347–49
  consequences of, 11, 14, 16, 19,
    206–7, 321
  effect on economy, 87–88, 405
  hard-line response, 331–36
  offensive response, 341–47
  soft-line response, 336–41
T'ien Chi-yün, 31
Tientsin, 382
Tina Jiyun. See T'ien Chi-yün
Ting Kuan-ken, 26, 27
Ting Pang-ch'üan, 208
T'ou-tzu chih-nan (A guide to
  investment), 37
Tsinan, Shantung, 382, 384
Turkmenistan, 236, 237, 287
Twelfth Party Congress, 43
Union of Soviet Socialist Repbulics
  (USSR), 201
  invasion of Czechoslovakia, 308
  relations with DPRK, 279
  relations with PRC, 309
  See also Russia
United Front Work Department,
  CCP, 376–77
United Kingdom-PRC talks on
  Hong Kong, 320–26
United Nations Organization, 310,
  312, 332, 344

United Nations Register of Conventional Armaments, 255
United States
  and Asian security, 226–27
  and cross-Strait relations, 220,
    353–55, 355–56
  and DPRK, 282
  and MFN status for PRC, 335
  military presence in EAP region,
    226, 238–40
  and PRC arms control, 257–58
  and PRC arms trade, 229
  PRC view of, 286–87
  recognition of PRC, 308–20
  seen as threat to Southeast Asia,
    245
  threatens sanctions against PRC,
    332
  and Tienanmen incident, 206–7
United States-Japanese Mutual
  Security Treaty, 238
Uzbekistan, 236, 287

Vietnam, 204, 205, 245, 247-248,
  251, 288

Wang Chien, 399
Wang Chien-hsien, 152
Wang Yung-ping, 383
Wan Li, 10
Washington Post, 334
Water Margin, 7
Wei Chien-hsing, 48
Wei Ching-sheng, 339, 340
Whan, Hupeh, 382
World Conference on Human
  Rights, 289, 346
Wuhan, 383

Wusih, 131, 132

Xiaowei Zang, 51n
Yang Shang-k'un, 343
Yeltsin, Boris, 202–3, 205, 234, 284

Zhao Ziyang. *See* Chao Tzu-yang
Zhirinovsky, Vladimir, 203n
Zhou Enlai. *See* Chou En-lai